Oxford Studies in European Law

General Editors: Paul Craig and Gráinne de Búrca

THE COHERENCE OF EU LAW

The Coherence of EU Law

The Search for Unity in Divergent Concepts

Edited by

SACHA PRECHAL
and
BERT VAN ROERMUND

OXFORD

UNIVERSITY PRESS

*This book has been printed digitally and produced in a standard specification
in order to ensure its continuing availability*

OXFORD
UNIVERSITY PRESS

Great Clarendon Street, Oxford OX2 6DP

Oxford University Press is a department of the University of Oxford.
It furthers the University's objective of excellence in research, scholarship,
and education by publishing worldwide in

Oxford New York

Auckland   Cape Town Dar es Salaam   Hong Kong   Karachi
Kuala Lumpur Madrid Melbourne Mexico City   Nairobi
New Delhi Shanghai Taipei Toronto
With offices in
Argentina Austria Brazil Chile Czech Republic France Greece
Guatemala Hungary Italy Japan South Korea Poland Portugal
Singapore Switzerland Thailand Turkey Ukraine Vietnam

Oxford is a registered trade mark of Oxford University Press
in the UK and in certain other countries

Published in the United States
by Oxford University Press Inc., New York

ISBN 978-0-19-923246-8

GENERAL EDITORS' PREFACE

This interesting and valuable set of essays explores an important theme, which is of relevance throughout EU law: the extent to which conceptual coherence is necessary for the EU legal order and the extent to which conceptual divergence threatens that legal order. The general premise is that the European legal order does indeed require convergence. Thus conceptual divergence is considered to be sub-optimal when it comes to threatening an essential presupposition of any legal order from an internal point of view, its unity.

The contributors note a number of factors that create an enhanced risk of divergence within the EU legal order, at least by way of comparison with the risk that pertains in national legal orders. These include: the fact that powers of application and enforcement of rules made by the EU are delegated to national authorities; that EU law has its own terminology, which may differ from that of the Member States; the difficulties of translation that flow from the EU's multi-lingualism; and that legal ideology can differ significantly as between Member States.

The initial hypothesis underlying the study was that there were many instances of conceptual divergence in EU law and that the EU suffered as a result. This was tested by considering the 'principles common to the legal orders of the Member States', and inquiring whether such 'common' concepts existed in reality, or whether we only seemed to have them. This led to consideration of a further question, which was whether we do in fact need such common concepts? The study acknowledges two divergent views in this regard. There is, on the one hand, the belief that there is a relatively clear, shared, and well-understood conceptual framework for European law, which constitutes an ultimately unifying perspective in spite of all apparent divergence. There is, on the other hand, the sceptical view, which maintains that there is no such framework, and that 'common concepts' are in reality based on misunderstanding and confusion and, hence, divergence, with the consequence that the unity of EU law is or will be illusory. The present study however explores a third hypothesis, which is that while there is no common conceptual core, the necessary unity and coherence of Community law can nonetheless be articulated and even reinforced through the use of divergent concepts.

The themes in the book are explored using perspectives from legal sociology, comparative law, European legal scholarship, and legal theory. The primary focus of the subject matter is, for exigencies of space and time, rights and discretion.

The book will be of interest to all those concerned with EU law and also to those with interests in legal theory, more especially as it concerns the inter-relationship of legal orders.

Paul Craig
Gráinne de Búrca

ACKNOWLEDGEMENTS

The papers presented in this volume are the result of a research project conducted in an international seminar group of scholars in European law, comparative law, and legal theory. Convened for a period of three years, it started out under the title of Binding Unity and Divergent Concepts in EU Law (BU/DC) at a workshop in Tilburg in April 2003. We wound up our discussions at a conference in Utrecht in January 2006. Most of the contributions were finalized in the winter of 2006–2007.

The larger part of the funds was provided by the Netherlands Organisation for Scientific Research (NWO), under the so-called Revitalization of Legal Research III call (SaRO III). The research is the result of collaboration between the law schools of Tilburg University and of Utrecht University, which both provided supplementary funding. We thank NWO as well as the two faculties of law involved for their support.

We would also like to thank Ms Rieneke Buisman (Utrecht University) and Ms Kay Caldwell (Glasgow) for their most welcome assistance with copy-editing texts, correcting linguistic errors, and checking references. Furthermore we are deeply indebted to Linda Senden (Professor of European Law at Tilburg University), Hans Lindahl (Professor of Legal Philosophy at Tilburg), and Thomas Vandamme (Lecturer in European Law at Amsterdam University). Without their generous investment of professional skills, enthusiasm, and tenacity our lives as co-ordinators of the project and as editors of this volume would have been far more difficult.

Sacha Prechal
Bert van Roermund

TABLE OF CONTENTS

LIST OF CONTRIBUTORS

Ricardo Alonso García is full-time Professor of Administrative and European Law at the Complutense University in Madrid, Spain. He has written numerous books and articles on EU law, in particular on the constitutional aspects of the interaction between EU law and national law. He is also an expert on Latin American integration systems (particularly South Common Market—MERCOSUR—and Andean Community—COMUNIDAD ANDINA).

Saša Beljin is Assistant Professor of German and European Public Law at the Westfälische Wilhelms-Universität Münster in Germany. European law is one of his main fields of work, especially the range of issues concerning the relationship between EC law and national law. In this field he has published a book on state liability for breaches against EC law (2000), and since 2002 he has written several articles as well as a casebook, mainly in cooperation with Hans D. Jarass.

Joxerramon Bengoetxea is Professor of Legal Theory at the University of the Basque Country in San Sebastian, Spain. He has been dealing with Lifelong Learning issues since 1998, when he was Deputy Minister for Employment at the Basque Autonomous Government, President of the Basque Foundation for Continuous Vocational Training, and President of the Basque Public Undertaking for the Promotion of Employment and Training. He has been coordinating the ELAP Network for the Basque Government for which he also acts as an occasional adviser on Lifelong Learning, namely contributing for the White Book since March 2004. Currently he is also Scientific Director of the International Institute for the Sociology of Law, which has its seat in the Basque Country (Oñati).

Michiel Brand obtained an LLM degree at the European University Institute in Florence, Italy in 2003 and is currently working as a lawyer at the Municipality of Eindhoven, the Netherlands.

Roberto Caranta is full-time Professor of Administrative Law at the University of Turin in Italy. He has written extensively on various aspects of European law and comparative law. His most recent works include a book on independent administrative authorities (co-edited with Mads Andenas and Duncan Fairgrieve, BIICL, 2006) and also one on public procurement

(Giappichelli, Torino, 2004). He is Director of the master's programme in Public Procurement for Sustainable Development, jointly organized by the University of Turin and ITCILO Turin.

Filomena Chirico is post-doctoral researcher at Tilburg Law and Economics Center (TILEC) in the Netherlands. She graduated from the Faculty of Law of LUISS University of Rome in 1999 and obtained a PhD from the University of Rome 'La Sapienza' in 2005 with a thesis on the *Antitrust analysis of dominance in Internet Governance*. She also holds a European Masters in Law and Economics awarded jointly by the universities of Berkeley (USA), Rotterdam (The Netherlands), and Hamburg (Germany). For a year she was the assistant of the ELEA Programme (European Law and Economic Analysis) at the College of Europe in Bruges. Her current research interests are competition law and policy, internet regulation, law and economics and telecommunications.

Emilios Christodoulidis has been Professor of Legal Theory at the University of Glasgow in Scotland since 2006. Previously, he taught at the University of Edinburgh. He holds degrees from the universities of Athens and Edinburgh. His research interests lie mainly in the areas of jurisprudence and legal philosophy, law and social theory, political and democratic theory, theory of constitutional law, and theory of industrial relations. His book *Law and Reflexive Politics* won the European Award for Legal Theory in 1996 and the SPTL Prize for Outstanding Legal Scholarship in 1998. He was a Visiting Professor at the European Academy for Legal Theory in Brussels between 1996 and 1998 and gave the seventh series of KOBE lectures in Japan in June–July 2002.

Tim Corthaut has been an Assistant at the Institute for European Law of the Katholieke Universiteit Leuven in Belgium since 2001. He obtained his LLM degree from Harvard Law School in 2005 and is conducting research into the EU *ordre public* for his PhD (with Koen Lenaerts as his supervisor). Currently, he is the case note editor for the *Columbia Journal of European Law*. He is also a lecturer in European law at the Louvain Institute for Ireland in Europe.

Ruth Dukes is Lecturer in Employment Law at the University of Glasgow in Scotland. Prior to joining Glasgow University, she was a PhD student and graduate teaching assistant at the London School of Economics. Her research interests lie in the areas of Labour law and industrial and employment relations. Her doctoral thesis charts the development of worker representation in the UK and in Germany throughout the twentieth century, and assesses the implementation of the Information and Consultation Directive (EC Directive 2002/14) in the UK. She is also a member of the Industrial Law Society and the British Universities Industrial Relations Association.

Michele Graziadei is full-time Professor of Comparative Private Law, Facoltà di giurisprudenza, Università del Piemonte Orientale in Italy. He teaches at the Faculté internationale de droit comparé and is a titular member of the International Academy of Comparative Law as well as a member of the executive committee of the Italian Association of Comparative Law. He has taken part in several international research projects and is now active in the 'Acquis group'. His publications are devoted to comparative law, legal theory, legal history, law and language.

Iñigo del Guayo Castiella is Professor of Administrative Law at the University of Almería in Spain. He publishes on issues related to administrative law, public economic law, and energy law. He has conducted research and has taught law in Spain and in several European and North American universities (Oxford, Leiden, Bochum, Sheffield, and Texas). He was Director of the Spanish National Institute for Public Administration (1999–2000). He has been a member of the Academic Advisory Group of the Section on Energy, Environment, and Natural Resources & Infrastructure Law of the International Bar Association since 1995 and a member of the Foundation for Regulatory Studies (Madrid), as analyst on gas regulation issues, since 1994. He was a permanent observer of the European Gas Regulatory Forum (1999–2003). He is a member of the Editorial Advisory Committee of the *Journal of Energy & Natural Resources Law*.

Niilo Jääskinen has been a Judge at the Supreme Administrative Court of Finland since 2000.

Martina Künnecke is a qualified German lawyer and has been a lecturer at the University of Hull in the United Kingdom since 2001. She obtained her law degree at Mainz University in Germany, and has trained as a lawyer in both the UK and Germany. She is a member of the Institute of European Public Law at the Law School and has published in the field of comparative constitutional and administrative law. Her most recent work, a monograph entitled *Tradition and Change in Administrative Law: An Anglo-German Comparison* was published by Springer, Heidelberg in 2007. She is also a fully qualified legal translator and a Member of the Chartered Institute of Linguists in London.

Pierre Larouche is Professor of Competition Law at Tilburg University in The Netherlands and Co-Director of the Tilburg Law and Economics Center (TILEC). He is also Professor at the College of Europe in Bruges, Belgium. He graduated from the Faculty of Law of McGill University in Montreal, Canada in 1990. Pierre Larouche clerked at the Supreme Court of Canada in 1991-1992. He obtained a master's degree from the Rheinische Friedrich-Wilhelms Universität Bonn in Germany in 1993. Thereafter, he practised law for three years with Stibbe in Brussels. Pierre Larouche worked together with Professor Walter van Gerven at Maastricht University in the Ius Commune Casebooks Project from 1996 to 2002 and he obtained his doctorate in 2000. His teaching and research interests include competition law, telecommunications law, media law, EC law, and the common European law of torts.

Koen Lenaerts is Judge of the Court of Justice of the European Communities and Professor of European Law at the Katholieke Universiteit Leuven in Belgium. Currently, he is also a member of the editorial board of the *European Law Review*.

Hans Lindahl is Professor of Philosophy at Tilburg University in The Netherlands. His research and teaching interests focus on legal and political philosophy, with special emphasis on issues pertaining to political representation, sovereignty, and (collective) reflexive identity, in particular in the context of the EU legal order. He looks at the reflexive structures of the concepts of place and time in (EU) law. He obtained a PhD in Philosophy at the Higher Institute of Philosophy of the Catholic University of Louvain in Belgium in 1994. Currently he holds a grant from the NWO for research into the normative foundations of European immigration policy. He is also Director of Research for the Department of Philosophy at Tilburg University.

Leonor Moral Soriano is Professor Titular of Administrative Law at the University of Granada in Spain, and Legal Adviser to the Ministry of Education. Her areas of interest are the provision of public services by public and private actors, the implementation of EC law by local authorities, and convergence/divergence strategies in legal systems. At the Granada Law Faculty she teaches EC law and economic administrative law to undergraduate students and implementation of EC environmental law to postgraduate students. She took her law degree at the University of Granada and her PhD studies at the European University Institute in Florence, Italy under the supervision of Professor La Torre. Marcial Pons has published her doctoral thesis on legal reasoning entitled 'Los precedentes judiciales'.

Leo Mulders is the former head of the Dutch language translation division at the Court of Justice of the European Communities.

Carmen Plaza Martín is currently full-time Profesora-Contratada Doctora of Administrative and European Law at the Law Faculty of Castilla-La Mancha University in Toledo, Spain. Previously, she taught at Complutense University in Madrid. She holds degrees from the universities of Essex (UK) and Complutense (Spain). She was a Visiting Researcher at Harvard Law School in 1995 and Legal Adviser to the Ministry of the Environment between 1996 and 1997. Her research and teaching interests focus on EC law, administrative law and environmental law, with special emphasis on issues related to the implementation of EC law by national authorities and on the impact of EC law in national legal orders. She is the author of many articles on EC and Spanish law and she has also published a book on European environmental law (Direcho Ambiental de la Unión European, 2005).

Sacha Prechal is currently full-time Professor of European Law at the Law Faculty of Utrecht University (Europa Institute) in The Netherlands, specializing in European administrative and constitutional law, and in the relationship between substantive and institutional law of the European Union. She has written numerous case notes and articles on EC law, in particular on EC equality law, on various aspects of the relationship and interaction between EC law and national law, and on problems related to EC directives, including *Directives in EC Law* (2005). She is also one of the authors of *Europeanization of Public Law* (2007), one of the editors of the *Common Market Law Review* and of the *Review of European Administrative Law*, as well as member of the editorial board of the *Utrecht Law Review*.

Matthias Ruffert is Professor of Public Law, European Law, and Public International Law at the Friedrich-Schiller-Universität Jena in Germany. His main research interests lie in European constitutional and administrative law, legal issues of globalization as well as the modernization of administrative law. He co-founded the Dornburg Research Group on New Administrative Law and co-edits (together with Christian Calliess) a major commentary on the EU and EC-Treaties (*EUV/EGV-Kommentar*, 3rd edn, 2007).

Linda Senden is Professor of European Law at Tilburg University in The Netherlands. She focuses in particular on institutional issues of EC law, including topics such as Community legal instruments, the quality of European lawmaking and European governance in a broader sense. She also has a special interest in European sex equality law. She wrote *Soft Law in European Community Law* (2004) and published *Co-actorship in the Development of European Lawmaking. The Quality of European Legislation and its Implementation and Application in the National Legal Order* (2005, with EMH Hirsch Ballin).

Thomas Vandamme taught European Institutional Law at Utrecht University in The Netherlands. Recently, he was appointed as lecturer in European Law at the University of Amsterdam. In 2005 he defended his PhD (University of Amsterdam) on the invalidation of the EC directive and the possible consequences for the validity of national implementation law. He also participates in the G.K. van Hogendorp Centre for European Constitutional Studies and is a member of the Dutch Association for European Law.

Bert van Roermund is Professor of Legal Philosophy at Tilburg University in The Netherlands. He has published extensively on various fundamental legal concepts and contemporary legal problems (constitutional review, democracy, European integration). His monograph *Law, Narrative and Reality* (1997; also in Spanish) concluded a period of research on law and language. Since 1997, he has focused on problems of authority and representation (sovereignty, identity, normativity, reconciliation) in supra-national contexts like the European Union and the World Trade Organization. He is currently leading a research programme on Legislation and Identity— Strategies of Authoritative Representation (2004–2009).

TABLE OF CASES

Court of First Instance

Opinions

NATIONAL CASES

France

Conseil d'Etat

Lower Administrative Courts

Germany

Bundesverfassungsgericht

Bundesgerichtshof

Bundesverwaltungsgericht

Oberlandesgericht

Ireland

Italy

Spain

Decisions of Ordinary Courts

United States

ABBREVIATIONS

BGB	*Bürgerliches Gesetzbuch*
BGH	*Bundesgerichtshof*
BU/DC	Binding Unity and Divergent Concepts in EU Law (Conference title)
ConsEur	Constitutional Treaty for Europe
CFI	Court of First Instance
CoR	Committee of the Regions
EC	European Community
ECHR	European Convention on Human Rights
ECJ	European Court of Justice
ECN	European Competition Network
ECOSOC	Economic and Social Committee
ECSC	European Coal and Steel Community
EEA	European Economic Area
EERF	European Electricity Forum of Rome (formerly of Florence)
EGRF	European Gas Regulatory Forum of Madrid
EIA	Environmental Impact Assessment
EOC	Equal Opportunities Commission
ERG	European Regulators Group
ERGEG	European Regulators Group for Electricity and Gas
EU	European Union
GATT	General Agreement on Tariffs and Trade
GG	*Grundgesetz*
IATE	Inter Active Terminology for Europe
IEM	Internal Energy Market
IGC	Inter-Governmental Conference
ILO	International Labour Organization
NGO	Non-Governmental Organization
NUTS	Nomenclature of Units for Territorial Statistics
NWO	Netherlands Organization for Scientific Research
OMC	Open Method Co-ordination
REGLEGs	Legislative Regions
SaRO III	Revitalization of Legal Research III
SE	*Societas Europaea*

SPD	*Sozialdemokratische Partei Deutschlands* (German Social Democratic Party)
TBT	Technical Barriers to Trade
TEC	Treaty Establishing the European Community
TEU	Treaty of the European Union
TPA	Third Party Administration
TRIPS	Trade-related Aspects of Intellectual Property Rights
VwVfg	Verwaltungsverfahrensgesetz
WTO	World Trade Organization

1

Binding Unity in EU Legal Order: An Introduction

Sacha Prechal and Bert van Roermund

At its core, this book makes a strong claim that flies in the face of postmodern defenders of pluralism in law: whatever conception one has of the European legal order, just as any other legal order does it requires a special kind of coherence, namely convergence. Much like a painting in perspective—indeed even a Mondriaan painting in multiple perspectives—it will not register as an 'arte-fact' without a sufficient number of 'depth clues'. These will be political depth clues, to be sure, but they are suggestive of motion towards a vanishing point holding the artefact together. Law requires unity, or rather the perception of movement towards (virtual) unity by the principal norm-setting agents involved, otherwise a legal order cannot deliver what it promises, namely to reduce, if not to end, conflict by authoritative decision-making. For that reason, its various elements (actions, procedures, roles, players, scenes, idiolects, etc) should be susceptible to being considered as pointing to final authority. Coercion is typical of law in society but only against the backdrop of such a final authority being largely accepted by those who are interested in having a legal order in the first place—not only state organs, but also private citizens, companies, NGOs, and pressure groups.

By necessity, there is one single final authority. Even when multiple agents claim to represent such authority, they will ultimately feel obliged, or challenged, to speak with one voice. This is not to say that a legal order is a unity by any account external to it. More often than not it is the product of political compromise, social and cultural heterogeneity, religious clashes, and economic antagonism. Despite the fact that there is usually some contested ground in most legal orders, those who conceive of such an order from an internal point of view, whether they are committed to it or detached from it, ie those who see it as a *normative* or *binding* order, cannot avoid construing it as a unity in terms of authority. They cannot be of the opinion that there is no final authority, or that that there is more than one. If either case were true, the law could not offer any guidance to its subjects, and would create perennial conflict.[1]

Legal concepts are needed to construe such patterns. We cannot do without them. It comes as no surprise, then, that the gradual convergence of concepts seems the preferred parameter in EU law,[2] and that conceptual divergence is considered to be sub-optimal. But what if divergence enters the legal stage under the guise of convergence? What if seemingly common concepts like 'rights', 'discretion', 'public order', or 'fault' are precisely the ones that cause misunderstanding, delay, harm, and conflict? What if the solution reiterates the problem?

For these and other reasons (to be explained below) the lures and limits of conceptual divergence in EU law are the central theme of this volume, in particular with regard to two widely used notions: rights and discretion. But an even more pertinent question is in the background of this topic: do we justifiably hold on to the presupposition that conceptual divergence jeopardizes the quest for unity? Could it not be the other way around, namely that—perhaps within certain constraints to be investigated in more detail—conceptual divergence is in fact a precondition favourable to unity, as it provides a manifold of pointers to a form of unity that is bound to remain virtual, a vanishing point that will always be constituent of the painting, but not part of what is painted?

[1] Note that accepting the binding unity of the law in principle does not commit one to either of the following doubtful theses: one always has to reconstruct the overall unity of the law before one can act according to the law; only a pre-established hierarchy of legal agents can establish the unity of the law; final authority can only be represented by one individual; any conflict can be solved by (final) authority. For a more elaborated argument of the thesis, cf B van Roermund, 'Authority and Authorisation' [2000] 19 Law and Philosophy, 210–222.

[2] B Markesinis, *The Gradual Convergence: Foreign Ideas, Foreign Influences, and English Law on the Eve of the 21st Century* (Oxford: Clarendon Press, 1994).

1 Conceptual divergence

First and foremost, let us try to capture our key term in a provisional definition. Note that conceptual divergence is not the same as linguistic variance.[3] The fact that Germans say *Vertrag*, the English *contract*, and the Dutch *overeenkomst* is not a matter of conceptual divergence. But suppose that the English idea of a contract were largely governed by the doctrine of consideration,[4] whereas the Dutch notion *overeenkomst* was entirely based on congruent declarations of will (promises) by the parties involved. Suppose, finally, that German lawyers recognized a legal relationship as a *Vertrag*, only if reasonable expectations were raised on either side of the deal.[5] Then all of that would be a *possible* source of conceptual divergence. We say 'possible' because from these differences themselves nothing follows. Divergence becomes legally meaningful only if, and to the extent that, it functions in arguing for conflicting courses of action as 'according to the law'. That is why Niilo Jääskinen opens part V of this volume with a forceful reminder from Scandinavian realism that our dealings with conceptual convergence should keep any belief in the 'metaphysical' unity of law at bay. Let us also point here to the plea made by Emilios Christodoulidis and Ruth Dukes for 'a discussion of unity unhampered by the misleading noises of uniformity', acknowledging throughout that 'merely contrasting unity to uniformity will not suffice'.[6] And indeed, far from hypostasizing petrified terminology 'in the books' we intend to focus on 'concepts in action'. Let us therefore define conceptual divergence in law as follows:

A legal term T is conceptually divergent between agents X and Y, if T is common parlance between X and Y, and if the sense and/or the reference of T yields meaning M_1 for X and M_2 for Y, such that X and Y are inclined to argue conflicting courses of action as lawful (or unlawful) under the legal order they are both committed to.

Some crucial features of this definition should be underlined. First of all, it purports to make clear that conceptual divergence is a relational concept: a concept is not divergent in itself, but in a relation between (at least) two agents. Second, these agents share a certain term or set of terms, so that conceptual

---

[3] For the relevance of this distinction, cf s 2 of ch 13 by H Lindahl.

[4] ie demanding that some form of mutual performance occurs before we accept that a legal relationship is contractual.

[5] We do not endorse *any* of these views on English, Dutch, or German contract law. The example is an artificial one, suggested for the sake of argument.

[6] cf E Christodoulidis and R Dukes, ch 17 p 399.

divergence arises against the backdrop of lexical convergence or translatability. Third, the definition takes issue with those who would argue that it is circular from the start, as it defines divergence in term of difference. If this were the case, it would prompt a lexical pursuit of sorts. Fortunately it does not. The definition does not hinge on the distinction between 'divergence' and 'difference', but on incompatible courses of action, reasons for action, and legal discourse articulating these reasons. Note that without some presupposition of ultimately binding authority, the concept of incompatibility would be meaningless. But then so would the whole notion of conflict.[7] Fourth, the definition leaves room for all sorts of factors that may cause conceptual divergence. It awaits and, indeed, anticipates various explanations for the phenomenon under investigation. Differences between legal cultures may well be one factor, but there may be others, and more important ones. Let us also stress one last point: conceptual divergence, if it is to raise any problems at all, is to be located within a legal order common to a set of agents from their internal points of view. Should we leave out the element of commitment to solving a common problem by law, conceptual divergence would boil down to variance between legal orders—a phenomenon that might be of interest from many points of view but not a practical one.

2 Conceptual divergence and European law

Conceptual divergence is clearly at odds with the promise of a legal order, as it allegedly jeopardizes the efforts of both legal officials and subjects to rewrite a pattern of general norms in terms of specific obligations and permissions. Initially this may seem to be a rather innocent problem, but as soon as it affects, for instance, higher order legal principles and, ultimately, the sources of authority that are required to make these principles binding upon subjects, it becomes a major difficulty. To a certain extent, this problem

---

[7] The relevance of this implication comes to the fore eg in ch 21 where Lenaerts and Corthaut argue that primacy only works to the extent that there is a conflict between two norms which both claim to be applicable. 'This actually implies two qualities the norms at issue must have: first, the norms must have some identifiable content, ie it must be possible to ascertain some behavioural standard for the actor to whom the norm is addressed. Second, the norm must be binding, in the sense that it vests a legally enforceable claim in another actor to ensure compliance with that standard. The extent to which this is the case differs depending on the legal instrument relied upon' (p 510).

exists in all legal orders—and there is no point in denying it.[8] First, as we have said, legal orders are political artefacts, and since politics is a clash of diverging forces, it is law that bears the cuts and bruises. Second, law evolves as a differentiating system, dovetailing into various branches such as public law and private law, civil law and company law, the law of torts and the law of contracts. A concept such as 'guilt', for instance, has well-known chameleon-like qualities depending on the differentiated area of law in which it is supposed being discussed Third, legal cultures produce conceptual frameworks in differing traditions of practical case-bound thinking that have proven to be as robust as they are resilient. The paradigm example, of course, is the divergence between common law and civil (or roman) law. But there are more of these resilient traditions. Within civil law, there is the tradition of the *Code civil*, still powerful in France, Belgium, and The Netherlands which contrasts with the tradition of *les gens de la justice*, suspicious of codification and fond of high-brow doctrine. There is the tradition of what has come to be known as *Wertungsjurisprudenz* (value–oriented legal thinking), in contrast with the tradition of social engineering that steers away as far as possible from morals or metaphysics.

There are a number of *prima facie* reasons why EU law in particular seems to be jeopardized by conceptual divergence:

- Multi-lingualism in EC legislation leads to incorrect, at times impossible, translations. These may incite lawyers to 'walk on the wild side' in advising or representing clients.
- EU law has its own terminology, different from Member States', jurisdictions. To a certain extent, it has developed outside of the system of checks and balance built into national legal traditions.
- While the law is enacted at the supra-national level, powers of application and enforcement are delegated to national authorities.
- Common education and common culture with respect to EU law are *in statu nascendi*, if not embryonic. They are certainly not part of the *acquis communautaire*.
- Socio-political constellations, aspirations, and ideologies differ greatly from one Member State to another.

---

[8] This issue was discussed specifically during a talk on the project I gave in a seminar hosted by my colleague in legal theory, Michel Troper (Paris X, Nanterre, Centre de Théorie du Droit, February 2004). I thank the participants and, in particular Professors Troper and Bazex, for sharing their views (BvR).

This may all be true, but why would it amount to something special in the context of European law? Why not say that here we meet the problems of comparative law writ large? Well, indeed, here we *do* meet the problems of comparative law writ large, and that is why expertise in comparative law was amply represented in our research group. But European law brings comparative law into a new perspective. Traditionally, comparative law is conceived in one of two ways.[9] Either it is seen as a peculiar branch of cultural anthropology applied to legal orders, ie an exercise in interpretive 'theory' as all social sciences are; or it is viewed as an extension of legal thinking beyond the confinements of one's own legal order and its doctrine, ie an exercise in practical thinking. Note that the latter often depends on a pedagogical, indeed a reflexive, view: one is supposed to learn from comparative law to the benefit of *one's own* legal order, or one expects to make legal things better *at home*, or one aims at promoting one's own solutions *abroad*. In other words, behind comparative law, as an extension of legal thinking proper, there is always a concern with domestic law as the point of departure and/or the point of arrival. Not that comparative law is biased in favour of domestic law; the point is that, even where it is sympathetic towards foreign law, the exercise is calibrated against a domestic system one can call 'one's own'. There is a form of radical reflexivity[10] involved in comparative law.

And it is this that poses a problem for the intersecting legal orders in European law, creating a need for and frustrating the common techniques of comparative law in one fell swoop: *it makes the core phrase 'one's own' seem meaningless.* From a normative point of view, ever since the all-famous decisions of *Van Gend&Loos* and *Costa—ENEL*, the first pillar of EU law, at least, has developed into what is usually called, a *sui generis* legal order. But the conceptual framework in which this *sui generis* character is to be accounted for is not a *sui generis* framework. This means that exercises in comparative law, as part of European law scholarship, are not calibrated against paradigms one may call one's own. Or, to put it in the memorable words of one of the linguistic specialists in our seminar group, Leo Mulders: in European law, no language is the original language. By analogy no conceptual framework is the original conceptual framework. The domestic ones are all equally original... or not. Indeed, our paradigms are lost, although they remain a

---

[9] See M van Hoecke (ed), *Epistemology and Methodology of Comparative Law* (Oxford: Hart, 2004) for a rich overview of the various epistemological views on comparative law, in particular the time-honoured discussion between legal doctrinal and social sciences views.

[10] As Charles Taylor would call it; cf C Taylor, *Sources of the Self: The Making of Modern Identity* (Cambridge: Cambridge University Press, 1989) 130 and *passim*.

presence and emerge where they are least expected. It is tempting to say that domestic and supra-domestic legal orders are all intersecting or overlapping. But how can we be sure that this in itself is not a domestic viewpoint, much like the discourse of the zodiac—only from our position on planet earth do stars compose intersecting line drawings of Pisces, Scales, Twins, etc—if it is not put to the test of conflict?

Finally, let us also face the fact that a predicate like 'the European legal order' is itself conceptually divergent. We do not have to remind our readership of the differences between the legal orders of the ECHR and the TEU, or of the differences between the various pillars of the latter. Suffice it to underline that this volume acknowledges the difference between, on the one hand, an EU legal order that encompasses the legal orders of the Member States as well as (where appropriate) those at infra-national level,[11] and, on the other, an EU legal order that is strictly limited to EU rules and decisions. The former context is surely more fitting for 'multi-level' or 'interlocking' law theories than the latter. And yet, in both contexts, with respect to law creation as well as (more importantly) with respect to implementation (transposition, application, enforcement), the EU and the national (or infra-national) legal orders are closely tied to one another. It is usually clear from the introductions of the respective papers in this volume which context they choose.

3 EU law endangered by conceptual divergence?

To sum up: (i) conceptual divergence is considered to be sub-optimal when it comes to upholding the unity that each and every legal order claims in order to pose as binding upon its subjects; (ii) there are at least *prima facie* reasons why the EC/EU legal order, when compared with national legal orders, faces an enhanced risk of conceptual divergence. But let us stress again: our hypothesis was not that conceptual divergence as such jeopardizes legal orders and should be removed from the face of the legal world. What we wanted to know was if, to what extent, and why conceptual divergence threatens the necessary preconditions for taking this internal viewpoint of binding unity with regard to European law.

We expected EU law to suffer from a great many instantiations of conceptual divergence. Note, however, that this is a double hypothesis: that there are

---

[11] cf the contribution by Bengoetxea, ch 18.

these many instantiations and that European law suffers from them. Moreover, and more importantly, we expected them to emerge at the very places where convergence is supposed to reside: in the 'principles common to the legal orders of the Member States', that the European Court of Justice (ECJ) often refers to as ultimately governing EU law. Such principles are often supposed to pave the road to unity in a specific sense: unification or 'harmonization' of laws. However, this strategy presupposes the very convergence of concepts we feared to be lacking in the first place. To break the circle, 'common concepts' on a higher level of abstraction are called for. Thus, our first question is this: Do we have these 'common' concepts, or do we only seem to have them?

Our second question, however, is a more radical one: whether we have them or not, do we need them? Believers in common concepts, on the one hand, think that there is a relatively clear, shared, and well-understood conceptual framework for European law, and that it warrants an ultimately unifying perspective in spite of all apparent divergence. In particular, this framework is believed to provide a semantic basis for 'communication' and 'negotiation' of different interests. It is alleged to be found in legislative instruments aiming at the harmonization or unification of EU law, or in the case law of the European courts. Sceptics, on the other hand, hold that there is no such framework; 'common concepts' turn out to be just so many sources of misunderstanding, confusion, and therefore divergence.[12] Thus, in the end, the unity of EU law will prove to be delusive. Our project as presented in this volume explored a third hypothesis. While there is indeed no common conceptual core (or at best one that exists at such an abstract level that it does not provide guidance for action), the necessary convergence of Community law can be articulated, strengthened, and even reinforced through the use of divergent concepts. Thus, the project aimed to stay clear, on the one hand, of the naive assumption that European integration is a process of real convergence without concomitant divergence, and, on the other, of the pessimistic assumption that there is a process of divergence without hope of real convergence.

---

[12] cf the Legrand–Van Gerven discussion, among other publications in P Legrand, 'European Legal Systems are not Converging' 1996 45 ICLQ, 52–81; 'On the Unbearable Localness of the Law: Academic Fallacies and Unseasonable Observations' (2002) 10 Eur Rev of Private L, 61–76. W van Gerven, 'Comparative Law in a Texture of Communitarization of National Law and Europeanization of Community Law' in D O'Keeffe (ed), *Judicial Review in European Union. Liber Amicorum in honour of Lord Slynn of Hadley*, vol 1 (The Hague: Kluwer, 2000) 433–445 and 'Comparative Law in a Regionally Integrated Europe' in AJ Harding, *Comparative Law in the 21st Century* (The Hague: Kluwer, 2002) 155–178.

The papers presented here address these topics along empirical, conceptual, and normative lines. In most essays these strands are intertwined, as they should be in legal argument. But this overall approach is coloured by four disciplinary perspectives: (i) legal sociology and socio-linguistics, (ii) comparative law, (iii) European legal scholarship, and (iv) legal theory. It is obvious that each of these disciplines has its own way of relating to the others, as well as of defining what counts as empirical data, conceptual problems, and normative questions. For instance, the behaviour of legal professionals (litigators, interpreters, civil servants) is the primary empirical domain for legal sociology and socio-linguistics, whereas the judgments of legal officials (representing the legislative, executive, and judiciary branches of the European legal order) are empirical grist to the mill of comparatists and other legal scholars. Again, when legal theorists ask conceptual or normative questions, they usually do this from a vantage point different from that of European law scholars, although the findings of the latter will be the point of departure as well as the point of return for the former. The reader will appreciate the balance we seek to strike between the specificity of disciplines and the integrity of an interdisciplinary enterprise.

By their very nature, the topics addressed in this volume seem to be a concern mainly for academics. Indeed, as Chapter 2 shows, most practitioners do not regard conceptual divergence as highly problematic. In their working environments, systematic investigations or routine procedures for detecting conceptual divergence are not of major concern. For example, Community legislation or case law is more often than not consulted in the 'native' language only—which is surprising, taken into account the multi-lingualism of EU law. But one should not jump to conclusions here. Most practitioners are perfectly on guard with respect to conceptual divergence, precisely because they sense its ambiguity with regard to the unity of the legal order as a whole. Often, conceptual divergence is conceived as instrumental to realizing private purposes: it may help to reach political compromise in legislation or it offers a good opportunity to lawyers, when advising their clients or representing them in litigation, to 'bend' the law in their direction. But interestingly, according to the same practitioners, divergent concepts need not necessarily undermine the unity of EU law. They may actually strengthen it, as national concepts then function as good 'transmitters' of EU law, a phenomenon that is also indicated at in several other contributions.[13]

---

[13] Eg, the 'escape valves' in ch 6 by Alonso, Moral, and Plaza, and ch 9 Brand in relation to discretion.

For instance, one of the causes of presumed conceptual divergence may lie in legal translation, a complex process where the person on the job is often caught between language and comparative law. Leo Mulders, in Chapter 3 warns lawyers and scholars not to lose themselves in an exegesis of terminological differences which may very well be caused by different terms being used by parties with different interests, in which case the difference often does not necessarily reflect a difference in concept. Also, a clear distinction is to be made between incorrect translation and impossible translation, the former being a work accident, whereas the latter arises from conceptual divergence. All this seems to corroborate the 'third hypothesis' ventured above.

4 'Rights' and 'discretion'

As the topic of conceptual divergence and binding unity with regard to European law is much too broad to manage within a limited period of time and in a limited research group, we focused on two concepts in particular: rights and discretion. The reasons for narrowing down the question to these concepts were twofold. First, previous research by the convenors of the research group gave rise to the expectation that these concepts are paradigmatically central *and* puzzling in European legal development. Second, it could be argued, from a theoretical perspective, that they are interrelated—an argument that is easily corroborated if one studies, for instance, (state-) liability in a European context.[14] Also, the interrelationship between the two comes to the fore when one explores to what extent judicial protection has to be conceived of in terms of protection of rights. Or is judicial protection equivalent to judicial review of the legality of governmental action? The answer, in turn, strongly influences questions of standing, or questions of what type of argument can be invoked by which party, issues that come back in various chapters of the present book.[15] Both aspects also encounter each other in Chapter 21 by Koen Lenaerts and Tim Corthaut, where they argue in favour of direct effect in a strict sense of the term, ie a technique which allows individuals to enforce their rights. The other forms of invocability, with primacy as the underlying principle, relate as a rule to controlling the exercise of often discretionary powers by national authorities or by EU institutions.

---

[14] cf ch 10 by Künnecke.
[15] In particular Beljin (ch 5), Alonso, Moral, and Plaza (ch 6), and Prechal (ch 7).

As it is indeed trivial to state that rights can be approached from many angles, one of the favourite approaches is to focus on fundamental rights. Linda Senden (Chapter 16) argues, *inter alia*, that transforming the EU into a political entity requires a certain degree of political unity. Common principles and rights at EU level are needed to articulate the necessary sense of European identity and solidarity. In other words, common concepts of (fundamental) rights contribute to legal unity which, in turn, serves as a basis for political unity in Europe. However, the rights debate in the EU and the Member States goes beyond the issue of fundamental rights. Both at Community and at national level we come across different efforts to translate legal positions under Community law into Community rights or, at least, to label these positions as such.[16] This has led to a proliferating, complex, and confusing 'rights discourse'. Not all legal systems 'create rights in the same way under the same conditions',[17] nor do they define rights in the same way. For instance, the rather rigid doctrinal definition of ('subjective')[18] rights in German law constitutes a filter for legal protection of legal subjects quite different from the rather loose concept of rights in common law (*pace* Hohfeld) or from the somewhat indolent view of rights in French law.

An amazing case in this respect is discussed by Martina Künnecke (Chapter 10). This case suggests that in German courts *Brasserie*-claims[19] can be relatively easily denied for lack of infringement of 'individual rights' that must be embedded in the Community law rule. By contrast, in claims applying German, autonomous, criteria (article 839 of the BGB), courts are specifically granted more leeway in determining whether individual rights are at stake. In other words, the EU law conditions are made more rigid by German courts. Another striking picture emerging from the papers is that while for instance in Germany a quite extensive discussion has been going on for years about how to accommodate so-called EU rights into the national

---

[16] A brief description of the context of this debate can be found in ch 5 (Beljin) and ch 7 (Prechal).

[17] W van Gerven, 'Of Rights, Remedies and Procedures' (2000) 37 CML Rev, 525.

[18] In English, the term 'individual rights' is often used as the equivalent of 'subjective rights', terminology that does not make much sense in English but is commonly employed in the civil law tradition. The term stems from the need to distinguish between 'law' and 'rights' as these two notions have been fused into one single word, eg, 'droit' in French or 'Recht' in German. Hence the distinction between 'droit objectif' and 'droit subjectif' or 'objektives' and 'subjektives recht'. Interestingly, in the English version of the Court's judgments the term 'subjective right' may appear from time to time. The same is true for—often continental—scholars writing in English. No doubt another source of misunderstanding!

[19] Joined Cases C-46/93 and C-48/93 *Brasserie* and Factortame [1996] ECR I-1029.

scheme of (public) subjective rights, in Spain, where the same notion of (public) subjective rights is common, the translation of EU rights into national legal concepts did not pose any problems worth noting.[20]

Michele Graziadei's chapter aims at clarifying the origins of the confusing rights discourse from a historical and comparative perspective. On the one hand, it covers the rise of national legal traditions concerning rights and their resistance to change. On the other, it shows the resilience of these traditions, which are mostly linked to the intellectual legacy of the nineteenth century and its twentieth-century aftermath. The author claims that this legacy is now in shambles, partly on account of the process of European legal integration. In particular the temptation to 'read' European law through the spectacles of national legal systems muddies the understanding of 'rights'. We will have to look beyond national traditions and stereotypes, and to think in terms of a common European legal culture.

One of the vital questions in this respect is precisely how strongly we should rely on national law and use comparative methods. Saša Beljin is largely sceptical about the usefulness of such an approach. In his investigation into rights in EU law, he finds that the differences between the coverage of rights or interests and their implications for legal protection in the Member States can hardly be explained by the fundamental differences between the systems. In almost all Member States, the concept of rights as well as the system of legal protection are very polymorphic, and therefore difficult to grasp. In his view, the notion of rights and their scope is influenced by a whole range of elements, which makes it difficult to draw general conclusions as to the decisive parameters based on comparative law.[21] He argues that an autonomous concept of EU rights is necessary. This does not imply that parallels between the concept of EU rights and the national legal concepts are totally out of question. But the significance of the national systems in the determination of a concept of EU rights is limited.

The question whether (and to what extent) we should seek inspiration from national legal systems or develop concepts that are neatly tailored to the purposes of EU law (and what if these concepts can be distorted again when referred back to national legal orders and read through 'national spectacles'?) is also central to the chapter by Sacha Prechal. It focuses on the so-called 'protective scope' of the provisions at issue. First, this notion is at the heart of the question as to whether or not a legal provision bestows a right

---

[20] cf Alonso, Moral, and Plaza (ch 6).
[21] cf Beljin, ch 5 p 93–94 and p 101.

on individuals. Second, however, the issue of protective scope has a much broader range and may emerge in discussions on the limits of national procedural autonomy and the concept of direct effect.

Another interesting feature which comes up independently in the chapters written from distinct national backgrounds, Chapters 5 (German) and 6 (Spanish), is the criticism of the European Court of Justice's (ECJ) case law under Article 230. The very limited access to European courts for private individuals, even in situations where their rights are at stake, is contrasted with the ECJ's requirement as to the judicial protection to be provided for EU rights at the national level. According to Saša Beljin, a possible explanation lies in the fact that rights and their judicial enforceability are two different issues. To what extent these coincide differs from one legal system to another. The Spanish authors are less benevolent when it comes to Article 230(4) case law and would prefer more convergence between European and national law in this respect.

Like rights, discretion has reached centre stage in EU law, and shows up in many different areas and contexts. At an earlier stage, we met with the observations made by Mertens de Wilmars, former president of the ECJ, who distinguishes between 'power of appraisal' and 'discretionary power' in ECJ legal argumentations. These concepts seem to square—on the surface at least—with the German distinction between *Beurteilungsspielraum* and *freies Ermessen*, the Dutch distinction between *beoordelingsvrijheid* and *beleidsvrijheid*, the Italian distinction between *discrezionalità/valutazione tecnica* on the one hand and *discrezionalità amministrativa* on the other. Roberto Caranta also refers to *Dorset Yacht v Home Office* in the UK,[22] when Lord Wilberforce advanced the distinction between operational decisions and policy decisions. However, Mertens de Wilmars immediately admitted that the distinction may appear artificial; many lawyers and legal bodies, even the ECJ in its case law, use the two terms interchangeably.[23] A fascinating argument put forward by Hans Lindahl in Chapter 13 is that this is the epiphenomenon of a much more basic fissure in any concept of discretion. Discretion invariably oscillates between 'the scope of legal power' (ie constitutional power) and 'the power over the scope of law' (ie constituent power). By bringing the twofold sense of discretion to bear on *Grogan*, the

---

[22] *Dorset Yacht v Home Office* [1970] AC 1004 (HL).

[23] J Mertens de Wilmars, 'The Case-Law of the Court of Justice in Relation to the Review of the Legality of Economic Policy in Mixed-Economy Systems' (1982) Legal Issues of European Integration, 1–16.

well-known abortion information case, Lindahl explains how the ECJ and the Irish Supreme Court play for time, negotiating divergence by deferring the unity of these legal orders. Note, however, that deferring unity in the reciprocity of this 'play' is precisely a mode of pointing to it, re-affirming it, and re-enforcing it within a shared time frame. In this sense, Lindahl's argument joins the efforts made by Christodoulidis and Dukes (Chapter 17), to search for 'unity without uniformity'.

Being another non- or ill-defined concept of EU law, discretion gives rise to confusion about the notion itself and to divergent results in application. The former is illustrated by the fact that problems with the concept of discretion begin as early as at the level of translation.[24] The latter is particularly striking if one looks at the distinctively different modes of judicial review which discretion triggers. This is true for both national legal systems and for EU law.[25] Roberto Caranta calls for more conceptual tidiness in the ECJ, arguing that the Tetra Laval litigation may be a turning-point in this respect. A less unstructured approach is not only important from the point of view of predictability at the EU level itself, ie the control of the exercise of discretion by EU institutions. It also has considerable impact on how (national) discretion is policed at Member State level or how EU law notions that are closely linked to discretion are fleshed out. The chapter by Martina Künnecke illustrates clearly how the requirement of a 'sufficiently serious breach' in state liability law is given different substance in Germany and in the UK. She points to the eight factors identified by Lord Clyde in *Factortame No. 5*, which were of influence to the ECJ and which should guide national courts in establishing liability under this principle. No single factor is a sufficient condition in itself, but one single factor may become decisive, depending on further circumstances. She observes a lot of uncertainty in German courts trying to deal with this case-law-based development of the principle, at least for the time being. But if we read her correctly, her explanations do not go in the direction of diverging conceptual frameworks, but in that of policy considerations entering judicial decision-making: 'The legal mechanisms are subservient to political or economic considerations'.[26] Bert van Roermund comes to similar conclusions: policy considerations at case law level are what matters most when divergent implications of 'discretion' are at stake, although it seems very difficult to deny that on a more abstract

---

[24]   cf chs 3 (Mulders) and 9 (Brand).
[25]   cf for instance chs 8 (Caranta) and 6 (Alonso, Moral, and Plaza).
[26]   Künnecke, ch 10.

level there is considerable agreement on the basic conceptual furniture dec-
orating contemporary 'europeanized' courtrooms. But then, he argues in a
more philosophical vein, it is this basic furniture of the concept of law itself
that is saturated with antinomies. These will continue to stir up conceptual
divergences amongst agents involved in enacting and applying law.

The 'policy thesis' seems to be corroborated by other contributions,
though with many caveats and constraints. Roberto Caranta (Chapter 8)
suggests that the ECJ's way of handling the notion of discretion differs
depending on whether liability concerns the EC institutions or the Member
States. Ricardo Alonso Garcia, Leonor Moral, and Carmen Plaza Martin
(Chapter 6) discuss in their chapter how the ECJ's understanding of discretion alters the scope of judicial review of discretion in Spain, in particular by
affecting the traditional substitution of an administrative decision by one of
the Court itself. Matthias Ruffert (Chapter 11) examines how Community
law changes the conditions which govern the exercise of discretionary power
by national administrations, in particular so-called post-decisional discretion. Interestingly, Community law does not only impose new limits, it may
also create some additional flexibility. Thomas Vandamme (Chapter 12)
discusses two less common dimensions of discretion, namely the role it plays
in the context of direct effect, on the one hand, and in relation to transposition of directives, on the other. Here the concept of discretion leads up to
the question as to whether national parliaments are still useful agents in the
transposition process. Despite the inherently different views in national law
on the link between discretion and the level of transposition legislation,
the chapter raises the issue as to whether 'direct effect discretion' might
represent a common 'minimum level' of discretion, justifying in *all* legal
systems the recourse to swift but less democratic lawmaking procedure. In
this vein, it may necessitate convergence.

5 Selected policy areas: instruments of convergence

Not surprisingly, even the self-imposed limits of two central, and interrelated, concepts were not tight enough to keep out a broader policy perspective. On the contrary, the more we concentrated on rights and discretion,
the more we found that policy areas are the important parameter of conceptual divergence. We were able to include examples from such diverse areas
as energy legislation, labour law, and constitutional law to substantiate this

claim, but probably many other examples could have been added to the list that would have been worth looking into.[27]

Iñigo del Guayo (Chapter 15) discusses the terminological and, more importantly, the conceptual problems that arose with the gradual emergence of an Internal Energy Market that has been taking place in Europe since the early 1980s, in particular regarding the notion of 'regulation'. With the rise of North-Atlantic neo-liberalism, elements of the American concept of economic regulation began to interfere with the European notion of public economic law, which in turn influenced domestic understanding of this branch of law in various unorchestrated ways. While the EC itself has contributed significantly to promoting the creation of a common regulatory culture, the very idea of regulation is still a much contested one, as it remains contingent upon diverging ideologies about the relationship between government and society. This was evidenced by the debate on 'services of general economic interest'—a phrase that seems utterly self-contradictory in some legal cultures (where 'general' means 'basic'), and utterly self-evident in others (where 'general' means 'public', and then 'governmental'). No wonder, then, that the call for 'regulation' by EC officials was understood differently by the different parties involved, with corresponding claims and defences regarding liability issues. Del Guayo expects more from regulation than from 'harmonizing' rule making, although the former includes the latter. Working one's way 'from function to organ' (as a Darwinist account of evolution would suggest), one will gradually discover the amount of governmental influence or distance required for the energy market to navigate the rocks of unfair competition. Diminishing ambiguity in legal terminology will come in the wake of piecemeal social engineering.

Linda Senden (Chapter 16) starts from the thesis that shared common values and fundamental rights not only help to forge legal unity, but also contribute to building a common transnational identity. In her chapter she explores how far EU law, and in particular case law, has contributed to converging concepts in the specific area of sex equality law. Her analysis focuses on two aspects. First, she demonstrates that there is indeed divergent interpretation of the equal treatment principle in the Member States, especially following the recent accession of twelve new members. While EU equal treatment law imposes a certain standard of equality and non-discrimination, does it also bring more unity into this area? Partly it does so through establishing common definitions, but much more crucial with a view to realizing this is the second aspect, namely the functioning of national courts and their dialogue with the ECJ. No

---

[27] cf also the few suggestions in ch 2.

doubt, judicial cooperation within the framework of the preliminary rulings procedure contributes to a higher level of convergence in EU law. However, when taking a closer look at the references for preliminary ruling made by national courts in the area of sex equality, the author argues that one should make a distinction between more fundamental, constitutional cases and more technical cases, the latter being less crucial with a view to realizing or preserving the unity of the EU legal order. The central question here is according to what criteria such a distinction can be made, whether these criteria can perhaps also be applied to other areas of EU law, and what consequences this could have for the organization of the preliminary procedure.

Building on Luhmann's analysis of the law as a system, Emilios Christodoulidis and Ruth Dukes argue (Chapter 17) that the moment of unity of a legal system arises through a certain 'gathering' of elements incongruous to, but therefore informative for, established law. Some organizing system principles decide whether the gates will be open for recovering elements from the environment and the filters they have to pass through. The unity of the system is strengthened—or undermined—by the extent to which new acts of interpretation can—or cannot—be imputed back to their organizing principles. Focusing on European labour law, the authors suggest that the unity of labour law across divergent European traditions, as manifested in the Treaties and the EC Charter of Fundamental Rights of 2000, is the commitment to the twin principles of democracy and dignity at work. Scrutiny of 'social dialogue', as stipulated under Articles 138 and 139 of the EC Treaty, and of 'soft law', indicates that a disjunction arises between these principles and their instantiation which undercuts the identity of European labour law. Communicative 'social dialogue', based on partnership, effectively disempowers workers by concealing the structural constraints in which that dialogue takes place. The subordination of social policy priorities to the imperatives of economic policy co-ordination has the effect of relegating fundamental principles of labour law to the domain of 'soft law', thereby breaking the articulation of levels of legal decision-making that alone makes sense of the unity of the law. To argue for the unity of European law is, *inter alia*, to argue for the unity of industrial democracy at the European level, in accordance with the principles of our European constitutions.

Joxerramon Bengoetxea (Chapter 18) approaches the guiding hypothesis of our research project from an unexpected angle. Instead of exploring how the legal systems of the Member States enter or penetrate Community law by way of divergent applications of seemingly unitary concepts, his chapter analyses how a constitutional feature of some Member States, in particular infra-state regionalism, penetrates the EU administrative and constitutional ethos by calling into question the sacrosanct principle that the Member States are the building blocks of the EU. Whereas for a long period of time European integration took for granted that the internal political organization of Member States is insignificant to the EU, macro-economic imperatives have led the EU to develop a regional policy of sorts. This policy received additional impetus from the interpretation of the subsidiarity principle by some Member States, which took it to comprise three levels of governance, not two: the EU, the Member States, and the regions. The emergence of the region as a new level of governance, as underscored by the negotiation of the Catalan statute of autonomy, has led to various forms of interregional dynamics, both within states and across states. While this dynamic offers new opportunities, it also requires identifying political and constitutional principles that are sufficiently flexible to be invoked by all actors at the three levels of governance, while still retaining some interpretative value. In this perspective, the author discusses the impact of interregional dynamics on the principles of the distribution of competences and equality, the open method of co-ordination, and representational practices on behalf of the citizen. These and related principles can guide the integration of the regional dimension in EU politics, thereby contributing to the binding unity of diverse entities.

Acceptance of conceptual divergence is not only inevitable but to a certain extent also beneficial. This is a recurring argument in the various contributions to this volume. To put it bluntly, we seem to differentiate between good and bad divergence, ie between divergence that leads to incompatible outcomes and divergence with the potential of flexible integration that helps to achieve unity. While on an abstract level contrasting the two is possible, on a concrete level divergence is Janus-faced. The emphasis then shifts to another question: how to ensure that good or innocuous divergence does not turn bad? Concepts at EU level which are sufficiently cohesive but not written in stone should allow for functional flexibility in the first place. Second, the technique of consistent EU law interpretation will contribute to bending national concepts in the direction of the ultimate perspective of binding unity. Third, there is a precondition to all this, ie comparative insight and skill—partly as a basis for building common but autonomous concepts, partly—and perhaps more importantly—as a tool to enhance perceptiveness of the possible different meanings and operationalizations of the concept in other legal systems.[28]

---

[28] A discrete but also interesting attempt at stimulating such perceptiveness is the casebook by HD Jarass and S Beljin, *Casebook Grundlagen des EG-Rechts* (Baden-Baden: Nomos, 2003), in which a number of leading EC-law cases are discussed from various national perspectives.

In the last part of this volume, three papers suggest, from radically different perspectives, a number of other instruments for overcoming the problem of conceptual divergence. Niilo Jääskinen (Chapter 19) considers the central problem of the research project from the perspective of Finnish analytical legal positivism. In his view, EU law studies may suffer from methodological flaws similar to those of traditional 'conceptual' legal science critiqued by analytical positivism. In EU law, many legal concepts such as 'Community right', 'Member State', and 'autonomous legal order' are used in argument as building blocks of premises from which legal consequences are to be derived. Such reasoning may easily become superfluous or circular, supporting unsustainable analogies or doctrines, and concealing teleological or value choices that should be submitted to open debate and scrutiny. The logical-analytic tradition aimed at formal or analytic concepts because it wanted to create legal terms that were universally applicable. Yet conclusions should be derived from legal sources and methodologically controlled argumentation, not from legal concepts.

Inspired by the regulatory competition approach, Filomena Chirico and Pierre Larouche (Chapter 20), after discussion of various solutions, advocate a 'marketplace of legal ideas', ie a market-like process where legal ideas are central and where members of the legal community are the main actors. In their chapter they examine first, from an economic analysis of law perspective, the reason why legal systems would diverge (in rulings as well as concepts); second, by using methods of comparative law and contextualization (ie placing the law in a broader context, including both the policy choices underlying it and its practical outcome), they address the question of what divergence is and how it can be detected. According to the authors, conceptual and explicit divergence is problematic only under certain conditions—in particular where the costs exceed the benefits—and occurs less often than is generally believed. In their view, the remedy may sometimes be worse than the disease.

Koen Lenaerts and Tim Corthaut (Chapter 21) bring primacy to the fore as a device that may help to overcome divergence. Obviously, primacy as a conflict rule helps to foster consistency in the sense that where two incompatible norms—a national and a European one—claim applicability, the national norm is excluded. This, however, is not the authors' main argument. In their contribution primacy features as a principle that may also help to overcome another divergence, specifically that in the ECJ's discourse about the invocability of norms in courts. As the authors convincingly argue, there is some confusion as to the EU norms' invocability—itself a crucial device for enhancing convergence—since there is apparently no agreement on the foundations of this invocability. This is an important point, which we gladly underline. Another vital instrument for handling divergence and diversity is the way in which administration of justice in the EU is organized, with the preliminary procedure through which national courts are instructed how to interpret and apply EU law as a special feature. On the one hand, the ECJ can only counteract divergence to the extent that the national courts refer issues to it. On the other hand, the ECJ bears a responsibility of its own to seize the opportunities that do occur to respond in a consistent manner to the issues raised. This delicate interplay, which is discussed by Senden in the context of sex discrimination in Chapter 16, is also one of the central issues in the chapter by Lenaerts and Corthaut. The authors note that the role of the ECJ is changing. Having established the abstract principles, the ECJ is increasingly confronted with more detailed questions, which seek guidance on how to apply these principles in concrete cases before the national court. The risk is obvious: taking into account the particularities of national laws and the facts of the case, in combination with the fact that the Court can decide only 'one case at a time', may affect the coherence of case law itself.

PART 1

Observations from Legal Practice

2

Experiences from Professional Practice: Some Steps towards Empirical Research

Sacha Prechal, Linda Senden, Bert van Roermund, and Thomas Vandamme

1 Introduction

One of the aims of the BU/DC project[1] was to establish the scope of the phenomenon of 'conceptual divergence' by gathering data from the daily practice and personal experience of legal professionals involved in European law. We aimed to get some clues as to how legal practice has to cope with this divergence, if at all. To this end we drew up a questionnaire and sent it out to practitioners in the field as well as to academics.[2] Rather than prompting them to score closed statements, we invited them to reflect freely on various topics. Of the sixty people contacted thirty-four respondents completed the questionnaire.

In this report, we give an account of the response to the questionnaire: how conceptual divergence is detected, perceived, and dealt with in legal practice, and how it is evaluated in the long run. We chose to drop the structure of the questionnaire and to present the outcome in a more thematic way, regrouping related issues where it seemed apt to do so. We use quantitative expressions loosely: roughly, 'few' means five respondents or fewer, 'some' means between six and sixteen, 'most' means more than sixteen. Where desirable and possible, we put the responses in a broader perspective and,

---

[1] For the organizational aspects see the Acknowledgements.
[2] The original questionnaire is attached to this report, Annex 1 p 37–43.

where appropriate, we include relevant information which emerged during the discussions in the seminar group.[3]

Thus, this report is of an indicative nature only and does not pretend to give a methodologically sound survey, let alone an explanatory account of how the issues involved are dealt with in legal practice. Moreover, it should be stressed that both the members of the seminar group and the respondents are people used to working in a European or international context. They are therefore perhaps more aware of the specific problems that occur in such a setting, including conceptual divergence. Whether and how the issues touched upon in this empirical exploration are perceived by agents working predominantly in a national context is a subject for further research. As some of the respondents wished to remain anonymous for professional reasons, personal details had to be erased from the report. Yet, as far as anonymity allowed, answers can be traced back to certain (categories of) professions.

2 Is conceptual divergence problematic?

Most respondents recognize the phenomenon. Some indicate that conceptual divergence is incidentally problematic but only few consider it a high priority problem. Thus, most of them regard it as a fact of life (a term actually used by a number of respondents). It is understood as well as accepted as an inevitable consequence of political compromise. One respondent also described some types/manifestations of conceptual divergence as 'accidental', for instance when the EU legislator uses the alternative Dutch terms *recht* and *wet* whereas the English term in both cases is *law*. The difference between the two Dutch terms is considerable.

In some cases the respondent acknowledged that the (relatively) unproblematic perception of conceptual divergence may be specific to the area concerned (notably agriculture and competition law). Agriculture is of course densely regulated by EC law (mainly through regulations), and so is competition law. As to competition law, it was interesting to note that, despite the fact that it is often practised in an international setting, conceptual divergence remains possible in this area too. An important example is the EC concept of 'universal service obligation' in the context of state aid, as this translates into different national concepts.

[3] Cf p vii (Acknowledgements) this volume.

Some respondents perceive conceptual divergence as a challenge, others point to the sometimes unexpected opportunities it creates. As to the challenge, it was noted that it is a particularly daunting task to plead a case in a foreign jurisdiction. In order to present the arguments in such a way that a judge will understand, one has to familiarize oneself with the concepts and be sensitive towards differences. Yet divergence may also offer manoeuvring space. At an individual level, this is the case when it enables lawyers to compare different solutions suggested by diverging concepts and to choose the concept that serves the interests of the client best. At a more general level, it may help to question old 'national' solutions and to 'rethink the issues'.[4]

The relatively low profile that conceptual divergence seems to have in the perception of most respondents may explain why one rarely finds references to it in explanatory memoranda of (European) legislation, in (European) case law, or otherwise.

3 Awareness and detection of conceptual divergence

The general picture is that conceptual divergence is encountered both in dealing with case law (attorneys, judges) and in rule drafting (civil servants) as part of an ongoing process of 'translation' (in the broad sense) in EU law. It is thus implicitly anticipated all the time and practitioners are permanently, though obliquely, aware of its potential effects. These effects are detected in a variety of specific situations, without any explicit strategy to pinpoint them. The mainspring may be, for instance, that a client's interests are at stake; or that one has to compare different language versions in order to adequately draft the transposition rules of a specific directive; or that one has a chance discussion on a case or on transposition with a colleague who happens to be qualified in a different jurisdiction. Often institutional and socio-political differences in 'real life', which should in fact be addressed on the basis of policy considerations and take into account political and social values ('teleological conflicts'), trigger instances of conceptual divergence. As one respondent put it, 'conceptual divergence is detected if and when it is beneficial'.

A more systematic awareness of the problem is present, not surprisingly, in the Legal Revisor Group of the European Commission. It is a specific, daily aspect of its work, since the Group has to assist legal draftsmen in order to

---

[4] See also s 5 below.

avoid problems at the stage of translation and to check legal drafts for consistency in different languages. In fact, the Legal Revisor Group was created
intentionally to ensure 'concordance' between the different language versions of Commission acts. More recently, however, the policy of the Group
shifted to concentrate on the correct legal drafting of the 'original', ie the
language in which the document is actually drafted in a particular version
of the act at issue.

Upon further inquiry, it appears that conceptual divergence is detected
in respect of all sorts of conceptual issues, ranging from broad principles to
very specific concepts. Examples of such wide-ranging general principles
are non-discrimination and proportionality,[5] which proved to be divergent
from EC law at least in UK, Belgian, and Finnish law. Conceptual divergence also occurs regarding the slightly more specific concepts of 'social
security' (Article 42, TEC) and 'worker' (Article 39, TEC). A very specific
example of conceptual divergence provides the concept of 'setting of cash',
which in Dutch law has a meaning that differs from the identical term used
in the Collateral Directive and in Dutch transposition law.[6]

A further distinction to be made in this regard is that between the
introduction of new legal concepts into national law, on the one hand, and
the influence of EU law on pre-existing national concepts, on the other. An
example of the first situation is the introduction of trade in greenhouse gas
emissions—something that proved troublesome in Germany, where this was
a foreign concept.[7] Similarly, legal mergers and scissions of companies or
transfer of an undertaking were new notions in The Netherlands. Important examples of the second situation are the concepts in procedural law of *ex
officio* application of (European) law and of public procurement. According
to some respondents, it is sometimes easier to deal with the introduction of
totally new EU concepts than with European concepts touching upon well-
established national notions, such as 'compensation', 'property', 'goods', 'partnership', 'unjust enrichment', the *'ne bis in idem*-rule', or the 'association to

---

[5] One should note that the term 'proportionality' also means different things *within* the context of EC law itself.

[6] See Parliament and Council Directive (EC) 2002/47 on financial collateral arrangements
[2002] OJ L168/43.

[7] See Parliament and Council Directive (EC) 2003/87 establishing a scheme for greenhouse gas emission allowance trading within the Community [2003] OJ L275/32 (*Treibhausgase-
missionshandelsrichtlinie*).

commit' (ie the notion of 'complicity' in criminal law).[8] Changing 'domestic' understanding of such concepts is sometimes harder than simply introducing a new concept. Against this background, one can understand guideline no 5 of the Inter-institutional Agreement on common guidelines for the quality of drafting of Community legislation,[9] according to which '[. . .] concepts or terminology specific to any one legal system are to be used with care.'

4 Dealing with conceptual divergence

As to the possible solutions to conceptual divergence, it follows from what we stated earlier that, first and foremost, not all respondents see a need for this, simply because they do not always consider conceptual divergence to be a problem. As already mentioned, some of the respondents who work for (international) law firms actually see conceptual divergence as a potential solution or 'tool' to help a case forward.[10] In other instances, conceptual divergence is not perceived as something that needs to be 'mended', because the national concept, although potentially different, is regarded to be broader in scope than the EU concept. But insofar as conceptual divergence *is* perceived as problematic, or at least undesirable, the respondents have put forward a number of solutions.

4.1 Ex ante *examination and* ex post *clarification of legislation*

Conceptual divergence may be prevented first of all by ensuring a better formulation or definition of concepts. Thus, a number of respondents advocate a better description of EU terms in contracts, national legislation, or in European legislation itself. In preparing new legislation the Commission may (and *should*) draft comparative tables on the situation in national law systems. Already, at this stage, instances of conceptual divergence may emerge, and they should be analysed and addressed in view of the legislative proposal to be made.

---

[8] cf the brief debate in the Dutch parliament about the scope of this notion in TK, 2000/2001, 27159, no 5, 17 November 2000, 3–4, which related to the implementation of Council Directive (EEC) 91/308 on prevention of the use of the financial system for the purpose of money laundering [1991] OJ L166/77.

[9] Parliament, Council, and Commission, Inter-institutional Agreement, 22 December 1998, on common guidelines for the quality of drafting of Community legislation, 1999 C 73/01.

[10] Although one respondent admitted that the way the legal counsel deals with conceptual divergence changes when he assumes the role of an adviser rather than a litigator.

It was also observed that early involvement of all stakeholders in drafting new legislation—including national administrations, legal draftsmen, lobbies, etc—may contribute to detecting and tackling problems of conceptual divergence,[11] in addition to preparatory work done by the Commission.

The Commission may also take on a 'didactic', informative role once legislation has been adopted, by issuing clarifying statements, communications, or notices. This is in fact a technique it uses already quite regularly. An example is the follow-up of the Directive on enforcement of intellectual property rights.[12] As the key notion of this Directive—'intellectual property rights'—was not defined, in order to prevent conceptual divergence on this issue,the Commission published a 'statement' in the *Official Journal* in which it gave a further definition of what is to be regarded as such a right.[13] Another example of *ex post* clarification, for the purpose of both transposition and application, is provided by the Interpretative Communication on waste and by-products, now annexed to the European waste legislation.[14] In the case of 'waste', it took quite some time before the Commission intervened for reasons of, *inter alia*, legal certainty. Yet, in other cases the risk of divergence may emerge much earlier, for instance at meetings with national experts on possible or already existing transposition problems.

Finally, several respondents also submit that ambiguity, vagueness or poly-interpretability is sometimes created on purpose, so as to facilitate political consensus or provide a space for socio-economic manoeuvring. This phenomenon is also referred to as 'constructive ambiguity'.

[11] The national structures for *ex ante* examination of European legislative proposals by different national stakeholders are far more developed in some Member States, such as Finland, than in others. Also views on how to improve *ex ante* examination, both at the European and the national levels, may differ quite a bit. cf on this EMH Hirsch Ballin and LAJ Senden, *Co-actorship in the Development of European Law-making: The Quality of European Legislation and Its Implementation and Application in the National Legal Order* (The Hague: TMC Asser Press, 2005) 74–78.

[12] Parliament and Council Directive (EC) 2004/48 on the enforcement of intellectual property rights [2004] OJ L157/45.

[13] Commission Statement (EC) 2005/295 concerning Art 2 Parliament and Council Directive (EC) 2004/48 on the enforcement of intellectual property rights [2005] OJ L94/37.

[14] European Commission, 'Communication on the Interpretative Communication on waste and by-products' COM (2007) 59 final. For questions which are not explicitly covered and defined by European legislation or other acts, one may seek assistance from EU terminology databases, such as <http://ec.europa.eu/eurodicautom/Controller> (with a test link to the IATE site, ie the Inter Active Terminology for Europe). Indeed, much depends on the quality of these databases.

4.2 *The use of different language versions*

Since conceptual divergence is strongly connected to the notion of a different (legal) language, one of the points raised in the questionnaire was whether different language versions of EU texts are being used in order to solve inter-pretation problems of European law. Most respondents point to the import-ance of comparing language versions of rules and rulings. Very few, however, revert to explicit exercises in comparative law as a necessary basis for either well-founded discussions with colleagues or readings of different language versions. We noted that those who did engage in such explorations are all involved in major law firms, where excellent research instruments and expert knowledge on other legal systems are available. Predictably, 'comparative lawyering' is also taking place within the services of the EU institutions, such as the Legal Service of the Commission. However, the primary aim of such an exercise is to find solutions to issues which are not explicitly addressed in EU law, in particular to fill a lacuna.

Comparable 'gap filling' also takes place at the ECJ, sometimes after recourse to the Court's Research and Documentation service.[15] Problems caused by linguistic differences are usually solved by the ECJ according to the adage that the provision at issue must be interpreted in the light of the general scheme and the purpose of the text of which it forms a part.[16] In any case, as to comparison of different language versions, it seems safe to assume that hardly anybody ensures that a text is consulted in all 20—at the time of research—official EU languages.[17]

The same picture also emerged from a recent legal comparative study performed by order of the European Association of Councils of State and Supreme Administrative Jurisdictions of the European Union on the qual-ity of European legislation and its implementation and application in the national legal order.[18] From this study, it has appeared that, as a rule, national courts only use the national language version of European legislation and

---

[15] See also s 4.4 below.

[16] cf, eg, Case C-1/02 *Privat-Molkerei Borgmann* [2004] ECR I-3219, which however makes clear that this rule of thumb does not always help.

[17] Comparison with the language versions of the 'new' Member States is an exercise that has to be carried out with caution. Initially, the terminology was not very stable in many respects. At the ECJ, for instance, in October 2003, a number of lawyer-linguists from these countries were hired with a view to creating new EU-terminology or improving on the existing terminology in earlier translations.

[18] Hirsch Ballin and Senden, see n 11 above.

have recourse to other language versions only in order to solve *serious* interpretation problems. The latter observation does not imply that national
courts have a common approach to recourse to other language versions. The
Greek and Austrian courts, for instance, are more prepared to have recourse
to other language versions than their Luxemburg and Portuguese counter-
parts. Where comparison does take place, it is usually limited to a small number of languages.[19]

4.3 *Informal and transnational cooperation*

Some respondents indicated that informal and transnational cooperation in
order to (try to) solve conceptual problems can be achieved by informal networks, mostly of colleagues (trained in other legal systems). Such networks
exist, as observed above, in major law firms and also in major (international)
companies. Similarly, national civil servants sometimes have their own networks, for instance as a result of 'implementation meetings' at the Commission, or of participation in Council working groups. In some cases such
cooperation, with the objective of discussing or preventing problems related
to conceptual divergence, may be provided for in EU legislation itself. In this
regard respondents referred specifically to the Directive on the enforcement
of intellectual property rights (2004/48) mentioned earlier.[20] In brief, these are
often personal networks of colleagues in the same or an adjacent professional
area—practising lawyers, company lawyers, or civil servants.

Another possible tool is correspondence with the Commission or the
Jurist-linguist group of the Council and with the legal services of the Council and the Commission, although, as one respondent observed, the EU
institutions are not always very eager to help.

As to national courts and their cooperation and mutual consultation, it
would seem that this is not very much developed. Consultation with colleagues from other jurisdictions at court level is virtually non-existent. In
some Member States, individual judges may consult colleagues from other
courts, but only in their own country. Contacts with the Commission are
rare, and so are informal contacts with the ECJ.[21] More recently, however,

---

[19] In The Netherlands eg, the English, French, and German versions. Hirsch Ballin and
Senden, see n 11 above, 91–93.
[20] See in particular Art 19 on 'Exchange of information and correspondents' Parliament and
Council Directive (EC) 2004/48 on the enforcement of intellectual property rights [2005] OJ
L94/37.
[21] cf Hirsch Ballin and Senden, see n 11 above, 101–102.

the Association of the Councils of State and Supreme Administrative Juris-dictions of the EU has started to develop a shielded 'discussion platform'—*Forum*—on its website, which could also be used for problems of lack of conceptual clarity or divergence.[22]

In the context of collaboration of lawyers originating from different legal systems within the (legal services of the) EU institutions, issues of possible conceptual divergence can emerge rather easily. According to some respond-ents, dealing with this is part of normal—daily—business. Problems are usually solved through discussion. Similarly, the ECJ and Court of First Instance (CFI), composed of members with roots in different legal systems, are often described as a 'comparative law laboratory'. Their work requires careful listening and incisive questioning, since in their deliberations these backgrounds 'come together'. Mutual understanding can sometimes be improved by having recourse to some less conventional methods: when the CFI was given jurisdiction under Regulation 40/94 on the Community trade mark,[23] each of the judges of one of the chambers of the CFI decided to write a brief note about 'their' national system of intellectual property rights protection, *inter alia*, in order to make their legal background in these matters more explicit.

4.4 *Obtaining a formal preliminary ruling*

As may be expected, a number of respondents point to the ECJ as the ultimate authority for solving problems of conceptual divergence under the prelim-inary reference procedure. Yet, the use of this procedure appears to vary quite considerably from one Member State to another. This points in the direction of the *acte clair* and *acte éclairé* doctrines being more eagerly applied in some Member States and more reluctantly in others, possibly also in cases of con-ceptual divergence.[24] Depending on the context, and against the background of imminent divergence, preliminary reference may cause the ECJ to opt for its own interpretation of a certain concept, in view of what it deems to serve EU law purposes best. This may, however, still rely heavily on (one of the) national understandings thereof. Alternatively, in some cases, profound

---

[22] See at <http://www.juradmin.eu/>.

[23] Council Regulation (EC) 40/94 on the Community trade mark [1994] OJ L11/1.

[24] See the annual reports of the Court of Justice and the Report of the European Association of Councils of State and Supreme Administrative Jurisdictions of 2002, which was dedicated to the use of the preliminary rulings procedure in the member countries.

differences in the understanding of a concept in national law may induce the ECJ to choose an autonomous interpretation.[25]

Apart from the argument of authority, it is also believed that the ECJ is in a much better position than a national court to resolve issues of conceptual divergence, *inter alia*, since it is easier for the ECJ to compare different language versions and to conduct comparative law research if necessary. Recourse to comparative law is an aid to the interpretation of EU law itself, generally with a view to filling out gaps. Instances of using comparative law for the purposes of interpreting existing terms are not very frequent; the Court seems to prefer to give EU law concepts an autonomous meaning, as long as no reference to national law is made.[26] Yet, in order also to establish the meaning of a European law provision, problems of (national) conceptual divergence are explored in a comparative law perspective. The Court may rely here on the studies of its Research and Documentation Service, which are not usually referred to explicitly, but which often find their way into the official ECR documents through the opinions of the Advocates General.[27] Advocates General may also embark on comparative law analyses;[28] sometimes the Commission does so, too, on its own initiative, or even the parties themselves.

5 Conceptual divergence, legal coherence, and binding unity

Some respondents consider that conceptual divergence entails high risks, but, as may be expected from previous answers, the majority does not think of conceptual divergence as constituting a serious threat to the legal coherence of EU law. One respondent regarded the possible divergence in procedural law a bigger threat to the effectiveness of EU law in the various legal systems than the divergence in concepts. Most respondents perceive the threat that conceptual divergence entails for legal coherence more as an incidental than as a structural

[25] cf K Lenaerts, 'Interlocking Legal Orders in the European Union and Comparative Law' (2003) ICLQ 896, referring to Case 59/85 *Reed* [1986] ECR 1283 as an example.

[26] cf, eg, Lenaerts, see n 25 above, in particular 894ff. See, eg, Case C-316/05 *Nokia*, Judgment of the Court of 14 December 2006, nyr.

[27] cf the Opinion of Advocate General Geelhoed in Case C-119/05 *Lucchini Siderurgica* Judgment of the Court of 18 July 2007, nyr (on *res judicata*).

[28] cf the Opinion of Advocate General Sharpston in Case C-467/04 *Gasparini* Judgment of the Court of 28 September 2006 nyr (on *ne bis in idem*) or the 'classic' Opinion of Advocate General Warner in Case 30/77 *Regina v Bouchereau* [1977] ECR 1999 (on *ordre public/public policy*).

problem in the EU legislative complex. In general, the risk is thought to be acceptable, either because it is unavoidable ('a fact of life') or because of the advantages national concepts may have for the effective application of EC law.

Thus, insofar as conceptual divergence is *not* problematic, national concepts are believed to function as good 'transmitters' of EU law into national legal orders and to adequately ensure the effectiveness of EU law. This function of concepts as transmitters comes to the fore particularly in the context of implementation of directives, and it is closely linked to the old question of what transposition method should be used.[29] As is well known, the choice of this method varies from Member State to Member State and depends in every individual case on several factors, such as the technical nature of the rules, the area of law, etc. A question that regularly occurs in the process of implementation is how to integrate the European rules and national law without disturbing the system, structure, and terminology of national law (and indeed, whether such integration is feasible and desirable at all). The articulation of European law in national rules may be facilitated through translation of EU law into national concepts which may perhaps differ, but which fit better in already existing national law. This can ensure that implementation goes beyond mere *paper compliance*. In that sense, national translation is favoured over national 'import' of EU concepts, unless European legislation specifically aims at introducing a fully-fledged, coherent, and uniform system in a particular field, as it attempted to do in the field of product liability.[30] From this perspective, one may also question the rather formal and legalistic attitude of the Commission—and to a certain extent also of the ECJ—who often seem to prefer literal incorporation of EU terminology into national law. Several respondents link the transmitting capability of national concepts to the instrument of the directive and to the trend of bringing more subsidiarity to European governance. Insofar as divergence occurs in the process of such 'transmission', it was suggested that a form of healthy 'competition of concepts' may even result from this, where the 'best solution' should win.[31]

---

[29] For an overview (with two case studies) see Hirsch Ballin and Senden, see n 11 above, 50–73.

[30] See Council Directive (EC) 85/374 on the approximation of the laws, regulations and administrative provisions of the Member States concerning liability for defective products [1985] OJ L210/29. It was literally transplanted into Art 6:185 and further of the Dutch Civil Code. In France, for instance, where 'copying in' is not used as method of implementation, the transposition of the same directive took place with a delay of almost ten years. One of the main reasons was that the implementation became part of an envisaged profound reform of the liability law of producers and professional salesmen. cf G Veney, 'L'introduction en droit français de la directive européenne du 25 juillet 1985 relative à la responsabilité du fait des produits défectueux' (1998) Recueil Dalloz 291–299.

[31] See also the contribution of Chirico and Larouche, ch 20.

Whereas the risk of conceptual divergence for the coherence of EU law is not to be exaggerated, it should not be seen as a negligible aspect of EU law. Thus, the usefulness of creating more awareness of (potential) conceptual divergence at both the EU and the national levels is not contested. In particular, the increasing efforts of the Commission to consult interested parties on proposed European legislation are welcomed. Most respondents stated that in this regard further improvements should be made on 'early detection' systems of conceptual divergence. However, at the same time, the obvious limitations in terms of resources or organizational possibilities are stressed as well.

Most respondents deem that 'ironing out' conceptual divergence by way of attempting to formulate common rules is not a viable alternative. Again, some regard this issue as overlapping with the question of whether the use of the regulation is to be favoured over using the directive. But it was then often pointed out that what really matters is to accommodate divergences, against the background of different legal and societal contexts, and to leave some space for conceptual divergence. Directives are believed to be 'brilliant instruments' for this purpose. In as far as uniformity of applicable legal rules *was* considered necessary (discarding conceptual divergence), some respondents referred to policy areas subject to wide-ranging, if not exclusive, EC competences such as the CAP, and fisheries and competition law. For example, in the area of competition law the problem now arising is that of conceptual divergence within the Member States on the modalities of claiming civil damages for violations of European competition law.[32]

Most respondents stress the political limitations that are self-evident in this regard, or point to the fact that common rules are no real solution, as conceptual divergence may persist nevertheless. The latter hypothesis is supported by reference to either conceptual divergence within the legal system of one Member State or to the problems the EC legislator faces in achieving uniformity. The latter became apparent when legislative draftspeople had to deal with different interpretation problems arising from 'uniform projects' such as the 'Societas Europaea' (SE), the new European company form established by Regulation 2157/2001.[33]

---

[32] All this due to the pressure of the European Commission, which encourages the sanctioning of competition law violations by these means. cf the European Commission, 'Green Paper on damages actions for breach of the EC antitrust rules' COM (2005) 672 and its follow-up at <http://ec.europa.eu.>

[33] Council Regulation (EC) 2157/2001 on the Statute for a European company [2001] OJ L294/1.

6 Research agenda

Investigating the responses to our questionnaire has uncovered some answers as well as raised new questions that may be the subject of further research. One respondent pointed to increased regionalism as a possible cause for increased conceptual divergence. An example could be the UK, as the new devolved legislatures of Scotland and Wales may feel more inclined to translate EU concepts into their own (sub-) national concepts.

Furthermore, numerous suggestions were made for further 'focus studies' on conceptual divergence. General fields were indicated such as environmental law, general principles such as 'proportionality' or more specific concepts such as 'ownership' (in civil law), 'sale' (a problem occurring during the implementation of the *droit de suite directive* into Dutch law),[34] 'legal privilege' (in competition law), or 'causal link' (does one follow the 'causa proxima' approach or the more Germanic 'adequate Verursachung') when dealing with the action for damages founded in Community law.[35]

Interestingly, many examples for further research were also mentioned in the sphere of criminal law, a relatively new area under EU influence. Indeed, as criminal law is more and more affected by EU law, conceptual divergence problems in this legal area may be expected to increase. The problems are reinforced by the fact that in many Member States criminal law is a well-established dogmatic and statutory system that adheres strongly to what civil law systems usually refer to as 'the principle of legality'. By its very nature, criminal law leaves less scope for interpretation and deviation than other areas of law.

According to some respondents, conceptual divergence may occur in relation to concepts such as *ne bis in idem*, or 'penalty' and 'sanction' (terms that are used interchangeably in EU law, much to the confusion of Dutch lawyers to whom they mean different things). Others are 'detention', 'confiscation' (a term that in Dutch legal language triggers the question of whether it is to be translated as *verbeurdverklaring* or *onttrekking aan het verkeer*) and, again, the concept of 'goods'. Whereas it was pointed out in the explanatory remarks relating to the questionnaire (see Annex 1) that 'goods' as a private/civil law term may cover

[34] Parliament and Council Directive (EC) 2001/84 on the resale right for the benefit of the author of an original work of art [2001] OJ L272/32. The Dutch implementation simply used the concept as laid down in Book 3 of the Dutch Civil Code which, for instance, also covers the situation where art is traded in goods with only a small additional money payment.

[35] See for instance the recent Case T-304/01 *Pérez*, Judgment of the Court of First Instance of 12 December 2006, para 109: applying the formula of 'certain and direct cause'.

diverging concepts (does it include land?), the same is true for 'goods' as a criminal law term. For instance, in Dutch criminal law it was translated as *voorwerp* which is arguably a narrower concept in Dutch than in other legal cultures.

Another factor that may be further investigated is the organizational or institutional side of dealing with conceptual divergence: how should national advisory bodies deal with the problem of advising on a proposal that is continuously amended in the European process of decision–making? Moreover, even if well organized co-ordinating structures are in place, national (democratic) scrutiny may not be as intense as one might hope . Problems of this kind may prevent conceptual divergence from being detected at an early stage.

Annex 1

Questionnaire for the research project 'Binding Unity and Divergent
Concepts in EU Law'

(Faculty of Law, University of Tilburg/Faculty of Law, University of Utrecht)

Preliminary observation

First we briefly sketch the context of the research project 'Binding Unity
and Divergent Concepts in EU Law.' This provides the background for the
separate parts of the questionnaire (A to D), which is then presented. This
questionnaire will be submitted to a broad spectrum of legal professionals,
including judges, attorneys, legislative draftsmen, company lawyers, legal
translators and lawyers working with or within the EU institutions. For this
reason, it is drafted in a somewhat elaborate way and in rather general terms.
As such, it may require small adjustments depending on the professional
situation of the person answering it and (in particular) it may turn out to be
impossible to answer all the questions.

Please read the questions taking into account the proviso 'where relevant' and do not consider them as a strait–jacket, but rather as a guideline
or instrument for identifying some of the conceptual divergence problems
encountered in the legal profession.

Context

1. The point of departure of the project is that the very system of EC/EU
law as it exists today is based on a close interconnectedness between the
European and the national legal orders.[36] In particular, the EU legal order
is contingent on national legal orders for its application and enforcement. As
is well-known, this relationship between Community law and national law,
both from the theoretical and practical perspectives, has generated a wealth
of legal writing about supremacy, direct effect, and other—often refined—
mechanisms which are supposed to safeguard Community law in its application and enforcement at the domestic level. Similarly, considerable attention

---

[36] For the sake of convenience we use the terms EU legal order and national legal order, without plunging into the discussion as to whether there are several but distinct legal orders which
are interrelated, whether or not there is a pluralist EU legal order, etc.

is paid to the process of harmonization of laws, implementation of directives etc, and the problems that this generates.

Although the present project partly builds upon these analyses, the approach is different: it looks at relatively unexplored aspects of the above-mentioned interconnectedness, namely how conceptual divergence may affect the unity of the EU legal order. We define conceptual divergence as: the same terms meaning different things in their domestic (national) legal context, with potentially different legal consequences.

To give a particularly glaring example of conceptual divergence, there is a very considerable difference between the British 'rule of law', the German 'Rechtsstaat' and the French *'état du droit'*, even though translators often assume that these terms mean the same thing. Similar observations can be made in respect of concepts such as 'public order'/*'ordre public'* and 'general interest'. Likewise, what is called 'rights' in common law countries is not covered by *'droits'* or *'Rechte'*, although it is impossible to use other words to translate 'rights'. Following on this, the scope of a right such as that of 'equality' or 'non- discrimination' may differ considerably from one Member State to another, ie be interpreted in a rather formal way or, to the contrary, in a more substantive way.

A more concrete example concerns the meaning to be given to the concept of 'discretion' in the context of the state liability procedure, which comes in as an element for the assessment of whether one can speak of a sufficiently serious breach of Community law; the broader the discretion or margin of appreciation is understood, the more difficult it is to pin the Member State down on a sufficiently serious breach. Yet, it is far from clear what the ECJ means by discretion in this context. According to some scholars, discretion must be understood here as 'the legal power to choose between two or more alternatives'.[37] This would then correspond to the German *'Ermessensspielraum'*, the term which is used by the Court in the German versions of the case law. This again would correspond with the Dutch concept of *'beleidsvrijheid'*. However, the Dutch versions of case law refer sometimes to *'beoordelingsmarge'*, a sort of equivalent of the French *'marge d'appréciation'*, which is again something else than *'pouvoir discrétionnaire'* or what should be in German *'Beurteilungsraum'*.

Another, more practical, example is provided for by Council Directive 93/13/EEC on unfair terms in consumer contracts and the interpretation of the term 'goods' which is used in Article 4 (1) of the Directive.

---

[37] HF Köck and M Hinstersteininger, 'The Concept of Member State Liability for Violation of Community Law and its Shortcomings: An Analysis of the Case Law of the European Court of Justice on this Matter' (1998) 3 Austrian Review of International and European Law 25.

According to this provision, 'the unfairness of a contractual term shall be assessed, taking into account the nature of the goods or services for which the contract was concluded [. . .]'. A question which arises in this connection is whether 'goods' within the meaning of this provision also include land. In the English version, 'goods' has a limited meaning and would not therefore extend to land. The references in the German text to '*Waren*' and in the Danish text to '*varer*' have the same meaning as the English term 'goods'. Under the new Dutch Civil Code, however, land could come within the scope of this term, and also the French term 'biens', the Italian, term '*beni*' and probably also the Spanish term '*bienes*' have a wider meaning and include land. This means that it could be concluded on the basis of the English, German, and Danish texts that land does *not* come within the scope of the Directive (and the implementing legislation) whereas this probably *would* be the case on the basis of the French, Italian, and Spanish versions. Crucially, there is no 'original' language in the EU, to carve out the conceptual framework from which others could be derived.

In this sense the project also builds upon another doctrinal debate. On the one hand, there are scholars who emphasize the mutual permeation and cross-fertilization of Community law and national law, which might give rise to a sort of common law of Europe (*Ius Commune*). Others, however, reject the idea of a common law of Europe and the convergence of legal systems, since, in their view, there are irreducible cultural differences between legal systems.

The present project should be situated somewhere in between. It does not share the pessimism of the latter group, namely that conceptual divergence will necessarily usher in politico-legal failure. On the other hand, the distinctive features of 'domestic' legal orders, emerging as they do in legal concepts, should not be underestimated either. Acknowledging these divergences, the project concentrates on the question of how to deal constructively with this distinctiveness in the EU legal context.

2. Put in other, more concrete, terms: the EU legal order, as any other legal order or system, requires compatibility, coherence and a certain level of unity. On the one hand, legal concepts in this system function as 'building blocks' and as 'conduits' between the European and national level. On the other hand, they also work as 'filters': seemingly clear and well-understood concepts, which are often believed to be common concepts, are, upon further analysis, less than clear, well-understood and common. They may result in a kind of 'veiled divergence'.

To understand the causes of this phenomenon the project looks, *inter alia*, at the communication between lawyers from different (national) legal backgrounds within an intelligible common field of Community law. The terms these lawyers use are seemingly clear. Yet, upon further consideration, the understanding of a certain term—even if defined for instance, by the ECJ—is influenced by the 'conceptual filters' of the lawyers' domestic legal thinking. The meaning and effects of apparently common, uniform concepts of Community law are explained, commented, elaborated upon, etc, by EC law specialists, and they bring their national legal background to bear on the exchange. Moreover, their audiences remain at the Member State level: the French usually write for the French, the Germans for the Germans, etc. To make sense for their respective audiences, they not only have to translate but also to transpose European law into a much more parochial legal framework. In this way, there emerges a set of national sub-doctrines or sub-concepts of what is believed to be a Community concept.

However, it also works the other way around. Divergences in the understanding of concepts are not only embedded at the national level and between the different legal systems; miscommunication and confusion also occur at the level of Community law itself. All actors on the Community's legal scene (individual judges, Advocates General, lawyers at the Commission and those 'negotiating' legislation within the Council) not only have knowledge of EC law; they also have their roots in specific national legal systems, indeed in specific legal cultures. Although, in an ongoing process of comparative lawyering, they seem to contribute to convergence by a unified discourse, using seemingly common terminology, this terminology, upon further consideration, may be less common than believed.

Indeed, we may expect these mechanisms for divergence to become more complex when more Member States enter the Union. This will increase pressure on the unity of the European legal order and it will have consequences for unifying mechanisms such as the 'preliminary rulings procedure' and the process of 'harmonization of laws'.

3. *The Questionnaire*

One of the aims of the project is to establish the scope of the phenomenon of 'conceptual divergence' by gathering data from 'day-to-day practices' or the personal insights of the legal agents involved and to identify and describe how legal practice copes with this divergence. This questionnaire is drafted for this purpose. Please note that it is meant in particular as an invitation to legal agents to reflect on the issues raised, and not as a quantitative survey.

The questionnaire is divided into four main groups of questions:

How can conceptual divergence be detected? (A)
How is it possible to cope with conceptual divergence? (B)
How should conceptual divergence in the EU legal context, and the EU's
  legal order's immanent need for unity, be evaluated? (C)
Is there any other relevant information? (D)

You are invited to respond to the questions by using, where appropriate, clear and concrete examples. Further references (to legal literature, case law and other documents) are also welcome.

A. How can conceptual divergence be detected?
Do you encounter conceptual divergence in your field? Are you aware of this possibility and do you actively attempt to identify cases in which conceptual divergence arises?

How is conceptual divergence detected in your profession or organization/institution?
Are there (standard) procedures or 'aids' to detect divergence in concepts?

For instance, do you use different language versions when you deal with an EU text?

Or, for instance, do you discuss EU law problems with your colleagues, both inside and outside your legal system?

Is there a kind of (informal) network you can turn to?

Do you make comparative law inquiries?

Is there a body to turn to for clarification?

Are there any other procedures, mechanisms etc that help to prevent 'hidden' divergence, ie which try to clarify the possible problems ex ante?

B. How is it possible to cope with conceptual divergence?
Is conceptual divergence perceived as a problem in your profession or organization/institution?

If not, why not? If yes, why?

To what extent for instance, does the 'translation' of EU law concepts into your national law lead to solutions which are not compatible with the ratio, purpose of the EU rules or legal principles?

Similarly, to what extent does the attempt to simply import concepts of European law into the national legal orders (thus ignoring conceptual divergence) lead to solutions which are not compatible with the spirit, ratio or purpose of the EU rules or legal principles?

Did EU law introduce certain concepts into your legal system which were earlier unknown, or did it strongly influence pre-existing national concepts?

Is the existence of divergence made visible in your work in one way or another? For instance, does it arise in considerations of judgments, in argumentations of charges, defences, or other legal instruments, in the explanatory memoranda of (implementing) legislation or in the parliamentary discussion about it?

Once (a presumption of) divergence is established, what are the next steps to be taken?

In other terms, how does your profession or organization/institution deal with instances of conceptual divergence?

Is the solution which is chosen for a problem of divergence explicitly justified, and who decides on it?

To what extent does transnational co-operation take place with a view to finding (common) solutions for conceptual divergence?

For instance, and again, is there a kind of (informal) network or a body you can turn to?

C. How should conceptual divergence in the EU legal context, and the EU's legal order's immanent need for unity, be evaluated?
In your opinion, is conceptual divergence a risk (great/small) for the unity and coherence of EU law?

Or are national concepts (and therefore also a degree of divergence), upon further consideration, an ideal device to transmit EU law into national legal orders and thus to accommodate divergent national approaches and respond to the particularities of the national legal system?

In other words, does the national re-conceptualization of EC law concepts contribute to the effective application of Community law in the domestic legal order?

Would you prefer a separate set of (uniform) legal rules for issues which concern EU law, in other terms, a body of a kind of federal law, encompassing substance, procedure and remedies?

If yes, why? If no, why not?

Do you think that the unity and coherence of EU law would be better served if the EU actors (legislator, judges, administration) better anticipated the problems linked to conceptual divergence—eg more (serious) comparative law work?

Do you think that the unity and coherence of EU law would benefit from an increased awareness of national legislatures, judges and administrations that they are 'co-actors' in the European legislative process rather than merely its 'consumers'? That is to say, that there is a stronger involvement and commitment of national actors/authorities, such as national legal draftsmen, in the early EU drafting and decision-making process.

D. Is there any other relevant information?
How much unity do we need in the EU, and in which respects?

Could you indicate any fields or cases of conceptual divergence which could be of interest for the present project?

Do you have any other observation to make on the subject, which has not been touched upon by this questionnaire?

3

Translation at the Court of Justice of the European Communities

Leo Mulders

To translate is one thing; to say how we do it, is another[1]

1 Introduction

According to the research proposal, one of the factors which may increase the risk of divergence, especially in concepts, in the EC/EU legal order is its multilingual nature, since it may lead to incorrect, at times impossible, translation. In this context, however, incorrect translations do not seem to be a real problem, since the proposition that a translation is wrong implies the possibility of a correct translation or at least a standard for evaluating the correctness or equivalence of a translation. The obvious solution in such a case is a correction. Nevertheless, some unfortunate translations may have a longer-lasting effect.

More serious are the problems caused by situations in which translation may indeed seem to be (nearly) impossible. Legal concepts are embedded in a legal order and the concepts used in the original language/legal order may not have a perfect equivalent in the target language/legal order. This is especially true in the context of the EU: at present twenty-seven national legal orders, the autonomous legal order of the Communities, and twenty-three official languages.

This chapter, which is of a more empirical character, will deal with some of the practical aspects of translation in order to make the various actors in the legal profession more aware of the intervention of translation in the judicial

[1] W Haas, 'The Theory of Translation' (1962) 37 Philosophy, 208.

process and of the possible consequences of this intervention. Indeed, to some extent the judicial decisions of the Court of Justice are produced by translators as far as the form/language is concerned, although the content is obviously decided by the Court. In reading these decisions one therefore has to be able to identify the specific linguistic aspects.

After a description of the language regime at the Court, the function of the translators ('lawyer linguists'), the translation service and the translation process, I will discuss some of the problems encountered during translation. Furthermore, I will analyse one of the topics of the project, discretion, from the point of view of a translator. Finally, conclusions will be drawn for the various legal actors (especially scholars).

2 The context of translation

2.1 *The language regime at the Court*[2]

The rules governing the language arrangements at the Court of Justice[3] are laid down in the Treaties, the Statute of the Court of Justice, and the Rules of Procedure.[4] Since the Treaty of Nice, the Rules of Procedure may be amended by the Council with a qualified majority instead of the previously required unanimity. The provisions of these Rules governing the language regime, considered too important to be amended with a qualified majority, are therefore raised to the level of rules of the Statute in order to maintain the requirement of amendment with a unanimous vote (EC Treaty, Article 290). For the time being these rules are still to be found in the Rules of Procedure (Articles 29–31), but they may only be amended or repealed in accordance with the procedure laid down for amending the Statute (Article 64 of the Statute). All the official languages may be used in procedures before the Court,[5] a right that the Member States are not likely to give up, particularly since it guarantees access to justice.

---

[2] See also DT Keeling, 'Language, Culture and Politics in the Life of the European Court of Justice' (1995) 1 The Columbia J of Eur L, 397 and L Sevon, 'Languages in the Court of Justice of the European Communities' in *Scritti in onore di Giuseppe Federico Mancini* (Milano: A. Giuffrè, 1998) 2:933.

[3] In general this term will include the Court of First Instance, which however has its own Rules of Procedure.

[4] For the most recent versions see the website of the Court, <http://www.curia.europa.eu>.

[5] For a long time, all the official languages plus one (Irish). The official languages are laid down in Council Regulation (EEC) No 1 determining the languages to be used by the European

A distinction has to be made between the language of the case (*langue de procédure*) and the internal working language of the Court. In principle, the language of the case is chosen by the applicant. In proceedings where the defendant is a Member State or a natural or legal person having the nationality of a Member State, it is the official language of that State. In a reference for a preliminary ruling it is the language of the national court. Where there is more than one official language in a country, the applicant may choose one of them.

The language of the case must be used in written and oral pleadings and supporting documents. The texts of documents drawn up in the language of the case are authentic. Therefore the authentic version of the judgments and orders of the Court is the version in the language of the case.

Some exceptions are permitted. Parties may jointly request authorization to use another language. In addition, one of the parties may request authorization to use another language. Such authorization may be obtained more easily for the oral than for the written procedure.

The Member States may use their own language in their pleadings. The Judges and the Advocates General may use a language other than the language of the case in their reports, questions at the hearing, or their Opinions.

From the beginning (1952) the Court has used French as its internal working language at its general meetings and its deliberations. Amongst the six original Member States it was the language most widely spoken. All the documents of the Court for internal use in the procedure (preliminary reports, reports for the hearing, and draft judgments and orders) are written in French. Many of those documents are therefore drafted by non-francophone Judges. A group of *lecteurs d'arrêt* ensures the quality of the French of the document and coherence in the terminology used. Where French is not the language of the case, the 'original' French version, which is not authentic, is regarded as a *traduction*.[6]

Economic Community [1958] OJ Spec Ed series I, ch 1952–1958, 59, which has been amended with every enlargement. However, Irish, one of the languages in which the Treaties are authentic, was only introduced as an official language by Council Regulation (EC) No 920/2005. According to Art 29 of the Courts Rules of Procedure, Irish is one of the languages that may be used before the Court, although in practice it never has been. The amended Regulation establishes a transitional period during which not all Community documents, legislation, and judicial decisions will have to be published in Irish.

[6] Since June 2004 not all decisions have been published in the Court Reports. The decisions that are not published are made available in the authentic and the French versions at the Court's website, see n 4.

The authentic version of the Opinions of the Advocates General is the language version in which the Opinion is written (the original version), usually the language of the Advocate General.[7]

2.2 *The lawyer linguists*

The legal translators, ie translators of legislation and case law, in the parlance of the EC/EU 'lawyer linguists', are an important group of legal actors in a multi-lingual environment like the EC/EU. Working anonymously, they make it possible for legislative and judicial decisions to be communicated to the public at large. Both the legislative and the judicial institutions employ lawyer linguists. In the legislative institutions they mainly verify translations of general translators as to their legal content. They are also responsible for ensuring consistency between the various language versions of legislative texts, where appropriate, in cooperation with national or Community civil servants involved in the drafting of the texts. Legislative texts, above all the Treaties, are usually authentic in all the Community languages in which they were adopted,[8] whereas individual decisions and some directives are authentic in the language of the case (competition, state aid) or of the Member State to which they are addressed.

At the Court the lawyer linguists are responsible for translation itself. They must all be trained in the law and some may in addition have a language or a translation degree and many are able to translate from five foreign languages or more. Every enlargement of the Communities results in a flurry of language courses to prepare translators for their new tasks. At present about 40 per cent of the Court's staff is involved in translation (both simultaneous interpretation during the hearings by interpreters[9] and translation of texts by lawyer linguists).

While translating the judicial decisions of the Court of Justice the lawyer linguists obviously follow with great fidelity the French version of the text. In general the 'translation' into the authentic version (if a language other than French) of a judgment or an order is supervised by the 'national' Judge or the Judge 'of the language': this supervision consists mainly in a verification of

---

[7] In the past, it was exceptional for an Advocate General to give his Opinion in a language other than his mother tongue. At present some Advocates General regularly present their Opinions in another language (usually French, English, or Spanish), in particular in an effort to accelerate procedures before the Court.

[8] Formally speaking therefore it is not correct to say that a certain language version of a Treaty, Regulation, or Directive contains a translation error, as is sometimes done.

[9] The interpreters do not have to have a law degree because of the specificity of their profession: translating orally and simultaneously.

the legal aspects of the authentic version since the translators are not present at the deliberations between the Judges and may therefore not be aware of all the nuances and intricacies of the reasoning underlying the decision.

2.3 *The translation service*

For every official language of the communities there is a translation division, bringing together translators of the same mother tongue (currently twenty-two divisions).[10] Translation is always carried out from the foreign language into the mother tongue. In some divisions there may be lawyer linguists of different nationalities and with a different legal training (Dutch/Belgian, French/Belgian, German/Austrian, English/Irish, Swedish/Finnish).

However, the current number of official languages—the penultimate enlargement added nine languages—makes it impossible to guarantee a sufficient knowledge of all the languages within each translation division. As a consequence, the Court has been obliged to create a system of relay translation, especially from and to the languages of the new Member States from Eastern Europe, or in more general terms from and to the smaller languages. In this system certain languages (English, French, German, Italian, and Spanish) are used for a first translation, which serves as a basis for the translation into the other languages.

2.4 *The translation process*

Translation is carried out in two directions. Incoming documents (mainly applications, pleadings, and observations) must be translated into the internal working language—French—when French is not the language of the case, and this is the main task of the French division. Furthermore, requests for preliminary rulings and communications of direct actions have to be translated into all the official languages for information purposes (to allow Member States or interested parties to decide whether to submit a statement in intervention or observations). Observations of intervening Member States may be submitted in the language of that State, and so will have to be translated into French and the language of the case. The Opinions of the Advocates General, and the judgments and orders of the Court are translated into all the Community languages for publication. The French translation of the incoming documents constitutes the foundation of the documents drafted in French by

---

[10]   There is as yet no Irish division, see n 5 above.

the members of the Court (reports for the hearing and judgments and orders). In 'translating back' from French into the language of the case, the translator will consult and use the original documents in order to render the arguments and observations of the various parties as much as possible in their own words, wherever the Court quotes the French translation of the original. The same is done if the Advocate General quotes from pleadings, etc.

Other foundations for the translation are legislation and case law. Whenever the Court quotes from legislation or case law, it is clear the translator must reproduce these quotations literally from the original. To this extent the translation process constitutes a form of reconstruction of reasoning in another language using the same 'building blocks' as the Court has used in drafting its decision. Explicit references are easy to find. Problems are caused by hidden quotations, not immediately recognizable as such. The author will usually indicate them. In those cases the quality of the cooperation between authors and translators decides the quality and reliability of the translation.

3 Concrete examples

It is clear that in the process described above, various problems may arise. In what follows, some of those problems will be described without any claim as to completeness. They are mainly based on personal experience.

3.1 *Problems caused by the procedure*

Some of the problems are caused by the fact that from the beginning the various parties in a case, even when expressing themselves in the same language, may use different terms. Even though the differences may be 'glossed over' when they are translated into French, they may return once the arguments are 'translated back' into the language of the case and various terms may occur within one decision even though this does not necessarily imply a difference in meaning or concept. Thus it may happen that in an English language case both the terms 'company' and 'undertaking' are used, the former in the pleadings of the lawyers of the applicants, using the more common national terminology, the latter in the pleadings of the Commission using the terminology of the Treaty (Article 81). The translator is not free to 'harmonize' the terms by using terms other than those of the parties. Where he renders the reasoning of the Court, however, he will use the terminology from the established case law wherever this is quoted by the Court, which in general will be closer to the original legal instruments. Some legal actors (scholars especially) do not realize this and may be tempted to draw unwarranted interpretative conclusions from this difference in terminology.[11]

In other cases a difference in terminology may be the result of variations in the translation of the pleadings in various cases: there is for instance no real difference between *concurrence effective* and *concurrence efficace* which both occur in the case law in French for 'workable competition'. Not every difference in terminology therefore reflects a difference in concept.

3.2 *General problems of comparative law*

Inevitably in translating terms from one legal order into the language of another, a lawyer linguist will be faced with problems of comparative law. Even within the same legal family problems may arise.

A case in point is *Dekker*,[12] concerning a reference for a preliminary ruling by the Netherlands Hoge Raad. Mrs Dekker's application for a job had been rejected because she was pregnant and she claimed damages on the ground of a breach of Directive 76/207/EEC on the implementation of the principle of equal treatment for men and women.[13] In The Netherlands, this directive had been implemented in various laws, which did not themselves impose a specific penalty for a breach of the principle, so that the general rules on non-contractual liability were applicable.

Article 1401 on non-contractual liability in the Netherlands Civil Code is based on article 1382 of the French Code: 'Tout fait quelconque de l'homme, qui cause à autrui un dommage, oblige celui par la faute duquel il est arrivé, à le réparer.' When drafting the Netherlands Code, which entered into force in 1838, the Dutch legislator decided to resolve an ambiguity in this formulation (does *faute* refer to an objective or a subjective element: unlawfulness or culpa?). He specified that damages could only be claimed in the event of an unlawful act (*onrechtmatig* was added, although according to many French lawyers at the time the condition of the illegality of the *fait* was implicitly

---

[11] For a detailed exegesis see PVF Bos and JHV Stuyck 'Concentratiecontrole naar EEG-recht' (1989) 37 SEW Tijdschrift voor Europees en Economisch Recht, 301, a discussion paper for a meeting of the Nederlandse Vereniging voor Europees Recht, and my intervention on this subject during the meeting as reported in 'Verslag van de vergadering van 27 mei 1989 te Baarn van de Nederlandse Vereniging voor Europees Recht' (1990) 38 SEW Tijdschrift voor Europees en Economisch Recht, 20.

[12] Case C-177/88 *Dekker* [1990] ECR I-3941.

[13] OJ L39/40.

included in *faute*). As a result of this clarification, the Dutch equivalent for *faute* (*schuld*) constitutes the subjective element of non-contractual liability ('any *unlawful* human act causing harm to another obliges the person through whose *fault* the harm has occurred, to make it good'; English translation as in *Dekker*). In this context the Hoge Raad asked: do the facts of the case constitute direct or indirect discrimination (unlawfulness) and, if so, is it acceptable to require evidence of *schuld* of the employer for the claim to be upheld? As in French *schuld* was translated by *faute*, the French version of the judgment and the Opinion (Mr Darmon being the Advocate General in this case) left some room for ambiguity as to whether the objective or the subjective element was meant. Even though a Dutch translator will always face this problem in translating *faute*, in this case the issue was sensitive, since Dutch was the language of the case.[14]

Another typical comparative law problem occurred in Case 85/78, *Hirsch*.[15] In this German case the issue was whether an application for an import licence could be cancelled and what the effects of such a cancellation would be for the purposes of Community law. The firm concerned claimed it had forgotten to ask in its application for the import levy to be fixed in advance and demanded that the levy be fixed at the rate applicable on the date it lodged the application. After fluctuations in the import levy, the import had become economically unattractive. When the intervention agency rejected the request, the firm contested the validity of the application because of an error in its declaration. On appeal it was decided in the firm's favour on the basis of an analogous application of the rules of German civil law concerning the cancellation of declarations of intent on the ground of error. In German law this type of error is known as *Erklärungsirrtum* (mistaken declaration), but in Dutch law it is not considered a legally relevant error that may result in annulment or cancellation of an application. Is it acceptable in such a situation to translate the German *Irrtum* as *dwaling*, the Dutch equivalent term? In the context of the case, there was no objection to doing so, since the problem of the effects of error with

[14] The decision of the Court that when the penalty chosen by the Member State is contained in the rules governing an employer's civil liability any breach of the prohibition of discrimination must in itself be sufficient to make the employer liable, without there being any possibility of invoking the grounds of exemption provided by national law, might at first sight be read as meaning that strict liability would have to be introduced in the Dutch regime on non-contractual liability. However, the Court only requires an adequate penalty for any breach of the Directive and it is the terminological framework of the case that obliges the Court to express itself in this way.

[15] Case 85/78 *Hirsch & Söhne* [1978] ECR 2517, with an Opinion by Advocate General Reischl, 2530. In this case a translator's footnote was used to clarify the issue.

regard to Community law may well arise in the Netherlands in a case where a relevant error in Dutch law is at issue.

3.3 *Different language versions/grammatical interpretations*

There is abundant case law of the Court on the interpretation of Community legislation that is drafted in more than one authentic language. According to the Court a comparison of the language versions is one of the elements in the interpretation of a provision of Community law. The case law may be summarized as follows: in the case of divergence between the language versions of a Community measure, the provision in question must be interpreted by reference to the purpose and the general scheme of the rules of which it forms part: ie a teleological, systematic, or possibly historical interpretation.[16] The Court therefore does not look for the highest common factor of the linguistic versions.

Translators, however, are faced with specific problems whenever they have to deal with differences in language versions. Whatever interpretation is proposed by a party or an Advocate General or decided upon by the Court, based upon a specific version, the translator has to find a way to render this reasoning or claim in his/her language, using the building blocks of 'his/her own' language version, even where the interpretation does not seem justified in this language.

A well known example is EC Treaty, Article 81. In the French version (*affecter le commerce entre Etats membres*), *affecter* is a neutral term, contrary to the Dutch, German, and Italian versions (*ongunstig beïnvloeden, beeinträchtigen,* and *pregiudicare*), which seem to require an adverse effect on trade. Not surprisingly, in the case *Grundig and Consten*,[17] concerning a request for annulment of a decision of the Commission which declared a sole distributorship contract contrary to the (then) Article 85 of the EEC Treaty, both Grundig and the German Government claimed that the Commission should have shown that trade would have been greater without the contested agreement. Accepting the arguments of the Commission, the Court replied that the fact that an agreement encourages an increase, even a large one, in the volume of trade between States is not sufficient to exclude the possibility that it may 'affect' such trade. The dilemma faced by a Dutch translator is: should *affecter* be rendered in a neutral way by dropping the *ongunstig*, in order to bring the Dutch in line with the interpretation of the Court, or should the terms be left as they are, because they occur as such in the Treaty and in view of the

---

[16] See of many: Case C-36/98 *Spain v Council* [2001] ECR I-779, para 49.
[17] Joined Cases 56/64 and 58/64 *Grundig and Consten* [1966] ECR 299.

fact that, in German and Italian, such a simple solution is not possible. It is interesting to note that even many years after *Grundig and Consten*, on the basis of their own language version of the Treaty, lawyers may still invoke the argument that trade increased as a result of an agreement which according to a Commission decision was in breach of EC Treaty, Article 81.

Major problems arise where reasoning is based on a specific term which may only be valid in one or more language versions, while in other versions a term used is not fully equivalent or sometimes even does not occur. Insofar as translator's footnotes are allowed in Opinions of an Advocate General, the problem can be solved relatively easily.[18] However, such footnotes are not permitted in the Court's judgments. In such cases square brackets may be used to introduce the term required in the rule to be interpreted. Other cases require inventiveness on the part of the translator.

Article 14a of Regulation No 1408/71 on social security lays down the special rules applying to persons who are self-employed. A self-employed person reads in Dutch 'degene die ... werkzaamheden *anders dan in loondienst* uitoefent', and in French in a comparable way: 'la personne qui exerce *une activité non salariée*'. In a Dutch case, the Hoge Raad asked the Court how *loondienst (salariée)* in this article had to be interpreted in order to allow it to interpret *anders dan in loondienst (non salariée)*. In English the *loondienst* might with some imagination be recognized in the 'employed' of 'self-employed', but in Spanish, which uses two different concepts (*por cuenta ajena* for employed and *por cuenta propia* for self-employed), this is not possible. First, therefore, the Spanish translator has a problem in rendering the intricacies of the question into Spanish. Next, the assertion in a Spanish Opinion[19] that the expression *por cuenta ajena* does not occur in this article may be true for the Spanish, but it cannot be translated by simply using the equivalent terms in the Dutch language version of the article. In such a case the solution is not a translation but an adaptation ('adapted from the Spanish').

What should be done if something is not a question that will arise in the language into which the translation is made? In *Spain v Council* cited above (footnote 16) the Court had to decide if the Council was competent to conclude the Convention on cooperation for the protection and sustainable use of

---

[18] Alternatively, an Advocate General facing a comparable problem when discussing an argument which does not really work in his language may give linguistic information in a footnote, which will not always be translated if the problem does not arise in the target language.

[19] Case C-340/94 *De Jaeck* [1994] ECR I-464, Opinion, para 11.

the River Danube.[20] The Council Decision approving the conclusion of this Convention was based on Article 130s(1)—now Article 175(1)—of the EC Treaty, obliging the Community to take action in order to achieve the objectives referred to in Article 130r (quality of the environment). According to Spain, the appropriate legal basis was Article 130s(2)—now Article 175(2) of the Treaty—under which the Council is to adopt *inter alia* 'measures concerning management of water resources'. The Council claimed that a clear distinction had to be drawn between water management, concerning the quality of water, and the management of water resources in Article 130s(2), dealing with the quantitative aspects of water management. The legal issue in this case was that on the basis of Article 130s(1) the Convention could be approved with a qualified majority, as opposed to the unanimity required under Article 130s(2). In particular, after having compared the various language versions, the Court agreed with the Council that 'the concept of management of water resources ... covers only measures concerning ... the management of water in its quantitative aspects' and that only those measures were to be adopted on the basis of Article 130s(2). This question, over which the parties, the intervening governments, and the Court spilt a fair amount of ink, would never have arisen on the basis of the Dutch version of the Treaty (*kwantitatief waterbeheer*). Leaving aside the interesting question of how this term got into the Dutch authentic version of this article, in the Dutch translation of this judgment a tautology had to be avoided, because otherwise in Dutch the Court would have needed a number of pages to state the obvious. After consultation with the chambers of the reporting Judge it was decided to hide the tautology by dropping the *kwantitatief* wherever possible.

3.4 *Unfortunate translations*

As stated above, incorrect translations do not have to be a real problem in the context of the research project. Nevertheless it may be of interest to point out some unfortunate translations and their possible causes.

An interesting problem arose in the context of cases concerning damage caused to individuals as a consequence of an infringement by a Member State of the rights conferred by Community law on individuals, or concerning the repayment of national charges that are incompatible with Community law. In the absence of Community rules on the subject, it is for the Member States to lay down the relevant rules. According to well-known and

---

[20] Council Decision 97/825/EC concerning the conclusion of the Convention on cooperation for the protection and sustainable use of the river Danube [1997] OJ L342/18.

consistent case law of the Court, these rules should be in conformity with *inter alia* 'the principle of effectiveness'. In the English version of the most frequently cited judgments it is specified as: these rules should 'not render virtually impossible or excessively difficult' the exercise of these rights. In French this *principe d'effectivité* is expressed as 'qu'elles [modalités, règles, conditions] ne rendent pas pratiquement impossible ou excessivement difficile l'exercice des droits …'.[21] 'Virtually' is an acceptable translation of one of the meanings of *pratiquement*, namely *virtuellement, presque*. However, in this sense it is a neologism, which, even if generally used, for language purists would not be correct. The correct first meaning of *pratiquement* is *dans la pratique*. In later judgments the Court also uses the unambiguous *en pratique impossible*,[22] probably to clarify the point. In the English version referred to above, the difference between 'virtually impossible' and 'excessively difficult' seems very small; it may even mean the same. 'In practice impossible or extremely difficult' would render the French more correctly.

This is one of the pitfalls for translation: minor changes in quotations from previous case law. In this case the change lifts an ambiguity. However, even in the authentic Dutch version the formula from *Francovich* is repeated, since the passage was indicated as a quotation, but the difference in the French had not been noticed or identified as such.[23]

Other pitfalls are quotations that are not identified as such. This happens also in the legislative process. Quite regularly, various regulations or directives on the same subject-matter use different terms, whereas at least one of the languages, presumably the version that served as the basis for negotiations, uses the same terminology. It may even happen in the EC Treaty. The French 'égalisation (des conditions de vie et de travail) dans le progrès' in Article 117 (old), in the Chapter on Social provisions, is more or less repeated as 'harmonisation, dans le progrès, des conditions …' in Article 118a (old) which was added by the Single European Act. The English is close to the French: 'harmonization while improvement is being maintained' in Article 117 becomes 'harmonization … while maintaining the improvements made' in Article 118a.

---

[21]   Since Case 199/82 *San Giorgio* [1983] ECR 3595 and Joined Cases C-6/90 and C-9/90 *Francovich* [1991] ECR I-5357.

[22]   Advocate General Jacobs mentioned this more or less as an aside in his Opinion in Case C-90/04 *Haahr Petroleum* [1997] ECR I-4085, para 172. Since this Opinion, the Dutch translation has in principle rendered *pratiquement* as *in de praktijk*. The English versions still seem to use 'virtually' although one also finds 'in practice'.

[23]   Case C-312/93 *Peterbroeck* [1995] ECR I-4599 and Joined Cases C-430/93 and C-431/93 *Van Schijndel* [1995] ECR I-4705.

This concordance was probably not brought to the attention of all 'translators' of the Single Act. At least in Dutch, Article 117 diverges strongly from Article 118a 'onderlinge aanpassing *op de weg van de vooruitgang*', respectively 'harmonisatie *bij de verbetering* van de ... omstandigheden' (*sic*). As a consequence, any reasoning of the Court based on the double occurrence of *dans le progress* in those articles may cause serious translation problems.[24]

3.5 Discretion

To finish the discussion of examples, I would like to make some observations on 'discretion', one of the main topics of the project, from the perspective of a translator. The contributions to this project have mainly been drafted in English, whereas the judgments of the Court quoted in the contributions were originally drafted in French. 'Discretion' is regularly used as a translation for (i) *pouvoir d'appréciation, marge d'appréciation* or *pouvoir discrétionnaire*. In the exercise of this *pouvoir* the institutions may be called upon to (ii) *apprécier les effets, apprécier une situation* or, as it is sometimes referred to, *évaluer les faits*, and in this process they may run into an (iii) *erreur d'appréciation*. The Court in its judicial review regularly indicates that it cannot (iv) *substituer son appréciation* for that of the institution concerned. In the French version of the case law therefore the Court formulates its rulings around the verb *apprécier* and the noun *appréciation*. This verb–noun relationship may get lost once it is rendered into other languages. Some random research on English translations shows that in general the terms under (i) are rendered with 'discretion', the terms under (ii) with 'appraise' or 'assess', those under (iii) with 'error in the appraisal', and those under (iv) with 'appraisal'. Even though the English is relatively consistent, discretion and appraise or appraisal do not have the same relationship of verb–noun. In Dutch it is possible to use *beoordeling* and *oordeel*, more or less the same verb–noun relationship and meaning as in the French. Is this also possible in other languages? The wide variation of terms mentioned in the chapter by Michiel Brand (footnote 8) seems to suggest otherwise.

In this specific case it seems advisable for the translators to remain as close as possible to the words used by the Court, and perhaps even to distance themselves from the doctrinal debates on the various elements and aspects of discretion in order to avoid nuances from a national legal order being

---

[24] Case C-84/94 *United Kingdom v Council* [1996] ECR I-5755, on Council Directive 93/104/EC concerning certain aspects of the organization of working time [1993] OJ L307/18. In this politically sensitive case, the Dutch translation was made in close consultation with the Dutch Judge.

introduced into the Court's case law through their translation. Translations which are closer to the French leave room for an autonomous development of the concept in Community law. It is for the Court to decide if some national elements should be integrated into the Community concept. These elements may then be commented upon by scholars, identifying the various aspects of the concepts used or not used, after verification that the conclusions reached are supported by the French version.

4 Conclusions and recommendations

According to Article 33 of the Vienna Convention on the Law of Treaties, the text of a treaty authenticated in two or more languages is equally authoritative in each language and the terms of the treaty are presumed to have the same meaning in each authentic text. Even though in practice some language version(s) may have served as a basis for negotiation or as the original during a legislative process, this does not make this/these version(s) more important than the other version(s). It is one of the tasks of the international judicial institutions to determine the meaning of the concepts used.

However, with regard to the case law of the Court of Justice of the European Communities a distinction should be made between an original version (French), the authentic version (the language of the case), and the translations. Legal actors having to interpret concepts in the case law of the Court, are well advised to consult not only their language version of the judgment or order, but also the French version and, if possible, the authentic version. Close reading of judgments in only one language may be risky. A variation in terms used does not necessarily imply a difference in meaning. It matters whether those variations occur in the French, in the authentic version, or in a translation. This is the only way to determine whether a difference in terminology is the result of a deliberate decision by the Court or is the result of translation, with the small proviso that even a difference in the French might be the result of translation of the procedural documents into French.

Within the Communities, where communication between the national and international levels depends on translation, all the legal actors concerned should be aware of the possible effects of the intervention of translation and of the conditions which have to be fulfilled for translators to be able to produce reliable translations of good quality. It should be borne in mind that translators do not always have at their disposal all the necessary information and, because of workload, do not always have the time needed for very detailed research. They depend to a large extent on the authors.

Parties should produce concise and clearly written pleadings which take into account the fact that they have to be translated: it may be difficult to find satisfactory translations for national 'legal jargon', and obscurity in meaning may be aggravated by translation.[25]

Although the translation directorate is one of the services of the Court, a certain level of autonomy for translation is inevitable, since it is impossible for the Court (its twenty-seven Judges and eight Advocates General) to supervise closely the daily work of a service of around 750 people. Neither is it practicable for the Court to deliberate on all the language versions of its decisions (as is still possible in the Benelux Court), nor to take all possible linguistic problems into account during its deliberations, quite apart from the fact that not all the Judges participate in the formation deciding the case. The Court as author should therefore provide the translators in all circumstances with accurate information on quotations or on nuances or differences in concepts or quotations that have been introduced deliberately. In general, whenever terms or concepts have been the subject of debate or play an important role in the case, adequate information will be the best guarantee for a reliable and equivalent translation, which for many legal actors is their only source of information on the case law of the Court.

If this chapter has contributed to a better understanding of the practical difficulties regularly met by the lawyer linguists at the Court, and of the problems caused by translation, it may also have contributed to a clearer delimitation of divergences in concepts, insofar as it helps to clarify where a difference in terminology may be the contingent result of the intervention of translation.

[25] Notes for the guidance of Counsel, January 2007, <http://curia.europa.eu>, point 14(a).

PART II

Rights

4

Rights in the European Landscape: A Historical and Comparative Profile

Michele Graziadei

1 Introduction

The making of European polity over the centuries has produced a stock of key ideas that are today shared across Europe. The notion that citizens have rights that are protected through adjudication is one of these key ideas. The European construction created in 1957 by the six original Member States of the European Economic Community depends upon this idea to the extent that the working of community law today cannot be explained without it. The European Convention on Human Rights signed in 1950 is based on the same premise, insofar as the text of the Convention allows individual complaints regarding the violation of human rights.

Upon closer examination, however, the rich common heritage underlying these foundational texts shows that the central notion of a right—deployed in countless instances by lawyers and lay people alike—remains controversial. The role that this notion should play in the legal system is controversial too. In fact, the variety of points of view that emerge across Europe on these issues is such that simply to go beyond the general opening statements of this chapter is to embark on troubled waters.[1]

This contribution aims to clarify the origins of the difficulties described above. It assumes that a historical and comparative treatment of the topic

---

[1] My attempt to delve into these waters is: M Graziadei 'Diritto soggettivo, potere, interesse' in G Alpa *et al*; R Sacco (ed), *Il diritto soggettivo in Trattato di diritto civile* (Torino: Utet, 2001) 3–102.

may help to address them. The following pages therefore investigate several chapters in legal history that either highlight the importance of rights in the actual working of legal systems, or else challenge their importance. These chapters fit within the wider European framework which contains a variety of approaches to the topic. This essay therefore also covers national legal traditions concerning rights and their resistance to change. The main underlying argument is that the resilience of these national traditions in Europe is primarily linked to the intellectual legacy of the nineteenth century and its twentieth-century aftermath. That legacy is now a shambles. This unpleasent diagnosis has been around for a long time, but little has been done so far to remedy it. This contribution advances the argument that in this field, as in other fields, finding a cure requires looking beyond national traditions and stereotypes and recognizing that it is by far more productive to think in terms of a common European legal culture.[2]

2 Legal rights and individual liberty: the gaze of the nineteenth-century classics

'Toute société dans laquelle la garantie des droits n'est pas assurée, ni la séparation des pouvoirs déterminée, n'a pas de Constitution'.[3]

With this article, the French *Déclaration des droits de l'homme et du citoyen* of 1789 effectively set the stage for nineteenth-century debates over rights in Europe. The Declaration imposed the protection of rights as the principal test to assess the features of political union among citizen. Its text contains provisions dedicated to several fundamental rights, and the doctrine of separation of powers was then conceived as the most effective guarantee of those rights. In historical terms, the Declaration was the death knell for the *ancien régime* in Europe, despite the subsequent Restoration. But the Declaration (like so many other documents of that kind) did not answer the single most

---

[2] S Prechal, *Directives in EC Law* (2nd edn, Oxford: Oxford University Press, 2005) ch 6, on directives as the sources of rights, has provided inspiration in this respect. See also M Aziz, *The Impact of European Rights on National Legal Cultures* (Oxford: Hart, 2004). While the present essay reached the stage of galley proofs I hit upon FE Bignami 'Creating European Rights: National Values and Supranational Interests' (2005) 11 Columbia J Eur L, 241. This brilliant article makes a fundamental contribution to the analysis of key points related to my theme.

[3] Art 16 *Déclaration des droits de l'homme et du citoyen*. I will not attempt to survey the historical questions related to this fundamental document.

important question that should be posed before using the notion of a right as a working tool. What is a right? And second, what does one mean by speaking of a right? Politicians have the luxury of leaving these questions unanswered; lawyers, who have to work with them, must tackle them.

It is well known that among the many notions explicitly framed by Roman jurists we do not find definitions of, or speculation on, this concept. Hence, the repository of Roman law provided only enough raw materials to frame the notion, or to decide its meaning.[4] Medieval and early modern legal science used the concept in a number of contexts and proposed definitions of it.[5] But nineteenth-century legal science could begin anew the exercise of reflecting on rights because it had already witnessed the rapid decline of the natural law idea that linked the concept of law (*ius*) with that of justice (*iustum*). The decline of natural law distanced the nineteenth century from previous centuries. In the new age, the main theoretical problem which kept mainstream legal thought busy was how to reconcile law and liberty, rather than law and justice, as had been the case in previous ages.[6] The notion of a right was discussed and developed, first of all, to provide an answer to this fundamental question. In the following pages, I will concentrate on this aspect of the story. I will not try to address the historical dimensions of the important tradition that in the latter part of the nineteenth century and in the first half of the twentieth century pursued the theme of justice through arguments about community, solidarity, and social approaches to the law. This 'social' theme will only be approached in the light of its contemporary relevance at the European level, and this is mostly linked to the ambivalent notion of social rights (see below, section 8).[7]

---

[4] But see now C Donahue Jr, 'Ius in the Subjective Sense in Roman Law: Reflections on Villey and Tierney' in *A Ennio Cortese*, vol 1 (Rome: Il Cigno, 2001) 506.

[5] B Tierney, *The Idea of Natural Rights: Studies on Natural Rights, Natural Law and Church Law 1150–1625* (Atlanta: Scholars Press, 1997). M Kriechbaum, *Actio, ius und dominium in den Rechtslehren des 13. und 14. Jahrhunderts* (Ebelsbach: Aktiv, 1996). On the emergence of the notion of '*subjectives Recht*', which had an original meaning different from that commonly accepted today: A Guzmán Brito, 'Historia de la denominación del derecho-facultad como "subjetivo"' in O Condorelli (ed), *Panta rei. Studi dedicati a Manlio Bellomo*, vol 2 (Roma: Il Cigno, 2004) 525.

[6] For a different way to frame this theme see the classic essay by I Berlin, *Two Concepts of Liberty* (rev edn 2002, Oxford: Clarendon Press, 1958).

[7] The complex motives that originated the above-mentioned social approach to the law cannot be explored here, but several excellent contributions cover the topic from different perspectives: D Kennedy, 'Three Globalizations of Law and Legal Thought: 1850–2000' in D Trubek and A Santos (eds), *The New Law and Economic Development: A Critical Appraisal* (Cambridge: Cambridge University Press, 2006) 18; F Ewald, *Histoire de l'État-providence* (Paris: Grasset, 1996) and P Grossi, *An Alternative to Private Property: Collective Property in the Juridical*

The work of Savigny, both because of its clarity and because of its great influence, is paradigmatic of the approach that in the nineteenth century linked rights to liberty. According to Savigny, a right is the sphere in which the individual will 'rules independently of any other will'.[8] The notion of a right therefore partakes of the task which is the task of law in general, that is to establish 'an invisible boundary, inside which the existence and the activity of each can enjoy a space that that is free and secure'.[9] But according to this theory rights derive from the law, rather than from natural law concepts of justice. Rights are just one aspect of legal relationships, which are relationships among persons governed by the law.[10] The immediate philosophical precedent of this outlook on rights is Kant's proclamation that the law is simply the whole of the conditions under which 'the voluntary actions of any one person can be harmonized in reality with the voluntary actions of every other person, according to a universal law of freedom'.[11]

This approach restates in other terms the Lockean idea that the law exists to protect (absolute) rights. In England we witness the same transition. Blackstone's *Commentaries*, first published in 1765, still linked the protection of rights and the establishment of human laws to natural law:

For the principal aim of society is to protect individuals in the enjoyment of those absolute rights, which were vested in them by the immutable laws of nature; but which could not be preserved in peace without that mutual assistance and intercourse, which is gained by the institution of friendly and social communities. Hence it follows, that the first and primary end of human laws is to maintain and regulate these *absolute* rights of individuals.[12]

The treatment of the topic by John Austin in 1832 is clearly different:

Consciousness of the Nineteenth Century (Chicago: University of Chicago Press, 1991). The Study Group on Social Justice in European Private Law is now reviving this legacy. On the impact of this move in today's Europe: U Mattei and FG Nicola, 'A "Social Dimension" in European Private Law? The Call for Setting a Progressive Agenda' (2007) 7 Global Jurist, Frontiers, Art 2. Available at <http://www.bepress.com/gj/vol7/iss1/art2>.

   [8] FC von Savigny, *System des heutigen Römischen Rechts*, vol 1 (Berlin: Veit, 1840) para 52.
   [9] Von Savigny, see n 8 above, para 52. This notion goes back to Donellus, at least.
   [10] Von Savigny, see n 8 above, para 4, 52.
   [11] I Kant, *The Metaphysics of Morals* (Cambridge: Cambridge University Press, 1996; first published 1797) 230. On rights in Kant's philosophy: AD Rosen, *Kant's Theory of Justice* (Ithaca: Cornell University Press, 1993) 82–114.
   [12] W Blackstone, *Commentaries on the Laws of England*, vol 1 (Chicago: University of Chicago Press, 1979; first published 1765) 120.

But the final cause or purpose for which government ought to exist is the further-ance of the common weal to the greatest possible extent. And it must mainly attain the purpose for which it ought to exist, by two sets of means: *first*, by conferring such rights on its subjects as general utility commends, and by imposing relative duties (or duties corresponding to the rights) as are necessary to the enjoyment of the former: *secondly* by imposing such absolute duties (or by imposing such duties without cor-responding rights) as tend to promote the good of the political community at large, although they promote not specially the interests of determinate parties.[13]

Nonetheless, even though the intellectual climate of the age was positivistic, law could still be conceived as a system of rights. Indeed, by separating each individual entitlement from every other, rights are still conceived of as the cor-nerstone of the legal system, as later legal German legal authors proclaimed.[14] On the basis of this foundation, several generations of scholars in Germany extolled the notion of a right as central to an understanding of what the law is, and drew attention to it. This approach was certainly not linked to the pecu-liar conditions of German law in the nineteenth century; it could therefore be imitated, and was actually echoed, elsewhere.

In Italy, the teaching of the German writers had a wide resonance which was first linked to the spreading of the Pandectists' teaching of the Roman law, but then took a more general character as it spread to the treatment of Italian law in its different branches. But even outside the circle of Romanist legal systems the German reflection on rights had a substantial influence. In England, Austin's jurisprudence adopted it and thus inaugurated a stream of works on jurisprudence that spilled plenty of ink over the notion of a right—to the benefit of English readers—at a time when German legal sci-ence provided inspiration for English students of jurisprudence. Yet, though Austin and some of his followers stressed the importance of developing a systematic approach to the law, in England the idea had less influence out-side the sphere of jurisprudence. In England, therefore, rights did not suc-ceed in gaining status as a building block of the legal system. Indeed, the few attempts to recast the law in systematic form were unsuccessful, as per-haps was to be expected, given the weakness of the institutional tradition, the lack of a powerful academic profession, and a certain taste for pragma-tism.[15] Nonetheless, English, legal theory accepted the idea that rights were

[13] J Austin, *The Province of Jurisprudence Determined* (Cambridge: Cambridge University Press, 1995; first published 1832) 224.

[14] See, eg, I Bekker, *System des heutigen Pandektenrechts*, vol 1 (Weimar: Böhlau, 1886) para 18, 46.

[15] On the link between rights and the systematic treatment of the law see: P Birks, 'Introduc-tion' in P Birks (ed), *English Private Law* (Oxford: Oxford University Press, 2000) xxxvff. On the

essentially spheres of liberty, free from interference by others. A classic expression of this idea can be found in one of the foundation texts of political liberalism, the celebrated essay *On Liberty* (1859) by John Stuart Mill who, like Savigny, justified this assumption by arguing that such liberty was to be respected so long as it did not interfere with the liberty of others.[16]

3   Legal rights and utilitarian considerations: of rights and interests

Though the success of the theory that rights exist to protect individual freedom was immense, even such immense success should not obscure other approaches that have had a lasting influence. At the beginning of the nineteenth century the most remarkable of these alternative approaches superintended the birth of the French civil code. Later on in the same century, it was revived by Rudolf von Jhering, who embraced it in an effort to defeat the idealism of the Pandectists' approach to the law.

The drafters of the French civil code knew all too well that any revolution unravels the basis of civil life though it may lead to the installation of a new order. A recurrent question in the debates leading to the adoption of the civil code was therefore what cement could keep society together after the collapse of the old order. The question had no obvious answer when tackled from an idealistic standpoint. But where all ideals fail, the appeal to personal interest may still contribute profitably.[17] Portalis, a leading light among the makers of the French civil code, was clear on this point: 'C'est sourtout par l'intérêt qu'on retient les hommes'.[18] The new legislation relied on self-interest 'puissant mobile des actions humains'[19] to provide some of the cement of society. This

---

impact of the academic contribution to the development of English law: N Duxbury, *Jurists and Judges: An Essay on Influence* (Oxford: Hart, 2001) and A Braun, *Giudici e Accademia nell'esperienza inglese. Storia di un dialogo* (Bologna: Il Mulino, 2006).

[16]   JS Mill, *On Liberty* (New York: Norton, 1975; first published 1858) 11–13, 87.

[17]   Landmark studies in this field include: F Niort, *Homo Civilis: Contribution à l'histoire du Code civil français* (Aix-Marseille: Presses Universitaires d'Aix-Marseille, 2004); XD Martin, *Human Nature and the French Revolution: From the Enlightenment to the Napoleonic Code* (New York: Berghahn, 2001) and S Solimano, *Verso il Code Napoléon: il progetto di codice civile di Guy Jean-Baptiste Target (1798–1799)* (Milano: Giuffrè, 1998).

[18]   JEM Portalis in PA Fenet (ed), *Recueil complet des travaux préparatoires du Code civil*, vol 12 (Paris: 1827) 268.

[19]   Tribunal d'Appel d'Agen in Fenet, see n 18 above, vol 6, 35.

was a necessary step because the law is not made 'pour un monde imaginaire, mais pour les hommes tels que les a formés la nature'.[20] Therefore the civil code could ultimately be understood as a law based on the mix of 'un corp de lois destinées à diriger et à fixer les relations de sociabilité, de famille et d'intêret qu'on entre eux des hommes qui appartiennent à la même cité'.[21] These relationships unite individuals who would otherwise be as isolated as grains of sand. Within this picture, individual will responds to the appeal of interests; rights must obey the same logic.

Though these ideas invite speculation about the place of Bentham's utilitarianism in the development of the codification project, the intellectual legacy backing them was very much in touch with the French tradition of thought rooted in Jansenism. That tradition suggested the possibility of snatching good from evil by re-evaluating the role of egoism as a positive factor in social and economic interaction.

In the second half of the nineteenth century, the revolt against will theories of rights that was launched by Rudolf von Jhering was very much inspired by the same theme. Jhering argued that the substance of legal rights is the interest that lies at their roots.[22] In his view, the protection of the right is provided by the legal system is introduced only to permit the satisfaction of that interest, as a means to that end—to paraphrase the title of one of his books. This doctrine attacked the idealistic approach to rights of mainstream German legal doctrine. Jhering dethroned individual will from the place of honour that Savigny and his followers (like Windscheid) had given it. But far from being universally accepted, Jhering's iconoclastic approach met substantial resistance. In the twentieth century, Kelsen rejected it on the basis of arguments that are directly reminiscent of nineteenth-century legal formalism.[23]

---

[20] JB Treilhard in Fenet, see n 18 above, vol 9, 556.

[21] JEM Portalis in Fenet, see n 18 above, vol 6, 35.

[22] R von Jhering, *Geist des römischen Rechts auf den verschiedenen Stufen seiner Entwicklung*, vol 3.1 (Leipzig: Breitkopf & Härtel, 1874–1878) para 60, 317ff. For an enlightening discussion of this theme in the context of a full analysis of Jhering's legal philosophy: N Duxbury, 'Jhering's Philosophy of Authority' (2007) 27 Oxford J of Legal Studies, 23. On the relationship between Jhering and Bentham: H Coing, 'Benthams Bedeutung für die Entwicklung der Interessenjurisprudenz und der Allgemeine Rechtslehre' (1968) Archiv für Rechts und Sozialphilosopie, 69. What about the possibility of rights held for the interest of beneficiaries, such as those held by a trustee, under the theory advanced by Jhering?

[23] H Kelsen, *Hauptprobleme der Staatsrechtslehre entwickelt aus der Lehre vom Rechtssatze* (Tübingen: Mohr, 1911) 576.

4 A common nineteenth-century theme: the lack of constitutional protection of individual rights and the subsequent rise of judicial review of legislation

By the early twentieth century the consequences of the nineteenth-century rejection of natural law and the parallel growth of legal positivism were beginning to become manifest. The ascent of positivism and the decline of natural law had removed all the traditional checks on the lawmaking power of sovereigns. In nineteenth-century Europe, therefore, rosy discourses about rights faced the reality of the unlimited lawmaking power of governments. In this context, rights could have only a restricted meaning. Rights existed only insofar the political will expressed in legislative acts did not rule otherwise. How could rights then be entrenched and protected from encroachments deriving from the exercise of legislative power? In Europe, the question had no obvious answer because rights were not yet considered as checks of the lawmaking power of the legislature. Solemn proclamations of rights at the constitutional level did not yet work as judicially enforceable tests of the limits of legislative power.

In nineteenth-century Britain, the need for such checks and tests was not apparent, given the assumption that British arrangements especially favoured liberty.[24] A tradition going back (at least) to the seventeenth century held that Britain had invented the effective protection of fundamental rights, or liberties, through the establishment of the rule of law. The influence of this tradition was apparent in Blackstone's approach to the subject and is clearly reflected in Dicey's classic work on the English constitution.[25] Dicey's *Introduction to the Law of the Constitution*, unlike Blackstone's work, appeared at a time when written constitutions providing for the formal guarantee of rights were already enacted in many countries. Yet, for Dicey, the absence of formal guarantees of rights—despite the principle of the sovereignty of parliament—was a minor point, in the light of the English constitutional tradition and its adherence to the rule of law.

On the continent, fear that the enforceability of fundamental rights proclaimed in constitutional charters could lead to terror, as had happened in

---

[24] On this point I rely on: AWB Simpson, *Human Rights and the End of the Empire: Britain and the Genesis of the European Convention* (Oxford: Oxford University Press, 2001) 18ff, 23ff.

[25] On Dicey see s 5 below.

revolutionary France,[26] loomed large behind the idea that proclamations of fundamental rights at the constitutional level could not be enforced in courts of justice. Eventually, the more moderate American version of constitutionalism arrived in Europe, and provided an alternative to Jacobin notions of fundamental rights and popular government. This in turn effectively established judicial review of legislation as a means of guaranteeing constitutionally protected rights. Thus, between the end of the nineteenth century and the beginning of the twentieth century, the Viennese jurist Georg Jellinek, the foremost public law scholar of the age, looked to the American constitutional experience and to its Puritan background as a source of inspiration to approach the idea of judicial review of legislation.[27] This was eventually realized in Austria by his former student—Hans Kelsen. A way of thinking that had first blossomed in the USA had come to Europe.

After the Second World War, the judicial review of legislation became a feature of many national legal systems in continental Europe, though both the UK and France (*inter alia*) for different constitutional reasons have chosen alternative ways of ensuring respect for rights. In historical terms, the birth of judicial review of legislation was clearly a step beyond the judicial control of administrative action that had been established in several European states during the nineteenth century. National systems of judicial review in the European continent are, by and large, not organized along the lines of the US experience, however. One could therefore argue that the closest functional equivalent of that model in Europe is the judicial disapplication of national legislation (court precedents, administrative acts, etc) that is contrary to overriding European Community sources. Even legal systems that do not allow judicial review of legislation under the national constitution have opened the doors to this check.

5 Some scepticism about rights: duties and remedies as ways to avoid the language of rights in England

While on the European continent lawyers were busy with the question of how to protect rights from the absolute power of the legislature, in England

---

[26] How French constitutionalism overcame that initial phase is illustrated by J Bell, *French Constitutional Law* (Oxford: Clarendon Press, 1992) 20ff.

[27] D Kelly, 'Revisiting the Rights of Man: Georg Jellinek on Rights and the State' (2004) 22 Law and History Rev, 493.

the notion of a right as a proper tool to adjudicate claims attracted growing scepticism.[28] Despite the fact that nineteenth-century works on jurisprudence in England discussed the concept it was not prominent in the adjudication of private claims. On the contrary, in the latter part of the century, the birth of an academic literature dealing with rights was accompanied by strong doubts about the real value of the concept as a tool to adjudicate claims. Possibly as a reaction to the contact with continental legal theory, leading figures in the common law world questioned its utility and relevance. In the 1870's both Fredrick Pollock and Oliver Wendell Holmes rejected the idea of conceiving of rights as the building blocks of the law. This move was an open criticism of Austin's jurisprudence, which by the last quarter of the nineteenth century was considered to be a rough pioneering effort rather than the ultimate word on the subject.

Fredrick Pollock, one of the major figures among the jurists of the Victorian age, was explicit on the point:

So far as it is worth while to indicate any general preference in classification, and other things being equal, duties appear to come in the natural and logical order before rights, for it is of the essence of the law to assign rules of conduct, and the rule of conduct which did not affirm some kind of duty would not be a rule. [29]

On the other side of the Atlantic, Holmes, a leading figure of Anglo-American jurisprudence, was even sharper:

---

[28] The general theme is addressed by several valuable contributions: S Whittaker, 'The Terminologies of Civil Protection: Rights, Remedies and Procedures' in B Pozzo and V Jacometti (eds), *Multilingualism and the Harmonization of European Law* (The Hague: Kluwer, 2006) 45–60; P Legrand, 'European Legal Systems are not Converging' (1996) 45 ICLQ, 52, 70–71; G Samuel, 'Epistemology, Propaganda and Roman Law: Some Reflections on the History of the Subjective Right' (1989) J of Legal History 161 and '"Le droit subjectif" and English Law' (1987) CLJ, 264; FH Lawson, '"Das Subjektive Recht" in the English law of Torts' repr in FH Lawson, *Many Laws* (Amsterdam: North-Holland Pub Co, 1977) 176. A related intriguing theme is why English law never accepted a doctrine of abuse of rights. P Catala and JA Weir, 'Delicts and Torts: A Study in Parallel' (1962) 37 Tulane L Rev, 221, 237, argue that, as English courts declared rights so restrictively, 'there is little need for an equitable temperance of their exercise'. For a second look at the question: M Taggart, *Private Property and Abuse of Rights in Victorian England* (Oxford: Oxford University Press, 2002) 145ff. Of course, in England as elsewhere, legal philosphers have often been more willing to reflect on rights than on other categories. This explains why twentieth-century English legal philosophy has nonetheless greatly contributed to the continuing relevance of rights in jurisprudential terms (and thus to their relevance for the development of the law in general).

[29] F Pollock, *A First Book of Jurisprudence for the Students of the Common Law* (2nd edn, London: Macmillan, 1904) 73–74 and 'Law and Command' (1872) L Magazine and Rev, 189.

Duties precedes rights logically and chronologically. Even those laws which in form create a right directly, in fact either tacitly impose a duty on the rest of the world, as in the case of patents, to abstain from selling the patented article, or confer an immunity from a duty previously or generally imposed, like taxation. [. . . .] Another illustration is, that, while there are in some cases legal duties without corresponding rights, we never see a legal right without either a corresponding duty or a compulsion stronger than the duty.[30]

Again, these ideas are not peculiar to the common law world, but in England they took firmer roots and became popular because of the context in which they occurred. The context was marked by the relevance of the notion of duty in the historical emergence of the tort of negligence, and by the positive appraisal of the notion of 'remedy', as opposed to 'right', in the reconstruction of the history of English law and of its unwritten constitution.[31]

By the middle of the nineteenth century, English law held that liability in negligence required the existence of a duty of care and of the breach of it.[32] Both requirements remained central in the law of negligence throughout the twentieth century as a consequence of the generalization of the duty of care accomplished by *Donoghue v Stevenson*.[33] Despite occasional doubts about its utility, the notion of duty thus became dominant in the litigation of negligence cases. Indeed, English courts are reluctant to give prominence to the language of rights in negligence cases even where that language would fit the facts.

An instance of this attitude is documented by *Stovin v Wise*.[34] Here, the Court rejected the claim for damages suffered by the victim of a traffic accident. The accident happened as a consequence of the failure of an

---

[30] OW Holmes, 'Codes and the Arrangement of the Law' (1870) American L Rev, 3–4 and 'The Arrangement of the Law: Privity' (1873) 7 American L Rev, 46.

[31] A further point to keep in mind, which will not be discussed here as it would require extended treatment, is linked to the structure and the language of the law of property. The English law of property is not centered on the image of *dominium* and the prerogatives of the owner of an asset. Hence, contrary to what happens in the civil law tradition, the notion of a right could not easily develop on the basis of *dominium*, as it did in continental Europe, despite Blackstone's vision of the right of private property as an 'absolute right': Blackstone, see n 12 above, 2. Once more, the language of property law speaks of 'interests' even where a civil lawyer would rather speak of rights: cf G Samuel, 'La notion d'intérêt en droit anglais' in G Ost and M van de Kerchove (eds), *Droit et intérêt* (Bruxelles: Facultés Universitaires Saint-Louis, 1990) 405, 435.

[32] *Vaughan v Menlove* (1837) 3 Bing NC 468; *Langridge v Levy* (1836) 2 M & W 519; affirmed (1838) 4 M & W 337; *Winterbottom v Wright* (1842) 10 M & W 109. On this development: PH Winfield, 'Duties in Tortious Negligence' (1934) 41 Columbia L Rev, 41.

[33] *Donoghue (or McAlister) v Stevenson* [1932] AC 562 (HL).

[34] *Stovin v Wise* [1996] AC 923 (HL). This case is part of a constellation of more recent cases holding that there is no general right to claim damages from a public body unless the body has

administrative authority to exercise its public law powers to order the removal of a hazard on land adjacent to a highway which was maintainable at public expense. The Court could easily have reached this conclusion by holding—as many judges on the continent would have done—that the claimant had no *right* to compel the administration to take action. The Court preferred instead to reason in terms of lack of *duty* of the defendant towards the claimant, and from a comparative perspective the difference is telling.[35] In the English context considered here rights are incidental to the existence of the duty of the defendant towards the plaintiff and of the breach of that duty. Of course, there are also indications that this view of the English scene is somewhat stereotypical. In other respects, English courts recognize the possibility of resorting directly to the language of rights to decide tort cases. Before the age of rampant legal positivism, strong statements to the effect that rights must be protected and that remedies are fashioned to protect rights were considered with some sympathy. The eighteenth-century *locus classicus* is *Ashby v White*.[36] Mr Ashby was prevented from voting at an election by the misfeasance of a constable, Mr White, on the apparent pretext that he was not a settled inhabitant. Lord Holt CJ, whose judgment was upheld by the House of Lords, remarked:

If the plaintiff has a right, he must of necessity have a means to vindicate and maintain it, and a remedy if he is injured in the exercise or enjoyment of it; and indeed it is a vain thing to imagine a right without a remedy; for want of right and want of remedy are reciprocal [. . .]. My brother Powell indeed thinks, that an action upon the case is not maintainable, because here is no hurt or damage to the plaintiff; but surely every injury imports a damage, though it does not cost the party one farthing, and it is impossible to prove the contrary; for a damage is not merely pecuniary, but an injury imports a damage, when a man is thereby hindered of his right.

Far from being dead letter, this precedent has been applied over and over in the last three hundred years, though in *Watkins v Home Office*[37] the House of

---

assumed a separate duty of care towards the claimant, eg, in the fire brigade, the education service, or the National Health Service.

   [35] Compare the language of the ECJ in Case C-216/02 *Österreichischer Zuchtverband für Ponys, Kleinpferde und Spezialrassen* [2004] ECR I-10683, involving the review of administrative discretion, which clearly focuses on the lack of rights, rather than the absence of duty.

   [36] *Ashby v White* (1703) 2 Ld Raym 938, 3 Ld Raym 320.

   [37] *Watkins v Home Office* [2006] UKHL 17 (HL). For analysis see R Stevens, 'Torts, Rights and Losses' (2006) LQR 565.

Lords refused to follow it by holding that the denial of right is not actionable in damages without proof of consequential loss.

In the nineteenth century 'right' also featured prominently in the litigation concerning the tort of inducing a breach of contract. The leading case of *Lumley v Gye*[38] concerned a suit by an impresario against another impresario for procuring the breach of the exclusive contract with the prima donna Miss Johanna Wagner, the niece of the composer. The preferred reading of the case today is that 'if you procure the commission of an actionable wrong by another then you are liable for that actionable wrong. The responsibility for the actionable wrong is a form of secondary liability.'[39] This opinion is supported by the judgement of Whitman J. 'It was undoubtedly prima facie an unlawful act on the part of Miss Wagner to break her contract, and therefore a tortious act of the defendant maliciously to procure her to do so.'[40] But the alternative reading of the case is just as interesting. According to this, the gist of the action was the violation of a right. 'It is clear that the procurement of the violation of a right is a cause of action in all instances where the violation is an actionable wrong, as in violations of a right to property, whether real or personal, or to personal security . . . .'[41] In the twentieth century this line of thought brought about the expansion of the tort, until this development was questioned by the Master of the Rolls in *Law Debenture Trust v Ural Caspian Oil*.[42]

These decisions warn about the risk of indulging in the stereotype that would simply deny the importance of the notion of a right in the analysis of the English law of torts. Nonetheless, it is true that the judicial attitude that often prefers the language of duties and remedies over that of rights is present, and it is not present by accident, since it is the manifestation of a self-conscious attitude, which finds typical expression, for example, in *Kingdom of Spain v Christie, Manson & Woods Ltd*:

In the pragmatic way in which English law has developed, a man's legal rights are in fact those which are protected by a cause of action. It is not in accordance, as I understand it, with the principles of English law to analyse rights as being something separate from the remedy given to the individual. [. . .] in the ordinary case to establish

---

[38] *Lumley v Gye* (1853) 2 E & B 216, 238.

[39] *Credit Lyonnais Bank Nederland NV v Export Credit Guarantee Department* [2000] 1 AC 486, 496 (Lord Woolf MR); see now *OBG Ltd v Allan* [2007] UKHL 21.

[40] *Lumley v Gye* (1853) 2 E & B 216.

[41] *Lumley v Gye* (1853) 2 E & B 216, 232 (Earle J).

[42] *Law Debenture Trust v Ural Caspian Oil* [1995] 1 All ER 157, 167 (CA).

a legal or equitable right you have to show that all the necessary elements of the cause of action are either present or threatened.[43]

This attitude reflects a respectable tradition that owes much to the nineteenth-century appraisal of the distinctive English path to the development of the law. Maine first called attention to the fact that remedies historically precede rights.[44] Maitland followed him when he maintained that forms of action were the essential key to explaining the historical development of the English law. He held that it was wrong to underrate this aspect of English legal history, as if it were secondary, simply because the forms of action were part of English legal history rather than of Roman law.[45] Dicey provided the salient political meditation on the subject by comparing the English constitution with the constitutions enacted on the other side of the Channel:

> The Englishmen whose labours gradually built up the complicated set of law and institutions which we call the constitution, fixed their minds far more intently on providing remedies for the enforcement of particular rights or (on what is merely the same thing looked at from the other side) for averting definite wrongs, than upon any declaration of the Rights of man or of Englishman. The *Habeas Corpus* Acts declare no principle and define no rights but they are for practical purposes worth a hundred constitutional articles guaranteeing individual liberty.[46]

The strength of the English constitution was based on: 'that inseparable connection between the means of enforcing a right and the right to be enforced which is the strength of judicial legislation'—a connection that in Dicey's opinion was wholly lacking under other constitutional regimes.[47] This stance reveals a certain diffidence towards the philosophical traditions that provided the intellectual background of the American and the French

---

[43] *Kingdom of Spain v Christie, Manson & Woods Ltd* [1986] 1 WLR 1120, 1129 (Nicolas Browne-Wilkinson VC). B Rudden, 'Torticles' (1991–2) 6/7 Tulane Civil L Forum, 105, brilliantly shows how this way of thinking fits into the English legal tradition in the law of torts.

[44] HJS Maine, *Dissertations on Early Law and Custom* (London: John Murray, 1883) 389: 'So great is the ascendancy of the Law of Actions in the infancy of Courts of Justice, that substantive law has at first the look of being gradually secreted in the interstices of procedure; and the early lawyer can only see the law through the envelope of its technical forms.'

[45] FW Maitland, *Why the History of English Law is Not Written* (London, 1888) and HAL Fisher (ed), *The Collected Papers of Frederic William Maitland*, vol 1 (Cambridge, 1911) 480, 485.

[46] AV Dicey, *Lectures Introductory to the Study of the Law of the Constitution* (London: Macmillan, 1885) 212.

[47] Dicey, see n 46 above, 199. Dicey's target was the French constitution of 1791.

revolutions. By the end of the twentieth century, the limits of Dicey's vision had become apparent, however.[48]

The enactment of the Human Rights Act 1998 was the occasion to take a fresh look at the role of rights in the law. In the field covered by the Act, it is simply impossible to ignore the fact that the law speaks of rights and of their protection. The diffidence that traditionally surrounded the notion of a right is replaced by the recognition that the language of the Act requires English lawyers to engage with the notion of a right.[49] Furthermore, doctrinal analysis devoted to tort law and to the law of remedies shows that the choice in favour of alternatives to the language of rights in framing legal issues does not necessarily avoid vagueness and ambiguity in the development of the law. The role played by the concept of duty in the development of the law of negligence in English law is non-pervasive *and* troublesome because of its complex constitution. T Weir points to the possibility of equivocation '[. . .] between the duty being, on the one hand, the duty to take care not to cause damage and, on the other, the duty not to cause damage by failure to take care (which is not in all respects the same thing).'[50] 'Remedy' too is an ambiguous concept precisely because it results from the interplay between substance and procedure. When the distinction between the procedural part and the substantive part of the law concerning remedies is explored—and quite often this needs to be done for sound practical purposes—'remedy' often turns out to be another label for 'right'.[51]

6 *L'imagination au pouvoir*: but how much? The mixed blessing of rights in the civilian world

If English lawyers have had the occasion to ponder the mixed blessings of duties and remedies, their colleagues on the other side of the Channel have had the opportunity to reflect on the mixed blessing of rights.

As mentioned above, the proclamation and the recognition of rights by various legal sources do not automatically solve the problems related to their

---

[48] Simpson, see n 24 above, 35ff, 54ff.

[49] Whittaker, see n 28 above.

[50] T Weir, *A Casebook on Tort* (9th edn, London: Sweet & Maxwell, 2000) 14, who provides the best concise analysis of the concept, notes that this confusion complicates a situation that is 'fluid, to say the least'.

[51] See P Birks, 'Rights, Wrongs, and Remedies' (2000) OJLS, 1 and R Zakrzewski, *Remedies Reclassified* (Oxford: Oxford University Press, 2005).

justiciability. In continental Europe, the awareness that an open issue exists in this respect goes back to the debate over the effects of the proclamations of rights contained in the constitutions enacted after the Second World War. With the enactment of those constitutions and the introduction of constitutional courts entrusted with the review of legislation, the third-party effects of those rights almost immediately became one of the most hotly debated features of the new constitutional landscape.[52]

Does the proclamation of rights at the constitutional level generate rights effective among private citizens *inter se* as well as against the State? This classic question now surely rings a familiar bell in broad areas of law. The international lawyer, the human rights lawyer, and the EC lawyer are well acquainted with the same problem, though the question takes a different shape in their respective fields of expertise.

Today, the debate over the effects of constitutional rights has reached the conclusion that they are capable of immediate effects in the relations of individuals *inter se*, as well as towards the State, except perhaps in relation to those social and economic rights that involve the exercise of discretion concerning the allocation of public expenditure—though this conclusion may also be questioned.[53] This is why some Members States (the UK and the Netherlands) pressed the drafters of the EU Constitutional Treaty (rejected by France and the Netherlands by referendum) to insert a provision in that text stating that the principles contained in it could not become the source of rights:

The provisions of this Charter which contain principles may be implemented by legislative and executive acts [. . .]. They shall be judicially cognisable only in the interpretation of such acts and in the ruling on their legality.[54]

This proposal is aimed essentially at foreclosing judicial lawmaking by the ECJ in the area of social and economic rights, as one commentator has remarked.[55] The thrust of such a provision shows that contrary to the

---

[52] For an instructive comparative study see S Garbaum, '*The "Horizontal Effect" of Constitutional Rights*' (2003) 102 Michigan L Rev, 388.

[53] This is a broad generalization that reflects the current understanding of the effects of the European Convention on Human Rights. For a survey of the state of the question in Europe on the verge of the accession process see the study commissioned by the European Parliament with special regards to social rights: ME Butt, J Kübert, and CA Schultz, 'Fundamental Social Rights in Europe' (SOCI 104 EN 2000) and for an instructive treatment see Aziz, see n 2 above, 97ff.

[54] Art II-112(5) Treaty establishing a Constitution for Europe. After a minor revision, the original EU Charter of Fundamental Rights was inserted into the Constitutional Treaty.

[55] S Prechal, 'Rights v Principles: Or How to Remove Fundamental Rights from the Jurisdiction of the Courts' in J W de Zwaan and AE Kellermann, *The European Union: An Ongoing Process*

conventional wisdom prevailing a generation ago, in principle, no barrier stands between the proclamation of rights at the constitutional level through the enactment of broad propositions, and their enforcement in legal proceedings. But, having said this, at the national level courts are still confronted with the need to respect—at least in form, if not in substance—the classical understanding of the doctrine of division of powers that restrains judicial activism by preventing judges from acting as legislators and administrators. At the supra-national level, however, this division of work is more difficult to defend. *Any* organ of the state may involve the state's responsibility for the breach of international obligations. Hence, the working of the judiciary and the action of courts may be scrutinized from an international point of view, no matter what the doctrine of the division of powers has to say about the distinction between parliamentary lawmaking, administration, and adjudication.

Across Europe, the twentieth century opened the doors to the recognition of new rights—social rights, environmental rights, etc. This change marked a turn in legal theory and raised new important and challenging questions. But the vision of individual rights that classical liberalism handed over to the previous century was not free from difficulty either. That is why by the early twentieth century the legacy of nineteenth-century legal theory on rights was under assault. The battlefield was the territory of tort liability, a minefield for the classical theory of rights in the legal system. This chapter of legal history imparts some lessons about rights that apply even to the new categories of rights that emerged during the twentieth century and that no one can afford to ignore.[56]

For present purposes, the focal point is the transition from a system of rules established for the protection of interests that the law specifies *ex ante* to an open-ended and flexible body of judicial methods and rules aiming at redressing harm caused by wrongdoing.

The comparative study of this subject often posits a fundamental difference between the French and the German approaches to tort liability.[57] The pillar

---

of Integration—Liber Amicorum Alfred E. Kellerman (The Hague: TMC Asser Press, 2004) 1. The pertinent case law of the ECJ is Case 43/75 *Defrenne v Sabena* [1976] ECR 455 and Case C-50/96 *Deutsche Telekom AG v Lilli Schröder* [2000] ECR I-743.

[56] Since 'duty' rather than 'right' is central to the English law of negligence the following pages do not cover English law. But there are reasons to believe that the pattern of development highlighted in the text could fit English law as well, once the notion of 'right' is replaced by that of 'interest'.

[57] Eg, D Howarth, 'The General Conditions of Unlawfulness' in AS Hartkamp *et al*, *Towards a European Civil Code* (3rd edn, Nijmegen: Ars Aequi Libri, 2004) 607. For a study focusing on the operative differences between these two approaches: M Bussani and VV Palmer (eds),

of the first approach is the Delphic provision of Article 1382 of the French civil code: 'Any act whatever of man which caused damage to another obliges him by whose fault it occurred to make reparation.' The second approach is enshrined in paras 823, 824, and 826 of the German civil code. These provisions join together different tests of liability (ie the violation of a right, the violation of a statute, and the violation of *bonos mores*). As far as rights are concerned, para 823 BGB includes a list of rights that goes back to the teachings of the natural law lawyers.

On paper, the distinction between the French and the German approaches is clear. The German approach emphasizes the idea that the defendant's conduct is unlawful when it invades interests that are protected as rights, indeed as absolute rights.[58] By enacting this requirement the German legislature made a conscious attempt to distance the German civil code provisions on torts from the vagueness of Article 1382 of the French civil code. After a narrow vote the Second Draft (*Zweiter Entwurf*) of the German civil code rejected the broad-brush approach of the French code because it was perceived to be too unspecific. Being so unspecific the argument went, the French code actually left to the judge the task of deciding what conducts were tortious or permissible. The drafters of the German civil code held that this was incompatible with the subordinate position of the judge vis-à-vis the legislature.[59] To be sure, this argument ignored the circumstance that delictual liability under French law at that time actually required the invasion of a right of the claimant (or the violation of a duty binding the world at large), despite the broad formula adopted by Article 1382 of the French civil code. Indeed, Article 1382 cc was often explicitly construed as a mere secondary norm, sanctioning the violation of a prior general duty to act or abstain, rather than as an independent ground of liability that could be invoked to generate new claims.[60]

Pure Economic Loss in Europe (Cambridge: Cambridge University Press, 2003); M Bussani and VV Palmer, 'Pure Economic Loss: The Ways to Recovery' in K Boele-Woelki and S van Erp (eds), *General Reports of the XVIIth Congress of the International Academy of Comparative Law* (Utrecht: Eleven International Publishing, 2007), 189ff.

[58]   R Zimmermann, *Roman Law, Contemporary Law, European Law* (Oxford: Oxford University Press, 2001) 57ff.

[59]   P Mossler, 'The Discussion on General Clause or Numerus Clausus during the Preparation of the German Civil Code' in EJH Scharge, *Negligence: The Comparative Legal History of the Law of Torts* (Berlin: Duncker & Humblot, 2001) 381ff. Note that the French civil code had been in force in several parts of Germany up to the entry into force of the German civil code.

[60]   See, eg, M Planiol, *Traité élémentaire de droit civil*, Vol 2 (4th edn, Paris: Librairie générale de Droit et de Jurisprudence, 1907) para 865ff.

Both in France and in Germany this view of tort law declined during the twentieth century. The idea that rights are essential keys for distinguishing between lawful and unlawful behaviour was first undermined by the theoretical and practical problems arising in the regulation of conflicting land use. In this area of the law, references to the notion of a right as a sphere of immunity from interference showed its limitations.[61] In the case of conflicting land use each owner claims protection in law on the basis of the right of ownership. The argument of an abuse of rights is the naive way out of the conundrum, providing abundant material for criticism of the famous French *esprit de clarté*.[62] In Germany, escape from the problems posed by conflicting land use disputes was found from another direction, with the removal of the problem from the field of tort law and the introduction in the civil code of a specific provision dealing with the regulation of conflicting land use (see now BGB paragraph 906).[63] The elaboration of the doctrine of abuse of rights in France did little to keep alive the idea that rights are the essential building blocks of tortious liability. If the abuse of rights theory is fully developed, as happened in France, rights cease to be essential notions in the jurisprudence of tort law. In this sense, even though it is stated that one of the functions of tort law is the vindication of rights, the fact that the violation of any legitimate interest of the claimant suffices to trigger tort liability explains why the notion of a right no longer has the function of determining the scope of protection in tort in France. Within this intellectual landscape rights can still work as defences. But rights as defences in the adjudication of tort issues is a minor issue when compared to that of rights considered as causes of action.

The relationship between tortious liability and rights under the German civil code has been no less problematic and controversial. The recognition of categories of rights unknown to the drafters of the code has been a source of tension within the legal system. Reliance on the concept of rights to expand the scope of delictual protection has been criticized because it stretches the notion

---

[61] J Gordley, *Foundations of Private Law: Property, Tort, Unjust Enrichment* (Oxford: Oxford University Press, 2006) 66ff.

[62] For the possibility of resorting to the idea of abuse of rights in this context: G Ripert, *De l'exercice du droit de propriété dans ses rapports avec les propriétés voisines* (Paris: Rousseau, 1902). Against it: M Planiol, *Traité élémentaire de droit civil*, vol 2 (7th edn, Paris, 1917) paras 871–872bis, 278ff.

[63] The seminal article was by R Jhering, 'Zur Lehre von den Beschränkungen des Grundeigentumers im Interesse der Nachbarn' (1863) 6 Jherings Jahrbücher, 81. This article is an early essay about balancing in adjudication, a theme which will grow in the twentieth century and that owes much to Jhering.

of a right unduly.[64] The provision, contained in paragraph 826 BGB, concerning harm deliberately caused to another in an immoral manner, has also been expanded to its limits, to provide an additional ground of protection to several interests not covered by paragraph 823. Inevitably, rights are to be balanced in the decision over liability and that balancing exercise regularly involves policy choices.[65] The upshot of this remark is that rights should be considered as reasons to reach conclusions about liability that must be tested against a widening number of factors.[66] In this intellectual landscape the notion of unlawfulness may also feature as a parasitic concept in the decision on the issue of liability.[67] Lastly, it should be noted that German law has often been willing to deploy contract law to achieve what it was impossible to achieve under tort law in consideration of the purely economic nature of the interest protected.

The story of rights in the field of tortious liability during the twentieth century is thus linked to the demise of the high jurisprudential vision of rights linked to the intellectual tradition represented by Kant, Savigny, and Mill. Their theories held that rights were spheres of liberty that granted to their holder 'an invisible boundary, inside which the existence and the activity of each can enjoy a space that that is free and secure'. The developments of tort law of the last century show that this is at best a metaphor of what rights are, but nothing more. Rights may be recognized and yet they may still not be protected against any kind of interference in any case (see below, section 7). The fact that the enjoyment of a right is impaired, or that the loss of a right is compensated by an award of damages, does not authorize the conclusion that the law enjoins the (wrongful) conduct, or that such conduct is actually prohibited under the law. But how to recognize this in formal terms? The way towards such formal recognition involved the recognition that rights are bound to interfere with one another. Kant, Savigny, and Mill did not seriously contemplate this possibility when they framed their

---

[64] L Raiser, 'Der Stand der Lehre vom subjektiven Recht im Deutschen Zivilrecht' (1961) Juristenzeitung, 465.

[65] BS Markesinis, *The German Law of Obligation: The Law of Torts* (3rd edn, Oxford: Oxford University Press, 1997) 68ff cites the contributions by Nipperdey, Von Caemmerer, Esser, and others, according to whom unlawfulness should be determined not by looking at the result of the action, but at the action itself, in the light of standards determined with regard to the social utility of the activity which caused harm.

[66] N Jansen, 'Duties and Rights in Negligence: A Comparative and Historical Perspective on the European Law of Extracontractual Liability' (2004) 23 OJLS, 443 and *Die Struktur des Haftungsrechts* (Tübingen: Mohr, 2003) (an essential contribution).

[67] cf C von Bar, *The Common European Law of Torts*, vol 2 (Oxford: Oxford Clarendon Press, 1998–2000) para 211ff.

doctrines about rights. They were content to provide an elegant intellectual model that ignored this very real possibility. They thus paid homage to the natural law tradition that they wanted to supersede in other respects. The twentieth century perspective is marked by the rejection of this nineteenth-century simplification.

7 The Hohfeldian moment and the breakdown of rights into elementary legal conceptions

In the history of ideas, nineteenth-century idealism gave way to theories of society that put a high value on competition as a factor of progress. At the beginning of the twentieth century the implications of these theories were being explored in different domains. To get a sense of the *Zeitgeist* it is worth citing a statement reflecting this creative moment in social theory:

When one savage catches the deer, and another the salmon, each may be forbidden to take the other's game by force. Each man has a right to the fruits of his own labour. In the actual state of things there is nothing of this charming simplicity. A man's wealth is not a definable material object, but a bundle of rights of the most complex kind; and rights to various parts of the whole national income, which are the product of a whole system of compacts. [. . .] To protect this property is to protect multifarious systems of rights accruing in all manner of ways, and to sanction the voluntary contracts in virtue of which the whole elaborate network of rights corresponds to the complex social order. The tacit assumption of the economists was that this order was in some sense 'natural' and law an artificial or extra-natural compulsion. Can the line be drawn?[68]

These remarks reflect a broader movement of ideas that spans the Atlantic. The rejection of nineteenth-century idealism is a common theme in the jurisprudence of Oliver Wendell Holmes.[69] But the formalization of this move and the further elaboration of the theme—with regard to the notion of a right—is commonly credited to Hohfeld, the Yale law professor who published two outstanding law review articles on 'Fundamental Legal Conceptions as Applied in Judicial Reasoning'.[70] In his work, Hohfeld focused on the consequences

---

[68] L Stephen, *The English Utilitarians*, vol 3 (London: Duckworth, 1900) 269. These are comments on JS Mill's essay *On Liberty*.

[69] See, eg, OW Holmes, 'Privilege, Malice and Intent' (1894) 1 Harvard L Rev, 1.

[70] WN Hohfeld, 'Some Fundamental Legal Conceptions as Applied in Judicial Reasoning' (1913) 23 Yale L J, 16. Part 2 of this essay discusses the distinction between legal and equitable

of the observation that the concept of a right is a complex one. In proceeding to the analysis of that notion he showed (rather surprisingly in the light of previous theories of rights) that there are certain kinds of 'rights'—labelled as privileges in his classification—that do not imply corresponding duties. The holder of these 'rights' is therefore exposed to the possibility of harm. This clarification was a major step in comparison with the previous jurisprudential tradition that imposed order through the law by making rights the correlative of duties. If the recognition of some 'rights' does not require the imposition of correlative duties then the legal system is open to the recognition of competing entitlements, granting no immunity from interference. This does not correspond to the Kantian picture of what a right is.[71]

Hohfeld's contribution to the analysis of rights can be characterized as the work of a forward-looking common lawyer. This last aspect of his contribution —the link with the common law tradition—must be stressed. His analysis of fundamental legal conceptions is squarely based on the idea that if the claimant is entitled to X, this legal position *must be related* to the defendant's position described either as the opposite or as a correlative of X. That is why criticism levelled at Hohfeld for the introduction of the negative term 'no-right' in his schema is inappropiate and misses the point. Each of these positions is distinct when the issue is understanding the outcome of a case. In fact, continental legal science did not ignore the relational aspect of rights. Savigny himself introduced this theme in his work. Much that is relevant to the key ideas underlying Hohfeld's jurisprudential work can also be found in previous works by continental authors. But the practice of looking at substantive law as a body of norms directing conduct, rather than as a set of rules to decide litigious issues before the Court, did not help in this respect.

The distinction between power, claim, and privilege was familiar to continental legal theorists working in the latter part of the nineteenth century, for example Bierling.[72] But the intellectual legacy of continental legal science that is present in Hohfeld's work should not obscure the innovative aspects of his contribution. Hohfeld discusses fundamental legal conceptions with

rights and rights *in rem* and *in personam*: (1917) 26 Yale L J, 710. Hohfeld's research generated a huge secondary literature that will not be discussed here.

[71] On this point see the important essay by J Singer, 'The Legal Rights Debate in Analytical Jurisprudence from Bentham to Hohfeld' (1982) 6 Wisconsin L Rev, 975, who also shows why the American legal realists were eager to underline and deploy Hohfeld's insight in their attack on legal formalism.

[72] ER Bierling, *Zur Kritik der Juristische Grundbegriffe*, vol 2 (Gotha: Perthes, 1883) 48ff.

no pretension of providing an overarching metaphysical view of the subject. His work cannot be the cornerstone of a legal system in which every question is, in a certain sense, decided before it is actually raised in court. He was fully aware of the effect of showing that privileges and duties are not connected by logical necessity. According to him this meant that 'Where there should be such concomitants rights (or claims) is ultimately a question of justice and policy, and it should be considered, as such, on its merits.'[73] The call for recognition that logical deduction cannot solve policy problems was in tune with the contemporary call for a realistic jurisprudence.

8 New rights for new subjects

The vision of rights prevailing in nineteenth-century law came under strong attack in the twentieth century not only because of the impossibility of producing closure in the law through the simple invocation of individual rights, but also because that vision was illusory for large sectors of the population. Legally enforced discrimination based on distinctions about race, gender, religion, language, ethnic origins, and social conditions restricted access to rights and justice throughout the nineteenth century and beyond. The twentieth century sanctioned discrimination on a large scale too. Within this landscape, the rise of modern European democracies could co-exist with limited rights and discrimination on a large scale both at home and abroad, in the colonies resulting from the expansion of European powers. To look back to this chapter of the law from a comparative and historical point of view is to discover how the law has worked to enforce criteria of exclusion that today are illegal, or to legitimate conducts that are now punished.

The theories of rights that have been discussed in the previous pages focused only on the rights of those who had full capacity to be recognized as right-holders. Even in respect that, it drew distinctions that are now repugnant. These theories were partial to an incredible extent. The attack on rights that tyrannical regimes unleashed in the twentieth century paradoxically showed how precious rights were, despite their weak basis and the partiality shown in their recognition, both of which lay in the origins of the authoritarian state.[74]

---

[73] Hohfeld (1913), see n 70 above, 16, 36.

[74] M La Torre, *La 'lotta contro il diritto soggettivo': Karl Larenz e la dottrina giuridica nazionalso-cialista* (Milano: Giuffrè, 1988).

Hence the importance of the recognition and protection of fundamental rights not only at the national level, but also in the interests of the construction of the European area of freedom, security, and justice.[75]

Since the Second World War, the need to have less exclusion and more justice has been addressed by making those rights that were once the privilege of a minority accessible to the majority, and by expanding the list of rights that make up citizenship to include social rights as well as so-called third-generation rights, such as the right to a clean environment.[76] In the last fifty years the demand for access to rights has thus become more pressing than ever. For the contemporary theory of rights this in turn reflects the need for the law to reject idealized models and to approach individual rights starting from the complexity of real-life experience, in terms of personal needs, capabilities, attitudes, and aspirations.[77] This approach to complexity can be assisted by empirical research, if necessary. A social dimension is included that is not fully captured by the language of individual rights and that belongs to the social dimensions of civic communities.[78] For its citizens, Europe, as a political entity, has added one more source to the established list of forbidden sources of discrimination: nationality.[79]

---

[75]   The establishment of the European Union Fundamental Rights Agency under Regulation (CE) No 168/2007 marks formal recognition of this centrality (cf <http://ec.europa.eu/justice_home/fsj/rights/fsj_rights_agency_en.htm>). About rights as a way to overcome Europe's democratic deficit see: R Bellamy, 'Still in Deficit: Rights, Regulation, and Democracy in the EU' (2006) 12 Eur L J, 725.

[76]   The work of TH Marshall, *Citizenship and Social Class and other Essays* (Cambridge: Cambridge University Press, 1950) which introduced the notion of social citizenship is now assessed by P Breiner, 'Is Social Citizenship Really Outdated?', a paper presented at the annual meeting of the Western Political Science Association, 2006. P Costa, *Storia della Cittadinanza* I–IV (Rome-Bari: Laterza, 1999–2000) and *Storia della cittadinanza* (Rome-Bari: Laterza, 2005) shows the present dimensions and of the history of the idea behind Marshall's essay.

[77]   cf G Calabresi, *Ideals, Beliefs, Attitudes and the Law: Private Law Perspectives on a Public Law Problem* (Syracuse, NY: Syracuse University Press, 1985). This topic is at the centre of A Sen's 'capabilities approach' to individual autonomy.

[78]   RA Macdonald, *Lessons of Everyday Law* (Montreal: McGill-Queen's University Press, 2002) and 'Legal Republicanism and Legal Pluralism: Two Takes on Identity and Diversity' in M Bussani and M Graziadei (eds), *Human Diversity and the Law* 43ff (Bern: Stämpfli, 2005). On this perspective, at the European level: S Fredman, 'Transformation or Dilution: Fundamental Rights in the EU Social Space' (2006) 12 Eur L J, 41; S Deakin, 'Legal Diversity and Regulatory Competition: Which Model for Europe?' (2006) 12 ELJ, 440; C Joerges and F Rödl, '"Social Market Economy" as Europe's Social Model?' (European University Institute, working paper, Law, 2004/2008).

[79]   cf N Reich, 'The Constitutional Relevance of Citizenship and Free Movement in an Enlarged Union' (2005) 11 Eur L J, 675. But there is a tension between the right of free movement and the Member States' interest in the safeguarding of national welfare systems: K Lenaerts and

At the European level, this policy unfolds from the combined effect of supra-national institutional design and the emerging political will to combat exclusion in its many forms.[80] Against this backdrop, the judicial discourse about rights in Europe cannot always be rephrased in the familiar terminology of national law. This should not be a source of concern because there is no reason why the law at the European level should be cast in the same conceptual mould that delivered national constitutions and legislation, or inspired judicial lawmaking by national courts.

9 National traditions, national stereotypes, and rights under EC law: some (interim) conclusions

The notion of a right is part of a common European heritage, but that heritage is compatible with (and is actually made up of) the manifold approaches to that concept that have emerged at the national and at the supra-national level. One of the purposes of this chapter has been to show that the efforts aimed at bringing clarity and order into the law have created a concept with multiple meanings that are all well attested in legal theory. The case law of the European Court of Justice is a testimony to this fact, as has been rightly noted.[81]

Furthermore, the concept shows an inherent indeterminacy, like other key legal concepts. Confronted with this complex situation, the first alternative

T Heremans, 'Contours of a European Social Union in the Case-law of the European Court of Justice' (2006) Eur Constitutional L Rev, 101.

[80] J Schmitt and B Zipperer, 'Is the US a Good Model for Reducing Social Exclusion in Europe?' (2007) 37 International Journal of Health Services, 15 show that on most measures of inequality, poverty, health, education, crime, and punishment, the US does not fare well compared to the much better funded welfare states in Europe. Furthermore, the US performs poorly in two areas where its superiority is usually simply taken for granted: incorporating traditionally disadvantaged groups into the paid labour force and providing opportunities for economic mobility. For futher data and reflections on the point: EC Commission 'Social Inclusion in Europe 2006' (available at <http://ec.europa.eu>); J Morijn, 'Balancing Fundamental Rights and Common Market Freedoms in Union Law: Schmidberger and Omega in the Light of the European Constitution' (2006) 12 Eur L J, 15; G de Búrca and B de Witte (eds), *Social Rights in Europe* (Oxford: Oxford University Press, 2005); D Caruso, 'Limits of the Classic Method: Positive Action in the European Union After the New Equality Directives' (2003) 44 Harvard Intl L J, 331.

[81] Prechal, see n 2 above, 97ff; W van Gerven, 'Of Rights, Remedies and Procedures' (2000) 37 CML Rev, 501–536 and C Hilson and TA Downes, 'Making Sense of Rights: Community Rights in EC Law' (1999) 24 ELR, 121.

would simply be to do away with it. This proposal would probably gain support from a radical point of view. After all, there is no lack of scepticism about the utility of the concept (or about the individualistic values that it symbolizes). Yet the remedy may be worse than the disease: consider the fate of the concept under authoritarian visions of society.[82] On the other hand, it is also true that belief in rights has not prevented the rise of Fascism, Nazism, or Stalinism. Replacing the concept of rights with other concepts (such as that of duty) does not necessarily yield superior results in terms of a more transparent legal discourse either.

A first general lesson therefore is that we have to muddle through the mess.[83] We should do so in the awareness that thinking in terms of a common legal culture which consists of different components is far more productive than insisting on the virtues of purism. This awareness helps because it uncouples national traditions and national stereotypes: they are not the same thing.

A further point concerns the case law of the European Court of Justice. The Court speaks the language of individual rights in deciding on the liability of the Member States for failure to implement directives. I will touch on this aspect only to address some difficulties that learned commentators have experienced in reading this important branch of community law. In *Brasserie du Pêcheur* the Court enumerates three conditions for the Member State's liability under this heading.[84] Those are (i) a sufficiently serious breach, (ii) of a rule intended to confer rights on individuals, and (iii) a direct causal link between breach and damage. These conditions are both 'necessary and sufficient to found a right in individuals to obtain redress'.[85] The crucial question that is often raised is: when do we have a rule intended to confer rights on individuals?

To be fair, a first point should be conceded. The Court may well maintain a degree of indeterminacy on this aspect that leaves some members of its audience unsatisfied. The previous sections of this chapter have documented the complex reasons that judicial discretion has emerged as a major difference

---

[82] FI Michelman, 'Justification (and Justifiability) of Law in a Contradictory World' in JR Pennock and JW Chapman (eds), *Justification* (New York: New York University Press, 1986) 1404.

[83] D Kennedy, *A Critique of Adjudication: (fin de siècle)* (Cambridge: Harvard University Press, 1997) 334, can therefore rightly claim that 'Having lost one's faith in rights discourse is perfectly consistent with, indeed often associated with, a passionate belief in radical expansion of citizen rights against the state.'

[84] Joined Cases C-46/93 and C-48/93 *Brasserie and Factortame* [1996] ECR I-1029.

[85] Joined Cases C-46/93 and C-48/93 *Brasserie and Factortame* [1996] ECR I-1029, para 66.

between the legal landscapes of the nineteenth and the twentieth centuries. It is only fair to recognize that the European Court of Justice is doing here what other judges have done before at national level when they have left the door open to a degree of discretion. This choice is not a mere consequence of the Court's awareness of the need to facilitate the translation of its language into the language of the laws of the member states.[86] Contemporary notions of legality imply attitudes towards judicial discretion that are different from those of other ages. But, having conceded the point, the question is still open. Is it possible to gain a better understanding of what this general formula implies?

The comparative and historical enquiry carried out so far leads us to reject the temptation to read the Court's work in the light of the backdrop provided by the laws of the Members States. A lawyer's mind in Europe even today still owes (too) much of its training and its understanding of the subject to the national dimension of the law. One example is sufficient to make the point. Some commentators hold that the German experience with paragraph 823 II BGB should guide the interpretation of the formula: 'rule intended to confer rights on individuals' that is central to the reasoning of the Court in *Brasserie du Pêcheur*. This provision of the German civil code allows claims for damages based on the violation of a protective norm, if that norm intends to remedy the mischief of which the claimant was a victim. The case law of the Court does not match German law on this point, however. The Court adopts a more liberal stance here because it goes further in protecting the claimant than German law does.[87] Recent steps made by the ECJ in the direction of a more cautious approach do not fundamentally alter this picture.[88] The Court's choice of distancing itself from the German experience is not a mere show of independence from the national law for its own sake, however.[89] The decisive point is that the Court is sanctioning the State's failure to act under a test of liability that is dominated by considerations based on *effet util* rather

---

[86] On this point Prechal, see n 2 above, 112, 118ff, where she notes that there is a good deal of uncertainty involved in the distinction between general and individual interest.

[87] Prechal, see n 2 above, 122. T Eilmansberger, 'The Relationship Between Rights and Remedies in EC Law: In Search of the Missing Link' (2004) CML Rev, 1199, 1225ff, points out the mismatch, but pleads strongly for the adoption of the *Schutzweck* approach, at least as a means to select protected interests.

[88] Case C-222/02 *Peter Paul* [2004] ECR I-9425.

[89] Note that the question of the effect of the violation of a criminal or administrative statute on civil responsibility shows a remarkable degree of divergence among some of the major national legal systems if the enquiry is carried beyond the level of superficial resemblances: Howarth, see n 57 above, 620–621.

than on a primary preoccupation with the claimant's rights. This is typical of the legal regime of State responsibility under international law. The distinction between right and remedy, which the ECJ draws in the context of the same type of litigation, is also linked to the international dimensions of the law concerning State responsibility and should be assessed in that light as well. When invoking the national experience, comparative law teaches us at least to keep in mind that this experience is usually more variegated than most national lawyers would like to admit. Until the lesson is brought home, the advice is, therefore, to proceed with caution.

5

Rights in EU Law

Saša Beljin

1 Introduction

1.1 *Use of the term 'rights' in the EU context*

One frequently encounters the term 'rights' both in primary and secondary EU law. Perhaps the clearest contemporary example lies in the fundamental rights listed in the Charter of Fundamental Rights. But there are numerous further examples. And the European Court of Justice (ECJ) itself has used the term in hundreds of rulings. They can be classified historically in the order in which they have arisen in the case law.[1] One can also attempt to arrange them according to viewpoints and factors as regards content. The ECJ emphasizes EU rights especially in three contexts: judicial enforceability, the liability of the Member States and the Union, and finally regarding the requirements for the implementation of directives.

Enforceability in national courts and the EU courts

Since EU law is for a large part implemented by the Member States, judicial protection predominantly occurs when brought before the Member State courts. As the case law has repeatedly emphasized, they are obliged effectively to protect the EU rights: it is the responsibility of the Member States to warrant the protection of EU rights in the absence of EU legal

---

[1] T Eilmansberger, 'The Relationship Between Rights and Remedies in EC Law' (2004) 41 CML Rev, 1202–1231.

provisions.[2] The protection is the responsibility of the courts of the Member States within the order of national law which must observe the limits of effectiveness and equality.[3] The implementation of rights in directives must ensure the possibility of relying on them before the national courts.[4]

The significance of EU rights for judicial protection on the EU courts level is by far less explicit in case law. Nor has this question received a great deal of scholarly attention.[5] There are, on the other hand, numerous examples which show that EU rights are relevant for judicial enforceability at the EU courts. This is obvious for any liability action against the Community. And with reference to the action of annulment according to EC Treaty, Article 230, the ECJ has emphasized that 'individuals are entitled to effective judicial protection of the *rights* they derive from Community law'.[6] However, this protection bears clear limitations because the ECJ requires the plaintiff to exhibit a high degree of concern, in accordance with EC Treaty, Article 230 (4).[7] But there is a connection between the protection of rights and the action of annulment.[8]

Liability

Rights play an important role when considering the liability of Member States for breaches of EU law. The ECJ states that 'it follows from the requirements inherent in the protection of the rights of individuals relying on Community

---

[2] Case 33/76 *Rewe* [1976] ECR 1989, para 5; Case 45/76 *Comet* [1976] ECR 2043, para 11–18 and Case C-224/01 *Köbler* [2003] ECR I-10239, para 46.

[3] Case C-13/01 *Safalero* [2003] ECR I-8679, para 49 and Case C-482/01 *Orfanopoulos and Oliveri* [2004] ECR I-5257, para 80.

[4] Case C-131/88 *Commission v Germany* [1991] ECR I-825, para 6; Case C-365/93 *Commission v Greece* [1995] ECR I-499, para 9 and Case C-478/99 *Commission v Sweden* [2002] ECR I-4147, para 18.

[5] Eg, A Ward, *Judicial Review and the Rights of Private Parties in EC Law* (Oxford: Oxford University Press, 2000), 202ff, 288ff, 332ff. Limited to the national systems of judicial protection eg Eilmansberger, see n 1 above, 1199; A Epiney, 'Primär- und Sekundärrechtsschutz im Öffentlichen Recht' (2002) 61 Veröffentlichungen der Vereinigung der Deutschen Staatsrechtslehrer, 396, n 162.

[6] Case C-263/02 P *Jégo-Quéré* [2004] ECR I-3425, para 29 (emphasis added) and Case C-50/00 P *UPA* [2002] ECR I-6677, para 39.

[7] cf Case C-263/02 P *Jégo-Quéré* [2004] ECR I-3425, paras 33ff, 36; Case C-50/00 P *UPA* [2002] ECR I-6677, paras 40, 44 and cf de lege lata and de lege ferenda C Koch, 'Locus standi of Private Applicants under the EU Constitution: Preserving Gaps in the Protection of Individuals' Right to an Effective Remedy' (2005) 30 ELR, 511ff.

[8] See s 3.3 below.

law that they must have the possibility of obtaining redress in the national courts for the damage caused by the infringement of those rights'.[9]

Regarding the liability of the EU in accordance with EC Treaty, Article 288 (2), the ECJ has also gone over to using the term 'rights', now requiring the violation of a legal norm that aims at granting rights to the individual.[10] Previously, the ECJ had required that the violated norm serve the purpose of protecting the individual, without explicitly speaking of rights.[11]

Implementation of EU law and miscellaneous

The purpose of EU rights is not limited to judicial protection and liability. The national implementation of directives must not only secure judicial protection, it must also be conducted in such a manner that 'the persons concerned are in a position to know the full extent of their rights *and*, where appropriate, to rely on them before the national courts'.[12] According to EC Treaty Article 253, the requirement to give reasons for a (general or individual) EU Act is also geared towards the plaintiff. In order to preserve his rights, he has to be aware of the core reasons for the act *and* Community Courts have to be enabled to exercise their jurisdiction.[13] The Court of First Instance (CFI) appropriately speaks of a double target.[14]

1.2 *Questions*

Neither EU legislation nor the ECJ have ever fundamentally identified the basic characteristics of EU rights nor the criteria by which to determine them. Such an outline could be deemed dispensable because all national legal systems know similar terms. The fundamental concept of a right can be described as somebody being entitled by law to demand something from the other.[15] However, the term exhibits diverse conceptions and contents within the same legal order as well as between different legal orders.[16] Therefore,

---

[9] Case C-224/01 *Köbler* [2003] ECR I-10239, para 36.

[10] Case C-76/01 P *Eurocoton* [2003] ECR I-10091, para 97 and Case C-234/02 P *Ombudsman v Lamberts* [2004] ECR I-2803, para 49.

[11] Case 238/78 *Ireks-Arkady* [1979] ECR 2955, para 9.

[12] Case C-194/01 *Commission v Austria* [2004] ECR I-4579, para 39 (emphasis added) and Case C-296/01 *Commission v France* [2003] ECR I-13909, paras 54ff.

[13] Case T-180/01 *Euroagri* [2004] ECR II-369, para 41.

[14] Case T-124/02 *The Sunrider* [2004] ECR II-1149, para 73.

[15] cf Case C-6/90 *Francovich* [1991] ECR I-5357, para 12.

[16] S Prechal, 'Direct Effect Reconsidered, Redefined and Rejected' in JM Prinssen and A Schrauwen (eds), *Direct Effect: Rethinking a Classic of EC Legal Doctrine* (Groningen: Europa Law Publishing, 2002) 20; M Ruffert, *Subjektive Rechte im Umweltrecht der EG* (Heidelberg: Decker,

when Member States refer to rights, very different things may be meant. It seems only too obvious that this can result in different interpretations of what EU rights actually are.

In reality, dealing with these rights can lead to problems that can go so far as to act contrary to the recognition of rights at the EU and the Member State levels. This is illustrated by an example stemming from environmental law. Although the ECJ has clarified that third parties must have the possibility of relying on the obligation to conduct an Environmental Impact Assessment (EIA) in legal proceedings,[17] German case law is rigid in its estimation that rights to file an action can be derived neither from the EIA-Directive nor from the German EIA-Act.[18] Can ignorance of the ECJ's jurisprudence be solely responsible for this contrast? Or can such contradictions be caused precisely by uncertainties regarding the notion of EU rights?

In the face of such problems, this chapter attempts to investigate the notion of EU rights, starting with a glance at the historical development of rights.[19] This constitutes our starting point for reflections on the relationship between rights and judicial protection, on the differences between rights and interests, as well as on the basic characteristics and determination of EU rights.

2 Historical development of rights

The term '(individual) right' was already in use in the *ius commune*, ie Roman (canon) law, but, since the nationalizing of jurisprudence has also been among the basic concepts of the nineteenth-century legal doctrine of private law in *all* legal orders.[20] If one traces its development in Germany, there has been a focus on the right of the individual in the German legal system since the period of Enlightenment[21], especially in the sphere of private law.[22] And

1996) 10, 12, 29ff, 89ff; S Prechal, *Directives in EC Law* (2nd edn, Oxford: Oxford University Press, 2005) 97 and J Coppel, 'Rights, Duties and the End of Marshall' (1994) 57 MLR, 864.

[17] Case C-435/97 *WWF* [1999] ECR I-5613, paras 69–71.

[18] Eg, OVG Lüneburg, Case 8 LA 206/03, Neue Zeitschrift für Verwaltungsrecht-Rechtsprechungs-Report 2004, 408; OVG Münster, Case 10 B 788/02, Neue Zeitschrift für Verwaltungsrecht 2003, 632ff.

[19] cf this volume, M Graziadei, ch 4.

[20] H Coing, *Europäisches Privatrecht 1800 bis 1914*, Vol 2 (München: Beck, 1989) 25, 270.

[21] J Hruschka, 'Kants Rechtsphilosophie als Philosophie des subjektiven Rechts' (2004) Juristenzeitung, 1085ff.

[22] Coing, see n 20 above, 43ff; A von Tuhr, *Allgemeiner Teil des Deutschen Bürgerlichen Rechts*, Vol 1 (Berlin: Duncker & Humblot, 1957) 53.

in German administrative law since the beginning of the twentieth century, individual rights have advanced to become a central legal concept.[23]

2.1 *Distinction between 'law' and 'rights'*

The development of the notion of rights in all of its different forms took place in two fundamental steps: the first was the emergence of a stricter distinction between *objective* law—in terms of the entire legal system—and *individual* rights. The dual meaning of the terms *Recht* and *jus*[24] as well as of the French term *droit* exemplifies the lack of strict distinction between the two concepts at the basis of juridical thinking. When referring to the right of the individual, French legal terminology adds the term *subjectif*—*subjektiv* in German—for the purpose of notional clarity. In contrast, there are the distinct terms 'law' and 'right' used in English legal terminology.[25]

2.2 *Distinction between rights and judicial protection*

In a second step, the right—in a substantive sense—was more significantly distinguished from judicial protection in respect of procedural law—a development that did not occur uniformly and simultaneously in all legal systems. Contrary to the minor degree of distinction that used to exist between substantive law and procedural law—as was the case in Roman and older common law—the nineteenth century witnessed a shift of the focus on 'actions' (without differentiation between procedural and substantive law) to the focus on law and rights in a substantive sense.[26] Rights and procedural law became more clearly separated. Since then, it has been possible to make a distinction between the creation of a right on the one hand and judicial protection on the other hand, both in continental European[27] and in common law.[28]

The distinction between rights and judicial protection is not merely theoretical, however. In practice, it is exemplified by the simple fact that quite naturally it is not always necessary to call upon help from the courts.

---

[23] S Kadelbach, *Allgemeines Verwaltungsrecht unter europäischem Einfluß* (Tübingen: Mohr, 1999) 368.

[24] Von Tuhr, see n 22 above, 54, n 2; H Coing, *Zur Geschichte des Privatrechtssystems* (Frankfurt am Main: Klostermann, 1962) 33–36.

[25] HD Jarass and S Beljin, *Casebook Grundlagen des EG-Rechts* (Baden-Baden: Nomos, 2003) 72.

[26] Coing, see n 24 above, 36ff, 50ff.

[27] M Ruffert, 'Rights and Remedies in European Community Law: A Comparative View' (1997) 34 CML Rev, 332ff.

[28] Prechal, see n 16 above, 106, n 92.

Whether or not rights have to be enforced by judicial protection depends on their implementation. In addition, further explanation is needed of the fact that judicial enforceabilty can exist without rights, just as—conversely—rights can exist that are not judicially enforceable.[29]

3   On the relationship between rights and judicial protection

3.1   *The problem*

Traditionally, despite their separation, rights and judicial protection are closely connected in legal debate, comparable to the estimation of rights in the context of judicial enforceabilty by the ECJ. A reason for this is that the enforcement of rights is a particularly significant instrument for their realization.[30] As a result, rights and judicial protection are often mentioned in one breath: 'rights and remedies', respectively 'material rights' and 'procedural remedies'[31] or 'rules of substantive law' and 'rights' on the one hand, and 'procedural rules to enforce those rights' on the other.[32]

Moreover, one faces the idea, at least in German legal writing, that rights and their enforceabilty run parallel, and that the notion of rights is to a large extent influenced by the respective model of judicial protection,[33] whatever that may mean in detail. However, since rights are not limited to judicial protection,[34] this approach is problematic. According to *EU* rights, the idea of parallelism between rights and their enforceabilty faces difficulties, because, as observed above, their protection lies to a large extent in the hands of the Member States but is also in part in the hands of the EU courts. Thus, several systems of judicial protection are juxtaposed for the protection of EU rights—that of the EU and those of the Member States. Due to the differences in judicial protection, there could be up to twenty-eight differently

---

[29]   See s 3.2 below.

[30]   Case C-224/01 *Köbler* [2003] ECR I-10239, para 33.

[31]   Eilmansberger, see n 1 above, 1199 and Ruffert, see n 27 above, 332.

[32]   See the Opinion of Advocate General Cosmas in Case C-261/95 *Palmisani* [1997] ECR I-4025, para 16.

[33]   Eg, M Reiling, *Zu individuellen Rechten im deutschen und im Gemeinschaftsrecht* (Berlin: Duncker & Humblot, 2004) 121 and Kadelbach, see n 23 above, 382.

[34]   Something different applies for mere rights of action.

articulated EU rights, notwithstanding regional differences within one Member State. Such a situation is difficult to conceive.

3.2 *National rights and their judicial protection*

Individual protection and general judicial control of legality

In the case of *national* rights it is difficult to summarize the interrelationship between judicial protection and rights in a few, tangible phrases, let alone to attribute to judicial protection a shaping effect on rights. This can be exemplified by means of two fundamental aspects that are often emphasized in the discussion on rights. The first aspect concerns the two basic models of judicial protection: the model of the 'protection of individual rights' and the model of 'general judicial control of legality'. Although neither the one nor the other model can—in its purest form—be encountered in any legal system, criteria to differentiate between the ideal types exist.[35] Individual protection focuses on the protection of the plaintiff's rights. Admissibility and giving the reasons for a judicial action are closely co-ordinated. Furthermore, the courts are bound to the plaintiff's application and judgments must be effective among the parties only. Regarding the model of (general) judicial control of legality, the purpose of proceedings is to review the (objective) legality of an action. Here, admissibility and giving reasons for judicial action need not be closely co-ordinated. There is also no obligation for the courts to be bound to the plaintiff's application and judgments must be effective *erga omnes*.

The practical differences in the range of norms that fall under judicial protection are limited. This is due first to the fact that differentiation is only relevant in those fields in which a right is not provided for by every legal provision. Traditionally, there is no such problem in private law. Private law serves specifically to balance private interests, and therefore regularly grants rights.[36] Consequently, the differentiation between law and rights is of minor relevance for judicial protection between private persons. The distinction does become relevant, however, for the legal relationships between the citizen and the State as well as judicial protection in this sphere. In this case, the sphere of law is larger than that of rights. Yet the consequences for judicial protection are limited. First, in models that prioritize the protection

---

[35] For a complete overview see Kadelbach, see n 23 above, 379–381 and Reiling, see n 33 above, 419–421.

[36] H Maurer, *Allgemeines Verwaltungsrecht* (16th edn, München: Beck, 2006) para 8: 7.

of rights, not only rights and not all rights can be enforced by legal action. Second, in systems of judicial control of legality not everybody can sue for everything. The plaintiff requires an entitlement to legal action. To summarize: in both systems there can be judicial protection without rights and rights without judicial protection.

Judicial protection without rights and rights without judicial protection

Germany, for example, is a prime example of the model of individual protection. A central factor is the guarantee of judicial protection in the German Constitution (*Grundgesetz*, GG) Article 19(4) which guarantees judicial protection for those whose rights have been impaired by public authority. Accordingly, the most important suits in Germany that can be filed at the administrative court are geared towards rights both in terms of admissibility and of the wellfoundedness of the action, in accordance with the Code of Administrative Court Procedure (*Verwaltungsgerichtsordnung*, VwGO) s 42(2) and s 113(1),(5).[37]

However, this does not imply that judicial protection must *always* be given when rights are impaired. Nor does it imply that judicial protection in Germany may be geared *only* towards the protection of rights. The existence of rights that are not legally enforceable can be illustrated by (general) procedural rights in Germany. This sort of procedural right is customarily only enforceable if the impairment of the procedural right is supplemented by the impairment of a substantive right.[38]

Legal exceptions to the precondition of rights for judicial enforceability are an example of judicial protection without rights. VwGO s 42(2) does not require the assertion of an individual (public) right without exception, but only 'insofar as no other legal provision is made'. The right of associations to take legal action under German environmental law is a good example.[39] Furthermore, the impairment of a right in terms of VwGO s 42(2) is naturally affirmed in cases of the addressees of a burdening individual act.[40] Determining concrete rights is practically irrelevant in these cases because the

---

[37] The administrative courts apply s 42 (2) VwGO to all types of legal claims.
[38] BVerwG, Case 4 C 5/95, *Deutsches Verwaltungsblatt* 1996, 681 and FO Kopp and WR Schenke, *VwGO* (14th edn, München: Beck, 2005) para 42: 95.
[39] R Wahl and P Schütz in FK Schoch, E Schmidt-Aßmann and R Pietzner (eds), *VwGO* (München: Beck, 2006) para 42(2): 42, 228.
[40] F Hufen, *Verwaltungsprozessrecht* (6th edn, München: Beck, 2005) para 14: 75ff.

addressee of a burdening individual act has wide-ranging rights of action, and an extensive examination into the justification takes place.[41]

In the system of judicial control of legality, the fact that there can be protection without rights is due to the fact that rights—as they are understood in Germany—play no significant role in that context. This shows that there can be judicial control without rights. However, rights are substituted by other attributes that restrict an individual's entitlement to legal action. In the French administrative process, an extensive examination can take place of the state measure which is being opposed, measured on the scale of the entirety of the law.[42] The accessibility to the complaint process is less objectively oriented, because it is also the case in France that not everyone can file a legal action for everything. For the most important type of claim—the *recours pour excès de pouvoir*—the plaintiff must have an interest, the so-called *intérêt à agir*;[43] and the 'interested' cannot confront every act.[44] The *effect* on the access to legal action through the courts, both for rights and interests is comparable, even if interests result in broader access to courts than rights. A comparable situation occurs in British law where the justification of legal actions against government bodies is examined on the basis of law.[45] In terms of admissibility, though, there is also the precondition of *locus standi* or 'standing' which exists when there is 'sufficient interest', in accordance with s 31(3) of the Supreme Court Act.[46] The content of this prerequisite ranges from a (factual) concern to rights that include European Human Rights.[47]

Furthermore, where no connection is required between right or interest in admissibility to the court on the one hand and illegitimacy in the justification of a legal claim on the other, judicial protection is generally broader

---

[41] H Sodan in H Sodan and J Ziekow (eds), *VwGO* (2nd edn, Baden-Baden: Nomos, 2006) para 42: 384ff.

[42] Epiney, see n 5 above, 373.

[43] J Gerkrath in Jarass and Beljin, see n 25 above, 185; Epiney, see n 5 above, 372 and CD Classen, *Europäisierung der Verwaltungsgerichtsbarkeit* (Tübingen: Mohr, 1996) 59.

[44] Reiling, see n 33 above, 49.

[45] cf F Lyall, *An Introduction to British Law* (2nd edn, Baden-Baden: Nomos, 2002) 165ff; Epiney, see n 5 above, 382.

[46] In detail MT Molan, *Constitutional Law: The Machinery of Government* (4th edn, London: Old Bailey Press, 2003) 302ff; B Thompson, *Textbook on Constitutional & Administrative Law* (3rd edn, London: Blackstone, 1997) 439 and T Ingman, *The English Legal Process* (10th edn, Oxford: Oxford University Press, 2004) 499.

[47] Epiney, see n 5 above, 380ff; Kadelbach, see n 23 above, 381, 385; Thompson, see n 46 above, 440ff; Ingman, see n 46 above, 499ff, and PP Craig, *Administrative Law* (3rd edn, London: Sweet & Maxwell, 1994) 489ff.

than the concept of rights.[48] Consequently, if a right or interest effects the admissibility of a legal claim, it can open the door to varyingly extensive legal scrutiny of its justification, both in terms of width (scale of control) and depth (intensity of control).

These examples show that the legal systems of the Member States contain elements of both individual protection and judicial control of legality. Thus the differences between the two fundamental concepts—'individual protection' and 'objective judicial control'—are in balance due to the respective designs of the requirements for action.[49] Since one encounters neither the one nor the other model in its pure form, the understanding of rights gains little from making reference to basic differences between the two systems.

Order between the granting of rights and judicial protection

A similar picture emerges when regarding the second fundamental aspect that is discussed in connection with rights—the chronological order of the granting of a right and judicial protection. It is repeatedly emphasized that in continental European legal orders substantive law constitutes primary law, while the possibility of enforcing its implementation is merely consequential and thus secondary.[50] The sentence *ubi ius, ibi remedium* applies.[51] In contrast, the situation in common law is distinguished by the traditionally strictly formal character of judicial protection. It is characterized by the causes in law and the legal consequences of judicial protection. Rights are the result of judicial protection, which is why rules of procedure are superordinate to substantive law.[52] Thus, the reversed phrase *ubi remedium, ibi ius* applies.[53]

However, the two approaches need not necessarily result in differences in practice. Rather, the tailoring of rights and of judicial protection is the

---

[48]   Epiney, see n 5 above, 411 and Wahl and Schütz, see n 39 above, para 42(2): 10.

[49]   Epiney, see n 5 above, 384, 421; Reiling, see n 33 above, 49, 531 and H Schulze-Fielitz in H Dreier (ed), *GG-Kommentar*, Vol 1 (2nd edn, Tübingen: Mohr, 2004) Art 19(4), para 34.

[50]   Coing, see n 20 above, 274ff; K Larenz and M Wolf, *Allgemeiner Teil des Bürgerlichen Rechts* (9th edn, München: Beck, 2004) para 18: 68; M Ruffert, 'Dogmatik und Praxis des subjektiv-öffentlichen Rechts unter dem Einfluß des Gemeinschaftsrechts' (1998) Deutsches Verwaltungsblatt, 69.

[51]   T Eilmansberger, *Rechtsfolgen und subjektives Recht im Gemeinschaftsrecht* (Baden-Baden: Nomos, 1997) 63, 64, 66. On EU rights T Heukels and J Tib, 'Towards Homogeneity in the Field of Legal Remedies: Convergence and Divergence' in P Beaumont, C Lyons, and N Walker (eds), *Convergence & Divergence in European Public Law* (Oxford: Hart, 2002) 113.

[52]   PS James, *Introduction to English Law* (12th edn, London: Butterworths, 1989) 63.

[53]   Eilmansberger, see n 51 above, 63 and also 60–62.

key: a legal order that bears extensive and general substantive rights does not confer a greater breadth of rights than a system that provides exhaustive opportunities of judicial protection, and vice versa.[54] Therefore, the *tailoring* of the rights and the possibilities of their judicial protection within a legal order are the key and not the (temporary) priority of either rights or judicial protection.

Trying to explore the range of rights and interests reveals the fact that the problems lie in the precise detail. For instance, in Germany who could claim that it is always possible reliably to determine whether a right is upheld or not? The actual situation resembles difficult casuistry[55] despite the existence of the 'theory of protective norms' (*Schutznormtheorie*) as a comprehensive instrument for the identification of rights.[56] In addition, development is ongoing, showing that the notion of rights cannot be understood as 'a fixed institution with selectively emphasized features'.[57] The bulk of judgments regarding the issue of rights and interests show that the situation in a Member State is far more differentiated than can be exemplified by fundamental differences alone. The sum of all individual provisions is by far more relevant to the practical outcome. In the light of the vast number of relevant provisions, it appears barely feasible to sketch *one* specific scope of rights and interests.

3.3 *EU rights and their judicial protection*

Judicial protection without EU rights and EU rights without judicial protection

Much like the situation in the Member States, the concept of EU rights is partly wider and partly narrower than that of judicial enforceability. Apart from the fact that Member States courts naturally protect both EU and national rights, the idea that *judicial protection* exists (and must exist) *without EU rights* also applies to (direct) legal protection by the EU courts. The concept of judicial protection is wider than the concept of EU rights because protection can also be achieved without them. This is at least the case for actions of a person against a decision addressed to that person. Locating rights is not the issue here, because—within the framework of the action of

---

[54] Judicial protection in British public law has significantly grown; see A Epiney and K Sollberger, *Zugang zu Gerichten und gerichtliche Kontrolle im Umweltrecht* (Berlin: Schmidt, 2002) 161.

[55] On the extensive case law in the sphere of neighbour protection in building law, Kopp and Schenke, see n 38 above, para 42: 98.

[56] On *Schutznormtheorie*, see s 4.1 below.

[57] Kadelbach, see n 23 above, 378.

annulment according to EC Treaty, Article 230(4)—the addressee is always authorized to file an action.[58] In the case of general acts and third-party judicial enforcements against decisions, the provisions require the addressees to be directly and individually concerned. Whether or not this is *only* the case when a right is violated remains to be explored.[59] Should this not be the case, then it can be deemed another example of judicial protection without EU rights by EU courts. Furthermore, the justification of a claim for action of annulment is *every* 'infringement of this Treaty or of any rule of law relating to its application'.[60] So there is no requirement for a connection between the concern (as examined in the admissibility) and the unlawfulness (as examined in the justification). This shows that the concept of EU judicial protection is wider than that of EU rights.

On the other hand, there are *EU rights without judicial protection*, meaning EU rights which need not be enforceable. In the case of the EU courts not every EU right needs to result in the direct possibility of bringing an action. This is clearly exemplified in case law. The ECJ recently stressed that the individual must have the opportunity to call upon judicial protection of those *rights* that he derives from EU law.[61] In doing so within an action of annulment, the ECJ has itself created a connection between EU rights and the possibility of suing before the EU courts. This connection is also incorporated in Article 47(1) of the EU Charter of Fundamental Rights which warrants an effective legal remedy against violations of EU rights. It should be remembered that in Germany the comparable guarantee of judicial protection of GG, Article 19(4) effected the orientation of judicial protection towards the protection of individual rights. However, an EU right does not always lead to the admissibilty of an action of annulment.[62]

It remains to be seen whether it is conceivable that there may be types of EU rights which are not enforceable before Member State courts—for example, in a situation comparable to that of procedural rights in Germany.[63] As a rule, one would have to reject this possibility, because one

---

[58]   cf M Burgi, in HW Rengeling, A Middeke, and M Gellermann, *Handbuch des Rechtsschutzes in der EU* (2nd edn, München: Beck, 2003) para 7: 55.

[59]   See s 4.3 below.

[60]   U Ehricke in R Streinz (ed), *EUV/EGV* (München: Beck, 2003) Art 230 EC, para 78 and Burgi, see n 58 above, para 7: 100.

[61]   For refernces see n 6 above.

[62]   As will be discussed below in this section.

[63]   Declining L Fichtner, *Rechte des Einzelnen im Recht der Europäischen Gemeinschaft* (Köln: Heymann, 2005) 83, 181.

key difference between procedural rights in EU law and in German law lies in the fact that those of the EU are *not* accessory to substantive rights.[64] Thus, the explanation used in Germany for the exclusion of judicial enforceability of mere procedural rights appears to be missing for EU rights. On the other hand, exceptions seem likely. Possible examples of rights which are not judicially enforceable are the rights of participation, which are stipulated in the directives to implement the Aarhus Convention (AC). The Convention, which is insufficiently transposed by the EU in this respect, differentiates in AC, Article 6 between the participation of the public concerned and the entire public.[65] AC, Article 9(2) requires only a right of action for the public concerned and not for the entire public, AC, Article 9(3) leaves it to the Parties of the Convention to provide further members of the public with a right of action. Consequently, EU law can contain a right of participation for everybody, which nevertheless need not be judicially enforceable by each and every person.

Effects of EU rights on judicial enforceability in EU courts

Although there are differences between the concept of EU rights and judicial protection, as described, the former have effects on judicial enforceability both in the courts of the EU and in national courts. Under EC Treaty, Article 235, in an action for liability the bearer of an entitlement to liability can enforce his right according to Article 288(2). Here, the entitlement according to Article 288(2) presupposes the infringement of an EU right.

With respect to the action for annulment according to EC Treaty, Article 230, the question occurs as to whether there is a link between the condition of *direct and individual concern* according to Article 230(4) and EU rights. One might think that direct and individual concern has nothing to do with rights, if only because of the wording. However, there are rulings which have addressed the issue of whether the individual is directly and individually concerned *in* (specific) *rights*, for example in patent rights,[66] in trademark rights,[67] or in rights to participate in proceedings.[68] Accordingly, there is the

---

[64] For further elaboration Kadelbach, see n 23 above, 415.

[65] cf C Walter, 'Internationalisierung des deutschen und europäischen Verwaltungsverfahrens- und Verwaltungsprozeßrechts—am Beispiel der Aarhus-Konvention' (2005) Europarecht, 328–330.

[66] Case T-213/02 *SNF* [2004] ECR II-3047, paras 68ff.

[67] Case C-309/89 *Codorniu* [1994] ECR I-1853, para 21 and Case T-370/02 *Alpenhaim-Camembert-Werk* [2004] ECR II-2097, paras 65ff.

[68] Case T-370/02 *Alpenhaim-Camembert-Werk* [2004] ECR II-2097, para 67 and Case T-27/02 *Kronofrance* [2004] ECR II-4177, para 34.

assumption of some link between EU rights and the direct and individual concern.[69]

The question whether rights are a *necessary* requirement for the right of action in accordance with EC Treaty, Article 230(4) is a different issue. Rights are *not* a necessary requirement for addressees of decisions. As was argued above, these persons are always entitled to bring an action in accordance with Article 230(4). And also in cases in which someone sues against a general act or a third party sues against a decision, the provisions that are actionable by action of annulment are not limited to EU rights. Instead, the ECJ repeatedly emphasizes factual elements without expressing a normative approach in its examination. This is the case, for example, for the (factual) market position and involvement in procedures such as the formal examination of state aids.[70]

Overall, EU rights play a role in enforceability in EU courts insofar that a (specific) right *can*—but does not have to—be meaningful. Direct and individual concern and rights are not identical, but there is a link: the impairment of rights is *one* possible way to argue in favour of direct and individual concern. One can thus differentiate three groups of individuals that are authorized to bring an action in accordance with EC Treaty, Article 230(4): the addressee of a decision being unrestrictedly concerned, the non-addressee being concerned in his rights, and the non-addressee being otherwise concerned.

Coming back to rights as a basis for direct and individual concern, case law shows that they are not a necessary requirement for filing an action of annulment. Merely the restriction of a right by a provision is insufficient to fulfil the conditions of Article 230(4).[71] The plaintiff will have to exhibit more than just a right in order to be individually affected.

Effects of EU rights on judicial enforceability in national courts

When an EU provision grants a right, the Member State must warrant the enforceability. This applies equally to directly applicable EU rights and to the implementation of EU rights in national law.[72] Because it is 'in principle,

    [69] cf Jarass and Beljin, see n 25 above, 205–207; Fichtner, see n 62 above, 289–301 and M Ruffert in M Ruffert and C Calliess (eds), *EUV/EGV* (3rd edn, München: Beck, 2007) Art 249 EC, para 69; cf also this volume, R Alonso, L Moral, and C Plaza, ch 6.
    [70] Eg, Case C-106/98 P *Comité d'entreprise de la Société française de production* [2000] ECR I-3659, paras 39–41 and Case T-158/00 *ARD* [2003] ECR II-3825, paras 62ff.
    [71] Case C-263/02 P *Jégo-Quéré* [2004] ECR I-3425, paras 37ff.
    [72] On the different ways in which EU rights can reach the individual, see s 5.3 below.

for national law to determine an individual's standing and legal interest in bringing proceedings'[73] the EU right must be equipped with criteria that grant a possibility to enforce the right in accordance with national law. In general, the Member State formulates—if legislative implementation is required—individual rights and in doing so creates the prerequisite for judicial enforceability, if this is necessary in the legal system concerned. Elsewhere, the affirmation of an interest must be warranted, if such is the precondition for judicial enforceabilty in the respective Member State.[74] There are EU provisions in which both of these possibilities are explicitly juxtaposed, ie they make rights dependent on either the impairment of a right *or* on sufficient interests.[75]

4 On the differences between rights and interests

4.1 *Overview of the legal situation in some Member States*

As has been shown, the Member States require either a right or an interest for access to court. The differentiation between rights and interests varies among the Member States. In Germany, rights also comprise legally protected interests that need only be differentiated from economical, political, aesthetic, or miscellaneous other interests.[76] If a right is not explicitly phrased, it needs at least to be determined—by means of interpretation according to the *Schutznormtheorie*—whether a legal norm is meant to serve not only general but also individual interests.[77] Therefore, the normative approach is

---

[73] Case C-13/01 *Safalero* [2003] ECR I-8679, para 50 and Case C-87/90 *Verholen* [1991] ECR I-3757, para 24.

[74] See s 3.2 above; cf also, this volume R Alonso, L Moral, and C Plaza, ch 6.

[75] Parliament and Council Directive (EC) 2003/35 providing for public participation in respect of the drawing up of certain plans and programmes relating to the environment [2003] OJ L156/17 inserted Art 10(a) in Council Directive (EEC) 85/337 on the assessment of the effects of certain public and private projects on the environment [1985] OJ L175/40 and Art 15(a) in Directive 96/61/EC, concerning integrated pollution prevention and control [1996] OJ L257/26. A comparable approach can be found in Art 12(1) Parliament and Coucil Directive 2004/35 on environmental liability with regard to the prevention and remedying of environmental damage [2004] OJ L143/56 with the supplementary option of whether the person is affected.

[76] Maurer, see n 36 above, para 8: 2, 5, 8.

[77] HD Jarass in HD Jarass and B Pieroth, *Grundgesetzkommentar* (8th edn, München: Beck, 2006) Art 19, para 37.

decisive,[78] and additionally restricts itself as far as possible to *one* norm,[79] but in doing so also comprises (specified) interests.

In contrast, the difference between rights and interests is underlined more clearly in France. A normative connection is not a required precondition for an interest—the interest in question need *not* be protected by law. Rather, the plaintiff's affiliation to a group is sufficient: for example to the group of tax payers, residents, users of institutions, pupils, students, or civil servants.[80] In some circumstances, not even this is required, while on the other hand, there are cases in which some affiliations are insufficient.[81] What this means more specifically is difficult to estimate. The literature describes the main difference as follows. Rights concern the assertion of legal norms whose protective intention needs to be determined (if necessary by interpretation). In contrast, in the case of interests, the only relevance is whether they are factually concerned.[82]

Another difference might possibly lie in the legal consequences. While interests serve as a form of defence, rights can effect legal consequences that have more than merely defensive functions, such as obligation and liability. This is, however, barely advantageous for the determination of rights and interests in a legal order.

4.2 *Legal and factual factors*

One cannot make as clear a distinction between legal and factual elements as one is led to believe by the comparison of normative intention on the one hand and factual concern on the other. Initially, regarding interests that function as a precondition for judicial enforceabilty, the concern lies in a legal appraisal of whether there is in fact the required interest for the suit in question.[83] This becomes especially clear in the requirement of a *sufficient* interest, which indicates that not every factual interest need in fact suffice. The methods employed in this legal assessment are certainly distinct: in the case of rights the method lies in the interpretation of norms, while in the

---

[78] Wahl and Schütz, see n 39 above, para 42(2): 50.
[79] Reiling, see n 33 above, 155.
[80] U Hübner and V Constantinesco, *Einführung in das französische Recht* (4th edn, München: Beck, 2001) 115.
[81] Classen, see n 43 above, 60.
[82] Epiney, see n 5 above, 385 and Classen, see n 43 above, 83.
[83] D Ehlers, *Die Europäisierung des Verwaltungsprozeßrechts* (Köln: Heymann, 1999) 53.

case of interests it lies in the assessment of facts rather than in the search for normative intentions.

It is, however, not the case that Germans concentrate entirely on determining the intention of a norm, while in the case of interests in other legal systems this is out of the question. Thus, *Schutznormtheorie* does not exclude factual aspects: the factual relevance can become important when dealing with the question of the scope of a right, when the norm does not define in detail the intended factual and personal protective purpose.[84] Here, the scope of a right is not derived merely from the norm itself, but instead its attributes are not fixed and are thus reliant on case-specific evaluation. With this in mind, the less normative content a right has, the more it depends on factual circumstances.

On the other hand—at least for an external observer—for one's affiliation to a group in terms of the French *intérèt'*, it seems plausible that the explanation of this interest also makes reference to legal provisions, for example tax provisions that define different groups of tax payers, or local provisions that determine who is in fact a local resident.[85] In short, one can put on record that rights and interests are not opposites in terms of being purely legal and purely factual judgments.

4.3 *On the extent of rights and interests*

Even when methodological differences are taken into account, they cannot explain whether rights or interests tend to be affirmed more or less generously. There is a customary assumption that the sphere of interests is wider in many Member States than the sum of rights in Germany.[86] Since the requirements for the intensity of the interest may vary, it is by all means plausible to believe that the sphere of interests in one Member State is narrower than the sphere of rights in another. In Germany, for example, despite the approach of the protective norm theory—which in general is perceived as being strict—some assume generous practice with a wide range of legally protected interests.[87] It would be interesting to examine the widespread

---

[84] Reiling, see n 33 above, 173–179 and Kadelbach, see n 23 above, 375ff.

[85] For a closer look cf Fichtner, see n 62 above, 203.

[86] C Calliess, 'Feinstaub im Rechtsschutz deutscher Verwaltungsgerichte' (2006) Neue Zeitschrift für Verwaltungsrecht, 2ff; Fichtner, see n 62 above, 124, 202ff and Classen, see n 43 above, 59ff, 82.

[87] Kadelbach, see n 23 above, 377ff.

belief of there being more interests than rights on a case-by-case basis. Such tightly focused investigations, however, are few and far between.[88]

Regarding EU rights it would be particularly interesting to examine *why* rights or interests are wider or narrower. To date, no efficient explanation has been found. Factors such as the historical development and constitutional tradition, the role of administration and courts, or the fundamental position of the citizen within the state are named as reasons.[89] Some also refer to 'historical coincidences'.[90] Such reasoning has little significance for the concrete application of law.

In summary, rights and interests are determined to some extent in methodologically differing ways. How narrow or wide they are is unlikely to be solely attributable to this. Thus, one cannot derive a great deal from the terms 'right' and 'interest'. This applies the more where there are EU rights which pick up the differences between the Member States and alternatively require a sufficient interest or an infringement of a right. In so doing, on the one hand, the EU legislator reacts to the differences between rights and interests in the Member States. On the other hand, both concepts appear to be equally appropriate to transposing the *same* EU right into national law. One may wonder if this works only with rights to action. Thus, in the end, one achieves as little understanding of EU rights from the comparison between rights and interests as one does from an examination of the relationship between rights and judicial control.

5 Basic characteristics of EU rights

5.1 *Advantages of an autonomous concept of EU rights*

On this basis, when dealing with EU rights it is advisable not exclusively to explore differences in and parallels to national systems by comparative means, for such differences or parallels reveal little about the concept of EU rights. Since it is already very difficult even to pinpoint the key attributes of every individual Member State's national concept, one certainly cannot expect them to disclose too much knowledge of the concept of EU rights. On

---

[88] Eg, Epiney, see n 5 above, 365–386; Classen, see n 43 above, 40–52, 59–65; and regarding environmental law, Epiney and Sollberger, see n 54 above.

[89] Epiney, see n 5 above, 364, 385ff and cf also Prechal, see n 16 above, 112.

[90] Kadelbach, see n 23 above, 369.

the contrary, by overemphasizing national concepts one would unnecessarily burden an examination of EU rights with the insecurities and differences of the Member States.

This does not exclude the possibility of parallels between the concept of EU rights and elements of the national concepts of rights. The character of EU rights must nonetheless be autonomous. This means that the EU model can—without obligation to do so—bear similarities to certain aspects of established Member State models. It can also unite various elements from different national concepts.

In addition, being aware of the national concepts is important in the detection of possible differences between the national concepts and EU rights and the detection of possible differences in understandings. From this perspective, elaborating the characteristics of EU rights is to some degree inseparable from the respective national approaches, which are necessarily influenced by national ideas, at least to some extent. Insights into the national concepts are a starting point: no more and no less than that. However, exploring the concept of EU rights must go beyond this and should lead to an autonomous notion. Apart from that, the significance of the national systems in the development of a concept of EU rights is limited to their being a mechanism of implementation that is subordinated to EU law, ie the Member States have to set and apply the necessary (procedural and material) rules.

5.2 *Substantive notion and normative approach*

Substantive notion

On the basis of the case law of the ECJ and CFI one can remark, first of all, that EU rights are not a purely procedural notion but also a substantive one, because they are not of importance in terms of judicial enforceability alone. Judicial enforceability concerns only the enforcement of a right, not its existence. The substantive nature of EU rights should not be obscured by the previous case law of the ECJ which prioritized the procedural possibilities of rights rather than their factual and personal scope.[91] This substantive nature does not rule out that an EU provision can grant a mere right to participation in legal procedures or a right of action.[92]

The differentiation between the (substantive) granting of EU rights and their (procedural) enforcement is especially important because rights can be

---

[91] cf Classen, see n 43 above, 78 and Reiling, see n 33 above, 302.
[92] cf the example discussed in s 4.3 above.

granted in one legal order, whereas judicial protection is offered by another. The right is thus granted by EU law, while its protection occurs through national law, insofar as taking direct legal action before the EU Courts is not possible or unless EU law makes exceptional requirements of judicial protection at Member State level. There is only *one* model of EU rights, while simultaneously, there are different conceptions of judicial protection.

EU rights can also be said to be a substantive notion in the sense that they largely derive from substantive (written or unwritten) law and not from procedural EU law, of which there is not a great deal anyway.

Normative approach

The rights of the individual are derived from EU provisions. So the normative approach is another characteristic of EU rights,[93] namely the requirement of a legal norm of the EU to indicate whether (to whom and to which extent) a right is granted. The normative approach can be recognized in the method of the ECJ for determining rights. It examines both the wording and the purpose of a provision.[94] Therefore, one can define EU rights as the normatively protected position of an individual.

The normative approach of EU rights is, however, shaped quite differently from the way it is in German law, for the normative connection at EU level is less intense. It is sufficient that an EU legal act, for example a directive—including the recitals in the preamble—generally indicates that the individual is intended to have rights.[95] Single elements of a provision are less relevant for granting an EU right. At least this is true for the question of *whether* an EU right is granted. In contrast, the normative approach can be more intensive for the scope of a right.[96]

There is no contradiction between the normative approach and the existence of EU rights that refer to rights *or* interests. The EU norm clarifies that a right *is* intended. Additionally, it can determine *who* is entitled to it and *what* it grants—but it need not regulate this in all details.[97]

---

[93] Also Reiling, see n 33 above, 311.

[94] cf Case C-37/98 *Savas* [2000] ECR I-2927, paras 39, 46, 51ff and Joined Cases C-178/94, C-179/94, C-188/94, C-189/94, and C-190/94 *Dillenkofer* [1996] ECR I-4845, paras 34–36.

[95] cf Joined Cases C-178/94, C-179/94, C-188/94, C-189/94, and C-190/94 *Dillenkofer* [1996] ECR I-4845, paras 37, 39 and Jarass and Beljin, see n 25 above, 179.

[96] See s 6.3 below.

[97] See s 6.3 below.

5.3 *How EU rights reach the individual*

Implementation, direct application, and interpretation of national law

There are several ways for EU rights to reach the individual. One must distinguish this from the question as to whether an EU legal act contains a right[98] and from the effect of EU rights on judicial enforceabilty.[99]

One possibility is the direct application (in respect of direct effect)[100] of EU rights. The ECJ occasionally equates the notion of rights with the possibility of 'relying' on these norms in court.[101] This can lead to misunderstanding in two ways. First, the notions of direct applicability and of EU rights are not identical, because direct application does not require individual rights as a precondition and vice versa.[102] And second, the ways in which EU rights reach the individual—including the route of direct application—apply independently of the question of whether or not a right needs to be judicially enforceable.

Other EU rights stem from EU law but need to be implemented by means of national provisions.[103] The possibility exists, however, of interpreting national provisions—in conformity with EU law—in such a way that they grant rights. The implementation does not always need to result in an explicit right. It can also result in an obligation serving individual interests, as long as it clearly covers the extent of the EU right both personally and in substance. However, due to the requirements concerning the implementation of directives, explicit rights in directives should be implemented by explicit national rights.[104] Upon implementation EU rights are national law, while in terms of their content they remain EU rights, at least insofar as the content of the right is specified in EU law. In cases when EU law provides for minimum rights, the content of the right remains EU law within the scope of the minimum right.

---

[98] Prechal, see n 16 above, 96.

[99] See s 3.3 above.

[100] The terms, direct applicability' and, direct effect' are used interchangeably within this text.

[101] Case C-37/98 *Savas* [2000] ECR I-2927, para 38 and Case 8/81 *Becker* [1982] ECR 53, para 25.

[102] cf Ruffert, see n 68 above, Art 249 EC, paras 66, 108. See for details the next subheading below.

[103] Prechal, see n 16 above, 96. Also Ruffert, see n 27 above, 322.

[104] For details cf HD Jarass and S Beljin, 'Die Bedeutung von Vorrang und Durchführung des EG-Rechts für die nationale Rechtsetzung und Rechtsanwendung' (2004) Neue Zeitschrift für Verwaltungsrecht, 8ff.

The categories of directly applicable EU rights and those to be nationally implemented can overlap. This becomes clear in cases where directives provide for rights: a right provided for in a directive can be directly applicable until it is implemented.[105]

Relationship between EU rights and direct applicability

Direct application is just one *technique* by which a right that is stipulated in EU law can be brought to the individual. An EU provision that has no direct effect can very well contain rights. For example, rights against private persons in directives have no direct effect due to the limits of horizontal directive effects.[106] Another example is a directive that is not precise enough to be directly applied, but which stipulates the granting of a right in national law. This was relevant in the case of a directive that stipulated a right for employees in the event of the insolvency of their employer, but did not identify the person liable to provide the guarantee.[107]

On the other hand, whether a directly applicable provision always grants a right is not yet entirely clear. This is, in part, assumed in the literature,[108] notwithstanding the question *who* can enforce the right.[109] One may argue for this, that the ECJ affirms a right just by reference to precedent cases on direct applicability.[110] On the other hand, the ECJ emphasizes the difference between the direct obligation of state authorities and the possibilty of the individual relying on a directly applicable provision.[111] From this, one can conclude that direct application is first an objective phenomenon concerning the duties of public authorities within Member States. This can—without obligation to do so—be supplemented on a second level by the issue of rights.[112] From this, one can also draw the conclusion that an individual right cannot be a necessary precondition for direct application.[113] Further-

[105]   Eg, Case C-354/98 *Commission v France* [1999] ECR I-4927, para 11 and Jarass and Beljin, see n 25 above, 64.

[106]   cf HD Jarass and S Beljin, 'Grenzen der Privatbelastung durch unmittelbar wirkende Richtlinien' (2004) Europarecht, 718.

[107]   Case C-6/90 *Francovich* [1991] ECR I-5357, paras 26ff.

[108]   Eg, Ruffert, see n 50 above, 71.

[109]   cf the Opinion of Advocate General Kokott in Case C-127/02 *Landelijke Vereniging tot Behoud van de Waddenzee* [2004] ECR I-7405, para 138.

[110]   Joined Cases C-46/93 and C-48/93 *Brasserie and Factortame* [1996] ECR I-1029, para 54 and Case C-150/99 *Stockholm Lindöpark* [2001] ECR I-493, paras 35, 30–32.

[111]   Case C-431/92 *Commission v Germany* [1995] ECR I-2189, para 26.

[112]   Jarass and Beljin, see n 25 above, 166.

[113]   cf HD Jarass and S Beljin, 'Unmittelbare Anwendung des EG-Rechts und EG-rechtskonforme Auslegung' (2003) Juristenzeitung, 771 and Ruffert, see n 68 above, Art 249 EC, paras 94–97.

more, one can conclude that one does not face different types of direct applicability but the consequences of the same direct applicability for the obligated State bodies, on the one hand, and the persons relying on the direct application, on the other.[114]

6 Criteria for determining EU rights

6.1 *Explicit and non-explicit EU rights*

In accordance with the normative approach, whether or not an EU provision grants a right depends on what it aims to regulate and thus on the content. In this, it is possible that an EU provision *explicitly* provides for a right. The search for an explicit right therefore ranks first.[115] Numerous provisions of EU law contain such explicit rights. Examples are both the fundamental rights of the EU and many directives and regulations within secondary legislation.[116] However, the use of the term 'right' is not obligatory. Rather, one often encounters the term 'entitlement', as is the case, for example, in Article 7(6) of the so-called Deposit-Guarantees Directive.[117]

However, norms that do not *explicitly* formulate a right can be interpreted in such a way that they do in fact grant rights. The ECJ noted this for fundamental freedoms long ago: 'Rights arise not only where they are expressly granted by the Treaty, but also by reason of obligations which the Treaty imposes in a clearly defined way upon individuals as well as upon the Member States and upon the Institutions of the Community.'[118] A further practical example for non-explicit rights is the directive about information in the field of technical standards and regulations.[119] Such non-explicit rights raise the question of how to recognize whether and possibly upon whom the obligation in question grants a right.

---

[114] Ruffert, see n 68 above, Art 249 EC, para 101.

[115] Case C-222/02 *Peter Paul* [2004] ECR I-9425, paras 27, 41.

[116] Eilmansberger, see n 51 above, 68–70 and HG Fischer, *Europarecht* (3rd edn, München: Beck, 2001) para 6: 38, 40.

[117] Parliament and Council Directive (EC) 94/19 on deposit-guarantee schemes [1994] OJ L135/5. On the right stipulated in this provision see Case 222/02 *Peter Paul* [2004] ECR I-9425, paras 26ff.

[118] Case 26/62 *Van Gend&Loos* [1963] ECR 1.

[119] Case C-443/98 *Unilever* [2000] ECR I-7535, para 51.

6.2 Differentiation of non-explicit EU rights (the 'whether' of granting a right)

Criteria stemming from EU law

Whether an EU right is granted—if it is not explicitly stated in the text of a norm—depends on what the norm aims to regulate. Since the granting of rights occurs within the legal order of the EU, EU law delivers the criteria and the standard for the test of whether and to whom an EU legal act confers a right. Scholarly discussion on whether the EU right is determined according to criteria of the EU or by national criteria[120] can only decide in favour of the former if the argument follows on from the autonomous concept of EU rights. However, this does not rule out the possibility that *one* of the criteria for the determination of EU rights can be whether the Member States grant rights through comparable provisions.[121]

Direction of protection as the most important aspect

Provisions on the allocation of powers between the EU institutions grant *no* rights to individuals because they are not designed for the individual's protection but to protect the balance between EU institutions.[122] Furthermore, an EU provision with the sole purpose of providing the Commission with information grants no individual rights. Such a legal act only concerns the relations between the Member States and the Union.[123] A state's duty of supervision in the sphere of deposit guarantees also grants no right. A different right does exist in this particular field, however.[124]

One can infer from the explanations given by the ECJ and CFI that emphasis is placed on whether the individual is meant to be protected by the legal norm (that is, emphasis on the purpose of the legal norm), and whether the individual is involved in the legal relationship that the norm aims to regulate. First of all, this clarifies that the (often controversially) debated question as to whether the protection of individual interests is a precondition for the granting of an EU right[125] needs to be answered in the positive.

---

[120] cf Jarass and Beljin, see n 25 above, 178ff.

[121] Case C-222/02 *Peter Paul* [2004] ECR I-9425, para 44.

[122] Case C-282/90 *Vreugdenhil* [1992] ECR I-1937, para 20 and Joined Cases T-64/01 and T-65/01 *Afrikanische Frucht-Compagnie* [2004] ECR II-521, para 116.

[123] Case C-380/87 *Enichem Base* [1989] ECR 2491, paras 19–24 and Case C-194/94 *CIA* [1996] ECR I-2201, para 49.

[124] See s 6.3 below.

[125] cf Jarass and Beljin, see n 25 above, 177ff.

If this was not the case, then every binding requirement that is regulated in an EU provision would have to grant a right. However, the ECJ does not go this far.

Regarding the purpose of a legal provision, use of the word 'protection' is a main indicator for a granting intention.[126] If the act serves to protect the individual or a subject of protection that benefits the individual, then the act contains at least *one* right. In this way, the ECJ justified the granting of rights on the grounds that an EU provision serves to 'protect human health in particular',[127] to 'protect human beings against the effects of lead in the environment',[128] to 'protect public health',[129] to 'protect tenderers against arbitrariness on the part of a contract-awarding authority',[130] to 'protect consumers',[131] to 'protect the Community' s groundwater',[132] or to 'protect depositors'.[133]

However, the term 'protection' need not be explicitly stated. It is sufficient if, for example, a legal norm serves other objectives that are advantageous for the individual, such as the free movement of goods.[134] In addition, the objective of protection can be very general, just as long as it includes the individual, as is exemplified by the protection of human health or the movement of goods.

In the light of the case law up to now, it is unclear whether there is—next to the examination of protection—an independent criteria of a legal relationship that is regulated by the respective provision.[135] As was pointed out above, the ECJ has justified the denial of a right with the fact that the provision in question solely concerns the legal relationships between the Member State and the Community. But the key question is *why* this is so. For there are provisions whose contents are obligations of the Member States to the Commission, but which still contain a right. One can find directives in

---

[126] See also Ruffert, see n 68 above, Art 249 EC, paras 64, 68 and C Calliess, 'Kohärenz und Konvergenz beim europäischen Individualrechtsschutz' (2002) Neue Juristische Wochenschrift, 3578ff.

[127] Case C-361/88 *Commission v Germany* [1991] ECR I-2567, para 16.

[128] Case C-59/89 *Commission v Germany* [1991] ECR I-2607, para 19.

[129] Case C-58/89 *Commission v Germany* [1991] ECR I-4983, para 14.

[130] Case C-433/93 *Commission v Germany* [1995] ECR I-2303, para 19.

[131] Joined Cases C-178/94, C-179/94, C-188/94, C-189/94, and C-190/94 *Dillenkofer* [1996] ECR I-4845, paras 35ff.

[132] Case C-131/88 *Commission v Germany* [1991] ECR I-825, para 7.

[133] Case C-222/02 *Peter Paul* [2004] ECR I-9425, paras 26, 38.

[134] Case C-194/94 *CIA* [1996] ECR I-2201, paras 40ff, 48–50.

[135] cf Prechal, see n 16 above, 115–118.

which private parties are not part of the relationship, their rights or obligations not mentioned.[136] Such a directive can nonetheless grant the individual
a right because it serves the free movement of goods, and therefore—in the
end—also serves the individual.[137] As a consequence, the normative purpose
is also relevant when determining the legal relationships that are covered by
an EU provision. Finally, the criterion of legal relationships does not have an
entirely individual meaning. One could perhaps differentiate two categories
of provisions. Provisions regulating relationships of a private party always
grant rights. Where private parties are not part of the legal relationship, the
question as to whether rights are granted depends on the protective purpose
of the provisions.

Overall, the criteria for the granting of an EU right are generous. There
are few EU legal acts from which one cannot derive any right. However,
this is limited by the fact that when it comes to legal acts containing explicit
rights, no further rights are drawn from respective provisions of that legal
act.[138] This concerns the *scope* of the rights that stem from the directive in
question, rather than the question of whether any rights are granted. The
scope of the limitation will depend on how often the EU legislator stipulates
explicit rights.

Reasons for granting EU rights and significance of the functional aspects

The criteria for granting an EU right could be influenced by the *reasons*
for doing so. There is a widespread thesis that the granting of EU rights is
geared less towards the interests of the individual and more towards mobilizing him as an instrument for enforcing EU law.[139] This functional orientation has the effect that *every* EU norm grants rights as long as it contains
only sufficiently unambiguous obligations. Quite apart from the fact that
the thesis of mobilizing or *functionalizing* the individual is also contended—
and that its significance is in the end relativized[140]—one must not fail to
register that the grounds for granting a right and the criteria for determining a right operate on different levels.[141] A mutual influence is not out of the

---

[136] Eg, Council Directive (EEC) 83/189 laying down a procedure for the provision of information in the field of technical standards and regulations [1983] OJ L109/8.

[137] Case C-194/94 *CIA* [1996] ECR I-2201.

[138] See for details s 6.3 below.

[139] J Masing, *Die Mobilisierung des Bürgers für die Durchsetzung des Rechts* (Berlin: Duncker &
Humblot, 1997); A von Bogdandy in E Grabitz and M Hilf (eds), *Recht der EU* (München: Beck,
2004) Art 288 EC, para 16 and for further references see Fichtner, see n 62 above, 185.

[140] Fichtner, see n 62 above, 219 and Reiling, see n 33 above, 365.

[141] Fichtner, see n 62 above, 18, 21 and Reiling, see n 33 above, 121, 148, 516.

question. However, reference to the functional orientation *on its own* can hardly explain why there are EU norms that grant no rights at all. This does not exclude the possibility of it being *one* of a number of criteria.[142] It is by all means possible that functional aspects can constitute the main argument for the granting of an EU right. For example, the ECJ has an eye on the effectiveness of an EU legal act[143] or on ensuring fair trading and the transparency of markets in the Community.[144]

6.3 *Scope of EU rights*

Difference between the granting of rights and their scope

The (general) protective purpose of EU provisions does not have significance in terms of their contents or their scope.[145] The determination of rights therefore requires two examinatory steps. This two-step test is recurrent in the jurisprudence of the ECJ. The first step is an examination of whether a Community provision *grants* a right or not, and the second aims at determining the scope of the right, ie whether or not the person in question can actually draw on it.[146]

The scope of a right can be of great practical relevance because a generous grant of a right can be put into perspective by restricting the scope of the right.[147] Since EU law grants rights quite generously, the more practically relevant question in the future may be *who* is entitled to the right and *what* it contains.

On the determinability of an EU right's scope

To date, the criteria for determining the personal and substantive scope of an EU right are not greatly developed. The ECJ has rarely addressed this issue.[148] One of only a few exceptions is a directive on the guarantee of deposits.[149] This may be attributable to the fact that EU provisions often make no or only limited statements as to who should be entitled to a right and what scope the right has as regards content. In the literature, this is

---

[142] See s 6.3 below.
[143] Eg, Case C-194/94 *CIA* [1996] ECR I-2201, para 48.
[144] Case C-253/00 *Muños and Superior Fruiticola* [2002] ECR I-7289, para 31.
[145] Case C-222/02 *Peter Paul* [2004] ECR I-9425, para 40.
[146] Case C-194/94 *CIA* [1996] ECR I-2201, paras 40ff, 48–50; similar Case C-162/00 *Pokrzeptowicz-Meyer* [2002] ECR I-1049, paras 18ff and Case C-222/02 *Peter Paul* [2004] ECR I-9425, paras 25ff.
[147] Reiling, see n 33 above, 169.
[148] Ruffert, see n 68 above, Art 249 EC, para 64.
[149] Case C-222/02 *Peter Paul* [2004] ECR I-9425, paras 25ff, 33ff.

sometimes pinpointed as *the* main deficit of EU rights.[150] However, the lack of outlining of rights in the directives is often deliberate. They often provide either for minimum rights, for the implementation of which the Member States retain a certain degree of discretion.[151] Alternatively, the directive requires 'sanctions' that are not defined in detail but which can also include rights.[152] In the light of such practice, the national legislator and the national executive have no choice but to deal with the problems that result from it.

First indications

The starting point for the question of *who* is entitled to a right has to be the group of people that is stated in the granting EU act. In some provisions, the circle of beneficiaries is more closely specified than in others, for example regarding the consumer, bidder, or depositor.

Problems arise when the circle of entitled persons is broad, especially in cases when everyone is protected. In such cases, the entitled persons can be determined by the degree to which they are (actually or potentially) concerned.[153] The following rule should apply in EU law as it does in national law: the *less* one can derive from the norm, the greater the significance of being concerned *factually*. However, how the latter is determined is again not clear. EU law grants a right to those who are 'affected or who have an interest'[154] without elaborating whether there is a difference and if so, what that difference is. In another provision, affectedness functions as a generic term for the parties concerned and entities with an interest.[155]

Those entitled need not be limited to those people who fall within the coverage of personal applicability of the legal act. An example is the principle of equal treatment of men and women in Directive 79/7, of which the scope covers discriminated people of both genders. In addition, the husband of a discriminated woman can deduce rights from the directive.[156]

---

[150] Eilmansberger, see n 1 above, 1245ff.
[151] Eg, Case C-303/98 *Simap* [2000] ECR I-7963, para 68 and Case C-283/94 *Denkavit International BV* [1996] ECR I-5063, para 39.
[152] Case 14/83 *Von Colson and Kamann* [1984] ECR 1891, para 18, 23 and Case C-180/95 *Draehmpaehl* [1997] ECR I-2195, para 24ff.
[153] Jarass and Beljin, see n 25 above, 181 and Ruffert, see n 68 above, Art 249 EC, para 69.
[154] Art 6(4) Parliament and Council Directive (EC) 2001/42 on the assessment of the effects of certain plans and programmes on the environment [2001] OJ L197/30.
[155] Art 2(f) Parliament and Council Directive (EC) 2002/30 on the establishment of rules and procedures with regard to the introduction of noise-related operating restrictions at Community airports [2002] OJ L85/40.
[156] Case C-87/90 *Verholen* [1991] ECR I-3757, paras 23, 26 and Case C-343/92 *Roks* [1994] ECR I-571, para 42.

Just because an EU provision protects the free movement of goods does not give any indication of whether this covers the manufacturer personally, the distributor, and/or the consumers. All of these groups are in fact covered as long as the use or marketing of a product is hindered.[157] This is, however, not the case with the use of a product by the public authorities, inasmuch as it is not liable to create an obstacle to trade.[158]

In order to determine the *substantive content* of a right, ie its substantive scope, the ECJ has to make grammatical, systematic, and teleological interpretations of the provisions in question. Indications for or against a certain content can be deduced from the recitals in the preamble to the legal act, if they—for example—explicitly rule out a right.[159] However, the ECJ additionally performs an interpretation of the provisions of the legal act in question.[160]

The existence of an explicit, selective right can—for systematic reasons—allow the conclusion that another provision within the same legal act does not grant a further right.[161] Should a number of legal acts concern the same subject and should one of these acts of law grant rights, then one can conclude that the other legal acts do not grant any rights.[162] In such cases, the *lex specialis* rule should apply. Does this lead to a result that an EU legal act without explicit rights grants more rights than an EU act where no explicit rights are stipulated? The answer to this question depends on the scope of rights in EU acts without explicit rights. Such rights need not be endless. This assumption is supported by the fact that in the past, the ECJ has refused to draw rights from a directive that (as a whole) served to protect humans' health, without indicating the speciality of other rights.[163]

From a teleological point of view, the ECJ inquires as to whether a certain substantive content of the right is needed in order to achieve the purpose of the legal act.[164] A directive that generally requires the interested party to be able to assert his rights in court leaves the Member States with discretion regarding the contents of these rights.[165] If the Member State opts for an

---

[157] Case C-226/97 *Lemmens* [1998] ECR I-3711, paras 32, 35.
[158] ibid, paras 36ff.
[159] Case C-222/02 *Peter Paul* [2004] ECR I-9425, para 31.
[160] ibid, paras 27–31.
[161] ibid, paras 29ff.
[162] ibid, para 45.
[163] Case 380/87 *Enichem Base* [1989] ECR 2491, paras 19–23.
[164] Case C-222/02 *Peter Paul* [2004] ECR I-9425, paras 42ff.
[165] Case 14/83 *Von Colson and Kamann* [1984] ECR 1891, para 18 and Case C-271/91 *Marshall* (Compare Ch 16 n 107) [1993] ECR I-4367, para 23.

entitlement to compensation, then this entitlement has to be efficient. The compensation has to be in appropriate relation to the suffered damages.[166] Equally, the legal consequences of entitlement to community liability must be appropriate and effective.[167] The complexity of a statutory duty and the vast range of interests that are to be protected while the duty is being pursued could be an argument against granting a right.[168] In general, effectiveness of an EU legal act does not only play a role for the question as to whether an EU provisions grants a right or not[169] but also in relation to the scope of the right.[170] Finally, it can be of relevance if comparable provisions at the national level grant rights.[171]

7 Results

The notion of EU rights must not be reduced to aspects of enforceabilty. The ECJ might emphasize the judicial enforceabilty of EU rights. Yet, it also stresses their relevance outside judicial enforcement. In addition, the limitation of EU rights to judicial protection is contradicted by the fact that judicial protection without EU rights exists and that there can also be EU rights without judicial protection. Furthermore, Member States' rights and their systems of judicial protection are multi-layered to a degree that renders it impossible to denominate the distinctive features of rights. Regarding EU rights, it must be added that they are enforced by up to twenty-eight systems of judicial protection—that of the EU and those of the Member States—or even more, depending on (regional) differences within a Member State. The clear distinction between EU rights and judicial protection does not rule out the possibility of EU rights affecting their enforceabilty before EU and national courts.

By juxtaposing rights and interests, again not much can be derived about EU rights. The fact that rights and interests are determined in a

---

[166] Case 14/83 *Von Colson and Kamann* [1984] ECR 1891, para 23 and Case C-180/95 *Draehmpaehl* [1997] ECR I-2195, para 25.
[167] Case C-373/95 *Maso* [1997] ECR I-4051, paras 36, 41 and Joined Cases C-46/93 and C-48/93 *Brasserie and Factortame* [1996] ECR I-1029, para 82.
[168] Case C-222/02 *Peter Paul* [2004] ECR I-9425, para 44.
[169] See s 6.2 above.
[170] cf Case C-174/02 *Streekgewest Westelijk Noord-Brabant* [2005] ECR I-85, paras 14–21.
[171] Case C-222/02 *Peter Paul* [2004] ECR I-9425, para 44.

methodologically different way does not lead to any conclusions regarding their scope. That applies all the more as there are EU rights picking up the differences between the Member States by requiring alternatively a sufficient interest or an infringement of rights. This shows that rights and interests are equally appropriate to transpose the *same* EU right into national law.

On this basis, when dealing with EU rights it is advisable not exclusively to explore differences in, and parallels to, national systems by comparative means, for such differences or parallels reveal little about the concept of EU rights. Since it is already very difficult even to pinpoint the key attributes of every individual Member State's national concept, one can certainly not expect them to disclose too much elucidation of the concept of EU rights. This does not exclude the possibility of parallels between the concept of EU rights and elements of the national concepts of rights, but the character of EU rights must nonetheless be autonomous. This means that the EU model can—without obligation to do so—bear similarities to certain aspects of established Member State models and can unite various elements from different national concepts. Insights into the national concepts are a starting point, no more and no less than that. However, an exploration of the concept of EU rights must go beyond this and should lead to an autonomous understanding. Apart from that, the significance of the national systems in the development of a concept of EU rights is limited to them being a mechanism of implementation that is subordinated to EU law.

EU rights are a substantive notion and not purely procedural because their relevance is not limited to their judicial enforceability. This does not rule out the existence of pure procedural rights or rights of action in EU law. EU rights are also characterized by the normative approach which means that they stem from EU provisions. So they can be defined as the position of an individual that is protected by law.

The criteria for the question as to whether a non-explicit right is granted can only be delivered by EU law. However, this does not rule out the possibility that *one* of the criteria for the determination of EU rights can be whether the Member States grant rights through comparable or similar provisions. In a first step, regarding the question as to whether an EU provision grants a right at all, a generally protective orientation of the EU act in its entirety is sufficient. EU rights can be recognized particularly when the act is intended to support the protection of specific groups of people or people in general. The case law of the ECJ and CFI is generous.

In a second step, the scope of a right requires clarification. The generous granting of EU rights gives rise to the belief that in future this step will be of more practical relevance. The criteria for determining the scope of a right are not well developed as yet because many EU rights are tailored to leave the details of defining that scope to the Member States. The starting point in determining *who* is entitled is the protected group of people. The more vaguely this group is defined, the more the entitlement depends on factual aspects of concern. In order to determine the range of *what* is covered in substance, the ECJ makes grammatical, systematic, and teleological deliberations. From a systematic perspective, the existence of an explicit, selective right can give reason to conclude that other provisions in the same legal act or in other legal acts on the same topic do not provide for further rights. The *lex specialis* rule applies in such cases.

Whether or not this leads to the assumption that an EU legal act without explicit rights tends to contain more rights than an EU legal act with explicit rights depends on the scope of non-explicit rights. This scope needs not be unlimited—especially if one aims at avoiding discrepancies with EU legal acts with explicit rights.

EU Rights and Discretion as Reflected in Spanish Public Law

Ricardo Alonso García, Leonor Moral Soriano, and Carmen Plaza Martín

1 Introduction: convergence and divergence, rights and discretion

The scheme according to which Community law confers rights and Member States provide the judicial remedy leads to two apparently contradictory requirements:[1] the need for uniform and coherent application of law versus subsidiarity and national procedural autonomy; and the need for legislative and judicial restraint versus the need for citizens to be able to enforce rights granted under Community law. Therefore, this scheme involves both convergence and divergence, for the effective application of Community law ought to be reconciled with the divergent systems of judicial (and administrative) protection of Community rights at Member States' level.

Convergence and divergence are symptoms rather than causes of the interaction between two different legal systems. Indeed, the question of the interaction of Community law and national law(s) is a question of legal pluralism and, in this sense, the normative answer to the question on how to deal with legal pluralism is the heterarchical organized configuration of legal authority.

---

[1] T Heukels and J Tib, 'Towards Homogeneity in the Field of Legal Remedies: Convergence and Divergence' in P Beaumont, C Lyons, and N Walker (eds), *Convergence & Divergence in European Public Law* (Oxford: Hart, 2002) 111–112.

In this scenario we witness a more deliberative mode of dialogue between actors occupying authoritative sites: the dialogue existing between the European Court of Justice (ECJ) and the national courts. Rights and discretion are analysed here to understand how this dialogue between heterarchical systems takes place, and to test how far this organization of legal authority is possible when the ECJ's strategies of convergence collide with the national constitutional framework.

From the point of view of the interaction between EC law and national legal orders, 'rights' and 'discretion' are key concepts for the implementation and enforcement of EC law by national authorities. They are essential for the functioning of this supranational 'autonomous' legal order that depends on national legal orders for the application of its rules, and the way they are handled has a deep influence on the development of EC law and national laws as interwoven legal systems.

Conceptual divergence of terms such as 'rights' and 'discretion' might be seen, in fact, as a handy corollary of Community legal order dependence on national legislative, administrative, and judicial structures and procedures for the implementation of EC law—which is the main variable affecting the 'homogeneous and uniform' application of EC Law.[2] In the context of the intertwined relationship between EC and national legal orders, the lack of Community definitions of 'rights' and 'discretion' makes it possible for these concepts to work as *escape valves*, hand-in-hand with the principles of national institutional and procedural autonomy, allowing national public authorities a certain degree of flexibility to accommodate better national legal structures, institutions, traditions, and procedures to the task of implementing and enforcing EC law.

To provide additional elements for the discussion on the phenomenon of conceptual divergence and legal convergence in the relationship of EC and national legal orders, this contribution focuses on the main features and problems that the concepts of 'rights' and 'discretion' pose in Spanish law and on how such concepts influence—along with the principles of institutional and procedural national autonomy—the process of implementing EC law by national authorities. It will also take a look at the way they are actually used in some EC instances and to what extent they diverge from the way in which they are used in Spain. This will allow a first assessment on how such

---

[2] See, eg, C Harlow, 'Codification of EC Administrative Procedures? Fitting the Foot to the Shoe or the Shoe to the Foot' (1996) 2 Eur L J, 5ff.

concepts may make it possible for Member States as well as EC institutions to achieve different results when applying EC law, and to what extent it can entail a breach in the unity of the Community legal system.

These issues will be explored in three parts. First, this chapter gives an outline of the relevance of the concepts of *rights* and *discretion* in Spanish law. Second, it deals with the notion of rights and discretion as developed by the ECJ's case law in order to identify parallels or differences, ie convergences and divergences in the way they have been conceived and are used in the Spanish legal system. Finally, it studies the reception of EC rights and discretion in Spanish public law. In particular, it focuses on the translation of EC rights into Spanish legal categories of rights, and their protection by Spanish courts and tribunal, and explores how the ECJ's notion of discretion alters the scope of judicial review undertaken by Spanish judges.

2 On rights and discretion in the Spanish legal order

2.1 *Rights and interests in Spanish law*

Within the Spanish legal order the legal position of individuals, vis-à-vis public authorities or other individuals, is determined by diverse positive and negative conditions. Among the different categories of positive conditions that individuals may enjoy according to Spanish public law the most relevant are the following: fundamental rights enshrined by the Spanish Constitution, mere individual rights,[3] and legitimate interests. All of them define spheres of individual powers that are the object of judicial protection, albeit the intensity of such protection varies among the different categories. Furthermore, the Constitution also sets out a list of 'Principles guiding social and economic policy', which will play an important role in the judicial review of public authorities' acts.

---

[3] *Derechos subjetivos* is the legal term used by Spanish legal doctrine to refer to what in English is called 'individual rights'. It should be noticed that it comprises different subcategories such as 'collective rights' as opposed to strictly 'individual rights', or 'public rights' as opposed to 'private rights'. See the Introduction for a reflection on the problems caused by the fact that the term 'right' is not always used in same fashion in the different national legal orders.

Fundamental rights, constitutional rights, and the 'Principles guiding social and economic policy'

The 1978 Spanish Constitution (hereinafter SC) enshrines in Title I, Chapter II a long list of 'Rights and Freedoms' which comprises not only different types and categories of rights, but also citizens' duties (Article 14 to Article 38 SC).

Section 1, 'On Fundamental Rights and Public Freedoms' (Articles 15 to 29) establishes traditional fundamental rights and freedoms, such as the right to life and to physical and moral integrity, the rights to freedom and security, freedom of ideology, religion and worship, the right to free expression, and the right to obtain effective judicial protection among others. To this group of rights and freedoms should be added the principle of equality and non-discrimination enshrined in Article 14 (or, in the language of rights, the right of every citizen to equal treatment before the law). They guarantee individual freedoms (*status libertatis*) and political rights to participate in the public life of the democratic state (*status activae civitatis*) and enjoy the strongest mechanism of protection according to Article 53(2) of the Spanish Constitution:

Any citizen may assert a claim to protect the freedoms and rights recognized in Article 14 and in Section 1 of Chapter Two (Articles 15 to 29) by means of a preferential and summary procedure before the ordinary courts and, when appropriate, by lodging an individual appeal for protection (*recurso de amparo*) to the Constitutional Court.

Section 2, 'On Citizens Rights and Duties', lays down a mixture of citizens' duties (such as the duty to defend Spain), public freedoms (such as free enterprise), and economic or social rights (such as the right to private property, the right to employment, or the right to collective labour bargaining). There is no special procedure for individuals to request the judicial protection of such rights and freedoms: they will not benefit from the special constitutional appeal envisaged in Article 53(2) SC and they will be safeguarded by ordinary judges following ordinary procedures.

Further, it also contains a list of the 'Principles guiding social and economic policy', which includes also some 'socio-economic and cultural rights' and some of the so-called 'fundamental rights of third generation' such as the right to a healthy environment, the right to access to culture, or the right to adequate housing (Articles 39 to 52 SC).[4] In spite of the fact that in some

---

⁴ On 'collective fundamental rights' also called 'fundamental rights of third generation', such as the right to a healthy environment, see G Haarscher, 'Les droits collectifs contre les droits de l'homme' (1990) 3 Revue Trimestrielle des Droits de l'Homme, 231–233; A Kiss, 'Définition

cases they are worded in terms of 'rights' they are conceived as principles which should guide the legislative, administrative, and judicial activity of public authorities in Spain (or as goals that public authorities should attempt to achieve): according to Article 53(3) SC, 'substantive legislation, judicial practice and actions of the public authorities' shall be based on the acknowledgement, respect and protection of such 'principles' and, therefore, they do not benefit from the special constitutional appeal of Article 53(2) SC. Furthermore, they may only be invoked in the ordinary Courts 'in accordance with the legal provisions by which they are developed'. They are, in short, not directly enforceable, as they need to be translated into subjective rights through implementing legislation adopted by Parliament or the executive.

They can be invoked, however, as legal arguments to review the constitutionality and, therefore, the legality, of public authorities' provisions and acts. In other words, the Constitution does not foresee a direct judicial protection of such 'principles/rights', but they can be used, however, as interpretative or review criteria for any statute, regulation, or administrative act, and to control the discretionary powers of public authorities that might influence the effectiveness of these principles. In these cases there should be at least a 'legitimate interest' affected by the action or inaction of a public authority for an individual to have *locus standi* in the national courts to challenge it.[5]

Individuals or legal persons who are affected by any violation of these constitutional rights and principles can seek relief in different ways:

1. When the infringement is due to an act of the legislature (a law or any other norm with the force of law such as law decrees or legislative decrees), by bringing an action before the Contentious-administrative jurisdiction against any administrative act or regulation applying such a law (in which case a preliminary ruling on the constitutionality of that law should be requested from the Constitutional Court in those cases in which the

---

et nature juridique d'un droit de l'homme à l'environnement' in P Kromarek (ed), *Environment et droits de l'homme* (Paris: UNESCO, 1989) 24 and WP Gormley, *Human Rights and the Environment: The Need for International Co-operation* (Leiden: AW Sijthof, 1976) 32–72.

[5] In the particular case of Art 45 SC, which states that 'Everyone has the *right* to enjoy an environment suitable for personal development, as well as the duty to preserve it', it has been argued that such a provision enshrines a 'universal legitimate interest' for everyone to enjoy an adequate environment that allows any individual not only to request the annulment of any illegal act or statute, but also the restoration of any damage caused to the environment: see L Ortega Alvárez, 'El concepto de medio ambiente' in L Ortega Alvárez (ed), *Lecciones de Derecho del Medio Ambiente* (4th edn, Valladolid: Lex Nova, 2005) 52ff.

ordinary court has doubts on the constitutionality of such a law or when it considers it unconstitutional).
2. When the violation is due to a governmental regulation or an administrative act, the plaintiff may question their constitutionality and, therefore, their validity, before the Contentious-administrative jurisdiction, which has jurisdiction to decide directly on the grounds of case (without requesting a preliminary ruling from the Constitutional Court).

As explained above, only if there is a fundamental right (as listed in Articles 14 to 30) at stake, will it be safeguarded by means of a preferential and summary procedure before the ordinary courts and, when appropriate, by lodging an individual appeal for protection (*recurso de amparo*) to the Constitutional Court.

Public individual rights and legitimate interests

In Spain effective judicial protection of individuals, enshrined in the Constitution of most EU Member States as a fundamental right,[6] is based—according to Article 24 SC—on the existence not only of 'rights' but also of 'legitimate interests' which were affected by a illegal action or regulation. As a matter of fact the right to effective judicial protection has experience in Spain, as it has happened in other European countries[7], a conceptual expansion in order to embrace not only the protection of classical subjective rights but also the protection of individual or collective legitimate interests that go beyond such a concept.

In the Spanish legal system a public individual right may derive directly from the Constitution, Parliamentary acts or administrative regulations,[8] from administrative decisions addressed to an individual (licences, permits, concessions, etc), or from a contract between an individual and the administration. A legitimate interest exists, on the other hand, when an administration's illegal action causes impairment or damage to the individual (a harm to her/his interests), or whenever the individual could obtain an advantage or benefit if such an illegal action were annulled. The existence of damage (or the loss of an advantage) gives the individual the 'right' to react in defence of

---

[6] Eg, Art 19(4) of the German Constitution.

[7] E Schmidt-Assmann, *La teoría general del Derecho Administrativo como sistema* (Barcelona: Marcial Pons, 2003) 229.

[8] Eg, Art 35 of Act 30/1992 on the Common Administrative Procedure that lists several citizens' rights.

his/her legal sphere against the illegal public action that causes it.[9] In short, no one is obliged to suffer the consequences of an illegal act, and in those cases procedural rights are conferred on individuals to request the courts for the annulment of such an act, pursuant to Article 71 of *Ley 29/1998 de la Jurisdicción Contencioso-administrativa* (hereafter Contentious-Administrative Jurisdiction Act).

From this point of view, the concept of 'legitimate interests' has been construed by leading Spanish scholarship (and accepted by the administrative courts) as *derechos reaccionales*, that is a public subjective right to react against the illegal administrative exercise of powers conferred on those persons who suffer an impairment in their legal position.[10]

Legitimate interests as a right to react against illegal administrative actions—something that fuses substantive and procedural rights—lead us to the issue of the procedural autonomy that Member States enjoy when applying EC law in general, and which national courts enjoy when protecting EC rights in particular: in Spain, in order to have *locus standi* to act before the court against an illegal administrative action, an individual or group has to claim either a 'subjective right' or an individual or collective 'legitimate interest' that has been affected.[11]

The main difference in the degree of judicial protection between subjective rights and legitimate interests is that whereas an individual claiming a right will always be able to request not only the annulment of the illegal act or regulation but also whatever measure is needed to ensure the full restitution of such a right, those who claim legitimate interests will only be able, in principle, to request the annulment of the illegal act or regulation, unless they can prove that—in accordance with Article 31.2 of the Administrative Jurisdiction Act—they have an adversely affected 'individualized legal

---

[9] The Spanish Constitutional Court sums up the state of Spanish case law on this concept in Case 73/2006 of 13 May 2006. For a doctrinal construction see E García de Enterria and TR Fernández Rodríguez, *Curso de Derecho Administrativo*, Vol 2 (10th edn, Madrid: Cívitas, 2006) 47.

[10] E García de Enterría, 'Sobre los derechos públicos subjetivos' (1975) 6 Revista Española de Derecho Administrativo, 427–445.

[11] As it has been noticed above since the 1978 Spanish Constitution, 'legitimate interests' are guaranteed within the realm of the fundamental right to effective judicial protection (Art 24 SC). This concept is wider than the former one of 'direct and individual interest' used by the pre-constitutional Administrative Jurisdiction Act of 1956 (this latter was very similar to the concept of 'direct and individual concern' used under Art 230 EC Treaty in order to restrict the *locus standi* for individuals to challenge the legality of an act of EC institutions (as it has been narrowly interpreted by the ECJ in cases such as Case C-50/OO P *UPA* [2002] ECR I-6677). Furthermore, Art 7(3) of the Judiciary Act 1985 made clear that the legitimate interests that are to be protected by the courts may be both 'individual' or 'collective' interests.

situation' that should be fully re-established (a condition which is in fact automatically fulfilled when any typical 'subjective right' is at stake).[12]

2.2 Discretion in Spanish public law

Spanish public law doctrine has elaborated three understandings of what discretionary power is and, in particular, administrative discretion:[13] (i) discretion as volitional margin of appraisal, (ii) cognitive discretion, and (iii) cognitive and volitional discretion.

Discretion as volitional margin of appraisal entails the power to choose between possible legal consequences—either foreseen or not. Here, legal norms are indeterminate as far as their legal consequences are concerned. Discretion as volitional margin to choose among legal consequences has been advocated by Luciano Parejo and Tomás-Ramón Fernández. For Parejo, 'the discretionary power does not belong to the cognitive realm but the volitional realm';[14] and for Fernández, the freedom to choose does not have to do with the premises of the norm that attributes discretionary powers; this freedom only concerns the election of legal consequences.[15] Despite their agreement on the notion of discretion, they strongly differ on the scope of judicial control of administrative discretion.

Discretionary power has also been considered as only belonging to the realm of the facts of legal norms because either the absence of the facts of a legal norm or its indeterminacy creates a margin of discretionary activity. Public actions entail either creating or determining the facts of the applied legal norm. Bacigalupo[16] argues, in favour of cognitive discretion, that determining the premises of the legal norm removes the possibility of choosing among two or more legal consequences, and leads to a single solution in the application of norms. He gives as his reason for defending this option the

---

[12] Art 70 and 31(2) of the Administrative Jurisdiction Act, cf Ortega Alvárez, see n 5 above, 54–57.

[13] See M Bacigalupo, *La discrecionalidad administrativa. Estructura normativa, control judicial y límites constitucionales de su atribución* (Madrid: Marcial Pons, 1997) for a compilation and critical study of the concept of discretion in Spanish law.

[14] L Parejo Alfonso, *Administrar y juzgar, dos funciones constitucionales distintas y complementarias: un estudio del alcance y la intensidad del control judicial, a la luz de la discrecionalidad administrativa* (Madrid: Tecnos, 1993) 122 (our translation).

[15] TR Fernández, *De la arbitrariedad de la Administración*, (4th edn, Madrid: Civitas, 2002) 247.

[16] Bacigalupo, see n 13 above, 191.

possibility of using objective criteria to control the exercise of discretion, whereas in the realm of volition discretion is rather difficult to scrutinize.

Finally, some authors have thought of discretionary power as arising not only because legal consequences are indeterminate (volitional discretion), but also because the facts as described by the norm (*supuesto de hecho*) are also indeterminate (cognitive discretion). Garcia De Enterría[17] and Sainz Moreno[18] reduce the realm of discretion to legal consequences and accept the existence of a margin of cognition, that is a margin in the application or appraisal (*Beurteilungsspielraum*) of the facts of the norm (premises of the norm). This is the so-called *margin of appraisal* that German doctrine elaborates to explain the application of undefined legal concepts.

Spanish law has embraced a notion of discretion intimately related to undefined legal concepts and the margin of appraisal within the realm of the facts of legal norms. According to this notion, the constitutional position of public administration includes its discretionary power (Articles 103 and 106 SC), that is it includes the existence of a margin of appraisal that is smaller or larger depending on the precise/imprecise legislation ruling administrative action. The constitutional position of the judiciary vis-à-vis public administration is also clear: judges not only control the legality of administrative actions, but they also scrutinize the effective protection of fundamental rights and legitimate interests (Article 24 SC). As a consequence, the existence of discretionary power does not exclude judiciary control since, in any case, public actions must conform to the principle of legality and with the protection of individual rights.[19]

In the Spanish Constitution, judges control the margin of appraisal attributed to public administration. However, it does not clarify the extent of this judicial scrutiny, which can vary from the mere annulment of public action to the substitution of public acts. For example a judge must not decide on the best location for a nuclear power plant but must decide whether the chosen location is acceptable from the point of view of planning law and environmental law. This kind of control leads to the annulment of public acts, which is sufficient in many cases to restore the legal position of individuals vis-à-vis public administration.

[17] E García De Enterría, 'La lucha contra las inmunidades del poder' (1962) *Revista de administración pública*, 159–205.

[18] F Saínz Moreno, *Conceptos jurídicos, interpretación y discrecionalidad administrativa* (Madrid: Civitas, 1976).

[19] This definitively closed the door which pre-constitutional legislation opened to 'political actions', that is actions of the government that by definition escaped from judicial control.

In this sense, TR Fernández and L Parejo are the protagonists of the Spanish doctrinal dispute on the extent of judicial review over public administration acts. For Parejo, the Spanish Constitution grants judicial control over administrative actions as a necessary consequence of the individual right to effective judicial protection (Article 24(1) SC). He holds that this entails the control of legality (Article 106 SC), that is supervising, censoring, and correcting the public administration's acts. The content, intensity, and extent of the judicial decision are up to the judge, who, however, cannot make a substitution for the scrutinized public action.[20]

On the other hand, for TR Fernández the protection of fundamental rights, among them the right to effective judicial protection (Article 24 SC), holds a preferential position vis-à-vis the principle of legality as applied to public administration actions (Article 106 SC). This means that the control of legality is sometimes not sufficient to restore individual rights that may have been violated by public actions, and the judge must therefore adopt a decision different from the mere annulment of public acts.[21]

These techniques of judicial control over administrative actions guarantee the supremacy of the law over both judges and public bodies. However, the following question still remains unanswered: if the effective protection of rights entails more than the mere annulment of administrative acts, does judicial scrutiny also entail the substitution of public actions by judicial decisions?

For the Spanish Supreme Court (Judgment issued on December 1st 1993) the substitution of the administrative act by a judicial decision is completely possible if there is no discretion, that is if the law provides all the features relevant to determining the content of the decision. This substitution, the Spanish Supreme Court goes on, is plausible within the control of legality and it is required for the effective judicial protection of rights. However, substitution is impossible where discretion exists and several solutions are therefore possible.[22]

The relevant question becomes whether there is discretion at all. To deal with this question, the notion of indeterminate juridical concepts has been used to argue that there is a single answer the judiciary is competent to

---

[20] Parejo Alfonso, see n 14 above, 48–49.

[21] Fernández, see n 15 above, 173.

[22] This position is also adopted by the Administrative Jurisdiction Act (*Exposición de motivos V*): it states that the inactivity of the public administration does not allow the judiciary to translate into precise commands all general and indeterminate empowerments and obligations to create a public service or to realize certain activities.

scrutinize (although this does not mean that there is a single specific and singular answer).[23] In other cases, the reduction of discretion comes through the density of regulation and the description of relevant facts. These are issues that relate to the existence of cognitive discretion. Finally, Beltrán De Felipe[24] also refers to the existence of bilateral or multilateral relations to appraise a reduction of discretion that makes the substitution of public acts possible. For example, in bilateral relations involving the individual and public administration, the judge may not only annul the disputed administrative act, but also establish the way in which the public body should act.[25]

3 On rights and discretion in EC law

3.1 *The concept and the protection of rights at Community level*

The ECJ case law on the existence of EC rights

The concept of rights is central to the case law of the ECJ on the application of EC law, and, in particular, on the implementation of directives. It is well known that it has been used by the ECJ to build up doctrines and principles which aim to encourage timely and correct implementation of directives by Member States, and to mitigate the serious handicap for the effectiveness of EC law that the lack or inadequate transposition of these Community acts into national law entails.

First the ECJ has used the concept of rights to draw (and strictly control) the limits of discretion that Member States enjoy in implementing EC Directives correctly into national law. When directives seek to regulate rights and obligations for individuals, they will work normally as an indirect source of

---

[23] In opposition to the 'one single answer' thesis largely defended by Professor Dworkin, here the claim to correctness as a normative claim elaborated by Professor Alexy is embraced. This is a vast discussion, which cannot be outlined here. However, in brief, for clarity, the main question explored by this contribution is that indeterminate legal concepts entail a claim to the correctness of the decision upheld.

[24] M Beltrán De Felipe, *Discrecionalidad administrativa y Constitución* (Madrid: Tecnos, 1995).

[25] If a person requests a permit to use arms, the public body is confronted with two decisions: either it grants the permit or it does not. If the permit is not granted, and the individual challenges this decision before the judiciary, the scope of judicial scrutiny, because of the bilateral nature of the relation, goes further than a mere annulment: the judge may consider that he/she has all the relevant features of the case and decide that the permit should be given. On the other hand, in multilateral relations involving a plurality of individuals, discretion is enhanced because it also increases the number of possible options, and as a result substitution is rather difficult.

such rights and obligations, as they will have to be concretized by national law implementing the directive. In such a task the principle of legal certainty has played a crucial role. According to well settled case law of the ECJ, when a directive intends to create rights and duties for individuals, the principle of legal certainty requires that it must be implemented in the national legal order with unquestionable binding force and with the specificity, precision, and clarity necessary for the persons concerned to be able to ascertain the full extent of their rights and duties, and to invoke them, if necessary, before the national courts.[26]

Further, it has clarified that 'Where, in particular, a directive is intended to create rights for individuals, it is indeed the case that Member States must lay down the provisions necessary to ensure that the persons entitled to exercise those rights enjoy judicial protection.'[27]

Therefore, a Member State will infringe its duty to implement EC directives properly when national law permits uncertainty as to the reach and scope of the rights (or advantages) that they intend to create for individuals, or when it does not provide adequate mechanisms for their judicial protection.

In order to transpose EC directives correctly, particularly when 'individual rights and obligations are at stake' the ECJ sets requirements and limits to national provisions according to the principle of legal certainty (binding legal force, clarity, and precision of national provisions). These are addressed in order to facilitate and, therefore, encourage individuals to pursue the protection of those 'community rights' in national courts through national law. Thus the ECJ attempts to strengthen the application of national provisions which transpose EC directives, and, therefore, indirectly, the effectiveness of directives.[28] In this regard it has been argued that

The main concern of the Court seems to be that the legal position of the individual must be safeguarded and, perhaps even more important, that Community law is simply applied, [. . .]. If this is true, the implication is that where the Court uses, in

---

[26]   See, eg, Case C-131/88 *Commission v Germany* [1991] ECR I-825; Case C-236/95 *Commission v Greece* [1996] ECR I-4461, para 13; Case C-197/96 *Commission v France* [1997] ECR I-1489, para 15; Case C-207/96 *Commission v Italy* [1997] ECR I-6869, para 26; and Case C-296/01 *Commission v France* [2003] ECR 13909, para 55.

[27]   Case C-340/96 *Commission v United Kingdom* [1999] ECR I-2023.

[28]   See C Plaza Martín, *Derecho ambiental de la Unión Europea* (Valencia: Tirant lo Blanch, 2005) 866ff, for an exhaustive analysis of the case law, especially in the field of environmental directives.

the context of its 'implementation case law' the term of right, it has nothing specific in mind.[29]

It should be taken into account, nevertheless, that in some national legal orders judicial review of public authorities' acts (or inaction) depends not only on a breach of legality by the administration, but also on individual 'rights' being injured.[30] In all those cases where the ECJ has declared that a directive is intended to create rights (*latu sensu*) for individuals this will entail, from the point of view of national law, open access to justice for individuals to defend the legal advantage or benefits that the directive intends to grant, whatever concept of rights exists in that national legal order.

The fact that a directive 'seeks to create rights for individuals', according to ECJ case law, has a number of important implications for national authorities, as it narrows down considerably the margin of choice that they might have when implementing a directive. Some legal instruments will not be adequate to ensure the correct implementation of those directives: for example administrative circulars, administrative practices, or new instruments that are developing in some fields such as environmental agreements among national public authorities and industry. It also makes it particularly difficult for a general legal context or general principles of law to suffice to ensure correct implementation of directives, particularly when they are very detailed, as is the case, for instance, in the field of EC environmental law. It also means that a particularly strict transposition of the terms and provisions of the directive is required, which does not leave much space for national law to accommodate the provisions of the directive to its own idiosyncrasies. It may in addition make it difficult for pre-existing national law to be a fully correct transposition of the new directive, even though this may have been enacted to achieve the same objectives as the latter.[31] Finally, it may require that procedural instruments be established to guarantee access to justice to the persons entitled to exercise those rights. All these limitations and requirements are introduced specifically to ensure that individuals can enjoy the 'advantages' or 'benefits' the directives intend to grant through national law.

Second, the concept of 'right' plays an important role in EC case law devoted to reinforcing the effectiveness of EC law in general, and of directives in particular, specifically through the principles of the direct effect

---

[29] S Prechal, *Directives in EC Law* (2nd edn, Oxford: Oxford University Press, 2005) 110.

[30] This is the case, for instance, in Germany, as analysed by Schmidt-Assmann, see n 7 above.

[31] Plaza Martín, see n 28 above, 874ff.

of EC law and state liability for breaches of EC law, and also through the requirement of effective judicial protection of community rights.[32] Directives may be (exceptionally) a direct source of rights when their provisions have direct effect according to the doctrine of the ECJ:

[. . .] wherever the provisions of a directive appear [. . .] to be unconditional and sufficiently precise, those provisions may [. . .] be relied upon as against any national provision which is incompatible with the directive or in so far as the provisions define rights which individuals are able to assert against the state.[33]

Further, the breach of an EC provision may give rise to a right to reparation (where three conditions are met: the rule of law infringed must be intended to confer rights on individuals, the breach must be sufficiently serious, and there must be a direct causal link between the breach of the obligation resting on the state and the damage sustained by the injured parties).[34] These principles—direct effect and state liability for breach of EC law—are addressed to satisfy the requirements of the full effectiveness of the rules of Community law and the effective protection of the rights that those rules confer.

Through all this case law the ECJ handles the concept of 'right' quite liberally, tacitly giving it fairly wide scope. In some Member States this has triggered a thorny discussion on the need to rethink traditional national concepts of rights when applying EC law.[35] Currently it is widely accepted that the concept of rights used by the ECJ may contain (national) concepts such as 'subjective rights', 'legitimate interests', or any other benefits that individuals might obtain from EC law to improve their legal position.[36]

Rights, interests and individuals' access to the European Court of Justice

As explained above, in national legal orders such as the Spanish legal order-the concepts of 'rights' and 'interests' are central to the rules on individuals'

---

[32] See further Prechal, see n 29 above, 99ff and Plaza Martín, see n 28 above, 1185ff.

[33] Eg, Case 8/81 *Becker* [1982] ECR 53.

[34] Joined Cases C-46/93 and C-48/93 *Brasserie and Factortame* [1996] ECR 1029, among others.

[35] Prechal, see n 29 above, 98ff.

[36] R Alonso García, 'Community and National Legal Orders: Autonomy, Integration and Interaction' in Academy of European Law, *Collected Courses of European Law*, Vol 7.1 (Dordrecht: Kluwer, 1999) 77ff; R Arnold, 'L'influence du droit communautaire sur le droit administratif allemand' (1996) L'Actualité juridique—Droit Administratif, 113–114; L Krämer, 'Direct effect of EC Environmental Law' in H Somsen (ed), *Protecting the European Environment: Enforcing EC Environmental Law* (London: Blackstone Press, 1996) 110; Prechal, see n 29 above, 111 and A Tizzano, 'L'influence du droit communautaire sur le droit administratif italien' (1996) L'Actualité juridique—Droit administratif, 136. See as well the Opinion of Advocate General Tesauro in Joined Cases C-46/93 and C-48/93 *Brasserie and Factortame* [1996] ECR 1029, para 33ff.

locus standi to challenge administrative acts or regulations. The same cannot be said, however, about individuals' access to the ECJ to challenge EC acts. As this section will sketch briefly, there are no signs of convergence at this point between national and Community legal orders.

The EC Treaty does not use terms such as rights or interests in order to regulate the standing of private parties who bring an action for annulment against a Community act. According to the fourth paragraph of Article 230 EC

[a]ny natural or legal person may . . . institute proceedings against a decision addressed to that person or against a decision which, although in the form of a regulation or a decision addressed to another person, is of direct and individual concern to the former.

The ECJ has traditionally maintained a very restrictive approach when examining private applicants' *locus standi* to challenge either Community decisions addressed to a third party or general acts which amount in substance to a decision. It follows from the case law of the ECJ that applicants who are not the addressees of an act may not claim that they are 'individually concerned' by it unless it affects them by reason of 'certain attributes peculiar to them', or by reason of 'a factual situation which differentiates them from all other persons and distinguishes them individually in the same way as the addressee of the act would be'.[37] Hence the narrow interpretation of the concept 'individual concern' upheld by the ECJ has severely reduced the opportunities of individuals' access to the ECJ to challenge general acts or decisions that are not directly addressed to them. Such a requirement does not equate to the concepts of individual rights or legitimate interests. The private applicants will have no standing before the ECJ to defend their rights or interests against an illegal community act if they cannot prove that such acts affect them in the same way as if the acts had been addressed to them. In other words, alleged adverse effects of a contested act on the applicants' interests (such as the interest in the protection of the environment of an environmental NGO) or on an individual right (such as property) might not qualify as 'individually concerned' for the ECJ.[38] Thus, Article 230 EC Treaty remains a provision designed to enable to some extent the judicial review of the legality of EC acts, but it is not simultaneously conceived as an adequate channel to protect the rights (or interests) of individuals.

[37] Eg, among others, Case C-50/00 P *UPA* [2002] ECR I-6677, para 36 and Case C-263/02 P *Jégo-Quéré* [2004] ECR I-3425, para 45.
[38] See, eg, Case T-94/04 *European Environmental Bureau (EEB)* [2005] ECR II-4919.

This strict ECJ conception of the requirement of 'direct and individual concern' has been widely criticized by legal commentators,[39] and even members of the ECJ have advocated a relaxation or even a change in the interpretation of the requirements for an 'individual concern' to provide adequate and effective judicial protection for individuals.[40] Notwithstanding, the ECJ has upheld its case law and has restrained itself to state that, taking into account the system for judicial review of legality established by the Treaty, it is for the Member States to set up a system of legal remedies and procedures that ensure respect for the right to effective judicial protection.[41]

3.2 *Discretion of Community institutions and judicial review*

As is the case for the concept of rights, there is no fully developed notion of discretion in EC law. However, this can be overcome by the analysis of judicial scrutiny: the scope of judicial review over the discretion of EC institutions will disclose the notion referred to by the ECJ. The result is not univocal: although the ECJ refers mainly to volitional discretion, that is the discretionary power of EC institutions in the realm of consequences, it also considers the existence of cognitive discretion, especially when the Commission must take account of complex features when making a decision. The ECJ, however, seems to take a clear position as far as the extent of judicial scrutiny is concerned: judgments concerning failure to act and Community liability show that the ECJ holds a strong position against the substitution of Community decisions by the Community judicature.

The notion of volitional discretion could relate either to the actions of public authorities or to the choice of possible consequences. In the first case, the legal norm does not oblige the public body to act (given the facts, X public bodies may adopt legal consequence Y); that is, the public authority enjoys a margin of volition to choose between either acting or not. In the second case,

---

[39] C Harlow, 'Towards a Theory of Access for the European Court of Justice' (1992) Ybk of Eur L, 228–229; A Arnull, 'The Action for Annulment: A Case of Double Standards?' in D O'Keeffe and G Slynn, *Judicial Review in European Union Law: Liber Amicorum in Honour of Lord Slynn of Hadley*, Vol 1 (The Hague: Kluwer, 2000) 189 and F Ragolle, 'Access to Justice for Private Applicants in the Community Legal Order: Recent (R)evolutions' (2003) 28 ELR, 90–101.

[40] See, eg, the Opinion of Advocate General Jacobs in Case C-358/89 *Extramet Industrie* [1991] ECR I-2501, paras 71–74; Case C-188/92 *TWD Textilwerke Deggendorf* [1994] ECR I-833, paras 20–23; Case C-50/00 P *UPA* [1994] ECR I-6677, paras 59–81; see the Opinion of Advocate General Ruiz-Jarabo Colomer in Case C-142/95 P *Associazione agricoltori della provincia di Rovigo and others* [1996] ECR I-6669, paras 40–41; and also Case T-177/01 *Jégo-Quéré* [2002] ECR-II 2365.

[41] C-50/00 P *UPA* [2002] ECR I-6677, paras 41–42 and Case C-263/02 P *Jégo-Quéré* [2004] ECR I-3425, paras 31–32.

the legal norm provides a margin of volition to choose between two (or more) determinate, or even indeterminate, legal consequences. Here, the public body must act within the framework of the attributed discretionary power.

In the ECJ's case law concerning Community institutions we can find examples of the first approach to volition discretion: wide leeway to appraise whether or not the institution ought to act. For example, in *European Parliament v Council* case[42] the European Parliament supported by the Commission addressed an action for failure to act against the Council. The reason was the failure to introduce a coherent common transport policy within the time limits established by ex-Article 75(2) EEC.

The ECJ stated that one conclusion could be easily drawn from the case (para 46), namely the lack of a coherent set of rules which could be regarded as a common transport policy for the purposes of Articles 74 and 75 of the Treaty (new Articles 70 and 71 EC). However, the ECJ held that the Council has discretion. This discretion, the ECJ stated, 'is limited by the requirements which stem from the establishment of the common market and by certain precise provisions in the Treaty such as those laying down time limits' (para 49). That is, the discretion does not refer to the decision on whether or not to act; it rather refers to the decision on 'the aims of and means for implementing a common transport policy' (para 49). Indeed, although the Council must act according to the Treaty and introduce a common transport policy, the Treaty does not determine the substance of that policy, and the Council has discretion to decide it.[43] The fact that the Parliament failed to state what measures the Council ought to adopt on the basis of the Treaty and in what sequence they ought to be adopted proves this broad discretion, at least to the ECJ.

This final finding of the ECJ, namely the broad discretion of the Council when deciding the content of the policy, invalidates the first conclusion it reached, namely the limited discretion to act and to introduce a transport policy. That is, although the Treaty compels the Council to act, the lack of definition of this intervention annuls the obligation to act, and therefore

---

[42] Case 13/83 *European Parliament v Council* [1985] ECR 1513.

[43] The ECJ says 'the Treaty leaves it to the Council to decide whether action in the transport sector must deal first with relations between the railways and the public authorities or with competition between road and rail. It is also for the Council to determine what priorities are to be observed in harmonizing the laws and administrative practices in the sector and to decide what matters such harmonization must cover. In that respect the Treaty gives the Council discretion', para 50.

there is no failure to act.[44] The consequence is clear: an apparent discretion to choose among options becomes the broad discretion to decide whether or not to act.

The level of discretion which Community institutions enjoy has also been explored in the framework of non-contractual liability:

The system of rules which the ECJ has worked out with regard to that provision takes into account, *inter alia*, the complexity of the situations to be regulated, difficulties in the application or interpretation of the texts and, more particularly, the margin of discretion available to the author of the act in question.[45]

The ECJ's point of departure is the application of the requirements of Community liability and state liability: 'The Court has stated that the conditions under which the state may incur liability for damage caused to individuals by a breach of Community law cannot, in the absence of particular justification, differ from those governing the liability of the Community in like circumstances'.[46] This refers to three conditions: the rule of law infringed must be intended to confer rights on individuals; the breach must be sufficiently serious; and there must be a direct causal link between the breach of the obligation on the part of state and the damage sustained by the injured parties.

In relation to the second condition, when it is applied to Community liability the ECJ states that 'the decisive test for finding that a breach of Community law is sufficiently serious is whether the Community institution concerned manifestly and gravely disregarded the limits on its discretion'.[47] This also implies that where that institution has only considerably reduced, or even no, discretion, the mere infringement of Community law may be sufficient to establish the existence of a sufficiently serious breach.[48]

Hence, for the ECJ, the decisive test for determining whether there has been a sufficiently serious breach is not the individual nature of the act (it is irrelevant whether the act is either administrative or legislative) but the

[44] In this sense, R Alonso García, 'Actividad judicial v. inactividad normativa' (2000) *Revista de administración pública*, 77.

[45] Case C-352/98 P *Bergaderm* [2000] ECR I-5291, para 40.

[46] Case C-352/98 P *Bergaderm* [2000] ERC I-5291, para 41, quoting Joined Cases C-46/93 and C-48/93 *Brasserie and Factortame* [1996] ECR 1029, para 42.

[47] Case C-352/98 P *Bergaderm* [2000] ERC I-5291, para 43, and in the same sense see Case C-312/00 P *Camar and Tico* [2002] ECR I-11355, para 54 and Case C-472/00 P *Fresh Marine* [2003] ECR I-7541, para 26.

[48] Case C-352/98 P *Bergaderm* [2000] ERC I-5291, para 44 and Case C-312/00 P *Camar and Tico* [2002] ECR I-11355, para 54.

discretion available to the institution when it was adopted: the mere illegality of individual or general acts does not prompt Community liability, especially when no account has been taken of the discretion of Community institutions.[49]

3.3 *Discretion of Member States as measured by the ECJ*

Does the ECJ maintain a similar standard of scrutiny over the exercise of discretionary powers by Member States under EC law? In relation to this issue, an analysis of the ECJ's case law leads to two conclusions. First, unlike in its attitude towards Community institutions, the ECJ is less generous when it determines the degree of discretionary powers that Member States enjoy under EC law; and second, the ECJ is reluctant to accept the possibility that EC law requires national courts and tribunals to substitute the legislature and executive choices with their own decisions when EC provisions leave Member States a margin of discretion for its implementation. This conclusion is certainly disturbing in legal systems such as the Spanish one, where, in some cases, the substitution of executive decisions by the judicature is accepted, and where the effective protection of rights, unlike the protection of legitimate interest, requires from the judiciary something more than the mere action of annulment of executive and legislative acts.

The discretionary power that Community law leaves to Member States has been analysed by the ECJ in the field of state liability, among others, although its definition is far from being univocal: it has been defined (i) as a margin of appraisal when transposing the directive, (ii) as the lack of discretion with regard the obligation to transpose the directive, (iii) as the possibility of choosing among given options, and (iv) as the leeway of Member States to choose among a large variety of solutions.

One of the best cases to analyse this variety of notions of discretion in the field of state liability is the *Francovich* case.[50] Here, the ECJ refers to two notions of discretion when assessing the discretionary power left to Member States by a particular directive, namely Directive 80/987/EEC on the protection of employees in the event of the employer's insolvency. When the ECJ analyses the content of the obligation set down in Article 5 of the Directive, it refers to the *broad discretion* given to Member States with regard to organization, operation, and financing of the guarantee institutions that the Directive establishes (iv). This proviso does not refer to a set of options

---

[49] Case C-312/00 P *Camar and Tico* [2002] ECR I-11355, para 56.
[50] Joined Cases C- 6/90 and C-9/90 *Francovich* [1991] ECR 1–5357.

Member States may choose among, since they have considerable latitude as regards the choice of means for achieving the results that directives seek. The ECJ also establishes that the Directive (Article 3) gives the Member State the *right to choose* (iii) among several possible means of achieving the result required by the Directive (para 17).[51]

To these two notions of discretion (right to choose the means to achieve the directive's aims, and right to choose among determined options) the ECJ attributes also different effects. For the ECJ, a broader notion of discretion excludes the application of the doctrine of direct effect (and, specifically, the substitution effect), and, therefore, as was stated in the *Francovich* case, the only door open is state liability for failure to transpose directives.[52] On the other hand, discretion as the right to choose among given options 'does not affect the precise and unconditional nature of the result required' (*Francovich* para 18), and therefore, it does not preclude the possibility of individuals enforcing rights before the national courts whose content can be determined with sufficient precision. Does this mean that the judiciary ought to substitute the public administration decision with one that complies with EC law?

The former question relates to the extent of judicial control that the ECJ recognizes for national judges under EC law. In this sense, the doctrine that the ECJ follows is very clear: national courts must review national authority decisions that are incompatible with Community law. However, the protection of rights conferred by Community law does not justify the substitution of national authority decisions by the national court and tribunals, even in the case of very reduced discretion. This doctrine has been elaborated in the framework of the effects of the doctrine of the direct effect of directives.

The landmark case concerning the extent of judicial review is the *Kraaijeveld* case,[53] which restores the *VNO*[54] doctrine settled by the ECJ in 1977. This

---

[51] In particular, Member States may chose among three options when determining the date prior to which the payment of outstanding claims should be made: (i) the date of the onset of the employer's insolvency; (ii) that of the notice of dismissal issued to the employee; and (iii) that of the onset of the employer's insolvency or that on which the contract of employment or the employment relationship with the employee concerned was discontinued on account of the employer's insolvency.

[52] Indeed, whereas the Commission held that, since the Directive envisaged as one possibility among others that the guarantee system could be financed entirely by the public authorities, the state should be the person liable for unpaid claims, the Court concluded, on the contrary, that it excluded the possibility of determining sufficiently precisely the person liable to provide the guarantee. This position has been analysed by R Alonso García, *El juez español y el Derecho comunitario* (Valencia: Tirant, 2003).

[53] Case C-72/95 *Kraaijeveld* [1996] ERC I-5403.

[54] Alonso García, see n 52 above, 160. Case 51/76 *Verbond van Nederlandse Ondernemingen* [1977] ECR 113.

case concerns the margin of discretion attributed to Member States by directives, such as Directive 85/337/EEC on assessment of the effect of certain public and private projects, that attribute broad discretion. In particular, the ECJ held that the fact that a Member State has discretion does not preclude judicial review on the question as to whether the national authorities exceeded it (para 59). This entails that judicial control over Member States' actions, when they exceed the limits of discretion, is limited to the action of annulment: the national court may examine on its own motion whether the legislative or administrative authorities of the Member State remained within the limits of their discretion and take account thereof when examining the action for annulment (para 60). This excludes any opportunity for the judiciary to substitute their own decision for that of the legislative or administrative authorities.

The *Brinkmann* case[55] goes further in this line of reasoning, since here the discussed Directive (on tax on tobacco) established three alternative means of achieving the Directive's aims. However, when the German Government adopted a fourth one, the ECJ did not accept the possibility of the national judge substituting the legislative and administrative decision by choosing one among the three given options, and held that the right to invoke the Directive does not amount to the right to substitute the national authority's decision with a national court decision.

Also significant is the *Upjohn* case,[56] which refers to cognitive discretion. In this case, the key question was not only whether Community law requires the national judge to substitute administrative or legislative decisions; it was also whether the national court must take account of the same facts as the national authority did, or whether it should take account of all relevant material of a particular case to proceed with the substitution. The EJC dealt with these questions by relying on two arguments: the principle of procedural autonomy and the practice of Community judicature. First, the principle of procedural autonomy supports the conclusion that the national judiciary may substitute its own assessment to protect rights deriving from Community law, if this is possible when protecting rights deriving from domestic law. However, the ECJ quoted its well-established case law on control of discretionary power exercised by Community institutions and held that when a 'Community authority is called upon to make complex assessments, it enjoys a wide measure of discretion, the exercise of which is

---

[55] Case C-365/98 *Brinkmann Tabakfabriken* [2000] ECR I-4619.
[56] Case C-120/97 *Upjohn* [1999] ECR I-223.

subject to a limited judicial review in the course of which the Community judicature may not substitute its assessment of the facts for the assessment made by the authority concerned.'[57] The consequence is that 'Community law does not require the Member States to establish a procedure for judicial review of national decisions revoking marketing authorisations . . . which involves a more extensive review than that carried out by the ECJ in similar cases'.[58]

If this conclusion is applied to the substitution issue, then Community law requires the review of national decisions that are incompatible with Community law. This review cannot be so intensive as to involve the substitution of the assessment of the facts, if this substitution is not possible as a matter of domestic law, even though substituting a legislative or administrative decision may fully grant the rights deriving from directives. This conclusion is striking. If a Member State has laid down procedural norms permitting the substitution of administrative decisions by national courts and tribunals, they are not encouraged by the ECJ to do this when assessing the compatibility of a national administrative decision with Community law. It also means that, if a Member State has laid down no such norms, the national court may fail in the protection of rights conferred by Community law where substituting the administrative decision is the only appropriate means of preventing the exercise of such rights from being rendered virtually impossible or excessively difficult.[59]

The ECJ also stands in the way of the possibility of national courts taking into account material and, in particular, scientific findings that may come to light after the adoption of an administrative decision, which may then be revoked. It is up to the competent administrative authority to assess this new material.[60]

---

[57]   Case C-120/97 *Upjohn* [1999] ECR I-223, para 34.

[58]   ibid, para 35.

[59]   In the *Upjohn* case, the ECJ held that a procedure for judicial review of national decisions revoking marketing authorizations and empowering national courts and tribunals to substitute their assessment of the facts, did not appear to be the 'only appropriate means' of preventing the exercise of rights conferred by Community law from being rendered virtually impossible or excessively difficult (Case C-120/97 *Upjohn* [1999] ECR I-223, para 25). The question, which remains unanswered by the ECJ, is whether Community law requires an intensive judicial review upon legislative and administrative decisions involving their substitution, if this is the 'only appropriate means' for fully granting and protecting rights conferred by Community law, even though no national procedural norms establish such means.

[60]   Case C-120/97 *Upjohn* [1999] ECR I-223, para 40.

4 EC rights and discretion as they reflect Spanish law

4.1 *The 'translation' and protection of EC rights in the Spanish legal system*

In the realm of Spanish public law there has not so far been any relevant doctrinal discussion on the concept of 'EC rights'—as the term is used by the ECJ—not even on its 'translation' into national legal categories when public authorities implement EC law. It seems that Spanish legal scholars have not felt the need to rethink, in the light of the ECJ case law, the concept of *derechos subjetivos públicos* (individual public rights), and it has just been peacefully assumed that whenever the Luxembourg Court uses the concept of individual rights it includes the Spanish notions both of individual rights and legitimate interests.[61] The main reason for this lack of debate in Spain may be linked to the further elaboration of the concept of legitimate interest as a sort of public procedural right, as has been explained above.

Not withstanding, EC rights may fit, when they are implemented and safeguarded within the context of Spanish law, into any of the diverse categories outlined above, and this has important consequences as to the type and degree of judicial protection that they will encounter.

First, within the realm of the Spanish Constitution, some EC rights may match one of the fundamental rights enshrined in its Title I, Chapter II, Section I (Articles 14 to 29) and therefore enjoy the reinforced constitutional protection established in Article 53(2) SC. A clear example is the right to equal treatment between men and women laid down in Article 141 of the EC Treaty and in several directives on gender discrimination at work adopted in the framework of social policy: they fit within Article 14 SC which forbids gender discrimination. In cases like this EC rights will be safeguarded, and breaches will be redressed and remedied, if necessary by the Constitutional Court through special constitutional appeal (*Recurso de amparo*).[62] On the other hand, other Community rights might only fit within one of the 'Principles guiding social and economic policy', such as the individual 'rights' contained in some EC environmental directives.[63] In such cases these 'rights'

[61] Alonso García, see n 36 above, 177.

[62] The Spanish Constitutional Court through the *Recurso de amparo*, among others, in cases 17/2003, 30 January 2003 and 203/2000, 24 July 2000, has protected equal treatment between men and women at work.

[63] As stated by the ECJ with regard to different directives on water protection (eg, Case C-131/88 *Commission v Germany* [1991] ECR I-825; Case C-360/87 *Commission v Italy* [1991]

will in principle fit within Article 45 SC, according to which 'Everyone has the right to enjoy an environment suitable for personal development, as well as the duty to preserve it,' but it will need further legislative implementation to be fully enforceable—unless the provisions of the directive concerned have direct effect. However, Article 45 SC can also be used by national courts, together with the relevant EC directive, as a parameter for the interpretation of any national statute. It can also be used to review the constitutionality, and therefore, the validity, of any statute or administrative decision, as it works as a general principle limiting the discretionary powers of public authorities.

Second, when an EC directive intends to create rights for individuals, those 'EC rights' may also be directly translated into the following legal categories of the Spanish legal order:

1. either into public subjective rights, which may be fully protected by national courts against the state (even by applying directly the provisions of an EC directive instead of national ones if such a directive has not been transposed in due time or it has not been transposed correctly but contains unconditional and sufficiently precise provisions);
2. or into legitimate interests which will allow the individual at least to invoke the EC provisions (if necessary) as a standard for review to set aside (or to annul) national measures contrary to EC directives.

Let us focus now on the cases of the (vertical) direct effect of directives. In those cases where a directive has not been (correctly) transposed into national law and is invoked by individuals against the state, once a Spanish Court accepts that those individuals have *locus standi* to challenge the administrative act or regulation which infringes a directive (either because they have a 'right' or a 'legitimate interest' at stake), the question as to whether the a directive intends to confer 'EC rights' upon them seems to be irrelevant to the Courts acknowledgement of the direct effect of its provisions. Thus, the Spanish Supreme Court has admitted the 'direct effect' of EC directive provisions that leave a wide margin of discretion to the Member States and do not properly define 'rights'. In other words, it accepts direct effect in terms of invocability.

This was the case, for instance, with Article 4(2) of Directive 85/337/ CEE on Environmental Impact Assessment (EIA)[64]—the same provision

---

ECR I-791, and Case C-298/95 *Commission v Germany* [1996] ECR I-6747), air pollution (eg, Case C-361/88 *Commission v Germany* [1991] ECR I-2567 and Case C-59/89 *Commission v Germany* [1991] ECR I-2607), and wild birds (Case C-415/01 *Commission v Belgium* [2003] ECR 2081).

  [64] Council Directive (EEC) 85/337 on Environmental Impact Assessment (EIA) [1985] OJ L175/40.

as at issue in *Kraaijeveld*,[65] *WWF*,[66] *Linster*,[67] and *Delena Wells*[68]—which was applied by the Supreme Court in order to annul several administrative acts which did not comply with the required EIA, as the Spanish authorities exceeded the margin of discretion allowed by the directive.[69] It should be noticed that in *Kraaijeveld* and the following cases the ECJ approached the question of the effects of Article 4(2) EIA Directive from the perspective of its 'invocability' by individuals to request the judicial review of national acts or provisions. The fact that the ECJ did not pronounce on whether or not such a provision confers 'rights' on individuals—and did not expressly declare its 'direct effect'—has triggered renewed academic discussion on whether 'a "legality review" a la *Kraaijeveld* is a form of direct effect or not'.[70] As stated above the Spanish Supreme Court has not shown, however, any doubt about answering on terms of 'direct effect' those requests for annulent of administrative decisions contrary to the provisions of the EIA Directive whenever a legitimate interest was invoked.

There are, however, other potential problems that should be taken into account. One of the main difficulties which might arise when an individual requests the judicial review of administrative acts which infringe certain directives (such as the environmental directives) does not relate to the fact that 'EC rights' might be 'translated' into either 'subjective rights' or 'legitimate interests'. In certain cases the main problem might stem from the distinction between: (i) 'individual or collective legitimate interest', which allows individuals to request judicial protection against illegal administrative acts, on the one hand; (ii) and the mere 'general public interest', which is considered a task for public authorities only, on the other, as there are no procedural channels, in principle, for individuals to ask for judicial review of illegal actions by the administration whenever they undermine such public interests.[71]

In our opinion, once the ECJ has expressly declared that the objective of a given directive is to confer 'rights' on individuals (as is the case, for example, in several environmental directives), national judges can no longer presume that those EC provisions (or the national law adopted to implement them) are

---

[65] Case C-72/95 *Kraaijeveld* [1996] ECR I-5403.

[66] Case C-435/97 *WWF* [1999] ECR I-5613.

[67] Case C-287/98 *Linster* [2000] ECR I-6917.

[68] Case C-201/02 *Delena Wells* [2004] ECR I-723.

[69] Spanish Supreme Court Judgements of 1 April 2002 and 27 November 2002 (RJ Ar 2002\10395 and 2002\10394).

[70] Prechal, see n 29 above, 101.

[71] Only in those cases where an Act expressly regulates the *actio popularis*, can anyone request, without having to prove a right or a legitimate interest, the judicial review of administrative actions.

intended merely to protect the general public interest and should recognize, at least, that (individual or collective) legitimate interests might be at stake.

4.2 *Positive claims against national authorities' failure to act*

So far we have referred to administrative actions contrary to EC directives and the direct application of the latter either as the rules governing the case, or as the rules to review the legality of a national measure. But what happens in cases of positive individual's claims against the national authorities' failure to act?

Specific problems might arise in Spain in cases where an individual wishes to invoke a directive to challenge an illegal administrative omission or failure to act. In a first approach to this issue, Article 29 of the Contentious-Administrative Jurisdiction Act might be read to suggest that in such cases it is not enough for an individual to have a legitimate interest which gives him/her *locus standi* to act in a court: it has to be proved that the directive confers a substantive 'right' on the individual, and that EC provisions have established this in unconditional and precise terms.

The most complex question refers, however, to the limits of national judges' powers in those cases in which there is a normative gap in an area in which an unimplemented directive leaves Member State a certain margin of discretion.

According to the ECJ in *Von Kolson and Kamman,*

[. . .] the Member's States obligations, arising under a directive, to achieve the result envisaged by the directive and their duty, under article 189 of the Treaty, to take all appropriate measures, whether general or particular, to ensure full fulfilment of that obligation, are binding on all the authorities of Member States including, for matters within their jurisdiction, the Courts.[72]

However, the ECJ seems to maintain in cases such as *Brinkmann* that the national judge may not—as a matter of Community law—assume the role of the legislature or the executive of the Member States in their lawmaking capacity in the presence of a margin of discretion.[73] It has been argued,

---

[72] Case 14/83 *Van Colson and Kamann* [1984] ECR 1891 at para 26.

[73] Given the complementary role that the principle of liability of Member States for breaches of EC law plays (Joined Cases C-6/90 and C-9/90 *Francovich* [1991] ECR I-5357), it may be the case that the ECJ has reduced the efforts demanded of national judges to reinforce the applicability of Community law at a national level through direct and interpretative effects. Alonso García, see n 52 above, 165ff.

nevertheless, against such restraints imposed on the national judges by the ECJ, that if the expression 'for matters within their jurisdiction' used in *Von Kolson* is interpreted in the sense 'of competences to hear and resolve the cases before them', national judges should, in the framework of the specific conflicts in which they intervene, proceed to 'implement the directive judicially', even when a margin of discretion exists, as long as the objective to be achieved is perfectly clear and precise in the directive.[74]

4.3 *Divergence in the control of discretion*

The Spanish case law on the direct effect of directives is not univocal. Although applicants more often invoke the direct effect of directives before the judiciary, the 'substituting direct effect' has little success among Spanish judges, and only the 'reviewing direct effect' seems to be applied.

A very good illustration of the problem is the Judgment of the High Court of Justice of Valencia (*Tribunal Superior de Justicia de la Comunidad Valenciana*) issued on 21 April 2001 (484/2001). The case arose when the council of Masamagrell in the Valencia Autonomous Region approved an action plan for urban development and classified a wetland area as 'land qualified for urban development'. This decision was challenged before the High Court of Justice of the Valencia Autonomous Region, which started its reasoning by stating that specifying land use is not a matter of discretion or *ius variandi* on behalf of the public administration. Rather, it is a matter of legality, that is a matter of assessing whether the administrative act should, according to the law, have classified the land use either as 'qualified for urban development' or as 'unqualified for urban development'. By so arguing, the High Court of Justice of Valencia neglected both volition and cognitive discretion. Indeed, there is no discretion on legal consequences because, if the disputed area could be legally considered as wetland, then the only possible classification of land use is that of specially protected land unqualified for development; nor is there the recognition of cognitive discretion, since for the High Court of Justice of Valencia, the disputed area must be classified according to legal-technical criteria leading to a single correct answer. This reasoning implies that, in cases where administrative discretion is reduced to zero, the judiciary may substitute the public administrative decision by classifying as 'land unqualified for urban development' an area that public administration has previously declared as 'qualified for urban development'.

---

[74] Alonso García, see n 36 above, 120ff.

Due to the environmental relevance of the case, the High Court of Justice of Valencia assessed the legality of the administrative decision in the light of Community law, and in particular, Directive (EEC) 79/409 on the protection of wild birds, and Directive (EEC) 92/43 on the protection of habitats. The High Court of Justice considered, first of all, the effects of the direct effect of directives. It differentiated directives that establish a clear command and leave no margin of appraisal to Member States from directives which are imprecise and provide national authorities with the possibility of choosing among several options in order to transpose them. In the first case, the judge, said the High Court of Justice, must apply the Community proviso; however, in the second case, the directive has a negative or annulment role. Hence, for the High Court of Justice of Valencia, the 'reviewing direct effect' of directives excludes the possibility of the judiciary substituting their own for the administrative decision, and limits the scope of judicial review to the annulment of challenged measures. This implies that if the High Court of Justice of Valencia considered the above-mentioned Directives as having only a reviewing direct effect, it could not change the classification of the land use, although according to Spanish case law this is possible when there is neither volition nor cognitive discretion, ie administrative discretion is reduced to zero.

The High Court of Justice of the Region of Valencia held that neither the habitats Directive nor the birds Directive could have direct effect. This was because the disputed area was neither included in Natura 2000, nor was it considered a Community Interest Area as a prior stage to being designated a Special Protection Area. (Nevertheless, it was the view of the High Court, that it *should* have been included in the Natura 2000 catalogue since some of the vegetal species of the area known as *Marjal de Rafaell-Vistabella-Masamagrell* were included in the habitats Directive.) Leaving aside whether this interpretation is correct under Community law, for the High Court of Justice of Valencia the final classification of the disputed wetland was a matter of internal law, and in particular the Special Protected Areas Act of the Region of Valencia that designated all wetland areas as special protected land not qualified for urban development. The High Court of Justice concluded that it was incorrect to classify the disputed area as 'land qualified for urban development', and that the correct classification for urban planning purposes was that of 'special protected land not qualified for urban development'. Hence the High Court of Justice not only annulled the disputed measure, it also substituted the public administration decision, grounding its conclusion on domestic law rather than Community law.

Because the High Court of Justice of Valencia substituted the public administration decision as a matter of domestic law, rather than as a matter of the direct effect of directives, it is difficult to judge from the above case whether the scope of judicial review of Spanish judges and Community judges diverges when the direct effect of directives is applied to annul a public administration decision. Indeed, as stated above, the substituting direct effect of directives has had little success among Spanish judges, and only the 'reviewing direct effect' seems to be applied, and then in only a few cases. Despite this lack of empirical data, the case analysed above contains some hints as to how the Spanish judiciary understands the scope of judicial review with regard to administrative acts when the direct effect of directives is at stake. If the directive contains precise and unconditional commands, the Community proviso will rule the case; if that is not the case, the national judge will apply the Community proviso as a criterion to reviewing the case, excluding the possibility of substituting the annulled administrative act with the court's decision. However, this is not the case if domestic law is applied, because the scope of review, in cases of lack of volition and cognitive discretion, is not limited to the annulment of public administration decisions: the judiciary substitutes the disputed decision though its own judgment based on legal-technical issues.

5 Conclusion

By analysing the deliberative dialogue between the ECJ and the Spanish courts concerning the use of 'rights' and 'discretion', we have seen that the definitions of these concepts are not always on the side of EC law. However, this does not undermine recourse to 'rights' and 'discretion' to guarantee the effectiveness of EC law. Indeed, the ECJ has used the concept of rights primarily to strengthen the implementation of EC law, and to mitigate the impact on the EC legal system of Member States' infringements such as late or incorrect transposition of directives through the invocation of 'EC rights' by individuals before national courts. The ECJ has also used the notion of discretion to enhance the scope of judicial scrutiny by national courts, which, under certain circumstances, are concerned not only with the protection of 'Community rights' but also with the conformity of public administrative acts with EC law.

The way in which the ECJ has handled the concept of 'right' in its case law, tacitly giving it a fairly broad scope, allows for such a concept to fit within different national legal notions and for national procedural autonomy to provide diverse channels and levels of judicial protection. Thus, Community rights, when they come to be implemented and safeguarded in the context of Spanish law, might translate into any of the diverse categories of 'rights' and 'interests' outlined above, and this has important consequences as to the type and degree of judicial protection that they will enjoy. In other words, the lack of a precise concept of 'EC rights' grants national public authorities as much flexibility as is needed to accommodate better national legal structures, institutions, traditions, and procedures in the task of implementing and enforcing EC law. Indeed, such a degree of 'divergence' in the use of concepts such as 'rights' allows national and EC legal orders to interact, avoiding rigidities or conflicts that could lead to a more problematical implementation of EC Law in the Member States. Thus, it could be argued that divergence as to the extent of this concept might lead to overall convergence between national and EC legal orders, or may at least prevent more serious ruptures between them.

There are, however, some limits to the flexibility that Member States enjoy in accommodating EC rights in national legal categories. For example, once the ECJ has expressly declared that the objective of a given directive is to confer 'rights' on individuals (as is the case with several environmental directives), national judges can no longer presume (as they did traditionally) that the national law which implements such an EC directive is adopted only to protect the 'general public interest'. In Spain, judicial protection under the 'general public interest' cannot be requested in principle by individuals, with the few exceptions where an act expressly allows for the *actio popularis*. In contrast, Member States must recognize that legitimate interests, whether individual or collective, are at stake in order to allow individuals or groups to request judicial protection against infringement of such 'Community rights'. Further, the translation of EC rights into either rights or interests is likely to create special problems in Spain with regard to the judicial control of illegal administrative omission or failures to act which undermine EC rights, as in these cases it is not sufficient for an individual to have a legitimate interest; it must be proved that the directive confers a (substantial) 'right' on the individual, and that EC provisions have established this in unconditional and precise terms.

The reception of the ECJ's notion of discretion by Spanish judges is also problematic because, unlike in EC law, in Spanish law the constitutional position of the judiciary vis-à-vis public administration involves controlling the legality of administrative actions, and scrutinizing the effective protection of fundamental rights and legitimate interests (Article 24 SC). As a consequence, the existence of discretionary power does not exclude judiciary control since, in any case, public actions must conform to the principle of legality and the protection of individual rights and legitimate interests. This means, as the Spanish Supreme Court has stated, that the scope of judicial review must be enhanced to allow for substituting the administrative act with a judicial decision if the law provides all the relevant features to determine the content of that decision.

This domestic notion of discretion is difficult to accommodate in cases concerning illegal administrative omissions or failures to act that undermine the implementation of EC law, and particularly the implementation of EC directives. In these cases the main question is to what extent Spanish judges could (or should) take a decision that implies a 'judicial implementation' of such a directive, even if a margin of discretion exists as to the means of achieving this objective, and the objective to be achieved is precise and unconditional.

The ECJ, however, in an exercise of convergence, has applied the same scope of judicial scrutiny over discretion on both Community institutions and national judges: it is opposed to the substitution of Community decisions/national administrative acts by the Community judicature/national judges. However, it has missed the opportunity to harmonize the judicial protection of rights derived from directives. The ECJ has not encouraged an intensive level of judicial scrutiny of Member States' discretion—something that already exists in Spain—even though the substitution of a legislative or administrative measure may be the only appropriate means of ensuring that the exercise of rights conferred by Community law is not rendered virtually impossible or excessively difficult.

Further, there is a clear sign of divergence in relation to rights and discretion as used by the ECJ in Community matters and in the domestic arena. First, it should be noted that whereas in the Spanish legal order the concepts of 'rights' and 'interests' are central to the rules on individuals' *locus standi* to challenge administrative acts or regulations and to open access to justice to individuals (and therefore, also to protect 'EC rights'), the same cannot be said with regard to individuals' access to the ECJ. On this point there is not the slightest sign of convergence between national and Community legal orders. Second, the ECJ is rather generous when determining the amount of discretionary powers that Community institutions enjoy under EC Law, and rather less so when the Member States are being scrutinized.

Hence, by analysing the dialogue between EC law and EC judges, on the one hand, and domestic law and national judges, on the other hand, we observe the existence of convergence and divergence patterns both in the protection of rights and in the judicial scrutiny of discretion. This, far from undermining the dialogue between EC law and domestic law, proves that if the relation between EC law and domestic law were dominated by either divergence or convergence, we would no longer witness a heterarchical organized configuration of legal authority.

7

Protection of Rights: How Far?

Sacha Prechal

1 Introduction

Protection of rights has always played a central role in European Community law. When, early in the 1960s, the ECJ pronounced that Community law creates rights for individuals which national courts are obliged to protect,[1] it created a direct link between the individuals in the Member States and the EC legal order, long before such a link was more formally laid down in the provisions on European citizenship. By recognizing the creation and existence of such rights and by providing for their protection, the Court has also put a powerful device in the hands of individuals for the enforcement of Community law as such. Similarly, the existence and use of these enforceable rights has contributed—and still contributes—to the unity of the EU legal order, at the very least in the sense that unilateral deviation by the Member States from Community law rules may be countered by private individuals, as well as by actions of the Commission and—less often—other Member States.

Not without some cynicism can it be observed that the European Court of Justice (ECJ) benefits from the language of individual rights in order to ensure that the requirements which it formulates in relation to the full effectiveness of Community law are more readily accepted in national legal orders and by national courts.[2] After all, the protection of individual citizens' rights

---

[1] Indeed, starting with Case 26/62 *Van Gend & Loos* [1963] ECR 1.

[2] In particular, if one compares how the ECJ deals with direct actions brought by individuals against the institutions. cf for instance A Arnull, *The European Union and its Court of Justice* (2nd edn, Oxford: Oxford University Press, 2006) 639–644. See on this tension also in this volume Beljin, ch 5, p103–104, Alonso *et al*, ch 6, p136–138.

seems a much more laudable project than merely stipulating that Community law must be complied with and that the Member States must be controlled. Interestingly, it would seem that, for the purpose of their enforcement in the domestic legal order, the use of rights is from time to time even reinforced by reference to the fundamental character of certain rights.[3]

In any case, it is no secret that Community law is not only concerned with the protection of the rights which individuals derive from it, but also with giving full effect to the rules in question. In many cases, the concern for protection of the individual and for full effect of the rules at issue may lead in opposite directions.[4] Decisions which safeguard the full effectiveness of Community law and which find against the individuals concerned are probably not much less frequent than those finding in their favour.[5] Similarly, in some cases the Court relies primarily on the full effectiveness of Community law rather than on effective judicial protection of the individuals concerned.[6] On the other hand, in numerous cases protection and full effect are two sides of the same coin. In this sense, protection of the individual and the full force and effect of Community law are two intimately linked issues.

In this context, it is striking that for a long time there was apparently no need to define or even explore the notion of rights. The creation of rights was often equated with the direct effect of Community law, and the legal consequences resulting from the application of the relevant provisions were a matter for national law. National legal systems absorbed, translated, and accommodated the application of Community law provisions. What really mattered was that these provisions were applied and the position of the individual protected, regardless of the qualification of the effects of the Community law provision under national law.[7] Obviously, there were—and are—considerable differences in the approach with regard to rights within the Member States. Moreover, qualification also depends on the type of procedure in which the provisions were relied upon.

[3] See, for instance, Joined Cases C-397/01 to C-403/01 *Pfeiffer* [2004] ECR I-8835 and in fact also Case C-144/04 *Mangold* [2005] ECR I-9981.

[4] For instance in the field of VAT.

[5] A salient example is the protection of legitimate expectation in the area of state aids. The level of protection is here lower than under national law alone. cf this volume, Ruffert, ch 11, p261–264.

[6] cf for instance Case C-253/00 *Muñoz* and Supertor Fruiticola [2002] ECR I-7289.

[7] Note, however, the relatively early discovery of the problem *effet utile d'effet direct*, which is at the heart of the 'articulation' between Community and national law. See J Mertens de Wilmars, 'L'efficacité des différentes techniques nationales de protection juridique contre les violations du droit communautaire par les autorités nationales et les particuliers' (1981) Cahiers de Droit Européen, 381.

Things started to change in the 1990s as a result of a number of factors and to this day the debate about rights and related issues continues unabated. In section 2, I briefly—and in very general terms—sketch the context of the debate. Next, I address one of its central topics, namely the protective scope of the provisions at issue. This issue is at the heart of whether a legal provision bestows a right on individuals (section 3). However, the issue of protective scope ranges further and may emerge in discussions about the limits of national procedural autonomy and the concept of direct effect (section 4). This chapter will show that Community law is still in search of a coherent and clear approach to the role and range of the protective scope of the rules concerned. Finally, in section 5, I briefly reflect on how this debate could or should evolve in the future, and how legal scholarship could contribute to this.

Throughout the discussion of all these issues I also hope to illustrate how national legal perceptions both complicate the debate and, at the same time, may also help to distil the elements which may be useful for finding solutions within the EU legal order. For instance, these elements may lead to an autonomous definition of rights.[8] Yet any indication of how to understand the notion of rights or how to tackle the issue of the scope of protection, even if these become autonomous Community law matters, must be understood and operationalized within a specific—domestic—conceptual framework. The latter will differ from Member State to Member State. Insight into the national legal systems is necessary to avoid misunderstandings between lawyers from different legal traditions, who 'meet' each other in the context of European law.

2 The context of the rights debate

As mentioned hitherto, although the term 'right' has been used regularly by the Court in its earlier case law, this term only became controversial in the 1990s. Which parameters established whether Community law provisions confer rights on individuals, how, and when? A number of factors are involved.

---

[8] cf the definition given by W van Gerven, 'Of Rights, Remedies and Procedures' (2000) CML Rev, 502. It is to an important extent based on findings made in the context of the *ius commune* project on tort law. See W van Gerven *et al*, *Cases, Materials and Text on National, Supranational and International Tort Law: Scope of Protection* (Oxford: Hart, 1998). On the necessity of an autonomous definition, see this volume, Beljin, ch 5, p108–109.

The debate began in Germany, at least in part. After a number of judgments in the area of environmental law, it was realized that the German concept of rights was perhaps too narrow when compared to what the ECJ wanted. According to established ECJ case law, when a directive is intended to create rights for individuals, the implementing measures must be such as to enable the individuals to ascertain the full extent of their rights and, where appropriate, to rely on them before the national courts. In a number of cases brought by the Commission against Germany on issues related to air quality and the protection of groundwater,[9] the Court found that these directives were intended to create rights for individuals, since the directives at issue were enacted—*inter alia*—with a view to protecting human health, or they laid down specific and detailed provisions, the purpose of which was, according to the Court, to create rights and obligations for individuals. Under German doctrine this was less evident. In particular, it was difficult to reconcile this case law with the German condition that it must be possible to establish an *abgegrenzten und beschränkten Personenkreis*.[10]

Closer consideration suggests that, in this type of case, the main concern of the Court seems to be that the legal position of the individual must be safeguarded and, perhaps even more importantly, that Community law is simply applied. How this position is further qualified under national law (eg, as one of individual rights or protected interests) is primarily a matter for the national legal order. The implication of this could very well be that where the Court uses the term 'right' in the context of its 'implementation case law', it has nothing specific in mind. Nevertheless, in Germany this was one of the important catalysts for the debate on the difference in scope of 'German' and 'European' rights, whatever the latter may mean.[11] At stake was whether the German concepts had to be changed under the influence of Community law. Numerous studies have been devoted to whether it is necessary to revise traditional national legal concepts of 'subjective public rights' as well as the key notion of German judicial protection, namely the *Individualrechtsschutz*.[12]

---

[9] Case C-131/88 *Commission v Germany* [1991] ECR I-825; Case C-361/88 *Commission v Germany* [1991] ECR I-2567, and Case C-59/89 *Commission v Germany* [1991] ECR I-2607. These judgments were subsequently confirmed in three judgments brought by the Commission against France: Case C-13/90 [1991] ECR I-4327; Case C-14/90 [1991] ECR I-4331; and Case C-64/90 [1991] ECR I-4335 (summary publications). cf also Case C-58/89 *Commission v Germany* [1991] ECR I-4983, and Case C-298/95 *Commission v Germany* [1996] ECR I-6747.

[10] cf G Winter, 'Individualrechtsschutz im deutschen Umweltrecht unter dem Einfluss des Gemeinschaftsrechts' (1999) Neue Zeitschrift für Verwaltungsrecht, 468.

[11] See on the notion of EU rights, this volume, Beljin, ch 5.

[12] cf for instance M Ruffert, 'Dogmatik und Praxis des subjektiv-öffentlichen Rechts unter dem Einfluss des Gemeinschaftsrecht' (1998) Deutsches Verwaltungsblatt, 69; Winter, see n 10

A second factor fuelled this debate, namely, the Court's case law on State liability. The case law has triggered a broader discussion on the concept of a right in Community law, since one of the conditions for liability is that the rule of law infringed must be intended to confer rights on individuals. It was striking that, in contrast to its case law under Article 288 of the EC Treaty, the Court did not merely require that the provisions of the directive aim to protect the individual.[13] On the contrary, it later imported the requirement of 'a right' into the Community liability regime and, arguably, made this more stringent.[14]

The Court's case law does not provide much guidance as to the assessment of this condition, and the few criteria it suggests are applied loosely. Doctrinal differences and divergent jurisprudential traditions come to the fore in the scholarly debate. Some have used a Hohfeldian analytical framework to clarify the Court's rights language, and to describe more precisely the legal relationships and the specific legal effects involved.[15] Others have given a very general and 'tentative' definition,[16] or criticized the Court's approach.[17] The debate and its intensity also differ between Member States.

Although the debate has not been as extensive everywhere as in Germany, writers based in other legal traditions have voiced concerns about the inherent ambiguity of the terms deployed by the Court, discussing, for example, whether the Court refers to the stricter or more narrow concept of a *droit*

---

above, 467; D Triantafyllou, 'Zur Europäisierung des subjektiven öffentlichen Rechts' (1997) Die öffentliche Verwaltung, 192; F Schoch, 'Individualrechtsschutz im deutschen Umweltrecht unter dem Einfluss des Gemeinschaftsrechts' (1997) Neue Zeitschrift für Verwaltungsrecht, 457; S Hölscheidt, 'Abschiedt vom subjektiv-öffentlichen Recht?' (2001) Europarecht, 376 and U Baumgartner, *Die Klagebefugnis nach deutschem Recht vor dem Hintergrund der Einwirkungen des Gemeinschaftsrechts* (Berlin: Rhombos-Verlag, 2005).

[13] cf G Bebr, 'Comment on Joined Cases C-6/90 and C-9/90 *Francovich*' (1992) CML Rev, 575.

[14] cf Case C-352/98 P *Bergaderm* [2000] ECR I-5291 and more recently, for instance, Case C-198/03 P *CEVA* [2005] ECR I-6357.

[15] See, in particular, C Hilson and TA Downes, 'Making Sense of Rights: Community Rights in EC Law' (1999) ELR, 121. cf also the Opinion of Advocate General Van Gerven in Case C-70/88 *Parliament v Council* [1990] ECR I-2041, para 6, which pointed out the necessity to conceive 'rights' in the widest sense of the term, namely as right, power, and prerogative.

[16] cf, for instance, Van Gerven (2000), see n 8 above, 502. In his view, 'the concept of rights refers [...] to a legal position which a person recognized as such by the law ... may have and which in its normal state can be enforced by that person against ... others before a court of law by means of one or more remedies ...'.

[17] cf T Eilmansberger, 'The Relationship between Rights and Remedies in EC law: In Search of the Missing Link' (2004) CML Rev, 1199.

subjectif, or whether in the Community context the protection of a legitimate interest would suffice for it to be labelled as a 'right'.[18]

In Italy, the Court's case law on State liability had to be reconciled with the traditional—and somewhat nebulous—distinction between 'subjective' rights and 'legitimate interests'.[19] Under domestic law, an infringement of a rule which generates 'only' a legitimate interest cannot lead to damages. In particular, State liability for the failure to implement a directive posed problems since, as a matter of national law, no 'subjective' right could be identified in such a context, and, consequently, Article 2043 of the Italian civil code could not serve as a basis for such liability.[20] Note that the distinction between 'subjective' rights and 'legitimate interests' is not merely relevant for the question of State liability. It also determines, *inter alia,* the jurisdiction of ordinary and administrative courts and may be relevant for the rules on evidence.[21] It is therefore not surprising that the distinction shows up, from time to time, in preliminary references to the ECJ.[22]

Even in the UK, or to be more precise, in the English legal system, where the issue of rights is not really of primary concern,[23] the *Three Rivers* case addressed the question of when Community law creates a right for an

---

[18]   Often without explaining what the difference between a right and a (legitimate or mere) interest is. cf M Pâques, 'Trois remèdes à l'inexécution du droit communautaire: utilité pour l'environnement?' (1996) Revue de droit international et de droit comparé, 199–201 and MP Léger, 'Libres propos sur l'application effective du droit communautiare de l'environement' in GC Rodriguez Iglesias (ed), *Mélanges en hommage à Fernand Schockweiler* (Baden-Baden: Nomos, 1999) 299, in particular 328.

[19]   cf on this, for instance, R Caranta, 'Government Liability after Francovich' (1993) CLJ, 286–291 and F Zampini, 'Responsabilité de l'État pour violation du droit communautaire: l'exemple de l'Italie' (1997) Revue française de droit administratif, 1042–1044.

[20]   At least this was the mainstream line of the argument. This problem, furthermore, was the background to the Legislative Decree, which, after the ECJ's judgment in Francovich, not only implemented Directive 80/987, but also provided for compensation of individuals, which suffered damage due to this belated implementation. For a discussion of this see G Anagnostaras, 'State Liability v Retroactive Application of Belated Implementing Measures: Seeking the Optimum Means in Terms of Effectiveness of EC Law' (2000) Web Journal of Current Legal Issues (Issue 1) <http://webjcli.ncl.ac.uk/2000/issue1/1.html>.

[21]   For instance in the litigation about the pollution of the Cava river, if a 'subjective' right had been established, the evidence presented by the administration could have been reviewed by an independent expert, while in the case of legitimate interests such a review was not permitted. cf M Gnes, 'Recent Developments in Italian Judicial Activism: The Impact of EC Law on the Administrative Judges' (1998) Eur Rev of Public L, 792–801.

[22]   Starting with Case 13/68 *Salgoil* [1968] ECR 453. cf also, amongst others, Case C-380/87 *Enichem Base* [1989] ECR 2491 and Case C-236/92 *Comitato* [1994] ECR I-483.

[23]   cf this volume, M Graziadei, ch 4, p71–77 and—in brief—S Prechal, *Directives in EC Law* (2nd edn, Oxford: Oxford University Press, 2005) 104.

individual.[24] The case concerned, *inter alia*, a claim, based on Community law, for damages incurred by several thousand depositors as a consequence of the collapse of the BCCI. The Bank of England, in its capacity of banking supervisor, allegedly acted in breach of the First Banking Directive.[25] According to the House of Lords, there were two distinct routes which could be followed: one based on the principle of direct effect (the *Becker*-type liability), and one based on the principle of State liability (the *Francovich*-type liability). However, it was not necessary to distinguish those two. The conditions to be satisfied under both types of liability 'are so closely analogous that they can be taken to be . . . the same'.[26] Next, the Lords proceeded to analyse the two 'critical questions', namely whether the First Banking Directive entails the grant of rights to individual depositors and potential depositors, and whether the content of those rights is identifiable on the basis of the provisions of the Directive. The Lords found that the Directive contained no provision which entailed the granting of rights to individuals.

Although this finding of the House of Lords does not seem to be correct from a Community law perspective—the dicta about two routes by which damages can be claimed are highly questionable, to say the least—it does show another intimate link,[27] namely the relationship between the debate on rights and the—older and to a large extent separate—debate on the meaning and scope of direct effect. Like rights, direct effect has turned out to be an ambiguous notion, which also seems to be coloured by national perceptions.[28]

For the purposes of this contribution it suffices to recall—very briefly— that there are, broadly speaking, two different notions of direct effect.[29] The first is direct effect in a *narrow* sense. This notion is defined as the capacity of a Community law provision to create rights for individuals. The existence of an individual right is often equated with direct effect. However, various scholars have pointed out that direct effect may also be understood as a

---

[24] *Three Rivers District Council v Bank of England* [2000] 3 CMLR 205. cf also *Bowden v South West Water* [1999] 3 CMLR 180 (CA) briefly discussed below, in s 3, p167–168.

[25] Council Directive (EEC) 77/780 on the co-ordination of the laws, regulations, and administrative provisions relating to the taking up and pursuit of the business of credit institutions [1977] OJ L322/30.

[26] *Three Rivers District Council v Bank of England* [2000] 3 CMLR 205, 230, no 45.

[27] On this see S Prechal, 'Member State Liability and Direct Effect: What's the Difference After All?' (2006) Eur Business L Rev, 299–316.

[28] cf P Craig and G de Búrca, *EU Law: Text, Cases, and Materials* (3rd edn, Oxford: Oxford University Press, 2003) 178 and S Prechal, 'Does Direct Effect still Matter?' (2000) CML Rev, 1047.

[29] For a more detailed discussion, see Prechal, n 23 above, 99–106.

broader concept than the mere creation of rights. In this view Community law provisions can be invoked or relied upon for a wide variety of purposes, for example as a defence in criminal proceedings or as a standard for review of the legality of a Member State's action in administrative proceedings, including the control of the use of discretion by the Member States.

More recently, this debate has received new impetus, last but not least because of the exclusion of direct effect under the Third Pillar in relation to decisions and framework decisions. Seen against this background, there is a certain interest in defining direct effect as narrowly as possible as this would mean that other methods of giving effect to EU law—consistent interpretation, state liability, perhaps even a 'simple' setting aside—are *not* excluded.

According to some, direct effect should be brought back to its true proportions, ie to be considered as 'the technique which allows individuals to enforce a subjective right'.[30] As a consequence, such a narrow definition should enable individuals to rely on EU framework decisions or decisions for the purposes of the control of legality and of setting aside incompatible national law. In this predominantly 'Franco-Belgian' line of thought, supremacy and not direct effect is then often put forward as the main rationale for this type of invocability.

An additional source of confusion is that in several State liability cases the ECJ simply stated that the relevant provision of Community law created rights for the purposes of establishing liability, because the Court had previously found that the provision at issue created rights in the sense of having direct effect.[31] This may be true to a certain extent. Direct effect in the *narrow sense* and creation of rights will often coincide; the provision can thus *have* direct effect and *define* rights. However, this is not always necessarily the case. Community law provisions may confer rights upon individuals, or at least may be intended to do so, without being directly effective.[32] Moreover, if direct effect is understood in the *broad sense*, it refers to the ability to rely on a provision of Community law for a variety of purposes, and not necessarily the ability to claim a right. In brief, the concept of direct effect and the creation of rights should be considered separately.

[30] K Lenaerts and T Corthaut, 'Of Birds and Hedges: The Role of Primacy in Invoking Norms of EU Law' (2006) ELR, 310. cf also their contribution to the present volume, ch 21.

[31] cf Joined Cases C-46/93 and C-48/93 *Brasserie and Factortame* [1996] ECR I-1029; Case C-5/94 *Hedley Lomas* [1996] ECR I-2553; and Case C-150/99 *Stockholm Lindöpark* [2001] ECR I-493. cf also Eilmansberger, see n 17 above, 1225–1227.

[32] cf for instance Case T-415/03 *Cofradía de pescadores de 'San Pedro' de Bermeo* [2005] ECR II-4355, where the CFI distinguishes, in para 86, four different options of how rights may be conferred upon individuals.

Finally, ambiguities about the notion of rights and the protection pre-scribed under Community law may emerge in relation to another line of case law. The Member State and, in particular, national courts are required, on the basis of EC Treaty, Article 10, to protect the rights of individuals derived from Community law.[33] They are often told that this protection must be effective. It seems that what really matters here is, primarily, the full applica-tion of Community law provisions as such, as opposed to the protection of any specific rights; the scope of the protection required seems much broader.[34] However, at the national level, such requirements may cause problems in terms of domestic (procedural) law, such as who should be given standing and which pleas are admissible in a concrete case.

3 The protective scope and existence of rights

Thus far there has hardly been any indication in the Court's case law of what it means by the first condition of State liability, and especially by the term 'right'.[35] In some cases the issue was treated as obvious; in others, the ECJ also relied on the preamble and the intentions laid down therein.[36] One could add the confusing dicta that equate direct effect and the creation of rights.[37] The few cases about the question of rights suggest that relevant parameters concern, in particular, the ascertainability of individual rights. In other words, individual rights must be determinable with sufficient precision as regards their content and the beneficiaries of the rights.[38] The more explicit the rule,[39] and the less discretion left to public authorities,[40] the better.

[33] cf the case law that started with Case 33/76 *Rewe* [1976] ECR 1989 and Case 45/76 *Comet* [1976] ECR 2043.

[34] In fact the protection required seems to include any challenge, before national courts, of the legality of national measure; if necessary even in order to consider—indirectly—the validity of a Community measure. cf Case C-50/00 P *UPA* [2002] ECR I-6677.

[35] For a discussion with some comparative notes see also J Jans *et al*, *Europeanisation of Public Law* (Groningen: Europa Law Publishing, 2007) in particular 336–344.

[36] cf for instance C-91/92 *Faccini Dori* [1994] ECR I-3325 and Joined Cases C-178/94, C-179/94, C-188/94, C-189/94, and C-190/94 *Dillenkofer* [1996] ECR I-4845.

[37] See above, s 2.

[38] cf the Opinion of Advocate General Tesauro in Joined Cases C-178/94, C-179/94, C-188/94, C-189/94, and C-190/94 *Dillenkofer* [1996] ECR I-4845, para 18 and Case C-140/97 *Rechberger* [1999] ECJ I-3499, para 22.

[39] cf Case C-222/02 *Peter Paul* [2004] ECR I-9425, para 41.

[40] cf Case C-127/95 *Norbrook Laboratories Ltd* [1998] ECR I-1531, para 108 and, very explicitly, Case C-216/02 *Österreichischer Zuchtverband* für Ponys, Kleinpferde und Spezialrassen [2004] ECR I-10683, para 36.

Another central issue is the protective scope of the relevant provision(s). As was observed in legal writing, when the Court requires, in view of state liability, that the infringed provision must have intended to create rights, it aims at introducing the concept of 'relative unlawfulness', a *Schutznorm* which is common to the non-contractual liability regimes of several Member States.[41] This means, succinctly, that only the breach of a rule creating rights for individuals concerned, or intended to create rights or, at least, protect their interests, can give rise to a right to reparation. In other words, the scope of protection of the infringed norm must include the harmed interest of the claimant.

The thesis that links a right to an interest, in the sense that rights are viewed as protecting individual interests, goes back to Jhering, and continues to enjoy widespread support.[42] In this sense the protection of individual interests is an element of the concept of rights. Concretely, it implies that it is necessary to establish whether the legal rules at the source of the alleged right exist to protect a specific or individual interest, rather than to only protect the general (or public) interest. This translates, with respect to the *addressee* of the norm, into whether his or her obligation exists vis-à-vis the general public or also specifically with regard to a certain person. In addition to this 'personal' scope of protection, one may distinguish a substantive scope as well, to wit not only whose interests are protected but also which interests are protected, and to what extent.[43]

As to the personal scope, the problem is that the distinction between general and more specific individual interests is not black and white, but rather a matter of degree. It is by no means clear how strict this requirement of protection of individual interest is in Community law. Apparently this depends on the different contexts in which cases have been decided thus far.[44] The discussion on this issue has been complicated by a number of dicta about environmental directives, which, in the context of infringement proceedings,

---

[41] cf D Simon, 'Droit communautaire et responsabilité de la puissance publique. Glissements progressifs ou révolution tranquille' (1993) Actualité juridique-Droit administratif, 237; W van Gerven, 'Non-contractual Liability of Member States, Community Institutions and Individuals for Breaches of Community Law with a View to a Common Law of Europe' (1994) Maastricht J of Eur and Comparative L, 16. cf also M Ross, 'Beyond Francovich' (1993) MLR, 55, who points out that in English law the norm violated must impose a duty which is owed to the plaintiff, 62.

[42] cf for instance Eilmansberger, see n 17 above, 1236–1245. However, see in this volume Graziadei ch 4, p69.

[43] Usually, this inquiry implies a two-stage approach: the existence of protective scope at an abstract level and, second, the concrete question as to the protection of the interest at stake of the individual concerned (the 'who' and 'what' question). cf on this Beljin, this volume ch 5 p117–120.

[44] For a discussion of the flaws in the case law see Eilmansberger, see n 17 above, 1231ff.

were said to create rights for individuals.[45] In any case, it has been submitted that the Court's case law is less strict than, for instance, German or Austrian law.[46] In particular, German legal scholars often point out that the Court of Justice is more readily satisfied that a provision also aims at the protection of an individual interest than would be the case for a German court applying the German *Schutznormtheorie*.[47] Until recently, it seemed that it sufficed that the protective scope of a Community law rule included an individual interest. It was not deemed necessary to include individual interest as a specific aim of protection.

In *Dillenkofer*,[48] the Court relied on the fact that the preamble repeatedly refers to the purpose of protecting consumers. Moreover, the aim and wording of Article 7, the particular provision which the court had to interpret, included the protection of consumers. The fact that the Directive intended to ensure other additional objectives (freedom to provide services and fair competition) did not detract from this finding. In case C-144/99 the Court dealt with Directive 93/13, regarding unfair terms in consumer contracts. Taking its point of departure in one of the aims set out in the preamble, namely 'to safeguard the citizen in his role as consumer when acquiring goods and services under contracts which are governed by the laws of Member States other than his own', the Court held that the Directive intended to accord rights to individuals.[49] In Case C-478/99 the Court also accepted that the same directive aims at creating rights for individuals, but this time on the basis of a number of specific provisions.[50] In the area of public procurement, the Court stressed that Directive 92/50 on the award of public service contracts[51] was adopted with a view to eliminating barriers to the freedom to provide services, hence that it intended to protect the interests of traders who wish to offer services to contracting authorities in other Member States.[52] This, too, seems to point in the direction of individual rights, even

[45] cf above for the origin of the German discussion referred to here. Arguably dicta about intended creation of rights in the implementation context cannot be transposed to liability cases.
[46] cf for a discussion, for instance, HD Jarass and S Beljin, *Casebook Grundlagen des EG-Rechts* (Baden-Baden: Nomos, 2003) 176–190.
[47] cf for instance Hölscheidt, see n 12 above, 386–389.
[48] Joined Cases C-178/94, C-179/94, C-188/94, C-189/94, and C-190/94 *Dillenkofer* [1996] ECR I-4845.
[49] Case C-144/99 *Commission v The Netherlands* [2001] ECR I-3541.
[50] Case C-478/99 *Commission v Sweden* [2002] ECR I-4147.
[51] Council Directive (EEC) 92/50 relating to the co–ordination of procedures for the award of public service contracts [1992] OJ L209/1.
[52] Joined Cases C-20/01 and C-28/01 *Commission v Germany* [2003] ECR I-3609.

though the main objective of the Directive is to remove barriers in the field of free movement of services.

The judgment of the Court in *Peter Paul* marks a reorientation of the case law, as it tightened considerably the individual interest requirement.[53] The central issue of this case was, briefly, whether certain banking directives included a right for depositors to have national 'supervisors' take supervisory measures in their interest. If that were the case, a national rule according to which the supervision of credit institutions was only a matter of public interest, and hence barred individuals from claiming damages in case of defective supervision, had to be set aside. Note that the issue of 'rights' and individual interest emerged here in the context of direct effect and supremacy. Under German law, liability could be incurred under Paragraph 839 of the *Bürgerliches Gesetzbuch*, in conjunction with Article 34 of the *Grundgesetz*. However, this liability regime—liability for breach of official duty—requires a breach of 'official duty . . . as against a third party', that is, a duty which exists in any case as against the injured party. In the case at hand, there seemed to be no liability under German law because the 'supervisor', the *Bundesaufsichtsamt*, exercises the functions assigned to it solely in the public interest.

The Court denied the existence of 'a right to supervisory measures' on the part of the depositors. The objective of the directives was harmonization, deemed necessary to secure the mutual recognition of authorizations and prudential supervision systems. Although the preambles asserted that the protection of depositors was one of the objectives of the harmonization, and although the relevant directives laid down a number of supervisory obligations of the national authorities vis-à-vis credit institutions, this was not enough to establish the existence of the right sought by the depositors. The Court stated:

it does not necessarily follow either from the existence of such obligations or from the fact that the objectives pursued by those directives also include the protection of depositors that those directives seek to confer rights on depositors in the event that their deposits are unavailable as a result of defective supervision on the part of the competent national authorities.[54]

---

[53] Case C-222/02 *Peter Paul* [2004] ECR I-9425. A comparable restrictive approach can also be found in the case law of the CFI. For instance, the principle of sound administration as such does not confer rights upon individuals, although it can hardly be denied that this principle also exists for the protection of individual citizens. cf Case T-196/99 *Area Cova* [2001] ECR II-3587 or Case T-193/04 *Tillack* [2006] ECR II-3995.

[54] Case C-222/02 *Peter Paul* [2004] ECR I-9425, para 40.

The main arguments were that:

- there was no express rule granting such rights;
- the co–ordination of the rules on liability in case of defective supervision was not necessary for the purpose of the harmonization;
- banking supervision is a very complex activity, including protection of a plurality of interests;
- one of the directives already provided for minimal protection of depositors in the event that their deposits were unavailable.

The finding that, under the directives, the depositors had no right to compensation beyond the minimum protection mentioned above, was also decisive for the next question, namely State liability under Community law in the event of defective supervision on the part of the supervisory authorities. The Court was brief on that: as there was no such right conferred on depositors, the first condition for State liability was not met.

The judgment in *Peter Paul* illustrates that, in the question of whether certain legal rules, for example directives, create rights for individuals, general dicta in the preamble must be complemented by more specific provisions, such that the particular interests and the class of persons protected under the rules at issue can be identified. The question is indeed whether this judgment marks a new approach in general or whether it should be limited to the area of liability in case of defective banking supervision. As compared to mainstream case law in the field of State liability, this is a step backwards, due to the narrow interpretation of the 'rights-requirement'. The main reasons for this change may reside in policy considerations and financial implications.[55]

The reasoning of the ECJ in *Peter Paul* comes close to that of the House of Lords in the *Three Rivers* case.[56] The directive at issue in that case was 'a first step in a process of harmonization,' and as such was concerned with 'the removal of barriers' to the fundamental freedoms guaranteed by the EC Treaty, not with the creation of rights for individuals. Another example of the rather reserved position of English courts is *Bowden*.[57] The case concerned an action brought by a shell fisherman. He claimed that he had been driven out of business because his fishing waters had been classified under

---

[55] cf M Tison, 'Do Not Attack the Watchdog! Banking Supervisor's Liability after Peter Paul' (2005) CML Rev, 639, in particular 668–670.

[56] *Three Rivers District Council v Bank of England* [2000] 3 CMLR 205, already briefly discussed above, in s 2.

[57] *Bowden v South West Water* [1999] 3 CMLR 180 (CA).

a directive and because of pollution of the waters. As to his claim under the Shellfish Waters Directive,[58] the Court of Appeal accepted that the relevant provisions were at least related to the plaintiff's activities, and that if there was a failure by the United Kingdom to implement or to comply with the requirements of this Directive, this could have contributed to the loss of the plaintiff's fishing grounds. However, a breach would be a breach of an obligation 'owed *to the public in general*' (my italics), and there was nothing to tie such a breach to specific rights of individuals nor was there a provision which would enable the content of such rights to be ascertained. Accordingly the Court of Appeal held that there was no basis for a claim for damages.[59]

A contradiction in national approaches can be found in relation to the belated transposition of Directive (EEC) 91/676 ('Nitrates Directive').[60] In the Netherlands, several environmental organizations claimed, *inter alia*, compensation for damages incurred due to the costs related to the purification of ground– and surface–water, which had high concentrations of nitrate. The case was dismissed. The Court of Appeal recalled that, as a matter of Community law, the provisions at issue must be intended to create rights for individuals. According to the Court of Appeal, the provisions relied upon by the claimants did not meet that requirement. The Directive does not impose upon the State an obligation to safeguard a specific level of water-quality which could be enforced by an individual. The provisions do not meet the *Schutznorm* requirement as applied in Dutch liability law either.[61]

This judgment seems to be at odds with a case decided in France. In 1995 the *Tribunal d'instance* in Guingamp had ordered the *Société Lyonnaise des Eaux* to pay compensation to 176 subscribers to its drinking water distribution network on account of the excessive nitrate content of the water it distributed. Next, the *Société* brought proceedings in the *Tribunal administratif* in *Rennes* in order to obtain compensation for the State's late transposition

---

[58] Council Directive (EEC) 79/923 on the quality required of shellfish waters [1979] OJ L281/47.

[59] In the light of the 'German implementation cases' discussed here above, the question may be raised whether the Court of Appeal did not come too easily to its conclusion.

[60] Council Directive (EEC) 91/676 concerning the protection of waters against pollution caused by nitrates from agricultural sources [1991] OJ L375/1 (Nitrates Directive). In Case C-322/00 *Commission v The Netherlands* [2003] ECR I-11267 the ECJ found that the Netherlands failed to fulfil its obligation under this directive.

[61] Court of Appeal, The Hague, 21 October 2005, *Waterpakt*, M en R 2006/1, no 4, with comment J Jans.

of Article 5 of Directive (EEC) 91/676. The *Tribunal administratif* accepted this argument and found the State liable.[62]

The conditions for State liability, as laid down in the case law of the Court of Justice, are, as is well known, minimum conditions in the sense that they are sufficient to give rise to a right for reparation. However, the national legal systems may offer better protection for the individual concerned. In this sense the individual will be better off if a national liability system is more flexible, and does not impose a strictly construed and applied requirement of 'rights'. The judgment of the Spanish Tribunal Supremo in the *Canal Satélite Digital* case is exemplary for this approach.[63] The case dealt with state liability concerning legislation on satellite television decoders that was not compatible with the free movement of goods and services.[64] According to the Supreme Court,

the principle of state liability must always be interpreted extensively so as to favour the protection of the individual against the actions of the state. This interpretation derives on the one hand from the objective character of such liability under internal law and on the other hand from the fact that it is a means of mitigating the deficiencies of other channels of protection of these interests. It would not be reasonable to reduce the individual's right to effective judicial protection to the benefit of the infringing state. The pro-individual interpretation of state liability can be inferred from the fact that the conditions set out by the Court of Justice do not prejudice the application of any less restrictive national rules. This is particularly important in the sphere of our national legal system, in which the institute of state liability is of an objective nature. It is therefore sufficient to be in presence of an individualized, illegal harm and of a causal link between the infringing act and the harm to engender this state liability.[65]

Finally, a special category of cases regards obligations of a procedural character. It is difficult to imagine how, for instance, a breach of an obligation of notification could give rise to a right of individuals and therefore to reparation.[66] However, it is not entirely obvious that this type of breach a

---

[62] Tribunal Administratif, Rennes, 2 May 2001, XIXth Report on monitoring the application of Community law; COM(2002) 324, Annex VI, Section 3.

[63] Tribunal Supremo, 12 June 2003, *Canal Satélite Digital SL v Administracion General del Estado*, discussed by S Martínez Lage and H Brokelman, 'The Liability of the Spanish State for Breach of EC Law: The Landmark Ruling of the Spanish Tribunal Supremo in the Canal Satelite Digital Case' (2004) ELR, 530–545.

[64] Case C-390/99 *Canal Satélite Digital* [2002] ECR I-607.

[65] English translation from Martínez Lage and Brokelman, see n 63 above.

[66] cf Case C-380/87 *Enichem Base* [1989] ECR 2491; Case C-159/00 *Sapod* [2002] ECR I-5031; or Case C-72/02 *Commission v Portugal* [2003] ECR I-6597.

priori excludes liability. Whether or not there should be state liability may
depend on the legal consequences of such a notification and their objective,
such as whether the procedure also serves the protection of the individual
interest of the person concerned. In some cases, there can hardly be any
doubt. The most obvious example of this is indeed the public procurement
directives.[67] Similarly, the Court accepted liability in *Wells* for the breach of
an essentially procedural obligation, namely the failure to carry out an environmental impact assessment. This would suggest that the Environmental
Impact Assessment Directive confers rights upon individuals.[68] On the other
hand, in relation to Directive 83/189 (notification of technical standards),[69]
the Court pointed out that this Directive does not 'define the substantive
scope of the legal rule on the basis of which the national court must decide
the case before it. It creates neither rights nor obligations for individuals'.[70]

4 Broader applications and implications of the protective scope requirement

The protective scope requirement is, to begin with, intimately linked to
the existence of a right. That is not the end of the story, however. First,
there is the issue of protection of an individual interest—the application of
a *Schutznorm*—in the context of direct effect. In Germany, for instance, with
Individualrechtsschutz as one of the basic principles, the creation of rights
was initially considered to be a condition of direct effect. Later the debate
in German legal writing led to the distinction between 'subjective direct

---

[67] cf also Case C-19/00 *SIAC* [2001] ECR I-7725; Case C-243/89 *University of Cambridge*
[2000] ECR I-8035; and Case C-433/93 *Commission v Germany* [1995] ECR I-2303, where the
Court held that the rules regarding participation and advertising in public procurement directives are intended to protect tenderers against arbitrariness on the part of the contract-awarding
authority.

[68] Case C-201/02 *Delena Wells* [2004] ECR I-723, paras 66–69.

[69] Council Directive (EEC) 83/189 laying down a procedure for the provision of information
in the field of technical standards and regulations [1983] OJ L109/8.

[70] Case C-443/98 *Unilever* [2000] ECR I-7535, para 51. Nevertheless, in the *Canal Satélite
Digital* case, the Spanish Tribunal Supremo found, basing itself on the ECJ's judgment in Case
C-194/94 *CIA* [1996] ECR I-2201, that Arts 8 and 9 of Council Directive (EEC) 83/189 laying
down a procedure for the provision of information in the field of technical standards and regulations [1983] OJ L109/8 were actually intended to confer rights on individuals. On this ground it
rejected the argument of the Spanish state to the contrary. See Martínez Lage and Brokelman,
see n 63 above.

effect', which remains conditional upon the existence of an individual right, and 'objective direct effect', a new form of direct effect which is not conditional upon the existence of an individual right.[71]

However, the condition of protective scope, which, as was demonstrated above, is closely linked to the issue of rights, slipped into the discussion on direct effect in the aftermath of the *CIA-Security* judgment and was by no means limited to Germany.[72] In that judgment the ECJ ruled that national measures on technical standards enacted in a Member State without respecting the notification requirement under Directive (EEC) 83/189 were inapplicable. The question which subsequently arose was the following: who is allowed to rely on this inapplicability?[73] Does this condition include a drunken driver prosecuted for driving under the influence of alcohol, and who has been tested by means of certain equipment manufactured on the basis of technical standards which were not notified to the Commission? According to the Dutch government before the ECJ, and Advocate General Fennely in the *Lemmens* case,[74] only those persons whose interests are intended to be protected by the Directive's provisions may invoke that Directive before the national courts. Both contended that the invocability of the Directive was reserved to those persons who have an interest in the free movement of goods. Unfortunately, the Court did not decide this issue in *Lemmens*. The judgment is not clear on this point and can be interpreted in many ways. While some read it as confirming a link between invocability and an interest requirement,[75] others find that the Court's judgment is inconclusive in this respect.[76]

[71] cf M Ruffert, 'Rights and Remedies in European Community Law: A Comparative View' (1997) CML Rev, 307–336, in particular 320, with further references. cf also G Winter, 'Die Dogmatik der Direktwirkung von EG-Richtlinien und ihre Bedeutung für das EG-Naturschutzrecht' (2002) Zeitschrift für Umweltrecht 2002, 314, referring to a judgment of the Federal Administrative Court, which seems to accept that the creation of rights is a consequence of direct effect and not a condition.

[72] Case C-194/94 *CIA* [1996] ECR I-2201.

[73] Note that this is not a matter of standing but a matter of what pleas may validly be submitted.

[74] Case C-226/97 *Lemmens* [1998] ECR I-3711 and see also Hilson and Downes, see n 15 above, 131ff, who are also 'smuggling' an interest requirement into the concept of direct effect.

[75] cf Van Gerven, see n 8 above, 508; K Lenaerts, 'Redactionele Signalen' (1998) 46 SEW Tijdschrift voor Europees en Economisch Recht, 269. On the lack of clarity of this judgment see also the comment by R Streinz, (1999) 39 Juristische Schulung, 599–600 and R Abele, (1998) 9 Europäische Zeitschrift für Wirtschaftsrecht, 571–572. It might be that it was exactly this kind of consideration that lay behind the question of the Hoge Raad in the *Streekgewest*-case, discussed below.

[76] cf T Koopmans SEW Tijdschrift voor Europees en Economisch Recht (1999), 338 (case note on *Lemmens*). In my view, the ECJ delimited the scope of the consequences of the violation at issue, ie the non-applicability, rather then the circle of persons who may rely on the Directive.

The case law of the Belgian *Conseil d'Etat* reveals the close interrelation between these issues, or at any rate that they are *perceived* as having such an interrelation.[77] In some cases, direct effect was more or less equated to the creation of rights and, subsequently, the conditions for direct effect determined the admissibility of the claim. This implied that where parties sought to vindicate individual rights,[78] the relevant provisions had to be directly effective. The *Conseil d'Etat* subordinated the review of the question of whether the claim is well founded to the preliminary question of whether the provisions relied upon are unconditional and sufficiently precise. When, however, an environmental association brought an action, the *Conseil d'Etat* did not seem to require that the provisions relied upon had to be directly effective. An explanation here may be sought in the fact that, by bringing a case, a non-profit organization acts in the general interest. Since these types of action are viewed as aiming at the maintenance of the 'objective legality', and thus focus upon the control of legality as such, they are no longer linked to some kind of individual interest. Consequently, the conditions for direct effect, which apply in more 'individual oriented cases', are dropped.

At any rate, introducing a *Schutznorm* requirement for the purpose of 'invocability' of Community law provisions amounts, in my opinion, to an unnecessary restriction at the Community law level, which thereby effectively adds a new condition for direct effect. The same holds for the creation of rights as an additional condition of direct effect. The same risk is also inherently present in efforts to narrow down (again) the notion of direct effect.[79] In particular, there is no need to introduce an additional limitation at the level of direct effect because provisions of domestic law may already limit either access to the courts or the admissibility of certain submissions. Thus it is for the application of domestic law requirements that interpretation

---

cf also Case C-127/02 *Landelijke Vereniging tot Behoud van de Waddenzee* [2004] ECR I-7405 where the Court uses neutral terms, namely that the obligation of the Directive 'may be relied on by those concerned', para 66. cf also Case C-213/03 *Pêcheur de l'étang de Berre* [2004] ECR I-7357, 'any interested party is entitled to rely on [the] provisions [at issue]', para 47.

[77]   cf P Gilliaux, 'Rapport belge, Les directives communautaires: effets, efficacité, justitiabilité' in *XVIII congrès FIDE—Stockholm 3–6 juin 1998, Congrès FIDE. 18* (Stockholm: FIDE, 1998).

[78]   In original version: ' requêtes ayant pout objet de préserver ou de mettre en cause des situations subjectives ou indirectement des droits . . .'. Gilliaux, see n 77 above, 104.

[79]   For a brief comment on these efforts see S Prechal, 'Direct Effect, Indirect Effect, Supremacy and the Evolving Constitution of the European Union' in C Barnard (ed), *The Fundamentals of EU Law Revisited: Assessing the Impact of the Constitutional Debate, Collected Courses of the Academy of European Law* (Oxford: Oxford University Press, 2007) 44–47.

of EC law and, where necessary, the protective scope of its provisions may become relevant. Similarly, a national court may raise preliminary questions about the possible interpretation of the Community law rules if the issue of rights is of importance for the case before it, either as a matter of State liability or because the qualification is necessary for national law purposes.[80] However, here we are dealing with the content of the measures, not with their direct effect as such. These considerations bring us to the second topic to be discussed, namely the role that the question of protective scope plays in the context of national (procedural) autonomy.[81]

The issue of the existence and the scope of protection arises in this context in the sense that it may also determine questions like standing, and the admissibility of certain pleas, or that it might otherwise limit the category of persons which may benefit from the rules.[82] The measure of strictness in applying a *Schutznorm* requirement depends basically on which view on the function of legal protection prevails, ie the 'subjective' or the 'general' view of legality. According to the former, judges are primarily responsible for the protection of individual citizens. Judicial intervention serves primarily to protect individual rights or at least individual interests. According to the latter, judges have a wider responsibility for controlling the legality of government action. Hence judicial review is perceived as a matter of public interest. Most legal systems are situated somewhere in between these two extremes.[83]

In Germany, for instance, the existence of an individual right is, as a rule, a prerequisite for bringing an action in a national administrative court. From a Community law perspective, however, such a requirement may unduly restrict access to the courts. For instance, in the wake of the Court's judgment in *Courage*,[84] the German Competition law (*Gesetz gegen Wettbewerbsbeschränkungen*) had to be amended in order to make private enforcement more effective. Initially, only the immediate contract partners could bring

[80] As was the case in, for instance, Case C-222/02 *Peter Paul* [2004] ECR I-9425 and Case C-216/02 *Österreichischer Zuchtverband* für Ponys, Kleinpferde und Spezialrassen [2004] ECR I-10683.
[81] Procedural in brackets since the qualification whether a matter is a procedural one or substantive is a matter of national law.
[82] cf also the Opinion of Advocate General Mengozzi of 29 March 2007, in Case C-429/05 *Rampion and Godard*, Judgment of the Court of 4 October 2007, nyr which makes clear that the divide between the protection of general interest and the protection of individual interest is relevant for the question whether certain provisions have to be applied *ex officio* or not.
[83] cf for instance DA Lubach, 'Convergerende tendensen in het Europees bestuursrecht' (2004) Nederlands Tijdschrift voor Bestuursrecht, 249-259. See also this volume, Beljin, ch 5 p97–100.
[84] Case C-453/99 *Courage* [2001] ECR I-6297.

an action for damages. The law did not make such actions available for suppliers, consumers, or contractors on a subsequent market level; these were not deemed to be within the scope of the protection provided by the competition rules. Following the amendment, a much broader category of persons may bring claims.[85]

Similarly, the case of the *Verband Deutscher Daihatsu-Händler* clearly illustrated the limitations which may result from this way of thinking.[86] The case concerned the implementation of Article 6 of Directive (EEC) 68/151 (First Company Law Directive).[87] The publication of annual accounts is obligatory under the Directive. Appropriate penalties must be provided for by the Member States in case of a failure to do so. In Germany, the proceedings for the imposition of a fine in the form of a periodic penalty payment could only be brought by a member or creditor of the company, the general works council or the company's works council. The *Verband* did not qualify as such, and its application was initially dismissed. However, in a preliminary procedure the ECJ made clear that such a restriction was not permitted under the Directive, since the Directive aims at the protection of a much larger category of persons.

An *Individualrechtsschutz* is also the starting point in Austria, as became patently clear in C-216/02.[88] In this case, the *Zuchtverband für Ponys* could only secure standing if it had a 'judicially protected right to ensure that a new organisation of breeders be refused recognition, if certain conditions are fulfilled'. The ECJ held that the relevant provisions of Decision 92/353[89] could not be interpreted as creating such a right. The problem was apparently not so much the protective aim of the Decision but rather that such an interpretation would amount to doing away with the discretion that the Article at issue granted to the competent authorities of the Member States. However,

---

[85] Under Art 33(3) and (1) GWB, compensation can now be claimed for by the party concerned, defined as those competitors or other market participants that are affected. Not surprisingly, this give rise to new interpretation questions. See for instance M Lutz, 'Schwerpunkte der 7. GWB-Novelle' (2005) Wirtschaft und Wettbewerb, 718–732, at 727–729.

[86] Case C-97/96 *Verband deutscher Daihatsu-Händler v Daihatsu Deutschland* [1997] ECR I-6843.

[87] Council Directive (EEC) 68/151 on co–ordination of safeguards which, for the protection of the interests of members and others, are required by Member States of companies within the meaning of the second paragraph of Article 58 of the Treaty, with a view to making such safeguards equivalent throughout the Community [1968] OJ, English Spec Ed 1968 (I), 41 (First Company Law Directive).

[88] Case C-216/02 *Österreichischer Zuchtverband* für Ponys, Kleinpferde and Spezialrassen [2004] ECR I-10683.

[89] Commission Decision (EEC) 92/353 criteria for the approval or recognition of organizations and associations which maintain or establish stud-books for registered equidae [1992] OJ L192/63.

the case also indicates that the ECJ accepted the rather rigorous standing requirement in Austrian law.

Even in legal systems where access to the courts is not dependent upon the existence of an individual right as such, it may still be some form of 'individual interest' which underpins standing rules. In Dutch administrative law, for instance, access to complaints and appeal procedures is reserved for so-called 'interested parties'. According to Article 1:2 of the General Administrative Law Act (GALA), an interested party means a person whose interest is directly affected by a decision. In order to have standing, the person must have a sufficient interest in the proceedings. In telecom law, Article 1:2 initially did not cover competitors. When it appeared that this was untenable in the light of Article 4 of the Telecom Framework Directive,[90] the District Court in Rotterdam re-interpreted the notion of the 'interested party' of Article 1:2 in order to provide standing for competitors.[91]

As to actions which focus upon the protection of collective interests, such as in environmental law or consumer protection, effective access to the courts may well be denied in Member States with restricted 'subjective' standing rules, unless a special provision has been enacted for this type of case. This is also the main rationale behind the Community stimulating broader standing rules through its legislation.[92]

Furthermore, the protective scope of a rule may also emerge at a later stage in a procedure, namely when the admissibility of the pleas becomes an issue. By this I refer to whether a party to a proceeding should also aim at protecting his/her interests, when, for instance, such a party relies on a provision to defend him/herself. Or, to put the question differently, would it be sufficient to enter a purely 'objective' illegality plea based on, for instance, the incompatibility of the relevant national rules with a Community law provision? This is also a feature that differs from Member State to Member State; moreover, it often depends on the nature of the proceedings in which the provisions are relied upon, ie administrative, criminal, civil, etc.[93]

---

[90] Parliament and Council Directive (EC) 2002/21 on a common regulatory framework for electronic communications networks and services [2002] OJ L108/33.

[91] District Court, Rotterdam, 7 January 2002, *Versatel/OPTA*, Mediaforum 2002/3, Jur no 9.

[92] However, these rules still often rely on national law, by making reference to 'organizations regarded under national law as having a legitimate interest'. cf for instance Art 11 Parliament and Council Directive EC 2005/29 on unfair business-to-consumer commercial practices [2005] OJ L149/22 or Art 7 of Council Directive (EC) 2000/43 on non-discrimination on grounds of race [2000] OJ L180/22.

[93] Moreover it may be considered either as a procedural issue or as a part of the judgment on the substance.

A lively discussion has been taking place in the Netherlands for some time as to whether a *Schutznorm* requirement should be introduced in the GALA. One of the main reasons for this is efficiency, in particular the reduction of the case load of the courts. Furthermore, it was argued, in the course of a recent evaluation of the GALA, that the current situation leads to an improper use of the right of appeal.[94] As was explained above, in Dutch administrative law, in order to have standing, the plaintiff must have a sufficient interest in the proceedings. The decisive criterion is whether the decision challenged affects his/her interests. Similarly, if the court finds that the administrative order is in violation of the law, the court will quash the contested decision. For this purpose it is irrelevant whether the breached statutory provisions are intended to protect the interest of the plaintiff. Some scholars in the Netherlands prefer the introduction of a *Schutznorm* requirement at the stage of the pleas, rather than the standing rules.[95] The former must protect the interest of the plaintiff. Indeed, Community law arguments are taken on board in this discussion, and academic doctrine is divided on the question as to whether and in particular *to what extent* Community law allows for such an introduction.[96]

Standing and the admissibility of pleas are, in my view, matters which are primarily governed by provisions of national (procedural) law. From the point of view of Community law, these national (procedural) provisions are subject to the well-known principles of equivalence and effectiveness or, where appropriate, effective judicial protection.[97] These principles may imply prohibiting the application of a *Schutznorm* requirement in order to deny certain parties the right to rely on Community law provisions. A clear indication to that effect can be found in the judgment in *Streekgewest Westelijk Noord-Brabant*.[98] In this case, the Dutch Supreme Court asked the following: 'May only an individual who is affected by a distortion of cross-border

[94] Report of the Commission 'Evaluation Dutch General Administrative Code II' (Algemene wet bestuursrecht II) 18 (the so-called Commissie Boukema).

[95] VAR-Commissie Rechtsbescherming, *De toekomst van rechtsbescherming tegen de overheid. Van toetsing naar geschillenbeslechting* (Den Haag: Boom Juridische Uitgevers, 2004) 102.

[96] For a brief discussion in English see S Prechal and R Widdershoven, 'The Dutch General Administrative Law Act: Europe-proof?' (2008) European Public L (forthcoming).

[97] cf recently Case C-432/05 *Unibet*, Judgment of the Court of 13 March 2007, nyr.

[98] Case C-174/02 *Streekgewest Westelijk Noord-Brabant* [2005] ECR I-85. cf also the Opinion of Advocate General Kokott in Case C-127/02 *Landelijke Vereniging tot Behoud van de Waddenzee* [2004] ECR I-7405, paras 138–143. On the other hand, see also Case C-157/02 *Rieser* [2004] ECR I-1477, paras 43, 44, which seems to limit the circle of persons who may rely on the Directive at issue.

competition as a result of an aid measure rely on the last sentence of Article 93(3) of the EC Treaty . . . ?'. The Court called attention to the fact that rules relating to the determination of an individual's standing and legal interest in bringing proceedings may not undermine the right to effective judicial protection.[99] Subsequently it held that

[a]n individual may have an interest in relying, before the national court, on the direct effect of the prohibition on implementation referred to in the last sentence of [the old—SP] Article 93(3) of the Treaty, not only in order to erase the negative effects of the distortion of competition created by the grant of unlawful aid, but also in order to obtain a refund of a tax levied in breach of that provision. In the latter case, the question whether an individual has been affected by the distortion of competition arising from the aid measure is irrelevant to the assessment of his interest in bringing proceedings. The only fact to be taken into consideration is that the individual is subject to a tax which is an integral part of a measure implemented in breach of the prohibition referred to in that provision.

In my opinion, this statement means that the protective scope of (what is now) Article 87(3) TEC covers more persons than competitors only.

Another illustration of the fact that under Community law the protective scope has to be construed more broadly than might be the case under national law alone can be found in cases on Article 39 TEC and in particular on the question of who may rely on this Article. In *Clean Car Autoservice*,[100] in relation to the question whether an employer could rely on this provision, the ECJ found that there is nothing in the wording of Article 48, as it then was, to indicate that parties other than workers could not rely on it. The ECJ referred to the full effectiveness of that Article, which entails the employer's entitlement to engage workers in accordance with the rules governing freedom of movement for workers. More recently, this finding was confirmed in the *ITC* case.[101] A private-sector recruitment agency may, in certain circumstances, rely on the rights directly granted to Community workers by Article 39 TEC since this contributes to the effectiveness of the right of workers to take up an activity as an employed person, and to pursue such activity within the territory of another Member State without discrimination.

---

[99] Under reference to Joined Cases C-87/90 to C-89/90 *Verholen* [1991] ECR I-3757 and Case C-13/01 *Safalero* [2003] ECR I-8679. In fact, this reference is a bit peculiar since Streekgewest was not concerned with standing or bringing proceedings but with whether a certain argument could be relied upon.

[100] Case C-350/96 *Clean Car Autoservice* [1998] ECR I-2521.

[101] Case C-208/05 *ITC* [2007] ECR I-181.

In this case again the German government argued that the agency cannot rely on Article 39 and Regulation No 1612/68, as it does not fall within the scope of application *ratione personae* of those provisions.

Summing up, in the first place, a limitation to the application of a *Schutznorm* lies in the requirements of effectiveness and effective judicial protection. Second, it is submitted that where the ECJ has established that a provision creates rights or, at least, aims at protecting the individual interest of the person concerned, there is an obligation to give effect to these findings at the domestic level in terms of standing and admissibility of the pleas, or for any other purposes of judicial protection.[102] This principle holds even if, under national law, the position of the individual concerned would not be defined as one of bestowal of rights or protection of individual interests. In other words, if it is possible to establish under Community law that a right is conferred upon individuals, or that the provision has the intention to do so, an appropriate remedy must exist and this may imply, for instance, that the person must be given standing.[103] Finally, ECJ jurisprudence makes clear that the Court gives a rather liberal interpretation to Community law provisions, often stretching their protective scope beyond what would be the case under national law alone.

5 How far?

The previous sections illustrate, I hope, that a form of protective scope approach (I do not dare to call it a 'doctrine' yet) is only slowly emerging in European Community law. There are still a number of questions about its substance and modes of application. These will no doubt be partially answered on a case-by-case basis. However, I submit that legal scholars can

---

[102] Note that this type of obligation may also follow from the treaty or from EU legislation. In Case C-295/04 *Manfredi* [2006] ECR I-6619, where the ECJ seems to have accepted, in para 59, an *actio popularis* under Art 81(2) TEC, at least as far as the invalidity is concerned, which may be invoked by any individual. Also, cf for instance, Council Directive (EC) 2002/21 on a common regulatory framework for electronic communications networks and services [2002] OJ L108/33, already mentioned above; Council Directive (EEC) 89/665 on the co–ordination of the laws, regulations and administrative provisions relating to the application of review procedures to the award of public supply and public works contracts [1992] OJ L209/1; and Case C-26/03 *Halle* [2005] ECR I-1.

[103] Certainly in a situation where no other legal remedy would exist otherwise. cf Case C-432/05 *Unibet*, Judgment of the Court of 13 March 2007, nyr, in particular para 41.

contribute by reflecting on these developments and help to mould an appropriate doctrine in view of the application and enforcement of EU law.

As indicated above, there are two distinct but nevertheless closely related problem areas. The first concerns the field in which communitarization takes place. By this I refer to the fact that certain notions are employed in Community law and are also given substance at that level. The notion of rights is an example of this. The extent of the protective scope requirement in this context is to be established by the ECJ or, where appropriate, by the EU legislator. The meaning given to these notions is an autonomous one. It should not be left to national legal systems, since this will make the notions too divergent. A solid legal order cannot be constructed on the basis of 'building blocks' which are too divergent.

Second, there is the realm of national (procedural) autonomy. Here Community law does not provide the substance, but merely poses limits. In concrete and simplified terms, the question is this: how strict a *Schutznorm* requirement does Community law grant to the Member States? Just as with the question of 'rights', the arguments in both case law and legal writing are by no means clear.

Although I have contrasted the area of communitarization with area of national autonomy, there is also a link between the two: the way in which protective scope is given shape as a matter of Community law will probably in turn influence the limits imposed on national (procedural) autonomy. Arguably, a broad concept in the context of Community law may imply that a strict *Schutznorm* requirement under national law cannot be accepted. The converse holds as well, at least in the sense that a strict conception of protective scope at Community law level may make it easier to introduce a strict *Schutznorm* at national level. The relationship between the two is even tighter in those legal systems or situations where the existence of a right also determines the issues which are theoretically within the realm of national autonomy, such as standing.

In the light of how national legal systems work and develop,[104] ignoring or denying the whole question of protective scope is certainly not a realistic option. The idea of protective scope is—in one way or another—embedded both in national law and, to a certain extent, in Community law, both in the literature and in the lawyer's habit of mind. It provides a method of

---

[104] cf a general trend of 'subjectivization'. On this see, for instance, Lubach, see n 83 above, 259 and KP Sommermann, 'Konvergenzen im Vewaltungsverfahrens- und Verwaltungsprozessrecht europäischer Staaten' (2002) Die öffentliche Verwaltung, 142.

establishing who is entitled to bring a certain type of action or the existence of an individual right. No legal system seems to be really sympathetic to *actiones populares*, unless there are specific reasons for making such a choice.

The key question in Community law is, in my opinion, not so much whether there should be a protective scope doctrine.[105] It is rather how strict that protective scope should be. When searching for an answer, we may partly draw on experiences in national law, provided the lessons to be drawn from this are not limited to only one or two legal systems. Yet, perhaps even more importantly, this problem is inextricably related to the question of how EC law should operate. Is it a system that aims primarily at the protection of individuals? Or is it concerned with the legality of Member States' actions, as perceived from Community law point of view? In other words, is it concerned with controlling the compatibility of the behaviour of the State and domestic public authorities with Community law? Or should it rather aim at a mixture of both?

As I pointed out in the Introduction (section 1), Community law is concerned with both protection of the individual and its full effect: 'It is the responsibility of the national courts in particular to provide the legal protection which individuals derive from the rules of Community law and to ensure that those rules are fully effective.'[106] This two-track approach may set limits to further 'subjectivization' of both Community and national law.[107]

It may also be translated into other terms, as was for instance done in Germany: here the conferral of rights is primarily functional. Where the ECJ says that rights are created for the benefit of the individual, it is not so much concerned with the protection of the interests of the individual as such, but rather uses or mobilizes the individuals for the enforcement of Community law.[108] Some seem to have taken this approach a stage further, and argue in favour of a Euro-specific theory of subjective rights, which should go beyond the economic component and should be extended to collective and diffuse rights, especially in social and ecological matters. Accordingly, they say, it

---

[105] cf Eilmansberger, see n 17 above, who argues strongly in favour of introduction of a protective scope or purpose in order to provide a solid basis for the relationship between a right and the remedy which is, in his opinion, missing in Community law.

[106] cf Joined Cases C-397/01 to C-403/01 *Pfeiffer* [2004] ECR I-8835, para 111.

[107] cf also J Jans, *Doorgeschoten? Enkele opmerkingen over de gevolgen van de Europeanisering van het bestuursrecht voor de grondslagen van de bestuursrechtspraak* (Groningen: Europa Law Publishing, 2005) 4–5.

[108] cf Beljin, this volume, ch 5 p116–117, with further references.

should include consumer rights, social rights, ecological rights, and citizens' rights.[109] In all these cases, individuals should be given enforceable rights.

In any case, the full effectiveness dimension implies that the protective scope requirement should not be too stringent. Both the EU and individuals have an interest in the application of Community law provisions by their Member States. Individuals should still be regarded as guardians of this law and help to ensure that Member States comply with their Community obligations and fulfil their duties. In the past, this role has played a crucial part in the construction of the Community legal order, helping to preserve its unity and to ensure its effectiveness. This need persists.[110] Furthermore, private enforcement[111] of public law standards is necessary in EC law for other reasons. Formal enforcement and control is increasingly laid in the hands of national authorities/supervisors. Yet these may still have a 'national protectionist reflex', or just simply act inadequately. An illustration of this is the *Muñoz* case, in which the legal basis for the injunction was predominantly the *effet utile*, both general and specific in the sense that it was linked to the purpose of the common quality standards. The reference to rights in that case was effectively an obligatory mantra indicating that persons may rely on the provisions at issue, and that the courts have to apply these.[112] Comparable observations can also be made in a broader perspective, such as those made in relation to implementation, which is from beginning to end—from transposition to application and enforcement—in the hands of national actors, whose interests may differ from those of the EU.

In brief, due to the particular context in which Community law operates, effectiveness as the rationale for the determination of protective scope makes sense. What is necessary is not to dismiss *effet utile* as a basis for this determination of protective scope, but rather to get a clear picture of how much weight should be given to the various elements—control or protection—that characterize the role of the courts in the context of Community law.

[109] cf N Reich, '*System der subjectiven öffentlichen Rechte*' in the *Union: A European Constitution for Citizens of Bits and Pieces, Collected Courses of the Academy of European Law*, Vol 6.1 (The Hague: Martinus Nijhoff Publishers, 1995) 163ff, in particular 164.

[110] cf also the developments in the Third Pillar, such as the introduction of the principle of EU loyalty in Case C-105/03 *Pupino* [2005] ECR I-5285.

[111] This term does not refer here to 'private law' litigation only but rather to (public law) cases brought 'by individuals'.

[112] Similarly, the cases relating to Council Directive (EEC) 83/189 laying down a procedure for the provision of information in the field of technical standards and regulations [1983] OJ L109/8, have been decided along the *effet utile* line, ie the full effectiveness of the preventive system laid down in the Directive, rather than as a matter of protection of interest of traders.

This brings me to a final remark, which in turn calls for a certain mitigation of the full effectiveness argument. This chapter has shown that at an abstract level, there seems to be agreement about the need and function of a *Schutznorm* in both national and Community law. As usual, it is the concrete interpretation or operationalization of the concept that leads to different legal consequences. While the fleshing out of protective scope at the level of Community law plays a role in maintaining the unity of the law, at the same time the effects of this fleshing out upon the elaboration of protective scope and related notions as they exist in the various Member States must be carefully taken into account. Serious disruption of the unity of national law will, at the end of the day, endanger the acceptance of notions coloured by EC law and therefore also the unity and coherence of EC law itself.

PART III

Discretion

8

On Discretion

Roberto Caranta

1 Introduction

Discretion is a technical term found in most European legal systems.[1] In very general terms, discretion is the room for choice left to the decision maker by some higher ranking source or authority. Courts see that the decision maker stays within the boundaries of discretion. Discretion is thus a sort of residual concept: discretion is what is left outside judicial control. The issue is whether and to what extent discretion is reviewed. Legal systems have diverged widely on whether to leave the rule maker and the decision maker alone or to place some constraints on them. 'Discretion' is the term of choice to describe this no-go zone for courts, but 'merits' is also sometimes used. Courts, on their part, have devised ways to infiltrate this preserve. Different legal traditions have developed different tools to deal with discretion and this in the end has led to divergent readings of the same idea of discretion. Discretion should be understood as a product of history.[2]

Discretion stays at the fault line between two time-honoured principles: the rule of law and the separation of powers.[3]

---

[1] According to JM Woehrling, 'Le contrôle judictionnel de l'administration en Europe de l'Ouest' (1994) 6 Eur Rev Public L, 362, the review of discretion is the central question of administrative justice systems.

[2] Various legal systems are analysed and compared in V Parisio (ed), *Potere discrezionale e controllo giudiziario* (Milano: Giuffré, 1998).

[3] Some aspects of this relationship are analysed by AW Herringa, 'The Separation of Powers Argument' in R Bakker, AW Herringa, and F Stroink, *Judicial Control: Comparative essays on Judicial Review* (Antwerp: Maklu, 1995) 27 and especially 52ff.

The main idea behind absolutism was that the ruler was above the law. Revolutions were about bringing rulers under the law's empire. Courts were to uphold the rule of law, making sure that rulers did not overstep the boundaries set for them by the law. Since the nineteenth century, European states have professed their allegiance to the rule of law; the Germans found a name for this—Rechtsstaat (French *État de droit*, Italian *Stato di diritto*). To make sure that rulers behaved, the American and French revolutions introduced another principle: the separation of powers. Provision XVI of the *Déclaration des droits de l'Homme et du Citoyen* adopted by the French National Assembly in August 1789 states that 'Toute société dans laquelle la garantie des droits n'est pas assurée ou la séparation des pouvoir déterminé n'a point de constitution'.

Courts being less popular in post-revolutionary France than in post-revolutionary England, the separation of powers started to work against them. A string of statutes were passed to restrict the powers of courts vis-à-vis the executive power. Vindication of the rule of law was entrusted to the *Conseil d'Etat*, an emanation from the executive branch which slowly grew into an administrative court.[4] French history shows the tension between the rule of law and the separation of powers, the former calling for accountability, the latter for unchallenged exercise of public powers. And Britain developed a theory of the supremacy of Parliament which in the end benefited the executive and led to judicial self-restraint.[5]

Different readings of discretion are the result of the peculiar evolutionary paths followed in different legal systems to solve the tensions between conflicting constitutional principles. Conceptual divergences increased when many countries adopted judicial review of legislation. Some countries, for example England and France, have been less ready to do away with the supremacy of Parliament,[6] but even in those legal systems which have embraced judicial review of legislation, democratic principles force the courts to respect some freedom of choice by parliaments.[7]

The Community courts have the task of reviewing discretionary decisions taken by both Community institutions (under EC Treaty, Articles 230, 232, and 234, and under Article 288, on the one hand) and by the Member States

---

[4] See P Sandevoir, *Études sur le recours de pleine juridiction* (Paris : LGDJ, 1964) 51ff.

[5] See Lord Irvine of Lairg, 'Judges and Decision-makers: The Theory and Practice of Wednesbury Review' (1996) PL, 59.

[6] On France see again Herringa, see n 3 above, 28ff and D Rousseau, 'Pour une Cour constitutionnelle?' (2002) Revue du droit public, 363ff, and on Britain J Alder, *Constitutional and Administrative Law* (5th edn, Basingstoke: Macmillan, 2005) 186ff.

[7] E Malfatti, S Panizza, and R Romboli, *Giustizia costituzionale* (Torino: Giappichelli, 2003) 303.

(under Articles 226 and 234, on the other). So far, they have failed to commit themselves to a coherent approach to discretion. This could be intentional, since it allows the courts to adjust their decisions to the real or perceived idiosyncrasies of each case but leads, to say the least, to unpredictability.

Different traditions of judicial review of discretionary powers in certain legal systems will be contrasted in order to develop a reference framework for the understanding of the Community courts' case law. Legal analysis of discretion at European level is at its inception, and it may benefit from the experience accrued in the Member States. In turn, Community law influences national laws; the forms of this relationship are conditioned by the approach to discretion prevalent in each Member State.

2 Some national modes of judicial review

It is impossible to give a detailed comparative assessment of the modes of judicial review of discretion. Some instances will be enough to give the feeling of how differently the Rule of Law and separation or powers may compromise to give life to different readings of discretion.[8]

2.1 *Germany*

As a reaction to Nazi dictatorship, in the past sixty years German courts have strived to restrict the margins of unchallengeable discretion allowed to executive authorities. Courts recognize discretion only when it is expressly granted by Parliament.[9] Generally, however, the presumption is that there is only one legal way to give execution to statutes, and consequently courts fully review the application of general clauses and vague terms such as 'public interest', 'public security', and so on.[10] Even when some freedom for the decision maker (*Beurteilungssplielraum* and *Ermessen*) is allowed, fundamental rights and general principles of administrative action limit discretion.[11] More specifically, courts are ready to hear challenges as to the proportionality of

---

[8] A useful reading is CD Classen, *Die Europäisierung der Verwaltungsgerichtsbarkeit* (Tübingen: Mohr, 1996) 175ff. See also this volume, Alonso, Moral, and Plaza, ch 6.

[9] G Nolte, 'General Principles of German and European Administrative Law: A Comparison in Historical Perspective' (1994) 57 MLR, 196ff.

[10] H Maurer, *Allgemeines Verwaltungsrecht* (14th edn, München: Beck, 2004) 147ff and Classen, see n 8 above, 176ff.

[11] Maurer, see n 10 above, 141.

the decision taken; under the strict proportionality text (*Verhältnismässig-keit*), the decision under review must not only be necessary and appropriate to meet the ends laid down by the lawmaker, it must also be proportional in the strict sense, meaning that the burden placed upon private parties must not be too heavy when compared with the general interest fulfilled. Invasive review is coupled, and this is a German peculiarity, with the power conferred to courts under given conditions to take decisions in the place of the administrative authorities.[12] Conversely, the breach of procedural rules is more easily condoned.[13] It is fair to say that the stringency of review is compensated for in Germany by the strict limits placed on standing. Indeed, rights only, not lesser interests, give access to judicial protection.[14]

The German Constitutional Court sees itself as the guardian of fundamental rights and freedoms. Since 1951, it has read the equality principle enshrined in the Constitution as imposing a reasonableness requirement on lawmaking. The Court does not hesitate to give a hard look at legislative choices checking their proportionality,[15] so much so that its interventions have at times met with strong criticism.[16]

2.2 *France*

The concept of discretion is a familiar one in French administrative law. Discretion is the power to make choices between different courses of action that are all consistent with the applicable rules. Discretionary powers are opposed to *compétence liée*, that is a situation where the conditions for the exercise of administrative functions are laid down in the applicable legislation without leaving any room for choice.[17]

The *Conseil d'Etat* has developed different tools to review discretionary decisions. *Recours pour excès de pouvoir* is the main avenue for judicial review but legality issues may also arise in actions for damages. Discretion is

---

[12]   Classen, see n 8 above, 177.
[13]   Nolte, see n 9 above, 197ff.
[14]   Classen, see n 8 above, 44 and Woehrling, see n 1 above, 363.
[15]   J Luther, 'Ragionevolezza e Verhältnismässigkeit nella giurisprudenza costituzionale tedesca' (1993) Diritto e società, 307.
[16]   Nolte, see n 9 above, 192ff; for the criticism see E Benda, 'Das Kruzifix-Urteil ist zu apodiktisch' (1995) Zeitschrift für Rechtspolitik, 427 and H Sendler, 'Liberalität oder Libertinage?' (1993) Neue Juristische Wochenschrift, 2157.
[17]   R Chapus, *Droit administratif général*, Vol 1 (15th edn, Paris: Montchrestien, 2001) 1055ff and see also 1057, where the *opportunité* (merits) is defined as 'ce qui reste hors contrôle et dont l'étendue dépend de l'évolution del la législation et de la jurisprudence'.

relevant when dealing with the *illégalité relative aux motifs de l'acte* and—to a lesser extent—with *détournement de pouvoir*. *Détournement de pouvoir* was the tool devised in the nineteenth century to strike down decisions affected by abuse of power, that is decisions taken for illicit private gain or in pursuit of public goals different from those envisaged in the enabling legal provisions. It has to do with the frame of mind of the decision maker; it depends on circumstantial evidence and it is hard to establish in less than blatant cases.[18]

The *illégalité relative aux motifs de l'acte* may take three different forms: the *erreur de droit*, the *erreur dans la qualification juridique des faits*, and the *erreur de fait*. The *erreur de droit* has mainly to do with a mistake in the way a provision has been construed. *Erreur de fait* has to do with simple facts: the decision maker may be wrong in establishing the existence or inexistence of some relevant factual situation. What is characteristically French is the *erreur dans la qualification juridique des faits*. It has to do with complex factual situations whose legal appreciation may leave room for debate. The leading case is *Gomel*; a permission was refused because the proposed building was considered incompatible with the monumental perspective of the square in which it was to be built; the *Conseil d'Etat* held that it had the power to verify whether the square could be characterized as a *perspective monumental*.[19] Here it is not just a question of pure fact; the decision has to be taken according to loosely worded legal texts. Other complex situations may be reviewed in the same way, such as whether a meeting can detrimentally affect law and order or whether wearing a headscarf at school is compatible with the *laïcité* principle of public education.[20]

The depth of judicial review varies according to the subject matter under review.[21] Discretionary power is reviewed with different degrees of intensity, with the review at times being somewhat peripheral, and with the courts at other times taking a hard look at administrative decisions. *Contrôle restreint*—also called *contrôle minimum*—includes *erreur manifeste d'appréciation*; the idea is that even when the decision maker enjoys margins of discretion, the decisions will be struck down when manifestly wrong. *Erreur manifeste d'appréciation* is similar to the English 'unreasonableness' of *Wednesbury*;[22]

---

[18]   ibid, 1048ff.

[19]   CE, 14 April 1914, *Gomel*, Recueil des arrêts du Conseil d'Etat (Lebon) 1914, 488 and *Recueil Sirey* 1917, part 3, 25, note by M Hauriou.

[20]   Many instances are found in Chapus, see n 17 above, 1044ff.

[21]   ibid, 1055 and see also JM Woehrling, 'Le contrôle juridictionnel du pouvoir discrétionnaire en France' in Parisio, see n 2 above.

[22]   *Associated Provincial Picture House Ltd v Wednesbury Corporation* [1948] 1 KB 223 (CA) 234.

only grossly mistaken decisions will be affected by it.[23] These days, *contrôle minimum* is exceptional, and concerns mainly the review of promotions of public servants and police decisions, including those on migrants.[24]

Contrôle normale, covering the *erreur dans la qualification juridique des faits*, is the rule.[25] Exceptionally, French administrative courts allow themselves *contrôle maximum*; in *Ville nouvelle Est* the *Conseil d'Etat* affirmed the legality of expropriations needed to build a new town but held that a zoning decision could not be considered to be in the general interests when inconveniences to the citizens, financial burdens, and other cons outweigh the pros.[26] The *théorie du bilan*, also known as *bilan coûts advantages*, was born.[27] Courts have shown their readiness to take a very hard look to administrative decisions in areas of such expropriation procedures. These are difficult cases of discretion, concerning as they do the balance between conflicting public and private interests.[28] Today *contrôle maximum* is at times referred to as proportionality control and analysed according to the lines of German *Verhältnismäßigkeit*; administrative action must be both capable of and necessary to attaining the public good and, more importantly, the benefits must override the drawbacks.[29]

The review of legislation performed by the *Conseil constitutionnel* is more restrained; the same possibility of checking the existence of *erreur manifeste d'appréciation*, corresponding to *contrôle minimum*, is hotly debated.[30]

[23] Chapus, see n 17 above, 1066 and for a different view A De Laubadère, 'Le contrôle juridictionnel du pouvoir discrétionaire dans la jurisprudence récente du Conseil d'Etat français' in G Vedel and M Waline (eds), *Mélanges offerts à Marcel Waline: le juge et le droit public* (Paris: LGDJ, 1974) 531ff.

[24] Again Chapus, see n 17 above, 1062ff.

[25] C Debbasch and JC Ricci, *Contentieux administratif* (8th edn, Paris: Dalloz, 2001) 788ff.

[26] CE Ass, 28 May 1971, *Fédération de défense des personnes concernées par le projet 'Ville nouvelle Est'*, Recueil des arrêts du Conseil d'etat (Lebon) 1971, 409, conclusion by G Braibant.

[27] Chapus, see n 17 above, 1074.

[28] Administrative decisions are rarely if ever quashed on this ground, but we are advised not to conclude that the *Ville nouvelle Est* case has no practical bearing on administrative action: Chapus, see n 17 above, 1078.

[29] ibid, 1074ff.

[30] L Favoreu, 'Conseil constitutionnel et ragionevolezza: d'un rapprochement improbable à une communicabilité possible' in *Il principio di ragionevolezza nella giurisprudenza della Corte costituzionale* (Milano: Giuffré, 1994) 221ff and DG Lavroff, *Le droit constitutionnel de la Ve République* (2nd edn, Paris: Dalloz, 1997) 237.

2.3 *Italy*

The late 1930s to the early 1940s were the defining moment for scholarly discussions on discretion in Italy. Costantino Mortati adopted a somewhat wide notion of discretion.[31] In his opinion, discretion was the room to manoeuvre which is left to the decision maker through open-ended rules, that is rules referring to undetermined legal concepts. Instances can be found in rules empowering public authorities to uphold public good, law and order, etc.[32] Mortati's works were clearly influenced by contemporary German scholarly writings on *unbestimmte Rechtsbegriffe*, translated in Italian as *concetti giuridici indeterminati*.[33] Massimo Severo Giannini claimed that discretion had to do with the choice between possibly conflicting public and private interests, ie policy choices.[34] Choices made according to other rules, be they technical or scientific, are not discretionary: here lies the main operative distinction between the two theories.[35]

Giannini's theory commanded a broad following in the scholarly world, but administrative courts—which are charged with reviewing administrative decisions—stick to a quite generic idea of discretion. They review the legality of administrative decisions (*legittimità*) but steer clear of their merits (*merito*), meaning they cannot substitute their views for those of the decision maker. A broad and generic concept of discretion correspondingly extends the realm of what is said to be the *merito*. Review of discretion is in principle peripheral, tangent. It is performed though the *eccesso di potere*. *Eccesso di potere* was initially read as the French *détournement de pouvoir*, that is the perverse use of official powers to attain illegitimate ends. Since it is difficult to say to what end a decision was taken, courts began to find situations when *détournement* was to be presumed. Even when no duty to give reasons was laid down in legislation, administrative courts quashed administrative decisions when reasons were not given; the rationale was that if no reason was

---

[31] A seminal work was C Mortati, 'Potere discrezionale' in M D'Amelio and A Azara, *Nuovo Digesto Italiano*, Vol 10 (Torino: UTET, 1939) 76ff.

[32] Mortati's works have been analysed by G Azzariti, 'Discrezionalità, merito e regole non giuridiche nel pensiero di Constantino Mortati' (1989) Politica del diritto, 347ff.

[33] The following theory of *unbestimmte Rechtsbegriffe* in Italy has been traced by D De Pretis, *Valutazione amministrativa e discrezionalità tecnica* (Padova: CEDAM, 1995).

[34] The defining work was MS Giannini, *Il potere discrezionale della pubblica amministrazione* (Milano: Giuffré, 1939).

[35] Giannini's theory has been analysed by GF Scoca, 'La discrezionalità nel pensiero di Giannini e nella dottrina successiva' (2000) Rivista trimestrale di diritto pubblico, 1045ff.

advanced to encroach on citizens' rights, this could only be because no permissible reason existed. Courts have gone a long way down this road, finding *eccesso di potere* when reasons, even when given, are considered insufficient, when different standards are applied to what appear to be similar cases, and when facts have been misunderstood.

Other instances are more problematic, most notable among them *ingiustizia manifesta*, that is a manifestly wrong decision: the fear here is that the courts could be seen as stepping into the shoes of the decision maker. It is much easier for courts to strike down manifestly wrong decisions, maintaining that the reasons given for them are either insufficient or inconsistent.[36]

In the end, courts do not usually go into the merits of the case. They stick to the surface. Matters of procedure and form are consequently of great relevance.[37] Proportionality review is still rather an exception, even if the reference to the general principles of Community law recently added to the Administrative Procedure Act 1990 could change this.[38] The approach favoured by the Italian courts is still far less intense and far less structured than the French one, even if some recent trends in case law seem to vindicate Giannini's ideas. Peripheral review is more and more limited to those cases concerning true policy choices. When it comes to the assessment of complex factual situations, courts are now ready to give them a hard look, at times having recourse to expert witnesses.[39]

Legislation is reviewed by the *Corte costituzionale*. Article 28 of L 11 Marzo 1953, n 87, expressly forbids the Court to interfere with policy or discretionary decisions by Parliament. The Court, however, has drawn from Article 3 of the Constitution—laying down the equality principle—the power to strike

---

[36] The case law is analysed by C Marzuoli, 'Discrezionalità amministrativa e sindacato giudiziario: profili generali' in Parisio, see n 2 above, 91ff.

[37] Cases are referred to in R Caranta, 'Procedural Errors and Substantive Legality in Italian Administrative Law' in KH Ladeur (ed), *The Europeanisation of Administrative Law* (Aldershot: Ashgate, 2000) 40ff.

[38] One case is TAR Lombardia, Sez III, 5 May 1998, n 922, Foro amministrativo 1999, 2452, note I Zingales, 'Disapplicazione da parte del giudice amministrativo di prescrizioni regolamentari dei bandi di gara contrastanti con normativa primaria e con il principio di proporzionalità' and proportionality is routinely used in cases concerning fines, where administrative courts enjoy full jurisdiction, and in other specific sectors: see A Sandulli, 'Eccesso di potere e controllo di proporzionalità. Profili comparati' (1995) Rivista trimestrale di diritto pubblico, 329.

[39] Cons St, Sez VI, 23 April 2002, n 2199, Foro amministrativo CdS 2002, 1007, note N Rangone, 'Intese nel mercato assicurativo e sindacabilità dei provvedimenti antitrust' (2003) *Giurisprudenza commerciale*, 170, and note R Caranta, 'I limiti del sindacato del giudice amministrativo sui provvedimenti dell'Autorità garante della concorrenza e del mercato'.

down manifestly unreasonable statutes.[40] The Court also checks the balance of interests struck by the lawmaker along the proportionality principle;[41] it is doubtful whether this review can still be considered marginal, but the case law is far from consistent.[42]

2.4 *England*

England has come to epitomize the mode of marginal review.[43] Courts have developed a doctrine of judicial self-restraint in deference to the sovereignty of Parliament and democratic institutions.[44] The main focus is on procedure, not on the substance of administrative decisions.[45]

Courts are ready to review factual assessments and the construction placed by the decision maker upon factual terms used by the lawmaker. In *Ripon (Highfield) Housing Confirmation Order 1938 White and Collins v Minister of Health*, the Court of Appeal quashed a compulsory purchase order. The relevant statute did not permit the taking of 'part of any park, garden or pleasure ground' and the authority had decided that the land did not qualify under this provision, but the court held otherwise. The court pointed out that the word 'park' in the Housing Act 1936 was used in its popular sense (instead of a technical and legal sense) as recorded in the *Oxford English Dictionary* to mean 'a large ornamental piece of ground usually comprising woodland and pasture, attached to or surrounding a country house or mansion, and used for recreation, and often for keeping deer, cattle or sheep'.[46]

Concerning discretionary powers, English courts refrain from intervention in all but the most extreme instances. They set a clear distinction between appeal and review. Appeal is going into the merits of a case, substituting the court decision in place of the one taken by the competent official.

---

[40] Eg, point 4 of Corte cost, 12 July 1995, n 313, Giurisprudenza costituzionale 1995, 2439, note E Gallo 'In tema di "oltraggi": le distinzioni normative fra le varie specie resistono al controllo di legittimità costituzionale' and see generally *Il principio di ragionevolezza nella giurisprudenza della Corte costituzionale*, see n 30 above.

[41] For references and discussion see GF Ferrari, 'Il principio di proporzionalità' in Parisio, see n 2 above, 127ff.

[42] For a recent appraisal see Malfatti, Panizza, and Romboli, see n 7 above, 303ff.

[43] F Stroink, 'Judicial Control of the Administration's Discretionary Powers (*le bilan executive—juge administrative*)' in Bakker, Herringa, and Stroink, see n 3 above, 81.

[44] Lord Irvine of Lairg, see n 5 above, 60ff.

[45] Woehrling, see n 1 above, 364ff.

[46] *Ripon (Highfield) Housing Confirmation Order 1938* [1939] 2 KB 838.

This is not for the courts. Review is much more restrained.[47] The standard of review was set in *Wednesbury*.[48] Lord Greene MR held that courts can be allowed to interfere with administrative decisions only insofar as the authority has come to a conclusion 'so unreasonable that no reasonable authority could have ever come to it'. His Lordship further contends that 'The power of the court to interfere in each case is not as an appellate authority to override a decision of the local authority, but as a judicial authority which is concerned, and concerned only, to see whether the local authority have contravened the law by acting in excess of the powers which Parliament has confided in them.'[49] Outside the provinces of European law, English courts have refused to embrace proportionality review.[50] The same has been the case with 'substantive' legitimate expectation; according to the Court of Appeal, it is for the decision makers, within the bounds of *Wednesbury* unreasonableness, and not for the courts, to decide whether expectations should be protected or whether the broader public interest is strong enough to override them.[51]

The reluctance shown by the English courts to give administrative decisions close scrutiny a hard look may be due to the absence of specialized courts:

The fact that the ordinary courts possess jurisdiction means that there is a more reserved attitude in testing and more regard for the discretionary powers of the administration. In continental administrative law, the courts are often manned by judges with professional background in administration. These judges are more inclined to subject the decision to intensive testing. There are a number of additional factors, such as the British tradition of inquiries (preventing rather than curing).[52]

---

[47] T Allan, 'Freedom of Speech and Judicial Review' (1991) NLJ, 683.

[48] For a discussion see Lord Irvine of Lairg, see n 5 above.

[49] *Associated Provincial Picture House Ltd v Wednesbury Corporation* [1948] 1 KB 223 (CA) 234 and the decision was reaffirmed by Lord Diplock in the case *Council for the Civil Service Unions* [1984] 3 All ER 935 (HL) 951.

[50] *R v Secretary of State for the Home Department, ex p Brind* [1991] 1 AC 696; see S Boyron, 'Proportionality in English Administrative Law: A Faulty Translation?' (1992) 12 Oxford J of L Studies, 237. A recent case involving ECHR law was *Huang v Secretary of State for the Home Dept* [2005] 3 All ER 435 (CA); see also Alder, see n 6 above, 383ff and S Mirate, *Giustizia amministrativa e Convenzione europea dei diritti dell'Uomo* (Napoli: Jovene, 2007) 389ff.

[51] *R v Secretary of State for the Home Department, ex p Hargreaves* [1997] 1 WLR 906; C Forsyth, 'Wednesbury Protection of Substantive Legitimate Expectations' (1997) PL, 375; TRS Allan, 'Procedure and Substance in Judicial Review' (1997) 56 CLJ, 246 and English and Community approaches are contrasted by PP Craig, 'Substantive Legitimate Expectations in Domestic and Community Law' (1996) 55 CLJ, 289.

[52] Stroink, see n 43 above, 87.

Whatever the reason, the attitude is quite straightforward: 'It is important at the outset to be clear about the limits of judicial intervention over discretion: it is *not* for the courts to *substitute their choices* as to how the discretion ought to have been exercised for that of the administrative authority.'[53]

English law still lacks the refined analysis of the different discretionary powers we find on the continent. Even the distinction between operational decisions and policy (or discretionary) decisions which was advanced by Lord Wilberforce in *Dorset Yacht v Home Office*[54] has met with resistance.[55] In other words, to say the least, English analysis moves along lines which are not familiar on the other side of the Channel.[56] Finally, apart from cases involving European law, English courts do not perform judicial review of legislation.[57] The days of Chief Justice Coke have yet to return.[58]

3 Some preliminary comparative conclusions

Most European legal systems have evolved well past the generic notion of discretion as the room for choice left to the decision maker by some higher ranking source or authority. Usually, different phenomena are clearly distinguished: ie policy decisions linked to the weighing of conflicting private and public interest (henceforth discrI, or discretion proper); decisions involving complex factual evaluations (discrII); and decisions involving the interpretation of complex and/or unclear legal rules (discrIII).

Moreover, even as the European countries differ markedly as to their modes of judicial review of discretionary decisions, a few patterns seem to be emerging. First, judicial self-restraint is greater when the courts are confronted with decisions taken by Parliament rather than by executive bodies. Second, and possibly with the exception of England, marginal or limited review is usually deemed appropriate in discrI and perhaps in some cases in discrII situations only. This seems to be the case in the Netherlands too: judicial self-restraint is appropriate when the courts are reviewing the

---

[53] PP Craig, *Administrative Law* (4th edn, London: Sweet & Maxwell, 1999) 579.

[54] *Dorset Yacht v Home Office* [1970] AC 1004 (HL).

[55] *Rowling v Takaro Properties Ltd* [1988] AC 473.

[56] Eg, Craig, see n 53 above, 507.

[57] In *R (on the application of Williamson) v Secretary of State for Education and Employment* [2005] 2 All ER 1 (HL) the legality of Section 548(1) of the Education Act 1996 was reviewed against Art 9 of the European Convention on Human Rights.

[58] See *Dr Bonham's Case* (1610) Co Rep 113b and *Day v Savadge* (1614) Hob 85, 97.

weighing of interests.[59] The separation of powers argument does not apply to the interpretation of rules, difficult as this may be, since this is the preserve of lawyers, courts included. It is barely effectual when factual situations, complex as these may be, are involved; factual assessments are the preserve of technicians, not of politicians, and courts may avail themselves of expert witnesses if the need arises.[60] Third, the intensity of judicial scrutiny of discretion may vary according to other factors, such as the sensitivity of the subject matter in relation to the general interest or the involvement of fundamental rights.

Finally, intensity of review seems to be growing, proportionality review being more and more accepted as a ground for scrutinizing discretionary decisions:[61] 'It is evident that the principle of proportionality provides the courts with many tools for reviewing administrative action much more comprehensively than on the basis of the criterion of "*willekeur*" ("willekeur" is literally translated arbitrariness, conceptually coming close to *Wednesbury* unreasonableness).'[62]

4 Liability actions

4.1 *An almost ideal test tube*

Liability actions are an almost ideal field for a comparative review of discretion at European level and for two reasons. First, the liabilities of both Community institutions and Member States follow the same rules.[63] 'It is settled case-law that the conditions of liability for infringements of Community law are the same in the case of liability of Community Institutions [. . .] and in the case of liability of the Member States'[64]; 'the tort rules laid down in the two lines of case law, one relating to Community institutions and the other

---

[59] See Stroink, see n 43 above, 82.

[60] Concerning the Netherlands see again Stroink, see n 43 above, 83ff.

[61] Woehrling, see n 1 above, 375ff.

[62] Stroink, see n 43 above, 84.

[63] Joined Cases C-46/93 and C-48/93 *Brasserie and Factortame* [1996] ECR I-1029, paras 42, 55; the Court followed the conclusions by Advocate General Tesauro; and see also, concerning actions under Art 288, Case C-352/98 P *Bergaderm* [2000] ECR I-5291.

[64] HG Schermers and DF Waelbroeck, *Judicial Protection in the European Union* (6th edn, The Hague: Kluwer, 2001) 540 (see also 206).

relating to Member States, are used by the Court, *back and forth*, as a source of inspiration'.[65]

Second, discretion plays a central role in the case law on liability for breach of Community law.[66] The standard test for liability of European institutions was laid down in *HNL v Council and Commission*[67] which gave full development to some ideas already present in *Zuckerfabrik Schöppenstedt*.[68] In *HNL* the European Court of Justice (ECJ) held that Community institutions can only exceptionally and in very special circumstances incur liability for legislative measures which are the result of choices of economic policy (discrI). In other words, a serious and manifest breach is needed. In *Brasserie du Pêcheur and Factortame*,[69] the ECJ strongly linked the requirement of a manifest and serious breach to the degree of discretion enjoyed by the decision maker.[70] *Bergaderm* confirmed that discretion was centre stage.[71]

Given this starting point, one would expect to find discretion dealt with consistently in liability cases, whether they are brought against Community institutions or Member States.

4.2 *Liability of Community institutions*

In cases concerning the liability of Community institutions, the Community courts have been quite eager to recognize the existence of wide margins of discretion. In *Bergaderm* the Commission had amended Council Directive (EEC) 76/768 on the approximation of the laws of the Member States relating to cosmetic products, limiting the permissible amount of bergamot essence in sun protection products. *Bergaderm*, whose products exceeded the new limits, went into liquidation and sued the Commission for damages claiming that the decision to amend the Directive was vitiated by many procedural

---

[65] W van Gerven, 'The Emergence of a Common European Law in the Area of Tort Law: The EU Contribution' in D Faigrieve, M Andenas, and J Bell (eds), *Tort Liability of Public Authorities in Comparative Perspective* (London: British Institute of International and Comparative Law, 2002) 132.

[66] G Vandersanden, 'Le droit communautaire' in G Vandersanden and M Dony (eds), *La responsabilité des Etats membres en cas de violation du droit communautaire* (Bruxelles: Bruylant, 1997) 42 and A Arnull, 'Liability for Legislative Acts under Article 215(2) EC' in T Heukels and A McDonnell (eds), *The Action for Damages in Community Law* (The Hague: Kluwer, 1997) 148.

[67] Joined Cases 83/76, 94/76, 4/77, 15/77, and 40/77 *HNL v Council and Commission* [1978] ECR 1209.

[68] Case 5/71 *Zuckerfabrik Schöppenstedt* [1971] ECR 975, especially para 11.

[69] Joined Cases C-46/93 and C-48/93 *Brasserie and Factortame* [1996] ECR I-1029, para 55.

[70] ibid, paras 45ff.

[71] Case C-352/98 P *Bergaderm* [2000] ECR I-5291, paras 43ff.

mistakes, infringed the requirements of proportionality, and was not based on sound science. Affirming the judgment of the Court of First Instance (CFI), the Court of Justice held that in delicate and controversial cases the Commission needed to have sufficiently broad discretion.[72]

It is doubtful whether there really is wide discretion in setting the permissible limits of potentially harmful ingredients. There are no policy decisions to be taken. The challenged decision was taken following the advice of the Scientific Committee on Cosmetology. Policy arguments were already settled when the precautionary principle was accepted in Community law: technical choices may err on the side of caution when adjudicating on the safety of a given product, but they are still technical—not policy—choices. This case should be classified as discrII; the concept of 'broad discretion' is not appropriate.

Bergaderm is a somewhat perplexing case for another reason. *HNL* stressed that the fact that a decision is invalid is not in itself sufficient to establish liability. No-illegality liability is admitted under specific and restrictive circumstances only.[73] Normally, illegality is a necessary condition for liability. In *Bergaderm* the Court of Justice affirmed the decision by the CFI upholding the legality of the measure taken by the Commission. There was no breach of Community law and the Court could have spared time and effort by showing that it was neither manifest nor serious.

In *Dieckmann & Hansen* the Commission had revised a decision allowing the import of caviar from Kazakhstan for reasons of concern about sanitary conditions in that country.[74] *Dieckmann & Hansen*, which had imported Kazakh caviar for decades and had made some advance payments for more, went into liquidation and sued the Commission for damages. The plaintiff claimed that its legitimate expectations not to see the relevant rules changed overnight had been breached by the Commission, which also failed to make temporary arrangements to allow a smooth transition.

The CFI considered that in relation to the common agricultural policy Community institutions have discretionary powers which correspond to their

---

[72] Joined Cases C-46/93 and C-48/93 *Brasserie and Factortame* [1996] ECR I-1029, para 66.

[73] Due to the influence of French legal jargon, no-illegality liability is usually called no-fault liability; in Case T-195/00 *Travelex Global and Financial Services Ltd* [2003] ECR II-1677, para 161, the CFI practically doubted the admissibility of no-fault liability and according to C Stefanou and H Xanthaki, *A Legal and Political Interpretation of Article 215(2) [new Article 288(2)] of the Treaty of Rome: The Individual Strikes Back* (Aldershot: Ashgate, 2000) 87, liability for lawful acts is part of the *acquis communautaire*.

[74] Case T-155/99 *Dieckmann & Hansen v Commission* [2001] ECR II-3143.

political responsibilities, which include ensuring a high level of protection of the health of consumers.[75] Consequently, it held that, in abruptly banning imports of caviar, the Commission did not overstep the boundaries of its discretion. Given the paramount importance of the protection of human health, the Commission was entitled to act as it did. The case is quite similar to *Bergaderm*. There was no breach of Community law. The CFI allowed broad discretion, both for the lawmaker and the decision maker, but actually the policy issue had been settled long before: 'protection of public health must take precedence over economic considerations'. The Commission acted in a discrII situation, making a ministerial rather than a policy discretion.

Liability issues have also arisen in the context of public procurement contracts passed by Community institutions.[76] *Renco* had taken part in the procurement of general renovation and maintenance works in the Council's buildings in Brussels; the contract was to be awarded based on the most economically competitive offer.[77] *Renco's* offer was held to be abnormally low and was excluded after being discussed at some length. The firm sued the Council asking for compensation for the harm suffered as a result of the allegedly unlawful conduct of the Council in the award procedure. The CFI, in choosing the standard applicable to the liability claim, held that the Council has broad discretion in assessing the factors to be taken into account when deciding to award a contract.[78]

The point is debatable. No choice had to be made between conflicting interests. All the procuring entity had to do was to choose the best bid. The Court very much emphasized the difficulties of the procurement, but it was just a somewhat complex contractual arrangement, as many procurements are. The facts of the case are conceptually distant even from those relevant in *Bergaderm* and *Dieckmann & Hansen*; the only interest at stake here is getting the best value for the Council's and the taxpayers' money. This is a case of very little if no discretion. However, all pleas of illegality raised by the applicant were found wanting. Again the liability claim failed not because the breach was not manifest and serious, but because no breach was found to have taken place. Community jurisdictions are quite ready to allow

---

[75] ibid, paras 47ff.

[76] Less recent cases are discussed by MH van der Woude, 'Liability for Administrative Acts under Article 215(2) EC' in Heukels and McDonnel, see n 66 above, 121ff.

[77] Case T-4/01 *Renco*, Judgment of the Court of 25 February 2003, nyr.

[78] Case T-4/01 *Renco*, Judgment of the Court of 25 February 2003, nyr, para 62.

Community institutions wide margins of discretion and consequently to apply severe liability standards. Quite often, however, no breach is found.[79]

The liability of Community institutions is rarely accepted. In *Camar*, a number of Italian firms which used to import bananas from Somalia claimed that the extreme rigidity of the Commission in managing transitional arrangements for the banana quota system had precluded them from buying their goods elsewhere when the deterioration of the situation in Somalia made imports impossible. The CFI held that in principle the Commission has broad discretion when assessing whether transitional measures are necessary. On the facts of the case, however, the CFI found that the Commission had committed a manifest error of appraisal in considering that Camar was capable of overcoming the difficulties. The manifest and grave disregard by the Commission of the limits placed on its discretion was a sufficiently serious infringement of Community law.[80]

In devising and managing the quota system the Council and the Commission often have to take into account many conflicting public policy considerations. In this case, however, the Commission simply had to manage transitional arrangements. This case should be categorized as one of very limited discretion, a discrII situation. Be that as it may, while in the cases discussed so far the courts found no illegality and therefore no liability, in *Camar* the action was successful on both counts.[81]

Dole is a different case.[82] Dole marketed bananas from Columbia, Costa Rica, Nicaragua, and Venezuela when Council Decision (EC) 94/800 and Council Regulation (EC) 478/95 were in force. Following protracted litigation, both those legislative measures were considered invalid because they discriminated between different categories of operators.[83] According to the CFI, the institutions enjoyed broad discretion 'by virtue of the international dimension and the complex economic assessments involved in the

---

[79] A few banana cases show the same pattern Joined Cases T-64/01 and T-65/01 *Afrikanische Frucht-Compagnie* [2004] ECR II-521 and Case T-139/01 *Comafrica*, Judgment of the Court of 3 February 2005, nyr.

[80] Joined Cases T-79/96, T-260/97, and T-117/98 *Camar and Tico v Commission and Council* [2000] ECR II-2193. The decision was upheld by Case C-312/00 P *Commission v Camar and Tico* [2002] ECR I-11355, para 54.

[81] See also Case T-178/98 *Fresh Marine* [2000] ECR II-3331.

[82] Case T-56/00 *Dole Fresh Fruit International*, Judgment of the Court of 6 March 2003, nyr.

[83] Case C-122/95 *Germany v Council* [1998] ECR I-973 and Joined Cases C-364/95 and C-365/95 *T. Port* [1998] ECR I-1023.

introduction or amendment of a Community import scheme for bananas'.[84]
The situation was an extreme type of discrI. Even if the reasons given to
support the legislative measures were not firm enough to withstand judicial
review,[85] they could not be held to be manifestly unreasonable: there was a
breach, but it was neither manifest nor serious.[86]

To sum up the findings from the analysis of the case law, Community
courts are very wary of finding against Community institutions in liability
actions. This is so because they tend to allow these institutions wide discretion in situations where most national legal orders would allow considerably
less. Consequently, most of the time, no breach is found, let alone a serious
and manifest one. Purported wide discretion leads to marginal review which
in turn leads to liability being discounted. The misreading of discretion thus
has a redundancy effect: first, by limiting judicial review and second (and
consequently), by restricting liability.

4.3 *Liability of Member States*

The attitude of the ECJ is different in *Francovich*[87] in relation to liability
for breach of Community law by Member States.[88] The notions of liability
for breach of Community law and its constituent parts, manifest and serious
breach and discretion included, are Community law notions.[89] The ECJ is
responsible for their design. In principle, it is for the national courts to find
whether the conditions for liability are met on the facts of each case.[90] This
would seem to extend to whether a breach is manifest and serious in those
cases where this further characterization is necessary to establish liability.[91]

---

[84] Case T-56/00 *Dole Fresh Fruit International*, Judgment of the Court of 6 March 2003, nyr,
para 75; the export licence system was one of four aspects of the Framework Agreement; the
Framework Agreement was the result of complex and delicate international negotiations in
which the Community had to reconcile divergent interests. The Community had to take into
account not only the interests of Community producers, but also its obligations to ACP States
under the Lomé Convention and its international obligations under the GATT.

[85] Case C-122/95 *Germany v Council* [1998] ECR I-973 and Joined Cases C-364/95 and
C-365/95 *T. Port* [1998] ECR I-1023.

[86] Joined Cases C-364/95 and C-365/95 *T. Port* [1998] ECR I-1023. The CFI adduces additional arguments in the subsequent part of the decisions, which need not to concern us here.

[87] Joined Cases C-6/90 and C-9/90 *Francovich* [1991] ECR I-5357.

[88] Stefanou and Xanthaki, see n 73 above, 1.

[89] Vandersanden, see n 66 above, 19ff and MP Chiti, *Diritto amministrativo europeo* (2nd edn,
Milano: Giuffré, 2004) 115ff.

[90] Eg, Case C-302/97 *Konle* [1999] ECR I-3099, para 58ff.

[91] Eg, Joined Cases C-46/93 and C-48/93 *Brasserie and Factortame* [1996] ECR I-1029, para
58; Case C-392/93 *British Telecommunications* [1996] ECR I-1631, para 41; van Gerven, see n 65

In *Brasserie du Pêcheur and Factortame* the ECJ felt impelled to come to the rescue of national courts, giving them some indications.[92] In *Brasserie du Pêcheur* a law limiting the permissible ingredients in beer manufactured and/or sold in Germany was at stake. *Factortame* arose from provisions restricting, on the grounds of nationality and residence, the possibility of owning, operating, and manning fishing boats flying the British flag. According to the Court, some of the breaches imputed to the German statute could not be 'excused' even in the light of the then existing case law. The same applied to some of the violations of Community law relevant in *Factortame* such as the nationality requirement, while some doubts were allowed as to whether the breach due to the reference to the residence requirement could be considered manifest and serious.[93]

It is apparent from the reasoning of the Court that what was at stake is discretion in a very weak sense (discrIII). All problems stem from the question whether or not the obligations imposed on Member States by the Treaty were clear enough at the time the decisions infringing Community law were taken or kept in force. According to *Brasserie du Pêcheur and Factortame*, to assess whether the breach is manifest and serious enough to give rise to liability, a number of factors may be considered, including the clarity and precision of the rule infringed, whether the infringement and the damage caused was intentional or involuntary, whether any error of law was excusable or inexcusable, and whether the position taken by a Community institution may have contributed towards the adoption or maintenance of national measures or practices contrary to Community law.[94] There is no room for policy choices to be made by the Member States (discrI). Nor are choices delegated to Member States (discrII). In the end there is only one correct application of Community law, and it is the one chosen by the ECJ. The degree of discretion enjoyed by national authorities is directly appraised by the ECJ. Often, so is the 'seriousness' of the breach.[95]

---

above, 132ff and T Tridimas, 'Liability for Breach of Community Law: Growing Up and Mellowing Down?' (2001) 38 CML Rev, 159. English case law is analysed by M Amos, 'Eurotorts and Unicorns: Damages for the Breach of Community Law in the United Kingdom' in Faigrieve, Andenas, and Bell, see n 65 above, 121ff; on Italy Chiti, see n 89 above, 547ff; and on Spanish case law S Martínez Lage and H Brokelmann, 'The Liability of the Spanish State for Breach of EC Law: The Landmark Ruling of the Spanish Tribunal Supremo in the Canal Satélite Digital case' (2004) 29 ELR, 530.

[92] Joined Cases C-46/93 and C-48/93 *Brasserie and Factortame* [1996] ECR I-1029, para 58.

[93] ibid, para 59ff and see Vandersanden, see n 66 above, 38.

[94] Joined Cases C-46/93 and C-48/93 *Brasserie and Factortame* [1996] ECR I-1029, para 56.

[95] But see Case C-424/97 *Haim II* [2000] ECR I-5123 and Case C-63/01 *Evans* [2003] ECR I-14447, para 87.

The same is true of *British Telecommunications*.[96] Judicial review and damages were sought against the decision by the government to list some telephone services provided by British Telecommunications as falling under the application of Council Directive (EEC) 90/531 on utilities' procurement. The Court found that the Directive did not give Member States this power. As to damages, the Court again felt that it had all the necessary elements to characterize the breach and to answer the question of liability in the negative. The relevant provisions are said to be imprecisely worded and reasonably capable of bearing the interpretation given to it by the United Kingdom in good faith. Indeed, that interpretation, which was also shared by other Member States, was not manifestly contrary to the wording of the directive or to the objective it pursued. This again is a case of weak discretion (discrIII). When a Community law provision may be read in different ways, Member States cannot be found liable just because they happen to choose a construction which later may not be the one getting the Court's stamp of approval.[97]

A more recent case is *Köbler*.[98] Mr Köbler applied for the special length-of-service increment for university professors. He claimed that, although he had not completed fifteen years service at Austrian universities, he had completed the requisite length of service if the duration of his service in universities of other Member States of the European Community was taken into consideration. The *Verwaltungsgerichtshof* referred the case to the Court of Justice. The Registrar of the Court asked the referring court whether, in the light of a subsequent judgment,[99] it thought it necessary to maintain its request. Believing that the precise categorization of the special length-of-service increment was a question of national law leaving no more room for Community law questions, the *Verwaltungsgerichtshof* withdrew the reference and dismissed Mr Köbler's application on the ground that the special length-of-service increment was a loyalty bonus which justified a derogation from the rules on freedom of movement. Mr Köbler brought an action for damages. The Austrian court raised new preliminary questions. The ECJ held that the referring court had been wrong in characterizing the litigation as a matter of national law and that, as a matter of Community law, Mr Köbler had been discriminated against. As to liability in such a case, the Court held that some factors had to be taken into account. These included the degree of clarity and

---

[96] Case C-392/93 *British Telecommunications* [1996] ECR I-1631.
[97] See also Joined Cases C-283/94, C-291/94, and C-292/94 *Denkavit International BV* [1996] ECR I-5063.
[98] Case C-224/01 *Köbler* [2003] ECR I-10239.
[99] Case C-15/96 *Schöning-Kougebetopoulou* [1998] ECR I-47.

precision of the rule infringed, whether the infringement was intentional, whether the error of law was excusable or inexcusable, the position taken, where applicable, by a Community institution, and non-compliance by the court in question with its obligation to make a reference for a preliminary ruling under the third paragraph of EC Treaty Article 234.[100]

Even if the Court of Justice seems quite careful to avoid excessive intrusion in the national adjudication system, the discretion it is ready to allow to national courts does not go beyond the discrIII type.[101] This is sufficient to limit liability to manifest breaches.[102] The ECJ accordingly ruled out liability because Community law did not expressly cover the point whether a measure for rewarding an employee's loyalty to his/her employer could be justified and because the correct solution is not obvious. The decision to withdraw its reference—which was prompted by the Registrar of the Court of Justice— although it was found to be wrong and therefore in breach of Community law, was not regarded as being manifest in nature and thus as sufficiently serious a breach.[103]

In many cases, however, the Court is not ready to concede even limited discretion, making Member States strictly liable in the sense that no further enquiry as to whether the breach is manifest and serious is necessary.[104] In other words, when not enjoying any discretion, national authorities are liable for every breach of Community law, any breach being sufficient to establish liability.[105]

In the second *Larsy* case Gervais Larsy, a Belgian national established in Belgium near the French border, was a self-employed nursery gardener in Belgium and France. He applied for retirement pensions from both the Belgian and the French authorities. These were granted, but when the Belgian pension fund realized the existence of a French pension, it curtailed the benefits originally accorded to Larsy. The decision withstood judicial scrutiny.

---

[100] Case C-224/01 *Köbler* [2003] ECR I-10239, para 55.

[101] A different view is shared by AS Botella, 'La responsabilité du juge national' (2004) 40 Revue trimestrielle de droit européen, 303ff, who contends that the Court did away with *marge d'appréciation* in this case.

[102] M Breuer, 'State liability for judicial wrongs and Community law: the case of *Gerhard Köbler v Austria*' (2004) 29 ELR, 248, 250 and the author points out at the differences in the approach by the Advocate General, 246.

[103] Case C-224/01 *Köbler* [2003] ECR I-10239, para 122ff and see also Case C-424/97 *Haim II* [2000] ECR I-5123.

[104] A Ward, *Judicial Review and Rights of Private Parties in EC Law* (Oxford: Oxford University Press, 2000) 99.

[105] The leading case is Case C-5/94 *R v Ministry of Agriculture*, Fisheries and Food, ex p *Hedley Lomas Ltd* [1996] ECR I-2553, paras 28ff.

A similar case concerned Gervais Larsy's brother, Marius Larsy. This time, however, the national court sought advice from the ECJ. The Court held that the relevant Community law provisions had to be interpreted as meaning that the rule against overlapping benefits in that provision did not apply where a person had worked in two Member States during one and the same period and had been obliged to pay old-age pension insurance contributions in those States during that period.[106] At that point Gervais Larsy reinstated his demand for a full pension. This having been met only *pro futuro*, he appealed asking for his full pension to be reinstated retroactively and also asking for damages. The Belgian pension authority was now ready to reinstate the full pension for all the time it had been curtailed, but it resisted the damages denying the existence of any wrongful act. A number of questions were raised under Article 234 EC.[107] Concerning damages, the Court though it again had all the necessary information to assess whether the facts of the case constituted a sufficiently serious breach of Community law. It held that the Belgian pension authority was bound by the first Larsy case and enjoyed no discretion fully and retroactively to reinstate the pension. It went on, remarking that 'in circumstances such as those which led to the main proceedings, the competent national institution had no substantive choice'.[108]

Without discretion, liability is easily engaged by the simple breach of Community law. This was also the case with many judgments concerning the late or non-implementation of EC directives.[109] In *Dillenkofer*[110] the Court held that failure to take any measure to transpose a directive within the period laid down for that purpose constitutes *per se* a serious breach of Community law.[111]

Ultimately, the Community Courts are quite ready to recognize broad discretionary powers to Community institutions, that is discrI situations. At times this finding could be seriously doubted.[112] The ECJ is far less

---

[106] Case C-31/92 *Larsy* [1993] ECR I-4543.

[107] Case C-118/00 *Larsy* [2001] ECR I-5063.

[108] Case C-118/00 *Larsy* [2001] ECR I-5063, para 41.

[109] Case C-127/95 *Norbrook Laboratories Ltd* [1997] ECR I-1531 is not clear-cut, but see para 88.

[110] Joined Cases C-178/94, C-179/94, C-188/94, C-189/94, and C-190/94 *Dillenkofer* [1996] ECR I-4845.

[111] ibid, para 29.

[112] A Ward, 'More than an 'Infant Disease': Individual Rights, EC Directives, and the Case for Uniform Remedies' in J M Prinsen and A Schrauwen (eds), *Direct Effect: Rethinking a Classic of EC Legal Doctrine* (Groningen: Europa Law Publishing, 2002) 56ff writes of 'a marked propensity toward categorising challenged instruments as "wide discretion" measures'.

enthusiastic about discretion when it comes to the liability of Member States. At most, discrIII is allowed. This may again be excessive in some cases. Member States often enjoy some discrII when implementing directives. They must achieve the aims laid down in the directives, but are responsible as to the means. There may be an equivalency of different means to achieve a given result, but the ECJ is often quite trenchant as to the alternative means proposed by the national governments.[113]

5 Judicial review of discretion in proceedings under EC Treaty, Article 230

5.1 *General remarks*

Liability of Community institutions is hard to establish mainly because the Courts are quite ready to concede wide margins of discretion to those institutions and (consequently) stop short of taking a hard look at their decisions. This is not limited to damages actions and extends to proceedings under Article 230 EC, the main, but far from the only, avenue for challenging Community acts. Courts' attitude to discretion is normally developed in direct actions as opposed to collateral challenges, such as damages actions— and the developments in Article 230 case law may harbinger a different take on the issues arising from review of discretion.

French administrative law played a major role in the framing of European readings of discretion. Article 230 is worded along French lines. *Incompétence*, *vice de forme, violation de la loi*, and *détournement de pouvoir* were traditionally the grounds of actions for *excès de pouvoir*.[114] French case law added that formal violations could lead to the annulment of the contested decision only if they concerned *formalités substantielles*, which is somewhat of a *contradictio in adjecto* given the usual opposition between form and substance in law, but is to mean that annulment is precluded in case the formal requirements breached do not have an impact on the content of the decision taken.[115]

---

[113] See Joined Cases C-6/90 and C-9/90 *Francovich* [1991] ECR I-5357; Joined Cases C-178/94, C-179/94, C-188/94, C-189/94, and C-190/94 *Dillenkofer* [1996] ECR I-4845; and Case C-140/97 *Rechberger* [1999] ECR I-3499, a case which turned on causation rather than on manifest and serious breach, deserves similar consideration.

[114] Chapus, see n 17 above, 1020.

[115] ibid, 1932.

The problem is that Article 230 applies to the review of validity of quite different kind of decisions, both regulatory and adjudicatory, legislative, and administrative. This unfortunate situation stemmed from the original failure to recognize that the then EEC Treaty, unlike the ECSC Treaty, was not a *traité loi* but a *traité cadre*, and some rules enacted under it, even if they go under the name of 'regulations' and are referred to as (part of) secondary law, are rather legislative in their nature. This failure may explain some difficulties in the building of a coherent judicial review system. Much of the activity of Community institutions is rule making activity; Member States are at times even referred to as the secular arm of Community institutions.[116]

Generally speaking, the Courts are quite restrained in their approach to judicial review. 'In Community law, as in any other democratic legal order, the principle of separation of powers applies. The Court of Justice must apply the law. It is not a political body and should therefore not substitute its own assessment to that of political Institutions'.[117] Review is therefore marginal, the courts being ready to recognize wide margins of discretion when dealing with European institutions. *Détournement de pouvoir* (misuse of power) is restrictively read according to the French tradition, and very rarely (if ever) established.[118]

Review is limited even when Community courts apply a review standard like the proportionality principle, as was shown in a recent case concerning the common agricultural policy.[119] The Court of Justice's reasoning is somewhat woolly. It starts repeating the old refrain that the Community legislature has wide discretion where the common agricultural policy is concerned, corresponding to policy choices (discrIII).[120] Only manifest mistakes could then lead to the nullification of Community legislature. The Court then changes track, referring to proportionality and holding that 'where there is a choice between several appropriate measures, recourse must be had to the least onerous, and the disadvantages caused must not be disproportionate to the aims pursued'.[121]

---

[116] K Lenaerts, 'Regulating the Regulatory Process: "Delegation of Powers" in the European Community' (1993) 18 ELR, 28.

[117] Schermers and Waelbroeck, see n 64 above, 397.

[118] Recently Case T-168/01 *GlaxoSmithKline Services Unlimited v Commission*, Judgment of the Court of 27 September 2006, nyr.

[119] Case C-310/04 *Spain v Council*, Judgment of the Court of 7 September 2006, nyr and the Court draws from Case C-189/01 *Jippes* [2001] ECR I-5689, para 80.

[120] ibid, para 96.

[121] ibid, para 99.

Proportionality review is far from marginal. The discretionary choice is restricted to an option for the least onerous measure, which moreover must not be disproportionate to the ends pursued by the institution. Indeed, proportionality entails a close examination of whether a certain end justifies the means.[122] The Court of Justice, however, reads the requirement that the measure must not be disproportionately very narrow. In its view,

98 bearing in mind the wide discretion enjoyed by the Community legislature where the common agricultural policy is concerned, the lawfulness of a measure adopted in that sphere can be affected only if the measure is manifestly inappropriate in terms of the objective which the competent institution is seeking to pursue.

99 What must be ascertained is therefore not whether the measure adopted by the legislature was the only one or the best one possible but whether it was manifestly inappropriate.

The proportionality principle, which in Germany is the tool of choice for strict monitoring of discretionary powers, is considerably watered down in the review of Community legislation.[123] The same is true in those sectors where Community institutions are directly charged with the adjudication of Community law. One such area is the law of competition: even though a decentralization process has taken place in the past years, the Commission still plays a central role in the enforcement of competition law.[124]

5.2 *Tetra Laval*

The attitude displayed by Community Courts to judicial review of individual measures was shaken up in *Tetra Laval*.[125] Acting under Article 81 EC, the Commission blocked a proposed merger in the food packaging industry involving Tetra, the leading firm in carton packaging, and Sidel, a firm providing plastic packaging, at a time when technological developments were

---

[122] Nolte, see n 9 above, 193.

[123] Generally Nolte, see n 9 above, 197 and see also A Egger, 'The Principle of Proportionality in Community Anti-dumping Law' (1993) 18 ELR, 366.

[124] See S Kingston, 'A "new division of responsibilities" in the Proposed Regulation to Modernise the Rules Implementing Articles 81 and 82 EC? A warning call' (2001) Eur Competition L Rev, 340 and T Jones 'Regulation 17: The Impact of the Current Application of Articles 81 and 82 by National Competition Authorities in the European Commission's Proposals for Reform' (2001) Eur Competition L Rev, 405.

[125] Case C-12/03 P *Commission v Tetra Laval BV*, Judgment of the Court of 15 February 2005, nyr.

making plastic appropriate for various types of beverages previously sold in carton. According to the Commission, the two entities operated in distinct but closely related and potentially converging markets having a growing number of common customers. This could give Tetra the leverage to induce its customers to switch to Sidel's products and reduce incentives to adjust prices and innovate to face the threat posed by plastic packaging.

Tetra brought an action under Article 230 EC.[126] It claimed that the modified merger had (i) no appreciable anti-competitive horizontal or vertical effects and (ii) no appreciable anti-competitive conglomerate effect. Furthermore, it claimed (iii) that the assessment by the Commission of the applicant's commitments was inadequate, and (iv) that the Commission had failed to give sufficient reasons for the contested decision.[127]

The CFI was ready to accept that the Commission enjoyed discretionary powers when deciding whether or not to give the green light to a proposed merger:

As a preliminary point, it must be recalled that the substantive rules of the Regulation, in particular Article 2, confer on the Commission a certain discretion, especially with respect to assessments of an economic nature. Consequently, review by the Community judicature of the exercise of that discretion, which is essential for defining the rules on concentrations, must take account of the discretionary margin implicit in the provisions of an economic nature which form part of the rules on concentrations.[128]

Having said this, the CFI performed a rather incisive review, finding multiple manifest errors of assessment in the way the Commission relied on the horizontal and vertical effects of the modified merger to support its analysis on the creation of a dominant position.[129] The Court also imposed on the Commission an onerous burden of proof as to the demonstration of anti-competitive conglomerate effects. The Court observed that 'effects of conglomerate-type mergers are generally considered to be neutral, or even beneficial, for competition on the markets concerned'. Consequently it held that it was for the Commission to produce convincing evidence of the anti-competitive

---

[126] Case T-5/02 *Tetra Laval BV* [2002] ECR II-4381.

[127] ibid, para 81.

[128] ibid, para 119; to this effect the following cases were quoted: Joined Cases C-68/94 and C-30/95 *France and Others v Commission* ('Kali and Salz') [1998] ECR I-1375, para 223, 224; Case T-102/96 *Gencor v Commission* [1999] ECR II-753, para 164, 165, and Case T-342/99 *Airtours v Commission* [2002] ECR II-2585, para 64.

[129] Case T-5/02 *Tetra Laval BV* [2002] ECR II-4381, paras 132, 140ff.

effects of a specific conglomerate-type merger[130] and according to the Court, such evidence was not provided.[131] Further, considering that the anticipated dominant position was to emerge only in the future, the Court observed that the Commission's analysis of the future position 'must, whilst allowing for a certain margin of discretion, be particularly plausible'.[132] Following a detailed examination of the conflicting arguments of the parties, the Court held that the Commission, even if its analysis were not 'vitiated by a manifest error of assessment',[133] had not proven its case 'to the requisite legal standard'.[134]

The damning review of the Commission's decision goes on for pages and pages, but the language is the same all though the judgment: 'the Commission committed an error',[135] which at times—but not always—is said to be 'manifest';[136] the Commission's prediction 'is not plausible',[137] 'the contested decision does not adduce evidence that suffices in law',[138] or 'does not provide sufficiently convincing evidence'.[139] By contrast, discretion is the (almost) absent word from the judgment, being mentioned only on the two occasions given earlier.[140]

The *Tetra Laval* judgment may be read in different ways. On the one hand, one could claim Community law is following the same evolutionary path already trodden by French administrative law. In an earlier phase, a decision could be struck down only if the decision maker had committed an *erreur manifeste d'appréciation*; today, this is so only in case of *contrôle restreint*. In cases of *contrôle normal* any mistake will make the decision void. On the other hand, one could read the 'mere' errors listed as stepping stones to a 'manifest mistake' case, and indeed the latter is referred to in many of the closing paragraphs of the reasoning of the Court and in the final paragraph of the judgment itself.[141]

---

[130] ibid, para 155, and the Court is here quoting and following its precedent in Case T-342/99 *Airtours v Commission* [2002] ECR II-2585, para 63.

[131] Case T-5/02 *Tetra Laval BV* [2002] ECR II-4381, para 160.

[132] ibid, para 162.

[133] ibid, para 223.

[134] ibid, paras 216, 223.

[135] ibid, paras 234, 245, 269, 293, 297.

[136] ibid, para 283, 308, 335, 336.

[137] ibid, para 246, and at other times, certain factors have been 'overestimated': eg, 288; or assessment and/or analysis are inadequate: eg, 287, 294.

[138] ibid, para 251 and similarly paras 307, 325, 332, where the decision is said to come short of the 'requisite legal standard'.

[139] ibid, para 254 and similarly paras 256, 261, 269, 271, 277, 278, 292, 305ff.

[140] ibid, paras 119, 162.

[141] ibid, para 336.

On appeal, the issue of the bounds of judicial review was raised. Advocate General Tizzano, thought that 'examination by the Community judicature of the complex economic assessments made by the Commission must necessarily be confined to verifying whether the rules on procedure and on the statement of reasons have been complied with, whether the facts have been accurately stated and whether there has been any manifest error of appraisal or misuse of powers'.[142]

Then quoting the ECJ's decision in *Kali and Salz*,[143] he contended that the rules applicable to the policing of mergers 'confer on the Commission a certain discretion, especially with respect to assessments of an economic nature' and 'consequently, review by the Community judicature of the exercise of that discretion, which is essential for defining the rules on concentrations, must take account of the discretionary margin implicit in the provisions of an economic nature which form part of the rules on concentrations'.[144]

In other words, the accuracy in the assessment of simple facts may be fully reviewed, while in complex factual situations only manifest mistakes will be relevant.[145] In the latter situation, the Community Courts have to respect the broad discretion inherent in that kind of assessment and may not substitute their own point of view for that of the body which is institutionally responsible for making those assessments.[146] Judicial review is possible mainly through the imposition on the Commission of the duty to investigate the case thoroughly and to give articulate reasons for its decision.[147]

Having laid down the bounds of judicial review, Advocate General Tizzano opined that the CFI had 'plainly overstepped' them on many occasions.[148] Nevertheless, he considered that the procedures followed and the reasons given in the contested decision were riddled with such shortcomings as not to be able to withstand judicial review even if it were confined in more strict bounds.[149]

---

[142] ibid, para 83 and the Court quotes Joined Cases C-204/00 P, C-205/00 P, C-211/00 P, C-213/00 P, C-217/00 P, and C-219/00 P *Aalborg Portland and Others v Commission* [2004] ECR I-123, para 279.

[143] Joined Cases C-68/94 and C-30/95 *France and Others v Commission* ('Kali and Salz') [1998] ECR I-1375.

[144] Case T-5/02 *Tetra Laval BV* [2002] ECR II-4381, para 84.

[145] ibid, see also para 85.

[146] ibid, para 86.

[147] ibid, see paras 87ff.

[148] ibid, para 94.

[149] ibid, see, eg, paras 126, 134, 141ff.

The ECJ sided with the CFI. The reasoning in *Kali and Salz*,[150] to which Advocate General Tizzano referred, was qualified to a relevant extent:

> Whilst the Court recognizes that the Commission has a margin of discretion with regard to economic matters, that does not mean that the Community Courts must refrain from reviewing the Commission's interpretation of information of an economic nature. Not only must the Community Courts, inter alia, establish whether the evidence relied on is factually accurate, reliable and consistent but also whether that evidence contains all the information which must be taken into account in order to assess a complex situation and whether it is capable of substantiating the conclusions drawn from it. Such a review is all the more necessary in the case of a prospective analysis required when examining a planned merger with conglomerate effect.[151]

Having briefly analysed some of the parts of the CFI judgment singled out for criticism by the Commission, the ECJ held that the lower court had correctly carried out its review, having set out the reasons why the Commission's conclusions seemed to be inaccurate, in that they were based on insufficient, incomplete, insignificant, and inconsistent evidence.[152]

Contrasting the ECJ's terse reasoning with the conclusions by Advocate General Tizzano one could conclude that the Court has embraced what the French would call *contrôle normal* in discrII situations. Some doubts are still possible as to the scope of this evolution in the law, since the specific nature of the assessment needed in this case required—as the Court itself is ready to concede—a particularly firmly reasoned decision and demanded a correspondingly severe standard of judicial review.

5.3 *Glaxo*

A more recent decision may have fine-tuned the *Tetra Laval* approach and made it more palatable. Glaxo had notified the Commission of its 'General Sales Conditions of pharmaceutical specialities to authorized Spanish wholesalers' with a view to obtaining negative clearance or an exemption under Article 81ff EC. The agreement set lower prices of sale for pharmaceutical products whose purchase was financed by Spanish social security funds, by Spanish public funds, or through pharmacies and Spanish hospitals. Higher

---

[150] Joined Cases C-68/94 and C-30/95 *France and Others v Commission* ('Kali and Salz') [1998] ECR I-1375.

[151] Case T-5/02 *Tetra Laval BV* [2002] ECR II-4381, para 39.

[152] ibid, para 48.

prices applied otherwise. The agreement had the scope to prevent parallel imports from Spain to England, where prices were higher. The Commission refused both the clearance and the exception and Glaxo lodged an action under Article 230 EC.[153]

Issues of discretion were raised with reference to the application of Article 81(3) EC. It provides that the provisions of Article 81(1) EC, forbidding agreements in restraint of trade, may be declared inapplicable, *inter alia*, in the case of any agreement which contributes to improving the distribution of goods or to promoting technical or economic progress. It also allows consumers a fair share of the resulting benefit, and does not impose restrictions on the undertakings concerned which are not indispensable to the attainment of these objectives. Nor in such undertakings does it afford the possibility of eliminating competition in respect of a substantial part of the products in question. The granting of an exemption is a discrI decision, involving the comparison and balancing of conflicting private and public interests.

The Court treads carefully, accepting that, insofar as it is faced with complex economic assessments, the review is confined to verifying whether the facts have been accurately stated, whether there has been any manifest error of appraisal, and whether the legal consequences deduced from those facts were accurate. Thus it is not for the Court to establish whether the evidence relied on is factually accurate, reliable, and consistent, whether it contains all the information which must be taken into account for the purpose of assessing a complex situation, or whether it is capable of substantiating the conclusions drawn from it. Moreover, the Court cannot substitute its own economic assessment for that of the institution which adopted the decision the legality of which it is requested to review.[154]

Even if *Tetra Laval* is duly referred to, caution seems to be the catchword. The Court however delves very deeply into the reasoning of the Commission and comes to the conclusion that insufficient reasons were given to rebut the arguments advanced by Glaxo to support its request. According to the Court, the Commission could not have merely rejected Glaxo's arguments outright on the ground that the advantage described would not necessarily be achieved. It was also required to examine, as specifically as possible in the context of a prospective analysis, whether it seemed more likely that the

[153] Case T-168/01 *GlaxoSmithKline Services Unlimited v Commission*, Judgment of the Court of 27 September 2006, nyr.
[154] ibid, paras 241ff.

advantages would be achieved than that they would not in the particular circumstances of the case and in the light of the evidence submitted to it. Nor was it entitled to consider, in a peremptory manner and without providing proper arguments, that the factual arguments and evidence submitted by Glaxo were to be regarded as hypothetical.[155]

The CFI is only apparently more restrained here than in *Tetra*. Its review of the reasoning is very attentive and equally damning. Along with Italian case law, *Glaxo* shows that courts, even when appearing not to go into the merits of a case, can go a long way in reviewing discretion just by scrutinizing the reasons given.

6 Conclusion

These most recent cases could show a new readiness on the part of Community Courts to review more stringently the decisions taken by Community institutions. This in turn could increase the chance of success on damages actions.

However, as novel as these judgments may be, they are still very unstructured from the point of view of the analysis of discretion. Community Courts still pay lip-service to supposedly broad discretion; they do not distinguish between different types or degrees of discretionary decision as most national courts do. This leaves plenty of doubt as to whether and to what extent review has changed. Is the evolution of case law, if any, limited to some specific areas, such as competition law, or is it more general? Case law does not articulate the answers.

This is unfortunate. Marginal or intensive reviews are not an end in themselves. Different considerations speak for or against any position taken.[156] What is important is to distinguish the different meanings of discretion in a consistent way. Conceptual sloppiness leaves us with the feeling that Community Courts apply double standards when reviewing Community versus national measures—as is the case concerning liability actions— hardly a tenable position in times of mounting discontent against European institutions.

---

[155] ibid, paras 301ff.
[156] Stroink, see n 43 above, 81.

Moreover, many national courts look at Community case law to develop domestic standards of judicial review and bring them into line with the requirements of the Community law principle of effective judicial protection. This becomes unduly difficult when the Community case law itself is fuzzy. National courts are left to fend for themselves. Divergences between Community law and national laws are not really dealt with and this could ultimately undermine effective judicial protection.

National traditions do not move on exactly the same lines when reviewing discretion, but most legal systems converge in distinguishing policy choices from complex factual assessment and the difficult task of legal interpretation. These categories of discretion deserve differentiated approaches because the balance of power between courts and decision makers which they involve sees a decreasing justification for judicial self-restraint. Policy choices are felt to be the preserve of the decision maker to a much greater extent than interpretation choices. Consistency in case law would be enhanced if Community Courts were to accept this simple truth, word it clearly, and abide by it.

9

Discretion, Divergence, and Unity

Michiel Brand

1 Introduction

There is no doubt that discretion is one of the most important, problematic, wide-ranging, and pervasive concepts within law and legal doctrine. This makes it a challenging task to write a useful and comprehensive discussion of it.[1] No such daring attempt will be made here, as this chapter merely maps out and considers some of the main points and characteristics associated with discretion. In particular, the aim will be to try to lay bare the relations of discretion with conceptual divergence and, ultimately, how this may relate to the attainment or stimulation of unity within a legal system.

2 A closer look at the concept of discretion

The concept of discretion is controversial, provoking passionate discourse in which it is either extolled or vigorously condemned.[2] One reason for this

---

[1] cf M Rosenberg, 'Judicial Discretion of the Trial Court, Viewed from Above' (1971) 22 Syracuse L Rev, 635: 'To speak of discretion in relation to law is to open a thousand doorways to discussion. The concept is pervasive and protean, with intimations of both power and responsibility. Even when confined to judicial settings, it manifests itself in numberless ways. Whatever the court, wherever it sits, the judge soon finds himself talking, wondering and, at times, thinking about discretion and its implications.'

[2] cf GC Christie, 'An Essay on Discretion' (1986) Duke L J, 747: 'If there is little agreement about the meaning of discretion, there is even less agreement about its desirability. Indeed, participants in the judicial process and observers of that process take a schizophrenic view of discretion. Sometimes they praise it and sometimes they execrate it.' Rosenberg, see n 1 above, 642,

is that discretion is often placed on the boundary between the 'rule of law' and the 'rule of man', or as KC Davis phrased it: '[w]here law ends, discretion begins, and the exercise of discretion may mean either beneficence or tyranny, either justice or injustice, either reasonableness or arbitrariness'.[3]

At the same time discretion is arguably *inherent* in a legal order, since '[t]he vagaries of language, the diversity of circumstances, and the indeterminacy of official purposes are', as HLA Hart has reminded us, 'considerations which guarantee discretion some continuing place in the legal order and make its elimination an impossible dream'.[4] This is of course only half the story. Discretion can also be *intended* in the sense that it is, explicitly or implicitly, delegated to agents as a means of escaping the rigidity of a detailed system of legal rules and allowing for necessary flexibility in relation to particular cases at hand. Contrary to how it is sometimes presented, it thus seems false to regard discretion either merely as a strictly peripheral phenomenon of a legal order naturally committed to the absolute supremacy of the rule of law, or as a necessary evil brought about by the opacity and incompleteness of legal rules.[5] Rather, discretion must be regarded as a concept that also has certain virtues and that has a useful role to play *within* a legal system. In fact, it could even be argued that *all* legal power is discretionary to a greater or lesser extent.[6]

Discretion is a broad and permeative concept that can hardly be framed in a conclusive definition.[7] It is noteworthy that European jurisprudence uses the concept of discretion with a very large degree of terminological imprecision. Reference is made indiscriminately to a wide mixture of terms

---

gives a nice example of the latter: 'Lord Camden called discretion the law of tyrants. He said that "in the best it is oftentimes caprice"; and in the worst, "every vice, folly and passion to which human nature can be liable." '

[3] KC Davis quoted in M Künnecke, 'Judicial Review of Discretionary Powers in England and Germany', presented at the BUDC conference, Tilburg University, 2004.

[4] DJ Galligan, *Discretionary Powers* (Oxford: Clarendon Press, 1990) 1. In fact, the decrease in the regulatory capacity of law, the vagueness of language, and the consequent existence of discretion, become increasingly apparent 'with the growing complexity of life', something that Bikle noted as early as 1933: HW Bikle, 'Administrative Discretion' (1933) 2 George Washington L Rev, 3.

[5] Which is, of course, not to deny the natural tension that exists between the rule of law and discretionary authority.

[6] H Lindahl, 'Public Policy as a "Boundary Concept": Discretion and Divergent Demarcations of the Public Realm', presented at the BUDC conference, Tilburg University, 2004, 2. See also Lindahl's contribution to this volume, ch 13.

[7] In the words of Galligan, see n 4 above: ' [D]iscretion is not a precise term of art, with a settled meaning, nor is it a concept which, when found to be present, leads to fixed consequences', 54.

to denote discretion[8] and these different terms are often even used alongside each other within the *same* judgment or Advocate General's conclusion, thereby sometimes bypassing national-doctrinal differences between discretionary concepts. An example of the latter is the conclusion of Advocate General Geelhoed in Case C-378/00 *Commission v Parliament and Council* (concerning a dispute over the choice of procedure under the second comitology decision) where the Advocate General refers consecutively to *beoordelingsvrijheid* (para 77, in the English version 'power of assessment') and to *beleidsvrijheid* (para 93, in the English version 'freedom in matters of policy'), thereby seemingly overriding the supposed doctrinal divergence between the two concepts. All this certainly adds to terminological and conceptual confusion, although it has to be said that this confusion is often just as much apparent at the level of national law.[9] However, it also has to be admitted that the difference between the two terms on the national level should not be overstated either.[10]

Even though it has to be acknowledged that there are many different and sophisticated theoretical distinctions to be made within the concept of discretion—such as between stronger and weaker senses of discretion[11]— *generally* speaking the term could be described as 'a certain amount of freedom, occurring in the adjudication of disputes or in the creation/application/interpretation of legal rules, that must remain within certain (legal, judicial, and political) margins'. These margins or boundaries of discretionary power are very important as they prevent discretion from effectively

---

[8] Eg, English: 'discretion', 'discretionary powers', 'margin of discretion'; German: *Ermessensbefugnis, Ermessensspielraum, Beurteilungsermessen, Beurteilungsspielraum*; Dutch: *beslissingsvrijheid, beoordelingsbevoegdheid, beoordelingsvrijheid, beoordelingsmarge, discretionaire bevoegdheid, beleidsvrijheid* and Italian: *potere discrezionale, liberta di valutazione, liberta d'apprezzamento*.

[9] S Prechal, 'Noot bij Dillenkofer' (1998) 2 SEW Tijdschrift voor Europees en Economisch Recht, 68.

[10] Schwarze remarks, with regard to Dutch law, that 'both ideas carry the same meaning' and that '[a]lthough there is no express distinction between discretion and scope for appraisal, the two are distinguished in practice', J Schwarze, *European Administrative Law* (London: Sweet & Maxwell, 1992) 292.

[11] As elaborated in RM Dworkin, 'The Model of Rules' (1967) 35 The U of Chicago L Rev, 32ff. Dworkin holds that there are two weak senses of discretion: first, when the standards an official must apply cannot be applied mechanically and thus demand the use of judgment; and second, in the situation in which an official has final authority to make a decision that cannot be reviewed and reversed by any other official. These two weak senses of discretion are contrasted with the strong sense, according to which an official is *not* bound by any standards set by a higher authority. Dworkin's strong and second weak senses of discretion correspond with Rosenberg's distinction between, respectively, primary and secondary judicial discretion: Rosenberg, see n 1 above, 637ff.

amounting to extra-legal arbitrariness. The issue is therefore to what degree discretion is subject to control. In this context, judicial review can be considered the primary mechanism that ultimately determines whether an authority can use discretion and, if so, what the boundaries of that discretion might be.[12] Indeed, the working of the judiciary and the review it undertakes is *itself* an exercise of discretion.[13] Even though this might seem a truism for most lawyers, it is not an uncontroversial statement in view both of the assertion many an average judge might make that he/she is no more than 'la bouche qui prononce les paroles de la loi',[14] and the related claims of some scholars who tend to view the legal order as a 'gapless system' which allows for hardly any discretion on the part of judicial authorities.[15] Here we assume, however, that judicial discretion is an inextricable feature of any legal system. It has to be noted strongly that, even though this judicial discretion is 'at the top of the legal ladder' and in some cases appears to be very extensive, it definitely has to respect certain boundaries as well.[16]

----

[12]   There are also other sets of officials that can set limits to the exercise of discretion, such as the senior authority that delegates discretionary powers to lower ones. It is the judicial branch, however, that has the most important role in this regard, since 'from a legal point of view, it is often the courts that determine the meaning and scope to be given to discretionary authority', Galligan, see n 4 above, 23.

[13]   See, eg, O Wiklund (ed), *Judicial Discretion in European Perspective* (Stockholm: Kluwer Law International, 2003). Bodenheimer nicely describes, and places in temporal perspective, the different attitudes towards judicial discretion, which range from outright denial to unlimited acknowledgement. It is argued here that judicial discretion certainly exists, thus leading us to a rejection of the position of outright denial. It could be held, however, that the position of unlimited acknowledgment, such as adhered to, eg, on the view of legal realism, reaches too far since '[t]his view breeds cynicism by portraying the judiciary as an autocratic body of officials who impose their social preconceptions on the parties and the public at large', E Bodenheimer, 'Hart, Dworkin, and the Problem of Judicial Lawmaking Discretion' (1977) 11 Georgia L Rev, 1171.

[14]   Montesquieu, *L'esprit des lois*.

[15]   An example is Dworkin, see n 11 above. He contested Hart's formalistic positivism, holding that to adopt a Hartian rule of recognition entails that principles are not binding law and thus manifest themselves merely in an 'extra-legal' quality. By necessity, this means that in 'hard cases', where he/she quickly finds him/herself running out of law (in its limited positivistic conceptualization), a judge must use discretion in the strong sense, meaning that he/she is not bound by any legal standards. Dworkin, on the other hand, adopts a more encompassing view of the law by recognizing principles as being intra-legal. This means that law can never run out and that accordingly, a judge cannot avail him/herself of discretion except in its most trivial sense (namely that of the exercise of judgment in relation to open-textured rules, a sense of discretion Dworkin dismisses as a tautology: see n 11 above, 35).

[16]   See, eg, A Barak, 'The Nature of Judicial Discretion and its Significance for the Administration of Justice' in Wiklund, see n 13 above, 19ff, distinguishing between a number of procedural and substantive limits to judicial discretion.

3 Discretion and conceptual divergence

At first sight, being a broad and fairly universal concept, discretion does not easily suggest ways of discussing conceptual divergence. This is also the conclusion reached by Bert van Roermund, who stated that he is 'inclined to think that, admittedly at a fairly high level of abstraction, the picture of discretion is a rather converging one'.[17]

On the other hand, however, discretion can be seen as the *pivotal example of a concept that creates and stimulates* divergence. After all, in its basic form, discretion provides the freedom to proceed along *divergent* routes in *similar or identical* situations, provided of course that certain outer normative boundaries are respected. Exploring, then, the links between discretion and divergence, two general categories pop up in which the two coincide. The first appears under the heading of conceptual divergence as regards discretion *itself*; the second concerns *related* conceptual divergence.

3.1 *Conceptual divergence*

It is useful here to recall briefly the exact meaning of 'conceptual divergence', as concisely expounded by Van Roermund.[18] Pointing out that conceptual divergence does not amount merely to linguistic variance, he comes up with the following definition:

A legal term T is conceptually divergent between agents X and Y, if T is common parlance between X and Y, and if the sense and/or the reference of T yields meaning M_1 for X and M_2 for Y, such that X and Y are inclined to argue conflicting courses of action as lawful (or unlawful) under the legal order they are both committed to.

This allows us to put things in better perspective. Whereas, following Van Roermund's definition, it becomes almost immediately clear that conceptual divergence is hardly discernible as regards the *positive* side of discretion—with its fairly general and universal definition—it comes to the fore more distinctly in relation to its *negative* side or the *bandwidth* of discretionary authority. In fact, it has been convincingly argued that focusing on the negative side—ie as we saw above, on the intensity of judicial review which ultimately sets the

---

[17] B van Roermund, 'Discretion, its Margins and the Margins of the Margins', presented at the BUDC conference, Tilburg University, 2004, 4. See also the Introduction to this volume.
[18] Van Roermund, see n 17 above, 1.

boundaries of discretionary action—allows us to flesh out a clearer *positive* concept of discretion.[19]

Conceptual divergence as to the *scope* of discretion can be seen to occur in two different senses. First, in a weak sense, meaning that the materialization of the scope of discretion within the different Member States diverges on the level of *specific legal areas*, ie the question which exact areas are under the 'reign' of discretion and in which areas its influence is minor or negligible. Especially relevant, however, is conceptual divergence in the strong sense, namely the differing views on the *general and theoretical* level as to the bandwidth of discretion.

Conceptual divergence in the weak sense

Just one example of this category can be found in the area of liability, an area that is intimately connected with discretion. It seems that divergence exists especially with regard to the question of *judicial* discretion and the connected issue of whether a State could possibly be held liable for failures—or, if one likes, the manifest infringement of discretionary boundaries—of its judicial branch. A starting point is the important judgment of the European Court of Justice (ECJ) in *Köbler*;[20] in which the Court confirmed that 'the principle according to which the Member States are liable to afford reparation of damage caused to individuals as a result of infringements of Community law for which they are responsible is also applicable where the alleged infringement stems from a decision of a court adjudicating at last instance'.[21] Even though this might seem obvious with regard to the Court's earlier case law,[22] it is

---

[19] L Moral Soriano and D Sarmiento, 'Contribution on Discretion', presented at the BUDC conference, Tilburg University, 2004: 'Why is the notion of discretion so malleable? Is it an empty construct, or simply an open-ended rule with a particular sensitivity to context? We understand that discretion can only be explained in opposition to the scrutiny of discretionary action. Only by means of control, the edges of discretion are shaped. Conceptual debate can only be developed under this dual perspective: what do public authorities consider to be within the area of discretion; and what do controlling powers understand to be such limits. Thus, normative and administrative activity must be viewed in the light of judicial scrutiny. With a *negative* perspective towards discretion, we can flesh out a *positive* concept.'

[20] Case C-224/01 *Köbler* [2003] ECR I-10239. See further the commentaries by AJC De Moor-Van Vugt, 'Note on Case C-224/01 Gerhard Köbler and Republik Österreich' (2004) 11 Tilburg Foreign L Rev; B Krans, 'Het arrest Köbler: aansprakelijkheid voor schending van EG-recht in rechterlijke uitspraken' (2004) 79 Nederlands Juristen Blad, 571–576; and E Steyger, 'De gevolgen van de aansprakelijkheid van de Staat voor rechterlijke schendingen van EG-recht' (2004) 10 Nederlands Tijdschrift voor Europees Recht, 18.

[21] Case C-224/01 *Köbler* [2003] ECR I-10239, para 50.

[22] In Case C-46/93 and C-48/93 *Brasserie and Factortame* [1996] ECR I-1029, para 32, the Court stated that the principle of State liability 'holds good for any case in which a Member State

however a rather controversial area considering the special place and function of the judiciary as well as the possible consequences of the acknowledgement of State liability for judicial infringements of Community law. After all, the principles of legal certainty and *res judicata* stand in the way of an all too swift and easy grant of judicial liability. The Court acknowledges this and carefully holds that 'State liability for an infringement of Community law by a decision of a national court adjudicating at last instance can be incurred *only in the exceptional case where the court has manifestly infringed the applicable law.*'[23] This reluctant, hands-off attitude of the ECJ in the *Köbler* case shows the Court acknowledging a relatively wide degree of judicial discretion for the national courts. The Court's deferential attitude towards the issue of liability of Member States for failures of the judiciary seems *largely* consonant with the restrictive approach taken by the national legal systems. Nonetheless, it is to be noted that the *Köbler* regime is still *less* strict than the regime in the Netherlands,[24] which should consequently be revised. Even though the *Köbler* formulation is restrictive, it *does* open a (perhaps more theoretical than realistic) prospect of a system of Member State liability for judicial infringements of Community law which is presumably still more generous than the regime existing in most Member States. In a contentious area such as this, it is to be expected that most national regimes—and more research could be done on this issue—are even more careful in their approach than that taken by the ECJ, which points to a certain amount of specific conceptual divergence.

Conceptual divergence in the strong sense

A much clearer example of conceptual divergence can be found in general and doctrinal differences with regard to the concept of discretion. The most obvious example is the situation in Germany,[25] which is an interesting object of study for enquiries into discretion.[26]

In Germany, the bandwidth of discretion granted to the administration is significantly smaller than that in other European countries. The distrust of

breaches Community law, *whatever be the organ of the State whose act or omission was responsible for the breach*' (emphasis added).

[23] Case C-224/01 *Köbler* [2003] ECR I-10239, para 53 (emphasis added).

[24] Hoge Raad, 3 December 1971, NJ 1972, 137, with annotation.

[25] See Y Arai-Takahashi, 'Discretion in German Administrative Law: Doctrinal Discourse Revisited' (2000) 6 Eur Public L, 69; Schwarze, see n 10 above, 270ff and Künnecke, see n 3 above.

[26] As Arai-Takahashi, see n 25 above, notes: 'It seems that in no other European country have such complex and in-depth principles governing administrative discretion been developed as in Germany', 69.

administrative discretion has its origin in Nazi history, in which executive and administrative authorities dominated, leaving the judiciary virtually powerless. There was a reaction in the post-war period, which saw the emergence of the idea of a *Rechtsstaat* characterized by strong emphasis on judicial review and a consequently narrow scope of administrative discretion. The principle of the constitutional state, as embodied in *Grundgesetz* (GG), Article 20(3) [27] and the right to effective judicial review, expressed in Article 19(4) GG,[28] 'create a general presumption in favour of strict legal controls on the administration and against the free use of discretionary power within the law'.[29] From this follows the requirement of the *express authorization* of discretion. This entails that when the legislature has left out code formulations such as 'can' or 'may', the administrative authority simply cannot avail itself of discretion.

German legal doctrine distinguishes between three different elements of administrative action, namely *Tatbestand* (the constituent elements of a provision), *Subsumtion* (the application of the interpreted concepts to the concrete facts), and *Rechtsfolge* (the appraisal and determination of a certain legal effect). The interesting point is that administrative discretion can, theoretically, *only* take place within the third phase of administrative action. This means that the *interpretation* of legal provisions allows for *one* correct outcome only, and that the courts have the final authority to make this determination. This is the case even when it concerns so-called *unbestimmte Rechtsbegriffe* or undefined legal concepts. Thus the court can fully review the specific interpretation given to such concepts by the administrative authority and then substitute it with their own. This dogmatic distinction—significantly limiting administrative discretionary freedom—is softened by the granting of *Beurteilungsspielraum* or 'margin of appraisal' in the interpretation of certain undefined concepts.[30] It should be noted, however, that a certain level

---

[27] 'Die Gesetzgebung ist an die verfassungsmäßige Ordnung, die vollziehende Gewalt und die Rechtsprechung sind an Gesetz und Recht gebunden.'
[28] 'Wird jemand durch die öffentliche Gewalt in seinen Rechten verletzt, so steht ihm der Rechtsweg offen. Soweit eine andere Zuständigkeit nicht begründet ist, ist der ordentliche Rechtsweg gegeben. Art 10 Abs. 2 Satz 2 bleibt unberührt.'
[29] Schwarze, see n 10 above, 272.
[30] See, eg, BVerwGE 39, 197. In this case, it concerned a statutory clause requiring a 'tendency to pervert youth' which was a condition for the Federal Scrutiny Agency to determine whether a certain publication presented a danger to young people. The *Bundesverwaltungsgericht* then stated that '[t]he idea that in applying the concept of a tendency to pervert, only one correct solution is possible, is found to be a fiction', cited by Schwarze, see n 10 above, 274. See, however, BVerfGE 83, 130 (Josefine Mutzenbacher case) 1990.

of *Beurteilungsspielraum* is only recognized exceptionally and in very limited circumstances, making this notion in fact largely academic.[31]

This stringent approach in Germany can be contrasted with the view taken by the UK courts and the ECJ. In the case of England, Künnecke states that:

In England the constitutional framework is characterised by the principle of Parliamentary sovereignty which in traditional terms limited the reviewing powers of the judges to the protection of the legislative intent. It is not for the judges to second guess an authorities' decision, the judges' function lies in the assurance that Parliament's will has been carried out. This principle is the basis for the judicial restraint, which has traditionally been applied.[32]

The room for judicial intervention is thus significantly smaller, and the scope for administrative discretion larger, in England than it is in Germany. The ECJ also displays a more deferential attitude than the German courts. One illustration is the case of *Upjohn*,[33] in which the Court held:

According to the Court's case-law, where a Community authority is called upon, in the performance of its duties, to make complex assessments, it enjoys a wide measure of discretion, the exercise of which is subject to a limited judicial review in the course of which the Community judicature may not substitute its assessment of the facts for the assessment made by the authority concerned. Thus, in such cases, the Community judicature must restrict itself to examining the accuracy of the findings of fact and law made by the authority concerned and to verifying, in particular, that the action taken by that authority is not vitiated by a manifest error or a misuse of powers and that it did not clearly exceed the bounds of its discretion.[34]

The system of judicial review that exists in Germany can readily be criticized for being too strict and it can be said that, when compared to the line taken by the English courts and the ECJ, the review approach of the German courts 'places itself in splendid isolation'.[35] Intensive judicial control leads to delays in judicial procedures and is not suited to dealing with complex cases. In the words of Schwarze:

The sheer rigour of the tests to which undefined expressions are subjected and the restrictive treatment of the legal notion of the scope for appraisal create a very

---

[31] Schwarze, see n 10 above, 275.
[32] Künnecke, see n 3 above.
[33] Case C-120/97 *Upjohn Ltd* [1999] ECR I-223.
[34] ibid, para 34.
[35] Künnecke, see n 3 above.

rigid and inflexible review system, with an inner logic which compels the courts in certain cases—for example, those concerning the approval of major technical installations—to reach a final decision in a subject area so complex that it is bound to tax the ability of even the most knowledgeable appeal body.[36]

The differences in the views on the desirability and scope of administrative freedom that were hinted at above can be traced back to the constitutional outline of a legal system. More specifically, the rationale for divergence can be found in the position of the judiciary vis-à-vis the other authorities within a legal system. Where the judiciary is assertive, the scope for discretion left to agents is accordingly small. In systems where the judge is more swiftly and easily inclined to annul an administrative decision; where he/she rigorously checks—and is often prepared to overrule—decisions made by lower courts; and where he/she is committed to scrutinizing closely pieces of legislation for their constitutionality, the general bandwidth of discretion is more strictly circumscribed than in a system that principally distrusts in-depth and presumed-intrusive judicial review. This point is also made, with regard to administrative discretion, by Jürgen Schwarze, who remarks 'that discretion is not merely a question of administrative practice, but in essence touches on a matter of principle, namely the inter-relationship which prevails among state-authorities'.[37] According to Schwarze, this also means that any possibilities for and efforts towards further approximation are clearly limited for '[i]t is to be expected that the constitutional separation and balance of powers among the Parliament, the administration and the courts, which in some cases has taken centuries to develop and which has contributed to the various theories of discretion, will prove resistant to change and will hamper efforts to achieve convergence among the various administrative law rules'.[38]

3.2 *Related conceptual divergence: public policy and public order*

Above, I described some *direct and immediate* links between discretion and conceptual divergence. Next to that, there are also divergent instantiations of discretion to be found in concepts *related* to discretion.[39] In this respect one can think of key terms such as 'public order' or 'public policy', vaguely formulated concepts that leave decision-making authorities a broad margin

---

[36] Schwarze, see n 10 above, 276.
[37] ibid, 294.
[38] ibid, 294–295.
[39] Van Roermund, see n 17 above, 8.

of discretion. These notions are very important, for in the cases where they are found to be present, the national and supra-national authorities can claim a wide range of powers.[40] Often, they provide a justification for 'deviating' from the law. Examples include the possibility offered in EC Treaty, Article 30 of derogating from the free movement of goods for reasons of 'public morality, public policy or public security [. . .]', and the possibility of invoking 'public order' as a means of restricting fundamental rights embodied in national constitutions[41] and the ECHR.[42]

It is interesting to explore the way in which the ECJ deals with these concepts. In Case 41/74 *Yvonne Van Duyn v Home Office*, the ECJ adopts a rather ambiguous stance, stating that

The concept of public policy in the context of the community and where, in particular, it is used as a justification for derogating from a fundamental principle of community law, must be interpreted *strictly*, so that its scope cannot be determined unilaterally by each Member State without being subject to control by the institutions of the Community. Nevertheless, the particular circumstances justifying recourse to the concept of public policy may **vary from one country to another and from one period to another**, and it is therefore necessary in this matter to allow the competent national authorities *an area of discretion* within the limits imposed by the Treaty.[43]

A unilateral determination of the scope of public policy is thus out of the question and must be controlled by Community institutions, but at the same time this does not prevent the Court from saying that temporal and spatial differences can mould the concept of public policy in many different ways, giving national authorities a considerable margin of discretion in the matter.

---

[40] ibid, 14.

[41] Eg, the Dutch Constitution, Art 8: 'The right of association shall be recognised. This right may be restricted by Act of Parliament *in the interest of public order*'; or Art 13 of the German Constitution, safeguarding the inviolability of the home, which states in its restriction clause para 7 that 'Eingriffe und Beschränkungen dürfen im übrigen nur zur Abwehr einer gemeinen Gefahr oder einer Lebensgefahr für einzelne Personen, auf Grund eines Gesetzes auch zur Verhütung dringender Gefahren für die *öffentliche Sicherheit und Ordnung* [. . .]'.

[42] Eg, Art 9(2) (ECHR): 'Freedom to manifest one's religion or beliefs shall be subject only to such limitations as are prescribed by law and are necessary in a democratic society in the interests of public safety, *for the protection of public order*, health or morals, or for the protection of the rights and freedoms of others.'

[43] Case 41/74, Yvonne van Duyn v Home Office, [1974] ECR 1337, cons. 18. Emphasis added.

In Case 36–75 *Rutili v Minister for the Interior*, the Court inverts its formulation by first stating that 'by virtue of the reservation contained in Article 48(3) [presently 39(3) EC Treaty], Member States continue to be, in principle, *free to determine the requirements of public policy in the light of their national needs*' (para 26, my emphasis), after which the Court repeats the reservation as regards national unilateral determination made in *Van Duyn*. A further attempt to put some flesh on the conceptual bones of 'public policy' is then made in Case 30/77 *Regina v Pierre Bouchereau*, in which it is added that,

in so far as it may justify certain restrictions on the free movement of persons subject to community law, recourse by a national authority to the concept of public policy presupposes, in any event, the existence, in addition to the perturbation of the social order which any infringement of the law involves, of *a genuine and sufficiently serious threat to the requirements of public policy affecting one of the fundamental interests of society*.[44]

This is a circular reasoning in which the Court in effect is saying that 'restrictions from public policy only hold if and when requirements of public policy seriously matter'.[45]

Public policy, seen from both the European and the national angle, is a 'boundary concept'[46] that is inversely proportional. Where the European Court of Justice is controlling the sphere of national public policy by sanctioning or rejecting national invocations of public policy, it is at the same time shaping, ie reducing or enlarging respectively, *European* public policy. The ECJ in this respect is adopting a careful approach that gives itself, as well as the Member States, considerable leeway. It does not go much further than the trivial statement that public policy is spatio-temporally determined, making the notions of national and European public policy discretionary concepts *par excellence*. Moreover, the Court does not give any concrete substantiation of European public policy, contenting itself with its circular reasoning in *Bouchereau* and with its statement in the case of *Jany* that 'Community law does not impose on Member States a uniform scale of values as regards the assessment of conduct which may be considered to

---

[44] Case 30/77, Regina v Pierre Bouchereau, [1977] ECR 1999, para. 35. Emphasis added. This formulation was repeated in, eg, Joined Cases 115/81 and 116/81 *Adoui and Cornuaille* [1982] ECR 1665 (in which the Court, more sensibly I would hold, spoke merely of 'a genuine and sufficiently serious threat affecting one of the fundamental interests of society', para 8) and Case C-348/96 *Calfa* [1999] ECR I-11.

[45] Van Roermund, see n 17 above, 14.

[46] Lindahl, see n 6 above.

be contrary to public policy'.[47] This situation is, however, far from strange since it is by definition impossible to turn a *discretionary* concept like 'public policy' or 'public order' into a tightly and clearly circumscribed notion that is subject to strict supervisory control by the ECJ (though a German lawyer might disagree here). On the other hand, it cannot be claimed that 'public policy' is left completely anchorless, for certain guidelines in the Court's treatment of public policy can certainly be discerned.[48]

Finally, what is noticeable is that the ECJ—in a way similar to the terminological confusion with regard to discretion referred to above – in some cases seems to make little distinction between the notions of 'public order' and 'public policy'.[49] Nevertheless, some claim that, at least within the context of the ECHR, the two notions most certainly have a different meaning, in the sense that the term 'public policy' (considered equivalent to the French *ordre public*) is significantly broader than the notion of 'public order'.[50] Any such difference should, again, not be overstated however.

In conclusion it can be stated that the vital concepts of 'public policy' and 'public order' are truly discretionary concepts that quite easily allow for national divergences in application. The ECJ—as final arbiter in determining what is to be understood with European and thus national 'public

---

[47] Case C-268/99 *Jany* [2001] ECR I-8615, para 60.

[48] Eg, to give the complete quotation from para 60 of Case C-268/99 *Jany* [2001] ECR I-8615: 'Although Community law does not impose on Member States a uniform scale of values as regards the assessment of conduct which may be considered to be contrary to public policy, conduct may not be considered to be of a sufficiently serious nature to justify restrictions on entry to, or residence within, the territory of a Member State of a national of another Member State where the former Member State does not adopt, with respect to the same conduct on the part of its own nationals, repressive measures or other genuine and effective measures intended to combat such conduct.'

[49] In Case C-268/99 *Jany* [2001] ECR I-8615, eg, the English text of the case refers in para 61 'to public order within the context of the Association Agreement between the Communities and Poland and that between the Communities and the Czech Republic'. One sentence later, it refers to 'public policy' again, implying that both concepts are considered as being one and the same. Oddly enough, the Association Agreements do not mention the term 'public order' once, but merely refer to 'public policy'. Another two examples include Case C-405/01 *Marina Mercante Española* [2003] ECR I-10391, para 36 and Case C-463/00 *Commission v Spain* [2003] ECR I-04581, para 34, where the Commission in its submission before the Court in both cases refers to the notion of 'public order' as a justification for, respectively, the freedom of movement for workers and the free movement of capital/freedom of establishment, whereas the TEC instead refers to 'public policy'.

[50] AMF Loof-Donker, EM Peeters, and PH Van der Tang-Van Loenen, 'De openbare orde: een te nemen horde? Kanttekeningen bij de wijze waarop de Nederlandse wetgever omgaat met het begrip 'openbare orde' als doelcriterium voor de beperking van grond- en mensenrechten' (1994) 19 NJCM-bulletin, 503.

policy' or 'public order'—has not posited any clear guidelines on the matter (nor can it realistically do so), thus reserving for itself as well as for the Member States a wide margin of discretion in an important area where power is at stake.

4 Divergence and unity

Most importantly for the hypothesis of the project, research could be done on the question as to whether discretion can be conceived as *a concept that may, in certain circumstances, trigger or maintain the existence of divergence in order to uphold the unity of a legal system.* This question is of course particularly apposite in a system that is composed of widely diverging places and value systems, like the EU. One is also naturally inclined to affirm the connection between divergence and unity, since the EU legal order is centred around divergence (enhanced co-operation, a Europe of multiple speeds, consistent calls for a centre of gravity or *avant garde*, etc). Although those forms of divergence are different from the conceptual divergence that is the object of our inquiry, the two are, I believe, closely connected.

In this respect, discretion can take a prominent place as a concept intimately connected with divergence that provides the freedom to follow alternative routes within a bound framework. In other words, discretion can give the necessary *room* to *existing* divergences within the EU system, for example with regard to the invocation of the concept of 'public policy'. As Hans Lindahl indicates in his paper,[51] divergent circumstances are not only the *precondition* of discretion, they can also be the very *result* of discretion. After all, judicial control of discretion is discretion itself. Divergence is not a priori given fact but may also be generated by setting the limits to discretion.

It should be pointed out that on some fronts the likely existence of discretion on the part of the Member States is foreclosed by a strict Community judicature. For instance, in the field of liability, which is closely linked with discretion, the ECJ could be considered to employ a double standard, in the sense that it is 'more ready to cry discretion' when liability claims are brought against Community institutions than when they are made against the Member States, where it adopts a more stern attitude. It has even been argued that this double standard reaches beyond liability law alone and is

---

[51] See n 6 above.

part and parcel of a wider judicial attitude that accredits little discretion to the Member States.[52]

On the other hand however, the Court of Justice—as an institution that should always have the unity of the European legal system in mind—is certainly generously willing to grant ample room for discretionary freedom to Member States in certain areas. Looking at the *Koebler* case, for example, here the ECJ sets extensive boundaries for national judicial discretion thus opening up the possibility of national divergence. It seems realistic to assume that it did so *inter alia* to safeguard the unity of the EU legal system, preventing uneasy tensions between itself and the national judiciary. A clearer example is the *Grogan* case.[53] The ECJ, using its judicial discretion, grants Ireland a certain margin of discretion in order to protect its constitutional system which recognizes the right to life of the unborn. (Note however that it is not the ECJ but Advocate General van Gerven who speaks about 'public policy' in this case.) Community law retreats on this point for the benefit of national constitutional integrity so as not to intrude too much on the Member States' legal systems and preventing the revolt of a Member State that could jeopardize the EU's unity. Following the distinction between *uniformity* and *unity*, it could be held that the *uniformity* of EU law is not a sacred value. EU law is not being enforced *coute que coute* and its 'uniformity' is 'sacrificed' in the interests of divergence and, ultimately, unity.

Discretion is thus a concept that relates strongly to divergence, subsidiarity, and decentralization. It could therefore be held that the granting of discretion from above by the ECJ often involves the *sustenance* as well as the *creation* of divergence, in many cases for the sake of upholding the unity of the EU system. Obviously, this is not strictly *conceptual* divergence rather it is divergence (or diversity) in the more general sense.

---

[52] R Caranta, 'On Discretion', presented at the BUDC conference, Tilburg University, 2004. cf this volume, ch 8.

[53] Case C-159/90 [1991] ECR I-4685.

10

Divergence and the *Francovich* Remedy in German and English Courts

Martina Künnecke

1 Introduction

The entanglement of national and supranational legal systems is a phenomenon which requires the management of diversity. The *Francovich* doctrine is a prime example of this complex relationship.

In *Brasserie du Pécheur SA v Germany* the European Court of Justice set out the conditions for a Member State's liability: there had to be a sufficiently serious breach of a rule intended to confer rights on individuals, and a direct causal link between breach and damage.[1] The criteria for determining the extent of reparation in the realization of the *Francovich* remedy are set by national courts, provided that national rules for the evaluation of damages comply with the familiar principles of equivalence and effectiveness. This means that national courts have a double function: they are asked to apply the Community criteria and, as far as other aspects of liability are concerned, they have to handle the case under their national law. However, entrusting national legal systems with this task involves risking 'national reflexes of legislators and judges in the Member States'.[2] It has been stated that 'the application of national law bears the risk of diverging decisions' in this area

---

[1] Joined Cases C-46/93 and C-48/93 *Brasserie and Factortame* [1996] ECR I-1029, para 51.

[2] W van Gerven, 'The Emergence of a Common European Law in the Area of Tort Law: the EU Contribution' in D Fairgrieve, M Andenas, and J Bell, *Tort Liability of Public Authorities in Comparative Perspective* (London: British Institute of International and Comparative Law, 2002) 128.

of law[3] and that the diversity of legal cultures and legal mentalities sets limitations to a uniform approach.[4] It has been argued that 'there are indeed considerable differences in style between the European legal systems'.[5] In their chapter Pierre Larouche and Filomena Chirico discuss potential difficulties in the tackling of divergence through harmonization. They state that the legal system can treat the 'harmonized' area as a form of foreign body (*Fremdkörper*) and seek to isolate it.[6] This isolation of a harmonized area of law may lead to odd results where national and EU law are applied alongside each other. In an attempt to sanction the European Court of Justice (ECJ) and the principle of Member State liability it has been argued that 'there is a temporarily more successful option, that of inaction at national level'.[7]

Despite guidance provided for the ECJ and academic commentators, references to the ECJ concerning the liability of Member States for breaches of Community law provide evidence of uncertainty over the application of the condition in the Member States.[8] Uncertainties exist as to the legal nature of the remedy which, it is argued, may leave scope for the isolation of the remedy within national legal systems. Further, this chapter assesses that even within Member States the courts have taken different views on the application of the criterion of a 'sufficiently serious' breach. In addition, the interlocking of Member State liability and domestic tort remedies against public authorities for potential breaches of Community law appears to vary across the Member States. This grey zone may lead to divergence in the approaches of Member States. An assessment of decisions taken by all Member State courts would be an even more interesting though difficult undertaking. However, many cases in the lower courts are not reported and linguistic limitations hinder such a project.[9]

This chapter assesses to what extent the common law system differs from a codified system in the application of the *Francovich* principle and to what

---

[3] W Wurmnest, *Grundzüge eines europäischen Haftungsrechts* (Tübingen: Mohr, 2003) 55.

[4] W van Gerven, 'Bringing (Private) Laws Closer to Each Other at European Level', January 2005, <http://www.law.kuleuven.ac.be/ccle/staff_pub.php>, 4.

[5] ibid.

[6] Larouche and Chirico, this volume, ch 20, p 468.

[7] L Talberg, 'Supranational Influence in EU Enforcement: The ECJ and the Principle of State Liability' (2000) 7 *J of Eur Public Policy*, 117.

[8] See, for instance, Case C-63/01 *Evans* [2003] ECR I-4447 and Case C-160/01 *Mau* [2003] ECR I-4791.

[9] A Barav, 'State Liability in Damages for Breach of Community Law in the National Courts' in T Heukels and A McDonnell, *The Action for Damages in Community Law* (The Hague: Kluwer, 1997) 376.

extent this results in divergence. The chapter concentrates on a comparison of the English and German law of state liability. Since the rulings in *Factortame* and *Brasserie*, between 1996 and 2006 there has only been a modest number of decisions in England[10] and Germany.[11] The reputation of the German Federal High Court (BGH, *Bundesgerichtshof*) with regard to the application of Member State liability had been shaped by its ruling following the ECJ judgment in *Brasserie du Pecheur*. The court held that no liability had arisen as the prohibition on the designation *Bier*, which was a sufficiently serious breach, had not caused damage. In respect of this provision no proceedings had been taken by the German authorities.[12]

2 Defining the remedy

2.1 *Germany*

The *Francovich* decision initiated significant discussion among German academic commentators over the nature of the new remedy for breaches of Community law. The majority view follows the *Bundesgerichtshof* (BGH), the highest court in civil matters, in asserting that Member State liability is a *sui generis* remedy. The majority view argues that it is a Community law remedy

---

[10] *Bowden v South West Water and another* [1998] 3 CMLR 330; *R v Ministry of Agriculture, Fisheries and Food, ex p Lay and Gage* [1998] COD 387; *Boyd Line Management Services Ltd v Ministry of Agriculture, Fisheries & Food* [1999] EWCA Civ 1129 (30 March 1999); *R v Department of Social Security, ex p Scullion* [1999] 3 CMLR 798; COD 345–426; *Matra Communication SAS v Home Office* [1999] 1 CMLR 1454; *Nabadda and others v City of Westminster and others* [2001] 3 CMLR 39; *HJ Banks & Co Ltd v The Coal Authority, The Secretary of State* [2002] CMLR 54; *Betws Anthracite Ltd v DSK Anthrazit Ibbenburen GmbH* [2004] 1 CMLR 12; *Bavarian Lager v Department of Trade and Industry* [2002] UK Competition L Rep 160; *Phonographic Performance* [2004] 3 CMLR 31; and *Alderson v Secretary of State for Trade and Industry* [2004] 1 All ER 1148.

[11] LG Bonn, 6 September 1999, 1 O 221/98 ZIP 1999, 1592; LG Bonn, 16 April 1999, Az: 1 O 186/98; LG Bonn, 25 October 1999, Az: 1 O 173/98; OLG Köln, 15 July 1997, Az: 7 U 23/97; OLG Köln, 26 November 1998, Az: 7 U 55/96; OLG Köln, 25 May 2000, Az: U 178/99; LG Hamburg, 6 August 1999, Az: 303 O 48/99; OLG Karlsruhe, 15 April 1999, Az: 12 U 273/98; LG Berlin, 9 April 2001, Az: 230650/00; BGH, 14 December 2000, Az: III ZR 151/99; BGH, 9 October 2003, Az: III ZR 342/02; BGH, 28 October 2004, Az: III ZR 294/03; BGH, 2 December 2004, Az: III ZR 151/99; and BGH, 20 January 2005, Az: III ZR 48/01.

[12] BGHZ 134, 30; *Brasserie du Pêcheur v Germany* [1997] 1 CMLR 971; BGH, 24 November 2005, III ZR 4/05; and for a case comment in English, see E Deards, 'Brasserie du Pêcheur: Snatching Defeat from the Jaws of Victory' (1997) 22 ELR, 620.

which is separate from other national remedies for governmental liability.[13] The codified national law (Article 34 Basic Law in connection with Section 839 BGB) is perceived as inappropriate to accommodate the Community law remedy. Therefore, the separation is more appropriate than a new remedy in national law.[14] On the other hand, the minority view argues that the basis for the remedy is founded entirely on national law.[15] These differences in approach are sometimes perceived as being of merely academic interest.[16] However, this section aims to show that the separation of national tort law from a European remedy fails to achieve the Europeanization of German tort law in this area. In some cases this may lead to a degree of undesirable divergence in the application of the European remedy.[17]

A decision by the BGH illustrates this point.[18] The case was concerned with damage which occurred due to the levy of inspection fees on meat products. Even though the fees had actually been incurred during the inspection,

[13] I Saenger, 'Staatshaftung wegen Verletzung europäischen Gemeinschaftrechts' (1997) 37 Juristische Schulung, 869; S Detterbeck, 'Staatshaftung für die Missachtung von EG-Recht' (1994) 85 *Verwaltungsarchiv*, 185; A Hatje, 'Die Haftung der Mitgliedstaaten bei Verstößen des Gesetzgebers gegen europäisches Gemeinschaftsrecht' (1997) 32 Europarecht, 303; F Ossenbühl, 'Staatshaftung zwischen Europarecht und nationalem Recht' (1995) 2 *Festschrift für Everling*, 1037; T von Dannwitz, 'Die gemeinschaftsrechtliche Staatshaftung der Mitgliedstaaten' (1997) 112 Deutsches Verwaltungsblatt, 6; and J W Hidien, *Die gemeinschaftsrechtliche Staatshaftung der EU-Mitgliedstaaten* (Baden-Baden: Nomos, 1999) 37ff.

[14] HG Fischer, 'Die gemeinschaftsrechtliche Staatshaftung' (2000) 32 Juristische Arbeitsblätter, 352.

[15] M Herdegen and T Rensmann, 'Die neuen Konturen der gemeinschaftsrechtlichen Staatshaftung' (1997) 161 Zeitschrift für das gesamte Handelsrecht und Wirtschaftsrecht, 551; R Streinz, 'Staatshaftung für Verletzungen primären Gemeinschaftsrechts durch die Bundesrepublik Deutschland' (1993) 4 Europäische Zeitschrift für Wirtschaftsrecht, 599; H Maurer, 'Staatshaftung im europäischen Kontext' (1996) *Festschrift für Karlheinz Boujong*, 597; HD Jarass, 'Haftung für die Verletzung von EU-Recht durch nationale Organe und Amtsträger' (1994) 47 Neue Juristische Wochenschrift, 882; D Ehlers, 'Die Weiterentwicklung des Staatshaftungsrechts durch das europäische Gemeinschaftsrecht' (1996) 51 Juristenzeitung, 778; M Nettesheim, 'Gemeinschaftsrechtliche Vorgaben für das deutsche Staatshaftungsrecht' (1992) Die öffentliche Verwaltung, 1000; C Henrichs, *Haftung der EG-Mitgliedstaaten für Verletzung von Gemeinschaftsrecht* (Baden-Baden: Nomos, 1995) 140; J Geiger, 'Die Entwicklung des europäischen Staatshaftungsrechts' (1993) Deutsches Verwaltungsblatt, 471; R Wittkowski, 'Der "MP Travel Line"—Konkurs im Lichte der Francovich- Rechtsprechung des EuGH' (1994) Neue Zeitschrift für Verwaltungsrecht, 326ff; S Kopp, 'Staatshaftung wegen Verletzung von Gemeinschaftsrecht' (1994) Die öffentliche Verwaltung, 205; and D Classen, 'Anmerkung zum Urteil des BGH vom 14.12.2000' (2001) Juristenzeitung, 459.

[16] HJ Wolff, O Bachof, and R Stober, *Verwaltungsrecht*, Vol 2 (6th edn, München: Beck, 2000) 581.

[17] See Wurmnest, see n 3 above; F Schoch, 'Staatshaftung wegen Verstoßes gegen Europäisches Gemeinschaftsrecht' (2002) 24 Juristische Ausbildung, 840.

[18] BGHZ 146, 153.

they were higher than the basic rate stipulated in Directive (EEC)85/37 and the corresponding Council decision. The German law on hygiene of meat (*Fleischhygienegesetz*) had stipulated that it was within the competence of the federal states to pass legislation for the levy of higher fees for inspections under certain circumstances. However, no such law had been passed in the case in question. The claimant had to take out a loan to finance the fees and claimed he had suffered a loss of DM85,000. He claimed that the levy was in breach of domestic and EU law. The claimant was successful in the lower and higher civil courts, but failed in the BGH.

Rights in Community law and the German requirement

In the above-mentioned case the court based its reasoning on two separate heads of tort, namely EC and national law based, and denied a claim in damages for both remedies. As to the claim based on Community law, the court argued that the separate head of Member State liability is not fulfilled as the Directive and the Council decision in themselves were not designed to confer a right on the individual. According to the Directive, the federal states were entitled to deviate from the basic rates through legislation. On the other hand, it denied the existence of individual rights under the Community remedy because the claimant had no right to expect lower fees. This approach is questionable because the BGH ignores the decision by the ECJ, which held that the decision of the Council (Article 2 I (EEC) 88/408) could be relied on by individuals wishing to challenge higher fees.[19] Despite this, the BGH decided that due to the lack of the breach of a Community right, the claim based on *Francovich* should fail.

As to the claim based on national law, it should be pointed out that Section 839 of the Civil Code and Article 34 of the Basic Law require that the official duty must be owed to *a third party*. Whether a person is a third party in this sense depends on whether the object of the duty is directly to safeguard the interests of that person. If for instance a policeman remains inactive while a theft is being committed, he is in breach of his official duty towards the owner because his power to interfere is conferred on him not merely in the interest of the general public, but at the same time in the interest of each single individual. In each case it has to be decided whether according to the object and the legal provisions of the official task the affected interests should have been protected. Three conditions have to be met in order to establish a duty towards a third party. First, the official duty must be capable

---

[19] Case C-156/91 *Mundt* [1992] ECR I-5567.

of protecting individuals; second, the plaintiff has to belong to the protected group of people; and, third, the damage must be included in the protective effect of the duty.[20] The establishment of such a duty owed to a third party is extremely difficult. The determination of which duties are capable of protecting third-party effects is left to the courts and the decision on this issue is crucial for the success or failure of an action. The fact that Section 839 of the Civil Code does not spell out official duties which confer rights on individuals illustrates that the courts are given some leeway as to how to interpret the concept of duty.

The BGH did not modify the German governmental liability remedy to comply with the conditions set out by the ECJ. Rather, it opted for an 'artificial' separation of Member States' liability and a second review under the stricter, purely domestic conditions of Article 34 of the Basic Law in connection with Section 839 of the Civil Code.

In applying the German law of tort, the court came to the conclusion that the duty towards a third party according to Section 839 of the Civil Code was violated. The domestic tort provision in German law, therefore, proved to be easier to establish. This divergence between the application of the *Francovich* criteria and a claim under domestic law causes concern. In BGHZ 146, 153 the court had no difficulty in holding that such a duty was owed toward the claimants. It is not clear at all how the BGH reached this decision. It denied the applicant the right in the context of the Community remedy, but held that in the context of the domestic remedy, a duty was owed for the protection of a third party. The claim ultimately failed under domestic law because the required fault element was not fulfilled.

The fault requirement in German tort law

Unlike the condition of 'sufficiently serious breach', the German head of tort requires that the official be at fault whilst in breach of his or her official duty. Article 34 of the Basic Law and Section 839 of the Civil Code do not contain a catalogue of official duties. Official duties may stem from any legal source. In the courts the requirement of official duty has been interpreted very liberally. Examples are the duty to act lawfully, as contained in Article 20 of the Basic Law, and the duty to exercise discretionary powers. The review of discretionary powers was originally limited to extreme cases of arbitrary exercise of the discretion. 'The *Reichsgericht* constantly held that the courts should not interfere with discretionary power. The courts could only decide

---

[20] F Ossenbühl, *Staatshaftungsrecht* (5th edn, München: Beck, 1998) 58.

in cases where the public body acted outside the ambit of its discretionary power.'[21] However, the control of the exercise of discretionary powers has been extended by the highest court in civil matters so that it now includes the failure to exercise discretionary powers, excessive use of discretionary powers, or incorrect exercise of discretionary powers parallel to the grounds of review in the review of an administrative act. A discretionary decision may thus be reviewed by a court in an incorrect public case even if it is within the ambit of discretion. However, the court will not go into the question as to whether the decision taken by the public body was 'right' (*Richtigkeitsprüfung*) but will consider only whether the decision seems plausible (*vertretbar*). The test for plausibility allows far more control than was sanctioned in the past, but it still does not mean that the court is substituting its own judgment for that of the administrative authority.[22]

The courts review the erroneous use of discretion (*Ermessensfehlgebrauch*), the excessive use of the exercise of discretion (*Ermessensüberschreitung*), and the omission of the use of discretion (*Ermessensnichtgebrauch*).[23] The landmark case is the decision of the BGH in 1979, when it found a breach of an official duty in the course of the exercise of a discretionary power even though the breach did not amount to an obvious level of abuse.[24] There is a clear trend towards a quasi strict governmental liability.[25] In this light BGHZ 146, 153 appears even more artificial and unconvincing as it emphasizes the fault requirement under national law.

The dualistic concept of governmental liability, ie the separation of the European remedy from the application of the domestic head of tort, led in this case to the denial of liability due to the application of the fault principle, a condition which features in a much weaker form within the condition of 'sufficiently serious breach'.[26] Moreover, it is not clear at all how the BGH came to the conclusion that the applicant had no rights under Community law standards so that the claim based on EC law failed at an early stage. On the other hand, the court was willing to proceed with the claim under purely German law and held that an official duty was owed to the claimant.

---

[21] ibid, 45.
[22] ibid, 63.
[23] ibid, 46.
[24] BGHZ 74, 156.
[25] See G Brüggemeier, 'From Individual Tort for Civil Servants to Quasi-strict Liability of the State: Governmental or State Liability in Germany' in Fairgrieve, Andenas, and Bell, see n 2 above, 571.
[26] Schoch, see n 17 above, 840.

However, as explained above, the fault requirement under German law was the stumbling block. The BGH therefore reduced the scope of protection under European law, and this may not be in line with the principle of equivalence. The European Court has repeatedly held that the protection of European rights, if left to national law, should not be less favourable than the protection of purely domestic rights.

The arguments for a Europeanization of the national remedy rather than the artificial separation of national and European law are threefold. First, the lack of legislative competence in the field of governmental liability does not permit the creation of an entirely new legal remedy. Second, the ECJ was entitled to give guidance on how to modify existing national governmental tort law. Third, the principle of indirect administration of Community law requires the application of national law. Accordingly, modified national law is applicable to breaches of Community law through national authorities.[27] It has been argued that the BGH merely paid lip-service to the Community law remedy and then denied the claim on the grounds that the provision which was allegedly breached gave no rise to individual rights. At the same time the BGH ruled, however, that there existed an official duty which also protected the interests of the claimant under German law. Further, the BGH declined to refer to the ECJ the question of whether the claimant had a protected right under EC law. This can be seen as a violation of the principle of lawful judge under Article 101 I 2 of the Basic Law.[28]

So far, the approach of the German court has not changed. In another case in December 2004, the BGH held that the Federal Republic of Germany was not liable because of to the domestic provision concerning the competences of national authorities. It held that the *See-Berufsgenossenschaft* was liable under German law. Liability under the European remedy was not assessed in full. Again, it applied rigid separation between European law and domestic law.[29]

The consequences of this approach are not easily verified. However, in BGHZ 146, 153 a more convincing result might have been induced at an earlier stage. Instead, the claimant remained largely unsuccessful. The case was finally settled in October 2004 with the claimant agreeing to pay €35,000 to the defendant authority, having gone back and forth several times.[30]

---

[27] ibid.
[28] ibid, 841.
[29] BGH, 2 December 2004, III ZR 358/03.
[30] OLG Karlsruhe, 7 October 2004, 145 I B 1397/05.

2.2 *United Kingdom*

It is now well established in English case law that the liability for breach of
Community law is to be understood as a breach of statutory duty. This had
also been considered in the *Factortame (No 5)* decision.[31] Lord Hobhouse
relied on previous case law, ie *Garden Cottage Foods*[32] and *Bourgoin v MAFF,*[33]
and held that the duty was imposed by way of the European Communities
Act 1972. The recent decision in *Phonographic Performance Ltd v Department
of Trade and Industry,*[34] which was concerned with the alleged incorrect transposition of the Rental Rights and Related Copyrights and Related Rights in
the Information Society Directive (2001/29) confirms this. The court made
important statements as to the nature of the claim. It held that a claim in
damages for breach of Community law 'gives rise to a correlative right in one
who has suffered such damages' and that 'such a right is not discretionary'.[35]
The Crown had argued that the cause of action is *sui generis* which as a result
'ought to be pursued in a public law claim' in proceedings for judicial review.
Such a procedure 'will enable the court to exercise control over the claims
and the periods for which they may be pursued'. The Crown argued that in
this case the court should strike out the claim as an abuse of process. The
court held that this interpretation of the nature of the claim would be 'to
subject the rights of an individual to discretion and a time limit much more
restrictive than those normally appropriate to a private law claim for breach
of statutory duty and would itself constitute a breach of Community law'.[36]

Despite the fact that the courts have ruled that the European remedy
should be considered a breach of statutory duty it is still not clear whether
the term is used in a wide non-technical sense or whether it refers to the traditional tort. More recently it has been argued that 'the Euro tort is simply to
be classified as a tort in domestic proceedings and the repeated references to
breach of statutory duty are a redundancy'.[37] The creation of torts such as
the Euro tort as a breach of statutory duty has been described as 'obscure'.[38]
There is little academic discussion on the precise meaning of the breach of

---

[31] *R v Secretary of State for Transport, ex p Factortame* [1998] 1 CMLR 1353.
[32] *Garden Cottage Foods Ltd v Milk Marketing Board* [1984] AC 130.
[33] *Bourgoin v MAFF* [1986] QB 716.
[34] *Phonographic Performance* [2004] 3 CMLR 31.
[35] ibid, para 47.
[36] ibid, para 50.
[37] K M Stanton, 'New Forms of the Tort of Breach of Statutory Duty' (2004) 120 LQR, 329.
[38] Stanton, see n 37 above, 340.

statutory duty in this context.[39] It is not irrelevant though. With a view to the recovery of pure economic loss the distinction is crucial: the traditional breach of statutory duty allows such a recovery more liberally, the tort of negligence does not.[40] A separation of domestic law and a free standing cause of action in Community law as seen in German cases do not feature in the English decisions. In conclusion, the more flexible British approach may be more prepared to accommodate the European remedy in its domestic system of torts and provide an effective protection of Community law rights. The avoidance of founding a claim on Member State liability can also be witnessed in English courts. In the case of *Nabadda*[41] the claimants, Swedish students in the UK, sued for damages because they had been denied a full grant from a local authority towards their education. The claimants founded their claim on the entitlement to damages under the Race Relations Act 1976 and argued that it should be disapplied in part as it contravened Community law. To avoid the condition of sufficiently serious breach, which in this case was harder to prove, the claim was not based on the European court's case law on Member State liability.[42] However, this case differs from the approach the BGH took. The applicants were of course under no obligation to base their claim on *Francovich* principles if another legal basis would be more likely to produce a liability. However, their claim was unsuccessful.

3 National courts and the condition of 'sufficiently serious breach'

The ECJ's ruling that it is within the Members States' courts' competence to apply the criterion of a 'sufficiently serious breach' to establish Member State liability has empowered domestic courts to take difficult policy decisions. The ECJ clarified that the condition was met if 'there was a manifest and grave disregard by the Member State of its discretion'.[43]

---

[39] See, however, P Craig, 'The Domestic Liability of Public Authorities in Damages, Lessons from the European Community?' in J Beatson and T Tridimas (eds), *New Directions in European Public Law* (Oxford: Hart, 1998) and M Hoskins, 'The Rebirth of the Innominate Tort' in Beatson and Tridimas, see above, chs 6 and 7.

[40] ibid, 341.

[41] *Nabadda and others v City of Westminster and others* [2001] 3 CMLR 39.

[42] ibid, para 8.

[43] Joined Cases C-46/93 and C-48/93 *Brasserie and Factortame* [1996] ECR I-1029.

Despite this clarification of the condition, there is a potential for divergent approaches in the Member State courts on the interpretation of 'discretion' and how it should be reviewed. Discretion in this context is not to be understood in the strict technical and complex sense as developed in German administrative law.[44] Discretion is to be understood in a wider sense than that, including margins of appreciation by the deciding bodies, which may not be based on legislative provisions granting such discretion. The precision and clarity of a rule breached becomes a guiding tool.

As is well known according to the case law of the Court, a breach is sufficiently serious when, in the exercise of its legislative powers, an institution or a Member State has manifestly and gravely disregarded the limits on the exercise of its powers:

The factors which the competent court may take into account include the clarity and precision of the rule breached, the measure of discretion left by that rule to the national or Community authorities, whether the infringement and the damage caused was intentional or involuntary, whether any error of law was excusable or inexcusable, the fact that the position taken by a Community institution may have contributed towards the omission and the adoption or retention of national measures or practices contrary to Community law.[45]

Establishing that the breach is serious requires the application of a test which is concerned with 'discretion, good faith, reasonableness and the behaviour of related actors, namely the Commission and other Member States'.[46] The Court further decided that 'where the Member State or the institution in question has only considerably reduced, or even no, discretion the mere infringement of Community law may be sufficient to establish the existence of a sufficiently serious breach'.[47] In other words, the *Brasserie* criteria apply in discretion and non-discretion cases alike.[48] It has been remarked that there is a 'strange circularity to such an approach'.[49]

According to the case law this enquiry is one for the national Member States' courts. The ECJ has shown a less interventionist approach in more recent decisions. It has taken commentators by surprise that the Court of

---

[44] Ossenbühl, see n 20 above, 507.

[45] Joined Cases C-46/93 and C-48/93 *Brasserie and Factortame* [1996] ECR I-1029, para 56.

[46] T Tridimas, 'Liability for Breaches of Community Law, Growing Up or Mellowing Down?' in Fairgrieve, Andenas, and Bell, see n 2 above, 150.

[47] Case C-352/98 P *Bergaderm* [2000] ECR I-5291, para 44.

[48] See Case C-118/00 *Larsy* [2001] ECR I-5063.

[49] C Hilson, 'The Role of Discretion in EC Law on Non-contractual Liability' (2005) 42 CML Rev, 681.

Justice has not provided any further guidance on the seriousness of the breach.[50] The reason for this may have been the interconnection with domestic law. The Court made it clear that

> The discretion . . . is that enjoyed by the Member State concerned. Its existence and its scope are determined by reference to Community law and not by reference to national law. The discretion which may be conferred by national law on the official or the institution responsible for the breach of Community law is therefore irrelevant in this respect.[51]

3.1 *German courts*

A decision by the Berlin *Landgericht* in April 2001 has been cause for concern as regards the application of the requirement of sufficiently serious breach.[52] This decision reflects insecurity in applying Member State liability. The decision concerned the incorrect transposition of Directives (EEC) 68/151 and 78/660 into Section 335 of the German Commercial Code (*Handelsgesetzbuch* 1985) on the co-ordination of safeguards. The safeguards are required by Member States of companies (within the meaning of the second paragraph of Article 58 of the Treaty), in order to protect the interests of members of the company and others, and also with a view to making such safeguards equivalent throughout the Community. The facts of the case are complicated. In the course of proceedings related to the return of property under the German property claims law (*Vermögensgesetz*), the claimant sought disclosure of the balance sheet and profit and loss account of the defendant, a limited company (*B-GmbH*). Reunification of East and West Germany has created the possibility of filing restitution or compensation claims for property in Germany which was expropriated by the Nazi government during the Second World War and by the East German government after 1949. The claimants argued that Section 335 of the German Commercial Code incorrectly transposed Article 6 of the first Directive which requires Member States to provide for appropriate penalties in the case of a failure to disclose the balance sheet and profit and loss account as required by Article 2(1)(f). The German court decided that the failure to interpret the Directive correctly was based on an excusable error and therefore not sufficiently serious. More interesting is the reasoning of the

---

[50] ibid.
[51] Case C-424/97 *Haim II* [2000] ECR I-5123, para 40.
[52] LG Berlin, 9 April 2001, Az: 23 0 650/00.

court with regard to the discretion left to the Federal Republic in incorporating Directive (EEC) 68/151.

Very early decisions by the ECJ in respect of directive (EEC) 68/151 pointed towards a wider interpretation of the first Directive, ie that everyone should be entitled to view the annual accounts.[53]

In 1998 the ECJ decided that the Federal Republic of Germany had failed to fulfil its obligations under the EC Treaty and those Directives. It had failed to provide for appropriate penalties in cases where companies limited by shares fail to disclose their annual accounts, as prescribed in particular by Directive (EEC) 68/151.[54] Only 10–15 per cent of all companies disclosed profit sheets (based on 1991 data) illustrating that the penalties imposed were unsuitable for achieving the purpose of the Directive.[55]

The German government argued in C-191/95 that 'because of the very large number of small and medium-sized limited liability companies, it would be disproportionate to the purpose of the system defined in Article 54(3)(g) of the Treaty to take legal action against them'.[56] However, the Court referred to previous rulings and held 'that a Member State may not plead internal circumstance in order to justify a failure to comply with obligations and time limits resulting from rules of Community law'.[57]

The *Landgericht Berlin* German court held that the incorrect implementation of a directive does not in itself amount to a sufficiently serious breach. It held that the Member State enjoyed a certain amount of discretion in implementing the directive and could therefore only be held liable in damages if the legislation is entirely erroneous and unsuitable to fulfil the aim of the directive. Nevertheless, it has been argued that the Federal Republic of Germany exercised its discretion erroneously in that it chose an insufficient sanction.[58] The court was criticized for its insecurity in dealing with EC law matters.[59] The *Landgericht Berlin* interpreted the guidance given as to the interpretation of the Directive in a very wide manner. It held that the principle of

---

[53] Case 32/74 *Haaga* [1974] ECR 1201 and Case C-136/87 *Ubbink Isolatie BV* [1988] ECR 4665.

[54] Case C-191/95 *Commission v Germany* [1998] ECR I-5449.

[55] S Leible, 'Haftung der Bundesrepublik wegen nicht ordnungsgemässer Umsetzung der Publizitätsrichtlinie durch para 335 a HGB' (2001) Europäisches Wirtschafts- und Steuerrecht, 563.

[56] Case C-191/95 *Commission v Germany* [1998] ECR I-5449, para 65.

[57] ibid.

[58] H Hirte, 'LG Berlin: Keine Haftung der Bundesrepublik für Schaden wegen unrichtiger Umsetzung der EG Bilanzrichtline', <http://www.rws-verlag.de>.

[59] Leible, see n 55 above.

subsidiarity had allowed such a wide interpretation of the Directive. At the time of the drafting of the Directive in question,[60] however, the principle of subsidiarity had not been incorporated into the EC Treaty.[61] Further, the judgement of the ECJ in *Daihatsu* [62] had set out clear guidelines. Therefore, it is questionable how the *Landgericht* reached the decision that the Federal Republic of Germany acted in good faith.

3.2 *UK courts*

In English law, it remains difficult to assert a claim for damages against public authorities. 'The basic premise is that an ultra vires act per se will not give rise to damages liability. For the plaintiff to succeed the claim must be capable of being fitted into one the recognized causes of action which exist.'[63] The major ones are negligence, to some extent nuisance, breach of statutory duty, and misfeasance in public office. However, to succeed in any of such claims the plaintiff has to overcome a variety of hurdles which have been developed by the courts in order to avoid a flood of cases trying to establish liability in damages.[64] In this light, the approach of English courts in matters relating to breaches of Community law provides an interesting contrast.

Lord Hoffmann stated the position in English law in the case of *Stovin v Wise*, a case which concerned the alleged negligence of a public authority in omitting road works to improve the visibility at a crossroads. The trend of [English] authorities [on negligence] has been to discourage the assumption that anyone who suffers loss is *prima facie* entitled to compensation from a person (preferably insured or a public authority) whose act or omission can be said to have caused it. The default position is that he is not.[65]

In contrast, EC law is described as 'a fertile source of ideas regarding the liability of public bodies …'. The jurisprudence of the ECJ is considered as 'far more sophisticated than that found in England' and a considerable

---

[60] Council Directive (EC) 68/151 on co-ordination of safeguards [1968] OJ L065/8.

[61] J Thietz-Bartram, 'Der Betrieb' (2002) 5, 260, <http://www.der-betrieb.de>.

[62] C-97/96 [1997] *Daihatsu* ECR I-68423.

[63] Craig, see n 39 above, 83.

[64] For comparative analysis see D Fairgrieve and S Green, *Child Abuse Tort Claims against Public Bodies* (Aldershot: Ashgate, 2004) and BS Markesinis, *Tortious Liability of Statutory Bodies: A Comparative and Economic Analysis of Five English Cases* (Oxford: Hart, 1999).

[65] *Stovin v Wise* [1996] AC 923, 949 (HL) referred to in Public Law Team, Law Commission, 'Monetary Remedies in Public Law—A Discussion Paper', October 2004, <http://www.lawcom. gov.uk>.

influence on domestic English law is expected.[66] Lord Hoffmann's statement in *Factortame (No 5)*[67] indicates a rather different approach in EC law matters from those concerned purely with domestic law: 'I do not think that the United Kingdom ... can say that the losses caused by the legislation should lie where they fell. Justice requires that the wrong should be made good.'[68]

In *R v Department of Social Security, ex p Scullion*,[69] decided just three months before the House of Lords gave its ruling in *Factortame (No 5)*, the High Court took a textbook approach to the application of the guiding principles of the ECJ and held that the government was liable for the incorrect transposition of Directive 97/7 on the progressive implementation of the principle of equal treatment for men and women in matters of social security. The High Court assessed various factors and took a 'basket or global approach, weighing the various factors which include the clarity of the Directive to be transposed'.[70] First, the government failed to seek legal advice as to whether discrimination in the different qualifying ages for Invalid Care Allowance was within the scope of Article 7(1) of the Directive. The clarity of the Directive to be transposed was considered. Article 7(1) of the Directive gave Member States discretion, but its scope was unclear. However, a number of previous judgments had clarified the position. Discrimination in retirement ages could not be justified in the interests of financial equilibrium since Invalid Care Allowance was a non-contributory benefit. The government had acted deliberately and the fact that the Directive was unclear did not mean that its breach was not sufficiently serious. The High Court held further that where legislative discretion was conferred on Member States, a restrictive approach to liability was to be applied. However, the discretion in Article 7(1) was conferred for the purpose of determining pensionable age and once that was achieved it conferred no broad discretion in relation to other benefits

Whilst the mere breach of Community law will not be enough to fix the state with liability, the mere fact that the state is able to advance an arguable case in litigation does not mean that the breach is not 'sufficiently serious'. Given the lack of precision in many directives it will not be too difficult for a government to construct some argument in favour of a particular interpretation.[71]

---

[66] ibid, 49.
[67] *Factortame V* [2000] 1 AC 524, 548.
[68] ibid.
[69] *R v Department of Social Security ex p Scullion* [1999] 3 CMLR 798.
[70] ibid, 42.
[71] ibid, 64.

The breach of the Directive was held to have been sufficiently serious. The judgment had great financial implications because of the number of persons concerned.[72]

In England the most important precedent with regard to the condition of sufficiently serious breach in this context is the case of *Factortame (No 5)*.[73] Lord Clyde held on 28 October 1999 that 'no single factor is necessarily decisive'. He identified eight factors which were of influence to the ECJ and which should guide national courts in their decisions:

> The importance of the principle which has been breached; the clarity and precision of the rule breached; the degree of excusability of an error of law; the existence of any relevant judgment on the point; the state of mind of the infringer, and in particular whether the infringer was acting intentionally or involuntarily; the behavior of the infringer after it has become evident that an infringement has occurred may also be of importance; the identity of the persons affected by the breach; and the position (if any) taken by one of the Community institutions in the matters.[74]

Of particular interest is that behaviour after the act which gives rise to the claim of damages could be a factor in the decision-making process. He further held that 'no single factor is necessarily decisive, but one factor by itself might, particularly where there was little or nothing to put onto the scales on the other side, be sufficient to justify the conclusion of liability'.[75] 'This indicates a broad and equitable approach'.[76]

The British approach to the sufficiently serious breach condition displays a willingness to apply the conditions developed in the decisions of the ECJ quite carefully.[77] This is also evident in the case of *R v Ministry of Agriculture, Fisheries and Food, ex p Lay and Gage*,[78] where the Court of Appeal applied all *Brasserie du Pêcheur* and *British Telecommunications* factors. Regulation 1078/77 established a scheme whereby a farmer could enter into a non-marketing agreement with another Member State in which he/she undertook for a given period, and in return for a premium, not to dispose of either milk or milk products from his/her land, nor to allow any land comprising his/

---

[72] XVIIth Report on Monitoring the Application of Community Law COM (2000) 92 final, June 2000, <http://europa.eu.int/comm/secretariat_general/sgb/infringements/report99_en.htm>.
[73] *Factortame V* [2000] 1 AC 524, 548.
[74] ibid, 554.
[75] ibid.
[76] Public Law Team, see n 65 above.
[77] A Merris, 'Eurotorts and Unicorns' in Fairgrieve, Andeans, and Bell, see n 2 above, 121.
[78] *R v Ministry of Agriculture, Fisheries and Food, ex p Lay and Gage* [1998] COD 387.

her property to be used for milk production. In *Gage and Gage*[79] the ECJ had established that the national legislation was in breach of Community law. The question in *Lay and Gage* was whether the breach had been sufficiently serious. The Court of Appeal considered all the factors in *Brasserie du Pêcheur* as relevant, insofar as they arise on the facts of any given case, in determining the extent to which any given breach of Community law is sufficiently serious. The Court denied a claim for damages, holding that 'The defendant acted bona fides, and made an excusable mistake as to the interpretation of a legislative provision, which was not clear or precise.'[80]

The case of *Boyd Line Management Services Ltd v Ministry of Agriculture, Fisheries and Food*[81] concerned the quota of British fisherman in the Norwegian Sea. The claimant, Boyd Line Management, sued the Ministry of Agriculture, Fisheries and Food for damages because it could not use up all of its allocated quota after the EC had declared that the total quota for this region had been exhausted. In assessing whether the alleged breach was sufficiently serious the Court of Appeal considered the case of *Dillenkofer*[82] carefully, but denied the claim. No breach of Article 31 of EC regulation 2847/93 could be found as it does not 'require the defendants either to ensure that compensation is paid to owners of vessels who do not receive the whole of their internal quota, or to take steps to ensure that vessels who do not exceed their internal domestic quota [. . .].'[83]

4 Conclusion

In conclusion, it appears to be easier to achieve an integration of the *Francovich* remedy in English courts than it does in German courts.[84] In a more pragmatic case-by-case approach, English courts have successfully embedded the *Francovich* remedy into English law. Harlow remarks that 'the UK appears to be an exception to the reluctance noted in the text [referring to the decision by the German Federal High Court in *Brasserie du Pêcheur*]

---

[79] Case C-165/95 *R v Ministry of Agriculture, Fisheries and Food, ex p Benjamin Lay, Donald Gage and David Gage* [1997] ECR I-5543.

[80] *R v Ministry of Agriculture, Fisheries and Food, ex p Lay and Gage* [1998] COD 390.

[81] *Boyd Line Management Services Ltd v Ministry of Agriculture, Fisheries & Food* [1999] EWCA Civ 1129 (30 March 1999).

[82] Joined Cases C-178/94, C-179/94, C-188/94, C-89/94, and C-190/94 *Dillenkofer* ECR I-4845.

[83] ibid.

[84] See also C Harlow, *Understanding Tort Law* (3rd edn, London: Sweet & Maxwell, 2005) 65.

embracing the liability principle enthusiastically and dutifully applying it in the *Factortame* case'.[85] The political reaction was somewhat different. The UK government issued a White Paper on the 1996 IGC and proposed appeals procedures against judgments of the ECJ. The late 1990s were marked by concern about the increase of judicial review cases and the fact that 'national courts might emulate the judicial activism of the two European courts, fuelled by the fact that British judges were happy to admit that European jurisprudence had pushed forward the boundaries of domestic judicial interventionism'.[86] Resistance to European integration was felt at a political level rather than on a judicial level. Membership of the EU strengthened the role of the judiciary.

Divergence in the approaches to the Europeanization of existing tort law regimes for official wrongs is not necessarily surprising in a complex area of law that touches upon both private and public law. Pierre Larouche's theory of 'path-dependency' may be a helpful tool in attempting to explain the different approaches of English and German judges. Accordingly, legal systems evolve in different directions because their reactions to problems are dependent on different sets of information. Legal systems diverge as 'tipping' in the network or path-dependency determines their priorities almost irreversibly.[87]

The integration of Member State liability into British law has to be seen in the wider context of the changing role of the British judiciary since the 1960s and the extension of judicial review into many domains of executive activity. In the EU context, despite early assurances that the judges were merely interpreting British legislation, from the early 1970s the courts were getting involved into more than 'business as usual'.[88] It has been argued that the courts have started to develop 'their own principles of constitutionalism'.[89] In the context of the *Factortame* decision it has been argued that 'the courts are simply putting into effect or "catching up with" a widespread political consensus about the particular constitutional rights and principles they

---

[85]   ibid.

[86]   D Nicol, *EC Membership and the Judicialisation of British Politics* (Oxford, Oxford University Press, 2001) 221.

[87]   Larouche and Chirico, 'Conceptual Divergence, Functionalism, and the Economics of Divergence', this volume ch 20, p 468.

[88]   R Stevens, 'Judicial Independence in England: A Loss of Innocence' in PH Russell and DM O'Brien, *Judicial Independence in the Age of Democracy: Critical Perspectives from Around the World* (Charlottesville: University Press of Virginia, 2001) 169.

[89]   D Oliver, *Constitutional Reform in the UK* (Oxford: Oxford University Press, 2003) 102.

elaborate'.[90] Further, constitutional reform through legislation confirmed 'the process of the constitutionalization of government that was initiated by the courts independently of these reforms'.[91] The motivation of their Lordships with regard to the development of the principle of parliamentary sovereignty in *Factortame* has been described as an 'essentially secondary and reflective constitution-developing role'.[92] When 'New Labour' came into power in 1997 it initiated legislative reform of the House of Lords, devolution for Scotland and Wales, and the incorporation of the European Convention on Human Rights into English law. Much to the regret of the government today these legislative reforms entailed an increase in judicial power.

Willingness to embrace the new remedy on the part of the British judiciary may therefore well be based on the changes in the constitutional relationship between the judiciary and the other powers in the state, and an awareness of the need to make changes in the area of tort claims against public bodies.

The German position, on the other hand, is marked by a more reluctant attitude. The case examples have shown that the BGH does not favour a Europeanized version of the codified tort liability, possibly leaving this to the legislature. The cases show that German judgments are less closely phrased to the rulings of the ECJ. It has even been argued that the EU tort claim in the BGH decision of 14 December 2000 discussed above was treated less favourably than the claim under domestic law. The BGH avoids any adaptation of the German tort provisions in fear of thereby introducing liability for legislative wrongs into German national law.[93]

In German courts there is an element of uncertainty or reluctance in the application of the remedy at present. In terms of legal consequences, the German approach reflects a position of stagnation at domestic legislative level. The example of two German cases, the BGH[94] and *Landgericht Berlin*[95], has illustrated that the uniform application of the right to reparation for breaches of Community law may be compromised by national reflexes, an element of re-nationalization, or purely inaction on behalf of the national judiciary. Among the German judiciary, different approaches to the translation of the principle into domestic law reflect a degree of uncertainty.

---

[90] ibid, 102.
[91] ibid, 103.
[92] Nicol, see n 86 above, 195.
[93] BP Säuberlich, *Legislatives Unrecht und EU-Amtshaftungsanspruch* (Frankfurt am Main: Lang, 2005) 105.
[94] BGHZ 146, 153.
[95] LG Berlin, 9 April 2001, Az: 230650/00.

In 2004 the FDP (Liberal Party) addressed the question of reforming the principles of governmental liability in a parliamentary question. Some of the MPs argued that the system is mainly based on case law and that the process of modernization is taking place on a case-by-case basis. They were interested in how other European Member States deal with it, whether legislation was needed to tackle this increasingly complex area of law, and whether national remedies are comparable to the protection required under Community law.[96]

The BGH, in particular, has chosen a path which does not lead to the Europeanization of German tort law. The artificial separation of German governmental liability and the European remedy led to a decision in December 2000 which, as we have seen, is unconvincing in its arguments. The claim failed due to the high threshold of the fault requirement under German law—the condition that the ECJ clearly avoided within its conditions for Member State liability. If, like some, one advocates a *ius commune* of administrative or tort law throughout Europe, one might be concerned about a re-nationalization of the remedy from the German point of view. In this case the BGH treated Community law less favourably than the similar national law in contravention of the principle of equivalence or non-discrimination.[97] Interestingly, there is a more recent decision by the *Oberlandsgericht Köln*[98] which embraces a more open approach to the integration of the ECJ state liability case law. The issue at stake was whether the applicant's claim for compensation was prescribed. The court allowed the case to proceed for revision to the BGH and a decision is eagerly expected. There may be a need for more clarification of the position of the ECJ on how Member States should accommodate the remedy in their national legal systems.

The decision by the *Landgericht Berlin*[99] clearly shows that legal mechanisms are subservient to political or economic considerations. The claim in damages was decided in line with previous political considerations by the German government. The flexibility of the criterion 'sufficiently serious breach' clearly permits policy considerations to enter into the decision-making process. This makes it difficult to establish a principle of 'full

---

[96] Deutscher Bundestag, Kleine Anfrage, Drucksache 15/3859, 29 September 2004, <http://dip.bundestag.de/btd/15/038/1503859.pdf>.

[97] W van Gerven, 'Of Rights, Remedies and Procedures' (2000) CML Rev, 504.

[98] OLG Köln, 2 June 2005, 7U 29/04, <http://www.olg-koeln.nrw.de>.

[99] LG Berlin, 9 April 2001, Az: 23 0 650/00.

reparation' or a uniform 'Community remedy' as was acknowledged by the ECJ itself.[100]

The ECJ, however, should, not permit avoidance of the application of the European remedy altogether. Other ways of tackling divergence have been suggested, including the denial that there is a problem with divergence, reform of the preliminary reference procedure, a Community-wide code (of administrative law), a natural alignment of state practices, and the establishment of Community courts in a federal style.[101] Hopefully time will allow for a new generation of lawyers trained in a variety of jurisdictions to take a fresh look at these complex issues.

[100] See the Opinion of Advocate General Mischo in Joined Cases C-6/90 and C-9/90 *Francovich* [1991] ECR I-5357, para 80; see the Opinion of Advocate General Tesauro in Joined Cases C-46/93 and C-48/93 *Brasserie and Factortame* [1996] ECR I-1029, para 111; and see Opinion of Advocate General Cosmas in Joined Cases C-94/95 and C-95/95 *Bonifaci* [1997] ECR I-3969, paras 63 and 103–106.

[101] C Himsworth in P Beaumont and C Lyons, *Convergence and Divergence in European Public Law* (Oxford: Hart, 2002) 109.

11

Stability and Flexibility in Administrative Decision Making: The Community Law Influence on Discretion with Respect to Administrative Decisions in German Law

Matthias Ruffert

1 From Divergence to Unity? The so-called Europeanization of administrative law: an introduction

Since the nineteenth century at the latest, national administrative legal systems have been developing in divergent directions. At least two tendencies have caused more terminological divergence than in other fields of law, for example civil and commercial law which traditionally contain rules and principles to manage transnational relationships. The first strong factor has been the rise of dualism as the core explanation for the relationship between international and national law.[1] Administrative law was considered to be on the national side of the legal sphere and thus cut off from foreign and international terminological and conceptual developments, in particular in Germany. The second factor is the positioning of administrative law within national legal systems as part of the rise of positivism which can be detected

---

[1] cf C Tietje, *Internationalisiertes Verwaltungshandeln* (Berlin: Duncker & Humblot, 2001) 86ff; M Ruffert, 'Rechtsquellen und Rechtsschichten des Verwaltungsrechts' in W Hoffmann-Riem, E Schmidt-Aßmann, and A Voßkuhle (eds), *Grundlagen des Verwaltungsrechts*, Vol 1 (München: Beck, 2006) para 17: 12.

in both France and Germany—with the United Kingdom lagging behind due to common law peculiarities. The jurisprudential, legalist positivism of the *Conseil d'État* or the strict interpretation of statutes following the *Juristische Methode*—both may have enhanced the standing of public law within French and German legal scholarship, but they have been blind to external influence, let alone the fact that there has been no institution exerting that influence.[2] So how can diverging concepts be brought together in a degree of unity?

In historical terms, the development leading to more convergence is fairly recent. One of the most pertinent features of current German administrative law—if not the most important—is the process of Europeanization.[3] The influence of European Community law upon the administrative legal system has led to the reversal of Otto Mayer's famous dictum—perfectly embedded in late nineteenth-century positivism—about the contrast between the transitory nature of constitutional law and the continuity of administrative law (*Verfassungsrecht vergeht, Verwaltungsrecht besteht*),[4] as constitutional provisions have remained intact to a great extent whereas administrative legal principles and rules have been turned upside down in some areas.[5] Today, it can rightly be said that the theoretical 'digestion' of European Community law in administrative legal scholarship has—all in all—been accomplished. European law shows its omnipresence and is no longer considered to be an intervention in structures whose continuous growth needed a long time to take place.[6]

This state of play reflects a development in several phases.[7] In the beginning, the discovery of European Community law as such and of its influence upon administrative law was the result of the pioneer achievements of a few

---

[2] cf M Ruffert, 'The Transformation of Administrative Law as a Transnational Methodological Project' in idem (ed), *The Transformation of Administrative Law in Europe* (München: Sellier, 2007) 3, 9ff.

[3] For a general overview see M Ruffert, 'Die Europäisierung der Verwaltungsrechtslehre' (2003) 36 *Die Verwaltung*, 293.

[4] O Mayer, *Deutsches Verwaltungsrecht*, Vol 1 (3rd edn, Berlin: Duncker & Humblot, 1969) foreword.

[5] See already C Engel, 'Die Einwirkungen des europäischen Gemeinschaftsrechts auf das deutsche Verwaltungsrecht' (1992) 25 *Die Verwaltung*, 438.

[6] cf F Schoch, 'Die Europäisierung des Allgemeinen Verwaltungsrechts' (1995) 50 Juristenzeitung, 109.

[7] For this, 'phaseology' see E Schmidt-Aßmann, 'Strukturen des Europäischen Verwaltungsrechts: Einleitende Problemskizze' in Schmidt-Aßmann and W Hoffmann-Riem (eds), *Strukturen des Europäischen Verwaltungsrechts* (Baden-Baden: Nomos, 1999) 10ff and Ruffert, see n 3 above, 293ff.

authors in commentaries, basic monographs, new (at their time) journals, and series of academic publications in the 1960s.[8] The identification of a subject called *Europäisches Verwaltungsrecht*/European administrative law took place at the end of the 1970s and the beginning of the 1980s, a period marked by singular pioneer writings of which Jürgen Schwarze's *European Administrative Law* is certainly the most well known across the borders of jurisdictions.[9] This phase of reception of the administrative structures of the EC and of the relevant jurisprudence of the ECJ is marked by two dominant lines of thought. The first is the differentiation between the different forms of administration at EC level, ie direct administration by Community institutions and indirect administration by the Member States executing EC Law.[10] The second is the description and systematization of the general principles of law as developed by the ECJ for all forms of 'European' government.[11] Methodologically, this phase remains attached to EC Law categories such as primary and secondary

[8] The textbook by HP Ipsen, *Europäisches Gemeinschaftsrecht* (Tübingen: Mohr, 1972) is still a monolithical, encyclopedic reference work. Early development is also documented by Ipsen: HP Ipsen, 'Die Europäische Integration in der deutschen Rechtswissenschaft' in HC Rüßmann, *Entwicklungslinien in Recht und Wirtschaft, Akademische Reden der Rechts- und Wirtschaftswissenschaftlichen Fakultät der Universität des Saarlandes: 1988/1989*, Vol 2 (Stuttgart: Schäffer, 1990) 71. Early commentaries: H von der Groeben and H von Boeckh, *Kommentar zum EWG-Vertrag* (Baden-Baden: Lutzeyer, 1958–1960); E Wohlfahrt and others, *Die Europäische Wirtschaftsgemeinschaft: Kommentar zum Vertrag* (Berlin: Vahlen, 1960), and Journals: CML Rev (1963); Europarecht (1966); Publication Series (eg): Kölner Schriften zum Europarecht (1965).

[9] J Schwarze, *Europäisches Verwaltungsrecht* (2nd edn, Baden-Baden: Nomos, 2005). See by the same author: 'Tendencies towards a Common Administrative Law in Europe' (1991) 16 ELR, 3 and 'Tendances vers un droit administratif commun en Europe' (1993) 29 Revue trimestrielle de droit européen, 235, and S Cassese, 'Der Einfluss des gemeinschaftsrechtlichen Verwaltungs–rechts auf die nationalen Verwaltungsrechtssysteme' (1994) 33 *Der Staat*, 25. Of similar importance for the German literature: HW Rengeling, *Rechtsgrundsätze beim Verwaltungsvollzug des Europäischen Gemeinschaftsrechts* (Köln: Heymanns, 1977).

[10] First developed by Rengeling, see n 9 above, 9–11. cf further U Everling, 'Elemente eines europäischen Verwaltungsrechts' (1983) 98 Deutsches Verwaltungsblatt, 650, 653ff and later (with more differentiation) W Hoffmann-Riem, 'Strukturen des Europäischen Verwaltungs–rechts—Perspektiven der Systembildung' in Schmidt-Aßmann, see n 7 above, 322ff; W Kahl, 'Europäisches und nationales Verwaltungsorganisationsrecht' (1996) 29 Die Verwaltung, 343ff, and S Hegels, *EG-Eigenverwaltungsrecht und Gemeinschaftsverwaltungsrecht* (Baden-Baden: Nomos, 2000). Later, the level of administrative cooperation was added.

[11] cf Rengeling, see n 9 above, 67ff, 89ff; Schwarze, see n 9 above, 74–93, and later E Schmidt-Aßmann, 'Zur Europäisierung des allgemeinen Verwaltungsrechts' in P Badura and R Scholz (eds), *Festschrift für Peter Lerche zum 65. Geburtstag* (München: Beck, 1993) 517ff and A Bleckmann, 'Methoden der Bildung europäischen Verwaltungsrechts' (1993) 46 Die öffentliche Verwaltung, 837.

sources, and organs and modes of administration.[12] Only in systematizing the said general principles, does a new methodological perspective arise, as administrative law categories are introduced: procedural rights, legitimate expectations, proportionality in administrative decisions, etc.[13]

This phase could have been brought to a positive and peaceful conclusion in the subsequent one. However, the next phase (at the beginning of the 1990s) was a phase of conflict. The Mainz conference of the Public Law Association (*Vereinigung der Deutschen Staatsrechtslehrer*) in 1993 indicated that there were deep 'trenches' between the two 'camps': on the one hand there were those who declared that the structures of national administrative law were without value as such, and on the other, those who were sceptical about any Europeanization whatsoever.[14] The conflict was intensified as administrative legal scholarship became aware of the growing influence of European Community law.[15] Furthermore, in a series of judgments the ECJ 'attacked' the inner core of convictions about administrative law in Germany—such as the suitability of administrative circulars,[16] the role of individual rights,[17]

---

[12] Schweitzer, see n 10 above, 137; Grabitz, see n 10 above, 1776; Ehlers, see n 10 above, 605; Engel, see n 5 above, 437ff (but see on pages 455ff); E Klein, 'Vereinheitlichung des Verwaltungsrechts im europäischen Integrationsprozeß' in C Starck (ed), *Rechtsvereinheitlichung durch Gesetze* (Göttingen: Vandenhoeck & Ruprecht, 1992) 117 and 'Der Einfluss des Europäischen Gemeinschaftsrechts auf das Verwaltungsrecht der Mitgliedstaaten' (1994) 33 *Der Staat*, 39.

[13] See in particular the second volume of Schwarze's work, see n 9 above.

[14] M Zuleeg and HW Rengeling, 'Deutsches und europäisches Verwaltungsrecht—wechselseitige Einwirkungen' (1994) 53 Veröffentlichungen der Vereinigung der Deutschen Staatsrechtslehrer, 154 and 202. See in particular Zuleeg's statement no 31, 199, and the reactions by Vogel, 241, and Starck, 245ff. The accompanying paper by E Schmidt-Aßmann, 'Deutsches und europäisches Verwaltungsrecht—wechselseitige Einwirkungen' (1993) 108 Deutsches Verwaltungsblatt, 924, already tries to show ways out of conflict.

[15] See—different viewpoints—R Breuer, *Entwicklungen des europäischen Umweltrechts—Ziele, Wege und Irrwege* (Berlin: De Gruyter, 1993) and with its strong wording J Salzwedel and M Reinhardt, 'Neuere Tendenzen im Wasserrecht' (1991) 10 Neue Zeitschrift für Verwaltungsrecht, 947.

[16] *Commission v Germany* Case C-131/88 [1991] ECR I-825; Case C-361/88 [1991] ECR I-2567; Case C-58/89 [1991] ECR I-4983; and Case C-59/89 [1991] ECR I-2607. From the ambivalent reaction of German scholars see on the one hand T von Danwitz, 'Normkonkretisierende Verwaltungsvorschriften und Gemeinschaftsrecht' (1993) 84 Verwaltungsarchiv, 81ff; M Reinhardt, 'Abschied von der Verwaltungsvorschrift im Wasserrecht?' (1992) 45 Die öffentliche Verwaltung, 102; A Weber, 'Zur Umsetzung von EG-Richtlinien im Umweltrecht' (1992) 12 Umwelt- und Planungsrecht, 8; on the other hand, C Bönker, *Umweltstandards in Verwaltungsvorschriften* (Münster: Instituts für Siedlungs- und Wohnungswesen, 1992) 115ff and Schoch, see n 6 above, 119.

[17] cf only M Ruffert, *Subjektive Rechte im Umweltrecht der EG* (Heidelberg: Decker, 1996) 72ff.

the conditions for interim relief, the framework of state liability in tort,[18] and finally—something that will be developed further here—modifications in the stability of administrative decisions (see section 3 below).

Against this background, it is even more astonishing that since the middle of the 1990s the Europeanization of administrative law has become one of the subjects of public law. The acuteness of the conflict seems to have provoked scholars of German administrative law to develop concepts for its solution.[19] Now, the overall perspective has changed: there is no longer any conflict between 'Community lawyers' and 'administrative lawyers'; instead both are increasingly approaching the relevant subjects under the pan-European categories of administrative law (decisions, rights, discretion, etc) rather than specifically under those of Community law.[20]

2 Discretion *after* administration has made its decisions

The process described briefly above does not include the whole of general administrative law; instead there are particular areas of impact in which the influence of Community law can be shown and analysed in greater depth.[21] Among these is the question of stability and flexibility in administrative decisions. An analysis of these two aspects of post-decisional discretion integrates well into the central theme of the present volume under the heading of discretion.

Discretionary powers of government are characterized by a certain level of choice in taking administrative action or making decisions.[22] The limits of these powers are normally analysed in relation to coming to a decision or choosing how to act. However, it is also important to take into account the post-decision phase. In all jurisdictions, administrative decisions—whatever

---

[18] Joined Cases C-143/88 and C-92/89 *Zuckerfabrik* [1991] ECR I-415; Joined Cases C-6/90 and C-9/90 *Francovich* [1991] ECR I-5357, and Case C-280/90 *Emmott* [1991] ECR I-4269.

[19] See the voluminous and comprehensive works by M Brenner, *Der Gestaltungsauftrag der Verwaltung in der Europäischen Union* (Tübingen: Mohr, 1996); T von Danwitz, *Verwaltungsrechtliches System und Europäische Integration* (Tübingen: Mohr, 1996); A Hatje, *Die gemeinschaftsrechtliche Steuerung der Wirtschaftsverwaltung* (Baden-Baden: Nomos, 1998) and S Kadelbach, *Allgemeines Verwaltungsrecht unter europäischem Einfluß* (Tübingen: Mohr, 1999).

[20] cf Ruffert, see n 3 above, 298ff.

[21] cf Ruffert, see n 3 above, 302ff.

[22] cf M Ruffert, 'Bedeutung, Funktion und Begriff des Verwaltungsakts' in HU Erichsen and D Ehlers (eds), *Allgemeines Verwaltungsrecht* (13th edn, Berlin: de Gruyter Recht, 2006) para 20, 6.

the terminology may be—are at the end of a process with more or less complicated procedural steps. The core question for our purpose is to what extent administrative bodies have the discretionary power to change, withdraw, or revoke a decision after it has been made. How much discretion exists to create administrative flexibility—and what are its limits in guaranteeing the necessary stability?

In answering this question with respect to German administrative law, uniform European and domestic developments as well as divergent approaches between Community and national law must be explained. The dogmatic concept which characterizes the balance between stability and flexibility in German administrative law is the administrative decision—*Verwaltungsakt*. Taken from the French idea of *acte administratif*—though the French concept is broader, enclosing normative and contractual instruments—it was first of all intended as a vehicle for stability to guarantee the rule of law in particular cases.[23] However, the concept of discretionary flexibility was introduced since a *Verwaltungsakt* was considered to be freely revocable by the competent authority.[24]

The actual rule is laid down in section 43(2) of the *Verwaltungsverfahrensgesetz* (Administrative Procedure Act, abbreviated VwVfG):[25] a *Verwaltungs–akt* remains valid if it is neither withdrawn, revoked or cancelled in another way or if it expires for reasons of time or other reasons (ie independently of government action). Each of the alternatives—withdrawal, revocation, and cancellation in another way—is laid down in a specific procedure.

The discussion in the following sections explores how stability and flexibility in administrative decision making under German administrative law are influenced by different approaches in European Community law. Unifying tendencies are discussed, but remaining or even newly occurring divergence at the conceptual level is also highlighted.

---

[23] On the basis of the famous definition by O Mayer, *Deutsches Verwaltungsrecht* (1st edn, Leipzig: Duncker & Humblot, 1895) 64ff. cf M Engert, *Die historische Entwicklung des Rechtsinstituts Verwaltungsakt* (Frankfurt am Main: Lang, 2002).

[24] On this historical development: HP Ipsen, *Widerruf gültiger Verwaltungsakte* (Hamburg, Lütcke und Wulff, 1932); F Haueisen, 'Die Rücknahme fehlerhafter Verwaltungsakte' (1954) 7 Neue Juristische Wochenschrift, 1425; and F Becker and N Luhmann, *Verwaltungsfehler und Vertrauensschutz* (Berlin: Duncker & Humblot, 1963).

[25] Verwaltungsverfahrensgesetz (Admininistrative Procedure Act), Bundesgesetzblatt, Vol 1 (2003) no 4, 102; last amendment Bundesgesetzblatt, Vol 1 (2004) no 21, 718. An English translation by the Bundesministerium der Justiz (Federal Ministry of Justice) is provided under <http://www.bmi.bund.de>.

3 Stability by means of protecting legitimate interests

3.1 *Crystallization of jurisprudence in a statute of German Law*

The main form of cancelling *Verwaltungsakte* by the administration itself is by withdrawing (section 48 VwVfG) or revoking (section 49 VwVfG) them. The difference between these provisions can easily be described. Withdrawal concerns *Verwaltungsakte* which are contrary to the law, ie unlawful. Revocation is about cancelling or changing *Verwaltungsakte* which are in conformity with the law, ie lawful. Of course it makes a difference whether the *Verwaltungsakt* to be cancelled or changed is lawful or not, if a vested position is taken away from the citizen by the act of withdrawal or revocation.

The main obstacle to withdrawal or revocation is the protection of legitimate expectations. This principle was first of all recognized by the continuous jurisprudence of the Federal Administrative Court (*Bundesverwaltungsgericht*) as against free (ie discretionary) withdrawal/revocation.[26] When the general principles of German administrative law were codified in the 1970s, the rules as developed by this jurisprudence were statutorily fixed. Thus, there is a general time limit of one year for withdrawal and revocation: neither lawful nor even unlawful *Verwaltungsakte* can be withdrawn or revoked later than one year after the competent authority has learned of the facts that would justify withdrawal or revocation (sections 48(4), first sentence; 49(2) second sentence).[27] Over and above that deadline, there are obstacles to withdrawing unlawful and benificial *Verwaltungsakte* which are divided into two categories:

(i) Those which provide for the payment of money or other material benefit cannot be withdrawn if the beneficiary has relied upon the continued existence of the *Verwaltungsakte* and their reliance deserves protection relative to the public interest from withdrawal. This is generally the case if the said money or material benefit has already been used or relied on for financial disposition and is generally excluded in cases of fraud, bribery, undue information by the beneficiary, or awareness or grossly negligent unawareness of the unlawfulness (section 48(2) VwVfG).

(ii) Those which provide for another kind of benefit—such as a planning permission or a licence to run a certain business—can be withdrawn,

---

[26] For the development of the elder jurisprudence see H Maurer, *Allgemeines Verwaltungsrecht* (16th edn, München: Beck, 2006) para 11, no 21ff.

[27] Leading case on that deadline: BVerwGE 70, 356.

but the financial loss incurred through the withdrawal must be compensated for (section 48(3) VwVfG).

Revocation of lawful *Verwaltungsakte* is even more difficult as there must be
clear reasons for taking away a benefit that has been lawfully granted, and
thus there is a clear-cut catalogue to be strictly interpreted which states such
reasons (eg, the elimination of serious harm to the common good) in the
statute (section 49(2) VwVfG).

All in all, we can see a broad and complex limitation of the discretion to
modify administrative law decisions in retrospect. It should be noted—as a
matter of course—that all these limitations do not apply if a *Verwaltungsakt*
does not confer benefits upon individuals. Discretion would then remain
intact. Finally, besides revocation and withdrawal there is the right of
resumption of proceedings that can be triggered in the case of changing factual or legal circumstances, of new evidence, or in certain other instances by
the person affected (section 51 VwVfG).

3.2 *A general principle of law in Community law*

The principle of protection of legitimate expectations has found continuous
and long-term acceptance in the jurisprudence of the ECJ.[28] First of all, it
requires an action by the Community institutions that create expectations,
such as a normative activity—or a singular administrative decision. Furthermore, the protection of the said expectations must be legitimate: there
must be a tangible reliance upon the administrative decision, and the fact
that reliance would be deceived shall not have been foreseeable. In addition,
the reliance must have been caused by the decision itself, and finally the
common interest in departing from the decision must outweigh the interest of the person affected in protecting his/her expectations.[29] Structurally,
these requirements are in conformity with the principles of German law as
they have crystallized in the statute quoted.

In its concrete application, however, the content of the principle of legitimate expectations is different. The ECJ is not inclined to follow all the lines
of the German administrative legal rules, as their application would make
the implementation of Community law practically impossible. The main

---

[28] cf Schwarze, see n 9 above, lxxviiff—also with respect to the following requirements.
[29] cf, eg, Case 159/82 *Verli-Wallace v Commission* [1983] ECR 2711, para 8; Case T-123/89
Chomel v Commission [1990] ECR II-131, para 34 and Case T-251/99 *Lagardère v Commission*
[2002] ECR II-4825, para 139ff.

field of reference for this kind of divergence is the withdrawal of administrative decisions (*Verwaltungsakte*) granting state aids that are unlawful under Community law (see Article 1 lit f of Council Regulation (EC) 659/1999).[30] In this area, there are two main consequences.

First of all, the one-year deadline does not have to be respected if the Commission has decided that Germany as a Member State would have to claim the reimbursal of a subsidy (cf Article 14 of Council Regulation (EC) 659/1999)[31] because this would lead to the opportunity to slow down the implementation of the plea of reimbursement.[32] This has been accepted by the *Bundesverfassungsgericht* as constitutional due to the supremacy of EC law.[33]

Second, in weighing up legitimate expectations on the one hand and the principle of legality on the other, the Community interest has to be taken fully into account.[34] This means that the protection of legitimate interests is less important than the implementation of Community law not being rendered impossible or excessively difficult.[35] Generally, the Community

---

[30] Council Regulation (EC) 659/1999 laying down detailed rules for the application of Article 93 of the EC Treaty [1999] OJ L83/1.

[31] See n 30 above.

[32] Case C-24/95 *Alcan* [1997] ECR I-1591, para 37 and beforehand Case C-5/89 *BUG-Alutechnik* [1990] ECR I-3437, paras 18ff. From the subsequent national jurisprudence see BVerwGE 92, 81; BVerwG, Neue Zeitschrift für Verwaltungsrecht (1995) 706. cf DH Scheuing, 'Europäisierung des Verwaltungsrechts. Zum mitgliedstaatlichen Verwaltungsvollzug des EG-Rechts am Beispiel der Rückforderung gemeinschaftsrechtswidriger Beihilfen' (2001) 34 Die Verwaltung, 107 and for extreme criticism R Scholz, 'Zum Verhältnis von europäischem Gemeinschaftsrecht und nationalem Verwaltungsverfahrensrecht' (1998) 51 Die öffentliche Verwaltung, 261 (rightly against him M Winkler, 'Das "Alcan"-Urteil des EuGH—eine Katastrophe für den Rechts-staat?' (1999) 52 Die öffentliche Verwaltung, 148 and JA Frowein, 'Kritische Bemerkungen zur Lage des deutschen Staatsrechts aus rechtsvergleichender Sicht' (1998) 51 Die öffentliche Verwaltung, 807ff. See also Case C-209/00 *Commission v Germany* [2002] ECR 2002 I-11695, paras 34ff. Hatje, see n 19 above, 283, is right in pointing at the collusive cooperation of the Member State and the relevant company.

[33] BVerfG, Neue Juristische Wochenschrift 2000, 2015; BVerwGE 106, 328. See to this point J Suerbaum, 'Die Europäisierung des nationalen Verwaltungsverfahrensrechts am Beispiel der Rückabwicklung gemeinschaftsrechtswidriger staatlicher Beihilfen' (2000) 91 Verwaltungsarchiv, 201ff and A Gromitsaris, 'Neue Entwicklungen des Vertrauensschutzes bei Rücknahme und Rückforderung europarechtsrelevanter Beihilfen' (2000) 9 Thüringer Verwaltungsblätter, 97.

[34] Case 205/82 *Deutsche Milchkontor* [1983] ECR 2633, paras 32ff and Case 94/87 *Alcan I* [1989] ECR 175, para 12. .

[35] Kadelbach, see n 19 above, 476ff; HJ Blanke, *Vertrauensschutz im deutschen und europäischen Verwaltungsrecht* (Tübingen: Mohr, 2000) 550ff; D Triantafyllou, 'Zur "Europäisierung" des Vertrauensschutzes (insbesondere § 48 VwVfG)—am Beispiel der Rückforderung staatlicher Beihilfen' (1992) 11 Neue Zeitschrift für Verwaltungsrecht, 438; TS Richter, 'Rückforderung gemeinschaftsrechtswidriger Subventionen nach § 48 VwVfG' (1995) 48 Die öffentliche

interest prevails to prevent Member States from evading their Community law duties by relying on the legitimate expectations of the subject receiving the state aids.[36] In addition, legitimate expectations can only arise if state aids have been granted following the procedure under EC Treaty, Article 88(3),—ie if their granting has been duly notified to the Commission—a procedure which every company can inform itself by taking a look at the Official Journal.[37] Consequently, in state aid matters legitimate expectations in the case of illegal subsidies only arise very rarely, eg, if the Community institutions contribute to granting an unlawful subsidy.

3.3 *Interim conclusion*

To conclude this point, it can be noted that the existence of unity at the structural level does not guarantee convergence in each and every result, though differences will not necessarily create diverging concepts. Discretion *after* the decision has been made is restricted in both German and Community law through the principle of legitimate expectations, though the effective implementation of Community law is a topic which strongly modifies the results. If Community law calls for withdrawal of a benefit which is considered an unlawful subsidy, discretion is fettered by Community law influence.

4 Flexibility for effective implementation of Community law

4.1 *Non-beneficial administrative acts: discretion, stability, and flexibility*

The constellation of withdrawal of beneficial *Verwaltungsakte* has been discussed rather intensively in German administrative legal scholarship.

Verwaltung, 851; and R Polley, 'Die Konkurrentenklage im Europäischen Beihilferecht' (1996) 7 Europäische Zeitschrift für Wirtschaftsrecht, 303.

[36] Case C-5/89 *BUG-Alutechnik* [1990] ECR I-3437, paras 17ff and Case C-169/95 *Spain v Commission* [1997] ECR I-135, para 48.

[37] Case C-5/89 *BUG-Alutechnik* [1990] ECR I-3437, para 14; Case C-169/95 *Spain v Commission* [1997] ECR I-135, para 51; Case C-24/95 *Alcan II* [1997] ECR I-1591, para 25; BVerwGE 92, 86; OVG Münster, Juristenzeitung 1992, 1081; KP Sommermann, 'Europäisches Verwaltungs–recht oder Europäisierung des Verwaltungsrechts?—Inkonsistenzen in der Rechtsprechung des Europäischen Gerichtshofes' (1996) 111 Deutsches Verwaltungsblatt, 894; and with doubts E Pache, 'Rechtsfragen der Aufhebung gemeinschaftsrechtswidriger nationaler Beihilfebescheide' (1994) 13 Neue Zeitschrift für Verwaltungsrecht, 323.

Another Community law influence is a rather recent one and concerns the revocation or withdrawal of *Verwaltungsakte* that are non-beneficial. As already mentioned, these *Verwaltungsakte* can be withdrawn or revoked (for lawful or unlawful *Verwaltungsakte* respectively) according to the discretion of the competent authority. However, in these instances there must be a *right* for the citizen or company affected to have an administrative decision which negatively affects him withdrawn or even revoked. Generally, there is a right to have discretionary powers duly exercised (*Recht auf ermessensfehlerfreie Ermessensausübung*).[38] In the cases, as indicated, everyone has the right that the competent authority respects the inner and outer limits of discretion when deciding whether to cancel or modify a *Verwaltungsakt*, ie that it takes all circumstances into account and does not act in a discriminatory or disproportionate way. In extreme situations, according to the jurisprudence of the *Bundesverwaltungsgericht*, discretion is reduced to one possible decision only—which would be the object of the right of those concerned. Such extreme cases occur when if it would be unbearable for the affected, third parties, or the general public if the *Verwaltungsakt* were not withdrawn, or if the non-withdrawal were to amount to a breach of good faith.[39] Unlawfulness of the *Verwaltungsakt* in question is not enough, as a right would then exist in each and every case. This brings the jurisprudence on sections 48 *and following* in line with the content of section 51(1) VwVfG, which indicates those—albeit limited—cases in which there is a particular right to claim that an administrative procedure is resumed with the effect of giving a new material decision beyond withdrawal and revocation (cf section 51(5)).

4.2 *Limits of stability in cases of breach of Community law*

This legal framework has been considerably 'Europeanized' by the relatively recent decision in the Case of *Kühne & Heitz*, which concerned the reimbursement of export refunds.[40] The refunds had been paid on the basis of a classification of the goods which was later discovered to be wrong according to a judgment of the ECJ. The exporter thus claimed a reimbursement which could only be granted on the basis that the decision of classification was cancelled.

---

[38] cf Ruffert, see n 22 above, para D, no 15.
[39] BVerwGE 28, 127ff; BVerwGE 44, 336; BVerwG, Neue Zeitschrift für Verwaltungsrecht 1985, 265. cf also VGH Mannheim, Neue Zeitschrift für Verwaltungsrecht 1989, 884.
[40] Case C-453/00 *Kühne* [2004] ECR I-837.

The Court first of all made clear (and repeated) that legal certainty was a general principle of Community Law.[41] In this kind of case it meant that the reopening of administrative proceedings that had been ended by a final decision was not an obligation upon national authorities as a matter of principle. However, as under the relevant national (Dutch) law, administrative proceedings could generally be reopened under certain circumstances, the ECJ formulated a four-tier test which lays down the conditions under which the administrative body would be obliged by EC Treaty, Article 10 to reconsider its formerly final decision, taking account of the relevant Community Law findings.[42] First of all, there must be an opportunity for reopening in domestic law. Second, the administrative decision must have become final following the decision of a high court against the decisions of which there is no remedy. Third, the interpretation given to Community law by that court must be found to be contrary to Community law in the light of a subsequent ECJ judgment. Fourth, the person affected must make his/her claim immediately.

It can be submitted that conceptually, the *Kühne & Heitz* judgment coincides with the German position on stability as it is in conformity with the restriction of the instances of a duty to withdraw a final administrative decision—and as it formulates a special circumstance which would allow for such withdrawal: the necessity to achieve implementation of Community law, in particular an ECJ judgement.[43]

Some doubts, however, may remain. *Kühne & Heitz* could be read as more than a judgment on administrative decisions, but as one that calls into question the stability of final decisions generally, whether administrative or judicial. Further challenge against *res judicata*, ie stability of decisions of national courts, emanates from the new line of cases on State liability, in which it is held that as a matter of principle, Member States can be liable for manifest infringements of Community law by their courts of last instance.[44] Indeed, the issue was raised in the later case of *Rosmarie Kapferer v Schlank & Schick GmbH*, the facts of which, though amusing, are irrelevant with respect to the problem at hand.[45] The ECJ clearly differentiated between administrative and judicial decisions, attributing less stability to the former as compared

---

[41]   ibid, para 24.

[42]   ibid, para 25ff.

[43]   cf M Ruffert, 'Annotation on Case C-453/00 *Kühne*' (2004) 59 Juristenzeitung, 619.

[44]   Case C-224/01 *Köbler* [2003] ECR I-10239 and Case C-173/03 *Traghetti del Mediterraneo* [2006] ECR I-5177.

[45]   Case C-234/04 *Rosmarie Kapferer* [2006] ECR I-2585. The case is about a prize that was supposed to have been won by a consumer.

with the latter.[46] It is submitted that this is not just in conformity with what has been explained on German administrative law, but that it can be seen as a general perspective in Europe.

The problem has recently been treated in *i-21 Germany and Arcor v Germany*.[47] The plaintiffs are two major telecommunications service providers. They were charged considerable fees under the relevant German legislation and statutory instrument for their licences to operate telecommunications services The ECJ held that the fees (which were calculated and imposed by the German authorities in a way that took into account the regulatory body's general administrative costs linked to implementing those licences over a period of thirty years) were contrary to the relevant Article of Directive (EC) 97/13 on a common framework for telecommunications authorizations and licences.[48] This is a result that appears quite clear-cut.

The problem, however, was that the fees had been fixed in administrative decisions under German law (ie *Verwaltungsakte*) which could no longer be challenged at this point in time. The ECJ differentiated the situation from the one in *Kühne & Heitz* because the two telecommunications companies had never challenged the administrative decisions on fees, a challenge which *had* been made by hen-breeders against the Dutch hen and egg administration.[49] The differentiation is somewhat uncertain. Does *i-21 and Arcor* call into question what has been found here to be deducible from *Kühne & Heitz*? At least, the ECJ develops that 'the judgment in *Kühne & Heitz* is not relevant for the purposes of determining whether, in a situation such as that in the main proceedings, an administrative body is under an obligation to review decisions which have become final', while in *i-21 and Arcor* the question at hand was the duty to withdraw administrative decisions.[50] Are we to conclude that *Kühne & Heitz* is about the procedural issue of reopening the procedure only without any substantive core?

At any rate, the Court stresses the fact that the plaintiffs in *i-21 and Arcor* did not exhaust the available remedies, and turns to whether there could be

---

[46] ibid, para 21.

[47] Joined Cases C-392/04 and C-422/04 *i-21 Germany*, Judgment of the Court of 19 September 2006, nyr, 9.

[48] Parliament and Council Directive (EC) 97/13 on a common framework for general authorizations and individual licences in the field of telecommunications services [1997] OJ L117/15.

[49] Joined Cases C-392/04 and C-422/04 *i-21 Germany*, Judgment of the Court of 19 September 2006, nyr, para 53.

[50] ibid, para 54.

a duty to withdraw *Verwaltungsakte* if they were contrary to Community law and if they have become final. The ECJ applies the well-known tests of equivalence and effectiveness which modify Member States' procedural autonomy in the sense that the application of procedural rules may be neither less favourable than the application of those rules governing similar domestic situations, nor applied in a way that would render practically impossible or excessively difficult the exercise of rights under Community law.[51]

Starting with the principle of effectiveness, the Court held that the application of a deadline to challenge administrative decisions would not entail the ineffectiveness of the application of Community law, given that even after the deadline the said decisions *could* be revoked (the question was, however, whether this *should* happen).[52] The ECJ then concentrates on equivalence. As explained in the context of *Kühne & Heitz* a duty to withdraw arises under special circumstances—if it is 'outright intolerable' (*schlechthin unerträglich*) to uphold the *Verwaltungsakt* which is in breach with Community law.[53] This would mean that the national court has to check whether the maintenance of the fees would run counter to the national legal principles of equality, fairness, public policy, and good faith, or if it was manifestly incompatible with higher-ranking law.[54] Indeed, no difference was detected between (fictitious) proceedings governed only by national law and the proceedings at hand, and the principles of public policy, good faith, and fairness were not claimed to be applied differently according to the nature of the dispute.[55] However, the ECJ called into question whether the competent German court (the highest administrative court, ie the *Bundesverwaltungsgericht*) had applied the criterion of 'manifest incompatibility with higher ranking law' in a way that duly complied with the requirement of equivalence: 'where, pursuant to rules of national law, the administration is required to withdraw an administrative decision which has become final if that decision is manifestly incompatible with domestic law, that same obligation must exist

---

[51] As to this test cf W Kahl in C Calliess and M Ruffert (eds), *EUV/EGV-Kommentar* (3rd edn, München: Beck, 2007) Art 10 EC, para 31.

[52] Joined Cases C-392/04 and C-422/04 *i-21 Germany*, Judgment of the Court of 19 September 2006, nyr, para 61.

[53] See s 4.1 above.

[54] Translation of the ECJ of 'die im nationalen Recht geltenden Grundsätze der Gleichbehandlung, der Billigkeit, der guten Sitten oder von Treu und Glauben . . .'—which is partly a questionable one and thus a potential source of divergence!

[55] Joined Cases C-392/04 and C-422/04 *i-21 Germany*, Judgment of the Court of 19 September 2006, nyr, paras 67.

if the decision is manifestly incompatible with Community law'.[56] There are indeed indications that the imposition of a fee to cover estimated general administrative costs for a period of thirty years would ban competition in contravention of Directive (EC) 97/13 and would thus be manifestly incompatible with higher-ranking Community law. The ECJ left it to the German court to assess whether there really was that manifest incompatibility, though the indications of the Luxembourg court are quite clear.[57]

4.3 *Interim conclusion: a trace of divergence*

To sum up, a certain degree of unity is clearly sought by the ECJ in cases of a duty to withdraw administrative decisions. However, a trace of divergence remains. Also after *i-21 Germany and Arcor* it is not entirely clear whether there is a difference between the reopening of administrative proceedings and the withdrawal of a final decision.[58] For some jurisdictions, this might be irrelevant. Other administrative legal systems are more sophisticated—or over-complicated—and draw a clear distinction between the procedural matters and the decision on its merits. The Court does not tackle these divergences, but focuses on factual differences between the facts in the sense of distinguishing.

5 Outlook

It seems that, with respect to discretion after a decision has been made, ie in cases concerning stability and flexibility in administrative decision making, the impression of unity prevails. It should be noted, however, that the more complicated the regulation of a subject, the higher the risk of diverging concepts—and of a divergence that cannot be overcome. Thus, two dangers have to be taken into consideration—the danger of over-simplifying Europeanization on the one hand, and also the danger of exaggerated dogmaticism at Member State level on the other. If both dangers are carefully dealt with, continuing conceptual divergence can enrich a pluralist view of unity.

---

[56] ibid, paras 68ff.
[57] ibid, paras 70ff.
[58] cf also the differentiated position taken by G Britz and T Richter, 'Die Aufhebung eines gemeinschaftsrechtswidrigen nicht begünstigenden Verwaltungsakts' (2005) 45 Juristische Schulung, 200ff.

12

Democracy and Direct Effect: EU and National Perceptions of Discretion

Thomas Vandamme

1 Introduction: two types of discretion

Divergence of concepts, whether it is (deliberately) veiled or unveiled,[1] plays an important part primarily in the context of *application* and *enforcement* of EU law on the national plane. One of the key themes of the joint research project 'Binding Unity and Divergent Concepts in EU law' is the concept of 'discretion'. Indeed, there is no doubt that discretion as a concept may prove to be multi-faceted in the context of applying and enforcing European law in national legal orders. Van Roermund very lucidly enumerates different manifestations of discretion, some of which relate to concepts of discretion particularly relevant to the application and enforcement of EC law in the domestic systems, such as the discretion to choose operational concepts, to allocate the burden of proof, and more generally, the discretion embedded in the national procedural autonomy Member States (still) enjoy under *Rewe-Comet* jurisprudence.[2]

---

[1] In European lawmaking, it may be expected that divergence is tacitly agreed upon as a form of compromise, yet the possibility cannot be excluded that such divergence was truly unintentional. For more details see this volume, ch 2.

[2] See this volume, ch 14, van Roermund, 'Laws at Cross-Purposes, Conceptual Confusion and Political Divergence'. He builds further upon an earlier classification by H Somsen, 'Discretion in European Community Law, an Analysis of ECJ Case Law' (2003) 40 CML Rev, 1413.

However, it does not stop there. In this chapter I will attempt to add a further dimension to the research theme of discretion by expanding from application and enforcement of EU law to its *transposition* into national legislation.[3]

When national legislatures or executives transpose an EC directive into national law, they may or may not enjoy a certain amount of discretion left to them by the EC legislator. That discretion may (or again may not) trigger certain national procedures for swift lawmaking. In this chapter I will explore how far this type of discretion (perhaps best called *democracy discretion*) can be linked to another type of discretion, that used in the context of the direct enforcement of EC directives before national courts pursuant to *direct effect* (hereinafter called *direct effect direction*). It will be remembered that the basic criteria for direct effect, the tests of unconditionality and sufficient clarity, are strongly connected with a notion of discretion, or rather with the absence of discretion. Thus, in this chapter the concept of discretion will be looked at from two, quite different, angles: (i) that of direct effect, and (ii) that of trans-position. This double perspective allows a look at 'discretion' as supposedly embedded in one and the same EU act from opposite perspectives: the EU perspective and the national one. The following basic scenario may clarify this idea:

it is not unlikely that a national court directly applies Directive A (as a substitution norm, see *infra*) in deviation of national statute B that conflicts with Directive A. Later, Directive A may be transposed in national law by a procedure less democratic than usual: the government adopts governmental regulations that deviate from statute B, something it would normally not have been able to do under national constitutional standards protecting parliamentary laws such as statute B.

In the basic scenario mentioned here, it is discretion that is the determinant factor for the national court to directly apply Directive A. Furthermore, discretion, or rather, its absence, is also the determinant factor for having recourse to a less democratic national legislative procedure to transpose Directive A into national law (governmental regulation deviating from statutory law). Consequently, directive transposition on the one hand and directive enforcement/application on the other hand may both be strongly connected with what seems to be *discretion*, yet is obviously discretion from two quite different perceptions.

---

[3] See also Brand, 'Discretion, Divergence, and Unity', this volume, ch 9, who distinguishes between conceptual divergence on discretion itself and related conceptual divergence.

The basic question is whether these two qualifications of 'discretion' operating in these two different legal contexts could be somehow interrelated. For instance: when the European Court of Justice (ECJ) issues a preliminary ruling judging a directive's provision to be 'sufficiently clear and precise', does the Member State in its process of transposition consider this very same directive provision as one that, due to a lack of discretion, does not justify the 'full' democratic process of transposition? What this chapter will attempt to do is to explore whether these perceptions of discretion are indeed interrelated and, whether convergence between 'democracy discretion' and 'direct effect discretion' is conceivable.

2 Two perceptions of discretion interrelated?

'Direct effect discretion' is of course well known among lawyers, judges, and citizens. Member State discretion, or rather its absence, is after all the core element of the clarity and unconditionality test that the ECJ and national courts use to argue direct effect.[4] By contrast, 'democracy discretion' as a (possible) core element in the transposition context is less well-known and less studied by those interested in the effect directives produce in national law. Such difference in interest is well explained by the totally different 'environments' in which these concepts of discretion operate, one being 'top down' the other being 'bottom up'. No doubt there is less pan-European interest in researching the notion of 'democracy discretion' because it is regarded as typical to each individual Member State (part of its unique peculiarities).

For the sake of convenience and because it is the 'richest' instrument, the focus of this chapter will be on the transposition of the EC directive. A directive *must* be transposed, and it is still the legal instrument most used by the Community legislature and an instrument very much used by the Community executive. Despite criticism of the directive for the obvious reasons of it being slow and not guaranteeing uniform results,[5] it

---

[4] In as far as it is also an element for establishing liability for Member States or EC institutions (the sufficiently serious breach test) this will not be addressed here.

[5] See European Commission, 'European Governance, a White Paper' COM (2001) 428 final, in particular 11, 17. It calls into question the Amsterdam Protocol on Proportionality and Subsidiarity in this respect as the latter favours directives over regulations. However, the report also stresses the importance of the principle of 'proximity', a principle that may be understood as favouring the use of directives, 4. See also A von Bogdandy, F Arndt, and J Bast, 'Legal Instruments in European Union Law and their reform, A Systematic Approach on an Empirical basis' (2004) 23 Ybk of Eur L, 91–136.

may be expected that the EC[6] will continue to use it widely and hence will continue to draw heavily upon the lawmaking competences of national legislatures and executives.

As a preliminary point, it must be acknowledged that the topic of this chapter requires much more thorough research of national legislative practice than will be found below. Limitations as to time, accessibility, and resources have compelled me to be eclectic and cursory. Yet, it is hoped that this chapter induces others to take things further.

In the course of this chapter, I will first try to establish whether a possible convergence between discretion as operating in the context of direct effect and discretion as operating in the context of transposition is conceivable in the first place (section 3). I will then expand on the two different contexts as such, starting with transposition. Apart from the question of whether convergence is conceivable, I shall at that point also address the consequent methodological question of *how* to research such possible convergence. Then, in section 5, the context of direct effect will be further elaborated. Consequently, in section 6, I will discuss the outcome of certain investigations of 'cross-references' between these two types of discretion in Dutch legislative practice. In section 7, I, will try to draw the arguments together and present a provisional conclusion, or rather, a hypothesis on the actual and future relationship between 'direct effect discretion' and 'transposition discretion'.

3 Convergence conceivable?

When looking at the national 'perception' of discretion for transposition purposes ('democracy discretion'), it seems safe to assume that at this point unity is certainly not a *desideratum*. Quite the contrary: the question as to how the EU Member States give form to their domestic democratic and legislative process reaches the very core of national sovereignty. In this field, not convergence but divergence seems to be the *norm*. After all, this concept of 'democracy discretion' may be said to concern very basic respect for the 'national identities' of Member States, an adamant requirement and

---

[6] Or of course the EU when it issues framework decisions (see Art 34(2)(b) TEU). These, however, do not produce direct effect in the national legal orders, at least not as far as EU law is concerned, and are therefore less interesting in this respect.

prominent feature of EU law as set out in Article 6(3) EU and in Article I-5(1) of the Treaty establishing a Constitution for Europe (TCE).[7] It is precisely this divergence that underpins the whole concept of the directive as a more proportional instrument than the regulation.[8] In short: the choice of 'forms and means' in Article 249 EC explicitly aims to leave intact national preferences as to the appropriate democratic safeguards applicable to transposition and, consequently, the national perception of discretion in that respect.

As was stated before, 'discretion' also regards the very core of EC law, in particular when one deals with the question whether it can be directly invoked before a national court. At this point, it must be acknowledged that a comparison does not seem obvious when operating within these two contexts that are so fundamentally different. Directive *application* by national courts, and as a corollary, the discretion left by the directive that must be examined, only becomes relevant when transposition has not occurred, or at least not correctly. Thus 'direct effect discretion' seems only remotely connected to discretion in the *transposition* context, where it is a factor for determining the extent to which national democratic safeguards are applied.

However, different as apples and oranges may be, they are both fruit. Instead of emphasizing differences one may also focus on similarities. As long as that does not blind one to the differences, such an exercise may prove interesting and provide new insights. Consequently, it may be argued that, despite the differences between these concepts of discretion each operating in its own 'environment', they are, on a deeper level, both connected with a basic notion of *trias politica* and *checks and balances*.[9] In both contexts the same EC act is assessed on its discretionary contents and in both contexts, such (absence of) discretion is the vital element that may change the interrelationships between the three branches of national government.[10] There is a shift from both legislative and executive power to the judiciary (direct effect) and from the legislative power to the executive power (accelerated transposition, see below). An example may be derived from a debate held in the Dutch

[7] The latter Article has the innovative effect of explicitly requiring respect for the 'fundamental structures, political and constitutional' of the Member States. It also requires respect for regional and local self-government.

[8] See Art 6 of the Protocol on Subsidiarity and Proportionality to the Treaty of the European Community.

[9] See also Brand, this volume ch 9, p 226 quoting J Schwarze, *European Administrative Law* (London: Sweet & Maxwell, 1992) 292: 'discretion [...] in essence touches on a matter of principle, namely the inter-relationship which prevails among state authorities'.

[10] Possibly also between the national horizontal separations of powers, particularly in federated states.

House of Commons. Former Dutch Minister of Economic Affairs Laurens-Jan Brinkhorst boldly characterized the Dutch Parliament as an authority with a more *executive nature* in the context of transposition.[11]

To revert to the possible scenario mentioned previously: it is not unlikely that a national court may apply Directive A (as a substitution norm, see below) in derogation of statute B that is consequently implemented by the government in deviation of that same statute. In such a scenario the lack of discretion that, according to EC law, justifies the increased power of the court towards the legislature, according to national law itself also justifies the increased power of government towards the legislature. After all, increased governmental power is usually the result of taking recourse to an accelerated, less democratic procedure (see below).

4 Discretion and transposition

It was stated that discretion as the central element of the 'sufficient clarity and unconditionality' test for direct effect operates in a very different context from discretion as a justification for upholding national democratic safeguards. The former concept of discretion relates to the relationship between national courts vis-à-vis national legislatures or executives. The latter concept of discretion primarily deals with the relationship of national executives vis-à-vis national legislatures. All interrelationships between these national branches of government change in an EU context. In general, courts grow more powerful[12] and in many cases so does the executive (see for instance the *Fratelli Costanzo* case).[13]

At this point, mention may be made of a small victory for the legislature in at least one Member State. In the Netherlands the question arose whether courts should be able to order the legislature to legislate if EC law requires

---

[11] Moreover, he thought it to be very unbalanced that at the same time the Dutch Parliament's involvement as a legislative authority in influencing the adoption of EC directives is not well organized and, insofar as it is adequately organized, there is little eagerness on its part to use the existing possibilities to their maximum potential, a striking contrast with the UK, see TK, 2004–2005, 29474, no 8, 7 February 2005, 13.

[12] See however, for a possible exception Case C-224/01 *Köbler* [2003] ECR I-10239: a national court's actions conflicting with EC law may be subject to proceedings for damages.

[13] However, the idea was recently rejected that national executives should have the power to set aside possibly invalid EC acts (thus to provide so-called '*Zuckerfabik* protection'), an idea that can be regarded as '*Costanzo*-linked', see Joined Cases C-11/04, C-12/04, and C-194/04 *Nevedi*, Judgment of the Court of 6 December 2005, nyr.

this. In the *Waterpakt* case the Dutch Supreme Court finally settled this issue in favour of the legislature.[14] The common feature between these two different 'discretion contexts' is the fact that the national legislature is the one branch of national government whose position unavoidably weakens in a 'directive setting'.

There are various examples of national transposition where the legislature is sidelined. In France, for instance, it is not uncommon for directives to be transposed by means of an *ordonnance*, a temporary law adopted by the executive in a field that, according to the French constitution would normally prescribe a *loi* (statute). At a later stage, such French executive legislation would have to be 'ratified' by parliament. Also in the Netherlands, it is possible for the executive to be empowered to implement an EC directive in derogation of statutory law, under the proviso that eventually such an executive act would be 'ratified' by a statute.[15] This particular phenomenon has already taken greater flight in Belgium. In Belgium the (federal) executive is empowered to transpose directives in a number of fields by deviating from (federal) statutes, but here a 'parliamentary ratification' is not always required.[16] Finally, in the United Kingdom, widespread lawmaking powers have been delegated to the executive (see below) for transposition purposes whereby deviation from statutory law is possible for the majority of EC directives. In the UK, statutory clauses allowing for such deviation are, not without wit, designated as 'Henry VIII clauses', a term that in this chapter will be more generally applied to 'tag' this phenomenon as it occurs in the various national legal systems. Contrary to French, Belgian, and Dutch law, UK law does not require parliamentary 'ratification' of this type of transposition legislation.

This possibility of deviating from statutory law by later executive regulations is of course the most vivid example of transposition legislation (temporarily) changing national *trias politica* relationships. Yet, such changes may also be more subtle. For instance, the democratic institutional mechanisms may be kept intact, while being reduced to a quasi-formality. In the Netherlands in particular, this approach is suggested as the best solution to the problem of

---

[14] Hoge Raad, 21 March 2003, JB 2003, 120. The Supreme Court declined to ask for a preliminary ruling on this matter even though there were good grounds to do so.

[15] HJHL Kortes and KAE Vervloet, 'Versnelde implementatie: een dringende kwestie in te rustig vaarwater' (2006) 54 SEW Tijdschrift voor Europees en Economisch Recht, 94, 95, 97.

[16] Older Dutch legislation empowering the executive to deviate from a statute also does not request such later parliamentary 'ratification'.

swiftly implementing directives (see *infra*).[17] One could describe this as the 'substantive' acceleration of lawmaking as opposed to the 'formal' acceleration of lawmaking.

4.1 *Avoiding democratic leakage: the key to comparative research?*

How does one perform comparative research on discretion in relation to the issue of possibly less democratic, accelerated, transposition of directives into national law? One method of getting a grip on this matter is by bringing into the picture the phenomenon of 'democratic leakage'. Swiftly transposing a directive that leaves a great deal of discretion may empower the national executive to impose policies that can only be said to be remotely vested in the directive. It is suggested that one takes as a point of reference *the avoidance of democratic leakage*. Comparative research on this issue would become easier if one accepts as common ground that the 'leakage' of democracy in the transposition process between the adoption of the directive and its (swift) implementation is to be avoided.[18] Defining discretion is of course the crucial element in preventing such 'leakage' from occurring.[19] The more discretion that is arguably embedded in the European (directive) provision, the less acceptable swift implementation *should* then be.[20]

Against these different national backgrounds, the term 'discretion' in the transposition context necessarily harbours a further twenty-seven different views on discretion. That must be so. As stated before, the directive as an instrument is originally designed to leave intact the various viewpoints on discretion (supposedly) embedded in its provisions, in particular

---

[17] Also, the legislative process may be altered in ways that do not directly affect the legislature individually. In the Netherlands, all mandatory consultation requirements may be waived when the (parliamentary) act to be adopted is a transposition measure, see Art 1:8(2) of the Dutch General Administrative Code (Algemene wet bestuursrecht).

[18] See also B Steunenberg and WJM Voermans, 'De Bermuda-driehoek van de versnelde implementatie' (2005) RegelMaat, 205–217.

[19] See TAJA Vandamme, 'Alternative Lawmaking Procedures in the Netherlands for the Sake of Implementation of the EC Directive: A Question of Going too Far or Not Going Far Enough' in TAJA Vandamme and JH Reestman (eds), *Ambiguity in the Rule of Law: The Interface between National and International Legal Systems* (Groningen: Europa Law Publishing, 2001) 110.

[20] It is remarkable that in a recent study of the University of Leiden (commissioned by the Dutch Ministry of Justice) on the practices in several EU Member States on transposition of EC acts, the issue of 'democratic leakage' was hardly addressed whereas, in my view, it should play a key role in developing policy in this regard. See D Steunenberg and W Voermans, *De omzetting van Europese richtlijnen, instrumenten technieken en processen in zes lidstaten vergeleken* (Leiden: Universiteit Leiden, 2005).

in interaction with the national *trias politica* constellation. The notion of *trias politica* is, in the words of Koopmans 'one of the few systematic starting points in the area of public law'.[21] Thus, despite it being a good paradigm and a useful tool for comparative research, it is also clear that national views on *trias politica* and on checks and balances differ to start with.

The national constitutional constellations that form the context of (accelerated) transposition may differ to a great extent to begin with. Consequently, if in a certain Member State the executive in a particular field enjoys widespread powers, it may be expected that in that field, the executive will be able to implement a directive without much interference from Parliament. Yet, in another Member State, that same directive would be qualified as leaving considerable discretion and therefore justifying a full-fledged democratic transposition procedure. As *trias politica* has a different meaning and form in the various national legal systems, so does discretion in the context of transposition. This unavoidable divergence on 'democracy discretion' may be illustrated by highlighting the differences in this respect between the UK and Ireland.

4.2 *Divergence of democracy: the Anglo-Irish example*

It is not surprising that in the United Kingdom, a country with arguably one of the most powerful executives *anyway*, the process of transposition of directives is largely a governmental or ministerial affair. Related to that, it seems that in the UK, a directive that one could easily classify as leaving Member States much discretion may still be implemented in a swift and relatively undemocratic fashion, sidelining Westminster. Indeed, the fact is that in the UK, the majority of directives are implemented by executive lawmaking powers laid down in the European Communities Act 1972 (hereinafter 'ECA'), a statute granting Whitehall the power to adopt executive legislation ('statutory instruments') that implement a directive, without there being any limitation as to the amount of discretion the directive could still be said to contain. Article 2(2) ECA simply states that:

Her majesty may, [. . .] make provisions for the purpose of implementing *any Community obligation* of the United Kingdom (emphasis added).[22]

---

[21] See T Koopmans, *Courts and Political Institutions, a Comparative View* (Cambridge: Cambridge University Press, 2003) 11.

[22] The only parameters being set out in 'Schedule 2' of the European Communities Act 1972: new or increased taxation, legislation with retroactive effect, further sub-delegation or the introduction of serious criminal offences are outside the scope of the ECA.

A new balance between executive and legislature in the transposition context was struck by granting supervisory powers to the Houses of Parliament through a 'negative resolution procedure'. During a short period of time, either House may reject a draft statutory instrument proposed under the ECA, something that is however a rare occurrence. Furthermore, as earlier described, the ECA contains a 'Henry VIII clause'. Thus under these wide legislative powers, the British executive is allowed to deviate from existing statutes, a mechanism that may also be observed in UK law outside the context of transposition.[23]

Having said that, it is interesting to turn to the neighbouring Irish Republic, a country whose legal system resembles that of the UK in many ways but with quite a different view on discretion in the context of transposition. In Ireland a transposition mechanism was set up that looks very similar to that of the British ECA, at least at first sight. This Act, hereinafter to be referred to as the 'Irish ECA',[24] is conceptually similar to the British ECA in that these two Acts both delegate to the executive wide-ranging lawmaking powers for the transposition of directives. The Irish ECA clearly attempted to establish a balance between on the one hand facilitating the transposition process and on the other maintaining the solid influence of the Irish legislature (the *Oireachtas*). Under this mechanism, ministerial measures[25] retain their legal force unless explicitly overruled by the *Oireachtas*.[26] Thus, in a way very similar to what happens in the UK, a 'negative resolution' mechanism governs Irish transposition of EC directives.[27] A further resemblance to UK law is that the Irish ECA too contains a 'Henry VIII clause', allowing Irish ministerial decrees to deviate from statutes.

Yet, there is also an important difference between the wordings of the UK ECA and the Irish ECA. The latter clearly expresses awareness of possible

---

[23] See for instance the Child Support Act 1991 and the Deregulation and Contracting Out Act 1994.

[24] See C Gallagher, 'The Case of Ireland' in SA Pappas (ed), *National Administrative Procedures for the Preparation and Implementation of Community Decisions* (Maastricht: EIPA, 1995) 301–314.

[25] There is much de-concentration in Ireland among the Departmental Ministers. There is no concept of 'Order in Council'.

[26] The *Oireachtas* annulling a statutory instrument is a rarity, despite the vigilance of the *Oireachtas* Joint Committee on secondary Legislation of the European Communities. One of the reasons may be the weakened position of this committee due to the fact that it stops being in function whenever the Dail (the Lower House of the *Oireachtas*) is dissolved; see F Murphy, 'The Fifth *Oireachtas* Joint Committee on Secondary Legislation' (1990) ELR, 274–279.

[27] In the original Act, there was however a system of positive control. As that was held to be too cumbersome, it was abandoned within a year after Irish membership of the EEC and replaced by the present system of negative review.

'democratic leakage' in the transposition process. Whereas the UK ECA merely mentions 'any Community obligation' as a sufficient element triggering executive lawmaking power, its Irish counterpart maintains a more careful phrasing:

A Minister may make regulations for enabling (*directives*), to have full effect. Regulations under this section may contain such *incidental, supplementary and consequential provisions* as appear to the Minister making the regulations to be *necessary* (emphasis added).[28]

Thus, the Irish ECA only allows for the adoption of executive legislation that is 'incidental, supplementary and consequential'. Furthermore, despite this limitation as to the scope of the executive lawmaking power, the Irish ECA would still cross the line of what would normally be acceptable delegation of powers in an 'autonomous' Irish context as ministerial regulations may still deviate from statute law.[29] A prior constitutional amendment was therefore required, shielding the Irish ECA from unconstitutionality:

No provision of this Constitution invalidates laws enacted, acts done or measures adopted by the State which are *necessitated* by the obligations of Membership of the European Union[30]

Discretion, or rather the lack of it, was translated as 'necessity'. Not surprisingly, that criterion proved too vague to be a suitable delineation. Right after the adoption of the Irish ECA, it was argued that the obligations arising from the *mere duty to transpose* directives *necessitated* endowing the executive with wide legislative powers it normally would not have, including the power of altering or abrogating statutes of the *Oireachtas*. In other words, it was said that the Irish executive should have, to use UK terminology, 'Henry VIII powers'. Of course there were others who argued that the mere duty to implement directives leaving Member States the choice of 'form and methods' cannot be said to 'necessitate' such potentially widespread executive powers vis-à-vis the legislature.[31] In their view, such a reading of the Irish ECA in which, under the guise of 'necessity', considerable discretion could

---

[28] See s 3, paras 1 and 2 of the Irish European Communities Act.
[29] As made clear in *City View Press Ltd v An Chomhairle Oiliúna* [1980] IR 381, 399 (Supreme Court). See also J Casey, *Constitutional Law in Ireland* (3rd edn, Dublin: Round Hall Sweet & Maxwell, 2000) 221.
[30] See Art 29(4)(10) Irish Constitution (*Bunreacht na hÉireann*).
[31] See P Keatinge, *Ireland and EC Membership Evaluated* (London: Pinter, 1991) 214.

be exercisable by government would clearly violate the national *trias politica* constellation.[32]

In 1993, these opposing views were put to the test when the Irish Supreme Court was asked to review the constitutionality of the Irish ECA. In its *Meagher* ruling[33] it upheld the validity of the Act,[34] but not without issuing a certain 'instruction' as to the actual use of this power. A certain scrutiny was therefore interpreted into the terms of the Irish ECA. In the words of Justice Denham, an Irish Minister can only make use of the powers under the Irish ECA:

where the [. . .] situation is that the *principles and policies* were determined in the directive, then legislation by a delegated form is a valid choice.[35]

If, in the Irish perception, 'principles and policies'are left to the Member States to decide upon, transposition must be pursued by means of an Act of the *Oireachtas*. In that sense the Supreme Court does not treat the matter any differently from the general limitations in Irish constitutional law on delegation to the executive, the test being 'whether what is challenged as an unauthorized delegation of parliamentary power is more then a *mere giving effect to principles and policies* which are contained in the statute itself' (author's emphasis).[36] To top it off, Denham J added an argument relating to the futility of upholding the democratic safeguards in cases where the 'principles and policies' were determined by a directive:

That being the case the role of the Oireachtas would be sterile. It would be able solely to have a debate as to what has already been decided.[37]

---

[32] See Art 15(2)(1) Irish Constitution, vesting the sole legislative power to make or amend statutes in the *Oireachtas*.

[33] *Meagher v Minister for Agriculture* [1993] IESC 2 or [1994] 1 IR 329 (Supreme Court).

[34] Since this was a constitutional issue of reviewing the constitutionality of an Act of the *Oireachtas*, there were no dissenting opinions published, see Art 34(4)(5) of the Irish Constitution.

[35] See para 17 of the Supreme Court's ruling in *Meagher v Minister for Agriculture* [1994] 1 IR 329 (Supreme Court). Denham J (his colleagues agreeing) in the *Meagher* case, 365. He links it with the wording of the Irish European Communities Act itself limiting the minister's power to creating 'incidental, supplementary and consequential provisions'. At this point, the opinions are made public for it does not concern the constitutionality of statutory law. See *Meagher v Minister for Agriculture*, para 49.

[36] *City View Press v An Chomhairle Oiliúna* [1980] IR 381 (Supreme Court). See also L Prakke and CAJM Kortmann, *Het Staatsrecht van de landen van de Europese Unie* (Deventer: Kluwer, 1998) 379.

[37] *Meagher v Minister for Agriculture* [1994] 1 IR 329 (Supreme Court), para 88, 89.

This case provides a prime example of a national court guarding the national democratic safeguards against what can be called 'democratic leakage' while at the same time acknowledging that such safeguards must be reassessed in the light of the changing world, governed more and more by Brussels. The choice of the criterion of 'principles and policies' and its complementary criterion of 'incidental, supplementary and consequential decisions' seems to make sense although it is also true that such criteria will of course never be fully waterproof. The question of the 'margins of the margins' is of course inevitable with any kind of definition of discretion. That being said, the fact remains that whenever 'principles and policies' (whatever that may exactly entail) are determined by the directive, Denham J characterizes the implementing of statutory instruments as 'what is in essence subordinate legislation as delegated under Community law'.[38]

Thus, despite certain similarities between the Irish and the UK methods of transposition, they differ considerably in approach when it comes to the safeguarding of the position of the *Oireachtas*[39] as opposed to that of the Parliament of Westminster. Whereas the UK ECA is legally indifferent to the amount of discretion embedded in the directive, the Irish ECA tries to divide discretion into the categories 'principles and policies' on the one hand and 'incidental, supplementary and consequential decisions' on the other.[40]

The difference between the UK ECA and the Irish ECA reflects a difference in national *trias politica* relations. The Irish Constitution, much more than the British Constitution, attempts to grant the legislature *inalienable* rights that may not be waived in an EC context, at least not if, in that EC context, the Irish authorities are considered still to be endowed with a fair amount of discretion. The British view is more that of a sovereign Parliament that must be able to waive (or alienate) its right (by adopting the UK ECA in the first place). For is not temporarily abandoning sovereignty the ultimate proof of that very same sovereignty?[41] Against that background,

---

[38] ibid, para 92. Such a perception of the status of national law transposing a directive does not have a basis in EC law itself; see TAJA Vandamme, *The Invalid Directive: The Legal Authority of a Union Act Requiring Domestic Law Making* (Groningen: Europa Law Publishing, 2005).

[39] For those not familiar with Gaelic, this is to be pronounced *Irókthas*.

[40] See also N Travers, 'The Constitutionality of the Implementation of EC Directives into Irish Law Revisited' (1994) 88 Gazette of the Incorporated Law Society in Ireland, 99.

[41] See however, Laws LJ in *Thoburn v Sunderland City Council* [2002] EWHC 195, para 64 on parliamentary sovereignty: 'being sovereign, it cannot abandon its sovereignty'.

discretion plays a pivotal role in the Irish transposition context whereas it seems only of secondary interest in the UK context.[42]

This example of the UK constitutional system as contrasted with its Irish counterpart indicates clearly that a *horizontal comparison* between the various Member States as to their perception of the amount of discretion in a particular directive is quite difficult. The 'avoidance of democratic leakage' may be a key to comparison but it of course serves just as effectively as a key to demonstrate the differences. Any comparison of national perceptions of 'democracy discretion' can therefore only have a vertical, compartmentalized basis. The main question then is whether twenty-seven concepts of 'democracy discretion' may still converge (each from their own starting point) under the influence of a common EU concept of discretion as embedded in the doctrine of direct effect.

5 Discretion and direct effect

As stated earlier, EC law requirements of sufficient clarity and unconditionality both seem derivatives of the basic requirement of absence of discretion, the true 'ground' for direct effect. It is that absence of discretion that may induce national courts to apply the directive provision directly without crossing any national *trias politica* boundaries. Not surprisingly, there is an abundance of legal writing in which direct effect and the EC law conditions that trigger it are linked with notions of *trias politica*.[43]

The actual assessment of discretion in this context is obviously not easy. It requires a detailed analysis of each instrument to 'tag' its individual provisions as leaving more or less discretion, regardless of one's perspective. Sometimes, a directive's typology may give a first clue, but really nothing more than that. For example, a 'framework directive' (a term that sounds a bit like a pleonasm), introduced in the Amsterdam Protocol on Subsidiarity

---

[42] It must be noted that although *legally* there are no limitations as to the discretion still to be present in a directive, *politically*, the UK Government may be put under pressure not to use its powers under the ECA but rather to propose a bill to Parliament, as it did in the Milk Act 1983.

[43] See A Prechal, *Directives in EC Law* (Oxford: Oxford University Press, 2005) 252, 231, 244, stating that the conditions for direct effect are of limited value: 'in the final analysis the ultimate test is to be found in the doctrine of separation of powers'. See also P Pescatore, 'The Doctrine of "Direct Effect": An Infant Disease of community Law' (1983) ELR, 177 and PJG Kapteyn, P Verloren van Themaat, and R Barents, *Het recht van de Europese Unie en van de Europese Gemeenschappen* (Deventer: Kluwer, 2003) 427.

and Proportionality may be expected to leave a good deal of discretion.[44] Furthermore, a directive aiming at total harmonization may sooner be expected to leave less discretion than one prescribing minimum harmonization. As one scholar states: 'In case of total harmonization, Member States merely implement Community legislation and fulfil the task of "an executive agency".'[45]

Last but not least, directives in the 'tertiary layer' of EC law, usually adopted by the Commission under 'comitology scrutiny', may be expected to have direct effect sooner than basic directives. Yet, these are all 'rules of thumb' and a detailed analysis of every single provision of any kind of directive remains necessary.

The guidance of the ECJ on the matter is of course helpful. However, one must be careful in searching for such guidance in jurisprudence that regards the discretion in directives as being in a different context from that of direct effect. For instance, when reviewing the *validity* of the Biotechnology Directive in annulment proceedings under Article 230 EC, the ECJ drew a distinction between 'discretion' and 'room for manoeuvre'.[46] This concerned Article 6 of the Biotechnology Directive regarding the *ordre public* exception to patentability of biotechnological inventions. The 'room for manoeuvre' embedded therein did not amount to legal uncertainty for which the Directive could be invalidated.

It is not at all clear whether this lack of discretion (or rather 'room for manoeuvre') indicates that the provision at issue must be deemed to have direct effect, let alone direct effect in its manifestation of *Alternativ-Normierung*.[47]

---

[44] To either the national authorities or to the EC authorities. See for an official example: Parliament and Council Directive (EC) 2000/60 establishing a framework for Community action in the field of water policy [2000] OJ L327/1. See for an unofficial example Council Directive (EEC) 89/391 on the introduction of measures to encourage improvements in the safety and health of workers at work [1989] OJ L183/1.

[45] See SA de Vries, *Tensions within the Internal Market, the Functioning of the Internal Market and the Development of Horizontal and Flanking Policies* (Groningen: Europa Law Publishing, 2006). See more generally with respect to harmonization: N Bernard, 'The Future of European Economic Law in the Light of the Principle of Subsidiarity' (1996) CML Rev, 63.

[46] See Case C-377/98 *Netherlands v European Parliament and Council* [2001] ECR I-7079, paras 38–40.

[47] Likewise, similar reservation must be made when the ECJ regards the admissibility of individual complaints against a directive under Art 230(4) TEC, see for instance Case T-223/01 *Japan Tobacco and JT International v Parliament and Council* [2002] ECR II-3259, paras 51–56. The tobacco companies challenging the Tobacco Directive under Art 230(4) TEC were said not to be

The term *Alternativ-Normierung* presents a further complicating factor in the picture. When dealing with the question of direct effect, the absence of discretion may refer to a mere 'limit', a (minimum) boundary that may not be crossed by the national legislator or executive. It was this type of review of national measures that drew a lot of attention in the aftermath of the *Kraai-jeveld* case.[48] In this respect, the well-known distinction between the 'shield' and 'sword' function of direct effect may prove useful once again.[49]

It is the 'sword function' of the directive or direct effect as *'Alternativ-Normierung'* that is of most interest here.[50] Controversy may be more easily expected in relation to what Member States must do as opposed to what they can be forbidden to do. It may not be clear what their positive action should entail, but it will usually be quite clear what action or inaction is definitely off limits.

Thus, when direct effect manifests itself as *Alternativ-Normierung*, it is more delicate in terms of national *trias politica* than when it performs a legal review function. The chances are greater that the amount of discretion will have to be weighed on silver scales against national concepts of *trias politica*, and, uncannily for some, it may be the ECJ that balances those scales. Prechal also acknowledges the vital difference between these two functions of direct effect:

Arguably, for a positive application, thus for a fully fledged alternative, the national court will need 'more' and another type of guidance from the provisions at issue than when it is asked to proceed to review the legality.[51]

Therefore, the directive as *Alternativ-Normierung* is far more interesting as its intrusion into national *trias politica* constellations requires (or may be expected to require) a more detailed judgment on the amount of discretion the directive attributes to the national branches of government.

---

directly concerned as the Directive's terminology on the specific issue they contested explicitly left national authorities a certain discretion in how to apply it.

[48] Although it was far from a novelty; see Prechal, see n 43 above, 236, 237, who regards it as a species of legality review. See for a recent example of this mode of direct effect Case C-127/02 *Landelijke Vereniging tot Behoud van de Waddenzee* [2004] ECR I-7405, para 67 concerning Art 6(3) Council Directive (EEC) 92/43 on the conservation of natural habitats and of wild fauna and flora [1992] OJ L206/7 (Habitat Directive).

[49] See also Prechal, see n 43 above, 241 who identifies these two functions separately in the definition of direct effect: 'Direct effect is the obligation of a court or another public authority to apply the relevant provision of Community law *either as a norm which governs the case or as a standard for legal review*' (emphasis added).

[50] Or 'invocabilité de substitution', see Lenaerts and Corthaut, this volume, ch 21 p 510

[51] See Prechal, see n 43 above, 251.

6 'Cross-references' between concepts of discretion: Dutch legislative practice

In order to put matters to the test, a brief analysis of Dutch legislative practice regarding discretion for transposition purposes and its possible 'cross-reference' to direct effect discretion will be given here. The Netherlands might prove an interesting country in this regard as Dutch lawmaking practice is still struggling with the question of how to balance the requirements of transposition with the basic requirements of democracy.[52] A debate on this issue started a number of years ago at the time when the Dutch Government proposed a new statute allowing it to implement (telecommunications) directives by deviation of that same statute. In UK terms this would be an ordinary 'Henry VIII clause' (see above). Whereas such a clause is not regarded as unusual in British constitutional law, it is considered constitutional blasphemy by a number of Dutch lawyers.[53] Thus, this proposed telecommunications statute kick-started the fundamental debate on how the Dutch should strike the balance between national democratic safeguards and the duty to implement directives swiftly.

In terms of what was described above as 'democratic leakage' the question of discretion *should* be a key element in the Dutch discussion on introducing 'Henry VIII clauses'. Yet, discretion has not always been a prominent issue in this discussion.[54] It was, however, the key element in a recent debate in the Dutch House of Commons. Almost all parties in this debate (except for the Liberal Party) agreed that discretion was ultimately to be defined by Parliament, acting upon proposals from the government to implement it swiftly by means of executive legislation. It is interesting to note therefore that a national definition of what should be 'discretion' (as for instance in Irish law, see above) is rejected as such and replaced by an open ad hoc judgment of Parliament.[55]

---

[52] A balancing act, of course set against the backdrop of the inherent limited capacity of lawmaking institutions.

[53] See Kortes and Vervloet, see n 15 above, 97–98, restating that there is no *Kompetenz-Kompetenz* for the Dutch statutory legislator.

[54] Strikingly, in the Senate (the upper house of the Dutch Parliament) where the debate had started six years earlier, the issue of directive discretion was not mentioned at all. See the most recent debate in the Dutch Senate (which includes a good summary of what had been said and done in the foregoing six years) EK, 2004–2005, 29803, 1 February 2005, 14–645.

[55] Although there is still discussion on the operational issues involved, such as *how much* parliamentarians can adopt the negative resolution, calling for a statute instead of executive legislation. Another interesting aspect in this debate was that the issue of swift transposition

In general, debates on accelerated directive transposition into Dutch law hardly contain references to direct effect discretion. When one does find references to direct effect discretion, it is in another context from that of accelerated transposition. An example of such a different reference may be direct effect as a 'relaxing factor': in the Dutch parliamentary proceedings leading up to the adoption of the statute implementing Directive (EC) 2003/8 on access to justice in cross-border disputes, direct effect had a 'relaxing' influence of this type on the national lawmaking process.[56] A month before the deadline was to lapse (it being blatantly clear that this deadline was not going to be met) the Dutch Government informed parliamentarians that the expiry of the deadline 'would be no catastrophe as the directive will have direct effect from that date'.[57]

Incidentally, in this example the Dutch reference to direct effect is also interesting in the sense that, even today, there is no indication from the Community judicature that Directive (EC) 2003/8 is indeed directly effective.[58] One must therefore be aware that this remains a Dutch perception of an EU perception of direct effect (and thereby of discretion).

On occasions, one does find a genuine 'cross reference' to (possible!) direct effect in an accelerated implementation procedure. As said before, economizing on national democracy for lack of discretion may also take place without changing the formal (constitutional) lawmaking structures. This 'substantive' rather than formal amendment of the legislative process could be observed in the Netherlands when the statute was passed to (further) transpose the Habitat Directive into Dutch law.[59] Here the direct effect of this Directive was one argument to speed up the legislative process

was directly connected with the discussion on how to safeguard Dutch parliamentary influence in the EC negotiation process, see TK, 2004–2005, 29474, no 8, 7 February 2005.

[56] Another example may be Order in Council of 26 April 2001 transposing Parliament and Council Directive (EC) 1999/4 relating to coffee extracts and chicory extracts [1999] OJ L66/26, Bulletin of Laws and Decrees 2001, no 218. The explanatory memorandum mitigates the lapsing of the transposition deadline as the Directive's provisions have direct effect. Again, this is a Dutch assumption that was not confirmed in Case C-239/02 *Douwe Egberts*, [2004] ECR I-7007, the only case on this Directive. See also a reassuring statement of this kind coming from Justice Minister Donner in the parliamentary proceedings on the bill that was to transpose Parliament and Council Directive (EC) 2000/35 on combating late payment in commercial transactions [2000] OJ L200/35, EK, 2002–2003, 28239, no 5, 18 November 2002, 132.

[57] See TK, 2004–2005, 29712, no 5, 25 October 2004, 1.

[58] See Council Directive (EC) 2003/8 to improve access to justice in cross border disputes by establishing common rules relating to legal aid for such disputes [2003] OJ L26/41.

[59] For the time prior to the adoption of that statute, the Netherlands was sanctioned in Case C-441/03 *Commission v The Netherlands* [2005] ECR I-3043.

(but without altering it).[60] For the time being, however, the conclusion must be that in Dutch legislative practice, such 'cross references' are a rarity. Evidently, regarding other Member States, this matter calls for further research.

7 From diversity to unity and back again

Sometimes, the notion of direct effect is explicitly rejected as an indication of what the applicable democratic standards on the national level should be. The Belgian federal government wanted to implement Directive (EEC) 90/388 swiftly, setting aside a Belgian federal statute. The use of this 'Henry VIII clause' was controversial as the Belgian Council of State, advising on the proposed government decree, worded serious doubts as to the appropriateness of using such a tool to implement a directive that left 'too much discretionary powers' to the Member States. The Belgian Government disagreed with the Council of State, claiming that:

if the Council of State's objections were followed, the government could in fact use the clause [= The 'Henry VIII clause'] *only* for implementing directive provisions that have *direct effect*.[61]

A statement such as this, taking the negative perspective on direct effect, probably amounts to what is the highest achievable level of uniformity at this point. Arguably, a deviation from national democratic safeguards should be justified in all Member States when the directive produces a directly effective *Alternativ Normiering*. One could at that point imagine a convergence of that which seems to be impossible to convene: national perceptions of discretion that relate directly to national perceptions of democracy and *trias politica*.

It is therefore suggested that congruence between 'democracy discretion' and 'direct effect discretion' may at least be constructed. To take it one step

---

[60] See TK, 2004–2005, 28171, no 5, 2. That direct effect was later confirmed for merely one particular provision of the Habitat Directive in Case C-127/02 *Landelijke Vereniging tot Behoud van de Waddenzee* [2004] ECR I-7405, para 67. See for a very indirect 'cross-reference' to direct effect the statement of the Dutch Council of State that accepted that transposition by delegated Dutch legislation would be more appropriate if the directive concerned was itself based on delegated powers, see Advice of the Dutch Council of State of 8 April 2004, no WO3.04.0024/I.

[61] Royal Decree of 28 October 1996 concerning the transposition of obligations that stem from the Commission Directives regarding the free competition on the market of telecommunications services, *Moniteur belge* of 10 December 1996. See also Vandamme, see n 38 above, 269.

further, if any convergence on the idea of discretion is detectable, one may take that as a stepping-stone to arguing in favour of a convergence of the idea of *trias politica* itself. Whether all the actors concerned—the ECJ, the national legislatures, executives, and courts—fully realize this connection may be doubted and it is this doubt that was the incentive for this chapter.

Yet, although such a finding (direct effect discretion as the common baseline for twenty-seven varieties of democracy discretion) has the charm of simplicity, one must take due care of the possible divergence that may then take place on what provisions do indeed have direct effect. It would seem that at this point the EU judicature and the national legislators, executives, and courts do not necessarily agree. If direct effect—discretion (for the purposes of establishing *Alternativ-Normierung*) is to be a useful minimum yardstick for assessing discretion as an element in the democratic safeguards of EC transposition (whatever those may entail in the national constitutional systems) one must be aware that this will in many cases involve dealing with a national perception of an EC perception of direct effect. Those two perceptions will not always be congruent. As Prechal states it:

What seems to be a justiciable matter in the eyes of the ECJ may be considered differently by national courts who may fear the accusation of the *gouvernement des juges*.[62]

As illustrated above, this works both ways, as direct effect may also be assumed (in national legislative practice) in situations where the ECJ's agreement remains to be seen.

In conclusion, it is not unlikely that the concept of discretion may swing from complete diversity to a certain, convening, minimum concept of direct effect discretion only to swing back again to what could be *national expectations* of direct effect that show inherent divergence once again.

---

[62] See Prechal, see n 43 above, 253, with reference to J Mertens de Wilmars, 'De directe werking van het Europese recht' (1969) SEW Tijdschrift voor Europees en Economisch Recht, 62.

13

Discretion and Public Policy: Timing the Unity and Divergence of Legal Orders

Hans Lindahl

1 Introduction

EC Treaty, Articles 30, 39, 46, and 55 allow for derogation from the free movement of goods, persons, and services between the Member States of the European Community on grounds, amongst others, of public policy (see also Article 95(4) ECT pursuant to harmonization). Early on, the European Court of Justice (ECJ) acknowledged that the Member States enjoy a measure of discretionary power when invoking this derogation: 'the particular circumstances justifying recourse to the concept of public policy may vary from one country to another and from one period to another [. . .]'.[1] Yet, by indicating that the derogation must be strictly construed and that it would review the invocation thereof by the Member States, the Court also indicated that it was prepared to safeguard the unity of the EC in the face of divergent applications of the public policy derogation. It is tempting to view this case as an exemplary confirmation of the hypothesis concerning conceptual divergence, if not necessarily of discretion on its own, then, at any rate, in conjunction with public policy. But, as we shall see, it is highly doubtful that the discretionary exercise of the public policy reserve might illustrate conceptual divergence in the strong sense demanded by the hypothesis. There is, however, an alternative, legally and philosophically more rewarding reading of the relation between discretion and public policy. I propose to view discretion not only as the scope of legal power but also as power over the scope of the

[1] Case 41/74 *Yvonne van Duyn v Home Office* [1974] ECR 1350.

law. This reading of discretion, it will be argued, sheds light on the process by which the EC and its Member States negotiate the unity and divergence of their respective legal orders in the context of the public policy exception.

This chapter unfolds in five stages. Section 2 briefly dips into the case law of the discretionary exercise of the public policy reserve to show that there is little hope of confirming the hypothesis of conceptual divergence, either with respect to public policy or to discretion. The subsequent sections attempt to move beyond this impasse. Drawing on Hans Kelsen's analysis of the indeterminacy of legal norms, section 3 introduces the twofold sense of discretion noted above. Section 4 moves beyond the limitations of Kelsen's analysis, situating discretion in a general theory of constituent and constituted power. Section 5 examines public policy afresh in the light of this denser notion of discretion. Bringing the twofold sense of discretion to bear on *Grogan*, the well-known abortion information case, this section explores how the ECJ and the Irish Supreme Court play for time, negotiating divergence by postponing the unity of these legal orders. Revisiting *Grogan*, section 6 radicalizes the analysis of 'playing for time,' suggesting that the negotiation of divergence does not merely take place *in* time but is also and perhaps primarily about the unity *of* time, ie the unity of past, present, and future as the historical time of a collective.

2 Discretion and the public policy reserve

Van Duyn was the first case in which the ECJ was asked to interpret the public policy reserve with regard to the free movement of workers. At first glance, this case supports the view that the discretionary application of this reserve involves conceptual divergence. In effect, the Commission, in its written observations, argued that the concepts of public policy and personal conduct 'are concepts of Community law'. It went ahead to offer a pragmatic argument in favour of this view:

In practice, if each Member State could set limits to the interpretation of public policy the obligations deriving from the principle of freedom of movement of workers would take a variety of forms in different Member States. It is only possible for this freedom to be maintained throughout the Community on the basis of uniform application in all the Member States.[2]

---

[2] Case 41/74 *Yvonne van Duyn v Home Office* [1974] ECR 1344.

Advocate General Mayras strongly disagreed: 'I do not think [. . .] that it is possible to deduce a Community concept of public security. This concept remains, at least for the present, national, and this conforms with reality inasmuch as the requirements of public security vary, in time and in space, from one State to another'.[3] In his view, Member States have 'the sole power', within the exceptions contained by provisions such as the directive at issue in the preliminary reference, 'to take measures for the safeguarding of public security within their territory and to decide the circumstances under which that security may be endangered' (ibid). The Court, in its ruling, seems to steer a middle course between Mayras and the Commission: while agreeing with the former that the circumstances which justify recourse to the concept of public policy vary in time and place, it shares the latter's concern about the dangers arising from the unilateral determination of the scope of public policy by the individual Member States. In the Court's words, 'it is necessary to allow the competent national authorities an area of discretion within the limits imposed by the Treaty'.[4] Notice, before we turn to examine briefly the subsequent jurisprudential refinement of *Van Duyn*, that this case does *not* confirm the hypothesis of conceptual divergence, as formulated in the research project 'Binding Unity/Divergent Concepts'(BU/DC). It is true, of course, that the expression 'public *policy*' rings oddly in the ears of the legal scholar steeped in what is too expansively called the continental legal tradition. In effect, the expression stands in contrast to various continental equivalents, such as *ordre public, öffentliche Ordnung, orden público, ordine pubblico, ordem pública*, or *allmän ordning*, which display little or no linguistic variance. But, as Van Roermund points out, the hypothesis concerning a tension between unity and divergence involves conceptual rather than linguistic divergence.[5] In particular, the question at the heart of BU/DC is whether the very concepts that render possible the national application and enforcement of European law—in this case 'discretion' and 'public policy'—and are meant to ensure convergence between the national legal orders on issues of European law, actually give rise to divergent applications and enforcements of this legal order. Perusal of various legal orders does point to a certain amount of conceptual divergence, in the strong sense indicated by van Roermund. For

---

[3] Case 41/74 *Yvonne van Duyn v Home Office* [1974] ECR 1357.

[4] Case 41/74 *Yvonne van Duyn v Home Office* [1974] ECR 1350.

[5] 'A legal term T is conceptually divergent between agents A and B, if T is common parlance between A and B, and if the sense and/or the reference of T yields meaning M1 for A and M2 for B, such that A and B can use M1 and M2 to argue differing courses of action as lawful (or unlawful) under the legal order they are both committed to.' Van Roermund, this volume, Introduction, p 3.

example, German legal dogmatics distinguishes *öffentliche Ordnung* and *öffentliche Sicherheit*. Whereas the former embraces 'the totality of unwritten rules "the compliance with which is, according to the dominant social and ethical views, an essential condition for an orderly human life in community [. . .]" ', the latter covers written rules of law.[6] Accordingly, 'the concepts of *"öffentliche Sicherheit"* and *"öffentliche Ordnung"* are mutually exclusive' (ibid). This distinction is unfamiliar to French legal dogmatics, amongst others, which, at least in administrative law, encompasses *la sécurité, la tranquilité et la salubrité publiques* under the general notion of *ordre public*.[7] And if we turn to the notion of 'public policy,' we are told that it is

a very indefinite moral value sometimes appealed to by Anglo-American courts in justifying a decision. It has been said to be a principle of judicial legislation or interpretation founded on the current needs of the community. It normally prohibits and rarely creates: the standard phrase is 'contrary to public policy' [. . .]. In essence to declare something contrary to public policy is for the judge to declare that he thinks it wrong to allow it.[8]

It would no doubt be possible to hunt down additional conceptual differences if one took into account the different legal contexts in which this set of terms is used, such as civil law, international private law, criminal law, and the law of aliens. But, I submit, this would be of little or no avail. For, although there are divergent assessments by the Member States of the situations that justify invoking the public policy reserve, the concept of public policy they appeal to is, for the effects of European law, largely convergent. The Court took a first step in determining the concept of public policy in *Rutili*, by establishing that the personal conduct of a national had to consist of 'a genuine and sufficiently serious threat to public policy'.[9] It later sharpened this criterion, adopting a formulation that was to become the canonical form of public policy: 'a genuine and sufficiently serious threat to [. . .] one of the fundamental interests of society'.[10] *What* are the fundamental interests of society, and *what* are genuine and sufficiently serious threats to those interests? All of this varies from place to place and from time to time; but this divergence in the *assessment*

[6] F Fechner, 'Öffentliche Ordnung'—Reinaissance eines Begriffs?' (2003) 8 Juristische Schulung, 734, citing BVerfGE 69, 315 Neue Juristische Wochenschrift 1985, 2395.
[7] See, amongst others, E Picard, *La notion de police administrative* (Paris: Librairie Générale de Droit et de Jurisprudence, 1984) and P Bernard, *La notion d'ordre public en droit administrative* (Paris: Librairie Générale de Droit et de Jurisprudence, 1962).
[8] DM Walker, *The Oxford Companion to Law* (Oxford: Clarendon Press, 1980) 1015.
[9] Case 36/75 *Rutili v Minister for the Interior* [1975] ECR 1231.
[10] Case 30/77 *Regina v Pierre Bouchereau* [1977] ECR 2014.

of the situations that give rise to derogation from one of the four freedoms presupposes convergence concerning the *concept* of public policy.

The reason for this conceptual convergence is straightforward: by reviewing the invocation of the public policy reserve by the Member States, the ECJ is in a position to develop the main lines of the concept and control its discretionary application by the Member States. In effect, the Court moves to refine the rule laid down in *Van Duyn*, identifying and describing the limits that the Treaty imposes on the discretionary exercise of the exception by the Member States. It suffices, for the purpose of this chapter, to outline briefly how the Court introduces the principle of non-discrimination to limit the discretionary power of the Member States.

Yvonne van Duyn, a Dutch national, had been refused entry to the United Kingdom because she intended to take up work with a Scientology establishment in the UK. Although the government of the UK regarded the activities of the Church of Scientology as socially harmful, it had taken no steps to declare it illegal, or to dissuade British citizens from participating in its activities. The Court dismissed Van Duyn's written observation that the measure constituted discrimination on grounds of nationality, asserting that, in view of invoking the public policy reserve, it sufficed for the competent authorities of a Member State to 'have clearly defined their standpoint as regards the activities of a particular organization', without also having to declare those activities illegal, 'if recourse to such a measure is not thought appropriate'.[11] In the joined cases *Adoui* and *Cornuaille*, the Court quickly dropped this widely criticized interpretation of the public policy reserve, subordinating the invocation of the derogation to the principle of non-discrimination:

Although Community law does not impose upon the Member States a uniform scale of values as regards the assessment of conduct which may be considered as contrary to public policy, it should nevertheless be stated that conduct may not be considered as being of a sufficiently serious nature to justify restrictions on the admission to or residence within the territory of a Member State of a national of another Member State in a case where the former Member State does not adopt, with respect to the same conduct on the part of its own nationals, repressive measures or other genuine and effective measures intended to combat such conduct.[12]

The Court's refinement of the rule laid down in *Van Duyn* does not stop here; in addition to the principle of non-discrimination, the Court has appealed

---

[11] Case 41/74 *Yvonne van Duyn v Home Office* [1974] ECR 1350.

[12] Joined Cases 115 and 116/81 *Adoui and Cornuaille* [1982] ECR 1708. See also Case C-268/99 *Jany* [2001] ECR I-8682.

to the principles of proportionality and respect for fundamental rights in view of further limiting the scope of the discretionary powers exercised by the Member States pursuant to the public policy exception. But all of this is of secondary importance for the purpose of this paper; instead, two features that are more or less taken for granted in the foregoing survey require closer scrutiny. The first is that discretion concerns the *scope* of legal power; the second is that public policy concerns the discretionary power of the *Member States*. Although correct as far as they go, the following sections suggest that these assumptions offer neither a complete nor sufficiently complex picture of the role of discretion and its relation to public policy.

3 The indeterminacy of legal norms

Let us begin by considering the notion of discretion as the scope of legal power. One of Hans Kelsen's lasting contributions to legal theory has been to show that this conception of discretion is nested in a general theory of what he calls the hierarchical and dynamic character of the law. As he succinctly puts it, 'it is a legal norm that governs the process whereby another legal norm is created, and also governs—to a different degree—the content of the norm to be created'.[13] This implies, on the one hand, that a legal order is organized as a *Stufenbau*, a layered system of norms, and, on the other, that legal acts are, for the most part, acts of both law application and law creation. Indeed, the distinction between these two acts is not absolute, as legal dogmatics tends to postulate; most acts involve both the application of a higher-level norm and the creation of a lower-level norm. Only the first act of a legal order—the presupposition of the basic norm—and the last act of the chain that begins with the basic norm—a coercive act—elude this complex structure: the former is purely an act of law-creation, the latter one of law-application.[14]

I will shortly return to consider the 'first act' of a legal order. For the moment, however, let us consider more closely how Kelsen draws on this account of the dynamic and hierarchical character of a legal order to explain the notion of discretion. Notice, to begin with, that the passage cited at the

---

[13] H Kelsen, *Introduction to the Problems of Legal Theory*, trans BL Paulson and SL Paulson (Oxford: Clarendon Press, 1998) 63 (translation of the first edition of the *Reine Rechtslehre*).
[14] ibid, 71.

outset of this section already intimates how discretion fits into the ongoing process of norm-creation and norm-application, when Kelsen suggests that the higher norm governs 'to a different degree' the content of the lower norm. But only later, in the framework of a theory of interpretation, does Kelsen fully develop the notion of discretion. Drawing on the hierarchical character of the law, he notes that 'the relation between a higher and a lower level of the legal system [. . .] is a relation of determining or binding'.[15] After reiterating that the higher-level norm determines the process of creating the content of the lower-level norm he adds that this determination is necessarily incomplete, as the higher-level norm cannot determine every detail of the act that applies it. 'There must always remain a range of discretion (*Spielraum freien Ermessens*), sometimes wider, sometimes narrower, so that the higher-level norm, in relation to the act applying it [. . .] has simply the character of a frame to be filled in by way of the act'.[16]

The authority that issues it can directly intend the indeterminacy of a legal norm. Kelsen provides the examples of a health law that empowers the administrative agencies of a city to establish what precautionary measures must be taken to deal with an epidemic, or the criminal law that, having established that a certain act entails either a fine or a jail sentence, empowers the judge to decide which of the two is to be applied, as well as the severity of the respective sanction. These examples mesh well with the notion of discretion employed by the ECJ when it grants Member States an 'area of discretion' with respect to an assessment of the situation that justifies invoking the public policy reserve and the measures that must be taken to deal with this situation. But, Kelsen argues, discretion also encompasses those cases in which the indeterminacy of a legal norm is unintended, as when the applicable norm is ambiguous, such that the authority that is to apply the norm is confronted with various possible meanings. This is the bailiwick of interpretation proper, which has as its task the discovery of the 'frame of meanings' to be applied by an authority. In other words, to interpret a legal norm is to clarify it, and to clarify it is to draw out and fix—*feststellen*—the ensemble of meanings that defines the legal norm as a 'frame' of possible applications. What matters for Kelsen is that discretion kicks in both when the indeterminacy of the applicable norm is unintended and when it is directly intended. For, in both cases, 'the norm to be applied is simply a

[15] ibid, 77.
[16] ibid, 78. See also H Kelsen, 'Zur Theorie der Interpretation' in H Klecatscky *et al* (eds), *Die Wiener rechtstheoretische Schule*, Vol 2 (Vienna: Europa Verlag, 1968), 1363ff.

frame within which various possibilities for application are given, and every act that stays within this frame, in some possible sense filling it in, is in conformity with the norm'.[17]

This insight impinges directly on the problem of discretion in the framework of European law. One of the leading writers in the field has acknowledged that there is an 'intimate link between problems of interpretation and those of discretion'.[18] At the same time, however, Koopmans clearly distinguishes interpretation and discretion, contrasting two different ways in which the ECJ might have contributed to the *acquis communautaire*, the first being due to 'the powers expressly conferred upon it by the EC-treaty, powers of discretion or otherwise', the latter to 'the position the Court occupied in the institutional framework established by the treaty'.[19] According to Koopmans, the ECJ's contribution to the *acquis* can best be understood from the perspective of the second term of this contrast, that is as a matter of interpretation rather than discretion. For Kelsen, although the distinction between discretion and interpretation may have a certain dogmatic interest, it obscures the essential point: *all* norm creation is to some extent discretionary because *all* applicable norms are to some extent indeterminate. The real issue, he would say, is that the 'position' the Court occupies in the institutional framework of the treaties is relatively indeterminate. From Kelsen's perspective, this is the sense in which, as Koopmans puts it, there is an 'intimate link' between interpretation and discretion. This insight bears on the second of the assumptions identified at the end of the foregoing section: the ECJ's review of the public policy reserve in the light of Articles 30, 39, 46, and 55 ECT is as much a discretionary act as are the apposite acts of the Member States.

We will return to examine this point at a later stage of the argument. For the moment, I submit that Kelsen is on the right track when relating discretion to the constitutive indeterminacy of legal norms. A first question that arises, however, is whether his account of indeterminacy, as summarized heretofore, is sufficiently radical. In fact, there are good reasons to believe that, in a sense, Kelsen's legal norms are determinate through and through. For, on his view, it is the task of legal science to '[exhibit] on the basis of a critical analysis *all possible interpretations* (including the politically undesired ones and those not intended by the legislator or the contracting parties, yet

---

[17]   Kelsen, see n 13 above, 80.

[18]   T Koopmans, 'Methods of Interpretation' in O Wiklund (ed), *Judicial Discretion in European Perspective* (The Hague: Kluwer Law International, 2003) 75.

[19]   ibid, 83.

included in the wording chosen by them)'.²⁰ As a 'frame,' the legal norm is a closed and unchanging corpus of meanings, waiting to be discovered and ordered by legal science.

Clearly, Kelsen is anxious to define a legal norm as a pre-given frame of meanings (with the limit value of *one* meaning) available to cognition in order to contain the danger of arbitrariness.²¹ The prior determination of the content of legal norms allows Kelsen to argue that a discretionary act *applies* the higher-level norm to the extent that it 'stays within the frame', ie 'is in conformity with the norm'. Conversely, norm application is what renders an act discretionary. For if a legal norm were indeterminate in a radical sense, then there would be no difference between discretion and arbitrariness, nor would it be possible to speak of an act of norm-application. And in the absence of norm-application the law would forfeit its hierarchical and dynamic character; in short, the act would cease to be a *legal* act, becoming the manifestation of unbridled power. Returning to *Van Duyn*, Kelsen's appeal to the norm as a pre-given 'frame of meanings' aims to safeguard the idea that discretionary power implies 'margins'; without these margins, it would be pointless to *review* a discretionary act in view of ascertaining whether it is in accordance with or falls foul of the applied norm.

Yet, Kelsen intimates in the second edition of the *Pure Theory of Law* that this account of discretion is insufficiently radical. Having consistently held throughout his earlier work that legal interpretation aims to map the 'frame' of normative possibilities available to a legal norm, Kelsen suddenly asserts that authentic interpretation may give rise to a legal norm 'which lies entirely *outside* the frame of the norm to be applied'.²² This point is of the greatest importance because it suggests that 'indeterminacy is more than a problem within the scope of the norm, it is also a problem of delineating the scope itself'.²³ To put it another way, discretion does not only concern the choice of one among the possible applications of a higher-level norm; far more radically, it concerns what *counts* as a possible application of this norm in the first place.

²⁰ H Kelsen, *Pure Theory of Law*, trans M Knight (Berkeley: University of California Press, 1970) 356 (2nd edn of the *Reine Rechtslehre*) (emphasis added).
²¹ 'Contain,' rather than 'expunge,' the danger of arbitrariness, because, according to Kelsen, the choice of one among the various possible applications is a *decision*, in the strong sense of an act that cannot be rationally justified. This position stands in sharp contrast with Dworkin's view on discretion, amongst others.
²² Kelsen, see n 20 above, 354 (emphasis added).
²³ SL Paulson, 'Kelsen on Legal Interpretation' (1990) 10 Legal Studies, 151.

This insight brings back on board all of the problems Kelsen was anxious to jettison by contrasting discretion and arbitrariness. If discretion concerns the frame of possible applications, rather than the choice of one among these applications, in what sense, if any, can we still speak of norm-*application*? And if an act of norm-creation must be an act of norm-application to be legal, in what way, if at all, is it still possible to distinguish discretion from arbitrariness, and unbridled power from legal power? Can we still meaningfully speak of an act that *reviews* discretionary power, that is which authoritatively establishes whether an act of norm-creation remains within—or breaches—the 'margin' or 'area' allotted to it by the applicable norm? Even if we were prepared to consider this act as reviewing the exercise of discretionary power, would it not itself be discretionary in a way that is indistinguishable from arbitrariness?

We will return to consider these questions in the following section. For the moment, notice the implication of Kelsen's insight for our inquiry into discretion and public policy. I noted at the end of the foregoing section that the case law of the ECJ and the commentary on that case law take for granted that discretion concerns the *scope of legal power*. Accordingly, I enlisted Kelsen's support to outline the conceptual framework underlying this assumption. Yet an astonishing transformation takes place in Kelsen's analysis: if he begins by conceptualizing discretion as the scope of legal power, his account of indeterminacy 'develops' discretion, in the photographic sense of the term, revealing it as *power over the scope of the law*.

4 Constituent and constituted power

So, we now have to deal with two notions of discretion, rather than one, and, on the face of it, two notions that are mutually exclusive. A first step in making sense of the relation between these two notions is to reformulate Kelsen's insight by asserting that discretion as an act of instituted (or legal) power presupposes discretion as an act that institutes legal power. When viewed in this way, Kelsen's theory of norm-creation and norm-application effectively joins up with one of the most hallowed tenets of modern constitutional theory, namely the idea that *constituted* power presupposes a *constituent* power. On this reading, to speak of discretion as power over the scope of the law is to speak of constituent power, in the same way that to speak of discretion as the scope of legal power is to speak of constituted power. Everything turns on the idea that the latter 'presupposes' the former. Constitutional orthodoxy, for its part, interprets this presupposition as meaning that constituent and constituted powers are disjunctive and sequential terms.

However, does constitutional orthodoxy succeed in giving account of the *relation* between these two forms of discretion, as they manifest themselves in the ECJ's case law? To be sure, scholars and practitioners of European law may shy away from using the conceptual couplet 'constituent power/constituted power' because it is allegedly too close to nation–state politics and too far removed from the post-national politics of the EC. But the couplet resurfaces in the very term associated with the ECJ's constitutionalization of the treaties: the *acquis communautaire*. Indeed, when formulated in a European key, the question concerning the relation between constituent power and constituted power is this: how do the two manifestations of discretion play a role in acts of 'acquiring' the European Community, acts in the absence of which there would neither be an *acquis communautaire* nor a *communauté acquise*?[24]

Everything turns on the concept of time implicit in the relation between constituent and constituted power. Indeed, constitutional theory tends to understand power relations as temporal relations, ordered according to a linear scheme, where the scheme's starting point is an act of constituent power by which a community founds itself as a community. Once the new legal order has been instituted, constituent power gives way, albeit provisionally, to constituted powers, which are entrusted with the task of representing the constituent power, that is the people. This conception of temporality governs the assumption that constituent and constituted powers are disjunctive and sequential terms. Significantly, it also governs Kelsen's theory of discretion as the scope of legal power, which rests on a strictly sequential analysis of norm-application and norm-creation, such that a legal authority applies one of the pre-given meanings contained in the higher-level norm when creating a lower-level norm.

This conception informs Kelsen's bottom-line on legal interpretation: 'one cannot extract from a norm by way of interpretation what the norm never had'.[25] It also informs what it could mean for Kelsen that the norm issued by a legal authority is—or is not—'in conformity' with the applied norm. Importantly, his devastating insight that a posited norm may lie 'entirely outside' the applied normative framework continues to presuppose

---

[24] This section borrows from my 'Acquiring a Community: The *Acquis* and the Institution of European Legal Order' (2003) 9 Eur L J, 433ff.

[25] Kelsen, see n 13 above, 87.

that the legal norm—as a framework—is a closed and unchanging corpus of meanings, awaiting discovery and ordering by legal cognition. To put it another way, the crisis of the indeterminacy of legal norms is the crisis of representationalism and of the underlying theory of temporality that is supposed to guarantee the distinction between discretion and arbitrariness, constituent power and constituted power.

Cases such as *Van Gend&Loos* and *Costa v ENEL* suggest a more radical—even paradoxical—view on relation between constituent and constituted power. In effect, to constitutionalize the Treaties, the ECJ must function as a constituent power, exercising power over the scope of the law; but it only becomes a constituent power to the extent that it succeeds in presenting itself as constituted power, that is power within the scope of the law. The rulings that created an autonomous legal order retroject this creation onto a past which is held to function as the origin of the new legal order. The very rulings that give rise to a 'new' and 'own' legal order, to borrow the formulations of these rulings, transfer the birth of this order to the past, and then go ahead to assert that direct effect and supremacy are just 'implications' of that origin. Ultimately, then, the paradoxical relation between constituent and constituent power is the political-legal manifestation of the paradoxical relation between the represented and its representations: an act becomes the *origin* of a community through its *representations*. Note, moreover, that this paradox is by no means limited to the landmark cases mentioned above, even though they are perhaps its most well-known illustrations; it governs all cases of normative innovation, whether by the ECJ or other institutional actors of the European Community.[26]

My suggestion is that the paradox of representation clarifies the structure of discretional power and its relation to the indeterminacy of legal norms. The indeterminacy of legal norms entails, on the one hand, that their meanings do not exist independently of the acts that apply them, yet also, on the other, that their meanings are not simply the result of an act of norm-creation. Power is discretionary in the twofold sense of determining the scope of the law while claiming to act within the scope of the law. The paradox of representation implies that the act that *applies* a norm also *creates* its meaning. While one or the other of these two aspects of power may be more prominent in any given act of positing a legal norm, neither ever entirely cancels out the other, nor are they ever entirely reconciled. In

---

[26] Eg, an analogous paradox governs the Treaty of Rome. The very treaty that initiates the European Community claims, in its Preamble, to come second, as the legal order that gives institutional form to an ever closer union of the peoples of Europe . . .'.

particular, although the creative moment remains more or less concealed in run-of-the-mill acts of legal power, it suddenly becomes manifest in the acts that spark the genesis of legal meaning. Such inaugural acts involve a dislocation and recomposition of time, in its threefold modes of past, present, and future; in effect, the ECJ's reasoning in *Van Gend&Loos* reveals that every act that inaugurates a legal meaning initiates by anticipating in the future a 'past which has never been a present'.[27]

Crucially, and this is part of the paradox of representation, the initiative that founds a community only becomes such *retrospectively*. *Van Gend&Loos* and *Costa v ENEL* only become the constituent acts of a 'new' and 'own' polity to the extent that, by invoking direct effect and the supremacy of EC law, the national judiciaries and market citizens accept the ECJ's invitation to view direct effect and supremacy as 'implied' by the Treaty, that is accept the ECJ's invitation to view these rulings as the acts of a constituted power. Constituent power only becomes such when it has *successfully* claimed to be a constituted power; in other words, an act of 'acquiring' a community becomes such when it has come to be recognized as an *acquis communautaire*. Only from the perspective of an *acquis communautaire* is discretion merely the scope of legal power, and a legal norm a stable 'frame' of pre-given meanings, such that, as Kelsen puts it, 'one cannot extract from a norm by way of interpretation what the norm never had'. In short, the indeterminacy of legal norms entails that it is only retrospectively that an act that exercises power over the scope of the law appears to be either a discretionary act—an act within the scope of legal power—or an arbitrary act—an *ultra vires* act.

5 *Grogan*: playing for time

Having rendered the notion of discretion denser than is usual in legal dogmatics, we must now turn to the question of how this notion of discretion

---

[27] M Merleau-Ponty, *Phenomenology of Perception*, trans C Smith (Oxford: Routledge, 1989) 242. Although I cannot discuss this here, the concept of discretion I am advocating is different from the Gadamerian notion of *Applikation*, heavily indebted as it is to a dialectical conception of change and indeterminacy, let alone Dworkin's conception of discretion. See E Christodoulidis, 'Dworkin in South Africa and End of History Jurisprudence' presented at the Conference on the work of Ronald Dworkin, University of Cape Town, 2002 (on file with the author), for an exceptionally acute and convincing critique of Dworkin along lines that, in some respects, are similar to my own concerns with representationalism. For a critique of Gadamer's legal hermeneutics, see my 'Dialectic and Revolution: Confronting Kelsen and Gadamer on Legal Interpretation' (2003) 24 Cardozo L Rev, 769ff.

is related to the public policy reserve laid down in articles 30, 39, 46, and 55 ECT. In a first approximation, I will develop the idea that public policy is a privileged locus of the paradoxical relation between constituent power and constituted power at the heart of discretion. But this provisional formulation is too under-developed, on at least two counts. First, and drawing on an earlier insight, I want to show that public policy brings this paradoxical relation into play *twice*: the ECJ's act of reviewing the invocation of the public policy reserve is as much a discretionary act, in the twofold sense noted above, as are the apposite acts whereby the Member States derogate from the four freedoms. Second, at stake in both the discretionary invocation of the public policy reserve by Member States, and the review thereof by the ECJ, is the *unity* of these legal orders. In short, public policy is of particular interest for us in virtue of revealing that discretion, in the twofold sense of power over the scope of the law and the scope of legal power, ultimately turns on the problem of safeguarding the unity of the European Community *and* that of the national legal orders. For, of course, accommodating divergent national legal orders, by allowing them to derogate from one of the four freedoms, means safeguarding their claims to unity.

We will return to the first of these points shortly. For the moment, let us dwell on the problem of public policy and the unity of a legal order. As *Bouchereau's* canonical formulation puts it, public policy may be invoked in the face of 'a genuine and sufficiently serious threat to . . . one of the fundamental interests of society'. In other words, public policy is at stake when there is a genuine and serious challenge to the legal order of a Member State, a challenge that justifies suspending the application of a legal norm in view of safeguarding the order's unity. Crucially, although this issue remains largely implicit in scholarly analyses, the discretionary exercise of the public policy reserve can itself constitute a challenge to the unity of the EC. This is not surprising to the extent that invoking the public policy reserve implies derogating from one of the four market freedoms, each of which constitutes a 'fundamental interest' of the EC. Accordingly, every derogation from one of these freedoms raises *prima facie* a challenge to the unity of the EC. The ECJ's review of these derogations has, for this reason, the function of safeguarding the unity of the European legal order. The danger that always lurks in the Court's review of the public policy reserve is that a situation can ensue in which striking down the discretionary invocation of the reserve by a Member State, thereby securing the unity of the European legal order, can only be achieved at the cost of compromising the unity of a national legal order—*and vice versa*. Might this exceptional situation—this state of exception—reveal the most general conditions governing the discretionary process by which the EC and its Member States negotiate their unity and divergence?

Such a situation arguably presented itself in *Grogan*, the well-known abortion information case.[28] Relying on Article 40(3)(3) of the Irish Constitution, which acknowledged the right to life of the unborn, the Society for the Protection of Unborn Children (SPUC) brought proceedings in the High Court of Ireland against the officers of three student associations. They did so with a view to obtaining a declaration that the associations' publication of information concerning the availability of medical termination of pregnancy in the United Kingdom was unlawful. SPUC also sought an injunction restraining the publication and distribution of this material. In its reference to the ECJ, the High Court sought a preliminary ruling on whether abortion fell within the definition of services pursuant to EC Treaty, Article 60, and, if that were the case, whether a Member State could prohibit the distribution of the aforementioned material and whether there was a right at Community law for persons to distribute such material in a Member State which prohibits abortion under its constitution and criminal law. In its judgment, the ECJ held that, although abortion indeed qualified as a service under EC Treaty, Article 60, the link between the distribution of information about abortion and the appropriate services carried out in another Member State was too 'tenuous' to qualify as a restriction to the freedom to supply services in the terms of EC Treaty, Article 59. As a result, the Court also held that it had no jurisdiction to ascertain whether the prohibition of abortion fell foul of the freedom of expression and to receive and impart information, as per Article 10(1) of the European Convention on Human Rights.

It is highly significant, from the perspective of discretion, that the central issue raised by *Grogan* concerned the *scope* of Community law. Both the SPUC and the Irish government argued, with regard to the first question of the preliminary ruling, that abortion was not a service, in the terms of EC Treaty, Article 60, and, consequently, that it did not fall within the scope of the Treaty. In substance, their position was that abortion does not constitute an economic activity. The Irish government, in particular, held that 'the defendants distributed the information in question free of charge and for no consideration, and did not do so in the context of any economic activity

[28] Case C-159/90 *Grogan* [1991] ECR I-4685ff. For a thorough analysis of this case, see G de Búrca, 'Fundamental Human Rights and the Reach of EC Law' (1993) 13 Oxford J of Legal Studies, 283ff.

carried on by them'.[29] Grogan and the other defendants argued, to the contrary, that the distribution of such material fell within the scope of EC Treaty, Article 60, and that the prohibition to distribute this material breached Articles 59 and/or 62 of the Treaty. The core of their argument was that the right to receive information in one Member State about a service lawfully provided in another Member State implied 'an ancillary right at Community law for persons in the first Member State to impart such information. Otherwise the right to receive information and, indirectly, the right to obtain services in another Member State would be rendered meaningless and deprived of any real effect'.[30] As the distribution of material about abortion fell within the scope of Community law, the defendants further held that the prohibition breached fundamental rights laid down in the European Convention on Human Rights (ECHR), rights that, according to the ECJ's case law, are an integral part of the general principles of law protected by the Court. In short, both SPUC and the Irish Government, on the one hand, and Grogan and the other defendants, on the other, suggested that the unity of one of the legal orders could only be maintained by compromising that of the other.

The ECJ dealt with this quandary by declaring that the behaviour of the defendants did not constitute a restriction to the freedom to provide services, under the terms of EC Treaty, Article 59. This view was debatable, to say the least, in the light of an earlier case, in which the Court held that 'consumers resident in one Member State may travel freely to the territory of another Member State to shop under the same conditions as the local population. That freedom for consumers is compromised if they are deprived of access to advertising available in the country where purchases are made'.[31] As opposed to this earlier case, the ECJ asserted, *Grogan* involved a 'situation in which student associations distributing the information . . . are not in cooperation with the clinics whose addresses they publish'. So, the Court retrospectively reads the rule laid down in *GB-INNO-BM* as meaning that there would only be a restriction to the freedom to provide services if the relevant information were 'distributed on behalf of an economic operator established in another Member State'.[32]

The Court's reasoning provides a good illustration of the paradoxical relation between constituent and constituted powers. On the one hand, *Grogan*

---

[29] Case C-159/90 *Grogan* [1991] ECR I-4690.
[30] Case C-159/90 *Grogan* [1991] ECR I-4697.
[31] Case C-362/88 *GB-INNO-BM* [1990] ECR I-686.
[32] Case C-159/90 *Grogan* [1991] ECR I-4740.

testifies to the fact that the meaning of the applied rule is constituted as such in and through its applications. By introducing the distinction between forms of advertisement that involve a relation between the economic operator and the advertiser, and those that do not, the ECJ exercises power over the scope of the law, thereby acting as a constituent power. Yet, on the other hand, the meaning of the rule laid down in *GB-INNO-BM* is not simply the performative construct of *Grogan*. This second aspect becomes clear if one bears in mind that the rule of *GB-INNO-BM* was laid down from the perspective of the *consumer*, not from that of the economic operator or its potential advertisers; as both the defendants and Advocate General van Gerven argued, the former perspective, not the latter, is consistent with the aim of giving full effect to the freedom of providing services and, therewith, to the realization of a common market.[33] When seen in this way, the Court's distinction turns out to be arbitrary; its ruling exercises power over the scope of the law, but does not succeed in presenting itself as an act within the scope of the law. Indeed, as several scholars have argued, the distinction introduced by the Court undermines the freedom to provide services to the same extent that *Grogan* compromises the unity of the European legal order. This assessment is reinforced if one bears in mind that, by declaring that the behaviour of the defendants fell outside the scope of Community law, the possible breach of freedom of expression also fell beyond the ECJ's jurisdiction, even though, as the Court's case law insists, the fundamental rights contained in the ECHR are part of the general principles of law it is called on to protect.

This, however, is only part of the story. For, clearly, the ECJ's exercise of constituent power must be understood against the background of the thinly veiled threat of the Irish Supreme Court to support the prohibition sought by SPUC if the preliminary ruling were to prove favourable to the claims of the defendants, a threat which rendered pressing the public policy reserve by the Irish government. From this perspective, the ECJ's exercise of discretionary power over the scope of the law can be understood as a move to safeguard the unity of the European *and* Irish legal orders: by narrowing the scope of Community law, the ECJ effectively *abandoned* the behaviour of the defendants to the legal order of Ireland, allowing the Irish Court to qualify this behaviour in a way that safeguarded the unity of its legal order.

This legal sleight of hand allows the ECJ to play for time. *Grogan*, I submit, should be read as an act that safeguards the unity of the Community legal order

[33] See the Opinion of Advocate General van Gerven in Case C-159/90 *Grogan* [1991] ECR I-4713.

by *postponing* it with an eye to the unity of the Irish legal order. On one level, this means that the Court was wise not to grapple head on with the problem of freedom of expression in *Grogan*. For, shortly after this ruling, the Court in Strasbourg issued a ruling on the prohibition of abortion, which declared Ireland in breach of its obligations under the ECHR. Moreover, although the price to be paid for defusing a constitutional crisis was to compromise the full effect of the freedom to provide services, the ECJ surely banked on being able to redress this problem, at a later stage and in a less controversial case, formulating anew the rule about information pursuant to the four freedoms. No less importantly, the Irish High and Supreme Courts also played for time. In the earlier *Open Door* case, injunction had been sought against welfare clinics that provided non-directive counselling to women, including the option of abortion in the case of unwanted pregnancy.[34] Although the defendants brought forward the Community dimension of the case, both the Irish High and Supreme Courts held that the case fell outside the jurisdiction of Community law. In *Grogan*, to the contrary, the Supreme Court did not quash the High Court's referral to the ECJ, even though it was critical of the High Court's move. Although it intimated that it was ultimately prepared to uphold the prohibition sought by SPUC, by authorizing the referral to the ECJ, the Supreme Court was effectively *postponing* the unity of the Irish legal order with an eye to the unity of Community law.[35] Accordingly, the negotiation of divergence of the European and Member State legal orders draws on the capacity, deployed by discretional power, to play for time, in the sense of acts that postpone the unity of these legal orders. [36]

6 Negotiating unity and divergence: two temporalities

But these considerations on discretion and public policy do not go far enough. In order to show how the ECJ and the Irish Supreme Court negotiate unity and divergence by postponing the acts that authoritatively determine the unity of their respective legal orders, the *unity* of these orders has been taken

---

[34] *Attorney-General (SPUC) v Open Door Counselling* [1987] ILRM, 477 and [1988] ILRM, 19.
[35] See *(SPUC) v Grogan and others* [1990] 1 CMLR 689, cited by AM Collins and J O'Reilly, 'The Application of Community Law in Ireland 1973–1989' (1990) 28 CML Rev, 328.
[36] I am indebted here to Van Roermund's discussion of sovereignty in the EU as the deferral or postponement of sovereignty. See B van Roermund, 'Sovereignty: Unpopular and Popular' in N Walker (ed), *Sovereignty in Transition* (Oxford: Hart, 2003) 33ff.

for granted. It is to this issue that we must now turn: in what sense is the unity of a legal order at stake in the negotiation of divergence? Eschewing a full-blown answer to this question, this concluding section focuses on one, albeit fundamental, aspect of this general problem, an aspect that has been largely overlooked by the literature on European integration. In effect, the negotiation of legal divergence as postponing a determination of legal unity suggests that the unity of a legal order is not only secured or compromised *in* time; the negotiation of divergence is also—and perhaps primarily—about the unity *of* time, that is the unity of past, present, and future as the temporal modes of a collective. On this reading, it does not suffice to assert that public policy involves a threat to the unity of a legal order; most fundamentally, human behaviour raises an issue of public policy when such behaviour challenges the temporal unity of a polity, ie its capacity to make sense of an event by viewing it as a present integrated into a *whole* of past, present, and future. Thus, the exercise of discretionary power in the face of public policy ultimately confronts us with the divergence of *times*—of the collective temporalities of the EU and its Member States.

It is not surprising that the problem of legal unity does not manifest itself, in the first instance, as a problem of temporal unity. Yet more pointedly, the unity and divergence of legal orders is only possible if, in one sense, the unity of time is *not* a problem. I have in mind here Émile Benveniste's distinction between calendar and lived time.[37] It is clear, to begin with, that time appears, in the first instance, as that *in* which every imaginable legal order commences, unfolds its career, and reaches an end. This also holds, of course, for all legal orders taken together, which are related as prior, contemporaneous, or posterior to one another. Here again, while it might be possible to substitute the Gregorian calendar for another calendar, the very notion of a calendar implies a temporal *continuum*, and, as such, the necessary unity of the intervals that compose it.

From this perspective, 'what we call "time" is the continuity in which distinct blocks named events are serially disposed. For events are not time, they are *in* time.'[38] This mode of time is immediately evident in the case law on the public policy exception. The first page of the *Grogan* ruling announces that Advocate General van Gerven filed his Opinion on 11 June 1991, and that the ECJ rendered its judgment on 4 October 1991. Obviously,

---

[37] É Benveniste, 'Le langage et l'expérience humaine' in É Benveniste *et al* (eds), *Problèmes du langage* (Paris: Gallimard, 1966) 3–13.

[38] ibid, 6.

the ruling of the Irish Supreme Court is also dated, which means that these three events can be located in the single temporal continuum of calendar time. The very possibility that these two courts negotiate divergence by *postponing* their claims to unity presupposes that they understand their acts as located within a *single* temporal flux. Neither of the courts could have 'played for time' in the absence of calendar time, a time which they share as the unquestioned horizon of their acts. As Benveniste puts it, the reference points offered by dates 'give an objective position to events, and therefore also define *our* situation in relation to these events'.[39] Note, moreover, that *Van Duyn* also appeals to the objectivity of calendar time when asserting that 'the particular circumstances justifying recourse to the concept of public policy may vary [. . .] from one period to another . . '.

To be sure, it may be difficult to establish with any precision when one conception of public policy gives way to another; but this difficulty presupposes the experience of time as a single sequence of intervals in which all events of significance to any legal system can, in principle, be ordered according to the distinction between a 'before' and an 'after'. It is not surprising, then, that the literature tends to overlook time when making sense of the unity and divergence of legal orders. For such unity and divergence presuppose the unity of calendar time. The unity of a legal order can only be problematic, and this means, amongst others, that it must be secured in time, if, in a sense, the unity of time—its constitution as a continuum—is itself unproblematic. There is, however, a second mode of time, the time of an individual or a collective, which surfaces in Benveniste's comment that calendar dates 'define *our* situation' in relation to events. The quasi-indexical term 'our' is linked to a subject-relative form of time, which Benveniste calls 'lived' time. As Benveniste correctly points out, lived time, and more generally the time of a subject, is irreducible to the uniform and continuous sequence of measurable units of time made available by calendars. 'As a day is identical to another day, nothing says about this or that calendar day, taken in itself, whether it is past, present or future. It cannot be placed under one of these three categories other than by who *lives* time'.[40] The unity of calendar time manifests itself as the continuum of a before and an after; by contrast, past, present, and future can only appear as a unity to the extent that they are the temporal modes *of* an 'I' or a 'We', that is insofar as the members of a community attribute these modes to themselves as their *own* collective past, present, and future.

---

[39] ibid, 7.   [40] ibid, 8.

Both forms of time are indispensable if we are to make sense of the unity and divergence of legal orders. If, from the first personal plural perspective of 'We', past, present, and future are personal in virtue of manifesting themselves as *our* past, present and future, a calendar opens up a more or less impersonal time in which events are not only part of the history of a collective but also datable and recognizable as such for other collectives. Calendar time makes possible an interpersonal—an *intercollective*—temporality, such that dates not only make possible an impersonal past, present, and future, but also become the 'anchor points for all the meetings, the mutual efforts, the conflicts that we can say happen at the same time, that is, on the same date'.[41]

These general comments allow us to take a further step in explaining in what sense the actors in *Grogan*, in particular the ECJ and the Irish Supreme Court, 'time' the unity and divergence of legal orders. Consider, to begin with, the opening lines of the Report for the Hearing in *Grogan*, which marvellously blend together these two distinct forms of time:

Abortion has always been prohibited in Ireland, first of all under the common law, then by an 1803 Statute, the Offences against the Person Act 1839 and finally by sections 58 and 59 of the Offences against the Person Act 1861. The 1861 Act is still in force in Ireland, and was reaffirmed by the Oireachtas in the Health (Family Planning) Act 1979.[42]

The key here is the term 'always', which evokes both the unity of time made available by calendars and the unity of collective time. On the one hand, the passage evokes a sequence of dates that stretches back to a 'first' unit of time that is not dated but that is in principle datable. On the other hand, 'always' evokes a string of events that make up the past *of* a community in virtue of the acts of a legal organ that, legislating on behalf of a We, 'reaffirms' that past in the present and projects it into the polity's future. Crucially, 'always', as invoked by the Irish Government, the Irish Supreme Court, and SPUC, means that, in their view, accepting the legality of the activities of the defendants in *Grogan* would amount to breaching the unity of Ireland's collective history because those present activities are only compatible with the reaffirmation of a collective past if they are qualified as illegal.

Yet, on the face of it, qualifying these activities as illegal is tantamount to breaching the temporal unity of the *European* legal order. Reaffirming

---

[41] P Ricœur, *Time and Narrative*, trans K Blamey and D Pellauer, Vol 3 (Chicago: Chicago University Press, 1988) 108.

[42] Case C-159/90 *Grogan* [1991] ECR I-4686.

the *GB-INNO-BM* ruling, itself a reaffirmation of the freedom of services posited in the inaugural act of the European Community, seemed to require that the ECJ qualify the act by which the Irish authorities banned the distribution of material as illegal. At stake was not only a 'fundamental interest' of the European Community, but also its capacity to understand itself as the unity of a past, present, and future.

If the term 'always' plays a key role in the cited passage, by virtue of highlighting the two modes of temporality which, in conjunction, condition the possibility of conflict between the two legal orders, the term 'reaffirms' intimates the condition for negotiating, or more properly, *timing* the unity and divergence of these legal orders. Indeed, the 're' of 'reaffirms' is the 're' of 'representation'. To the extent that 're' does not refer to what supervenes or follows an original present and presence, but rather, as Merleau-Ponty puts it, to a past that was never a present, the ECJ could act as a constituent power by claiming to reaffirm the past. By asserting that the link between the distribution of information about abortion and the apposite services carried out in the United Kingdom was too 'tenuous' to qualify as a restriction to the freedom of services, the Court's reaffirmation of the Treaty deploys the paradoxical temporality of representation: the meaning of the *present*—the state of affairs brought to the Court's attention—is determined in an act that opens up a *future* by revealing a meaning the *past* only acquires retrospectively. So, the paradox of 'reaffirmation' is double in *Grogan*: the ECJ averts a breach of the Community's temporal unity by itself breaching this polity's temporal self-understanding; and this rupture takes place in the process of forging the three modes of time into a single history. This double paradox defines what it means to say that the ECJ's ruling *times* the unity of the European legal order in a way that accommodates the divergence of legal orders.

This chapter began as an inquiry into the public policy exception in Community law, with a view to ascertaining the role of discretion in securing the unity and divergence of the European and national legal orders. Inasmuch as discretion is not only the scope of legal power but also power over the scope of the law, it was suggested that this twofold sense of discretion is at work in the process of playing for time, by means of which authorities of the Community and national legal orders negotiate divergence by postponing the unity of their respective legal orders. This idea was subsequently taken a step further: the negotiation of divergence and unity of legal orders not only takes place 'in' calendar time but is also and primarily about the unity of collective time. It seems that the price that must be paid for this line of thinking is to lose contact with the issue that got it started in the first place: public policy.

Yet, on closer consideration, the line of inquiry I have been following not only begins with but also arrives at the problem of public policy. For if the unity of a legal order is at stake in public policy, does not a legal order's unity unfold as the unity of a collective history? If so, then the relation between the 'publicness' of public policy and temporality is much more intimate than meets the eye. For not only do the circumstances justifying the invocation of public policy vary 'from one period to another', as the ECJ asserted in *Van Duyn*, but securing the unity of collective temporality is also primordially a condition of publicness as such, that is a condition in the absence of which nothing could *appear* to the members of a community.

14

Laws at Cross-Purposes: Conceptual Confusion and Political Divergence[1]

Bert van Roermund

1 Introduction

The hypothesis of the research project reported in this volume is that basic concepts of EU law are conceptually divergent[2] in spite of their lexical similarity, due to the fact that they are rooted in, and revert back into, domestic legal frameworks that have cogent ways of their own of rewriting facts in terms of legal consequences. This chapter will argue that this hypothesis must be refined. Conceptual divergence is the epiphenomenon of two more basic forces: conceptual confusion and political divergence. There is a lack of conceptual clarity, indeed a lack of interest in conceptual clarity, pervading community as well as domestic law in our times. This absence seems both driven by and followed by divergent political pursuits from various legal agents, not all of them Member States. I will examine the concept of discretion as a paradigm case, acknowledging that other basic concepts must be investigated before any robust corroboration of my hypothesis can be claimed. I will explain that the evasiveness of discretion is largely accounted for by our confusion about what is called 'power' in law. Having straightened that out, I will turn to the mirror-image of discretion, liability for exceeding the constraints of legal power. I will show that the three constraints are in fact communicating vessels rather than cumulative conditions, ushering in

---

[1] Thanks go to Michiel Brand, Linda Senden, and Sacha Prechal for their comments on earlier drafts.

[2] cf the working definition given in the Introduction to this volume, p 3.

various considerations of policy. Finally, I will argue, on a more philosophical note, that the cause of theoretical confusion on discretion in the case of EU law has to be generalized: it is law's necessarily ambivalent relationship to power that should account for it.

2 Discretion: an initial set of phenomena

One should not underestimate the variety of phenomena that can be gathered under the umbrella of 'discretion' in various jurisdictions. Even a modest inventory would exceed the limits of this chapter. Striking a balance between this abundance and a customized selection, it is instructive to follow the argument submitted by Somsen[3] in analysing decision making in EC environmental law, and argue that his distinctions can be generalized to areas other than environmental law and EU law. Somsen focuses on supra-national vs national discretion in a number of different situations in the EU context,[4] which are neatly announced at the beginning of his paper as so many headings of his report. But I think it is illuminating to cast them in a more general mould, and paraphrase them in terms that can easily be transposed into other contexts, with environmental law providing useful illustrations.

1. A legal authority A has discretion if A has freedom to choose the legal basis for the norm she is to enact, in pursuit of her political goals. For instance, the choice of legal basis for (environmental) directives in the various provisions of the EC Treaty, even though it is guided by the 'centre of gravity' doctrine,[5] is itself an issue of competence attribution; and it is of immediate significance for national discretion in the subsequent process of implementation. For instance, the basis of EC Treaty, Article 95 (harmonization of the internal market) entails more specific and onerous consequences than the basis of EC Treaty Article 175 (environmental protection policy). Another example: to escape from

---

[3] H Somsen, 'Discretion in European Community Environmental Law: An Analysis of ECJ Case Law' (2003) 40 CML Rev.

[4] ibid, 1413.

[5] Case C-155/91 *Commission v Council* [1993] ECR I-939: the legal basis of an act is determined by its primary (rather than its ancillary) aims. Although this guides the choice, it by no means eradicates it.

the stringent regime of EC Treaty, Article 95, a certain pervasive move on the market (eg, involving genetic manipulation) may be brought under a less stringent directive provision facilitating mere technological adaptation of the directive. In addition the choice of one paragraph of a certain EC Treaty article may entail a co-decision procedure, while a second of the same article will entail a consultation procedure. Although the official doctrine is that the choice of legal basis for a certain act is not a discretionary matter for the institutions (it should rest on 'objective factors', subject to judicial review), the choice to pursue a strategy X or Y or Z cannot be ruled out.

2. A has discretion, if she has a degree of freedom in choosing the form and method of implementation of a norm issued by a higher authority. In the European context, the obvious example is the implementation of a directive, but one may also think of national administrations implementing formal statutory law. Somsen submits that these questions form a major part of the ECJ caseload. Obviously, failure to adopt implementing provisions altogether or within the set period of time[6] will not fall within the margins of discretion. Also, Member States appear to have no liberty to elaborate improvement programmes or plans that are not sufficiently 'organised and coordinated' to function as alternatives for specific standards.[7] They amount to obligations of result.[8] But one *does* struggle over the completeness and the accuracy of national implementing provisions (too little? too much?), in view of principles like legal certainty, *effet utile*, and uniform application of EC law.

3. A has discretion if she has liberty to issue, within her own jurisdiction, stricter versions of the same norms as the higher authority issued for the encompassing jurisdiction. For instance, Member States may adopt national standards of environmental protection (EC Treaty, Article 176)[9] that are more demanding and/or stricter than the communitarian standards, provided that these measures are compatible with the EC Treaty (provisions such as Articles 28, 81, 82, and 86). This latter condition

[6] cf Case C-152/98 *Commission v The Netherlands* [2001] ECR I-3463 (scientific difficulties relating to the identification of the substances belonging to List II of Council Directive (EEC) 76/464 on pollution caused by certain dangerous substances discharged into the aquatic environment of the Community [1976] OJ L129/23 did not excuse failure to transpose the Directive).

[7] Case C-387/97 *Commission v Greece* [2000] ECR I-5047.

[8] Somsen, see n 3 above, 1451.

[9] Somsen mentions Art 175 Treaty of the European Community as the basis for EC directives silently referring to Art 176 as the basis for a higher national protection profile.

however often entails serious constraints on national discretion, for
instance in view of harmonization (either minimum or full).[10]

4. *A* has discretion if she has a choice to qualify her setting a certain norm
either as a *demanded* transposition of a higher norm or as a more *demanding*
imposition of a similar norm in her own jurisdiction. For instance, in
case of national imposition of more stringent norms, Member States
have to notify the Commission ex EC Treaty Article 176. Failure to do so
constitutes a substantial procedural defect rendering the norms in question not binding (on individuals). The problem arises whether a certain
national norm counts as a simple transposition of an EC directive or as
a more stringent norm of a Member State, and within what margins the
latter can decide.[11]

5. *A* has discretion if she enjoys a certain degree of freedom in using legal
techniques of 'designation' or 'classification' in order to rule on the legal
regime that will be applicable in the situation at hand. For instance,
these techniques are used in deciding which objects or activities are to
be governed by EC environmental law and which are not—with consequences for the extent to which individuals may enforce such provisions.
See the examples under (6). But then again, this freedom is limited.[12]
Normally, a directive entails criteria that have to be accounted for in
using the techniques mentioned.

6. In a similar vein, *A* has discretion if she has a choice of interpreting
operational concepts one way or another, thus purposively seeking or
avoiding certain legal consequences. Examples abound, eg, what qualifies
as 'waste', 'discharge', etc? Teleological interpretation of a directive often
casts a wide web over possible cases, but runs counter to demands of legal
certainty and specificity (*effet utile*). Interestingly, Somsen points to 'the
intrinsically observer-relative nature of the social concept of "waste"'
as a source of contention. 'It is a very fine line that divides "products"
(benefiting from unhindered circulation within the Community) from
"waste" (subject to a restrictive EC waste regime).'[13]

7. *A* has discretion if she has freedom to decide on the allocation of the
burden of proof for infringements of a norm, as well as on the required

---

[10]   cf Case C-324/99 *Daimler Chrysler* [2001] ECR I-9897.

[11]   See eg, Case C-159/00 *Sapod* [2002] ECR I-5031.

[12]   cf Case C-3/96 *Commission v The Netherlands* [1998] ECR I-3031.

[13]   Somsen, see n 3 above, 1437 with (justified) reference to JR Searle's seminal book *The
Construction of Social Reality* (New York: Free Press, 1995). A case in point is Case C-192/96
Beside [1998] ECR I-4029.

standard of evidence in case of non-compliance with a norm. Member States often have authority here, but they should exercise it 'in a spirit of genuine cooperation and mindful of each Member State's duty under EC Treaty Article 10 to facilitate attainment of the general task of the Commission, which is to ensure that the provisions of the Treaty, as well as provisions adopted thereunder by the institutions, are applied'.[14]

8. *A* has discretion if, in issues of enforcement, she enjoys a certain institutional and procedural autonomy. In *Brasserie*[15] it is stressed that reparation has to be made 'in accordance with the domestic rules on liability, provided that the conditions for reparation of loss and damage laid down by national law must not be less favourable than those relating to similar domestic claims' (equivalence or non-discrimination), and to the extent that these rules do not make reparation impossible or excessively difficult (effectiveness). However, the principles of national institutional and procedural autonomy are gradually yielding to jurisprudential and legislative pressure for supra-national intrusions. On the basis of principles of effectiveness and non-discrimination, the Court allows the Commission to sanction over-lenient sanctioning by Member States.[16] The limits are admittedly difficult to determine. For instance, Anagnostaras wishes to ask, to what extent, according to the ECJ's decisions in a series of cases,[17] a Member State 'should be allowed to choose the retroactive application of belated implementing measures as a remedy for the damage individuals might have sustained because of the violations of its EC law obligations'. As it happens, such application is possible under Italian law. In the cases under discussion, it would yield a protection of the rights conferred by the directive in question, equal to or better than an appeal to the *Francovich* doctrine, ie state liability.[18] If that is the case, it should be allowed, as it makes it easier for national judges to keep their middle position between loyalty to their domestic legislators and cooperation with the ECJ. But then, one should bear in mind that, typically, this road is viable only in cases where transfer

[14] Somsen, see n 3 above, 1445 referring to Case C-365/97 *Commission v Italy* [1999] ECR I-7773.

[15] Joined Cases C-46/93 and C-48/93 *Brasserie and Factortame* [1996] ECR I-1029, para 67.

[16] Eg, Case C-354/99 *Commission v Ireland* [2001] ECR I-7657.

[17] Joined Cases C-94/95 and 95/95 *Bonifaci* [1997] ECR I-3969; Case C-261/95 *Palmisani* [1997] ECR I-4025, and Case C-373/95 *Maso* [1997] ECR I-4051.

[18] G Anagnostaras, 'State Liability v Retractive Application of Belated Implementing Measures: Seeking the Optimum Means in Terms of Effectiveness of EC Law' (2000) Web Journal of Current Legal Issues (Issue 1), <http://webjcli.ncl.ac.uk/2000/issue1/1.html>.

of money is what the rights in question amount to. Belated payment will not do if these rights are of a substantive rather than a pecuniary nature. Moreover, one should not underestimate the role of the *Francovich* formula as an incentive for national states to monitor closely those EC law obligations that transposition of a directive imposes on private parties and public bodies under their jurisdiction. When it comes to robust protection of rights, *Francovich*[19] remains the safety net, and national procedural autonomy or discretion will be restricted.[20] It has not remained unchallenged, though, as the last section of this chapter will show.

3 The core of discretion

What are we to conclude from this variety of phenomena on the conceptual level? Instead of yielding to the worn-out answer that it all depends on context, let me maintain that it all depends on the level of abstraction. When, as in Somsen's argumentation, the practice of procedure, precedent, and liability is near, differences in detail matter considerably. I am inclined to think, however, that, admittedly at a fairly high level of abstraction, the picture of discretion is a rather converging one. Moreover, it is one that legal writing is rather familiar with. Galligan accurately describes this common core:

In its clearest and strongest sense, discretion means that in deciding whether to do [X] the official has some freedom of choice as to the standards and criteria which ought to govern his decision. To a greater or lesser degree they are left for him to determine as he thinks best. In making that determination, the official is not free of all constraints but must act reasonably and in good faith, have good reason for his actions, and follow certain procedures, including hearing the parties affected. The official could not be criticized, however, for not properly applying the standards, since to a large degree it is left to the official to decide what the standards should be.[21]

---

[19] Joined Cases C-6/90 and C-9/90 *Francovich* [1991] ECR 1-5357.

[20] 'Accession to the Communities entails a voluntary limitation of national sovereignty and any violation concerns obligations freely undertaken by the States through their representatives in the Council. Therefore, there is little justification for national courts to refuse the application of the *Francovich* case law, under a reasoning showing a manifest misunderstanding or even disregard of fundamental EC law principles and a willingness to subordinate the effectiveness of the EC legal order and the effective protection of the rights the latter intends to confer on individuals to the satisfaction of national interests.' Anagnostaras, see n 18 above.

[21] DJ Galligan *et al, Administrative Discretion and Problems of Accountability. Proceedings of the 25th Colloquy on European Law* (Strasbourg: Council of Europe Publishing, 1997).

Arguing from the reverse side of the coin, we arrive at similar conclusions. As Galligan also says at the beginning of his analysis, 'discretion consists not just in the authority to choose among different actions, but to choose amongst different courses of action *for good reasons*. The course of action cannot be separated from the reasons, and therefore the standard on which it is based.'[22] Thus, setting the standard for what counts as 'good reasons' for a certain course of action in a given case *C* is definitional of exercising discretionary power by authority *A* in *C*. However, it is also definitional of discretion that the capability of setting such standards for good reasons in *C* is itself authoritatively governed, in turn, by standards or 'margins' of a more general nature or a higher order. In short, discretion is part and parcel of the rules that are constitutive of legal power, ie of that specific legal 'can' that we vest in authorities when we call them legal authorities in the first place. These are not only state authorities, obviously. Parents, contracting parties, shareholders' assemblies, church leaders, and vice-chancellors—all of those who are 'in charge' in a particular domain have this specific ability that accrues to them by virtue of the institutional character of law. Thus, at the end of the day, discretion should find home in the definition of legal competence. Let us therefore use the concept of discretion in an effort to define legal competence, as follows. An agent *A* has legal competence if and only if:

1. there is a set of legally valid constitutive rules P of the form[23] '*A*'s doing *X* counts as *Y* in context *C*', where *X* is a legal decision and *Y* is tantamount to (co-referential with) a change in obligations of legal subjects other than *A*;
2. there is a set of regulative rules R governing accountability of *A* for doing *X* in *C* to another agent *B*, specifying types of the facts *F* that are to be the case, of conditions *G* that have to obtain, and of factors *H* that have to be taken into account;[24]
3. *A* has a margin of discretion in validly assessing not just values but also parameters ('standards') for variables *F*, *G*, and *H*, and/or in deciding whether to pursue a course of action ϕ rather than ψ in doing *X*, within the constraints deriving from P and R.

---

[22] DJ Galligan, *Discretionary Powers: A Legal Study of Official Discretion* (Oxford: Clarendon Press, 1990).

[23] See JR Searle, *Speech Acts: An Essay in the Philosophy of Language* (Cambridge: Cambridge University Press, 1969).

[24] In items (2) and (3) I inserted Galligan, see n 22 above, 20ff on 'a central sense of discretionary power' and see also Galligan, see n 21 above, 16 for a useful scheme of administrative decisions.

Conditions (2) and (3) entail that *A* has no discretion on the margins of her discretion: *A* has to comply with constraints of types *F*, *G*, and *H* as well as *X* imposed on her. Otherwise neither accountability nor judicial review would work, and discretion would be tantamount to arbitrary power. But also, (1) and (3) taken together imply that it is up to A whether an act-token φ falls within the act-type *X*, whether *f*, *g*, and *h* are values for *F*, *G*, and *H*, and (often) whether she is going to exercise the power conferred on her in the first place.

4 The source of confusion

Popular wisdom[25] has it that 'meaning is use' rather than definition. And indeed, my claim is that the definition in the previous section, though admittedly abstract, captures the core of how concepts like discretion and competence are used over a large range of cases from various Member States. Given the constraints of this chapter, let us test it against what is often seen as a paradigm case of conceptual divergence. Some jurisdictions, particularly, though not exclusively, German ones, make a distinction between two basic notions of discretion. Discretion allegedly dovetails into 'genuine discretion' as the power to choose between alternative and equally valid legal decisions on courses of actions to pursue, and 'quasi discretion' as the freedom to assess the best (or the one and only right) interpretation of an indeterminate legal term or rule.[26] Other jurisdictions are less sensitive in this respect. Their scholars will usually stress that (i) there is always a creative, law-setting element in applying a rule or assessing an indeterminate concept;

---

[25] That some ascribe to Wittgenstein on the basis of arguably limited reflection on his texts cf B van Roermund, *Het verdwijnpunt van de wet. Een opstel over symboolwerking van wetgeving* (Deventer: Tjeenk Willink, 1997).

[26] K Meessen in Galligan, see n 21 above, 107 observes that German doctrine insists on there being a difference of principle here between the two categories. For instance, genuine discretion is to be found in Art 87(3) (new) Treaty of the European Community, which gives the Commission discretion to declare certain forms of state aid to be compatible with the common market inspite of their distorting effect on competition. Assessing indeterminate legal terms is at issue in Art 81(3), where despite wording similar to Art 87(3) 'the rule obliges the Commission to exempt certain restrictive agreements from the prohibition spelled out in Art 81(1) once it has decided to regard such agreements as contributing to the improvement of the production of goods'. See also this volume, ch 9 in which Brand, points to the Dutch distinction between *beleidsvrijheid* and *beoordelingsvrijheid*. In ch 13, s 2 Lindahl offers an in-depth analysis of the distinction in light of Kelsen's theory.

(ii) there is always an element of compliance to higher standards in rule creation; (iii) the consequences of both aspects of discretion are equally binding upon, and can be equally invasive for, legal subjects; (iv) in the final analysis, as law is an order governed by authority rather than argument, the second element (power) prevails over the first (judgment). Thus, there is no point in denying that there is ample room for confusion and discussion here, which would perhaps explain the ECJ's broad spectrum of alternative phrases in these matters: margins of appreciation, discretion, liberty to decide, etc.[27] Here, indeed, is a term, 'discretion,' that may give rise to agents arguing different courses of action as 'valid law', as our definition of conceptual divergence stipulated. But the question remains whether it is the type of conceptual divergence and confusion this volume is trying to track down: divergence that would be caused by the lexical roots of common terms used both in differing conceptual legal frameworks and within their specific 'cultures'?

A hypothesis presents itself that has more explanatory power with regard to this source of confusion. Both jurisdictions that make the distinction between genuine and quasi-discretion, and jurisdictions that find it scholastic fail to make another, far more important distinction: the distinction between acting 'before the law' and acting 'on behalf of the law'. The former is tantamount to exercising some form of power, to which regulative norms of law apply. The latter is tantamount to exercising legal power binding upon others, to which not only regulative norms apply, but constitutive rules as well. So if I *walk* my dog in my neighbour's garden, my neighbour will refer to the regulative norms of law forbidding this type of behaviour. But if he ventures to *sell* my dog, I will confront him with two sets of rules: those constituting the legal competence that comes and goes with ownership and those regulating what owners should, may, and should not do. To put this another way, there are legal norms (i) that *regulate* all sorts of human behaviour (the unspecified 'can' we call powers, capabilities, etc), and there are legal norms (ii) that *constitute* or *define* types of institutional behaviour that count as imposing norms in certain situations (the legal 'can' we call competence). Given this distinction, we may easily see that there are also legal norms that, in turn, *regulate* types of *constituted* institutional behaviour (of norm setting or competence). Now, to operate with norms of *both* types (i) and (ii) one needs what was called 'quasi-discretion' a few paragraphs above.

An agent *A* has a decisional space in virtue of what it takes to follow a rule and interpret its terms in one way or another. There is, indeed, an

---

[27] See the papers by Caranta (ch 8), Brand (ch 9), and Künnecke (ch 10) in this volume.

indeterminacy inherent in any rule, any norm, or any set of norms taken together, to the extent that they are regulative.[28] Regulative rules do not guide our actions by giving thumbnail descriptions of the circumstances in which we should do what they say. They only speak to us if and when 'we have got the picture'—which is the main reason why, in law, we cannot separate the study of rules from the study of cases. 'Doing things by rules' calls for *judgment*, and in exercising judgment, *A* applies (respectively, complies with) a rule, reconfirming, resuming, refining, and renewing it in one fell swoop.[29] However, exercising the specific kind of power we call legal competence, as defined by constitutive rules, is a different matter. The freedom of action here does not strike us because it is such a peculiar kind of freedom, but because it is freedom in such a peculiar kind of action, namely norm setting action entirely constituted by the rules of an institution. Here is where discretion comes in, as the use of freedom in a realm of action that can only exist by virtue of law defining it. Contracting, convicting, legislating, prosecuting, bequeathing, and their ilk, exemplify a legal 'can' supervenient on human power in general, as they are bound up with law *being regarded as* a norm-creating institution. Typically, in exercising this power, *A* creates a rule that *counts as* imposing obligations upon others (or herself, in the case of legislation). But then, A has discretion to make rules in virtue of a competence, left to her,[30] attributed to her, or accruing to her by implication,[31] as the case may be, on the basis of what EU lawyers call *acquis communautaire*, but which is the basis of all lawmaking.

   To the extent that these very distinctions are bound up with law being an institution, they are characteristic of legal orders as such, regardless of cultural differences or conceptual idiosyncracies at more concrete levels. But the fact that they are basic does not prevent them from being disregarded for all sorts of practical, and in particular political, purposes. In this respect, the

---

[28] The last part of this phrase is added because I have argued elsewhere that constitutive rules can be analysed as default settings of regulative rules: B van Roermund and H Lindahl, 'Law Without a State? On Representing the Common Market' in Z Bankowski and A Scott (eds), *The European Union and Its Order: The Legal Theory of European Integration* (Oxford: Blackwell Publishers, 2000) 1–16.

[29] For an elaborated argument on the basis of Wittgenstein's theory of rule following cf Van Roermund, see n 25 above.

[30] In its decision of 26 November 2002 the CFI refers to this as a 'residual' competence, Case T-74/00, T-76/00, T-83/00 to T-85/00, T-132/00, T-137/00, and T-141/00 *Artegodan* [2002] ECR II-4945, para 142.

[31] cf L Corrias's MA unpublished thesis on 'Implied Powers in the EU' (Tilburg 2004). May be obtained from the author at email address: L.D.A.Corrias@uvt.nl.

concept of discretion shares a history with the other concept that is central to this volume, the concept of rights. The distinction between discretion as judgment in rule following and discretion as the exercise of a legal 'can' is exactly parallel to the distinction between a right in the sense of a claim or a 'subjective right' and a right in the sense of a legal power.[32] The fact that these two dimensions of discretion and rights often hunt in pairs (or 'are correlate') is not a sufficient ground to blur the distinction, as long as there are enough cases where they have to be kept apart for good reasons. After all, holding things apart is one way of holding them together.[33] When it comes to rights, most legal systems make the distinction when they need it: the right (claim) to enjoy the benefits of a property is distinguished from the right (power) to sell it. Similarly the freedom of judgment in following a rule has to be distinguished from the freedom of action in making a rule, although there is no point in denying either that the two often hunt in pairs or that exercising this freedom of action involves this freedom of judgment again.

By consequence, one should be careful to distinguish between the deontic modalities in which the norm-setting actions performed by authority A are involved, and the deontic modalities of actions that are part of the context in which A's power is to be exercised. For instance, it may be the case that, in a certain context C, A is *obliged* to use a certain power to do X if other agents do something forbidden, eg, to close a pub if there is drug trafficking going on. Then the margins of discretion for A shrink to the power to 'judge' that some premises constitute 'a pub' or to decide on the modalities of 'closing'. It may also be the case that A is *permitted* to use this power under these circumstances. Then A has wide(r) discretion; indeed he even exercises his power if he chooses not to close the pub. From the fact that A decides not to use his power to close the pub (as he is permitted to do) one should not infer that the trafficking is permitted—a fallacy often made in contemporary argumentation on administrative acquiescence. On the other hand, from the fact that A decides to use his freedom to set the law as 'a freedom to be influenced by factors other than the law' one should not infer that the law in the case at hand can be ignored or that a process of deliberation can be endlessly perpetuated.[34]

---

[32] The distinction is a familiar one in jurisprudence, acknowledged in civil law and common law systems.

[33] As my colleague Roger Shiner once said to me as we were climbing *il due torri* in Bologna.

[34] KO Hawkins with reference to RO Lempert, 'Discretion in a Behavioral Perspective: The case of a Public Housing Eviction Board' in KO Hawkins, *The Uses of Discretion* (Oxford: Clarendon Press, 1992) in Galligan, see n 21 above, 89.

5 Illustrations

To further illustrate, rather than to test, our rather candid definition above and its ensuing distinctions in a EU context, let us look again where discretion is of primary importance: EC Treaty Article 87 (1)–(3), where the prohibition of state support and its unconditional (para 2) and possible (para 3) exceptions are at issue. On the basis of para 3, the Commission will have competence to decide whether a certain form of state support is permitted or not. To this end, it has to settle certain standards, but in doing so it will, itself, have to comply with more general standards: it ought to take into account the general interest of fair competition on the common market in a certain domain, the principles of proportionality, subsidiarity, and effectiveness, etc.

Moreover, once an authority like the Commission has settled the standards for good reasons in C and once it has announced how it shall apply them in future cases similar to C, these announcements seem to become binding upon itself, even if they are not formal legal acts and even if they do not entail substantial exceptions to the rule in question. For instance, Article 87(3) gives wide discretionary power to the Commission in deciding whether specific forms of state support do or do not interfere with fair competition on the internal market.[35] Now the Commission, in order to avoid arbitrariness and to make its decision policy transparent, has given information on the criteria it is going to apply in certain policy sectors. Though these announcements were not legal acts and did not produce exceptions to the prohibition of state support on a par with Article 87(2) ECT, the question arises whether or not the Commission binds itself to these criteria in the exercise of its discretionary power.[36] Increasingly, the answer is in the affirmative. Thus, judicial review of discretion seems to be possible on at least two counts: the binding force of more general standards and the binding force of self-imposed criteria. But the deeper explanation, I submit, is that this is an example of the correlation between two different modes of 'doing things with rules': the Commission's exercise of judgment in complying with rules of the internal market and the exercise of competence in fulfilling its authoritative role.

---

[35] I realize that state support is a Community matter by default. But note that, in a sense, this is an application of the subsidiarity principle rather than an exception. It is from the highest level of authority that matters are attributed to lower levels.

[36] A Bleckmann, *Europarecht. Das Recht der Europäischen Union und der Europäischen Gemeinschaften* (Köln: Carl Heymans, 1997) and L Senden, *Soft Law in European Community Law* (Oxford: Hart, 2004) 420–436, with some salient examples in the state aid area.

As to the former, one could think of the principles laid down in Recommendation R (80)2 of the Committee of Ministers of the Council of Europe[37] concerning the exercise of discretionary powers by administrative authorities. Member States were called upon:

- to adhere to the lawful purposes of such powers, by refraining from pursuing a purpose other than that for which the power was conferred;
- to be objective and impartial, taking into account only factors relevant to the particular case and recognizing each factor's significance;
- to uphold equality before the law by avoiding unfair discrimination;
- to keep a sense of proportion, by maintaining a proper balance between the purpose pursued and any other adverse effect which an administrative decision might have on people's rights, liberties, or interests.[38]

As to the latter, the main issue here is transparency or openness, or what K Davis calls 'the seven instruments that are most useful in the structuring of discretionary powers': open plans, open statements, open rules, open findings, open reasons, open precedents, and fair informal procedure. 'The reason for repeating the word "open" is a powerful one: openness is the natural enemy of arbitrariness and a natural ally in the fight against injustice.'[39] Indeed, far from being arbitrary power, discretionary power is defined by institutional constraints.

6 More sources of confusion

Until now, the reasons we found for worrying about conceptual divergence sparking off from discretion had to do with theoretical confusion rather than legal disparity. It is quite probable, though, that divergent instantiations of 'discretion' find their causes in diverging ideas (in various legal orders) on concepts *related* to discretion, in particular about liability for administrative discretion. In EU law contexts, it does not seem to make much difference whether

[37] Council of Europe, Committee of Ministers, Recommendation R (80)2 concerning the exercise of discretionary powers by administrative authorities, 11 March 1980.

[38] See L Silveira's contribution to Galligan, see n 21 above, 53: he wishes to add reasonableness and good faith, and observes that these principles, though vague in nature, have proven to be powerful constraints on arbitrary power in a great number of cases in different countries See also Harremoes's contribution to the same volume, 181.

[39] KC Davis, *Discretionary Justice: A Preliminary Inquiry* (New York: John Wiley, 1969) 98. I owe the reference to L Silveira's paper referred to above. I should stress, however, that openness *in this sense* is a necessary and not a sufficient condition for justice.

we look at the institutions of the EC or those of the Member States. The Court, at least, consistently aims at treating these levels alike as far as liability is concerned. Whether it is always successful in this pursuit is a different matter.

As to the Member State level, discretion in EC law[40] is of course frequently discussed in the context of Member States' liability for the implementation of directives. On the basis of Article 249(3), EC Treaty directives oblige Member States to implement legal provisions in their respective legal orders, such that a certain result is obtained within a certain period of time. Member States have a freedom of choice between actions X, Y, or Z in complying with this obligation. They typically have discretion in matters of implementation, in the strong sense set out above, ie competence. As is well known, Member States are not only accountable for fulfilling their obligations before the institutions of the Community, they are also liable, in principle, to private persons for failing to achieve the said result.[41] Such liability ties in with various other doctrines in European law. Legal writing has observed that, for instance, liability for adequate transposition on the part of the Member States is the ultimate upshot of direct effect.[42] Alternatively we may say that it follows from 'the system of the Treaty'.[43] If and when in a certain case a Member State is liable to a private person for not (correctly) implementing a certain directive, then this person is entitled to damages from the Member State. On the other hand, one can easily see that a non-directly effective instrument, such as a directive, presupposes 'by definition, a great margin of discretion as to the way it will be transposed in the domestic legal order'.[44]

With regard to the Community level, there is a clear parallel between the liability of a Member State and that of EC bodies such as the Commission or

---

[40] Throughout this chapter reference to the law of the European Union should be read as 'giving examples', not as 'rendering sufficient evidence'. Thus, I refer to a singular case to illustrate a statement, rather than giving a full list. The statements, however, are derived from what I see as state of the art analyses by legal scholars, who deserve all the credit for mapping out both case law and statutory law. I can only hope that they will acknowledge my efforts to understand, from a philosophical point of view, what they are doing.

[41] Joined Cases C-6/90 and C-9/90 *Francovich* [1991] ECR 1-5357.

[42] A doctrine that is itself, in turn, the result of gradually convergent views on the binding effect of directives, the 'most useful effect' (*effet utile*) topos, and the preliminary reference procedure of Art 234 TEC. The obligatory reference for 'direct effect' is to Case 26/62 *Van Gend&Loos* [1963] ECR 1. For a critical analysis of direct effect, see A Prechal, 'Does Direct Effect Still Matter?' (2000) 37 CML Rev, 1047–1069, continued in A Prechal, *Directives in EC Law* (Oxford: Oxford University Press, 2005) 278–279.

[43] Joined Cases C-46/93 and C-48/93 *Brasserie and Factortame* [1996] ECR I-1029 and Joined Cases C-178/94, C-179/94, C-188/94, C-189/94, and C-190/94 *Dillenkofer* [1996] ECR I-4845, para 20.

[44] Anagnostaras, see n 18 above.

the Council, as one would expect, to be sure, if EU law is to respond to the requirement of unity in a legal order. Indeed, the liability of Member States for the implementation of directives is a sequel of the overall liability of the Community for its 'normative actions', as far as the Court is concerned. As the latter should not contradict the former,[45] one is *prima facie* permitted to infer liability criteria for the former from the latter or vice versa. In *Dillenkofer*[46] the ECJ succinctly reviews and summarizes these conditions in the light of its somewhat uneasy line of decisions since *Brasserie du Pêcheur & Factortame III*.[47, 48] They are threefold:

1. The violated directive attributes *rights* to private persons.
2. The Member State's violation of EC law is sufficiently qualified.
3. There is a *direct causal link* between the violation and the damage done to the private persons.

Note that these conditions are each of them necessary and jointly sufficient for liability of the Member State in question. In other words: these conditions are all necessary and no other conditions are necessary.

The first condition can be regarded as stating the sort of 'harm' that should be at issue. In order to come to grips with 'harm' from implementation of directives, the European courts, it seems, increasingly favour rights talk. It allows them to assess whether or not directives are implemented with sufficient coercive force, specificity, precision, and clarity; which, taken together, give meaning to the principle of legal certainty with regard to implementation.[49] Though many questions concerning the concept of 'rights' may be raised here, the two important points, as far as the ECJ is concerned, are: (i) that the result envisaged in the directive—either in its provisions or in its considerations, either in part or in whole—entails rights to be conferred upon private persons, and (ii) that the content of these rights can be established on the sole basis of the provisions of the directive.[50]

---

[45] See Joined Cases C-46/93 and C-48/93 *Brasserie and Factortame* [1996] ECR I-1029, para 42 and Case C-352/98 P *Bergaderm* [2000] ERC I-5291.

[46] Joined Cases C-178/94, C-179/94, C-188/94, C-189/94, and C-190/94 *Dillenkofer* [1996] ECR I-4845.

[47] Joined Cases C-46/93 and C-48/93 *Brasserie and Factortame* [1996] ECR I-1029.

[48] See also Case C-352/98 P *Bergaderm* [2000] ERC I-5291, para 41, 42; Case C-312/00 P *Camar and Tico* [2002] ECR I-11355, para 53, and Case C-472/00 P *Fresh Marine* [2003] ECR I-7541, para 25.

[49] Joined Cases C-46/93 and C-48/93 *Brasserie and Factortame* [1996] ECR I-1029, para 48.

[50] I refer to Beljin's contribution to this volume with regard to rights, ch 5.

The heart of the matter is condition (2): when is a Member State's violation of EC law 'sufficiently qualified'? Assuming that there is little difference with EC liability generally, again I concentrate on Member State liability for directives. Here, the ECJ seems to distinguish two situations. With regard to some aspects of the Member State's competence (legal power)[51] to implement directives, the competence is 'bound', ie the Member State is under an obligation to exercise this power in a certain way. For instance, the Member State is not free to tinker with the deadline of implementation, to ignore enforcement, or to disregard implementation altogether. Where there is a violation of EC law in terms of this bound competence, the legal consequence is strict liability on the part of the Member State. As the Court has already made clear in *Hedley Lomas*,[52] if the institution has a very limited or virtually no margin of appreciation, the violation of community law alone gives rise to liability. With regard to other aspects, however, liability will be attributed only if the Member State has clearly and seriously exceeded the limits of its normative competence.[53] The 'margin of discretion available to the author of the act' is dependent on factors like 'the complexity of the situations to be regulated',[54] 'the difficulties in the

---

[51] The conceptual relation between 'competence' and 'discretion' was dealt with earlier on in s 2.

[52] Case C-5/94 *R v Ministry of Agriculture, Fisheries and Food, ex p Hedley Lomas Ltd* [1996] ECR I-2553.

[53] Joined Cases C-46/93 and C-48/93 *Brasserie and Factortame* [1996] ECR I-1029.

[54] The specific terminology and the default arguments originate in ECSC times, when, apparently, French administrative law and German views on *freies Ermessen* were believed to be inspiring. It matured, however, in agricultural law, where the ECJ, typically, would refer to 'a complex economic situation', requiring (i) striking a balance between economic social financial political and other factors; (ii) accounting for the political pressure from the Member States rooted in national need to balance of similar factors; (iii) assessing the priority of some goals over others given that the official goals of the EC in a policy area are not always mutually consistent. R Barents, *The Agricultural Law of the EC* (Deventer: Kluwer 1994) and 'De communautaire rechter tegenover burocratie en politiek. De interactie tussen algemene rechtsbeginselen en discretionaire bevoegdheden' (1995) Rechtsgeleerd Magazijn Themis, 219–226. The Court is very open in stressing the 'political' nature of this discretionary power. It extends both to the choice of actions to be pursued and the facts to be taken into account. As to the former, the EC is free to decide in a certain complex situation: whether or not to take measures; to change or abolish measures already taken; and the order of measures—all of this regardless of how effective the measures in question prove to be after a certain lapse of time. As to the latter, the EC is free to ignore or address the (unequal) effects of the policy in individual cases.

application or interpretation of the texts',[55] or the 'very complicated scientific and technical facts'.[56]

As to condition (3) above I can be very brief. For all the intricacies of causation in the law, the conceptual differences between various legal traditions are largely restricted to criminal law,[57] and therefore of less concern to the European lawyer (at this point in time). Moreover, as Hart and Honoré report in the preface to the second edition of their majestic book,[58] the core of their analyses met with approval from academic representatives of various national jurisdictions. It is only fair to note that they did not refer to any German authors, in spite of the fact that the original edition spent the two last chapters mainly on German theories of causation, which were believed to be at variance with the common-sense approach of Anglo-American jurisprudence. Hart and Honoré also note the criticism they received from supporters of generalized risk theory such as Leon Green and Glenville Williams. I believe it is not an overstatement to claim that, increasingly, risk analysis and corresponding probability theory are crystallization points in contemporary approaches to causation, and that they are here to stay, at least in the eyes of those who object to reducing causation to normative imputation or ascription of responsibility. Although the theory is developing slowly, its direction is fairly clear, and to the extent that it is a new and computing one, it is less haunted by the alleged idiosyncracies of the various legal traditions.

As I have noted, there is no *prima facie* reason things would be different with respect to the liability of EC institutions. Let us have a closer look at the liability picture provided so far. It does not take a very thorough inspection to get the feeling that we are looking at something familiar. The conditions of liability (1)–(3) reveal a pattern that is deeply entrenched in both civil and common law legal thought. It comes down, I submit, to a series of variations on the theme of liability criteria in tort, as it can be inferred from various domestic jurisdictions, in both common and civil law systems. In tort law, according

---

[55] Joined Cases C-46/93 and C-48/93 *Brasserie and Factortame* [1996] ECR I-1029, para 43.

[56] Case C-120/97 *Upjohn Ltd* [1999] ECR I-223, para 34. Prechal kindly brought to my attention the judgment of the Second Chamber in Case C-278/05 *Robins and others*, Judgment of the Court of 25 January 2007, nyr, where the judge saw clear violation of Community law, but not 'qualified' (ie in a sense, not 'unlawful') enough to ascribe legal consequences in the sphere of liability. see para 72ff.

[57] HLA Hart and AM Honoré, *Causation in the Law* (2nd ed., Oxford: Clarendon Press, 1985) lvi, cf 431.

[58] ibid.

to a widely held view, liability can only be attributed (i) if there is harm done, (ii) if the harm done is unlawful (for instance a sheer violation of rights or negligence with respect to one's duty of care), and (iii) if there is a causal relationship between the unlawful harm and the actions of the defendant. The similarity between this time-honoured pattern and recent ECJ rulings is a striking one, with the provisions on the liability of Community institutions on the basis of EC Treaty Article 288(II) as an important intermediary. In the context of implementation of EC directives, as *Dillenkofer*[59] shows, a Member State can only be held liable on the basis of conditions that resemble classical tort doctrine. Condition (1) specifies (i), ie 'harm'; condition (2) specifies (ii), ie 'unlawfulness'; and condition (3) neatly reflects (iii), ie 'causality'.

This finding does not exactly point in the direction of conceptual divergence. On the contrary, it is evidence of sound conceptual convergence. At the same time, however, it comes in support of the argument of the chapter developed so far: theoretical confusion rather than divergence in conceptual frameworks is at the root of our problem. For the three conditions of the doctrine of liability in tort are renowned for not being completely mutually exclusive. To a considerable extent they overlap, or— perhaps a more elegant way of putting it[60]—they are like communicating vessels. For instance, in many contexts (though not in all) harm is unlawful by definition. If company *A* successfully competes on the market with companies *B* and *C*, *B* and *C* will suffer losses, but if the competition was fair, ie lawful, *B* and *C* will not claim to be harmed. Inversely, if no harm in the sense of (pecuniary) loss is to be claimed, judges will usually be reluctant to qualify certain acts as 'unlawful' behaviour, even if it has caused major emotional sorrow on the part of the plaintiff. Again, harm is analytically linked with what philosophers call agent causality: harm, typically, is not so much 'caused' as 'done', or at least not prevented by someone who acted unlawfully by not doing what he or she should do, or, at the very least, regarded beforehand as susceptible to being made 'undone' (insurance). Thus, legal subjects mostly have a choice of stressing rights being harmed or behaviour being unlawful or facts being acts, when it comes to arguing liability. If lawyers are puzzled by these modalities of argument, they should perhaps be advised to turn to jurisprudence rather than comparative law.

---

[59] Joined Cases C-178/94, C-179/94, C-188/94, C-189/94, and C-190/94 *Dillenkofer* [1996] ECR I-4845.

[60] I owe the expression to Veegens, HR 9 December 1960, NJ 1963, no 1 (conclusion Procureur-Generaal Langemeijer and with note DJ Veegens).

7 Political divergence

While it may be a challenging hypothesis that theoretical confusion, whether it concerns discretion or liability, is a major factor in explaining conceptual divergence, it only becomes falsifiable if we supplement it with an equally interesting hypothesis of how this confusion can come about. Unless one feels the need to picture lawyers as muddle-headed generally (which I for one do not), one would like to know more about the kind of uneasiness they feel and report as conceptual divergence. My conjecture would be that it is political divergence in EU law that, by and large, is responsible for conceptual divergence. In other words, conceptual divergence is an epiphenomenon of political divergence, emerging in at least two dimensions. The first dimension determines the disparity of EU policies; not all domains of EU decision making are (regarded as) equally central to the main concern by EU authorities themselves. The second one determines the disparity of legal subjects' policies (both Member States and others), using different conceptual inroads into EU law in order to mark and argue their respective interests.

To lend initial feasibility to this hypothesis, let us go back to the conditions to be taken into account when the use of discretionary power by EU and Member States' administrations comes under judicial review. The institutions of the Community, the institutions of the Member States and the various executing bodies on all levels, have discretionary powers that correlate with their respective, either exclusive or subsidiary competences. They are to be deployed in 'complex (economic) situations' and for the purpose of the Community's common wealth. It is natural to ask what principled limits are set to these powers? The answer will probably refer to principles like equality, respect for fundamental rights, legal certainty, and proportionality.

But—as Barents infers from his in-depth study of EC agricultural law[61]—these principles do not only govern the policy area in question. It also works the other way round. Where there is wide discretion, as in the area of agriculture, policy arguments will decide what is equal to what. Policy arguments will account for restrictions on fundamental rights. Policy arguments will require that certainty is a matter of foreseeing changes rather than extrapolating status quo. Policy arguments will decide what is proportional to what in making out which measures are necessary and sufficient to which purposes as seen from the overall purpose of the EC. Indeed, the principles,

---

[61] cf Barents, see n 54 above.

inversely, are governed by policy, and if one principle is violated, they are all violated.[62] So when it comes to the celebrated 'marginal review' of discretion, principles tend rapidly to lose their specific grip. They all boil down to a prohibition of arbitrary use of power, as all other more robust interpretations would usher in restrictions on discretion and undermine its allegedly beneficial use in complex (on the whole mainly economic) situations.

Note that this is a matter of degree. Some policy areas are less complex than others, others become regarded as [more] or [less] complex as time goes by, while others are even waiting to be discovered as policy areas in the first place. Indeed, what is and what is not recognized as a suitable issue on a political agenda is subject to change. The celebrated rise of the 'social question' in nineteenth-century Europe has proved paradigmatic[63] for the 'discovery' of new policy areas in our time, eg, environmental pollution, transnational crime, gender equality, or ageing. A recent study on judicial review of equality argued convincingly, for instance, that the ECJ sets the default margins of discretion for all authoritative bodies more narrowly in the areas of gender equality and equality of nationalities than in the area, most notably, of agriculture, where invariably wide discretion is said to be required.[64] Default standards of judicial review vary accordingly from strict to marginal. In either case, these default settings may be modified, referring to special facts and circumstances of the (types of) cases at hand: pressing 'common good' policy widens the margins of discretion even when rights are at issue, while fundamental rights narrow the margins of discretion in spite of political impetus.

Obviously, in areas where wide discretion is required, generally, by virtue of the political stakes involved, the ECJ finds the law supporting an overall top-down hierarchy from Council to national authorities. This indicates that at the end of the day, and at least as far as the Court is concerned, discretion is granted 'from above', rather than taken 'from below'. Note that this is not an inversion of the subsidiarity principle, but an application. As Somsen aptly puts it: it is not at the Member State level that one can decide whether a matter is to be dealt with at the Member State level.[65] Here is where the second dimension makes itself felt: the disparity of legal subjects' policies (both Member States and others), using different conceptual inroads into

---

[62] Barents (1995), see n 54 above.

[63] cf F Tanghe, *Sociale grondrechten tussen armoede en mensenrechten* (Antwerp: Kluwer, 1988).

[64] JH Gerards, *Rechterlijke toetsing aan het gelijkheidsbeginsel. Een rechtsvergelijkend onderzoek naar een algemeen toetsingsmodel* (The Hague: SDU, 2002).

[65] Somsen, see n 3 above, 1432.

EU law in order to mark and argue their respective interests as belonging to the lowest possible (ie their own) level when seen from the highest possible (ie the Community's) level. At least that is what they try to achieve. But as far as I can see, rather than going along with the conceptual cover-up, the European Court is in the habit of defusing these attempts by masterful tautologies. Let me give two examples.

It is of considerable importance in all sorts of legal contexts that citizens of the EU are under a common regime of 'public policy'. The reason is clear enough: both national and supra-national authorities can claim a wide range of discretionary powers if and when it can justifiably be said that 'public policy' is at stake. In fact, however, the very notion that should both justify and constrain the use of discretionary power is subject to conceptual divergence. In the procedures of Case C-30/77 (*Regina v Pierre Boucherau*), where national restrictions on free movement for reasons of public policy were at issue, the Commission took the view that each Member State has its own conception of public policy and that it has proven to be impossible to come to a shared definition. So it became the Court's duty to address, in a preliminary judgment, the question of what 'public order' can do to justify 'public policy'. It developed a sort of 'clear and present danger test by proxy'—in close analogy to the doctrine on free speech under the First Amendment as developed by the US Supreme Court[66]—that, I submit, is as circular as can be, thus leaving the Commission's problems where it found them. I apologize for inserting a rather long quotation from the ECJ's decision here, the excuse being that it makes things immediately clear.

The third question asks whether the words 'public policy' in Article 48 (3) are to be interpreted as including reasons of state even where no breach of the public peace or order is threatened or in a narrower sense in which is incorporated the concept of some threatened breach of the public peace, order or security, or in some other wider sense. Apart from the various questions of terminology, this question seeks to obtain a definition of the interpretation to be given to the concept of 'public policy' referred to in Article 48. In its judgment of 4 December 1974 the court acknowledged that the particular circumstances justifying recourse to the concept of public policy may vary from one country to another and from one period to another and it is therefore necessary in this matter to allow the competent national authorities an area of discretion within the limits imposed by the Treaty and the provisions adopted for its implementation. So far as it may justify certain restrictions on the free movement of persons subject to Community law, recourse by a national authority to the

---

[66] cf QL Hong, *The Legal Inclusion of Extremist Speech* (Nijmegen: Wolf Legal Publishers, 2005).

concept of public policy presupposes, in any event, the existence, in addition to the perturbation of the social order which any infringement of the law involves, of a genuine and sufficiently serious threat to the requirements of public policy affecting one of the fundamental interests of society.[67]

What the Court says, in effect, is that domestic restrictions (on free movement) in view of public policy only hold if and when requirements of public policy seriously matter. I have failed to detect what is conceptually informative here; which is why I regard it as a tautologous statement of sorts. But although it is conceptually empty, it is politically effective. By granting Member States discretionary power to restrict freedom of movement on the basis of their domestic concept of public policy, as long as they have *serious* reasons to do so, the Court does not grant them the opportunity to go by their own yardsticks of public policy. Quite the opposite. It may be the case that Member States have different ideas of what seriously matters when it comes to the interests of society: public morality, or even decency,[68] economic stability, political correctness, etc. But whatever the Member States will claim for themselves they will have to grant to the Community. If they wish to use their domestic versions of public policy in order to protect 'one of the fundamental interests of society', they have to acknowledge the constraints on their policies imposed by EU authorities for the very same reason. That is to say, at the end of the day, granting conceptual convergence in justification of political disparity will remain reviewable from community viewpoints. This is why the ECJ, in the same judgment, can emphasize the concept of public policy in the context of the Community. In particular, where it is used as a justification for derogating from the fundamental principle of freedom of movement for workers, it must be interpreted strictly, so that its scope cannot be determined unilaterally by each Member State without being subject to control by the institutions of the Community. The message seems to be: conceptual divergence is fine, but the ECJ will not tolerate abuse for domestic policies incompatible with EU policies.

   A second example to illustrate this can be derived, once more, from the twin issues of discretion and liability. In *Brasserie du Pêcheur*[69] the ECJ admits that

---

[67] Case 30/77 *Regina v Pierre Boucherau* [1977] ECR 1999, para 31–35.
[68] Though it happened outside Europe: think of 'Nipplegate' (February 2004) when Janet Jackson's breast was visible nationwide in the US for two whole seconds during her performance at the Super Bowl half-time show, being allegedly 'one of the most watched television moments in history'.
[69] Joined Cases C-46/93 and C-48/93 *Brasserie and Factortame* [1996] ECR I-1029, para 76.

'As is clear from the case-file, the concept of fault does not have the same content in the various legal systems.' Assuming that this concept, by virtue of whatever content, is part and parcel of the principles that govern non-contractual liability, one may well ask whether EC Treaty Article 288 contributes to the perspective of a unified legal order. The Court, however, evades the question by introducing, only a few lines further down in para 86, what it regards as a common general principle. 'Indeed,' it says, 'it is a general principle common to the legal systems of the Member States that the injured party must show reasonable diligence in limiting the extent of the loss or damage, or risk to bear the damage himself.' How can this be? Why would 'fault' be such a contested and diverging concept, if 'reasonable diligence' is not?[70] Why is it that 'reasonable diligence' can interpret 'fault', but not the other way around? There is no conceptually convincing argument to maintain that it cannot work both ways—which transforms the Court's statement into a tautology.

In these cases, I submit, the issues go beyond what authoritative decision or rule making could achieve in harmonizing the semantics of the terms. While in other cases it is certainly possible to settle minor conceptual divergences giving rise to litigation by authoritative rulings or doctrinal conventions, fundamental terms like 'fault' or 'public order' show that the terms that will have to give the explanation feature the same kind of divergence as the terms they purport to explain. But as in the first example, in spite of it being uninformative, the tautology is an effective one. It conveys the message: if you, Member States, insist on having your own conceptual framework, then you will not blame us for having one, too; and like you we will defend it if and when it will come under attack. So, on the basis of EC Treaty Article 288 (second paragraph)[71] non-contractual liability of the European Community is governed by 'the general principles that the legal systems of the Member States have in common', even if it can seriously be doubted whether there are these principles that are shared or 'common' in the sense of having the same content. They are perhaps shared or 'common' in a different sense: though they are not identical in each Member State, they provide sufficient incentives for legal subjects mutually to expect 'reasonable diligence' in socio-political behaviour under EU law.

But surely there is a reverse side to this political coin. There is often good reason, from the EU point of view, to grant Member States discretion in

---

[70] Earlier the Court asserts that Art 288 TEC (previously Art 215) itself expresses such a principle, Joined Cases C-46/93 and C-48/93 *Brasserie and Factortame* [1996] ECR I-1029, para 29.

[71] Before renumbering Art 215 TEC.

accordance with their domestic criteria of public policy or, for that matter, liability. Harlow mentions this when observing:

We frequently find that, when these [powers] are invoked, courts hesitate to impose civil liability for fear that its widespread imposition will inhibit public authorities from using their powers—in other words, that the deterrent effects of tort law will be too great. Yet in common law countries it is accepted in principle both that negligence is the basic principle of civil liability and that, consequently, negligence in the exercise of statutory power is actionable. These contradictory lines of reasoning have given rise to much difficulty and uncertainty in common law systems.[72]

Basically, the situation is the same in civil law countries: on the one hand there is a duty of care governing tort law and applying to public authorities on a par with other legal subjects, on the other there is reluctance to press state agencies too hard when they are exercising formal competence. Harlow goes on to observe that not all legal orders consider the same distinctions as well entrenched when it comes to liability. Not all think that the state is always at the end of the chain of wrongdoers, bearing as it were policy liability or 'secondary liability' where servants or employees have 'primary liability' for operational matters. Not all legal orders make a distinction between compensatory and punitive theories of liability as clear as the common law does (or did?). She also mentions, though, that recent English case law has become more sensitive towards 'the deterrent effects of liability', as they inevitably produce 'a detrimentally defensive frame of mind' with the administrative authorities.

The point is well taken, and it is quite revealing of post-*Francovich* liability. Discretion is invariably justified by the Court on the basis of two considerations:

First, even where the legality of measures is subject to judicial review, exercise of the legislative function must not be hindered by the prospect of actions for damages whenever the general interest of the Community requires legislative measures to be adopted which may adversely affect individual interests. Second, in a legislative context characterised by the exercise of wide discretion, which is essential for implementing a Community policy, the Community cannot incur liability unless the institution concerned has manifestly and gravely disregarded the limits on the exercise of its powers.[73]

---

[72] Galligan, see n 21 above, 156.

[73] Joined Cases 83/76, 94/76, 4/77, 15/77, and 40/77 *HNL v Council and Commission* [1978] ECR 1209, para 5, 6.

Consequently, with regard to *Francovich*,[74] Harlow believes that the Court went too far there, and that it is bound to redress and refine its own doctrine: 'To allow the creation of such a potentially widespread liability for losses flowing from use of national legislative power is certainly unwise.' She fears it will spark off reactions on government policy in other areas, as compensation of one group for loss from administrative decisions must be paid out of the same pocket as the money that should increase public wealth in the first place. This ushers in a large amount of strategic behaviour by parties on the market, which concepts, however convergent, cannot be contained within manageable limits.

Her conclusion seems relevant to the hypothesis of our project, at least from an economic point of view:

The numerous theories of state liability incorporate variant and conflicting objectives. Decisions which accord perfectly with one theory may sit odd with another. A deterrent theory of administrative liability, for example, will surely insist on the availability of exemplary damages in police malfeasance cases. Put into practice, the results inevitably conflict with theories which view resource-allocation as the legitimate prerogative of government. The importance of decisions about liability is capital because they impinge on the key governmental function of resource allocation; this is discretionary power at the highest and most political level. Such decisions may frequently also involve a major redistribution of collective resources, a matter on which political opinions vary; whether, for example, one welcomes the creation of new entitlements or sees the development as an unwelcome manifestation of the welfare dependency syndrome in modern society is largely a matter of one's political standpoint.[75]

In closing she remarks that these decisions also affect constitutional matters, in particular the balance of state powers in society.

8 Divergence in the concept of law

I have argued that under the pressure of political divergence of interests, the doctrinal convergence on the concept of discretion becomes fluid and gives way to confusion around distinctions one believed to be clear-cut and well-established. It is fashionable to blame this on the obsoleteness

---

[74] Joined Cases C-6/90 and C-9/90 *Francovich* [1991] ECR 1-5357.
[75] Galligan, see n 21 above, 164 (all three quotes in the previous sections).

of legal concepts[76] and to demand, indeed to supply, new ones. In alleged contradistinction to the old furniture, the new should be informed by social sciences, so that it will be less vulnerable to the political powers that be. Quite apart from my somewhat deviant assessment of conceptualism in law,[77] I submit that there is a deeper reason that doctrinal buttresses in law seem to collapse so easily under political pressure. This reason has to do with the ambiguity that is inherent in the concept of law at the most pertinent level one can think of.[78] The notion of discretion is particularly apt to bringing this ambiguity to the fore. Let me explain.

In an essay as early as 'The Model of Rules I'[79] Ronald Dworkin argued that discretion in the strong sense[80] is a tempting model for a positivist account of law. To be sure, Dworkin argues that it is a temptation one should not yield to, first and foremost because this strong sense of discretion does not convey (as positivists seem to think) that the official in question is free to decide without recourse to principles of substance underlying law in case rules run out. Nevertheless, the temptation of such a positivist account of law, lurking in the background of a quite received doctrinal concept, suffices to generate a series of tensions that is at the heart of what we think law is about. Masterfully depicted in Fuller's case of the speluncean explorers,[81] they were systematically accounted for by Radbruch in terms of Kantian 'antinomies'.[82]

In a nutshell, this account submits that the concept of law oscillates between the poles of equal treatment (under varying parameters of equality), policy considerations (in divergent terms of expediency), and warrants of certainty (provided by different guises of authority). As these poles mutually attract and repel each other, they generate the kind of energy in society we

[76] Scandinavian realism has been advocating this view for more than a hundred years now. see Jääskinen's contribution to this volume, ch 19.

[77] I happen to think that *Begriffsjurisprudenz* has been far more critical of the politics of the time than one usually thinks.

[78] A simpler phrase would have been: the concept of law 'as such', but that would trigger accusations of my being an 'essentialist'.

[79] R Dworkin, *Taking Rights Seriously* (London: Duckworth, 1978) 31ff.

[80] 'We use "discretion" sometimes not merely to say that an official must use judgment in applying the standards set to him by authority, or that no one will review that exercise of judgment, but to say that on some issue he is simply not bound by standards set by the authority in question'. ibid, 32.

[81] LL Fuller, 'The Case of the Speluncean Explorers: In the Supreme Court of Newgarth, 4300' (1949) 107 Harvard L Rev, 714–744.

[82] G Radbruch, R Dreier, and SL Paulson, *Rechtsphilosophie. Studienausgabe* (Heidelberg: Müller, 1999) 73ff.

call distributive justice. However, as soon as one isolates and hypostatizes one of them, it turns into one of the well-known ideologies of law: moralism, pragmatism, or positivism, ushering in the perennial clash of 'philosophies'. Now even if one is justifiably reluctant to take Radbruch's account as ultimate wisdom,[83] I submit that any competitive candidate theory will have to explain these conceptual antinomies as a factual 'logic' or 'grammar' of legal thinking in our culture.[84] On this hypothesis, the phenomenon of conceptual divergence under political pressure would receive an elegant but solid explanation, even to the point where divergence becomes predictable. While ideological divergence will predictably occur as more political pressure builds up, rotating the poles of the antinomies would be the model one could use to defuse the pressure. Discretion, for instance, would either be seen oscillating between the poles of, say, fair competition (equality), *effet utile* (expediency), and 'direct invocability' of EC (EU) law (certainty); or it would be seen petrifying at either one of these poles, transforming into acts of moral paternalism, market liberalism, or bureaucratic authoritarianism. Only the first of these alternatives would generate the positive energy Radbruch had in mind and which this volume refers to as 'binding unity'.

[83] One of the problems being that the concept of justice seems to have a job to do in the *definiens* as well as in the *definiendum*, bringing in serious risks of circularity.

[84] Although lots of caveats would pertain, one might point to the theatrical roots of legal thinking in western culture as we find them in Sophocles' *Antigone*.

PART IV

Policy Areas

15

Binding Unity and Divergence while Creating a Common European Culture of Energy Regulation

Iñigo del Guayo Castiella

1 The context of regulation

What is regulation? Why regulate? Who regulates? Is the regulatory function a rule making one, is it a function for enforcing rules, does it consist in supervising how those rules are drafted and enforced, or does regulation include all these three functions? Is regulation a branch of law? If regulation is understood to be a rule making function, for example, should every rule dealing with energy be considered a regulatory rule, from the rule on overcoming shortages in oil stocks, to the rule establishing the compensation to be paid to consumers whose supply has been interrupted for a period, and including the rule laying down the diameter gas distribution pipelines must have? In other words, are (legal) rules always to be considered *regulatory rules*, or are there legal rules of a non-regulatory nature?

For two reasons this chapter does not even try to answer those questions. On the one hand, a far reaching conceptual discussion would be involved, referring to the fundamentals of society and government, and the relation of one to the other, about which the available literature is overwhelming, and, on the other hand, there is too little space to deal properly with those issues. Instead, this chapter will try only to point out a number of problems arising from a lack of common understanding of what regulation is and what regulation should aim at within the efforts to create a European Internal Energy Market (IEM).

It is often assumed that the Anglo-American concept of economic regulation is equivalent to the continental idea of public economic law, and in a sense that may be true. But, from a number of perspectives, there are not enough grounds to reach such a conclusion. Whereas regulation seems to be based on the assumption of a clear distinction between the regulator (public) and the regulated (private), continental public economic law can be, in some countries and in some areas, based on the assumption that both the regulator and the regulated activity are of a public nature. This is not necessarily because companies operating in such areas are in public hands, but because the proper functioning of this sector is somehow considered to be the responsibility of public institutions, either because there is a constitutional right to be promoted, or because the activity is considered to be a public service.[1] In any case, it is worth underlining that regulation is a multidisciplinary concept (sociological, economic, legal, political, etc), and cannot be constrained within the realms of Law.

This chapter aims to analyse some terminological and conceptual legal problems arising from the efforts to build a true European Energy Market amidst the existence of both a significant number of disparate legal traditions within the EU in dealing with energy issues, and a reluctance on the part of Member States to give up their responsibilities in guaranteeing, among other aspects of the industry, the security of energy supply.[2] In particular, this chapter tries to underline that there are two main legal streams converging within the procedure to build a legal framework for energy at EU level. These are on the one hand, the system based on an Anglo-Saxon idea of economic regulation and energy regulation and, on the other, the systems of most continental countries based on the idea of public economic law, to which energy law belongs, convergence being hindered by a lack of common language, as well as of a true common legal tradition.

The idea of an IEM started to be strongly promoted in the early 1980s, at a time when in many countries policies of liberalization, deregulation, and privatization were being enforced as a response to a new stream of economic assumptions led by the governments of the USA and the UK. As a consequence a clear victory for the concept of economic regulation based on the Anglo-American legal system led to the inclusion of some of its typical

---

[1] I have made an attempt to draw a distinction between economic regulation and public economic law in Spain in I del Guayo, 'La regulación económica como alternativa' (2006) Revista Española de Derecho Administrativo, 227–254.

[2] For example, the dispute between Spain and the Commission on the take-over bid of the German energy giant E. On of the Spanish electricity utility Endesa.

techniques and institutions within the energy Directives and Regulations passed at a EU level. They were, in their turn, either unknown within some of the legal orders of the Member States, or the terms and expressions had another meaning or no precise legal meaning.

2 The Internal Energy Market

The 1996 Electricity Directive and the 1998 Gas Directive signalled an important step towards the creation of an IEM. They aimed to allow large users of electricity and gas to choose their supplier and indirectly, the electricity generator or gas producer or importer, from the whole range of energy companies active in the EU, thus opening these markets to competition. However, in 2001 the EC identified in its first Benchmarking Report significant obstacles remaining for new market players entering the market and for eligible customers really to benefit from competition.[3] In particular, the Report identified the following obstacles:

1. There was unequal implementation of the Directives, thus affecting consumer choice and distorting both competition and the competitive position of energy companies (since, for example, some of them are losing business to, or are vulnerable to take-over by, companies whose domestic markets are not fully open).
2. There was a lack of proper implementation of the Directives in Germany and France.
3. The detailed regulatory framework varies significantly and, in particular, in some Member States there are certain conditions relating to third party access (TPA) that are not conducive to a competitive market, which cause particular problems where there is insufficient unbundling of network operators.
4. In some countries network tariffs appeared relatively high at an aggregate level and required justification or modification, while for almost all Member States a few existing electricity generators had a dominant position in wholesale markets, a circumstance which made imbalance charges unnecessarily high.

---

[3] European Commission, 'Commission Staff Working Paper, First benchmarking report on the implementation of the internal electricity and gas market' SEC (2001) 1957, 35–37.

5. There were generally restricted opportunities for cross-border trade, for both electricity and gas, due to the lack of a cost-reflective tarification system and a lack of co-ordination of capacity allocation with insufficient information being made available.

6. The information collected by the EC indicated that, where properly organized and regulated, market opening does not lead to problems with security of supply or standards of service. Neither does it impede the promotion of environmental policy and renewables nor lead to unacceptable social consequences (such as the weakening of demand management and vulnerable customers' protection policies).

3 The European Gas and Electricity Forums, and their outcomes, as instruments of unity and convergence

The European Gas Regulatory Forum of Madrid (EGRF) and the European Electricity Regulatory Forum of Rome (formerly of Florence) (EERF) were set up by the European Commission to examine issues around the creation of true internal gas and electricity markets and to address cross-border trade in electricity and gas, in particular the tarification of cross-border gas and electricity exchanges, the allocation and management of scarce interconnection capacity, and other technical and commercial barriers to the creation of fully operational internal gas and electricity markets. In general terms, most aspects related to the IEM have been addressed by the Forums. However, some issues, such as public service obligations, have not been on the agenda because the Forums have focused mainly on liberalization issues.

Participants at the Forums are the European Commission, Member States, national regulatory authorities, transmission system operators, gas and electricity suppliers and traders, consumers, network users, and gas and power exchanges.

The Forums convene once or twice a year. The first meeting of the EERF was held in 1998, two years after the adoption of the 1996 Electricity Directive. The first meeting of the EGRF was held in 1999, one year after of the adoption of the 1998 Gas Directive. Both the EERF and the EGRF are consultative informal bodies of the European Commission and they do not have any regulatory powers, as such.

The main outcome of both Forums has been threefold: first, they helped to design the Gas Directive (2003) and the Electricity Directive (2003); second, they helped the European Commission to realize that there was a need not only for directives, but also for regulations, which were passed in 2003 (electricity) and 2005 (gas); third, the Forums adopted a number of guidelines on key issues of the energy market, which, in their turn, have either been incorporated into the Regulations or are being used as a mean of properly interpreting the legislation in force.

By means of the working methodology and the final outcome, which has led to the creation of the European Regulators Group for Electricity and Gas (ERGEG), the Forums have contributed strongly to the promotion and creation of a common regulatory culture.[4]

4 Energy and the regulatory debate

The Gas and Electricity Directives and Regulations (2003 and 2005) are directly aimed at creating an IEM, and not at laying down a regulatory framework for energy industries. However, the obstacles to reaching an IEM identified by the EU institutions and the ways of overcoming these problems envisaged by the Energy Directives and Regulations (such as TPA to the system), have had a strong impact on national key regulatory issues and, as a result, many aspects of energy regulation have become harmonized. In other words, neither the Gas and Electricity Directives nor the Electricity and Gas Regulations are direct regulatory instruments, but only indirect ones, and there is within them a regulatory harmonization to the extent that it has become inevitable that the emergence of an IEM for gas and electricity is facilitated.

Most of their provisions are not harmonizing ones, but are rather a further specification of the law of the Treaties in these two energy sectors. There are two provisions within both Directives which clearly are simultaneously both evidence of the lack of attempts at direct harmonization within them and a practical recognition that the Electricity and Gas Directives have indirectly harmonized a number of regulatory issues. These relate to the obligation

---

[4] See, further, L Hancher and I del Guayo, 'The European Electricity and Gas Regulatory Forums' in B Barton *et al* (eds), *Regulating Energy and Natural Resources* (New York: Oxford University Press, 2006) 243–261.

imposed upon the EC to monitor and review the application of the Electricity and Gas Directives, and to submit an overall progress report to the European Parliament and the Council before the end of the first year following their entry into force (and thereafter on an annual basis). On the one hand, this report will cover the extent to which the unbundling and tarification requirements contained in the Directives have been successful in ensuring fair and non-discriminatory access to the Community's electricity and gas systems. It is recognized, therefore, that at least two aspects of regulation have been subject to a degree of harmonization. On the other hand, it must address the need for possible harmonization requirements which are not linked to the provisions of the Directives (this is evidence that some requirements have been harmonized by the Directives—those linked to the provisions of the Electricity and Gas Directives—and some have not).[5]

The regulatory debate within the energy field has to do not only with a tension between centralization and subsidiarity,[6] but also with divergent ideologies about the relationship between government and society. This is shown by the existing debate on the services of a general economic interest, which is a relevant concept for energy issues. Within the debate on the adoption of a draft Constitution, there were ideological issues behind the discussion on whether to delete, amend, or keep the wordings of Articles 16 and 86 of the Treaty establishing the European Community. In general terms, the debate was twofold: on the one hand, between those favouring the increase in the powers of the EU over the definition and regulation of the services of a general economic interest, and those who thought those powers must be kept by Member States; and on the other hand, between those who pushed for a wider and more relevant role of the said services within the EU (by means, for example, of a concept of services of general interest and not only of services of general *economic* interest), and those who thought that the exemption from competition rules contained in Article 86 (2) must be kept within the existing limits, or even reduced. The result was a compromise, but with a small victory for those who were in favour of the maintenance of the word 'economic' in Article 86.[7]

---

[5] Art 28(1)(b) and (g) Parliament and Council Directive (EC) 2003/54 concerning common rules for the internal market in electricity and repealing Directive (EC) 96/92 [2003] OJ L176/37 and Art 31(1)(b) and (g) Parliament and Council Directive (EC) 2003/55 concerning common rules for the internal market in gas and repealing Directive 98/30/EC [2003] OJ L176/57.

[6] B Eberlein and E Grande, 'Beyond Delegation: Transnational Regulatory Regimes and the EU Regulatory State' (2005) 12 *J of Eur Public Policy*, 89–112.

[7] See I del Guayo, 'El futuro de los servicios de interés económico general en la Unión Europea' (2005) *Revista Argentina del Régimen de la Administración Pública*, 163–192.

5 Energy regulation within divergent legal cultures: a terminological and conceptual approach

In order to be able to draw proper conclusions from the achievements of the electricity and gas Regulatory Forums, one must also analyse what energy regulation means within the EU context, as here (as well as in many other areas of EU law) there is a 'Tower of Babel' reflecting different legal traditions with the result that crucial terminology in the energy field—such as 'regulation', 'licences', 'concessions', etc—has disparate meanings. I shall now address a conceptual issue as well as a terminological one within the EU, in the sense that the legal orders of many EU Member States are built on different principles from those on which the Anglo-American tradition of energy regulation is based, and, as a consequence, terminology also varies from one country to another. I now advance the idea that as a result of the process towards an IEM and, particularly, as a result of the EERF and the EGRF, in recent years many EU Member States have experienced neither new forms of energy regulation nor alternatives to traditional regulatory instruments, but instead have experienced energy regulation as an alternative itself, ie as an alternative response to their traditional approaches to market failures (including natural monopolies), based on similar principles to those of the Anglo-American concept of regulation and, ultimately, on similar terminology.

Legal and economic professionals and academics in the UK, the USA (and other countries whose law is influenced by them) seem to share an understanding—to the extent that it is possible—of regulation, including both economic regulation, which provides a substitute for competition in relation to natural monopolies, and social regulation, which deals mainly with two other types of market failures: consumer information and externalities.[8] Energy industries are subject to both kinds of regulation, but insofar as energy supply is a key element of the economy and there are uncontroversial natural monopoly elements when carrying out some energy activities (such as in transmission networks), the focus is on energy regulation as a form of economic regulation. Therefore, the kind of regulation which has been directed at energy industries since the late 1970s is primarily the regulation of competition, aiming to create conditions for energy markets operators

---

[8] AI Ogus, *Regulation: Legal Forms and Economic Theory* (Oxford: Hart, 1994) 5.

as if there were a true market. From now on I shall refer to regulation as the legal response to natural monopolies in favour of competition within energy markets—unless otherwise expressly stated—and this, in its turn, is the main sense in which regulation has been used in the IEM Directives and Regulations.[9]

The concept of regulation is based on the presumption that economic activities are run by individuals and companies—and so they must be, since *freedom of enterprise* is a constitutional fundamental right—and that allocative efficiency is primarily achieved by markets, since there is no regulation to enforce if there is no market. Actually, regulation has no role either in pure market systems (where governments do not feel themselves impelled to correct any market distortions), or in pure collectivist systems (where there are no markets). However, it is hard to find an example of a pure market system or a pure collectivist system due to the fact that on the one hand, markets tend to disappear if there is no form of regulation and, on the other, that extreme versions of collectivism collapsed in the twentieth century. In Anglo-American economic systems 'the aim (of regulation) is to correct perceived deficiencies in the market system in meeting collective or public interest goals',[10] ie the aim is to correct markets, not to exclude the existence of a market. Variations between countries with this understanding of regulation depend upon quantitative criteria (more or less regulation, more or less intervention) and not upon qualitative ones (markets are always considered to be the best instruments for allocative efficiency, and regulation somehow has an inevitable character).

In many EU countries, principles on which governmental intervention on the economy is based (particularly in energy industries) have not traditionally been those on which the Anglo-American concept of regulation relies. The economic systems of these EU countries belong to a market system model, in which market failures are also corrected by regulation and governmental intervention. They have *social market economies*, as does the EU itself,[11] where both economic and social regulation have paramount roles. From this perspective, there are no identifiable relevant differences with regard to regulation between these countries and the Anglo-American ones, and in the end, variations are only a matter of the degree of regulation exercised. However,

---

[9] Eg, Art 22 Parliament and Council Directive (EC) 98/30 concerning common rules for the internal market in natural gas [1998] OJ L204/1.

[10] Ogus, see n 8 above, 2.

[11] Art I-3(3) of the failure of the Draft Treaty establishing a Constitution for Europe.

I still identify a distinction between two traditions to do with different under-standings of the relations between the economy and the state, and of markets as the optimal instrument for allocative efficiency. This distinction arises from ideological principles, and is reflected in law and legal terminology.

In some European countries (particularly in Latin ones, such as France, Italy, Portugal, and Spain) the usual response to a natural monopoly chal-lenge is the creation of a public service, identified, in its turn (although not always) with a legal monopoly run by a public undertaking. Regulatory response to natural monopolies has three main forms: (i) public ownership, (ii) private ownership subject to external constraints in the form of price and quality regulation, and (iii) forcing firms desiring to obtain a monopoly to compete for it.[12]

It is important to note that the creation of a public service in some EU countries has not merely been the result of a regulatory response (the first of the three possible forms of economic regulation) but rather of a dom-inant school of legal thinking that the activity declared to be a public ser-vice must be provided by the state. These services belong to the province of what the constitutions of those countries designate as the 'Social State'. It is the legal responsibility of governments to provide citizens with minimal basic services (including some energy services). By creating a public service some governments in continental Europe have not only tried to overcome the inherent risks of natural monopolies, but they have also reversed the presumption on which economic regulation is based, ie the primacy of mar-kets. The UK together with the rest of Europe experienced the nationaliza-tion of energy industries after the Second World War, but this development in Britain was not the result of—and was not rooted in—legal theory, as in some continental European countries. There was no sense of the reversal of the primacy of markets, rather nationalization was based on practical grounds. It is widely acknowledged that Anglo-American legal systems lack the 'intellectualism' of some continental European ones.

In continental European countries issues to which energy regulation refers are termed economic public (or administrative) law.[13] In some EU Member States, regulation is an issue for the public administration itself to exercise as a branch of government, rather than for independent agencies, and is part of administrative law. In their law dictionaries and literature all of

[12] Ogus, see n 8 above, 5.
[13] *Wirtschaftsverwaltungsrecht* (Germany and Austria); *droit public économique* (France), or *derecho público económico* (Spain).

these countries have a word equivalent to the English 'regulation': *regulación* in Spain, *regolazione* in Italy, *regulação* in Portugal, *régulation* in France, *regulering* (or *regelgeving*) in the Netherlands, and *Regulierung* in Germany. But whereas in Anglo-American countries the term 'regulation' tends to have a relatively precise meaning, in these continental European countries the word has the same broad meaning as *regula, -ae*, the Latin word from which it is derived, and therefore regulation may be identified with 'law', insofar as law, in its turn, may be identified with rules. The words *regulación, regolazione, regulação, régulation, regulering* (or *regelgeving*), and *Regulierung* have traditionally referred, in principle, to whatever legal rules are in force in any sector, regardless of the institution which has produced them, regardless of their aims, and in particular regardless of whether they have been specifically addressed to natural monopolies.

In the legal orders of these EU continental countries there is a more precise legal term used to designate secondary legislation approved by governments as opposed to acts passed by Parliaments: *Reglamento* in Spain, *regolamento* in Italy, *regulamento* in Portugal, *règlement* in France, *verordening* (provincial or municipal) in the Netherlands, and *Verordnung* in Germany. This sense of the word 'regulation' also exists in the British tradition.[14] This is the meaning of the word as used in the Gas Directive,[15] by which Member States were asked to bring into force the laws, regulations,[16] and administrative provisions necessary to comply with the Gas Directive not later than 1 July 2004. This term was also chosen in those countries and in the UK to designate a specific form of EU secondary legislation, European Regulations (as a European legal norm distinct from European Directives).

To summarize, whereas in the English language 'regulation' may designate at least two different concepts, some European continental languages not only have two different words, as, for example, in French (*régulation* and *Règlement*), but do not use the word *régulation*, when applied to energy, in its accurate meaning of energy regulation aiming to provide a substitute for natural monopolies in energy, but rather as a synonym for norms related to energy. As a consequence, it was noted that often when English versions of

---

[14]   See HWR Wade and CF Forsyth, *Administrative Law* (7th edn, Oxford: Oxford University Press, 1994) 867 and PP Craig, *Administrative Law* (3rd edn, London: Sweet & Maxwell, 1994).

[15]   Art 31 Parliament and Council Directive (EC) 2003/55 concerning common rules for the internal market in gas and repealing Directive (EC) 98/30 [2003] OJ L176/57.

[16]   *Disposiciones reglamentarias* (Spanish); *disposizioni regolamentari* (Italian); *disposições regulamentares* (Portuguese); *dispositions réglementaires* (French); *bestuursrechtelijke* (Dutch); and *Verwaltungsvorschriften* (German).

European legislation and official documents used the term 'regulation' in the sense of a specific legal method to deal with natural monopolies, other languages used the term to designate secondary legislation. For example, when the English version uses the word 'regulation', the French version may use the word *Règlement*. The overall result of this was that dialogue and discussion became hard to maintain, and the goal of dealing with monopolies became submerged in terminology.

An example of such terminological and conceptual differences within the EU is found within the *Green Book on Services of General Interest*, which, when addressing TPA to energy networks in its Annex, states the following:[17]

In such cases, the mere application of common rules (eg, competition or public procurement rules) may prove insufficient and thus needs to be complemented by more intense and continuous sector-specific oversight (regulation).

Regulation in this paragraph is translated into *réglementation* (France), *regolamentazione* (Italy), *regulamentação* (Portugal), and *Verordnung* (Germany). In these four cases, each respective version of the *Green Book* uses the word which in those countries designates secondary legislation. It would seem that the *Green Book* is asking for the adoption of norms rather than for actual regulation, ie to adopt norms and take decisions to overcome abuses of the dominant positions of energy infrastructure companies and monopolistic tendencies. Only the Spanish and Dutch versions use *regulación*, and *regulering*, respectively.[18]

The tendency of the legal orders of some continental European countries to identify regulation with a set of norms, regardless of its aims, is also shown in the way 'regulatory framework' or 'regulatory environment' is designated in those countries:[19] *marco reglamentario* or *marco jurídico* (Spain), *cadre réglementaire* (France), *quadro normativo* (Italy), *quadro de regulamentação* or *quadro regulamentar* (Portugal), *regelgevingskader* (Netherlands), and *Rechtsrahmen* or *Regelungsrahmens* (Germany).

---

[17] European Commission, 'Green Paper on Services of General Interest' COM (2003) 270 final, Annex, 29.

[18] In this book, whenever the English version refers to 'regulatory authorities' (for example, paras 34, 35) or to *autoridade reguladora* (Portugal), other versions refer either to *autoridades de reglamentación* or to *autoridades reguladoras* (Spain); *autorités réglementaires* or *autorités de réglementation* (France); *autorità di regolamentazione* (Italy); *regelgevende instantie* (Netherlands); and *Regulierungsbehörden* (Germany).

[19] As, for example, in Recital 1 Commission Decision (EC) 2003/796 on establishing the European Regulators Group for Electricity and Gas [2003] OJ L296/34 and European Council, Presidency Conclusions of 23 March 2005, no 24, 7619/1/05 REV 1.

Despite the underlined divergent approaches, there has been an evolution and convergence, both in conceptual and terminology areas. One of the few places where the 1998 Gas Directive uses the word 'regulation' in the sense of economic regulation is Article 22:

Member States shall create appropriate and efficient mechanisms for regulation, control and transparency so as to avoid any abuse of a dominant position, in particular to the detriment of consumers, and any predatory behaviour.

The Spanish, French, Dutch, and German versions use the word *regulación, régulation, regulering*, and *Regulierung*, respectively, (possibly) in an attempt to follow Anglo-American terminology, whereas the Portuguese (*regulamentação*) and Italian (*disciplina*) versions used a word whose meaning is wider, since it covers a rule making concept, regardless of the aim of those rules, although their true meaning—rules to deal with monopolies—can be deduced from the context provided by the rest of the wording of Article 22.

However, following the development of the IEM and as a result of the work of the Forums, the new Article 25(8) of the Gas Directive has the same wording as Article 22 of the 1998 Gas Directive, but the terminology is now uniform, and even the Portuguese and Italian versions use the words *regulação* and *regolazione*, respectively.

Another example is provided by Recital 13 of the Gas Directive, where it is said there is the need for effective regulation, carried out by one or more national regulatory authorities, and the Spanish, French, and Portuguese versions of this provision use the closest word linguistically to the English word 'regulation'. Only the Italian version still uses the word *Regolamentazione*.[20]

6 The Dutch case: *regulering* and *regelgeving*[21]

Particular attention should be paid to the Dutch case, since as opposed to the use of the term *regulering* in the 1998 Gas Directive, in both Article 25

---

[20] *La existencia de una regulación eficaz, aplicada por una o más autoridades reguladoras nacionales* (Spanish); *l'existence d'une régulation efficace assurée par une ou plusieurs autorités de régulation nationales* (French); *a existência de uma regulação eficaz por parte de uma ou mais entidades reguladoras nacionais* (Portuguese); *de aanwezigheid van effectieve regelgeving, die door een of meer nationale regelgevende instanties wordt uitgevoerd* (Dutch); *der wirksamen Regulierung durch eine oder mehrere nationale Regulierungsbehörden* (German); and *l'esistenza di un'efficace regolamentazione, attuata da una o più autorità nazionali di regolamentazione* (Italian).

[21] This section is based on information which Professor Sacha Prechal kindly sent to me, on which I have only elaborated. I am in debt to Professor Prechal for her assistance in dealing with

and Recital 13 of the 2003 Gas Directive the word *regelgeving* (or *regelgevende instanties*) is used instead. Focusing on the Dutch case may help to further discuss and illustrate the need for a more accurate use of the concept of regulation in EU legal orders than in the British one. In particular, I shall focus on the change of the word *regulering*, used in Article 22 of the 1998 Gas Directive, for the word *regelgeving*, used in Article 25 of the 2003 Gas Directive. The aim of the following analysis is to try to demonstrate that using the word *regulering* would have been better than using the word *regelgeving*, but, of course, no definitive conclusion can be drawn on this issue, since both Dutch words may have a variety of meanings.

In principle, the English expression 'regulation' can be translated into Dutch by *regulering, regelgeving,* or *verordening*, depending in which context the English term is used. But, at the same time, it must be stressed that the real problem lies not in a linguistic problem, but rather in the fact that the idea of regulation itself does not properly exist in Dutch law, and in the fact that the fundamentals and assumptions on which British economic regulation is based differ considerably from those of Continental public economic law and in particular from Dutch public economic law.

Within the Dutch legal order, there is no strict distinction between the terms *regulering* and *regelgeving*, though the former seems to have a broader meaning than the latter, since *regulering* can also include self-regulation, contracts, etc. In any case, both are vague and imprecise terms in Dutch law. Indeed, *regelgeving* is usually used for law giving, rule making, or legislation, not only of parliamentary acts, but also of other generally binding rules, such as provincial legislation, or delegated legislation enforced by the government upon the request of Parliament.

In the Netherlands, the term *verordening* is used both for European Regulations (*EG Verordening*), and for internal regulations, but in this latter case mainly for provincial or municipality regulations based on a Parliamentary act, so that whenever an act provides that provinces or municipalities are required to do something, they are empowered to issue a *provinciale verordening* or *gemeentelijke* (municipal) *verordening*. The term is also used in the case of delegated legislation, though in such case the most common terms are *amvb* (*algemene maatregel van bestuur*) or *regeling*.

In this context, a number of problems arise in properly translating into Dutch the English expressions 'regulation' and 'regulatory authorities', which

the Dutch case, whose ideas I have tried to reflect in the text, but I must stress that any inaccuracy or error about the Dutch law is my sole responsibility. I am also thankful to the input given by Professor MM Roggenkamp and by Willemijn Pastoor, from the University of Groningen.

are used by, amongst other legal instruments,[22] the 2003 Gas Directive and the 2003 Electricity Directive. Regulation is often translated into *regelgeving*, but, as already noted, 'a regulation' (as a single juridical act) is translated into *verordening* (ie a piece of delegated legislation or provincial or/and municipal regulation, or an EC Regulation). The usual translation into Dutch of 'regulatory authorities' is *regelgevende instanties*.

The Anglo-American concept of regulation is related to a variety of instruments, including, of course, rule making, but the problem relies upon the fact that in Dutch economic law, such a broad concept of regulation does not really exist, and if a Dutch legal term was to be found to designate it, *regulering* would seem to be more appropriate than *regelgeving*.

One of the main issues is that according to EC secondary law, for example, the Electricity and Gas Directives, national regulatory authorities are not, necessarily, rule making bodies (ie bodies issuing rules which are generally binding). However, when transposing EC law into Dutch law, the English expressions 'regulation' and 'regulatory authorities' are translated, respectively, into *regelgeving* and *regelgevende instanties*, and one may presume, therefore, in accordance with Dutch legal tradition, that those *instanties* would be set up to issue rules of general application. But such a presumption is not necessarily valid within the internal Dutch legal order according to which there is a *trias politica* arrangement, ie a peculiar separation of powers, that prevents the unrestricted acceptance of *instanties* with such extensive power to make rules.

Behind that discussion is a more substantial one, related to the determination of the extent to which some Dutch public bodies, such as the competition authority or the telecom supervisor, do actually issue generally binding rules, since there is an obvious lack of parliamentary control. For instance, during the implementation of Directive (EC) 2002/21, there was an initial question about which body should be made responsible for carrying out 'regulatory tasks': the competent minister, the telecom supervisor (Opta), the Media supervisor (*Commisariaat voor de Media*), or possibly a combination of these executive bodies and Parliament? Some confusion in this respect was also caused by the White Paper on Governance and the Commission

---

[22] See, eg, Parliament and Council Directive (EC) 2002/21 on a common regulatory framework for electronic communications networks and services [2002] OJ L108/33 (Framework Directive); Parliament and Council Directive (EC) 2003/54 concerning common rules for the internal market in electricity [2003] OJ L176/37, and Commission Decision (EC) 2003/796 on establishing the European Regulators Group for Electricity and Gas [2003] OJ L296/34.

Communication on regulatory agencies.[23] It appears that some confusion is also due to the fact that in the EU translation/terminology databases (such as EuroDicAutom and the Inter-Agency Terminology Exchange or IATE) 'regulatory' is still translated as *regelgevend*. In addition to these points, what is labelled under EC secondary law as 'regulatory authorities' is being referred to in the Netherlands as *toezichthouders* (ie 'supervisory authorities'). *Regulering* would be another option, and this is perhaps linguistically the best translation, but it is also a very vague and imprecise term in Dutch law.

The consequence of what we have said about Dutch law is that even though one may think that in principle there are no legal consequences to be deduced from the fact that Article 25(8) of the 2003 Gas Directive (by which Member States are asked to create mechanisms for regulation to avoid the abuse of a dominant position), even though it has the same wording as the former Article 22 of the 1998 Gas Directive, uses *regelgeving* instead of *regulering*, there *are* relevant consequences from the point of view of the internal legal order of the Netherlands. The change from one word to another, insofar as the new term (*regelgeving*) is closer to the idea of rule making than the previous one (*regulering*), creates unnecessary problems in relation to the actual powers of such regulatory authorities.

7 Concluding remarks

The process for the creation of an IEM within the EU is simultaneously a source of legal confusion in the midst of divergent traditions and ideologies, and a fruitful way towards juridical convergence into a common regulatory culture. Assuming, with Darwin, that the function creates the organ, so in the EU the need to exercise a new regulatory function to set up a truly integrated and liberalized market for energy has driven the creation of regulatory authorities in national jurisdictions, and these must be confronted with constitutional exigencies of democracy, parliamentary accountability, and transparency.

The need for regulation and for 'independent' regulatory authorities is in conflict with the legal orders of some Member States of the EU, where the

---

[23] European Commission, 'European Governance, a White Paper' COM (2001) 428 and European Commission, 'Communication on the operating framework for the European Regulatory Agencies' COM (2002) 718 final.

functions developed by such regulatory authorities have traditionally been in the hands of governments and their public administrations, and even in the hands of parliaments. New legal measures at EU level stress the need for those regulatory authorities to be independent from the industries, but independence from government is not, as yet, an exigency of EU law, since it would obviously be constitutionally unacceptable for a number of countries. However, the kind of functions which such authorities are expected to develop in accordance with Energy Directives and Regulations is no doubt pushing towards a certain level of autonomy from government in both decision and rule making.

Behind terminological developments within EU law related to energy, one may assume a certain decree of conceptual convergence, and one may view the term 'regulation' as something different from rule making, though at the same time including it. It is not just that within the EU many different expressions were used to designate the same concept, whereas now there is a tendency to use common terminology. Beyond terminology there are also different understandings of regulation, and EU Member States now tend to share a basic concept of regulation as the substitute for competition in relation to natural energy monopolies, albeit subject to their national traditions. This conceptual convergence has been achieved by means of the political integration process within the EU, and in particular, by means of the gradual construction of an IEM. As a result, terminology is also becoming homogeneous. The fact that discussions at the Forums were held in English and that documents are available only in English has undoubtedly had an impact there.

The theory of systems, as developed by Luhmann,[24] emphasizes that the identity of a system is the result of that system's self-consciousness, at the same time as it dialogues and confronts its own properties with the characteristics of other systems. However the current situation in the EU is no more than that there are a number of separated energy systems, and therefore—with their own languages (including, of course, legal terminology and concepts) and techniques—the progressive integration of these systems would undoubtedly lead to a homogeneous regulatory culture. To underline the validity of the idea of self-consciousness of systems, we may have to look at how the problem of security of supply has suddenly come onto the preferential EU agenda. Although the Draft Treaty Establishing a Constitution for Europe is unable to provide a more ambitious wording to allow

---

[24] N Luhmann, *Das Recht der Gesellschaft* (Frankfurt am Main: Suhrkamp, 1995).

a true energy policy to emerge, a number of facts have opened the eyes of governments to the need for a common policy on energy. Indeed, the gas crisis between Russia and the Ukraine which endangered supplies to EU countries in January 2006, as most of the gas crossed the Ukraine, together with the electricity blackout suffered by millions of European citizens in November 2006 due to failure in the German transmission network have both contributed to spreading the idea that the security of Member States' energy systems depends on the security of the energy system of the EU as a whole. These facts, together with the increase in oil prices located *outside the system*, have pushed European leaders to look for new ways of allowing the EU to play a more active role in this area, while combatting some national misunderstandings of what security of supply really means. Actual integration of energy systems, for example by means of greater network integration, will gradually lead to a common regulatory culture, since a system develops its own language.

16

Conceptual Convergence and Judicial Cooperation in Sex Equality Law

Linda Senden

1 Introduction

The claim to the unity of the EU legal order is as old as the European integration process itself[1] and is in fact inherent in the very notion of a legal order, whatever its shape and whatever its relation to other legal orders.[2] The European legal order relies heavily on the national legal orders for ensuring this unity, through the effective day-to-day implementation of EU law by national legislators and executives and through its enforcement by national courts. The latter may have to resort to the preliminary ruling procedure of Article 234 EC in doing so, which as such provides a crucial mechanism for securing the uniform interpretation of European law throughout the EU.

We will reflect here first on what the claim to the unity of the European legal order actually implies. We will start from the thesis that shared common values and fundamental rights help to forge not only legal unity, but in turn also contribute to building a common transnational identity. 'Legal unity' in itself must be understood as a relative or variable notion, with the intensity or level of (conceptual) convergence actually aimed at dependent on the matter concerned (section 2). The extent to which conceptual convergence can actually be achieved, presupposes certain features of the national legal system, reflecting as such its convergence capacity (section 3). The chapter next explores the issue of conceptual divergence in the specific area of sex equality

---

[1] Case 26/62 *Van Gend & Loos* [1963] ECR 10.
[2] See Prechal and Van Roermund, this volume, Introduction.

law. While EU equal treatment law imposes a certain standard of equality and non-discrimination, does it also bring more unity into this area (section 4)? Partly it does through establishing common—minimum—definitions, but no doubt judicial dialogue between the European Court of Justice (ECJ) and the national courts is also crucial for realizing this. The possible unifying effects of this cooperation within the framework of the preliminary ruling procedure will be assessed both at a general level and in the specific area of sex equality law (section 5). On that basis, it will then be considered how the efficiency of the preliminary ruling procedure could be enhanced, in particular whether a distinction could be made between more fundamental and constitutional cases on the one hand and more technical ones on the other, the latter being less crucial with a view to realizing or preserving the unity of the legal order (section 6).

2 Enhancing unity

To what extent are divergent interpretations of European legal concepts, because they are channelled through already existing and possibly well-established national legal concepts, a threat to binding unity in the EU? As tempting as it may be for a lawyer to equate 'binding unity' here to 'legal unity', we must admit that it implies more than that. Legal unity is a means to the higher end of market unity, which in its turn is to be considered as an intermediate step towards ultimately realizing some form of political unity, be it in the form of a federation or otherwise. Over time, we have indeed witnessed a move beyond the internal market concept, as EU powers have extended in areas such as criminal law, social law, and migration law. The EU has also increasingly engaged in the fundamental rights discourse, to which the introduction of European citizenship has contributed. EU citizens are no longer to be considered mere—economic—market citizens, but may also derive rights from European law, for instance, in their capacity as students.[3] Yet, a politically united EU requires more and presupposes a sense of European identity amongst its citizens. Building a European, transnational identity, based on a sense of common destiny and belonging,[4] has

---

[3] Case C-184/99 *Grzelczyk* [2001] ECR I-6193 and Case C-209/03 *Bidar* [2005] ECR I-2119.

[4] W van Gerven, *The European Union: A Polity of States and Peoples* (Oxford: Hart, 2005) 2, under reference to N MacCormick, *Questioning Sovereignty: Law, State, and Nation in the European Commonwealth* (Oxford: Oxford University Press, 1999) 170.

proved to be one of the major hurdles or challenges in the European integration process.[5]

Law is the primary tool of the EU in meeting this challenge, which is very
much reflected in the observation of De Burca that EU law cannot build on
the 'underlying social solidarity', but that '[t]he process in the Community
sometimes appears as the reverse, in which an attempt is being made to *create*
solidarity through law, by declaring common principles and rights in the
hope that these will influence the legal systems of the Member States as an
integrating force'.[6] Indeed, this connects to a first major path along which
law may contribute to bridging the gap between the EU and its citizens and
to the creation of a European identity: the process of constitutionalizing
Europe, as a result of which our shared values and norms are confirmed and
enhanced.[7] Such values can be found in the EC and EU Treaties, secondary
legislation, and the case law of the ECJ, they are expressed in (unwritten)
general principles of law and come to the fore in the EU's commitment
to human rights, fundamental freedoms, and the rule of law in Article 6
Treaty of the European Union (TEU). The EU respects fundamental rights
as these are guaranteed by the European Court of Human Rights and as
they flow from the constitutional traditions common to the Member States.
The Charter of Fundamental Rights also contains shared values and norms
and is increasingly applied by the European legislator and both Community Courts,[8] even if legally still non-binding. The Constitutional Treaty for
Europe (hereafter ConsEur) reinforced this commitment by establishing
common Union values (Articles I2 and I3), by awarding legally binding force
to the Charter, and by providing not only for a legal basis, but even a duty for
accession to the European Convention on Human Rights (Articles I9(2)).

Paradoxical as it may seem, a second essential path for forging a European
identity is also to ensure protection of national identity and, in so doing, of
what divides us. If Europe is to be acceptable to its citizens, it must respect
and enable the protection of certain national values, norms, and traditions.

---

[5] See the 'no demos' thesis as posited by JHH Weiler, U Haltern, and F Mayer, 'European
Democracy and Its Critique: Five Uneasy Pieces' (1995) Jean Monnet Paper, available at <http://
www.jeanmonnetprogram.org>.

[6] G de Burca, 'The Language of Rights and European Integration' in J Shaw and G More
(eds), *New Legal Dynamics of European Union* (Oxford: Clarendon Press, 1995) 48–49.

[7] Shaw and More, see n 6 above, 41. In the same sense, Van Gerven, see n 4 above, 52 and LA
Geelhoed, 'Een Europawijde Europese Unie: een grondwet zonder staat?' (2003) SEW Tijdschrift voor Europees en Economisch Recht, 299.

[8] Case C-432/05 *Unibet*, Judgment of the Court of 13 March 2007, nyr.

The ConsEur acknowledged this in many different ways,[9] even by explicitly stressing some values the Member States do not (yet) share, such as the right to marry and to start a family (Article II69). Striking the right balance between respecting national values and norms and enhancing European ones also means that no more European legal unity should be created than is necessary.

This connects to a third path, which is to bring the European citizen closer to the European decision making process. This can be achieved not only through enhancing representative and participatory democracy,[10] but also by taking away the fear or impression of European meddlesomeness and over-regulation. European legislation that leaves more leeway for national policy choices and lawmaking may be beneficial in terms of creating more public support for the European integration process.[11] Legal unity should thus not be simply equated with uniformity[12] and can in fact be seen as a variable or relative notion. Depending on the legal basis in the EC Treaty, the intensity of European rule making may thus vary considerably from one area to another, ranging from the unification of law through regulations, via the harmonization of law through directives, to the mere co-ordination of policy or cooperation between Member States through recommendations or other soft law mechanisms. Whenever the legal basis leaves room for this, legislative powers conferred upon the EU are to be exercised with restraint, as the subsidiarity and proportionality principles require. This implies the choice of directives over regulations, framework directives over detailed directives, minimum harmonization over total harmonization, and soft law over legislation.[13] European legislation must thus be flexible enough to co-ordinate a multiplicity of national systems, as a result of which European (harmonization) legislation may only regulate certain aspects of the law or still leave room for the Member States to introduce higher standards.[14]

---

[9] In its motto 'united in diversity' (Art I8 TCE); the respect of national identities (Art I5); the recognition that we live in a pluralist society (Art I2); and the respect of the Union's rich variety in culture and language (Art I3(3) and Art III280(4)).

[10] Arts I46 and I47 TCE.

[11] cf the Protocol on the role of national parliaments, attached to the TCE.

[12] See Christodoulidis and Dukes, this volume, ch 17.

[13] Edinburgh European Council Conclusions of 1992, Bulletin EC 12-1992, 15 and Art 6 of the Protocol on Subsidiarity and Proportionality.

[14] EMH Hirsch Ballin and LAJ Senden, *Co-actorship in European Law-making. The Quality of European Legislation and its Implementation and Application in the National Legal Order* (The Hague: TMC Asser Press, 2005) 15.

3 The convergence capacity of national legal systems

3.1 *Some legislative hurdles to conceptual convergence*

The foregoing leads us to the understanding that there may already be a built-in limit to conceptual convergence at the European legislative level itself, in the sense that a certain piece of legislation does not aim at convergence at all or aims at establishing a European concept only as a minimum standard to be complied with by the Member States. As we will see below, this seems to be the case as regards the European concept of sex discrimination. Whether conceptual divergence must be considered problematic at all will therefore depend primarily on the contents and scope of the underlying European legislation.

Where conceptual convergence is aimed at, to some extent at least, another serious problem presents itself, namely that European concepts are rarely unequivocally defined in the legislation itself. In an ever-enlarging EU, conceptual vagueness at the legislative level must rather be taken as a fact of life despite all the efforts to improve the quality of the legislation, as this may be the only way to reach political agreement.[15] The step-by-step development of European decision making, its own legal language, multi-language regime, and the lack of *travaux préparatoires* contribute to the fact that European concepts often crystallize only over a certain period of time, usually with the substantial assistance of the ECJ. The need for a common understanding of certain Treaty concepts may also reveal itself well before any legislation has been put into place, as we will see in the next section. At the same time, one must also acknowledge that European legislation can never be tailor-made to all national legal systems, given their huge diversity in legal, political, economic, and cultural background. Conceptual tie-in problems are thus also a rather natural feature of the European landscape and it would be an illusion to think that conceptual convergence can be fully achieved at the legislative level.

This does not mean, however, that the national legislator cannot do anything to reduce such problems. She could put in an effort to translate European concepts into the common national legal jargon, instead of simply 'parachuting' these into the already existing national legislation. The latter may be attractive from the point of view of timely transposition, but it may

---

[15] Often referred to as constructive ambiguity. cf also this volume, ch 2.

just lead to shifting the problem to the national courts. This will be problematic particularly in Member States where positivist textual approaches to the law prevail and where national courts understate their own role in this process of transplanting and translating European concepts into their national legal system.[16] Likewise, simply using already existing national concepts to channel European concepts without adapting them to the semantics of European law also bears the risk of divergent interpretation. Indeed, these concepts have a proper meaning under national law and it might be tempting for courts to stick to that also in situations covered by the European law at issue.

3.2 *Convergence capacity of the national judiciary*

When the legislation falls short in providing sufficient conceptual clarity, it will often be up to the national court to ensure compliance with European concepts, as interpreted by the ECJ. What convergence capacity must the national judiciary provide for and how can this capacity be enhanced?

By imposing the duty of consistent interpretation upon national courts, the ECJ has actually presumed that national legal systems allow for a dynamic development of the law and an active role on the part of the judge. The obligation to interpret national law 'as far as possible' in conformity with European law would serve little purpose, if the national judge did not have any discretion in its interpretation of the law. Even though the national judge is not obliged to give a *contra legem* meaning to the national law,[17] he may be required to give a different meaning to this law from the usual one. It is one thing to state that the national court has to do this, it is yet another whether it is actually going to proceed to such dynamic interpretation.

At least three major pitfalls affecting the convergence capacity of the national legal systems can be identified in the application of the doctrine of consistent interpretation. First of all, the national judge must be *aware* that there is a problem of European law in a case before him, for instance he must know that a relevant rule or concept has an EU origin. Second, the judge must have sufficient *knowledge* of how to deal with this problem, both as regards the substantive aspects of the law (he must know the meaning of such rules or concepts) and as regards his duties as a *juge communautaire*

---

[16] Z Kühn, 'The Application of European Law in the New Member States: Several (Early) Predictions' (2005) 6 German L J, 568.

[17] Case C-105/03 *Pupino* [2005] ECR I-5285.

(he must know about the doctrines of supremacy, direct effect, and consistent interpretation). As such, he must be able to apply European law. Last but not least, he must be *willing* to act as a Community law judge and be prepared, if necessary, to seek assistance from the ECJ in the framework of the preliminary ruling procedure. These pitfalls are not only present in the recently acceded Member States,[18] but certainly also in the 'old' ones,[19] even if their seriousness may vary from one Member State to another.

Technically speaking, the first two pitfalls can be overcome relatively easily, by providing educational training and enhancing information support systems such as electronic databases and judicial networks. It is different for the third one. This may actually require fundamental changes in judicial culture and practice. This may not only concern constitutional courts that have difficulty in accepting the primacy of European law,[20] but more importantly also ordinary courts that have to ensure the day-to-day application of European law. How far these courts will go in this application, and in interpreting their national law so as to converge with European law, will depend primarily on the way in which the *trias politica* is understood in a Member State and how the role of the judiciary is perceived in relation to that of the legislator.

The views on this vary considerably between the Member States and even within states. What is regarded as creative interpretation in one legal system may be regarded as wholly unacceptable or an error in law in another.[21] With the accession of many Central and Eastern European countries, these divergent views have gained in importance and therewith also the problem of how to ensure uniform application and interpretation of European law throughout the Union. These countries have demonstrated a lot of flexibility in the process of implementing the *acquis communautaire*, but a number of factors complicates their effective judicial enforcement of the *acquis*.[22]

---

[18] Kühn, see n 16 above, 576.

[19] S Prechal, 'National Courts in EU Judicial Structures' (2007) Ybk of Eur L, 432–436.

[20] Eg, Kühn, see n 16 above, 573–574, discusses the different attitudes of the Polish and Hungarian Constitutional Courts in this respect. More general, see AE Kellermann *et al* (eds), *The Impact of EU Accession on the Legal Orders of New EU Member States and (Pre-)candidate Countries. Hopes and Fears* (The Hague: TMC Asser Press, 2006).

[21] C Kilpatrick, 'Gender Equality: A Fundamental Dialogue' in S Sciarra (ed), *Labour Law in the Courts. National Judges and the European Court of Justice* (Oxford: Hart, 2001) 58.

[22] For a comparative overview including also (pre-)candidate countries, see Kellermann, see n 20 above.

Without denying here that in the old Member States, also, restrictive views may exist on the scope of the national court's power of interpretation,[23] many new Member States thus share a tradition in legal argumentation which is oriented towards a mechanical application of the written law. As Kühn observes, such a legal positivist attitude and textual reading of the law contrasts highly with the use of persuasive discursive arguments that connect to the law's rationale and purpose, and does not make Central European judges likely candidates to apply the doctrine of consistent interpretation.[24] This tradition also implies that the ordinary judiciary is not used to applying either abstract legal principles or international law, since in the post-communist era constitutional courts have been entrusted with this.[25] This inexperience complicates their functioning as true Community law judges. The focus on a literal reading of the written law also brings with it the reality that there is little or no tradition of publishing, studying, and applying case law.[26]

The capacity of a national legal system to smooth out conceptual problems will thus depend greatly on the extent to which it is capable of addressing and overcoming these problems. Improving judicial cooperation may be one important way to do so, as will be discussed below.[27]

4 Converging concepts: 'discrimination' in sex equality law

Let me first return here, however, to the claim made in section 2 that binding unity can be enhanced through a stronger protection of shared human and fundamental rights. This claim will be further substantiated here, by first discussing the conceptualization and scope of the European principle of sex

---

[23] Eg, in the UK as a result of the doctrine of parliamentary sovereignty. See Z Bankowski and DN MacCormick, 'Statutory Interpretation in the United Kingdom' in DN MacCormick and RS Summers, *Interpreting Statutes* (Aldershot: Dartmouth, 1991) 396.

[24] Kühn, see n 16 above, 580. But there are of course exceptions to this, such as, eg, the Lithuanian Supreme Court and Supreme Administrative Court already confirming this doctrine before accession. See on this Jarukaitis in Kellermann, see n 20 above, 399–400.

[25] Kühn, see n 16 above, 580.

[26] ibid and T Ćapeta, D Mihelin, and S Rodin, 'Croatia' in Kellermann, see n 20 above, 83 signals this problem also in the candidate country Croatia.

[27] Another way could be improving the cooperation between the judiciary and the legislator, the latter following up on deficiencies that have been signalled by judges. Further on this, Hirsch Ballin and Senden, see n 14 above.

discrimination as it developed through time and next considering its reception in the Member States. Where the 'discrimination-equality' discourse varies from one Member State to another and these concepts have retained a proper meaning differing from the European one, can a contribution to binding unity still be made or does this require a broad, unequivocal, and uniform interpretation thereof in all Member States? What level of legal unity in the national protection of such shared European values is required from this perspective?

4.1 *Conceptualization and scope of the European principle of sex discrimination*

At the heart of the body of EU sex equality law, we find Article 141 EC (ex 119 EEC) which establishes the principle of equal pay for male and female workers for equal work or work of equal value. It refers to 'equal pay without discrimination', yet without giving a definition of discrimination. In secondary legislation, such a definition was also lacking for a long time. The first Directive to be adopted in this area in 1975, merely stated that 'all discrimination' arising from national rules regarding equal pay had to be abolished.[28] Even if one might have been tempted to think that it was thus left to the Member States themselves to establish what to understand by discrimination, the ECJ readily made it clear that this must be considered a self-standing concept of Community law. It did so in line with its earlier case law on the principle of non-discrimination on grounds of nationality in the framework of the market freedoms.[29]

For our purposes here, the following observations are of particular relevance as regards the conceptualization of the principle of non-discrimination on the grounds of sex. To begin with, this conceptualization did not come about overnight, but is the result of a very gradual process. Starting from the point of view that discrimination must be considered to occur if different rules are applied to comparable situations or when the same rule is applied to different situations,[30] the ECJ soon came to a broad interpretation of this concept. It did so, first, by recognizing the principle of sex equality—and the elimination of discrimination in this regard—as a fundamental human right, which forms

---

[28] Council Directive (EEC) 75/117 on the approximation of the laws of the Member States relating to the application of the principle of equal pay for men and women [1975] OJ L45/19.

[29] Eg, Case 152/73 *Sotgiu* [1974] ECR 153, concerning the application of the principle of non-discrimination on grounds of nationality in the area of free movement of workers.

[30] Eg, Joined Cases 117/76 and 16/77 *Ruckdeschel* [1977] ECR 1753.

part of the general principles of Community law. The directly enforceable right to equal treatment ensued from this,[31] even if limited in scope. Second, on a case-by-case basis, the Court then developed the distinctions between overt and disguised, hidden, or covert discrimination[32] and between direct and indirect discrimination.[33] In the beginning this led to some terminological and conceptual confusion and inconsistency and only after a series of cases[34] did the Court establish, in the *Bilka* case, a definition of indirect sex discrimination which it has since upheld. The Court thus ruled that:

Article 119 of the EEC Treaty is infringed by a department store company which excludes part-time employees from its occupational pension scheme where that exclusion affects a *much greater* number of women than men, unless the enterprise shows that the exclusion is based on objectively justified factors which are unrelated to any discrimination based on sex.[35] (*my emphasis*)

So, direct discrimination concerns very blunt forms of discrimination, where the sex of the person is the distinguishing factor, and indirect discrimination concerns situations where other criteria than sex are applied (such as part-time work) but leading to the same result by affecting one group substantially more than another. In principle, direct sex discrimination can only be justified if there is a written ground for this,[36] as the Court confirmed in the *Dekker* case,[37] but since then we have also seen instances in which the Court

---

[31] Case 149/77 *Defrenne (III)* [1978] ECR 1385.

[32] Case 152/73 *Sotgiu* [1974] ECR 153.

[33] Case 43/75 *Defrenne v Sabena* [1976] ECR 455.

[34] Case 129/79 *Macarthys* [1980] ECR 1275; Case 69/80 *Worringham* [1981] ECR 767, and Case 96/80 *Jenkins* [1981] ECR 911. For an account of this early jurisprudential development, see S Prechal and N Burrows, *Gender Discrimination Law of the European Community* (Aldershot: Dartmouth, 1990) 1–21.

[35] Case 170/84 *Bilka* [1986] ECR 1607, definition confirmed in Case C-167/97 *Seymour-Smith* [1999] ECR I-623, para 25.

[36] Which was only introduced in Art 141(4) Treaty of the European Communities by the Treaty of Amsterdam, pursuant to the Kalanke ruling and its aftermath. Council Directive (EEC) 76/207 on the implementation of the principle of equal treatment for men and women as regards access to employment, vocational training and promotion, and working conditions [1976] OJ L39/40 already contained a similar provision in its Art 2(4), now replaced by Art 2(8) of the revised Parliament and Council Directive (EC) 2002/73 amending Council Directive (EEC) 76/207 on the implementation of the principle of equal treatment for men and women as regards access to employment, vocational training and promotion, and working conditions [2002] OJ L269/15.

[37] Case C-177/88 *Dekker* [1990] ECR I-3941.

has deviated from this rule.[38] As the Court made clear in the *Bilka* case, indirect discrimination can also be objectively justified on grounds outside the written law, such as a real need on the part of the undertaking, as long as the national measure passes the proportionality test as well, referring to both its suitability and necessity. Many questions were still left unanswered, however, regarding the requirement of a comparator, the rigour of the objective justification test, and the required level of proof as to the discriminatory effect or disparate impact.[39]

Following on this, a further observation is that the process of conceptualizing sex discrimination has not been the sole prerogative of the Court. As from the mid-1970s, sex equality law has developed in interaction with the European legislator, which has further substantiated the sex equality principle in a number of harmonization directives. These concerned not only equal pay, but also equal treatment in employment, statutory and occupational social security, pregnancy and maternity, and the burden of proof. Initially, the concept of discrimination was left undefined in these directives,[40] the first definition only being introduced in 1997 in the Burden of Proof Directive, stating that: 'indirect discrimination shall exist where an apparently neutral provision, criterion or practice disadvantages *a substantially higher* proportion of the members of one sex unless that provision, criterion or practice is appropriate and necessary and can be justified by objective factors unrelated to sex' (my emphasis).[41] This can be seen as a first codification of the Court's case law, also referred to as the first generation of legal definitions.[42]

---

[38] See S Prechal, 'Equality of Treatment, Non-Discrimination and Social Policy: Achievements in Three Themes' (2004) 41 CML Rev, 533–551 and the case law she mentions in n 43.

[39] C Tobler, *Indirect Discrimination: A Case Study into the Development of the Legal Concept of Indirect Discrimination under EC Law* (Antwerp: Intersentia, 2005) 211ff.

[40] Apart from the one mentioned already in n 28, this was also the case in the aforementioned Council Directive (EEC) 76/207 on the implementation of the principle of equal treatment for men and women as regards access to employment, vocational training and promotion, and working conditions [1976] OJ L39/40 and the Council Directive (EEC) 86/378 on the implementation of the principle of equal treatment for men and women in occupational social security schemes [1986] OJ L225/40, as amended by Council Directive (EC) 96/97 amending Directive (EEC) 86/378 on the implementation of the principle of equal treatment for men and women in occupational social security schemes [1996] OJ L46/20.

[41] Art 2(2) of Council Directive (EC) 97/80 on the burden of proof in cases of discrimination based on sex [1998] OJ L14/6, as amended by Directive (EC) 98/52 on the extension of Council Directive (EC) 97/80 on the burden of proof in cases of discrimination based on sex to the United Kingdom of Great Britain and Northern Ireland [1998] OJ L205/66.

[42] Tobler, see n 39 above, 280.

A second generation of definitions is contained in the Race Directive and the General Framework Directive (adopted in 2000 on the basis of Article 13 EC) and in the revised Equal Treatment Directive (ETD) of 2002.[43] These definitions are based on the Court's more recent case law regarding the prohibition of discrimination on grounds of nationality[44] and read:

1) 'direct discrimination': where one person is treated less favourably on grounds of sex than another is, has been or would be treated in a *comparable situation*;
2) 'indirect discrimination': where an apparently neutral provision, criterion or practice *would* put persons of one sex at a *particular* disadvantage *compared with* persons of the other sex, unless that provision, criterion or practice is objectively justified by a legitimate aim, and the means of achieving that aim are appropriate and necessary. (*my emphasis*)

This definition appears less harsh than the one in the Burden of Proof Directive, in the sense that it does not seem to require the proof of statistical data to demonstrate that 'a substantially higher proportion' of women are affected by a certain rule. Yet, it does not go so far as to stipulate the unlawfulness of any national measure that is merely liable of being an obstacle to the objective of the improvement of the position of women, even if its formulation suggests that the possibility of being put at a particular disadvantage suffices and not that it has actually occurred.[45]

As regards the requirement of a comparator, this problem seems more apparent than real as far as indirect discrimination is concerned. That is, the above definition does not seem to impose the requirement of a real or hypothetical comparator, but rather proof that a national measure is liable to disadvantage one group over another. Strikingly, whereas this definition is directed towards comparing the—effect of the—treatment, the definition of direct discrimination is directed towards comparing the situation of those concerned. This is to be deplored, as in the case of direct discrimination, the situation of men and women is by its very nature often not comparable, the state of pregnancy being the clearest illustration of this.

The above development reveals that at one particular moment in time, different definitions of indirect discrimination applied side by side to different

---

[43] Parliament and Council Directive (EC) 2002/73 amending Council Directive (EEC) 76/207 on the implementation of the principle of equal treatment for men and women as regards access to employment, vocational training and promotion, and working conditions [2002] OJ L269/15.

[44] Case C-237/94 *O'Flynn* [1996] ECR I-2617.

[45] Tobler, see n 39 above, 286–287, calls this the liability approach. K Ahtela, 'The Revised Provisions on Sex Discrimination in European Law: A Critical Assessment' (2005) 11 Eur L J, 64–65.

aspects of sex equality law, and that the legislator has been lagging behind the Court in the process of conceptualizing and regulating equal treatment of men and women. Only after almost fifty years of European integration do we witness the firmer establishment of a concept of sex discrimination that applies more generally. This occurred with the adoption of the so-called Recast Directive in 2006,[46] which confirms the above definitions of direct and indirect discrimination and declares their applicability to the areas of equal pay, equal treatment, occupational social security, and burden of proof.[47]

Yet, a third observation must be that, despite this important step forward, it is still too early to say that the process of conceptualizing sex discrimination has been completed. For instance, it is not clear when the requirement of a 'particular disadvantage' may be considered fulfilled. At a more fundamental level, the question is still unanswered as to what extent the EU merely strives after the prohibition of discrimination, and thereby to what is called formal equality, or to what extent it also strives after establishing substantive equality in practice.[48]

This issue also connects to the scope of application of the European sex discrimination principle. A first aspect of this concerns the question of the situations and areas to which this principle actually applies. Even if sex equality has been recognized as a fundamental right and a general principle of European law, that does not mean that it is generally applicable in the Member States; it governs the actions of the Union institutions and those of the Member States only when they act within the scope of Community law.[49] This means that its application is thus still very much limited to the economic sphere, as Article 141 is limited to equal pay, the Recast Directive to access to employment, working conditions, and occupational

---

[46] Parliament and Council Directive (EC) 2006/54 on the implementation of the principle of equal opportunities and equal treatment of men and women in matters of employment and occupation (recast) [2006] OJ L204/23.

[47] As such also repealing Council Directive (EEC) 75/117 on the approximation of the laws of the Member States relating to the application of the principle of equal pay for men and women [1975] OJ L45/19; Council Directive (EEC) 76/207 on the implementation of the principle of equal treatment for men and women as regards access to employment, vocational training and promotion, and working conditions [1976] OJ L39/40; Council Directive (EEC) 86/378 on the implementation of the principle of equal treatment for men and women in occupational social security schemes [1986] OJ L225/40; and Council Directive (EC) 97/80 on the burden of proof in cases of discrimination based on sex [1998] OJ L14/6.

[48] The views on this differ, some criticizing the ECJ for not going far enough in this respect, others applauding the Court's achievements.

[49] Eg ,Case C-148/02 *Avello* [2003] ECR I-11613.

social security (Article 1), and other directives primarily to statutory social security and the position of working women during pregnancy and maternity. In this context, the ECJ has also been called upon to define the scope of concepts such as pay and occupational social security,[50] and even of 'sex' itself in cases concerning different treatment of transsexuals and same sex couples.[51]

Another aspect concerns the extent to which Member States must stick to the European concept of sex discrimination or may deviate from it. In this respect, it is important to note that the Recast Directive (another example is the Revised Equal Treatment Directive) only aims at ensuring a minimum level of protection. In its Article 27(1) it is thus broadly stipulated that: 'Member States may introduce or maintain provisions which are more favourable to the protection of the principle of equal treatment than those laid down in this Directive.' I agree here with the views expressed by Tobler and by Whittle that the Recast Directive thus not only allows for horizontal expansion, extending the applicability of the principle of equal treatment beyond the area of employment, but also for vertical expansion, by improving the level and quality of the protection that it affords.[52] This would mean then that Member States are not only allowed to uphold an already existing concept of discrimination but also to introduce a new one that, for instance, requires a lower level of disparate impact, is less lenient in the acceptance of objective justification, or does not require any comparison to be made. This would only be otherwise as regards issues falling within the scope of Article 141 EC itself, ie equal pay and occupational social security benefits. As regards derogations that are to the detriment of the equality principle and the position of claimants, this will only be allowed under the conditions set out in the directives, as interpreted by the ECJ. In this respect, it can also be observed that the course taken by the legislator has sometimes appeared difficult to reconcile with the Court's stricter interpretation of Article 141 EC, leaving less scope for derogation.[53]

---

[50]   Eg, Case C-262/88 *Barber* [1990] ECR 1889.

[51]   Eg, Case C-13/94 *P v S* [1996] ECR I-2143 and Case C-249/96 *Grant* [1998] ECR I-449.

[52]   Tobler, see n 39 above, 288 and R Whittle, 'The Framework Directive for Equal Treatment in Employment and Occupation: An Analysis from a Disability Rights Perspective' (2002) ELR, 303–326.

[53]   This occurred, eg, in respect of Council Directive (EEC) 86/378 on the implementation of the principle of equal treatment for men and women in occupational social security schemes [1986] OJ L225/40 and the judgment in Case C-262/88 *Barber* [1990] ECR I-1889.

4.2   *Convergence of national concepts of sex discrimination*

The above sketch of the European process of conceptualizing sex discrimination gives several clues to the conclusion that one must not cherish too high an expectation with regard to the level of convergence of national sex discrimination concepts. Given that a more consistent and broadly applicable definition has only been established in fairly recent years, conceptual clarity at EU level has come a long way. Obviously, the long and bumpy road of jurisprudential and legislative conceptualization of the European sex discrimination principle has complicated a safe and sound arrival and reception thereof in the national legal orders. The many preliminary questions referred to the ECJ in the area of sex equality (see Tables 16.1 and 16.2 below) are illustrative for the problems which the application of the European sex discrimination concept has caused in the legal practice of the Member States.

Since the direct and indirect discrimination concepts as contained in the European legislation must be considered to impose upon the Member States only minimum standards of protection, another conclusion must be that full convergence is not an objective. This is also corroborated by the statement in Article 27(2) of the Recast Directive, to the effect that the implementation of the Directive may 'under no circumstances be sufficient grounds for a reduction in the level of protection of workers in the areas to which it applies [. . .].'

Table 16.1 Number of preliminary references made per year in the area of sex equality law (1958–2006)

1970	1	(Defrenne I)	1987	1		1997	9
1975	1	(Defrenne II)	1988	7		1998	11
1977	1	(Defrenne III)	1989	6		1999	8
1979	1		1990	5		2000	5
1980	2		1991	14		2001	7
1981	2		1992	9		2002	10
1983	4		1993	15		2003	3
1984	5		1994	8		2004	3
1985	7		1995	11		2005	1
1986	1		1996	10		2006	8

Source: Table compiled on the basis of the *Bulletin Legal Issues in Gender Equality: Bulletin of the Commission's Network of Legal Experts in the Fields of Employment, Social Affairs and Equality between Men and Women*, No. 2/2007, and the overview of cases presented at the following website of the European Commission (last consulted 1 July 2007): <http://ec.europa.eu/employment_social/gender_equality/legislation/case_law_en.html>.

Table 16.2 Number and percentage of sex equality references per Member State in view of the total number of preliminary references made per Member State (1958–2006)

	Sex eq ref	Total ref	% of total	Population (m)
UK[1]	50	418	11.96	60.4
Germany	48	1542	3.11	82.5
Netherlands	22	666	3.30	16.3
Belgium	14	533	2.62	10.5
France	8	717	1.11	60.9
Austria[4]	8	288	2.77	8.3
Denmark[1]	7	111	6.30	5.4
Ireland[1]	6	48	12.50	4.2
Spain[3]	3	180	1.66	43.8
Greece[2]	2	117	1.70	11.1
Sweden[4]	2	63	3.17	9.0
Finland[4]	2	47	4.25	5.3
Italy	2	896	0.22	58.8
Portugal[3]	0	60	0	10.6
Luxemburg	0	60	0	0.5

[1] Acceded in 1973
[2] Acceded in 1981
[3] Acceded in 1986
[4] Acceded in 1995

Source: Table compiled on the basis of the Court's annual report of 2006 and the overview of cases presented at the following website of the European Commission (last consulted 1 July 2007): <http://ec.europa.eu/employment_social/gender_equality/legislation/case_law_en.html>.

Hence, transposition of these concepts may not give cause to a levelling down of the level of protection already afforded in a Member State.

It goes beyond the scope of this chapter to discuss the level of convergence effectively established in this area in all of the Member States, but on a general level it can be observed that the direction in which the European concept of sex discrimination has developed was quite revolutionary for almost all Member States, the UK being the major exception as it was already familiar with the application of the concept of indirect discrimination.[54] The fact that most Member States had to recognize in their legal

---

[54] M Bell and M Ilieva, *Equality, Diversity and Enlargement: Report on Measures to Combat Discrimination in Acceding and Candidate Countries* (Employment & Social Affairs. Luxembourg: Office for Official Publications of the European Community, 2003). S Prechal and A Masselot, *Legal Impact Assessment of the Equality Directives; A Report to the Commission* (Tilburg/Leeds, 2003) s 1.7.3.

order a far wider concept of discrimination than they were used to already triggered in that sense an important converging effect throughout the EU.

However, not surprisingly in view of the above, the way in which the concept has been established in national law has indeed varied quite a bit, as well as the interpretation and scope given to it. Some Member States have thus proceeded to insert general prohibitions and definitions of direct and indirect discrimination into the national legislation (Italy), whereas others have done so in a rather piecemeal way in different statutory acts (Germany), and still others have recognized it only in their Constitution and case law (Spain).[55] In doing so, some Member States have closely followed the Court's interpretation (Portugal), whereas others have given a very limited interpretation to this (Luxemburg)[56] or have in fact ensured a broader protection to the equality principle (Spain), for instance by not imposing any comparison (Finland).[57] One may be tempted to think that the laws of the twelve new Member States would show more coherence and convergence with European law concepts, since they had to implement the sex equality *acquis* as a 'big-bang' change to their national law, yet this does not seem to be the case. Even when some of these countries did pass entirely new legislation, various sources indicate that explicit definitions of direct and indirect discrimination may still be lacking or that they are not always consistent with those contained in the European legislation.[58]

Conceptual divergence is thus a given fact in this area of the law, which from a strictly legal point of view is not necessarily problematic since, to a certain extent at least, the law itself allows for this. But how are we to assess this from the point of view of enhancing binding unity in the EU? The recognition of the concept of indirect discrimination in all the Member States can in itself be seen as an important step towards both ensuring equality of treatment in law and preventing the circumvention of the non-discrimination principle by relying on formally neutral differentiation grounds.[59] As such, it has the potential to increase awareness of the existence of discriminatory

[55] Prechal and Masselot, see n 54 above.

[56] Prechal, see n 38 above, 536.

[57] Ahtela, see n 45 above, 71–72.

[58] A Sloat, 'Legislating for Equality: The Implementation of the EU Equality Acquis in Central and Eastern Europe' (2004) Jean Monnet Paper, available at <http://www.jeanmonnetprogram.org>; A Wilkowska, 'Implementation of Gender Equality Standards in Central and Eastern Europe—Mission (Im)possible?', available at <http://www.wccpenang.org>, 5; and Bell and Ilieva, see n 54 above, 39–40.

[59] In this sense Tobler, see n 39 above, 419 and Prechal, see n 38 above, 537.

situations in Member States, which may not be all that obvious to those concerned by it, both at the employers' and employees' level. Tobler states in this regard that the rationale behind the introduction of the concept of indirect discrimination was a concern to ensure the effectiveness of European sex equality law.[60]

In my view, the obligation to ensure a shared minimum level of protection against both direct and indirect discrimination, which nevertheless leaves room for a higher level of national protection, can still be seen as a contribution to binding unity in the EU. The conceptual divergence that is allowed for must be to the benefit of the individual claimant of sex discrimination, which also means that from the individual's point of view the interest of conceptual convergence should be put into perspective. Put differently, the conceptualization of the European sex equality principle as a fundamental right would not be very much at ease with the starting point that every legal system should uniformly keep to the level of the lowest common denominator the Member States can agree on. Furthermore, the development of European sex equality law 'in bits and pieces' over time shows that the level of protection it affords is enhanced little by little, just as its scope of application has gradually expanded.[61] This body of law has even had an important spill-over effect to other grounds of discrimination, in the sense that it has contributed to inserting a legal basis into Article 13 of the EC Treaty for taking measures to combat these. On the basis of this provision the aforementioned Race Directive and General Framework Directive were adopted, covering *inter alia* age discrimination and sexual orientation.

The biggest problem or challenge for enhancing binding unity in this area, in the sense of confirming and enhancing our shared values and norms, is thus not how to ensure full conceptual convergence on paper, but rather how to ensure full application and enforcement of the—minimum—rules that have been put into place. A high level of litigation and enforcement could be taken as an indication that a certain value is supported by society. However, as we will see in more detail in the next section, having put into place a solid legal framework for combating sex discrimination is by no means sufficient for a high level of awareness, commitment, and litigation.[62] This is also illustrated by the fact that despite having equal pay legislation in place

---

[60] Tobler, see n 39 above, 260ff.

[61] The term 'convergence' in itself already implies an element of time. See H Lindahl, ch 13 in this volume.

[62] Prechal and Masselot, see n 54 above.

for decades, the gender pay gap has not significantly decreased over this time and in certain respects even seems to be widening again.[63] We cannot but acknowledge that there is still a long way to go, both in the old and the new Member States,[64] before the values that we share on paper will become truly shared values in our minds and hearts. In other words, what is needed at this point in time is to bring about a convergence in the social understanding of, and attitude towards, the aims underlying the body of European sex equality law and what equal treatment of men and women means in practice. Only on that basis, can sex equality receive the legal and political commitment, priority, and protection it deserves as a fundamental right.

5 Judicial cooperation: the preliminary ruling procedure

In section 3 the doctrine of consistent interpretation was identified as a mechanism by which the national court can remove uncertainties in the law. In trying to reconcile a national concept with its European counterpart, the national court may have to turn for guidance to the ECJ and that is where the preliminary ruling procedure comes in as a unifying mechanism. We will first consider its unifying effects from a general perspective and then in the specific context of sex equality law.

5.1 *General unifying effects of the preliminary procedure*

It is generally accepted that the primary purpose of the preliminary ruling procedure of Article 234 EC is to enable national courts to ensure uniform interpretation and application of European law in all the Member States, as the ECJ had already stated in the *Rheinmühlen* case.[65] It confirmed this explicitly in its Information Note on references from national courts for a preliminary ruling.[66] To this end, the procedure is based on the idea of

---

[63] Report by the Commission's Network of legal experts in the fields of employment, social affairs and equality between men and women, 'Legal Aspects of the Gender Pay Gap', February 2007, available at: <http://ec.europa.eu/employment_social/gender_equality/legislation/report_equal_pay.pdf>, 7–8.

[64] In the latter, there may also be resistance against gender equality as a policy goal, because it was part of official communist ideology. See also Sloat, see n 58 above, 78–83.

[65] Case 166/73 *Rheinmühlen* [1974] ECR 33.

[66] Court of Justice, 'Information note on references from national courts for a preliminary ruling' [2005] OJ C143/01, point 1.

cooperation—and not hierarchy—between the ECJ and the national courts. Yet, the *Foto-Frost* and *CILFIT* obligations[67] condition this cooperation, by imposing that invalidity questions of European secondary law are always to be referred, whether a national court is ruling in last instance or not, and interpretation questions when the national court deals with a case in last instance. Despite voices in favour of loosening these requirements,[68] the ECJ can be said to have tightened them instead by establishing that Member States can be held liable for wrongful application of European law by national courts, including wrongful non-referral of a preliminary question.[69]

Nonetheless, the Note also confirms the national court's discretion in two respects. First, it is up to the national court to decide at what stage of the proceedings a question can be best referred, but the ECJ suggests that the national court only does so when it is able to define the factual and legal context of the question. Second, it is the national court which decides whether a ruling of the ECJ is necessary at all to enable it to give judgment. The Note confirms in this regard the *acte clair* and *acte éclairé* exceptions, even if it does not denote them as such (point 12). Quite strikingly, it does not refer to the conditions the Court formulated in the *CILFIT* judgment for the application of these two exceptions (such as comparison of language versions), which indicates that the national court is not to think too lightly that these exceptions apply. Furthermore, a national court against whose decision there is still a judicial remedy may itself decide on the correct interpretation of Community law and its application to the situation before it, 'in particular when it considers that sufficient clarification is given by the case-law of the Court'. The Court deems a preliminary reference particularly useful, 'when there is a new question of interpretation of general interest for the uniform application of Community law throughout the Union, or where the existing case-law does not appear to be applicable to a new set of facts' (point 13). So, the Court clearly hints here at 'auto-limitation'[70] by the national court and to its duty to function as a Community law judge in a fairly independent and self-responsible way, unless the uniformity of European law

[67] Case C-314/85 *Foto-Frost* [1987] ECR 4199; Case C-283/81 *CILFIT* [1982] ECR 3415.

[68] Even by Court members themselves, eg A Meij, 'Effective Preliminary Cooperation: Some Eclectic Notes' in EMH Hirsch Ballin, *The Uncertain Future of the Preliminary Procedure, Symposium at the Council of State, The Netherlands, 30 January 2004* (The Hague: Raad van State, 2004).

[69] Case C-173/03 *Traghetti del Mediterraneo* [2006] ECR I-5177. cf Lenaerts and Corthaut this volume, ch 21, n 64.

[70] For the use of this term, see Prechal, see n 19 above, 441.

is at stake. The call for auto-limitation is inspired by the high number of references made each year,[71] and the effects this has on the workload of the ECJ and on the through-put time of preliminary questions.[72]

In practice, there may be different understandings of the scope of the discretion thus left to national courts. Looking at the total number of references made by national courts of different Member States,[73] it appears that the 'reference density' may indeed vary quite substantially from one Member State to another, even if the figures are corrected for the size of population and the moment of accession. Comparing for instance the Netherlands and France, we can see that their figures are relatively close (666 versus 717), whereas the population of France is about four times larger. Portuguese and Luxemburg courts have both referred sixty cases, but the Portuguese population is twenty times larger. The UK and Italy have a more or less equal population, but Italy has referred twice as many cases. Austria, in its twelve years of membership and with 8.3 million people, has referred more cases (288) than Spain and Portugal together (240) in twenty-one years of membership and a joint population amounting to 54.6 million.[74]

This data triggers the question as to what factors, including outside the judiciary, may explain such differences, and these will be dealt with in section s.2. Another question it raises is the possible unifying effects of references made by one jurisdiction on the legal systems of the other Member States. Formally speaking, preliminary rulings only concern the national case and judge at issue, yet broader unifying effects occur as a result of the fact that, according to Article 220 EC and the Protocol on subsidiarity and proportionality, Community law applies as interpreted by the ECJ. The scope of these unifying effects will depend on the follow-up to these rulings given not only by national courts, but also by national legislators and executives. Portugal provides an interesting illustration of this: Portuguese courts have made no preliminary reference at all in the area of sex equality law, yet the Portuguese legislation follows the Court's case law closely.[75] The case law of the Court should thus be considered to form part of the *acquis communautaire*, as it must be complied with by Member States

---

[71] According to the annual reports of the Court of Justice, published on <www.curia.eu.int>, the figures since 2000 range between 200 and 250 each year.

[72] Yet, the Court's last annual report shows that over the past few years throughput time has slightly decreased from an average of 24 months to 19.8 months in 2006.

[73] In the period 1958–2006, leaving aside the Member States that acceded in 2004.

[74] Table 16.2 below.

[75] Prechal and Masselot, see n 54 above, 19, 22.

and acceding countries must implement it.[76] The increasing effect of binding precedent of the Court's case law ties in with this, as the Court itself as a rule now relies on and explicitly refers to its previous case law.[77] Acceptance of this quality of precedent is also imposed on national authorities as a result of the fact that non-compliance with the Court's case law can be a ground for state liability.[78] Finally, the discussion in section 4 shows that unifying effects can also come about in the sense that the legislator or the Member States proceed to the codification of the Court's case law in secondary legislation or in the Treaty itself.

5.2 *The preliminary procedure as a unifying mechanism in sex equality law*

As we have seen, the Court has played a pivotal role in the conceptualization of the principle of sex discrimination. It has only been able to do so as a result of the use which national courts have made of the preliminary procedure. Here the cross-national variation in sex equality references will be considered as well as the possible reasons behind this variation. On that basis, consideration will then be given to whether it is possible to establish criteria that would allow for a more efficient use of the preliminary procedure as a unifying mechanism.

Cross-national variation in references

Since 1970, when the first *Defrenne* case was referred to the ECJ, 193 sex equality cases have been submitted to the ECJ, of which 17 were infringement proceedings and 176 were preliminary references.[79] The latter amounts to about 3 per cent of the total number of references that have been made to the ECJ since 1958 (5765).

---

[76] Recently confirmed in Joined Cases C-231/06 to C-233/06 *Jonkman*, Judgment of 21 June 2007, nyr, in which the Court held that: 'Following a judgment given by the Court on an order for reference from which it is apparent that the national legislation is incompatible with Community law, it is for the authorities of the Member State concerned to take the general or particular measures necessary to ensure that Community law is complied with, by ensuring in particular that national law is changed so as to comply with Community law as soon as possible and that the rights which individuals derive from Community law are given full effect.'

[77] cf A Stone Sweet, *The Judicial Construction of Europe* (Oxford: Oxford University Press, 2004) on this.

[78] Case C-173/03 *Traghetti del Mediterraneo* [2006] ECR I-5177. cf Lenaerts and Corthaut, this volume, ch 21 n 64.

[79] Table 16.1. Five of these cases are still pending.

Most of the sex equality references were made by the UK (50), Germany (48), and the Netherlands (22), followed at quite some distance by a second group of Member States consisting of Belgium (14),[80] France (8), Austria (8), Denmark (7), and Ireland (6). A third group of Member States have made only very incidental references up to now: Sweden (2), Greece (2), Spain (3), Finland (2), and Italy (2). A fourth group, consisting of Luxemburg and Portugal, made no reference at all, despite many years of EU membership.[81] If we consider the above figures in the light of the total number of preliminary references that have been made per Member State, the following picture emerges:[82] Ireland and the UK take the lead (with respectively 12.5 per cent and 12 per cent), followed by a second group consisting of Denmark (6.3 per cent), Finland (4.2 per cent), the Netherlands (3.3 per cent), Sweden (3.2 per cent), Germany (3.1 per cent), Austria (2.8 per cent), and Belgium (2.6 per cent). A quite considerable third group of Member States scores very low: Greece (1.7 per cent), Spain (1.7 per cent), France (1.1 per cent), Italy (0.2 per cent), Portugal (0 per cent), and Luxemburg (0 per cent).

If we take the figures of the British, German, and Dutch courts together, it appears that they have accounted for about 69 per cent of the total number of references made in this area since 1958. Two of the original Member States have thus made a considerable contribution to the jurisprudential development of this body of law, whereas the record of other original Member States is very disappointing (Luxemburg, Italy). If one also takes into account that sex equality litigation before the ECJ only took off as from the mid-1970s, Portugal and Spain also show poor performance, quite in contrast with that of later acceding countries (Finland, Sweden, Austria).

Looking at the substance of the national references, another varied picture emerges. More than twenty German references have thus concerned indirect discrimination and part-time work and other forms of 'atypical' work—such as minor and short-term employment—regarding maternity rights, equal payment, and the social security of part-time workers (eg, *Bilka*). Other important references have concerned positive discrimination (*Kalanke*, *Marschall*), the equal treatment of women in military service (*Kreil*), and the effective enforcement of sex equality law (*Von Colson* and *Kamann*). British

---

[80]   Three of the 14 Belgian cases were only referred in 2006, by the same court and on the same matter; Cases 231-233/06, [2006] OJ C190/9–11, referred by the Brussels Labour Court. See also n 76 on these cases.

[81]   The twelve new Member States since 2004 are left aside here, as the time that has elapsed since accession is too short to expect many references to have been made.

[82]   Table 16.2.

references have concerned, in particular, equal treatment in social security, concerning pensionable age and equal pay (*Barber*), invalidity pensions and surviving spouses benefits, and maternity and pregnancy discrimination. British courts have also referred important questions on the equal treatment of transsexuals (*Richards, P v S*), same sex couples (*Grant*), equal treatment of women in the royal marines and the police force and the effective enforcement of sex equality law (*Johnston*). Dutch courts have referred mainly questions concerning equal treatment in social security (*Ten Oever*) and discrimination against pregnant women (*Dekker*). Danish courts have referred questions regarding equal value and the burden of proof (*Danfoss*), and pregnancy-related illness, whereas French courts have shown a particular concern with the night work of women (*Lévy*), and Spanish courts with pregnancy and maternity issues (*Gómez*).

Explaining cross-national variation

In trying to explain the different levels of the use of the preliminary procedure, two remarks are to be made in line with what has been argued already. First of all, the use of the preliminary procedure presupposes that the problems signalled in section 3 have been overcome to an important extent: national courts must have developed an adequate European 'reflex' and a European law 'toolkit' to go along with that.[83] In the area of sex equality law this still presents problems in most of the Member States. Second, the use of the preliminary procedure depends on the level of litigation; if there is hardly any national sex equality litigation, preliminary references are not likely to be made, the Portuguese situation being (again) a clear illustration of this. Overall, however, there is a rather low level of sex equality litigation in the Member States.[84]

There are some general factors accounting for this, such as the costs and the length of legal proceedings, but there are many other factors at play that are rather specific to sex equality law. Most importantly these include: the

---

[83] Prechal, see n 19 above, 435, under reference to M Darmon and JG Huglo, 'La formation des juges en droit communautaire' in M Dony and M Waelbroeck, *Mélanges en hommage à Michel Waelbroeck* (Brussel: Bruylant, 1999) 306.

[84] J Blom *et al*, 'The Utilisation of Sex Equality Litigation Procedures in the Member States of the European Community: A Comparative Study' (1995) Brussels, V/782/96-EN. For a brief and more recent overview see also the 'General Reports on Developments in EU Gender Equality Law' by the Commission's Network of legal experts in the fields of employment, social affairs, and equality between men and women, for the years 2004–2005, 2005–2006, and 2006–2007 respectively. The reports are available at <http://ec.europa.eu>. The UK and Ireland are significant exceptions to the low litigation rates.

prevalence of an individual justice system that may deter women from going to court for fear of victimization; the lack of institutional support systems such as special equality agents or bodies; the limited role of labour inspectorates or trade unions; a lack of interest in discrimination cases on the part of trades unions or among legal professions in general; the absence of collective enforcement mechanisms and strategic litigation possibilities such as class-actions; problems of proof; and unavailability of legal aid.[85] The level of litigation will also depend on the extent to which out-of-court settlement is possible through conciliation committees or equality opportunity commissions allowing for easily accessible, less costly, simpler, and faster resolution of disputes. The Dutch Equal Treatment Commission, for example, provides an important means of out-of-court settlement, issuing non-binding decisions, and is one of the main reasons why few discrimination cases actually get to court. The new Member States face additional problems, in the sense that there is still no real tradition of putting concrete mechanisms into place for the protection of human rights,[86] and there is also mistrust of the judicial system.[87] In a time of profound economic restructuring, sex equality is not a political priority in some of these countries, a situation that may be reinforced by the still rather conservative views of society on sex equality as such, a problem which also persists, to a greater or a lesser extent, in the old Member States.

When sex equality cases do get to court, reference activity also appears very much linked to particular features of the domestic legal systems. Without claiming to be exhaustive here, there are at least three important factors to be identified in this respect, which can be deduced from the extensive comparative research Kilpatrick has performed on this[88] and which are confirmed by other sources, such as publications of the Commission Network of legal experts on the application of Community law on the equal treatment of men and women.

The first factor concerns the basis and nature of the national legal sex equality discourse. The situations of Italy and Spain are illustrative. In Spain, there is a fairly wide range of litigation, directed by the Constitutional Court

---

[85] Blom, see n 84 above.

[86] Kühn, see n 16 above, 578.

[87] JH Anderson, DS Bernstein, and CW Gray, *Judicial Systems in Transition Economies: Assessing the Past, Looking to the Future*, Report for the World Bank, 2005.

[88] Kilpatrick, see n 21 above and C Kilpatrick, 'Community or Communities of Courts in European Integration? Sex Equality Dialogues between UK Courts and the ECJ' (1998) 4 Eur LJ, 121.

on the basis of the non-discrimination clause of the Spanish Constitution. Ordinary courts tend to follow this, rather than directly applying Community sex equality sources. The Constitutional Court itself has taken the course of following and applying Community law where it agrees with the ECJ and leaving it aside where it does not.[89] In Italy, the case law of the ECJ has made its way primarily via the legislative path, the definition of indirect discrimination in the equality law of 1991 being a transcription of the words used in the *Bilka* ruling and subsequent cases. As a result, 'the dialogue between Italian courts and EC sources therefore takes place largely through the mouthpiece of the Italian legislature', as Kilpatrick puts it.[90] The origin in European law of the national concepts of direct and indirect discrimination is very much blocked from the national courts' view and applied without any reference to EC law.[91] As European law is not brought into play in the national legal discourse, it is hardly surprising that hardly any references on its proper interpretation are made to the ECJ.

The second factor concerns the prevalence of a centralized or decentralized legal system. The British and German systems show interesting contrasts in this regard. In both of these countries, European sex equality law is far more present in the legal discourse, but is brought into play in different ways. In British sex equality litigation, institutional litigators such as the Equal Opportunities Commissions (EOC) and trades unions play an important role. They are often organized on a national level and pursue strategic goals, no less when bringing cases to court. Courts in their turn usually weigh up the appropriateness of a reference to the ECJ[92] and try to organize claims, as the background of the *Preston* case illustrates. This case actually concerned the position of 60,000 women, each of whom lodged a claim with an Industrial (now Employment) Tribunal, but only one single reference was made to the ECJ. The House of Lords did this only after having carefully considered its necessity in the light of other cases that had already been referred.[93] The Danish system can also be considered rather centralized, as six out of its seven preliminary references were brought by trades unions.

---

[89] Kilpatrick, see n 21 above, 96.

[90] ibid, 114. cf also Prechal and Masselot, see n 54 above, 21.

[91] Kilpatrick, see n 21 above, 113–114.

[92] T Tridimas, 'Knocking on Heaven's Door: Fragmentation, Efficiency and Defiance in the Preliminary Reference Procedure' (2003) 40 CML Rev, 38, has noted this as a more general feature of British references.

[93] Kilpatrick, see n 21 above, 48.

Kilpatrick typifies the German system as a decentralized and more pluralistic one, as institutions such as the EOC are lacking and German courts operate as their 'own small kingdom[s] with a local cast of characters (lawyers, judges, academics, etc)'.[94] In such a system, much will depend on the engagement of local personalities in sex equality issues. Besides the courts themselves, these include law activists (including lawyers and academics) and political parties.[95] This is indeed confirmed by the fact that the huge amount of references made by the Hamburg courts (eleven) and in North West Germany can be traced back largely to the efforts of just a few people.[96] French reference activity seems to have been steered in a similar way, building also on a rather isolated utilization of gender equality sources.[97]

Against this background, one can understand that in the UK the higher courts have mediated the arrival of European sex equality law, whereas in Germany first instance courts have shown the way.[98] The third factor ties in with this fact, relating to the approach that courts have developed towards the use of the preliminary procedure. It appears that the German lower courts have actually been more strategic, in the sense of using the procedure to 'rebel' against particular solutions adopted by higher courts, the ECJ included. This inter-court competition use of the preliminary procedure has appeared more of an accepted practice in Germany[99] than in the UK, where British courts have been less directed towards wishing to gain power vis-à-vis other national courts.[100] This is reflected not only in the high number of German part-time cases that have been referred to the ECJ, but also in the style of these references. These are characterized by repetition, aiming to a certain extent to put pressure on the ECJ to change its mind about a previous decision on a similar issue.[101] Danish courts can also be said to have

---

[94] Kilpatrick, see n 21 above.

[95] ibid, 50–51.

[96] N Colneric (former labour law judge and former judge of the ECJ), K Bertelsmann, and H Pfarr (both lawyers). Interestingly, the first two were also members of the aforementioned Commission Network.

[97] Some (former) French members of the aforementioned Commission Network are making a considerable contribution to this, including H Masse-Dessen, T Lanquetin, and C Pettiti.

[98] Kilpatrick, see n 21 above, 42–45 and the table of comparison presented there.

[99] ibid, 54.

[100] ibid, 40.

[101] Eg, Case C-457/93 *Lewark* [1996] ECR I-243 and Case C-287/93 *Freers and Speckmann* [1996] ECR I-1165 after Case C-360/90 *Bötel* [1992] ECR I-3589. Kilpatrick, see n 21 above, 47 typifies this as persuasive repetition, alongside same issue same court repetition and same issue repetition. Tridimas, see n 92 above, 39 refers to this as protest through cooperation, citing some Greek company law cases as illustrations of this.

tried to direct or influence the ECJ in its interpretation, by expressing in their references their preferred substantive meaning of the EC law at issue.[102] Both the somewhat more deliberate and reserved way of proceeding of British courts and, for instance, the reluctance of the Spanish Constitutional Court to refer any questions on issues it holds a different view on,[103] can be seen as demonstrations of a less confrontational style of communication. Yet, both styles and the ensuing high or low level of references may at times express the same thing: a disagreement or unwillingness on the part of national courts to accept the interpretation given by the ECJ.

Unifying effects

By resorting to the preliminary procedure with regard to many different aspects of sex equality law, it is clear that national courts themselves have made a crucial contribution to the broad development of this body of law. As such, they have also contributed to bringing about a certain level of convergence of this law in the Member States. Yet, it must be observed at the same time that this has occurred notably as a result of the dominant reference activity of the courts of just a few Member States. Some of these courts have sought to move the ECJ in a certain direction, for instance by repeating certain questions, and they have proved successful.[104] A limited number of national jurisdictions have thus been particularly influential in terms of the direction in which sex equality law has headed more generally in all, now twenty-seven, Member States. A consequence of this may be that European sex equality law 'fits' those jurisdictions better than others and that convergence may be more difficult to bring about. This may in fact be considered the case with regard to the concepts of direct and indirect discrimination.[105]

The foregoing is not to say that all references made by the most frequently referring jurisdictions have been equally important from the point of view of preserving the unity of the European legal order, nor that references made by the less frequently referring jurisdictions would not have made significant contributions to this unity. The *Danfoss* case, referred by a Danish court,[106] is a highly illustrative example of the latter, as it led the ECJ to conclude a reversal of the burden of proof in sex equality cases, later codified in the Burden of Proof Directive. Obviously, this ruling concerned an aspect of

---

[102] Kilpatrick, see n 21 above, 93.
[103] ibid, 105, 125.
[104] ibid, 47–48, 97.
[105] In this sense, Ahtela, see n 45 above, 71–72.
[106] Case C-109/88 *Danfoss* [1989] ECR 3199.

sex equality law that is relevant for all national jurisdictions. This also goes for other questions regarding effective enforcement,[107] and, for example, for questions on the discriminatory dismissal of pregnant women.[108] However, this is certainly not the case for all matters referred to the ECJ. Certain types of case can be said to address problems that are of a rather specific national nature (such as the night work issue in France), whereas others concern only partly commonly experienced problems. For instance, the problem of discrimination against part-time workers may be a very relevant issue in countries such as Germany and the Netherlands, but this is far less the case, for instance, in the Czech Republic and Denmark, which have a rather low level of part-time working women. Only where such cases lead the Court to more principled decisions having more general effects, such as in the *Bilka* case on the concept of indirect discrimination, are these of unifying importance.[109]

Whether the unifying capacity of the preliminary ruling mechanism is used to its fullest extent has appeared to depend not only on the courts themselves, but also on the role of non-governmental actors as public interest litigators, such as unions, equal opportunities commissions, and individual sex equality 'activists'. Their commitment and efforts make an invaluable contribution to the development, application, and enforcement of European sex equality law in the Member States. They can put pressure directly on national governments and legislators to make the necessary changes to law and policy, but they may also do so through the use of national courts and their emphasis on using the preliminary procedure. These actors are of crucial importance for bringing about the required changes in and convergence of social and political attitudes towards the goal of sex equality in the Member States.

6 Towards a more efficient unifying mechanism

The foregoing analysis leads me to a number of conclusions that will form the basis of some suggestions to enhance the efficiency of the use of the

---

[107] cf Case 14/83 *Von Colson and Kamann* [1984] ECR 1891 and Case C-271/91 *Marshall II* [1993] ECR I-4367.

[108] Case C-177/88 *Dekker* [1990] ECR I-3941.

[109] Case C-262/88 *Barber* [1990] ECR 1889 is also an example of a case that on the surface seemed to concern a rather national problem, but that had effects going far beyond that.

preliminary procedure in the light of its primary purpose of ensuring uniform interpretation and application of European law throughout the EU.

First of all, it shows us that we should be careful in developing views on reforming the preliminary procedure that are too abstract and theoretical and do not sufficiently take account of the actual reference activity of the national jurisdictions. The question of how to improve the efficiency of the preliminary ruling procedure is, only too often, merely considered from a general, top-down EU law point of view, focusing on the Court's workload and the resulting length of proceedings. It is within this context that suggestions are made for adapting the preliminary procedure and also that the plea for auto-limitation of national courts can be heard.

However, taking a bottom-up approach to this question, by taking the reference activity of the national jurisdictions in a certain area of the law as a point of departure, teaches us that there are different national realities hiding behind the use of the preliminary procedure. A general plea for auto-limitation denies this huge cross-national variation in reference density and the reasons underlying it. Depending on the situation in a particular Member State and what these underlying reasons are, the plea for auto-limitation may be misplaced or premature at the very least, and stimulation might be what is actually required. This applies not only to the situation of the new Member States, but for instance also to cases in which national courts refrain from making a reference because they wish to retain an interpretation that differs from that of the ECJ. More preliminary references may then point to positive changes in the attitude towards the application and enforcement of European law, which should not be discouraged.

The plea for auto-limitation is often linked to the plea that national courts should only make references that are useful from the point of view of the uniform application of European law. Such a plea fits in with the above top-down approach and also seems in denial of the national court's reality. To clarify, even though from the point of view of EU law the primary purpose of the preliminary ruling procedure is the uniform application of European law, we must admit that the concerns of the national courts for using it are usually of a very different nature and relate to other needs. From the analysis in section 5 we can infer that national courts may refer preliminary references with a view to properly fulfilling their job of ensuring legal protection of the interests of (a considerable number of) individuals (cf the British *Preston* case). National courts may also refer, or abstain from referring, with a view to protecting the national interest of upholding—their own interpretation of—the national law (Germany and Spain). As we have seen, the cross-national variation of preliminary references in terms of their substance also confirms that some cases are of national interest only or only of partly common interest.

So how realistic is it to demand from these national courts that they only refer preliminary questions that are of a general interest to the uniform application of Community law. Furthermore, how are the national courts to assess this difficult question in a given case, especially when they are still in a learning process and wishing to turn to the ECJ for guidance? Answering this question presupposes that they have an in-depth knowledge not only of European law but also of the legal systems of the other Member States. In an expanding and multilingual EU this is an impossible requirement to impose upon national courts. Against this background, it appears only logical that it is for the ECJ itself to decide what preliminary questions are of true importance for the uniform application and interpretation of European law, since it combines all the required expertise. At the same time, this background also induces the conclusion that the ECJ should remain easily accessible in order to meet the different concerns and needs of the national courts, whether or not these are of general, fundamental European interest. What does this mean then for the judicial organization of the preliminary ruling procedure?

In my view, two steps should be taken. First, criteria should be developed on the basis of which the Community Courts can distinguish between cases of general, fundamental European interest and those of a more national, technical nature. Second, what has already been provided for in the Nice Treaty should be put into practice, namely declaring the Court of First Instance (CFI) competent to deal with preliminary questions.[110] The CFI would be the Court deciding on the second category of cases, whereas the ECJ would deal exclusively with the former one. It would be most appropriate if the ECJ itself were to proceed to this filtering exercise, since it can be considered the most qualified institution for making the assessment of which cases concern fundamental aspects of European law and affect its uniform application in the EU. However, there should also be the possibility of referring a case back to the ECJ, if it is revealed before the CFI that what appeared to be a national or technical case does raise fundamental European issues affecting the unity of European law.[111]

---

[110] In the same sense P Dyrberg, 'What Should the Court of Justice be Doing' (2001) 26 ELR, 291–300 and Prechal, see n 19 above, 439.

[111] See the introduction by the Nice Treaty of Art 225(3) TEC and the *recours dans l'intérêt de la loi* that an Advocate General may initiate on the basis of Art 62 of the Statute for the Court of Justice.

What then could be basic criteria for distinguishing between cases of a fundamental European interest and those that are not? We can take as a starting point the fact that the ECJ already applies a filter mechanism, given that cases are decided by the Full Court (now of twenty-seven judges), the Grand Chamber (thirteen judges), or the small chambers (five or three judges). As Lenaerts and Corthaut note elsewhere in this volume, the Full Court is rarely convened[112] and it is the Grand Chamber that deals with the major cases. So, the bulk of cases is dealt with in very small chambers and one can assume that these cases do not generally present any new 'hot' issues from the point of view of European law.[113] Article 44 of the Court's Rules of Procedure provides just some basic rules for the assignment of cases to formations, stipulating that 'The Court shall assign to the Chambers of five and three Judges any case brought before it in so far as the difficulty or importance of the case or particular circumstances are not as such as to require that it should be assigned to the Grand Chamber.' It is the Judge-Rapporteur who makes a first assessment thereof, issuing a recommendation on this, whereas the Court decides on the assignment of cases. At any stage, cases may be reassigned to a bigger chamber. More insight is yet needed in the nature of the cases that are in practice assigned to and decided by the Grand Chamber.

The discussion in section 5 gives some further clues on how to distinguish fundamental European cases from more national and technical ones which can also be applied to other areas of law. To begin with, one can distinguish those cases that raised questions regarding the effective enforcement of sex equality law in the legal orders of the Member States, but that in fact also appeared relevant to the enforcement of European law more generally. Suffice it here to indicate the ruling in the *Von Colson and Kamann* case which established not only the duty of consistent interpretation, but also the entitlement to adequate compensation for a breach of European sex equality law. So cases concerning constitutional issues regarding the effect and application of European law in a national legal order (including supremacy, direct effect, consistent interpretation, effective legal protection) are obvious cases to be dealt with by the ECJ itself.

---

[112] According to Art 44 of the Court's Rules of Procedure the Full Court only decides on Art 16(4) Statute cases and on cases the Court considers to be of 'exceptional importance'.

[113] Figure 4 of the Court's annual report of 2006 shows the following figures, covering 444 cases completed in that year, also including direct appeals: Full Court (2); Grand Chamber (55); Chamber of 5 (278); Chamber of 3 (108); and President (1).

Another example of cases that would belong to the category of cases fundamental to European law are those involving the basic principles or concepts underlying a particular area of the law.[114] As these constitute core elements of substantive law, as we have seen for instance in respect of the concept of indirect discrimination, it would be up to the ECJ to provide for their definition or clarification. Once these concepts are fully crystallized, the CFI could deal with further preliminary questions related to them. This would cover questions that do not so much concern the European concept itself as the application of this concept to the case before the national court and in relation to the national law at issue.[115] For instance, must a monthly allowance be considered as 'pay' in the sense of Article 141 EC? [116] Even if one argues that a national judge should him/herself be capable of testing the national law in relation to such a concept or principle, some guidance may still be desired. However, it is inefficient for the ECJ to deal with such questions.

Third, cases that concern the scope of the application of substantive law can also be regarded as presenting a fundamental European interest. Sex equality law has shown interesting examples of this, not only in the purely economic sphere of whether occupational pensions are to be considered as pay under Article 141 EC (*Bilka*, *Barber*), but also in the more social sphere, where the Court was asked whether sex equality law encompasses sexual orientation (*Grant*, *P v S*) and about its applicability to the military (*Kreil*).

More generally, if references of the kind described above would involve clear repetition of issues that had already been decided and there is no reason for the Court to reconsider its earlier case law, these cases could also be left to be decided by the CFI. The same goes for questions that relate to situations that occur in only one or just a few Member States.

Redesigning the preliminary procedure in the above way would contribute to a reduction in the workload of the ECJ, while at the same time ensuring easy access to the Community Courts for national courts and considerably shortening the length of proceedings. In addition, in terms of the quality of judicial lawmaking, such a system allows for substantial gains. The limited capacity and resources of the ECJ would be better used, since dealing with (far) fewer cases would mean that the ECJ could dedicate more time to those cases that do involve issues of crucial importance to preserving

---

[114] cf Lenaerts and Corthaut, this volume, 21.
[115] cf Dyrberg, see n 110 above, 292.
[116] Case C-381/99 *Brunnhofer* [2001] ECR I-4961.

the unity of European law. Furthermore, it could do so as a Full Court, no longer operating in (small or Grand) chambers. This would not only be to the benefit of a more uniform, consistent, and well-reasoned development of European law,[117] as such it would also add to the credibility and acceptance of the Court's case law in the Member States.

---

[117] cf also the plea of Lenaerts and Corthaut in ch 21, p 514–515 for developing more consistency and building more coherent theory behind the Court's case law.

17

On the Unity of European Labour Law

Emilios Christodoulidis and Ruth Dukes

1 Unity, uniformity, identity: setting the terms

The concept of unity has come to be seen as pivotal but equivocal during the course of this research project. It appears in contra-distinction to two different concepts, and is at least implicated in the distinction between uniformity and diversity. What are we to make of that 'implication', except to comment on how unhelpful the notion of 'uniformity' is in this context? It is unhelpful because it begs the questions it is meant to address: *What* constitutes uniformity? What *measure* of diversity erodes it? What *degree* of variation is significant? What is the relevant threshold? One must assume after all *some* degree of difference or variation otherwise there would be no distinct legal entity to observe: the legal events or orders under scrutiny would simply fold into each other. If unity is what is in question, it appears that one hits an impasse along the 'uniformity' route sooner or later, because the concepts doing the hard work of tracking the tolerable level of variation that allows us to collect disparate events under the notion of a single order are distinctly *not* the pair uniformity/diversity. It is for this reason that one must disentangle from this the concept of unity and reorient it vis-à-vis identity.

Unity, to put it simply, is the way we understand identity over time. Unity allows us to understand law as *being* a system always in the process of *becoming*. That is why we consider that it is so useful to think of law—to use Joxerramon Bengoextea's wonderful formulation—as *a system a posteriori*.[1]

---

[1] J Bengoextea, 'Legal System as a Regulative Ideal' (1994) 53 Archiv für Rechts- und Sozialphilosophie, 65–79.

Unity then involves a certain act of inclusion of the disparate event. The act of norm creation—at whatever level this occurs, of judicial application or legislation—is then always-already in some sense preordained by the system. It is this that brings clearly into view the crucial distinction between unity and identity. Unity furnishes identity with a temporal dimension, submitting it to the hazards of time, and to the limit condition of entropy. Against that limit, and to the extent that it continues as a system, its identity is based on the continuous 'gathering' of new elements into the corpus of existing law, and that alone accounts for its unity.

Perhaps one could explore these important issues with the help of a 'pure science' of law, particularly the idea that imputation and representation articulate in a legally significant way to give us the 'objective meaning' of the law.[2] One could also perhaps combine this with Luhmann's account of how the unity of the law continuously operates to re-embed a legal system's basic distinctions in new contexts.[3] For Luhmann there will forever be centrifugal forces undermining the unity of the law. Some of the pivotal concepts discussed in the research project so far, eg, the divergent uses of discretion or the differential treatment of social rights, are centrifugal forces of precisely this sort. Yet against this move of differentiation, understood as the pull of local jurisdictions, Luhmann argues that there is a force of 'redundancy' at play that sets a threshold of 'tolerable'—for the system—variation. The unity of the law then depends on this gathering of incongruous elements [4] around its existing categories and descriptions, which are re-embedded as the legal system goes on.

There are of course a number of sometimes interesting objections to this understanding of unity. Unity, one objection goes, appears to be secured at the expense of 'plasticity' and experimentation with new concepts and, crucially for us, local variation. We would argue that that counter-positioning is in fact misleading. But it is also revealing in another way that has something important to tell us about the unity of EU law. Unity once divorced from uniformity involves a creative 'holding together' of

---

[2] H Kelsen, *Pure Theory of Law* (Gloucester: Peter Smith, 1989).

[3] For an early account see his much-discussed N Luhmann, 'The Unity of the Legal System' in G Teubner (ed), *Autopoietic Law: A New Approach to Law and Society* (Berlin: De Gruyter, 1988). For a more recent restatement see N Luhmann, *Das Recht der Gesellschaft* (Frankfurt a Main: Suhrkamp, 1993) translated as *Law as a Social System* (Oxford: Oxford University Press, 2004) especially chs 4 and 10.

[4] They must be 'incongruous' otherwise they would have no informational value for the system: information requires that the system be 'surprised' in some way.

confirmation and plasticity, a dialectic of past and future, with every legal act bringing the new and variable within the ambit or horizon of that which at every step re-establishes itself (and this establishment requires time!) as the law, *both* already present *and* new at every step.

A great deal more needs to be said about the precise meaning of this charged philosophical term 'unity', and in a way that picks up the thread more systematically and links it to our substantive discussion. We have so far set the scene for at least a discussion of unity unhampered by the misleading concept of 'uniformity'. And yet if it is indeed the temporal dimension of the legal system, the notion that its identity is caught up in time, that makes it so difficult to understand how something both *is* and *develops* simultaneously, merely contrasting unity with uniformity will not suffice. We will need to 'unpack' the notion in a way that reconciles variety over time with identity (perhaps more accurately 'idem-identity'[5]), in a way that comprehends the former as productive rather than erosive to the latter. Let us consider some familiar suggestions.

A first suggestion is to understand unity in terms of an *underpinning* or *substratum*: something that holds and supports variety from below. The customary way in which this understanding of unity is theorized is through the deployment of the distinction between *concept* and *conception*, the former an umbrella category whose very constancy allows the accommodation of the latter as a variety of ever-changing instantiations. Take Ronald Dworkin's *Law's Empire* as a typical example here. According to Dworkin, the practice that is law is defined as that which spans all its instantiations. It underlies and supports them from below, harbouring a certain diversity that, for Dworkin, is constructive, in the sense that it allows a practice both to remain the same—as concept—and be contested—as conception—at the level of its actual instantiations.[6] This, of course, also permits Dworkin the deeply suspect liberal move of immunizing law (*because* the concept is for him committed to integrity, the past, rights as entrenched, etc) from any radically

---

    [5] We would like to thank Hans Lindahl for his hugely insightful editorial intervention at this point. Borrowing from P Ricoeur's *Oneself as Another* (Chicago: University of Chicago Press, 1992), Lindahl insists on an analytical distinction between *idem-identity*, that is as what remains the same over time, and *ipse-identity*. The latter emerges in reference to common principles underpinning EU law, which presupposes the first-person plural perspective of a *We* as the unity of the legislative body. While the collective that has a joint or common interest in the act (for the sake of which its members act jointly) features in our discussion of European labour law (as the commonality of interest between managers and employees, below) it is the first notion of identity—idem-identity—that underpins our discussion of unity.
    [6] R Dworkin, *Law's Empire* (London: Fontana, 1986) especially 70–72.

different understanding of the concept itself, typically a more political understanding that might question commitment to entrenched advantage and entrenched distributions. Such rival theories are rebutted by Dworkin at the meta-level as having simply misunderstood the practice of law, as having misconstrued the fundamental features of the practice, as having belied, if you like, the concept itself of law.

We will say no more on this understanding of unity as guaranteed by the concept, because it cannot survive the challenge of the temporal. The concept itself cannot provide the intended stability. To underpin the practice it would need to be furnished with a stability of meaning that withstood the vagaries of time and the attendant slippages, which is a nonsense in the most basic terms of linguistic philosophy. *And*, if accommodating of those slippages, it would be too *under-determined* to perform the function of underpinning—of holding something fast from below.

A second, more useful way to approach the function of unity is provided by Wittgenstein's concept of 'family resemblances'. The introduction of the latter allows a certain loosening of the hold of the 'concept' over the 'conceptions', or of the general category over its concretizations, since it is no longer the case that the former ('concept') sets the necessary and sufficient conditions for the inclusion of the latter ('conceptions') within its ambit.[7] With 'family resemblances' no set of features need to be shared by all instances: instead 'overlapping resemblances pass from one case to another via intermediate cases'.[8] The notion relies on there being a significant overlap between cases where the criteria of what can be deemed significant need not meet any closed list of conditions.

We may wish to sharpen this account of unity by introducing *as constitutive* the dimension of time. Luhmann's systems theory is above all a theory of society that pivots on the key concept of time: his writings orient us to a meaning of phenomena as infused in time, or more accurately to processes of selection that channel and direct every social system's response to the complexity of the environment via the *handling* of its temporal self-adjustment. Time is a dimension of the meaning of law; it underlies its every operation and observation. Time furnishes expectations as anticipation of selected future events and immunization against non-selected others. It underlies

---

[7] For an analysis of Wittgenstein's notion see S Mulhall, *Inheritance and Originality* (Oxford: Clarendon Press, 2001) 84ff. For an application in the theory of criminal law see V Tadros, 'The Distinctiveness of Domestic Abuse' in A Duff and S Green (eds), *Defining Crimes: Essays on the Special Part of the Criminal Law* (Oxford: Oxford University Press, 2005) 119–143.

[8] Mulhall, see n 7 above, 84–85.

the dialectic of constancy and indifference on the one hand and receptivity on the other. It is constitutive of any system's linkage capacity (*Anschlussfähigkeit*) of operations to previous and to anticipated operations.

These are all suggestions that would require too much expository work for present purposes, so we will limit ourselves to some brief comments on relevant points. Crucial to the system's ability to maintain itself as a unity is 'redundancy', a term which Luhmann borrows from information theory to denote the system's tendency to reduce the element of surprise within it. The system thus opens itself to its environment in a controlled way. It receives information to which it must respond and in the process adjust, but in adjusting it returns to a state of order, re-establishing its unity as a system. It maintains itself as an 'island' of reduced complexity in a world of high complexity. So while change enters the system, it enters it in the form of information against a controlled horizon of what the system itself perceives as expectable. The system is 'redundant' 'in so far as it supports itself in processing information on the basis of what is already known [...]. Every repetition makes information superfluous which means, quite simply, redundant.'[9]

The legal system is principally a redundant order. In processing information on the basis of what is already known it supports itself, and self-referentially assimilates what is new to what already exists. Legal argumentation, says Luhmann, overwhelmingly reactivates known grounds. Information becomes confirmed in subsequent operations, gradually becomes entrenched in self-descriptions, and acquires orientation value for new arguments and condensation value for the system. Of course the assimilation cannot be complete. The system needs to react to a changing environment, and to this effect *variety* comes into play. Significantly, the practice of distinguishing and overruling 'occasionally invents new [grounds] to achieve a position where the system can, on the basis of a little new information, fairly quickly work out what state it is in and what state it is moving towards'. The reason it requires 'a special effort' to shake the redundancy of the system and stretch its imagination is that the system tends to

---

[9] N Luhmann, 'Legal Argumentation: An Analysis of Its Form' (1995) 58 MLR, 291. Also in Luhmann, *Law as a Social System*, see n 3 above: 'Cases that require a decision are concrete cases and that means they are different from each other. They provoke the system into acknowledging their differences. Argumentation picks up on that provocation and transforms it into redundancy (in terms of programmes and rules) that are tested, condensed and confirmed in relation to a greater number of possible applications. Argumentation evidently opts for redundancy, for economy of information and surprises'.

'reduce its own surprise to a tolerable amount and allow information only as differences added in small numbers to the stream of reassurances'.[10]

A great deal more can be said about the stream of reassurances, the connections of the positive values of the code—legal decisions building on legal decisions—and be included under the symbol of validity. In all this, and marking the moment of unity, is a certain 'gathering' rationalization around organizing principles. *The unity of the system is strengthened through redundancy, and conversely undermined—and in limit cases even eroded—if the new acts of interpretation can no longer be imputed to the system's organizing premises.* The system only continues—and in our discussion the system of European law emerges—only if the disciplining effect works and if the balance between redundancy and variety is maintained as productive for the system, allowing the activation of known grounds in every expansion onto new terrain.

This dialectic of the familiar and the new as contained within the unity of law is not of course confined to systems theory. Kelsen brilliantly argues that the new act is always already authorized by existing law, validity performing here the logically precarious act of containment: because what does interpretation *mean* if it means loyalty to the *existing* text? And Luhmann, deeply Kelsenian at this point, revisits this ground in *Das Recht der Gesellschaft*, in the chapter on legal argumentation: 'Interpretation is understood as an after-rationalization of the text, as our honouring the premise that the law-maker made a rational decision'; 'Arguments cannot—or cannot be seen to—change the law. They are effected under the symbol of validity: a valid interpretation is that which remains faithful to valid law'; 'With the help of *concepts*, distinctions can be stored and made available for a great number of decisions. In other words, concepts compound information, thereby producing the redundancy required by the system.'[11]

We have covered some distance to return to the idea of law as a system *a posteriori*; and to this *a posteriori* systematicity that we have given the name *unity*. Time shoots through it in a dialectic of anticipation and adjustment, a double movement of controlled release of alternatives and readjustment in view of these alternatives. Undergirding unity is a moment of containment of the new within the familiar, always-already authorized as such by the system in place.

But while unity implies *re*turn, *re*adjustment, *re*-grouping, *re*-ordering, *a posteriori* coherence, we also need to understand the other side of the process.

---

[10] Luhmann, see n 9 above.
[11] All in Luhmann, *Law as a Social System*, see n 3 above, 306ff.

What is it that destabilizes, forces variation, exerts pressure on the system to depart from protected equilibria? What forces restlessness on an order whose natural state is stability, inertia, the protection and guarantee of established expectations? What breaks and makes productive the tautology 'the law is what the law is'? Or, in less esoteric terms, what tests the unity of the system and calls its stable state into question? What allows the law to react to external pressure, to become responsive to political, moral, and economic demands, to regulate, and in the process, to reaffirm identity? We will call this moment that pulls against unity 'divergence'. The articulation of openness and closure that allows the system to exist over time depends crucially on the deployment of *the distinction between unity and divergence*.

But at the same time as setting that distinction as crucial, let us explore it at a level at which the binary concepts may allow us a political intervention. For this we move to the field of labour, to the legal regulation of labour, because it is in this context, and more specifically that of European labour law, that the concepts may furnish an intervention. The binding *unity* we are talking about is that of the European labour law;[12] the *divergence* is in the competing interests of capital and labour. We will ask the questions: In what sense precisely is the articulation of unity and divergence not problematic but instead productive for law? What are the ideological effects of this productivity? And perhaps most importantly for us: what strategic use can be made of the articulation —and at what level—of unity and divergence?

2 Binding unity—divergent interests

A divergence of interests between management and workers exists wherever the power to manage production is vested in someone other than the worker-producer. Often this divergence of interests is identified in terms of the conflict that arises over the division of the profits of an undertaking.[13] For Marx the divergence of interests is expressed as a conflict between capital and labour, which arises by reason of the nature of the social relations of

---

[12] Let us here introduce a caveat. The naming of 'it' as unitary subject is perhaps already an act of usurpation, an over-determination belying an incoherence too radical to be called to presence through the concept of European labour law.

[13] 'The war between the profit-maker and the wage-earner is always with us.' HB Higgens, *A New Province for Law and Order* (New York: Dutton, 1922) 1 cited in O Kahn-Freund in P Davies and M Freedland (eds), *Kahn-Freund's Labour and the Law* (3rd edn, London: Stevens, 1983) 27.

production intrinsic to capitalism. The capitalist acts to increase capital, but can only do so through the exploitation of wage labour. The worker sells his labour in order to gain the means to live; this is his only source of livelihood. Though he remains free to leave the employ of any particular employer, he 'cannot leave the whole class of purchasers, that is, the capitalist class, without renouncing his existence. He belongs [...] to the capitalist class.'[14]

The 'belonging' that Marx sets out to denounce is ironically of course the very thing that allows labour law to recast class conflict as a divergence of interests. If polarization is going to be productive for law, it must first be internalized. The cleavage that for Marx is fundamental to capitalist society is the very thing that, once internalized as divergence (of interests), becomes productive to capitalist society. We will concern ourselves here neither with the co-option nor with the *différend* it generates for a radical politics. Instead from within a social-democratic paradigm our intention here is to identify the organizing premises of the law that regulate labour relations.

Within this paradigm, the internalization of class conflict becomes productive in a specific sense. The focus on the division of profits as the primary locus of conflict allows space to posit some commonality of interest between workers and management, and to advocate cooperative labour relations in furtherance of those objectives which are shared. *It is this projected commonality that provides the pivot for the deployment of the term 'unity' and 'divergence'*, the commonality itself never in question. In that sense, recognition of the divergence of interests is at the core of constitutional provisions and labour legislation that seek to introduce elements of democracy to the management of industry and the workplace: the need for independent representation of worker interests arises for the very reason that those interests are not coincident with the employers'. For industrial pluralists, such as Kahn-Freund, the commonality of interest is limited to having some kind of negotiation or arbitration procedures in place for the regulation of (collective) conflicts, but the commonality is again implicit.[15] Through collective bargaining, and the type of 'conflictual partnership' relation that it engenders,[16] conflict is

---

[14] K Marx, *Wage Labour and Capital* (Moscow: Progress, 1952).

[15] '[The] one interest which management and labour have in common [...] is that the inevitable and necessary conflicts should be regulated from time to time by reasonably predictable procedures, procedures which do not exclude the ultimate resort to any of those sanctions through which each contending part must—incase of need—assert its power'. Kahn-Freund, see n 13 above, 27.

[16] Or *partecipazione conflittuale*: KW Wedderburn, 'Consultation and Collective Bargaining in Europe: Success or Ideology?' (1997) 26 ILJ, 7.

managed and contained (internalized), and a balance is, optimally, struck between the interests of both parties.[17]

It is indicative that in German labour law, the sphere of commonality of interest between management and workers at workplace level, defined as the *Betriebszweck* or *Betriebswohl*—'works objective' or 'good of the works'—has played a definitive role. Under the Works Councils Act 1920, employee representatives on the works councils were ascribed a dual role, to protect the economic interest of the employees, and to support the employer in the achievement of 'works objectives'.[18] Similarly, in the Works Constitution Acts of 1952 and 1972, works councils are placed under an obligation to 'work together' with the employer 'for the good of the employees *and of the works*'.[19] According to Kahn-Freund, the tendency of judges in the Weimar labour courts was to interpret the 'works objectives' as lying with the public interest in industrial peace, and to prioritize this interest above the 'partisan' aims of the employees and employers.[20] But the original idea underlying these legislative provisions was, rather, that employees and management share an interest in the success of the establishment; in increasing profits so that both wages and reinvestment are greater, and in securing the continuation of the establishment.

We have argued that the distinction between binding unity and divergent interests, and the specific mode in which that distinction is deployed in legal decisions, accounts for the rational 'holding together' of the system of (European) labour law. In our earlier discussion of the 'redundancy' that underlies unity we also argued that the unity of law is *undermined—and in limit cases even eroded—if the new acts of interpretation can no longer be imputed back to its organizing premises*. If redundancy (and with it unity) depends on a reflexive articulation of organizing principles and concrete norms, then in cases where that articulation is broken, or caught up in a process of such fundamental erosion that it is severely weakened, the very rationality—of our system of law, let alone its effectiveness, is undercut.

This is the condition we are currently faced with. In late capitalism, under conditions of globalization, it has become increasingly difficult to assume an area of shared interest between workers and management that might

---

[17] Kahn-Freund, see n 13 above, 28.
[18] Works Councils Act 1920, s 1.
[19] ibid, s 2 (emphasis added).
[20] O Kahn-Freund, 'Das soziale Ideal des Reichsarbeitsgerichts' (1931), reproduced and translated as 'The Social Ideal of the Reich Labour Court' in O Kahn-Freund, *Labour Law and Politics in the Weimar Republic* (Oxford: Blackwell, 1981).

underpin the pursuit of cooperative labour relations. In an ever-increasing proportion of private sector undertakings throughout Europe, there is little or no trade union presence; the dominant labour relation is the employment relationship between the individual employee and employer. In the absence of collectivities of workers, Kahn-Freund's assertion of a common interest in reasonably predictable procedures for the resolution of conflict collapses, *at most*, into an argument in favour of the institution of individual disciplinary or grievance procedures. Where labour is not organized, management has less to fear from conflict with the workforce and so, less to gain through compromise. Nor can it always be assumed that management will wish to secure the sustained success of the establishment or undertaking—the *Betriebswohl*. Forms of ownership of capital prevalent in late capitalism encourage management to prioritize short-term gains for shareholders, including those gains that might be made in the context of a liquidation or hostile takeover.[21]

Under UK law, managers are required, when making decisions regarding corporate structure, to prioritize shareholder value over other interests. That being the case, they are correspondingly less able to consider the long-term interests of other stakeholders, including employees.[22] If an increase in share price can be secured through the sale of all or parts of the undertaking, through relocation abroad, or through strategic liquidation, the attendant collective redundancies need not detain management.[23]

What do these trends signify and entail? In short, that the hollowing out of any assumed commonality of interests collapses the unity/divergence distinction (that pivots on that commonality), and *that* collapse in turn precipitates the disarticulation of legal regulation from its underlying principles. This gradual implosion 'undoes' labour law as an institutional achievement, subordinates legal protections to market imperatives, crucially undercuts the 'mediating responsiveness'[24] and 'reflexivity'[25] of labour law,

---

[21] We refer here, in particular, to *dispersed share ownership*—a form of ownership whereby the principal shareholders are insurance companies or pension funds that invest, through fund managers, on behalf of policyholders and beneficiaries.

[22] S Deakin and F Wilkinson, *The Law of the Labour Market* (Oxford: Oxford University Press, 2005) 336–338.

[23] As Marx put it, 'the body of capital can change continually without the capital suffering the slightest alteration'. Marx, see n 14 above, 29.

[24] See P Nonet and P Selznick, *Law and Society in Transition: Toward Responsive Law* (New Brunswick: Transaction Publishers, 2005).

[25] See G Teubner, 'Substantive and Reflexive Elements in Modern Law' (1983) 17 L and Society Rev, 239. Also R Rogowski and T Wilthagen (eds), *Reflexive Labour Law: Studies in Industrial Relations and Employment Regulation* (Deventer: Kluwer, 1994).

and forces industrial relations into the polarities of market fundamentalism[26] or anti-capitalist resistance.[27]

3 Europe's tradition of industrial democracy

But let us take things more gradually. Any discussion of the unity of European labour law has to confront the fundamental contradiction with which the global organization of markets presents it. We will attempt to identify the contradiction, a contradiction that is 'real' because it is rooted in real practices, and discuss the disjunction that cuts away at the unity of European labour law: the disjunction between organizing principle and actual practice. We will show that this disjunction operates to disarticulate fundamental connections that underlie the democratization of employment relations and the protection of workers against managerial prerogative and the capitalist drive for profit. We will then put forward an argument *against* that disarticulation and *about* (and *for*) the unity of law.

In the tradition of critical theory, a theorization of law is also a political intervention to sustain or interrupt the pattern of reproduction of industrial relations. The argument we attempt to make in defence of unity has a descriptive and normative side. On the descriptive side, the argument is that the best way to make rational sense of the system of European labour law is to see it in terms of the unity of general principle and individual statute and decision, of the European and the municipal, of citizen and employee. Normatively, an effort must be made, again in the defence of unity, to hold up current practices to the principles of industrial democracy they instantiate.

Underlying the unity of labour law across European traditions is the democratic-socialist aspiration of righting the fundamental injustice of the subsumption of labour under capital. This is traceable in the convergence of European political traditions around the ideals of co-determination, democratic control of the workplace, and producer-citizenship. Central to these traditions has been the aspiration to harness state power to promote social justice and social reform through the legal regulation of the political economy. What follows is the briefest of accounts of this 'original convergence' of traditions, its foundational principles, and their enactment as 'fundamental' in European constitutions and the treaties and charters of

---

[26] See RA Posner, 'Some Economics of Labor Law' (1984) 51 U of Chicago L Rev, 988.
[27] See M Hardt and A Negri, *Empire* (Amsterdam: Van Gennep, 2002).

the European Union. We will look then at the disjunction between principle and practice, and at what a discussion of unity might offer us in terms of redressing its effects.

The *German* tradition of worker democracy has its roots deep in socialist thought. From it has stemmed a legal tradition informed by the commitment to worker co-determination: to the principle that all workers should be represented collectively at the workplace and at industry level, and should participate collectively in managerial decision making on a range of work and personnel related issues. The essentials of the system were originally settled in the Constitution and other collective labour legislation of the Weimar Republic.[28] The figure of Hugo Sinzheimer, a labour lawyer and parliamentary representative for the Social Democratic Party (SPD), was pivotal to this development, and influential in the theorization and evolution of labour law across Europe. A brief explanation of his particular conception of *Wirtschaftsdemokratie* will serve as a useful starting point for discussion of the principles underlying European labour law.

Sinzheimer's writing on labour law was directed by a 'passionate will to social justice',[29] by a recollection of the worker as human being ('die Arbeit ist also der Mensch selbst'), and by a Kantian recognition of human dignity that acted to reveal the injury involved in subordinating labour to capital.[30] Where Sinzheimer broke with Marx, and with Luxemburg, Kautsky, and other of his contemporaries, was in his belief that social justice and democracy could be achieved within the confines of the parliamentary system. Sinzheimer taught that 'full democracy' would follow from the extension of democracy from the political sphere to the economic sphere: the constitutionalization of industry and, as one element of this, the workplace. For Sinzheimer, the role of labour law was understood in terms of achieving this constitutionalization of industry. Law was to be used by the state to 'call labour into community with property', to afford to labour a status, a 'starting position' (*Grundstellung*), equal to that of property and to create a sphere within which matters that had previously fallen within the employer's sole prerogative would come to be decided in community with labour.

Alongside property, there would appear *ipso jure* a second agent, with its basis not in property law but in labour law where labour would cease

---

[28] See further R Dukes, 'The Origins of the German System of Worker Representation' (2005) 19 *Historical Studies in Industrial Relations*, 31.

[29] O Kahn-Freund, 'Hugo Sinzheimer' in R Lewis and J Clark(eds) *Labour Law and Politics in the Weimar Republic* (Oxford: Blackwell) 73.

[30] H Sinzheimer, *Grundzüge des Arbeitsrechts* (2nd edn, Jena: Fischer, 1927) 8.

to be represented only through property and would become its own representative.[31] In providing labour with a status equal to that of property, labour law would secure for collectivities of workers a decision making power equal to that of the employers, and so would affirm the right, and ability, of workers to participate in managerial decision making. Having secured this status and power for labour, state law was to be regarded as having fulfilled its role. The actual regulation of industry and of the workplace would then proceed through the autonomous creation of law by the representatives of labour and property—the trade unions, works councils, employers, organizations, and individual employers.

Sinzheimer's proposals were included in Article 165 of the Weimar Constitution, which, in its opening lines, called workers, 'to participate, in community with the employers and with equal rights, in the regulation of wages and conditions of employment as well as in the overall economic development of the productive forces'. It is true that in the early 1920s, resistance in the private sector, together with disagreement within the SPD, meant that the economic constitution as Sinzheimer had envisaged it was not fully achieved.[32] At the end of the 1920s, renewed plans for economic democracy were rendered obsolete by the onset of world depression and the rise of Nazism.[33] The system of worker representation enacted in the period 1949–1952 did closely resemble that of the Weimar Republic,[34] though significantly, there was no equivalent of Article 165 in the Bonn Constitution, only a more limited 'freedom of association'.[35] The influence of Sinzheimer's thought nevertheless continued to be felt. The idea of the

---

[31] Sinzheimer, see n 30 above, 207–213.

[32] Statutory provision was made for the establishment of trade unions and works councils, and these remained a lasting feature of German industrial relations, but plans for district level workers councils and industrial councils were never implemented.

[33] These plans were formulated by the research institute of the German trades union congress and published in a pamphlet written by Fritz Naphtali as head of the institute: FP Naphtali, *Wirtschafsdemokratie: ihr Wesen, Weg und Ziel* (Frankfurt am Main: Europäische Verlagsanstalt, 1966). After 1945, a further attempt by the unions to institute *Wirtschaftsdemokratie* failed because of opposition, this time, from the US military government, and later the CDU-led federal government, which were united in their wish to re-establish a private capitalist economic order in the western part of Germany, and to suppress any possibility of a communist uprising. See E Schmidt, *Die verhinderte Neuordnung 1945-1952* (7th edn, Frankfurt am Main: Europäische Verlagsanstalt, 1977).

[34] Though with the CDU in power, the new system was less sympathetic to the claim of labour to participate in the management of industry than the Weimar system had been.

[35] Art 9(3): The right to form associations to safeguard and improve working and economic conditions is guaranteed to everyone and to all trades and professions. Agreements, which restrict or seek to hinder this right, are null and void; measures directed to this end are illegal.

constitutionalization of industry survived, most obviously, in the name of the act regulating works councils: the Works Constitution Act. And a constitutional basis for co-determination rights has been found in the fundamental commitment to the dignity of the person, to inviolable and inalienable human rights, and to the right of free development of personality that is contained in Articles 1 and 2 of the Bonn Constitution.[36] *Mitbestimmung* in its widest sense—the collectivization of labour and its participation in the regulation of the economy—was an integral element of the post-war social market economy.[37]

The struggle to introduce democracy to industry as a means of limiting managerial prerogative was not particular to Germany, but was mirrored throughout Europe.[38] While one cannot claim that there was uniformity across different countries when it came to the *enactment* of these principles in legal texts, the differences have typically been exaggerated.[39] It is well known, for example, that some countries have entrenched collective rights in the text of their constitutions while others have not. Italy is an example of the former, with the Italian Constitution declaring as early as section 1 that 'Italy is a democratic Republic founded on labour'; in section 4 that 'the Republic recognises to every citizen the right to work'; in section 35 that 'the Republic protects work in all its forms and applications'; and in sections 39 and 40 the freedom of association and the right to strike respectively. In France, the Preamble to the Constitution contains a declaration that everyone has the right to strike, the right to defend his interests by trade union action, and the right 'to belong to the trade union of his choice'. In contrast, the UK, with no written constitution, affords a limited degree of protection for trade unions and workers involved in industrial action, provided through statutory immunities rather than through positive rights.

---

[36] Mitbestimmungskommission, *Mitbestimmung im Unternehmen, Bericht der Sachverständigenkommission zur Auswertung der bisherigen Erfahrungen bei der Mitbestimmung* (Stuttgart: Kohlhammer, 1970). The Commission was set up to investigate worker rights to co-determination and to report to the *Bundestag*.

[37] M Glasman, *Unnecessary Suffering: Managing Market Utopia* (London: Verso, 1996).

[38] See generally, B Hepple (ed), *The Making of Labour Law in Europe: A Comparative Study of Nine Countries up to 1945* (London: Mansell, 1986).

[39] cf S Simitis, who argues that claims regarding the particularities of national labour laws are usually made for instrumentalist reasons, eg, to deny that the EC has legislative competence in a particular area: 'Die Entdeckung der "Rechtskultur" hat in Wirklichkeit sehr wenig mit der jeweiligen Regelung selbst etwas zu tun, dafür aber umso mehr mit dem Widerstand gegen den immer stärkeren Regelungsanspruch der supranationalen Instanzen und der sich gleichsam maximierenden Betroffenheit des eigenen Rechts'. S Simitis, 'Europäisierung oder Renationalisierung des Arbeitsrechts' in M Heinze and A Söllner (eds), *Arbeitsrecht in der Bewährung: Festschrift für Otto Rudolf Kissel* (München: Beck, 1994) 1111.

To focus too greatly on such differences, however, is to overlook the convergence of underlying principle. In the traditions of *English* labour law and of collective *laissez-faire*, we in fact find many of the same assumptions as we met in Sinzheimer's *Wirtschaftsdemokratie*. 'Collective *laissez-faire*' was the term coined by Otto Kahn-Freund, Sinzheimer's one-time student, to describe the English system of industrial relations and, in particular, the relative paucity of labour law in place in the UK until the mid-1960s. Like *Wirtschaftsdemokratie*, collective *laissez-faire* rested on the principle that industry was best regulated autonomously, by the trade unions and the employers, so that the primary role of law in industrial relations was to allow for and to set the limits of that autonomous regulation. This was done, in English law, through the provision in law of immunity from the common law liability—criminal, tort, and contractual liability—that would otherwise have attached to union activities. For the reason that the law acted only to provide negative protections, and no positive rights, for example, to form or be a member of a union, or to take industrial action, Kahn-Freund described the English system of industrial relations in terms of 'the retreat of law' from that sphere of human interaction[40]—working terms and conditions and the detail of the relationships between unions and employers were best decided without interference from the state, legal practitioners, or the courts.

But, of course, in one sense, the statutory immunities could equally be said to constitutionalize the economic sphere, fulfilling the same function as the Weimar Constitution's call to workers to participate in the regulation of industry. The role of labour law, in each case, was to exclude from the industrial sphere the otherwise inequitable consequences of the functioning of private law: to sanction the collectivization of labour and the withdrawal of labour power in enforcement of collectively reached agreements, thereby allowing for the autonomous regulation of industry by labour and management. In an earlier period of historical development, law provided space for individuals, as legal subjects, to act autonomously within the market, entering into agreements and acquiring and disposing of property, free from state interference. It now created space for collectivities of workers and employers to act autonomously in the economic sphere, entering into agreements to regulate industrial relations and employment conditions free from state interference.[41] To describe this function of labour law variously

---

[40] O Kahn-Freund, *Selected Writings* (London: Stevens, 1978) 9.

[41] F Böhm, 'Rule of Law in a Market Economy' in H Willgerodt and A Peacock (eds), *Germany's Social Market Economy: Origins and Evolution* (Basingstoke: Macmillan for the Trade Policy Research Centre, London, 1989).

as the retreat of law from industrial relations, or as the constitutionalization through law of the industrial sphere, represented, in this sense, only a shift in emphasis.

Variations of this type between states at the level of legislation underlie a shared commitment to the protection of Europe's workers that has withstood the reactionary adventures of Thatcherism and its replications across the continent, even if we are still reeling from the ferocious remnants of the market fundamentalism that held sway during those years. The roots of a social Europe go deep, held in the form of the commitments to the twin ideals of democracy and dignity at work, that mark the endeavour, as Karl Polanyi put it, to make society a distinctively human relationship.[42]

The commitment to these principles has informed the drafting of the treaties and charters of the European Union since its inception. The Preamble to the 1957 Treaty of Rome stated that the fundamental objective of the EEC was to improve the living and working conditions of its people. The 1961 European Social Charter of the Council of Europe formulated labour and welfare rights in terms of human rights and was approved in the Preamble of the Single European Act.[43] In 1989, the European Community adopted its own Charter of Fundamental Rights of Workers. Though itself lacking in legal force, this Charter became the blueprint for several measures which were made binding in the shape of Directives, and was cited in most labour-related instruments that followed in the 1990s. The more recent EC Charter of Fundamental Rights of 2000 is significant for its attempt to protect social rights on a par with classic civil and political rights.[44] The social rights listed in the 2000 Charter include the prohibition of slavery and forced labour (Article 5), freedom of assembly and association (Article 12), the right of collective bargaining and action (Article 28), fair and just working conditions (Article 31), prohibition of child labour and protection of young people at work (Article 32), and the right to choose an occupation and to engage in work (Article 15) (the latter placing emphasis on willingness to increase accessibility to the labour market). Each of these instruments offers a positive message: they seek to safeguard decent working

---

[42] K Polanyi, *The Great Transformation* (Boston: Beacon Press, 1944) 234.

[43] The signatories to the SEA declared themselves, 'DETERMINED to work together to promote democracy on the basis of the fundamental rights recognized in the constitutions and laws of the Member States, in the Convention for the Protection of Human Rights and Fundamental Freedoms and the European Social Charter, notably freedom, equality and social justice'.

[44] See generally S Peers and A Ward, *The European Union Charter of Fundamental Rights* (Oxford: Hart, 2004).

conditions and to provide a collective defence of interests against the forces of deregulation and decollectivization. As Spiros Simitis states with regard to the 1989 Charter, 'with these [principles], the Community has made a declaration of the road which it intends to follow'.[45]

It is at this point that we come to the disjunction between stated principle and the practice it informs and undergirds, a disjunction that takes the form of a real contradiction whose management has proven both difficult and, ironically, economically productive to the architects and managers of capitalist integration.

4 'Productive' pathologies: managing market utopia[46]

The development of European labour legislation has been shaped, since the Treaty of Rome, by the primacy of economic aims within the European model.[47] During the early stages of the EEC, the guiding philosophy was that market integration would bring as a matter of course a gradual harmonization of social systems, and working and living conditions. On that basis, legislation was focused almost exclusively on the creation of a legal framework suited to the establishment of a common market.[48] Since the Single European Act of 1986 there has been an ever-greater emphasis on the social dimension of the common market, culminating in 2000 with the passing of the Charter of Fundamental Rights. Notwithstanding these developments, legislative and other measures taken in pursuance of social goals continue to be legitimated in terms of economic as well as social policy. This has acted and acts still as a 'crucial constraint' on the development of EC labour law.[49]

---

[45] Simitis, see n 39 above, 1104.
[46] We borrow M Glasman's subtitle from his excellent *Unnecessary Suffering: Managing Market Utopia*, see n 37 above.
[47] P Davies, 'The Emergence of European Labour Law' in L McCarthy (ed), *Legal Intervention in Industrial Relations: Gains and Losses* (Oxford: Blackwell, 1992).
[48] S Simitis and A Lyon-Caen, 'Community Labour Law: A Critical Introduction to Its History' in PL Davies *et al* (eds), *European Community Labour Law: Principles and Perspectives: liber amicorum Lord Wedderburn of Charlton* (Oxford: Clarendon Press, 1996) 4–7.
[49] M Freedland, 'Employment Policy' in Davies, see n 47 above, 287. See also KW Wedderburn, 'Common Law, Labour Law, Global Law' in BA Hepple (ed), *Social and Labour Rights in a Global Context: International and Comparative Perspectives* (Cambridge: Cambridge University Press, 2002) 46–47.

A second institutional constraint on the development of EC labour law arises from the fragmented nature of the legal base, or competence, within the EC, for social policy law. With respect to collective labour law, the scope for legislative action is severely restricted by the exclusion of pay, the right of association, the right to strike, and the right to lock out from the legislative competence of the EC, contained in Article 137(5) of the EC Treaty.[50] On paper, the 2000 Charter of Fundamental Rights protects freedom of assembly and association, the right of workers to information and consultation within the undertaking, and the right to collective bargaining and action.[51] But since the Charter 'has no independent legal status, may not be interpreted in conflict with existing international and European human rights structures, [...] and creates no "new" rights',[52] it can be regarded only as a statement of policy or set of guiding principles, *not* as a new or supplementary basis for legislative action.[53] The case of collective bargaining is instructive in this context. Article 28 of the 2000 Charter of Fundamental Rights states: 'Workers and employers, or their respective organisations, have in accordance with Community Law and national laws and practices, the right to negotiate and conclude collective agreements at the appropriate levels and, in case of conflicts of interest, to take collective action to defend their interest, including strike action.' By reason of the Article 137(5) EC restriction, however, the right to take collective action falls outside Community law competence.

This inconsistency throws up a problem that is crucially relevant to the way we understand, and have been discussing, unity. A disjunction arises between the principle and its instantiation that undercuts unity and with it the very rationality of law. After all, a standard cannot be rationally subverted in its *own* instantiation. And in that respect, to the extent that the

---

[50] The Art 137(5) EC Treaty restriction applies only to action taken under Art 137. The possibility of legislation on collective labour rights on alternative EC Treaty bases—Arts 94, 95, and 140—is discussed: ACL Davies, 'Collective Labour Rights in the EU' in P Alston (ed), *Labour Rights as Human Rights* (Oxford: Oxford University Press, 2005) 196–198.

[51] Arts 12, 27, and 28 Charter of Fundamental Rights of the European Union respectively.

[52] B Hepple, 'Enforcement: The Law and Politics of Cooperation and Compliance' in Hepple, see n 49 above, 243. See further B Bercusson, 'Episodes on the Path towards the European Social Model' in C Barnard and S Deakin (eds), *The Future of Labour Law: liber amicorum Sir Bob Hepple QC* (Oxford: Hart, 2004). The relevant Treaty provisions are Arts II 111 and II 112 of the TCE.

[53] Bercusson hopes that, 'The European Court of Justice may be willing to recognise as protected by the EU Charter those fundamental trade union rights which all, or most, or even a critical number of Member States insist should be protected.' Bercusson, see n 55 above, 180.

natural continuity between the right to dialogue, the right to associate, and the right to strike is broken, with only the former entrenched in principle but the latter two still excluded from EC competence, European labour law limps along in a state of fragmentation that undercuts its rationality. As Lord Wedderburn puts it:

> If Community labour law does not carry even the commitment to fundamental labour standards, including rights to take action, its promoters are obliged to devise some alternative at Community level which can render the social dialogue effective as negotiation. Without some such guarantee, the dialogue will ultimately appear to workers to be a false prospectus, the script of a monologue echoing to serve the needs of multinational capital.[54]

If what has been proclaimed at the level of founding principle is in fact subverted at the level of legal regulation, the question of unity—to the extent that unity underlies the identity of the system—throws open the question of the rationality of European labour law. There are two principal ways in which this rationality deficit—the irrelevance of underlying principle to actual practice—has been addressed. The first is through recourse to 'social dialogue'. The second is in the deployment of the distinction between 'hard' and 'soft' law. We will say something about the poverty of both these rationalizations.

4.1 *Social dialogue*

First, let us address the attempt to 'salvage' law's founding principles by allowing them to mutate into procedural guarantees of 'social dialogue'. Not only is the mutation from substance to procedure problematic, but it is accompanied by a serious discrepancy between the rationale for the institution of the dialogic forum and the rhetoric around it. Let us look at this more closely.

Under Articles 138 and 139 of the EC Treaty, the Commission is obliged to consult management and labour on issues in the sphere of social policy. Under Article 139, management and labour may inform the Commission that they wish to initiate the procedure known as 'social dialogue'. This procedure allows them to remove the issue from the Commission for a period of nine months and seek to reach consensus on the content of the proposal. This modest proposal for a stalling device has triggered nothing

---

[54] KW Wedderburn, *Labour Law and Freedom* (London: Lawrence and Wishart, 1995) 406.

short of Habermassian fervour in some quarters. It has been hailed by some as nothing short of 'revolutionary';[55] it is seen as 'implementing a vision of social justice as a process of *reconciling the divergent interests concerned* rather than as a predetermined product'.[56] Underlying the fervour (and justifying the mutation) is the shift 'from substance to procedure' that has in the last couple of decades, at least, become paradigmatic of political action, and animating of the (democratic) principle of self-determination. Dialogue, in this model, preferably unconstrained or ideal, underlies processes of communicative exchange that constitute or 'interpellate' political actors in the public sphere. The democratic imperative, harboured in the principle of self-determination, is realized—imperfectly, perhaps, for now. But then the dialogic model has a self-correcting dynamic built into its very premise—in, and *as*, processes of dialogue, setting up in this instance communicative contexts where employers, managers, and workers can meet as 'partners' in production.

But this is a 'social dialogue' fraught with problems. It stumbles first and foremost on the issue of 'representativity'.[57] There is no effective representation of workers at the European level, so that there is no guarantee that affected parties will have a say in the dialogue. Nor is the question of the representativity itself subject to, and thus determined reflexively in, processes of dialogue. Some of these questions are identified by Keith Ewing in his excellent 'Democratic Socialism and Labour Law': 'What is the bargaining unit?'; 'Is any threshold of support required?'; 'What is meant by the employers' "duty to bargain"?'; 'How are disputes on these issues to be decided?'[58]

It is the last question in particular that points to the absence of any reflexive element in the process, an element that it is democratically imperative to establish. As envisaged, 'social dialogue' is to be conducted in the absence of any formal framework, in the absence of any procedural guarantees, and in the absence of bargaining structures that might regulate bargaining outcomes. It is conducted within a framework of decisions largely taken by others. The negotiating positions of the vulnerable partners are obviously undercut without the possibility of backing a claim with the threat of industrial action.

---

[55] F Maupain, 'Is the ILO Effective in Upholding Workers' Rights?' in Alston, see n 50 above, 89.

[56] Maupain, see n 55 above (emphasis added).

[57] Davies, see n 50 above, 225.

[58] K Ewing, 'Democratic Socialism and Labour Law' (1995) 24 ILJ, 104. Ewing raises his questions in respect of trade union recognition within the UK, but they are also relevant to the matter of social dialogue at the European level.

The cumulative effect of the multiple forms of disempowerment—the absence of any guarantees of effective bargaining power or representativity—leaves the speaking position of labour weakened or withdrawn in the process.

One might be excused therefore for pointing out the naivety of assuming that a constructive, undistorted, or communicative (as opposed to strategic) dialogue is feasible under these conditions. 'Social dialogue' imposes the format of communicative action upon a substrate of the antagonistic relations of classes. The substitution of a strategic (antagonistic) model for a communicative (partnership) one allows a triple displacement. Workers are prevented from backing their claims with the possibility of acting on them. They are also assumed partners in a dialogue whose natural end is consensus. Failure to reach it is attributed either to bad faith or to incidental rather than structural constraints. The naivety of the model of social dialogue looks rather more cynical in this light, an ideological technique of anticipation and substitution, and of symbolic simulation.

4.2 *Soft law*

What of the second attempt to address the disjunction between principle and practice in European labour law, through recourse to *soft law*? The term 'soft law' is used within an EC context to describe a multitude of non-binding governmental instruments including recommendations, opinions, Green Papers, White Papers, informative communications, action programmes, guidelines, and notices.[59] The use of such instruments has increased since the European Council of Edinburgh in 1992, where it was concluded that legislative and other state action had to be taken, wherever possible, at national level, in line with the principles of conferred powers, subsidiarity, and proportionality. If Community measures were deemed necessary, recourse should be had preferably to framework directives and not to regulations. Since 1992, this policy has been further confirmed in various statements, including the Protocol on subsidiarity and proportionality attached to the Treaty of Amsterdam and the 2001 Commission White Paper on European Governance.[60] The guiding idea is that where legislation at EC level is problematic, because of considerations of subsidiarity, or because agreement across

---

[59] Linda Senden has provided the following useful definition: 'Rules of conduct that are laid down in instruments which have not been attributed legally binding force as such, but nevertheless may have certain (indirect) legal effects, and that are aimed at and may produce practical effects.' L Senden, *Soft Law in European Community Law* (Oxford: Hart, 2004) 3.

[60] ibid, 20–21.

Member States cannot be reached, soft law instruments can be used instead to encourage cooperation and the achievement of commonality in goals and standards.

The acute problem that arises has to do with how subsidiarity at the national level can be made to work in any sense in tandem with common-ality at the European level. As is often the case the answer to a difficult question is elided in hyperbole. So some proponents of soft law claim that it should be regarded, in many situations, not just as second best to legislation, but as the first choice. Scott and Trubek, for example, emphasize its 'greater flexibility', pointing out that 'its involvement of a broader range of actors in less clearly delineated roles [shape] policies which are not necessarily bind-ing and which are less substantively prescriptive and more accommodating of diversity'.[61]

There is a simple, yet fundamental, conflation in this 'solution' between that which affords 'greater flexibility' and is thus more 'accommodating of diversity' on the one hand, and that which is 'less prescriptive' on the other. Principles are more general than rules, and thus more 'flexible' since they afford greater leeway in the interpretive options they offer and furnish, but that in itself has no bearing on the degree of their prescriptiveness. And yet it is precisely this conflation that allows proponents of 'greater flexibility', subsidiarity, and managerial 'freedom' to piggyback such policies on the 'flexibility' of 'soft law'. There is little doubt that this greater flexibility is purchased here at the expense of those common commitments that may have underpinned the protection of workers at European level. And similar defeatist or reductionist pronouncements abound in the literature.

Against the very real danger that there is no mechanism for checking the dangers of either 'race to the bottom' policies or the undesirable slippage in protection in respect of certain fundamental values, Grainne de Burca makes the important point that soft law has the potential to encourage unity, in the sense that we too have discussed it: that is, to address the tension between statements of fundamental and universal rights on the one hand and limited EC competences on the other.[62] She asks: 'Is there a way for constitu-tional values to be reflected and protected within soft law (and open method

---

[61] J Scott and D Trubek, 'Law and New Approaches to Governance in the EU' (2002) 8 Eur L J, 1 cited in G de Burca, 'The Constitutional Challenge of New Governance in the European Union' (2003) 28 ELR.

[62] ibid, 814.

of co-ordination[63]—OMC) processes, other than as flexible policy stand-ards, capable of being revised in any direction?'

Her proposal is that soft law, and OMC more generally, should be combined with the EC Charter of Fundamental Rights and that there are two ways in which this could proceed:

1. OMC processes could be used as a way of giving concrete contextual meaning to the various rights set out in the Charter. OMC could consti-tute a suitable vehicle through which the general and abstract guarantees of the Charter are given flesh in particular settings and the context of particular policies.
2. Charter rights could be used as 'ideal norms' in relation to which the outcomes of the OMC processes would be appraised, and as means of stimulating reform or revision of the standards which emerge when the outcomes are considered substantively unsatisfactory.[64]

De Burca's is a robust proposal for the constitutionalization of 'soft law' which would allow the holding up of current practices against the principles they instantiate. The generality of the principles allows the maintenance of variety at the level of concrete regulation, and their simultaneous entrench-ment by the confirmation and re-establishment of the core commitments underlying the unity of law.

Let us then reiterate both the objections to the trivialization of soft law and the necessity of the elevation and entrenchment of general principle above national regulation. As we have argued, it is one thing to acknowledge that current legal practice is (still) only an imperfect realization of its stated principles. It is quite another to rationalize bowing to corporate power in terms of a distinction between hard and soft law, or valid law and law that isn't quite that. The problem arises when these two are conflated. In turn the two arguments (i) that no instantiation ever exhausts—but inevitably falls short of—its aspiration, and (ii) that general principles make possible a

---

[63] De Burca defines the open method of co-ordination as follows: 'a strategy which leaves a considerable amount of policy autonomy to the Member States, and which normally blends the setting of guidelines or objectives at EU level with the elaboration of Member State action plans or strategy reports in an iterative process intended to bring about greater coordination and mutual learning in these policy fields. As yet, there is no one "open method", but rather a range of different kinds, all broadly sharing a number of characteristics but with variations and distinctive features according to the particular policy area'. ibid, 824. Soft law may be understood as one of the instruments associated with OMC.

[64] ibid, 833–4.

certain variety of concrete interpretations are collapsed into a quite different argument: that declaratory principles are to be contrasted with *jus cogens*. They become 'less prescriptive'; 'they fail to establish themselves as real recognised standards'; 'their aspirations have abated'.[65] But general principles are not deficient norms. They are real and they underlie real practices, validity spanning them both. If the practices don't stand up to the principles then they are mistakes. And it is the job of observers of legal practice to identify those mistakes, and the job of labour practitioners and judges to right them.

Note here another disturbing symmetry between two sets of distinctions. Built into the very idea of soft law as 'soft' is a subordination of social policy priorities to the imperatives of economic policy co-ordination. In the topography of the Community, competition is 'upstream' from welfare,[66] and there is a fear that this hierarchy may too often be mirrored in the distinction between soft and hard law. Look at some typical pronouncements: the European Social Charter 1961 failed to uphold social rights 'because it lacked enforcement mechanisms', or 'due to the reluctance of the Court to look to the interpretive standards that inform the legislation'. 'Even if construction or transport companies are exposed to cutthroat competition, for example, it is not possible according to the current interpretation of fundamental rights to define the opening-up of markets as such as an infringement of fundamental rights, even though the disruption of workplaces and workers' lives may be devastating.'[67]

What needs to remain clear is that the reference to fundamental principles of labour law as 'soft law' belies the importance of what is at stake. The validity of those principles makes them prescriptive. Their entrenchment elevates social policy priorities above economic interests. Their generality imports an important 'element of reflexivity' into the process. The operation of all law (including that of 'soft law') depends on the allocation of the code values 'legal' and 'illegal' to real situations awaiting regulation. This allocation is guided by programmes, some at quite concrete levels, some at more general levels. Of course the allocation of legality and illegality is simpler

---

[65] 'Formally, the [2000] Charter is merely a solemn proclamation by the European Parliament, Council and Commission [. . .]. It was at one point hoped that, although the instrument is not as yet legally binding, it could provide a new source of reference for the courts in the exercise of its [sic] fundamental rights jurisprudence. This aspiration has abated [. . .]'. T Novitz, 'The European Union and International Labour Standards' in Alston, see n 50 above, 228.

[66] GF Mancini, 'Labour Law and Community Law' (1985) 20 Irish Jurist, 2, 12.

[67] W Däubler, 'Instruments in EC Labour Law' in Davies, see n 48 above, 159.

when the programming is more concrete. And of course human rights, civil or social, as well as general principles, are in contrast poorly selective: their guidance value in terms of precise individual legal decisions is more limited. But at whatever level of generality programming occurs, whether through regulation, directives, statutes, or general principles, it nonetheless gains its quality as legal through its contribution in allocating, *in the last instance*, law's code values to events in the world. The danger is that in relegating these principles to 'soft law' we confuse what is poorly selective with what is invalid. Such relegation breaks the articulation of levels of legal decision making that alone makes sense of the unity of the law. Such relegation places its organizing principles outside the sphere of validity, and thus turns them into an irrelevance as mechanisms of redress in the disempowerment and dispossession suffered daily in the workplace.

5 Conclusion

Political will is required to meet the forces of global capital with international labour standards. Forging the unity of labour law at the European level is a distinct possibility, even if that political will has been absent so far. 'The problem with relying on the ILO [International Labour Organization] as the institution competent to devise and enforce these standards', writes Hugh Collins in a recent article, is that while 'it was useful for capitalist countries to assert international labour standards in their ideological battle with communism, they never intended this ideological weapon to become an effective instrument of labour legislation'.[68] We have argued instead that the recognition of these rights is part of the skeletal framework of European constitutionalism. Whether this 'represents the triumph of hope over experience' (Collins, above) depends, at one level, on how seriously we take the transformative opportunities that law itself makes available against the 'false necessity' of economic imperatives and market fundamentalism. At another level, however, this transformative opportunity is immanent, so we have argued, and a crucial corrective in restoring the rationality of a system by realigning its practices to its stated values—against the erosion of its

---

[68] Hugh Collins, 'The Future of Labour Law: liber amicorum Sir Bob Hepple QC' (2005) 68 MLR, 883.

autonomy, its subsumption under the logic of capitalism and the pathologies attendant upon the commodification of labour.

More specifically in terms of European *law*, we have put forward an argument for the unity of industrial democracy at the European level in accordance with the principles of our European constitutions. What we have argued is that unity requires us to hold our practices up to scrutiny in terms of the principles they are meant to instantiate. We have argued that there is a dialectic here that operates between setting the standards and interpreting the minimum requirements that those standards set. This distinction is similar to that between 'aspiration' and 'duty' wonderfully employed by Lon Fuller[69] to set the basis of any understanding of law which warrants the name. Unity alerts us to a crucial distinction between the limits of the tension that maintains the interplay between aspiration and standard, and the instantiations that betray the principles that underlie them.

In the former case, the tension is productive, and commands a constant attentiveness to standards that by their very nature exceed what can in each concrete case be actualized. But this is a tension that is crucially not a contradiction, such as encountered in practice in instantiations that belie the guiding principles—a contradiction which is replicated at the level of theory and redeemed through the vacuousness of social dialogue and the conflations that plague many discussions of soft law. In the latter case where instantiations belie the principles, the dialectic is broken, and with that the unity of the law goes under. And with it goes under any possibility of making sense of the law as a rational enterprise that depends for its rationality on holding together principles and their instantiations.

Of course any intelligent discussion of unity will accept that the temporal dimension makes any apparent fixity an illusion: as Edward Levi brilliantly captured it all those decades ago 'classifications change even as they [classifications] are made'.[70] Luhmann restated this in his discussion of unity, as we have seen. But just as there is a significant distinction to be drawn between relative truths and outright lies, there is also one to be drawn between (the variety of) instantiations and those that are not, because they give the lie to the principles of democratic empowerment and self-determination that undergird our legal systems, and give some hope for the redress of the manifest and latent injuries of class.

---

[69] In the first chapter of LL Fuller, *The Morality of Law* (New Haven: Yale University Press, 1978).

[70] E Levi, 'Towards a Theory of Legal Reasoning' (1934) U of Chicago L R, 503.

18

A Case of Multidirectional Constitutional Transplant in the EU: Infra-state Law and Regionalism

Joxerramon Bengoetxea

1 Introduction: state centrality and formal unity

In this chapter I would like to deal with one of the main objectives of the BU/CD project in a rather heterodox way. The hypothesis of the project is that the legal systems of the Member States enter or penetrate Community law precisely at such points where one is inclined to believe that unity is well established, a true normative *acquis*. The test ground for verification or falsification is rights and discretion, and the locus is conceptual divergence. If one finds that the same terms and notions of the treaties are being understood in different ways it might be because interpreters carry with them their own domestic legal preconceptions. My approach is slightly deviant in that I try to analyse how a constitutional feature of some Member States, that of infra-state regionalism, penetrates the EU administrative and constitutional ethos at a point which is quite unexpected: the sacrosanct principle that the Member States are the building blocks of the EU.

But, using the language of the project, my approach hinges on the formal *rights* of states under international or supra-national organization law and on States' *discretion*, meaning the constitutional autonomy to organize themselves internally as they see fit. These two principles bring unity or at least give an appearance of unity into the system—a unity without uniformity or a unity which consists in not looking into the internal structure of the Member States. Conceptual diversity originating in the interpreters' domestic preconceptions concerning infra-state governance may however play an important role in changing this appearance of unity. As a result international and supra-national organizations and their law will increasingly have to face infra-state governance, first as a matter of fact, and then as a legal challenge.

Many basic principles, perhaps the crucial constitutional principles, of the EU and the EC legal order take the Member States to be the main building blocks and the operational prerequisites of the supra-national legal system in Europe: the attribution of powers from the states to the EC (also known as the pooling of sovereignty); the representation of the Member States in the different institutions and the recognition of the legitimate defence of Member State interests in the Council, which is the legislator par excellence; the principle of state responsibility and liability (linked to the international law system based on the personality of the state), amongst others. The paradigm of this centrality is the Member States' veto right: no matter how small, a Member State can keep the whole Union on hold, in an issue requiring unanimity. This gives Union Member-Statehood a crucial formal power, which a small state could not even dream of having on its own in the international community.

Even if the Commission and the Court reintroduce supra-state[1] bureaucratic and discursive dynamics into the EU—more properly the EC system—and even if the European Parliament reintroduces a democratic or *demoicratic*[2] balance, the examples given should suffice to demonstrate the centrality of the state in any understanding of the EC, and even more so of the EU (considering the current Second and Third Pillars). The EU is altogether much more state-oriented and arguably less amenable to the strict criteria of the rule of law[3] than the EC. Statehood, and the formal sovereign equality of states is thus paradoxically reinforced by international and supranational organizations contrary to the previously dominant notion that the state is being undermined by European integration.

---

[1] The distinction first made by J Weiler, *Il sistema comunitario europeo* (Bologna: Il Mulino, 1985) has now become a classic.

[2] See S Besson and JL Martí (eds), *Deliberative Democracy and Its Discontents* (Aldershot: Ashgate 2006).

[3] See the Opinion of Advocate General Mengozzi in Case C-354/04 P *Gestoras*, Judgment of the Court of 27 February 2007, nyr and Case C-355/04 P *Segi*, Judgment of the Court of 27 February 2007, nyr, entrusting the courts of the Member States with the task of controlling the legality of acts adopted under the Third Pillar.

A corollary of the centrality of the state in the EC/EU legal system is the principle of the institutional and constitutional autonomy of the Member State. The State, regardless of its separation of powers among the state organs and its internal territorial structure and division of powers—be it centralized or federal—is responsible, as a whole, before the EC/EU. There is no requirement on the criteria that would need to be fulfilled by the Member State, besides the obligation to respect democracy, fundamental rights, and the rule of law. The form of state and the system of government is up to the Member States themselves. The regional phenomenon which has developed in federal or quasi-federal Member States and in some unitary Member States is therefore irrelevant, at least in principle, from the purely legal and constitutional perspective of European integration as it is embedded in the EC/EU. Theoretically at least, the level of governance upon which the EU is based and upon which it depends functionally is state governance. Infra-state governance may be a matter of fact, something the EU will have to *acknowledge* as a social, economic, and even political reality, but not something a Member State may be in any way *required* to integrate into its law and decision-making. Whatever relation the EC/EU might develop towards the infra-state levels of governance, it will be mediated—authorized, encouraged, and channelled—through State interlocutors.

This legal and constitutional state of affairs ensures the formal unity and equality of all Member States in the EC/EU. It is a binding unity for all legal systems, complex or simple, concrete or diverse, unicentric or polycentric. The EC/EU legal system acquires its unity by the principle that only states are represented: unity as uniformity. Uniformity is achieved not by the technique of imposing a common structure on all the Members, but by the fact that the supra-state or inter-state system will not look into the internal realities of the state and will not enquire below the state level of governance as those matters are left for the state legal system to determine. It is a form of non-interference with the formal sovereignty of the Member States, and it is this *blindness* to internal issues which predetermines a particular version of formal unity and equality, which the EU system shares with public international law.

The reality of infra-state entities producing law and having their status constitutionally enshrined in (some) Member State legal systems is itself a phenomenon which has had, still has, and will increasingly have a direct influence on the EC/EU as a system of governance through both law and policy. It will also have an indirect influence on the laws and policies of those Member

States where infra-state governance is limited to the municipal level and which do not constitutionally recognize, or have not until now recognized, the relevance of the regional dimension, above the local but below the state level. The uncomfortable question for the supra-state legal system of the EC/EU is how long it can postpone reckoning with this infra-state reality.

But the ensuing question, equally uncomfortable, is what happens when the very Member States present this infra-state governance level as a player that must interevene at the supra-state level, and when the EC institutions start dealing with the regions in order to ensure the effectiveness of EC law and policies, to ensure the functionality of integration. This is where a new challenge to an imaginary unity can obtain: in this process the principle which has been securing a formal unity of Member States, the institutional autonomy of the Member States, is not deleted, but it is transformed. The process of reversal and thus, of awareness to regional diversity, will be illustrated at the end of the chapter with a comment on a recent case in which the ECJ developed a theoretical framework for assimilating infra-state law adopted by constitutional regions and integrating it into the EC legal order. This is the *Azores* case[4] in the area of state aid and direct taxation.

By infra-state I mean the level of governance which is immediately below the state but above municipal governance. The term 'sub-state' or sometimes 'sub-national' is often used as well and I take it to be a synonym of infra-state, but my preference for this latter term is meant to match the use of the term 'supra-state' or 'supra-national' sometimes used to refer to levels of governance like the EU. We would therefore have infra-state or sub-national levels, the Member State or national level, the inter-state or international level, and the supra-state or supra-national levels. By infra-state *law* I mean public or private law made by the regions or even a specific regional legal order, different from that of the Member State, although constitutionally integrated in the Member State.[5] Just as the supra-state entity which is the EU makes law and designs policies according to its competences, so do the infra-state systems of governance and for that matter, the Member States. I shall try to explain the different expressions of these dynamics. Infra-state legal systems are a reality which simply cannot be ignored.

---

[4] Case C-88/03 *Portugal v Commission*, Judgment of the Court of 6 September 2006, nyr.

[5] The Azores judgment, analysed at the end of this essay, also opts for the term 'infra-state' and states some of the features of infra-state entities.

2 Multidirectional transplants

The EU is an interesting experiment in multi-level governance. Most of the instruments and techniques in this art of governance are legal norms, to the extent that the process of European integration has been, to a large degree, a legal integration—an economic integration through law. The subject was economics and the market, but the mechanisms were legal. A new legal order was created. It was to be expected, and it was sensible to expect that this legal order would receive important influences and direct legal transplants[6] from the legal cultures and systems of the Member States: the Treaty negotiators of the original Member States carried with them a whole code of legal concepts, sometimes visible and sometimes implicit in their legal cultures.

However, when one first approaches EC law and the Treaties, it is difficult to provide a list of conceptual links with national legal systems. Perhaps EC law was meant to be a new legal order and coinages of legal concepts in domestic traditions were seen as prejudicial to the necessary autonomous character of the concepts of EC law. If EC law was seen to be conceptually linked to a particular legal system, this would pose the threat of also linking it dogmatically to all the doctrine developed in the given domestic system around the legal concept in question. This again would pose the threat of extending those dogmatics to other domestic systems through the backdoor, without them having agreed to the terms. It was better then to avoid national interpretations of commonly agreed norms.

Another possible explanation for the lack of a clear genealogy of domestic concepts in EC law is that it is a law of economic freedoms. Dismantling regulative barriers to free movement of the main factors of economic activity—workers, goods, capital, companies—and ensuring fair conditions of competition and free trade were the leitmotiv of integration, and the generally shared leap of faith behind economic de facto solidarity was that this would contribute to peace. In a sense it was a new area for all Member States. The new approach was a strange mix of centralization and deregulation: Member States would lose their power to regulate the economy and the market to the centre, to Brussels,[7] but what Brussels ultimately required was to remove restrictions and to control the process. The state intervention

---

[6] On this concept see generally D Nelken and J Feest (eds), *Adapting Legal Cultures* (Oxford: Hart, 2001).

[7] See C Barnard, *The Substantive Law of the EU: The Four Freedoms* (Oxford: Oxford University Press, 2004).

in the economy had led to a frenzy of regulatory intervention in the economy and the market which originated in economic administrative law, but the new approach was one of structured deregulation. The EEC Treaty was almost self-sufficient in this sense. It was primarily a programme for removing barriers, and only secondarily a programme to introduce new common rules, and that is probably why little additional regulation or secondary legislation was needed in order to bring forward the teleology of eliminating barriers, something the Court of Justice did with relative ease in a dynamic and purposeful interpretation.[8] That the EC legal system ended up in a similar regulatory fever is arguably an inevitable consequence of any legal approach to the market and the economy. It is also due to the dominant regulatory culture which Community law and policy makers brought with them from their national legal cultures.[9] The attempt to reverse this second aspect has culminated in the new governance culture and the Lisbon Agenda.

Against very sensible expectations then, EC law neither clearly, nor openly, contains domestic transplants. It presents itself as an autonomous legal order—a law with its own language. What really came as a surprise was the opposite phenomenon— transplants moving from EC law to domestic legal systems. Indeed, it is surprising that it should be the newly created Community law and its concepts that should end up exerting an important influence on domestic laws, legal systems, and cultures. Such transplants are now part and parcel of the theoretical training in domestic law. These include direct effect, direct applicability, Member State liability for breaches of Community law (even domestic judicial liability for wrongful applications of EC law), provision of interim measures where rights might be in jeopardy, limits to procedural autonomy—like the duty to raise, ex officio, issues of EC law—institutional autonomy, equal pay for equal work, and competition law. They are not all regulated in the same way. Some of them have entered domestic legal orders through EC law. Some of these top-down influences might themselves be the result of the initial influence of a particular domestic law on EC law, which is then exported to other domestic systems. In fields such as

---

[8] This is one of the main points of my book *The Legal Reasoning of the European Court of Justice* (Oxford: Oxford University Press, 1993).

[9] See, in this sense, D La Rocca (ed), *Diritti e società di mercato nella scienza giuridica europea* (Torino: G. Giappichelli Editore, 2006). See also A von Bogdandy, 'The Contours of Integrated Europe: The Origin, Status and Prospects of European Integration' (1993) 25 *Futures*, 22–31.

transparency and environmental law or in areas such as anti-discrimination law, these multidirectional dynamics are quite notable.[10]

One such type of multidirectional transplant is regionalism. The regional transplant originates in domestic legal systems, or rather in some of the constitutions of the original Member States and those of the Member States that later joined the EC, as well as in the constitutional evolution of some Member States, original or adhered. Only a few Member States have decentralized regional systems: Germany, Belgium, and Italy make up half of the original Member States. Adding Spain and Austria makes one-third of the EU-15, and with the post-devolution UK, just over one-third, but slightly over a fifth of the current EU-25 (or EU-27). The others are unitary states, with a greater or weaker degree of local or municipal autonomy. The tendency is clearly one of diminishing representation, accentuated of course with the enlargement to Bulgaria and Romania, the EU-27. True, soft forms of regionalism exist in other Member States, but it is precisely this political phenomenon of new softer forms developing in formally unitary states that can be telling from the point of view of decentralized Member State constitutional influence on the EU and subsequently on unitary Member State constitutional systems.

It is quite striking that this phenomenon should have taken place at all when one considers, as it is generally considered, that the EU suffers from regional blindness[11] and that the dynamics of pre-subsidiarity integration are quite centripetal.[12] This means that the internal organization of a Member State—its unitary, federal, or decentralized structure—is insignificant to the EU. It is the Member State as a whole that is responsible for the observance of Community law and obligations, and it is the Member State as a totality that participates in the constitutional make-up of the EU. At least not officially, there is no third gender after the EU and the Member State.

The EU has nevertheless developed a special type of *regional* policy. This has been primarily motivated by economic reasons, more precisely for reasons of macro-economic governance. Two streams contribute to the

---

[10] See the interesting discussion of certain general legal principles 'travelling' both sides in X Groussot, *The General Principles of Community Law* (Groningen: Europa Law Publishing, 2006).

[11] See S Weatherill, 'The Challenge of the Regional Dimension in the European Union' in S Weatherill and U Bernitz (eds), *The Role of Regions and Sub-national Actors in Europe* (Oxford: Hart, 2005) 1–32.

[12] See W Wallace (ed), *The Dynamics of European Integration* (London: Pinter, 1990).

regional drive of the EU: cohesion policy and the constitutional recognition of the regions, implicit in the principle of subsidiarity and explicit in the Committee of the Regions (CoR). The EC first and the EU later have developed a policy to reduce disparities and to promote greater economic, social, and territorial cohesion. This ultimately links together the aims of creating an integrated well-operating market, reducing the gaps in income between rich and poor, the creation of new opportunities in innovative activities, and the establishment of networks linking regions, businesses, and people across the continent. This requires eliminating or at least reducing the following structural deficiencies in key factors of competitiveness: inadequate endowment of physical and human capital (of infrastructure and workforce skills), lack of innovative capacity, lack of effective business support, and low level of environmental capital (a blighted natural and/or urban environment). Countries and regions need assistance in overcoming these structural deficiencies and in developing their comparative advantages in order to be able to compete both in the internal market and outside. Equally, people need to be able to access education and training in order to develop their capabilities wherever they live, and this requires a territorial or regional policy. The EU cohesion policy was strengthened some fifteen years ago when the single market project was initiated precisely to meet these parallel needs. Such assistance is even more important now in the face of the widening of disparities which enlargement entails.[13]

On the other hand, the CoR was created in the Treaty of Maastricht to represent the regions of the Member States as a consultative organ. Not all Member States have regions. The Committee also represents cities from all Member States, a fact which could be interpreted as a weakening, rather than a strengthening, of the regional phenomenon, now watered down with municipalities. It is not easy to say how this organ will evolve in the constitutional future of the EU, given the weak emphasis on regionalism in the new Member States. In any case, some regions, the so-called legislative regions or REGLEGS, have made a call for this organ to be involved in the EC lawmaking process.[14] This could parallel the evolution of the lawmaking powers of the European Parliament, from consultation to co-decision.

---

[13] European Commission, 'A New Partnership for Cohesion Convergence Competitiveness Cooperation, Third Report on Economic and Social Cohesion' (Luxembourg: Office for Official Publications, 2004).

[14] J Nergelius, 'The Committee of the Regions Today and in the Future: A Critical Overview' in Weatherill and Bernitz, see n 11 above, 119–129.

Another possible evolution of the CoR is to recognize some legal force to agreements reached by the REGLEGs, a parallelism from the social dialogue, since, according to EC Treaty, Article 139:

should management and labour so desire, the dialogue between them at Community level may lead to contractual relations, including agreements [...] [which] shall be implemented either in accordance with the procedures and practices specific to management and labour and the Member States or at the joint request of the signatory parties, by a Council decision on a proposal from the Commission.

It could be envisaged that agreements adopted by the REGLEGS at the CoR, or outwith its specific procedures, be given special consideration by the Commission in a proposal for a Council decision, but this is a very unlikely hypothesis.

The Economic and Social Committee, often referred to as ECOSOC, has been in existence since the creation of the EEC and has contributed in many ways to the development of EC law and to its greater sensibility to issues of social and industrial relations. In addition to this sensibility a great constitutional leap forward was made when the Social Dialogue was recognized as a source of lawmaking within the EU. This was not located in the context of ECOSOC, but rather as an autonomous source of law in the social provisions of the Treaty, under Title XI, reflecting the social heteronomy of EC law. This constitutional formula giving legal force to collective agreements originating in industrial relations is a process that has probably been imported from the legal culture of some Member States, another interesting case of legal transplant. What is yet to be seen is whether the EU will see a development of regional law, supported by the Committee of the Regions but not generated by it, similar to the recognition of the lawmaking power of the social actors through social dialogue, supported but not generated by the ECOSOC and by the CoR.

Finally, *subsidiarity* was introduced in Maastricht as a constitutional principle to govern the relationships between the EC and the Member States in cases of shared or mixed competences. It was not explicitly meant to transcend the level of the central governments and penetrate the regional question in decentralized states. Some Member States—Germany, Austria, and Belgium—in fact interpreted the principle that way and even made a joint declaration attached to the Treaty of Amsterdam to the effect that they understood subsidiarity as a principle which decided which level should act and with what intensity in situations of shared competence between not two but three levels: the EU, the State, and the region. And this descending interpretation of subsidiarity prevails nowadays, especially after the debates in the Convention on the Future of Europe and the Protocol on Subsidiarity of the Treaty establishing a Constitution for Europe, with its important alert mechanism which can, arguably, already operate as a matter of practice.[15]

So, perhaps after all, for all its blindness, the EU does have a *regional vision*. This vision is being reinforced by many dynamics originating with different actors and stakeholders, some private, some public. Among these are the regions, and the constitutional regions are becoming new actors in the dynamics of integration. It might be interesting to analyse the role of these regions and the specific mode of governance they involve more closely in order to detect possible trends of conceptual divergence.

2.1 *Infra-state or regional governance*

We have explained top-down dynamics where domestic legal orders and constitutional systems are influenced by constitutional developments at the EU level, or by recognitions of institutions or specificities of some but not all of the existing Member States. We have also explained side-to-side dynamics where developments of one particular EC or EU institution influence other institutions at the same level, or where institutions or specific institutional arrangements at the domestic level inspire those in a different Member State. The top-down and side-to-side dynamics interact with other less institution-alized dynamics arising from sub-state or infra-state actors and from citizens and economic actors. Networks of regions sharing best practice in law and policy making are examples to the point and these are flourishing in differ-ent areas: employment, social policy, education, environment, transport, and urban planning. All these dynamics create a competing logic of change at all levels of governance. At the sub-state level they are sometimes referred to as 'regional governance'.[16] Different actors are defending different interests and sometimes clashing and competing with other actors at higher or lower levels on grounds of competence, definition of basic standards, and access to resources. Until not so long ago in the history of European integration, these competing dynamics obtained between actors located at the same level, ie between states. After the creation of the EC, they also developed between the state-national and the supra-national level. But this seems to

---

[15] F Morata, 'Subsidiariedad, regiones y Unión Europea' (2006) *Cuadernos Europeos de Deusto*, 73–94.

[16] A Rojo Salgado, 'La importancia de la dimensión regional para la buena gobernanza europea' (2006) *Cuadernos Europeos de Deusto*, 119–142.

be the very story of European integration: until now it has been possible to find compromises between these dynamics involving one or two levels. The new dynamics involve actors at more than two different levels with the result that new alliances can develop between the actors: sometimes regions might reinforce the claims and arguments of the supranational institution; sometimes regions compete between themselves; at other times regions and states might join forces against the Commission; and on other occasions still regions might be alone in defending certain interests against the state and the supra-national institutions. These dynamics will become even more complex when we introduce new, non-institutional actors such as NGOs, corporations, political groupings, financial interests, social actors.

The quest for coherence at all the levels of governance in order to ensure minimum legitimacy before the electorates leads to a quest for political and constitutional principles that can be flexible enough to be invoked by all actors at all levels while at the same time keeping some interpretative value. 'Subsidiarity'—a term which seems to encompass proportionality and decentralization—is one of these priciples. 'Community loyalty' is another, not unrelated to cooperation or co-ordination and with clear federal affiliation in the German *Bundestreue* principle. Together with these formal principles, two substantive sets of principles giving coherence and vision to the European project are 'the Lisbon Agenda'[17] and above all, the shared culture of 'fundamental rights', domestic genealogy. The latter is even becoming the most important coherence-seeking principle.

2.2 *Processes of change and complex dynamics*

There are many processes of change in the EU at all levels—institutional, economic and social policy, and constitutional, as well as at the international and globalization level. The EU tries to be an influential actor in all these processes and strives to generate synergies with its component entities, ie the Member States, but also with other actors and stakeholders. It is guided by a general maxim: whatever internal competition or struggle there may be to accessing power and spheres of influence, the end result should not be a decrease in the general power and influence of the EU as a whole: they should be Pareto efficient. Processes of change, as well as the polit- ical and constitutional dynamics guided by formal and material coherence

---

[17] J de Miguel Barcena, 'La dimensión institucional y democrática de la gobernanza económica europea: el Método Abierto de Coordinación' (2006) *Cuadernos Europeos de Deusto*, 23–42.

principles like the ones mentioned above can contribute to the legitimacy of the EU's effort to seek influence over the citizens of Europe, and perhaps even globally.

Until now these processes have been viewed as Europeanization but they have only been analysed at the national Member State level. The regional level was neglected in political maps of Europe; consequently, the regions asked to be part of the picture, in line with their relevance on the physical maps. Indeed, they are relevant because they are the component entities of the federal or decentralized Member States themselves, and because in the satellite view of the world, which puts physical and political maps in perspective, interregional cooperation could become a new transnational or supranational dynamics in the context of globalization. The regions are also relevant because of geopolitics, ethno-national conflicts in the EU and in Europe as a whole. European Frontiers are an increasingly important phenomenon that capture the attention of the EU, which may then become a potential actor in the resolution of conflict.[18]

These new inter-regional dynamics may contribute to the good governance of the EU meta-state entity, not only from an economic standpoint but also from the point of view of sustainable development, geographical (and geopolitical), cultural-educational, and social perspectives. But at the same time other processes may be neglected, for example local actors (cities and territories) or actors affected by deregulation and privatization. Europeanization is not the only ongoing process, and we need to look at different types of maps. These different maps and dynamics will be captured, somewhat superficially, in section 3.

It is revealing to analyse the specific geography of regional actors and their contribution to the process of integration. There are seventy-four legislative regions, known as REGLEGs, in the EU: these made up 56 per cent of the EU-15 but now make up only 43 per cent of the EU-25, even less of the EU-27. Their views are very strongly articulated in the constitutional debate in the Convention and in the Inter Governmental Conference (IGC). REGLEGs have focused on government and competences whereas non-REGLEGs, purely administrative divisions of a Member State into regions, and NUTS (Nomenclature of Units for Territorial Statistics) have

---

[18] On this topic, I have been inspired by Igor Filibi's doctoral thesis at the University of the Basque Country, 'La Unión política como marco de resolución de los conflictos etnonacionales europeos: un enfoque comparado' (2004). See also, by the same author, 'Nuevas escalas: retos conceptuales y políticos para la construcción de una democracia europea' (2006) *Cuadernos Europeos de Deusto*, 43–72.

focused on non-hierarchical network governance and structural funds. They can operate visibly and effectively at a level below the central governments, and sometimes purely statistical regions may be created simply for the purpose of benefiting from Structural Funds (the NUTS politics). Since EU enlargement to the east, the REGLEGs have become a more marginal phenomenon, but it is not impossible that a new version of non-REGLEG regionalism might arise in large Member States with a complex social fabric, territorial-ethnic diversity, and pronounced centralization. Combine all these in the Committee of the Regions, add some cities or macropolises, and what you get is a hodge-podge of differing interests and agendas, hard to comprehend and even harder to manage. The result is that the Committee of the Regions has become an unmanageable body, whether or not this was the original intention behind its creation in the Maastricht Treaty, its enormous complexity and diversity have become an easy excuse to deny regional claims at the constitutional level and to prevent regional initiative in EU constitutionalism.

The issues raised by the regional actors are manifold and only a selection will be analysed here. Regional interests vary greatly from one region to another and drawing generalizations beyond the institutional claims made by new actors like the REGLEGs is very difficult. I propose to take a look at one specific case—the Spanish—to see the complex dynamics of change taking place in the global European context.

In fact one should speak of this example in the plural because there are many different possible models in Spain: the Catalan model (symmetric, enhanced devolved powers); the Basque model (asymmetric, free association with the state); the Socialist Party model (symmetric, quasi-federal, with enhanced participation of the regions in European affairs); the United Left model (federal, with redistributive solidarity mechanisms at state-national level), and the Popular Party model (restrained devolution, recapturing powers for the centre, no regional participation in Europe, no external action for the regions). They are all competing in the ongoing discussions on the reform processes of the Statutes of Autonomy and the Spanish Constitution, a legal and political phenomenon which is closely linked to the wider European constitutional debate. The reform of the Statutes and of the Constitution are part of the process of relocation of states and infra-state entities in the new polycentric map of Europe and in the new global context of network governance.[19]

---

[19]   Compare in this sense two policy papers: European Commission, 'European Governance, a White Paper' COM (2001) 428 and Catalan Government paper, 'Governance for Sustainable Development in Catalonia: Concepts, institutional requirements and analytic elements' 2002, at <http://www.gencat.cat>, a pioneer at the Spanish level.

3 Regional dynamics in the EU

Initially, at their creation, the dynamics or processes of European integra-
tion were two-dimensional: there was the Community or the Union, and the
Member States. In this extreme simplification a major sub-state actor, the
regions, were forgotten or neglected and; the democratic legitimacy question was neglected. The Communities were to be run by governments in
Council and by a bureaucracy, the Commission, modelled upon the High
Authority of the European Coal and Steel Community (ECSC). A Court of
Justice would supervise the legality of administrative action, a process that
was really parallel to state intervention in the economy. Parliament was only
consulted. Integration was to take place in the free movement of the factors
of economic activity, and through the creation of an integrated free trade
area with a customs union and with uniform or harmonized rules on goods
and services.

The functionalist inspiration behind this economic model of integration
was put into practice relatively successfully and the spill-over effect of
integration affected new areas of regulatory activity: social, educational,
environmental, energy, financial, fiscal—practically all spheres of government, even those, like the criminal justice system or military administration which were thought to be immune to integration. The expansion into
new areas meant that the legal map of Europe was effectively taking over
the maps of the individual Member States. The influence of the EU was
seen everywhere: EC law entered areas of domestic law that had hitherto
sheltered in *legal bunkers,* and the EC became a presence in distant conti-
nents through aid projects, cooperation, and 'diplomatic' missions. The
institutional architecture and governance culture of the EC/EU adapted
accordingly. The resulting picture is one is which it is no longer easy to see
what matters are clearly the competence of the Member States and which
are clearly the competence of the EC. Consider an issue such as agriculture
and forestry: to what extent can a provincial parliament (a region within a
region within a state within the EC) adopt laws that affect the management
and demarcation of forests, their public use and economic exploitation, their
contribution to landscaping and heritage, or the public rights of servitude,
exploitation, and passage? Could one envisage the nightmare of a Common
Mushroom Policy developing in the EU and affecting those rights? A comparable situation has clearly already been developed as regards the fruits
of the sea.

If you add to this blurring of the map the fact that some Member States have federal or decentralized structures, then the complication is multiplied: decisions are being made at three different levels at least—infra-state, state, and supra-state—and sometimes they are being made on the same subject matter, eg, employment policy, social inclusion and protection, or education policy, but with varying degrees of normative intensity. Sometimes the EU recommends, sometimes it harmonizes via shared objectives, sometimes it dictates concrete norms. Sometimes the states implement, sometimes they execute, sometimes they dictate their own norms. The regions do likewise. Intergovernmental arrangements and the open method of co-ordination (OMC) have not helped to clarify the picture; in fact, they pose a challenge and threat of pre-emption in areas of infra-state competence in decentralized states. Areas of regional competence are thus being decided at the EU level by Commission initiatives, Council guidelines, and soft law. The discussion at Council level is rather opaque but the diffusion of procedural commitments to transparency and participation in EU networked governance has stimulated demands to widen the circle of actors involved in policy making at the European level.[20]

Achieving this result requires the use of principles that will reintroduce coherence and clarity. Enter the principles of subsidiarity and proportionality, the principle of cooperation, and the clear distribution of competences (who does how much of what). Four comments will be made about the principles that help us draw the political map.

(1) Seeing the distribution of competences as a zero sum is a defensive strategy that brings about a risk of confrontation and perhaps the loss of efficiency especially where party politics favour confrontation and competence becomes an instrument or an excuse for political cleavage or, worse, partisan struggle for power. The Catalan discussion around the new Autonomy Statute, finally adopted in 2006, has tabled proposals of water-tight or water-proof competences, ie a clear definition of exclusive legislative, regulatory, and executive competences, of shared competences and of executive competences. Some shared competences are being classified into sub-areas in order to draft who does what. The aim is to prevent their pre-emption by the so-called basic law common to all of Spain and to prevent the intervention of State administration in the execution of 'horizontal' competences like

---

[20] See CF Sabel and J Zeitlin, 'Learning from Difference: The New Architecture of Experimental Governance in the European Union', presented at the Arena seminar, University of Oslo, 2006.

general economic organization, guarantees of equality, prerogatives of *fomento*, or economic support. This confrontational approach to the distribution of competences as zero sums might be useful to clarify the picture, but with regard to shared competences it requires perfect co-ordination. It is also a system which is likely to involve and possibly erode an umpire such as a Federal Constitutional Court which will be expected to solve disputes and which will be called upon by infra-state, state, and supra-state entities alike in order to preserve their prerogatives.

(2) Sometimes the principle of equality is understood in a Cartesian way as though it necessarily means uniformity: ie that all infra-state entities should have exactly the same level of competence and the same capacities in their execution and design. This has become almost an ideology which is at odds with asymmetric federalism. In my view, this approach is flawed. All the component entities need not assume the same level of competence; the will and the technical and economic capacity to assume a given level of power should also count. A Member State may be particularly interested in assuming competence over fishing and co-ordinating this activity with other Member States. Another Member State, for example Luxembourg, will have no interest in fishing policy. An infra-state entity such as the Basque Country will have a clear interest and capacity whereas La Rioja may not, so why impose uniformity? The traditional Cartesian approach of the EC/EU has been linked to the principle of equality of Member States, but although this does simplify the constitutional political map, it completely disregards the geographical and socio-economic, even the cultural, maps: it imposes uniformity where there is diversity. This gives us asymmetric federalism at the internal Member State level or variable geometry at EU level, but it also gives new meaning to the second condition of subsidiarity, ie the added value of acting at a higher level. Subsidiarity may be one of those concepts that ensures unity precisely because it can accommodate complexity. The concept of equality in EC law may actually be transforming under the impact of uniformity and of diversity.

The first criterion of subsidiarity is to make decisions and act on them on a level as close as possible to the citizens as long as there is the capacity to act realistically and efficiently. It requires the will and the capacity to exercise competences. Capacity building may become a new criterion of subsidiarity or a new reading of efficiency. If a lower level lacks the capacity to carry out a competence then a higher level will act, but if the lower level is not given the funds to do so, then the higher level can retain the competence, which is what happens in the case of the debate on *transferencias* or devolution of powers.

Where a level has the competence but lacks the capacity and the resources, the higher level might be tempted to take over from the lower one. But what if the higher level has provoked this situation by reserving the resources, the know-how, the capacity, the information and statistics, or the level of interlocution and negotiation with other stakeholders? Is competence a discourse for protecting power or hiding power relations? These dynamics will probably not be mirrored in the EU as long as the resources it has are as scant as they currently are, but they may contribute to reinforcing its role as a policy booster: if the EC has few and limited resources, it might be tempted to develop a policy co-ordinating role, telling those who have the resources how they should use or not use them. The EC's general orientations on political economy and the OMC co–ordination can be understood in this way.

(3) The resulting picture is one of a polycentric Europe: there is no single centre but many capitals, many decision-making centres, which will need to be co-ordinated: 'Europe, in the process of polycentric symbiosis represents both the probability of national *decentrism* and the indispensability of heterogeneous rationalities of multiple political cultures.'[21] The previous discussion shows how important loyalty and cooperation have become.

It will be necessary to create a feeling of belonging to the same project, a sense of belonging to the polis of Europe, if there is going to be coherence amongst all the capitals. The Commission and the European Council probably sensed this need when the OMC[22] was launched, around the Lisbon objectives, as the new mantra of the EU cosmogony. OMC is really a co-ordination of Member State capitals, with assistance from the Commission, turned think-tank, but produces no binding norms, is accountable to nobody, and is immune to judicial control of legality. Regional actors and other public and private stakeholders are excluded from the process of co–ordination.

(4) But where do the citizens join in this picture? All this seems to be a discourse on enlightened governance—all for the citizen but without the citizen. Yet the citizen may after all be best represented through representative and deliberative democracy, rather than through diluted participation of the governance type. Citizens may be better served through norms that recognize enforceable rights than by policy desiderata embodied in soft law that judges

---

[21] Von Bogdandy, see n 9 above, 27.
[22] DM Trubek and LG Trubek, 'Hard and Soft Law in the Construction of Social Europe: The Open Method of Coordination' (2005) 11 Eur LJ, 343.

have no jurisdiction to review. Contrary to the classic interpretation of some of the principles of international law, in which States are the only legal subject, the Community specifically makes a place for the individuals who are actors in the common market by allowing them either direct (albeit still limited) access to Community judges or the option of invoking Community law before a national judge. The law is thus an effective weapon in the hands of private individuals,[23] considerably more so than policy.

When we complement the constitutional map with richer information like physical maps, tourist sites, and landscaping, economic, historic, climate dynamics, etc, and when we introduce other sub-state actors, and other players or stakeholders such as NGOs, trades unions, lobbies, territorial interest groups, and local authorities, we obtain even more complexity. 'The connection between national territory and political rule, along with the organizational principle of the sovereign nation-state—the dominant form of societal coexistence throughout the world—has been overcome.'[24] The new governance culture is said to have been conceived precisely for this type of multi-layered, polycentric entity based on the network and cybernetic models. Governance is a three-dimensional craft;

1. On the vertical dimension we find cooperation between administrations— supra-state, state, and infra-state (regions and cities)—and this takes us to multi-level governance. The way to monitor this governance is through a cooperational division or distribution or sharing of competences, through tripartite contracts, or by giving institutional support to the voice of the infra-state entities in the Community method, and making sure that the Court of Justice or another body invested with authority safeguards the prerogatives of all levels, including individual constitutional regions and the Committee of the Regions.

2. On the horizontal dimension we find cooperation between players located at the same level: inter-regional cooperation, inter-governmental cooperation, cooperation with other international organizations. An interesting dynamic may take place in relation to inter-regional cooperation. The EU is fostering this type of cooperation and encouraging agreements and factual solidarities between regions in different Member States. But the political culture in some Member States, and the constitutions of some

---

[23] JP Jacqué, 'Le rôle du droit dans l'intégration européenne' (1991) *Philosophie Politique*, 119–123.

[24] Von Bogdandy, see n 9 above.

of these, such as Spain, go against inter-regional cooperation within the State, on the argument that this would jeopardize internal coherence and equality, again understood as uniformity.

3. There is a third dimension which we could call inclusive or participatory governance. It is a matter of scale, degree, of intensity: how much intervention by binding law, how much recommendation and steering through soft law; how much de-regulation, etc. This is largely an ideological debate but it does require an enquiry into, and an identification of, existing forces' interests, and pressures, as well as the possibilities of action at legal level and repercussions of proposed actions within the normative sub-systems and their related sub-systems is turn. Inclusive regional, state, and supra-state governance looks at the multiplicity of stakeholders that can be involved in law and policy making, at processes of consultation, elaboration, implementation, application, and decision making, and at evaluation. The way to organize this is through notions of responsibility, legal and political accountability, access to relevant information and transparency, and possibility of control.

The notion of sub-state or infra-state actors does not take into account the full complexity of the governance picture: what about multinational companies or major investment groups, multinational mafias or organized crime, and fanatic movements? How does our supra-state/Member State/ infra-state map help us place these other real actors? How can the citizen control all these processes; and who is going to rescue the citizen? For the moment all that we have seems to be representative democracy—no equivalent interpretation of democracy has been devised for this new culture of governance. And this concept of governance will very likely be interpreted in different ways in the different administrative cultures of the EU. Is the citizen going to be empowered through these processes? What instruments does the citizen have to control the processes of change in governance? Furthermore, this projected move is not free of drawbacks: non-citizens could be completely forgotten. The prospect of protecting citizens and individuals by means of the Charter of Fundamental Rights was appealing. Now it awaits the courage of the European Council.[25]

---

[25] On the issues raised by this new governance culture, see G de Burca and J Scott (eds), *Law and New Approaches to Governance in the European Union and the United States* (Oxford: Hart, 2006).

4 The special case in the EU: the REGLEGs

Even the EU recognizes special cases and exceptions to uniformity and Member State equality, as exemplified in the case of the euro, the Schengen Accord, the social policy opt-out, the special protocols. These are often referred to as variable geometry or multiple speed integration, or enhanced or reinforced cooperation. The challenge for EU constitutional thinking is to what extent and in what way the EU can accommodate diversity and special cases within Member States: many of the isles (overseas territories or internal like Åaland), Scotland and its legal system, special provisions for East Germany, the special case of Northern Ireland, and many others. The principle of reality is powerful and unity-seeking solutions will eventually have to take it into account. They will do so most successfully by shying away from the notion of unity as uniformity and respecting the constitutional logo: united in diversity.

As we have seen, the principles are there to turn the EU into a coherent entity and bring a new unity—call it Community, meta-state, or federal union—an evolved form of statehood, unique in its own way but also leading the way for regionalization in our multilateral global world. If it has not yet developed fully in this direction this is simply because it lacks the unanimous will to do so. The following issue will inevitably arise: what if some European states wish to go further and move towards something that looks very much like a United States of Europe? What will be left of the federated Member States that make it up; and what of the nation–regions that make up those Member States?

We should not lose sight of the economic factors behind Europeanization and regionalization. Different actors may be protecting different interests and markets such as those of the mass media, trades unions, and industry. They are turned into stakeholders and become learning organizations in this complex picture of network governance. The processes of change that affect them and those that affect infra-state, state, and supra-state entities will result in new political maps we cannot properly anticipate. But if the guiding principles are clear and if they are generally shared, and especially if we insist on the protection of fundamental rights (liberal-political, socio-economic, environmental, educational) we can be assured that the end result will contribute to the legitimacy of the project.

Nations are projects in development; some are well established and still have formal hold of the machinery of the state, others are in the making and belong to multinational states. In some nations, institutions and consti-tutional arrangements will be paramount in driving the change; in others it will be a consociational or a cooperative network of stakeholders and polit-ical, cultural, and economic actors. In some nations, the top-down approach will gain ground whereas in others civil society will set the pace for political drive. What seems clear to me is that all entities in this polycentric picture will learn from the new governance culture and from its interaction with law. If they refuse to learn, they may be tempted to resort to the cosiness of national discourse, closing in on themselves and possibly blaming every-body else for whatever goes wrong with their national values.

If the EU comes to be seen as a project for the rebuilding of nation–statehood or for national liberation, this will be an indication that the dynamics mentioned in section 3 have not been grasped or understood or that they have been manipulated. Domestic constitutional orders may wish to protect internal or national identity and insist on respect for institutional autonomy. But the challenges of globalization, and the real erosion of state power and factual sovereignty will bring a plethora of social, economic, and political issues knocking on their doors, demanding solutions: talk of national constitutional identity will be little help.

Likewise, if the supra-state officials and intelligentsia think that regions and infra-state entities may be neglected, or if they consider that they may become allies in their dialectic tension with the Member States, they are clearly wrong. The legislative regions may very well feel that the European-ization of competences may disempower them. They may as a result favour a confrontational approach to the distribution of competences, access to the Court of Justice to protect them, and even re-nationalizing some EU competences rather than an approach based on additionality (subsidiarity) and partnership or cooperation. The REGLEGs will need to react with vision and intelligence. The new network culture of three-dimensional governance, which they despise, might come in handy after all.

As for the Commission, it seems interested in consultation with all sub-state actors and sees the Committee of the Regions as the proper organ for such consultation. It has so far expressed no *souci* or worries about its composition or its representative value. Even if this organ eventually intervenes in the legis-lative process and in policy making, it is still unlikely that the Commission will start questioning its composition. EC Treaty, Article 263 is too naive in its composition to introduce the concept that its members will either hold a mandate or be accountable to an elected assembly, and in any case the alternate members seem to be under no such representative requirement.

To my knowledge, no serious enquiry has been made to make sure this is the case, and the democratic deficit of this institution goes unnoticed.

There is little left of the third-level optimism which characterized the Lamassoure proposal for special status for the REGLEGs, the special case in the EU. Perhaps the regions share a perception of loss of control and power over decision making and citizen control, and linked with this a perception of a loss of identity and security in relation to the crisis of the welfare state and the loss of power of representative and democratic institutions to other less accountable agencies. We are back again to the need for coherent principles that give us a renewed vision we can all share. The integration of the regional dimension in EU politics and in the governance culture may contribute to the quest for this binding unity of diverse entities.

As for the Court of Justice, there are some signals that a positive evolution might be taking place. I am referring to the recent recognition of the REGLEG reality by the Court of Justice in its judgment of 6 September 2006 in the *Azores* case, C-88/03 *Portugal v Commission*. I shall briefly summarize the case and analyse the contribution of the Court on the issue of regionalism.

In 1999, the legislative body of the Azores Region adopted detailed rules for the adaptation of the national tax system to regional particularities, in accordance with powers which were devolved to it in that matter. Those rules included a reduction in the rate of income and corporation tax which applies automatically to all economic operators and which is designed specifically to enable undertakings established in the Azores Region to overcome the structural handicaps resulting from their location in an isolated region on the periphery of the Community. That tax scheme was notified late to the Commission and entered into force without authorization. The Commission decided that the measures constituted operating aid which could be authorized only if, in accordance with the Guidelines on national regional aid, they were justified by their contribution to regional development and were proportional to the additional costs they were intended to offset. The conditions were not fulfilled in the case of undertakings providing financial services to other undertakings of the same type, as such activities did not contribute sufficiently to regional development. Portugal challenged the classification of the measures concerned as state aid. The debate before the Court turned largely around both the issue of selectivity as favouring certain undertakings or the production of certain goods, and the extent regional measures should be considered as selective in relation to wider national measures.

What is interesting for current purposes is the Court's analysis of regional legislators. The Court observes that, in order to determine the selectivity of a measure adopted by an infra-state body which establishes a lower tax rate in part of the territory of a Member State, there must be an examination of whether that measure was adopted by that body in the exercise of powers sufficiently autonomous vis-à-vis the central power. There must also be an examination of whether that measure actually applies to all the undertakings established in, or all production of goods on, the territory coming within the competence of that body. The reference framework for determining whether a tax measure is selective may therefore be limited to the geographical area concerned, where the regional or local authority occupies a fundamental role in the definition of the political and economic environment under its competence, and in which the undertakings operate (paras 57, 58, and 66).

In this context, the exercise of sufficiently autonomous powers requires that the decision must have been taken by a regional or local authority which has, from a constitutional point of view, a political and administrative status separate from that of central government. Next, it must have been adopted without central government being able directly to intervene as regards its content. Finally, the financial consequences of a reduction of the national tax rate for undertakings in the region must not be offset by aid or subsidies from other regions or central government. The regional or local authority must assume the political and financial consequences of such a measure. The two aspects of the fiscal policy of the regional government of the Azores, the decision to reduce the regional tax burden by exercising its power to reduce tax rates on revenue, and the fulfilment of its task of correcting inequalities deriving from insularity are inextricably linked and dependent, from the financial point of view, on budgetary transfers managed by central government. In these circumstances, the Court found that the proposed measures must be assessed in relation to the totality of Portuguese territory, in the context of which they appeared to be selective measures, not general ones.

It is worth noting that several regional actors and multinational or federal Member States intervened in the process. Åland intervened in the administrative procedure before the Commission, and the UK and Spain intervened before the Court in support of Portugal. The following is an interesting report of some of the arguments put to the Court:

According to the United Kingdom Government, the assessment of a regional tax system for State aid purposes raises broader issues of regional autonomy of considerable constitutional importance. In particular, the United Kingdom's 'asymmetrical' constitutional system of devolution could be called into question, having regard to the position of Scotland and Northern Ireland. (48)

The Kingdom of Spain, also intervening in support of the Portuguese Republic, emphasises that devolution, where it exists, forms part of the Member States' constitutional framework. Following the Commission's arguments would result in upsetting this constitutional structure, particularly as policy concerning direct taxation remains within the specific competence of the Member States. (49)

In its statement in response to the United Kingdom's intervention, the Commission denies that the approach adopted in the contested decision may hinder the exercise by Scotland or Northern Ireland of the powers conferred on them in tax matters. (50)

Advocate General Geelhoed gave a very interesting opinion in which he carefully analysed the different hypotheses of regional action in the area of taxation. These debates were, again, reflected in the reasoning of the Court:

As the Advocate General pointed out in paragraph 54 of his Opinion, in order that a decision taken in such circumstances can be regarded as having been adopted in the exercise of sufficiently autonomous powers, that decision must, first of all, have been taken by a regional or local authority which has, from a constitutional point of view, a political and administrative status separate from that of the central government. Next, it must have been adopted without the central government being able to directly intervene as regards its content. Finally, the financial consequences of a reduction of the national tax rate for undertakings in the region must not be offset by aid or subsidies from other regions or central government. (67)

It follows that political and fiscal independence of central government which is sufficient as regards the application of Community rules on State aid presupposes, as the United Kingdom Government submitted, that the infra-State body not only has powers in the territory within its competence to adopt measures reducing the tax rate, regardless of any considerations related to the conduct of the central State, but that in addition it assumes the political and financial consequences of such a measure. (68)

In this judgment the Court recognizes a constitutional reality, ie the fact that certain Member States have complex structures which include regions with lawmaking powers equivalent to those normally attributed to Member States and which deserve special attention. These regional legislators are subject to EC law in the same manner as state-level legislators. The Court is therefore aware of, or is certainly not blind to, internal diversity within the

Member States. More than merely being aware of it, the Court will, if necessary, examine internal constitutional complexities to check whether its three conditions are fulfilled:

1. The region must be a constitutionally recognized regional or local authority with a political and administrative status separate from that of central government.
2. There can be no possible intervention from central government as regards the content of the measure.
3. There may be no offsetting of the financial consequences of a reduction of the national tax rate for undertakings in the region by aid or subsidies from other regions or central government.

True, this approach still respects the institutional autonomy of the Member States, but not in the sense that this autonomy can escape the scrutiny of the Court; it will not. In fact, the rationale of the Azores judgment inevitably leads to an examination of the internal constitutional setup of a region within a Member State. By way of conclusion, and going back to the opening part of this essay, we can say that the idea of infra-state bodies adopting laws within a Member State has now entered the legal order of the EC and it cannot be ruled out that it might actually penetrate other Member States with similar infra-state phenomena: regional or municipal authorities with a political and administrative status separate from that of central government.

PART V

Outlooks

19

Back to the *Begriffshimmel*?[1] A Plea for an Analytical Perspective in European Law

Niilo Jääskinen

1 Introduction

In the following my intention is to do something that the lawyers rarely do, namely to present and explain a theoretical approach that I personally find one-sided and out-dated, and to which I am not personally committed. In addition, I'll explore what kind of questions that approach would entail for the study of EU law. This approach is the Finnish analytical legal positivism in the forms it took from the 1950s to the early 1970s. It should be added that I could perhaps convey a similar message by using the early writings of HLA Hart or the Scandinavian, Italian, or Polish variants of analytical legal theory as my point of reference.

My reasons for this venture are as follows. Analytical legal positivism formulated a view on legal concepts and doctrines that may provide useful ideas for the development of EU law studies. I fear that EU law studies may suffer from essentialism and constructivism, ie from the 'metaphysical' methodological and theoretical flaws, for which analytical positivism so fiercely criticized traditional legal science.

---

[1] Rudolf von Ihering (1818–1892), also spelled von Jhering, was a great German legal scholar who accused his contemporary colleagues of inhabiting the *Begriffshimmel* ('the heaven of legal concepts') and thus neglecting the world of societal interests and purposes that is the real basis of the law. For an English translation see R von Ihering, 'The Heaven of Legal Concepts' in MR Cohen and FS Cohen, *Readings in Jurisprudence and Legal Philosophy* (Boston: Little Brown, 1951).

For analytical positivists legal questions do not have only one right answer. Legal concepts are mere linguistic devices for helping effective communication on legal matters. Consequently, there are no correct definitions or meanings of legal concepts, and it may be functional and useful to define and use them differently in different contexts.

From this perspective it is natural that there are all kinds of terminological and conceptual hurdles in a new multi-language legal system embracing divergent legal traditions such as EU law. They are not so important *per se*. However, behind conceptual or terminological problems often hide important teleological conflicts between actors and normative systems.

These teleological divergences can be political in the narrow sense of the concept. As such they can concern the constitutional issues of European integration or more mundane political conflicts relating to the legislative and economic policy choices of the EU. Teleological divergences may also refer to conflicts concerning ethical, economic, or social ends of action that are not 'political' in the sense that they relate to the political system. Examples of these broader teleological divergences include the tensions between legal certainty and the need to find just and equitable solutions to individual legal cases, and the tensions between the protection of individual interests and the effectiveness of economic regulation.

According to analytical legal positivism, the teleological issues should be addressed as such, ie on the basis of transparent policy considerations, not as linguistic or conceptual issues. Political and social values should be openly put on the table, not hidden behind quasi-legal argumentative facades.

The Savignyan objective of this project is to bring about binding European legal-scientific unity through common conceptual elaborations. This goal may actually increase the risk of essentialism, as it did in nineteenth-century Germany. Hence, the message of analytical legal positivism may be relevant for the study of European law even today. It underlines the need to rethink and redefine the traditional conceptual apparatus used in legal reasoning and legal science

2 Analytical legal positivism in Finland

Analytical legal positivism in Finland was an intellectual current that emerged after the Second World War and became prominent during the 1960s. It was mainly a school of thought or paradigm that tried to reform the theoretical and methodological framework of legal science even as it was inspired by a deeper legal-theoretical or philosophical interest. During the 1970s it gradually lost its position as the leading theoretical current, though a lot of actual legal science still reflects this tradition.[2]

Analytical legal positivism in Finland coincided in time with and was partly inspired by the second generation of Scandinavian legal realism, represented above all by the Dane Alf Ross.[3] However, Finnish analytical positivism lacked the ontological and value-theoretical premises of the Uppsala school of philosophy, so-called value nihilism, which had inspired the first generation of Scandinavian realists and still formed the background of the meta-legal theories of the second generation.

Instead of the Uppsala school, the philosophical inspiration of Finnish analytical legal positivism was derived from logical-analytic philosophy. That current formed the basis of the renaissance of Finnish philosophy that took place during the 1950s around such prominent logicians as Georg Henrik von Wright and Jaakko Hintikka.

Despite these differences, Finnish analytical legal positivism and the second generation of Scandinavian realists shared the view that legal science needed theoretical purification. It was seen that the leading doctrinal approaches, based on the models of the German *Pandektistik* of Puchta and Windscheid, in the field of private law, and its younger relation, the state law positivism of Gerber, Laband, and Jellinek in public law, were theoretically flawed and practically inadequate. It was considered that the general idea of the conceptual jurisprudence (*Begriffsjurisprudenz*) was based on dubious ontology. This general idea could be summarized as the exposition of the law, right in the objective sense, as a hierarchically organized system of concepts and principles that provides a well-ordered network of subjective rights covering all possible legal relations between legal subjects.

According to the analytical positivists, the traditional view seemed to lead to metaphysics, ie scientifically meaningless questions and pseudo-problems. They also saw it as reducing the task of legal science to the classification of

[2] cf, eg, A Aarnio, 'The Development of Legal Theory and Philosophy of Law in Finland' in A Aarnio, *Philosophical Perspectives in Jurisprudence* (Helsinki: Philosophical Society of Finland, 1983) 9–46, M Helin, 'On the Evolution of Argumentation in Finnish Private Law Research 1920–1960, (1989) 33 Scandinavian Studies in L, 140–166.

[3] On Alf Ross see H Zahle, 'Legal Doctrine between Empirical and Rhetorical Truth: A Critical Analysis of Alf Ross Conception of Legal Doctrine' (2003) 14 Eur J of Int L, 801–815 and A Aarnio, *Reason and Authority: A Treatise on the Dynamic Paradigm of Legal Dogmatics* (Aldershot: Dartmouth, 1997) 62–74.

subjective rights with little relevance to practical legal life or more general social development. The root of these problems was seen to lie in a fallacious understanding of the role of legal language and legal concepts.[4]

The main achievements of analytical legal positivism in Finland lay in the field of private law. There the school made its main theoretical advance, which was to develop a more refined conceptual apparatus to replace the traditional system of subjective rights.[5] This 'nominalistic' deconstruction of rights into the various correlative and opposite legal positions of the different parties created a more accurate conceptual system, and as a consequence, a more fruitful and analytic treatment of the complex legal situations typical to the modern law of property and credit.

In the field of administrative law the results were less convincing. This can be explained by the fact that public law legal relations often cover a plethora of different party positions and legal interests that cannot be translated into simple Hohfeldtian relationships.[6] However, this did not prevent enthusiastic young scholars from achieving in their studies, published around 1970, results that might also be interesting from the point of view of EU law. I mention two examples to illustrate the application of the analytic method in administrative law studies:

1. In 1971 Kari Sinisalo published a study on the general competence of the police.[7] He convincingly demonstrated that the supposed general power

[4] Perhaps I should add here that my first legal publication concerned the concept of legal science according to the German historical school of law. cf N Jääskinen, *Historiallisen koulun oikeustiedekäsitys* (Helsinki: Oikeustieteellisen tutkimuksen tutkimusprojekti, 1983). Therefore, I am fully aware that much of the criticism that the analytical positivists directed against the German conceptual jurisprudence was exaggerated and one-sided.

[5] WN Hohfeld's basic legal oppositions inspired this enterprise. WN Hohfeld published in 1913 an article entitled 'Fundamental Conceptions as Applied in Judicial Reasoning' where he claimed that the term 'right' covers eight basic ideas that can be grouped into pairs of opposite and correlative notions. The pairs of jural opposites are right (claim)/no-right, privilege/duty, power/disability, and immunity/liability. The jural correlatives are right/duty, privilege/no-right, power/liability, and immunity/disability. According to Hohfeld, in legal discourse it is necessary to understand which meaning of 'right' is used in order to avoid inconsistencies and fallacies. cf WN Hohfeld, *Fundamental Legal Conceptions*, ed WW Cook (New Haven: Yale University Press, 1966). For a recent analysis of Hohfeld's system see DT O'Reilly, 'Are There Any Fundamental Legal Conceptions?' (1999) 49 U of Toronto L J, 271–279.

[6] However, the Hohfeldian system has found applications in the study of constitutional law on fundamental rights both in Finland and abroad. See H Karapuu, 'Perusasioita perusoikeuksista' (1986) 19 Oikeustiede-Jurisprudentia, 67–124 and R Alexy, *A Theory of Constitutional Rights* (Oxford: Oxford University Press, 2002) 132–138 and 155–156.

[7] cf K Sinisalo, *Poliisin toimivallan määräytyminen* (Vammala: Suomalainen Lakimiesyhdistys, 1971).

of police authorities to take the necessary measures to maintain law and order was a typical aprioristic conceptual construction lacking support in the positive legal sources. He also showed that the traditional way of deducing the powers of authorities from the tasks entrusted to them is neither a logically nor a legally valid conclusion. Legal ends do not imply the existence of the legal means necessary for their achievement. An intervention in the liberty of citizens must be based on positive rules of competence, not on legal deductions.[8]

2. My second example comes from Toivo Holopainen's book on the position of municipalities in the state[9] published in 1969. For my purposes what is important is how Holopainen defined the problems connected with the concept of the state in legal discourse. He argued that the term 'state' has different meanings in different legal contexts. It is futile to try to find some common denominator or legal essence that would explain or unite these meanings. The 'state' that pays subsidies means a different thing from the 'state' that punishes wrongdoers or enacts statutes or resolves legal disputes or wages wars and concludes treaties. The 'state' that is in a privileged position legally as a constructor of waterways exhibits different phenomena from the 'state' that inherits from the deceased person in the absence of legal heirs and testament. In conclusion, traditional speculation as to whether local self-government is an emanation of the state or an autonomous source of public power does not lead legal scientific analysis to any fruitful directions.

During the 1970s, analytical positivism lost its position in Finland because it did not give satisfactory answers to the questions of legal pragmatics, ie the practical ways in which legal concepts are used in our reasoning and argumentation. 'Legal pragmatics' is a wider concept than legal practice as it refers to all the legally relevant societal discourses, not only to the judicial ones. It was found that the meaning of a legal concept cannot be derived from any logical or semantic analysis but is determined by its various uses in legal language games. For example, the concept of ownership entails different ideas when we discuss the technicalities of bankruptcy law than when the debate concerns constitutional protection against nationalization. Hence, for legal language pragmatics may more relevant than semantics. In addition, legal meanings seem to have a culturally determined frame of

[8] In my opinion, a similar critical conceptual analysis of the principle of *effet utile* of EU law or the implied powers doctrine might be interesting reading.
[9] cf T Holopainen, *Kunnan asema valtiossa* (Vammala: Suomalainen Lakimiesyhdistys,1969).

reference heavily influenced by the extra-legal moral and political traditions of the legal system in question.

The subsequent trends in Finnish legal theory adopted some kind of a communitarian understanding of legal language and legal concepts, emphasizing their common cultural and societal meanings and functions. It is sufficient to mention here the analytical hermeneutics of Aulis Aarnio, building on the theory or argumentation and Wittgenstein's later philosophy, and Kaarlo Tuori's critical legal positivism, emphasizing the layered structure of legal cultures and the importance of the deeper conceptual layers of law.[10]

3 The basic claims of analytical legal positivism and European law

Bert van Roermund's definition of conceptual divergence provides a useful starting point for illustrating the basic theoretical points represented by the analytical legal positivists. According to Van Roermund:

A legal term T is conceptually divergent between agents X and Y, if T is common parlance between X and Y, and if the sense and/or the reference of T yields meaning M_1 for X and M_2 for Y, such that X and Y are inclined to argue conflicting courses of action as lawful (or unlawful) under the legal order they are both committed to.[11]

To analytical legal positivism, the idea of arguing that differing courses of action are lawful/unlawful on the basis of meanings ascribed to legal terms represents a 'deduction from concepts' that is typical of the essentialist fallacy of traditional legal thought. The structure in this inference is the following:

If a certain legal fact (F) is subsumed under a certain legal concept (C), then all the legal consequences (c) that are understood as being inherent in the meaning of that concept become applicable also to the legal fact in question.

---

[10]   cf A Aarnio, *On Legal Reasoning* (Turku: Turun Yliopisto, 1977), *The Rational as Reasonable* (Dordrecht: Reidel, 1987), *Reason and Authority* (Aldershot: Dartmouth, 1997), and K Tuori, *Critical Legal Positivism* (Aldershot: Ashgate, 2002). A different path is taken by Raimo Siltala who proceeds from analytical positivism to a deconstruction of law, see R Siltala, *A Theory of Precedent: From Analytical Positivism to a Post-analytical Philosophy of Law* (Oxford: Hart, 2000).
[11]   See the Introduction to this volume, p 3.

To give an example, we can take 'Community law' as F and the concept of 'international law' as C. Then we can start to discuss the question of whether F is covered by C, that is if Community law is indeed a part of international law or not. If the answer is positive then all the legal consequences (c) inherent in the concept of international law would also apply to Community law; if the answer is negative, then they would not.

Why would an analytical legal positivist see the above-mentioned reasoning as invalid? His/her answer would be that the concept of 'international law' does not refer to a bundle of legal qualities or consequences but is merely the *name* of a certain normative order and/or a discipline studying it. Hence, no legal consequences of Community law can be derived from its conceptual classification or its 'nature' as international law/not international law.

For example, the choice of interpretation methods of Community law or determination of its domestic effects should not depend on or be argued on the basis of the answers given to this classificatory question. Accordingly, for example, the question of whether Community law order has direct applicability within the national law of the Member States is logically and legally independent of the question of whether Community law is better described as being an autonomous legal system or a sub-system of public international law. For an analytical legal positivist the last mentioned question thus represents a typical constructivist pseudo-problem, as Community law has direct applicability and direct effect and primacy because its only authoritative judicial interpreter, ie the European Court of Justice (ECJ), has so found on the basis of its constitutional charter, and because this jurisprudence has been approved by the supreme courts of the Member States.

According to analytical legal positivists, a Platonic legal reality inhabited by such objects as contracts, ownership, subjective rights, or legal persons, or corresponding generic properties like legal personality, admissibility of action, etc, does not exist. It is especially misleading to treat rights and duties as if they were material things or their properties.

Thus, the main methodological consequence of analytical legal positivism was that the concepts of subjective rights and duties became problematic. It was considered that these concepts did not have any empirical reference; moreover, that they did not posses any clearly defined meaning and that their practical function in legal discourse was dubious.

Hence, it was thought redundant and logically fallacious to use rights and duties as some kind of conceptual intermediaries between the legal facts and the legal consequences. For analytical legal positivists, subjective rights and duties can be a vehicle for *describing* normative relations, especially for systematizing or pedagogical purposes, but not a device playing an independent role in legal deductions.

The following is an example of this chain of reasoning applied to EU law. For an analytical legal positivist, a reference to the EU rights of the subjects concerned would add nothing relevant to the legal appreciation of whether an EU rule has direct effects or whether the liability for damages of a Member State could be based on it. This is the case because it is doubtful whether an affirmative answer to the question 'Does this EU rule intend to establish rights to private parties?' can be based on any other grounds than exactly on those that would directly justify an affirmative answer to the question 'Is it appropriate to apply this rule directly to the behaviour of this Member State vis-à-vis this private party or order the Member State to pay damages under these circumstances?'

Thus the analytic way would be that of separately determining the various legal effects of an EU rule, as the case may be, in the binary relations of

- private party/another private party in contractual relationship,
- private party/third parties,
- private party/national administrative authority,
- private party/Member State,
- private party/Community institution,
- Member State/Community institution

with the help of the legal correlatives of claim/duty, privilege/no-right, power/liability, and immunity/disability. Such analysis might show, for example, that the 'rights' provided for by the Treaty articles on fundamental freedoms are, in the first instance, privileges, to which corresponds the 'no-right' of intervention by Member States. Consequently, deducing from these provisions any claims or immunities of the private parties in relation to Member States would not be a matter of logic but of substantive legal reasoning based on teleological and systemic reasons.

The experience of many national legal systems also shows that the need for the effective legal protection of individuals against public authorities is much wider than the sphere covered by their 'rights'. In my opinion, it is rather artificial to speak about 'rights' when we ponder the legal protection an individual is entitled to on the basis of the principles of proportionality or good administration.

One of the main objectives of analytical legal positivism was to make visible the valuations and ideological elements that are inherent in legal concepts and legal reasoning. Most analytical legal positivists saw the idea of 'pure', ie value-free legal science, as impossible to achieve. However, given this inherently necessary teleology in law, it had to be made open and transparent. This meant that valuations determining choices between different interpretative alternatives had to be justified openly, preferably with reference to the factual societal effects of the alternatives and their practical importance.

4 Some inconclusive remarks

It is apparent that the needs of European legal science cannot be fulfilled solely with critical analysis of the type pursued by the Finnish legal analytical positivists, but there is plenty of room for more constructivist theory building and conceptual development. However, I think that current EU law studies could learn something from the Finnish analytical legal positivists or any similar school inspired by logical-analytic philosophy.

Let us first take the problem of making deductions from legal concepts. In EU law, legal concepts such as a Community right, direct effect, the supremacy of EU law, a Member State, an autonomous legal order, are often used in argumentation as something from which the legal consequences are derived. Analytical legal positivists were wrong when they claimed that this kind of reasoning is always fallacious. However, in many cases it may be.

First, it may be superfluous or circular. As I indicated above, in most instances the concept of a Community or Union right probably adds nothing relevant to the chain of reasoning. In fact it may conceal the logical circularity (*petitio principii*) of the argumentation. Further, many of the conceptual constructions may support unsustainable analogies or doctrines. My personal candidate for this category would be the broad definition of the concept of a Member State which occasionally leads to inconsistent and impractical results.

An essentialist understanding of legal concepts often supports legal theory building that does not offer the conceptual distinctions needed by the complexities of practical life. The on/off debate on the legal personality of the EU is (or was?) an example of this phenomenon. Legal concepts are also apt to conceal such teleological or value choices that should be put to open debate and scrutiny. The role that the principle of effectiveness (*effet utile*) plays in EU law could be an example of this.

So critical conceptual scrutiny of the basic doctrines of EU law would be welcome. Why do I then suggest that those who engage in that kind of project would be well advised to consult the logical-analytic tradition of philosophy? The reason for this is that the logical-analytic tradition aimed at formal or analytic concepts. For example, the analytical legal positivists of Finland wanted to break down traditional subjective rights and replace them with new formal concepts that would enable an analytic description of the various party positions emerging in complex legal relations. By doing this they wanted to create legal concepts that are universally applicable, ie concepts that would not entail any substantive legal propositions. The conclusions should be derived from legal sources and methodologically controlled argumentation, not from the legal concepts.

As I mentioned, Finnish analytical legal positivism lost its position to more communitarian approaches because of its inability to provide adequate methodological tools for the problems of legal pragmatics and the culturally determined conceptual structures of legal thought. That also meant that the cultural particularity of each legal system was emphasized in place of a universally applicable formal conceptual system. Unfortunately, such a communitarian way seems to be difficult to pursue insofar as EU law is concerned.

The very reason for this volume is the problem caused by conceptual divergence between our legal systems. As we lack a unified European legal culture, seeking conceptual structures from our inherited domestic frames of reference means that each of us brings along his/her own conceptual baggage to the common enterprise.

A better way of overcoming the conceptual divergences might be the creation of a more analytical and formal common conceptual apparatus for the interpretation and systematization of EU law. In practice this would require that instead of discussing the conceptual divergences that emerge when national meanings are attributed to European legal terms, we would try to develop common European law conceptual systems that are as independent of the national traditions as possible.[12] Bearing in mind the teachings of analytical legal positivism, however, we should understand that this conceptual system would not bring about binding unity, as unity of this kind can be the outcome only of sound and transparent legal argumentation and reasoning. For example, we could agree what we mean by legal 'homogeneity' but it is another question to decide how much legal homogeneity

---

[12] Actually this is something that is already reality in many fields of European law. Two examples of this are the concepts of an 'undertaking' and 'state aid' in European competition law.

EU law normatively requires. The latter question can only be answered on the basis of good legal reasons, ie a convincing combination of linguistic, systemic, and teleological arguments.

A consequence of this approach would be the necessity to 'translate' European legal discourse into national legal language with all the possible divergences that might occur between the Member States at the level of national pragmatics. However, this alternative would in any case give us a fair possibility of understanding each other when we discuss European law at EU level. At the national level, according to my experience, merely being conscious about the possible conceptual divergences between European and national law is often enough to overcome the danger of the misapplication of EU law. According to Jay Rosenberg, mature language users can speak both a language and a meta-language, and, in their meta-language, express norms of semantic correctness for their language.[13] I see no reason why this could not apply to EU legal discourse as well.

---

[13] See JF Rosenberg, *Linguistic Representations* (2nd edn, Dordrecht: Reidel, 1981) 43.

20

Conceptual Divergence, Functionalism, and the Economics of Convergence

Filomena Chirico and Pierre Larouche

1 Introduction

It is common knowledge amongst legal academics and practitioners that legal systems sometimes diverge. Over the years, law and economics scholarship has paid attention to that phenomenon under the heading of 'law and economics of comparative law' or 'regulatory competition'. Scholarship often assumes that convergence or divergence between legal systems is easily perceptible, ie that it can be seen in the face of the formal sources of law. For example, the applicable legislation of legal system *A* states that 'title to the goods sold passes to the buyer upon the conclusion of a valid contract', whereas the applicable legislation in system *B* states that 'title to the goods sold passes to the buyer upon delivery of the goods to the buyer'. Divergence is explicit and open. Economic actors can be expected to behave accordingly. As a consequence, the literature considers that, through their conduct, economic actors will also influence the evolution of legal systems in order to reach an efficient outcome as regards the appropriate level of convergence or divergence. If needed, legislative action (ranging from mild co-ordination to outright unification) can also address explicit divergence.

This chapter aims to take a broader perspective on issues of convergence and divergence between legal systems.

First of all, it takes a more complex view of convergence by relaxing the assumption that language is unequivocal: the same words can mean different things to different people, what we will call 'conceptual divergence'. In the case of the explicit divergence mentioned in the previous paragraph, divergence immediately springs to mind, and in a number of cases it actually reflects the deliberate choice to diverge.[1] In contrast, 'conceptual divergence' often lurks below the surface and is neither immediately perceptible nor entirely deliberate.

For the purposes of this chapter, the working definition of conceptual divergence put forward by Bert van Roermund[2] will be used:

A legal term T is conceptually divergent between agents X and Y, if T is common parlance between X and Y, and if the sense and/or the reference of T yields meaning M_1 for X and M_2 for Y, such that X and Y are inclined to argue conflicting courses of action as lawful (or unlawful) under the legal order they are both committed to.

In a case of explicit divergence, there is no doubt in the minds of the agents that there is divergence, whereas in the case of conceptual divergence, it may be that the agents believe that they are indeed using the same concept, since the label they are using is the same term, while they are in fact using diverging concepts. We will come back to this point later in this chapter: sometimes the standard analysis must be adapted to deal with conceptual divergence, but very often it makes no difference whether the divergence is explicit or conceptual.

Second, this chapter also takes into account a broader range of dynamic tools to address convergence and divergence. As mentioned at the outset, the literature so far (perhaps reflecting a private law bent) tends to rely primarily on the choice made by economic actors as regards the law governing, or applicable to, their legal relationships as a tool to reach an efficient outcome. While this tool is undeniably available and effective, it is also limited: economic actors cannot influence the law at will and, futher, legal issues are often peripheral to the choices made by economic actors. In this chapter, we want to suggest that there is also—or ought to be—a 'marketplace of legal ideas', ie a market-like process that centres around legal ideas in which members of the legal community are the main actors. Under certain conditions, this marketplace of ideas can provide wide-ranging and effective tools to deal with convergence and divergence.

---

[1] Between different legal orders or within a single order that allows this practice under certain circumstances, such as a federation.

[2] See the Introduction to this volume, p 3.

Against this background, this chapter deals with a number of basic issues. At the same time, it also illustrates a number of basic propositions that arise from economic analysis of the law.

First of all, this chapter examines why different legal systems diverge (section 2). This section illustrates the basic proposition that the existing state of affairs is not fortuitous and will usually turn out to be in equilibrium: in other words, that it is the outcome of various forces. At least, the 'spontaneous'[3] ordering of law (and of society) must be carefully studied on its merits, and if it indeed proves to be in equilibrium, then it may be adequate. Note that in the context of this chapter, the existing state of affairs is considered to be the legal systems as they exist at a given moment, with whatever levels of divergence or convergence may be present. We are therefore not dealing with the issue of 'unbridled' market forces versus 'discipline' from the law, but rather with the higher-level issue of difference between legal systems (each of which has had to solve the first-level issue of which laws, if any, are appropriate to dealing with various economic and social problems) and legal intervention to constrain that difference.

Second, this chapter touches upon methodology, ie what divergence is and how it can be detected (section 3). This section is not so much concerned with economic analysis of the law, but rather with the methodology of comparative law. It illustrates a more general proposition arising from any multidisciplinary ('law +') approach to the law, namely that it is crucial that the law be seen in a broader context, ie one that includes both the policy choices underlying it and its practical outcome. Third, the chapter explains under what conditions divergence should be seen as a problem (section 4). Finally, it explores possible solutions to the problem (section 5). The last two parts rest on another fundamental proposition from economic theory: almost every change involves a trade-off. In the words of Friedman, 'there is no such thing as a free lunch'. Jurists are notoriously weak here. We tend to focus on the downsides (disadvantages, costs) of the current situation and the upsides (advantages, benefits) of the envisaged change when deciding

---

[3] Of course, there is no such point of reference as a 'spontaneous' market economy at the scale and level of our large industrialized societies, as economists would sometimes claim. Economics tends to take for granted a set of basic laws which enables the market economy to work in the first place (usually the basic legal disciplines as they would be reflected in codes or the common law). 'Spontaneous' should perhaps be better read as 'bottom-up' in the context of this project.

Table 20.1 Complete decision matrix for legal change

	Costs	Benefits
Current	C_{now}	B_{now}
Change	C_{after}	B_{after}

whether to change (shaded grey in Table 20.1), often ignoring the upsides of the current situation and the downsides of the envisaged change.

Obviously, change should only be carried out if the benefits of change minus the costs thereof exceed the benefits of the current situation minus the costs thereof. In formal terms, change would be justified if and only if

$$B_{after} - C_{after} > B_{now} - C_{now}$$

and not merely because

$$B_{after} > C_{now}$$

The cost-benefit analysis just outlined extends to all sorts of costs and benefits,[4] not just to economic costs and economic benefits, which might be more easily quantifiable. Non-economic costs and benefits are equally important, and the mere fact that a choice also has non-economic implications—which is actually more the rule than the exception—does not render a cost-benefit analysis superfluous, quite the contrary.

2 Why would divergence occur?

When browsing through the legal literature, one cannot escape the impression that jurists are (at least) slightly biased against divergence. Convergence, harmonization, and even stronger phenomena such as unification are often perceived as positive developments in and of themselves. Even those who write in praise of divergence present it in such a fashion—calling upon irreducible cultural differences beyond apprehension[5]—that it seems to border

---

[4] The discussion on the goals of regulating is very wide. From the perspective of the economic analysis of law, see L Kaplow and S Shavell, 'Fairness versus Welfare' (2001) 114 Harvard L Rev, 961.

[5] P Legrand, 'A Diabolical Idea' in AS Hartkamp and EH Hondius, *Towards a European Civil Code* (Deventer: Kluwer, 2004) 245; P Legrand, 'European Legal Systems are Not Converging'

on the irrational, a line of argument which ultimately feeds into the bias against divergence.

Without dismissing the cultural argument as a whole, it seems more satisfactory to investigate what is behind certain choices of legal rules. Why would divergence occur at all? Using economic theory, divergence can be rationally explained on the basis of at least three lines of reasoning.

2.1 *Divergence as a rational but not deliberate phenomenon*

On this line of reasoning, divergence can be explained rationally, but does not necessarily result from deliberate choice on the part of those concerned. Two different strands of economic theory can be brought to bear here.

Informational imperfections

First, divergence can be explained by *informational imperfections* (or asymmetries) between various jurisdictions. The law progresses in great part as a result of outside pressure, which takes the form of new information about the world outside the law (eg, a new case never seen before, technological developments, social evolution) that the law must then process. Legal systems evolve within different informational environments. The comparative scholar will often observe that certain areas of the law are more developed in certain jurisdictions as a result of specific historical occurrences.[6] Similarly, larger jurisdictions tend to run ahead of cutting-edge legal developments because, statistically, novel cases will tend to arise there first. Furthermore, there will rarely be an obvious 'perfect solution' to a given legal problem that can immediately be singled out. Therefore, much as in economic activity, when it comes to the development of the law, decisions taken under asymmetric (and imperfect) information may lead different actors onto different paths.

Network effects

Second, network economics can also help to explain divergence. The starting point is the notion of *network effects*[7] (also presented as demand-side

---

(1996) 45 ICLQ 52, and G Teubner, 'Legal Irritants: Good Faith in British Law or How Unifying Law Ends Up in New Divergences' (1998) 61 MLR, 11.

[6] For instance, the doctrine of *Wegfall der Geschäftsgrundlage* in Germany as a result of the Great Depression.

[7] O Shy, *The Economics of Network Industries* (Cambridge: Cambridge University Press, 2001); MR Lemley and D McGowan, 'Legal Implications of Network Economic Effects' (1998) 86 California L Rev, 479; SL Liebowitz and SE Margolis, 'Network Externality: An Uncommon

scale effects): for certain products, the value of the product to the individual user increases as the number of users increases. The classical example is telecommunications: in the absence of interconnection, the value of a subscription to a network with 1,000 subscribers is much less than that of a subscription to an otherwise identical service provided over a network with 1 million subscribers. In telecommunications, network effects are strong, but the theory can also be applied more loosely to other phenomena, including fashion and language. It can be ventured that the 'market' for legal ideas is also subject to network effects:[8] the more members of the legal epistemic community subscribe to a given opinion, the more attractive it becomes, sometimes irrespective of its inherent validity.[9] The effect is not as strong as in telecommunications, of course, since some jurists—fortunately so in many circumstances—can still decide not to be swayed by the mere fact that the majority holds a certain view, and try to reverse network effects by convincing their peers to espouse another view.

More particularly, two specific properties associated with network effects can explain divergence. The first is called *tipping*:[10] a small movement in demand can trigger a snowball effect.[11] In the case of legal ideas, a single leading decision or a leading article at a given point in time can quickly lead to the emergence of a majority view. The second is called *path dependency*: once network effects have worked to the advantage of one firm, it becomes very difficult to 'change the course of history'.[12] In the case of

Tragedy' (1994) 8 *J of Economic Perspectives*, 133, and M Katz and C Shapiro, 'Network Externalities, Competition and Compatibility' (1985) 75 *American Economic Rev*, 425.

[8] A Ogus argued, for instance, that 'the acknowledged characteristics of "legal culture", a combination of language, conceptual structure and procedures, constitute a network which, because of the commonality of usage, reduces the costs of interactive behaviour'. See A Ogus, 'The Economic Basis of Legal Culture: Networks and Monopolization' (2002) 22 Oxford J Legal Studies, 420.

[9] Hence the practice of pointing to the majority and minority views when there is a controversy.

[10] See M Katz and C Shapiro, 'Systems Competition and Network Effects' (1994) 8 *J of Economic Perspectives*, 93.

[11] This lies at the heart of the commercial strategy of most firms active in sectors affected by network effects.

[12] The classical example, PA David, 'Clio and the Economics of QWERTY' (1985) 75 *American Economic Rev*, 332, is the QWERTY keyboard that, once established as a standard, could not be replaced by a more efficient alternative: the users had been trained in the QWERTY system and could not easily switch all together to the other system. See AW Brian, 'Competing Technologies, Increasing Returns, and Lock-in by Historical Events' (1989) 97 *Economic J*, 642, and SJ Liebowitz and SE Margolis, 'Path Dependence' in B Bouckaert and G de Geest (eds), *Encyclopaedia of Law and Economics* (Chatham: Edward Elgar, 1999).

legal ideas,[13] here also, once certain choices have been made and are deeply imbedded in the shared knowledge of the legal community, they are difficult to reverse. Path dependency can also show itself in a slightly different manner: when faced with a new kind of problem that needs an immediate remedy, legal systems tend to choose solutions that are 'familiar' to them; hence, different systems easily end up choosing different solutions.[14]

Accordingly, legal systems can display divergence as a result of discrete choices made differently in the past. Indeed, on many issues (for instance, the relationship between contract and tort law), if one goes sufficiently far back in time, the same or very similar debates can be found in each system until the point at which a choice was made. Network effects (including tipping and path dependency) amplify the consequences of these choices. Sometimes it suffices for a single leading author or court to choose option *A* in one system and option *B* in the other for these two systems later to evidence 'irreconcilable divergences' after network effects have done their work. The choices made might have been the best possible at that particular time in that particular legal system. However, this does not imply that such choices are still the best once time has moved or that it pays to reverse them without assessing the costs brought about by such change.

2.2 *Divergence as a rational, deliberate, and benign phenomenon*

The explanations above assume that divergence does not result from deliberate action. The more classical and traditional explanation for divergence, however, involves deliberate choices made by the members of a community as regards their legal system: in other words, *local preferences*. Because it is intuitive and well-researched, this explanation is only briefly summarized here, but this should not take away any of its power.

In essence, the legal system reflects the consensus of the community (or at least of the ruling class) on the balance to be reached between competing policy interests. Some trade-offs are involved, and they are not always

[13] For earlier applications of these economic concepts to developments in legal rules, see O Hataway, 'Path Dependency in the Law: the Course and Pattern of Legal Change in a Common Law System' (2001) 86 Iowa L Rev, 601; CP Gillette, 'Lock-in Effects in Law and Norms' (1988) 78 Boston U L Rev, 813, and MJ Roe, 'Chaos and Evolution in Law and Economics' (1995) 109 Harvard L Rev, 641. For a study of the effects of path dependency in corporate law, see K Heine and W Kerber, 'European Corporate Laws, Regulatory Competition and Path Dependence' (2002) 13 Eur J of L and Economics, 47.

[14] See U Mattei, 'Legal Systems in Distress: HIV-contaminated Blood, Path Dependency and Legal Change' (2001) 1 Global Jurist Advances, Art 4.

resolved in the same manner from one community to another. For instance, in a given community, more emphasis will be put on ensuring that injured persons receive compensation, while in another, the need not to overburden economic actors with liability claims will prevail. The laws of these respective communities will then most likely diverge.

2.3   *Divergence as a rational, deliberate, but less benign phenomenon*

A third line of argument builds on the previous one, but adds a twist. Whereas the previous account assumes deliberate decisions taken in good faith and with a view to the public interest, *public choice theory*[15] would consider the production of law as a market responding to general economic principles, for instance demand and supply models, price theory. Accordingly, the production of law will favour the interests which are best able to articulate their demand and offer a valuable counterpart to the producer of law. Public choice theory can be used to explain lawmaking in complex settings involving interest groups, lobbying, and other features of modern-day democracies.

Public choice theory can account for divergence as a rational and deliberate phenomenon. However, the outcome in each jurisdiction might be affected by market imperfections, including the presence of market power on the part of certain interest groups vying for the production of law, or information asymmetries (the interest groups know more than the lawmakers and choose to disclose only that information which serves their interest). The outcome is thus not necessarily in line with the general public interest in that jurisdiction. It could be ventured that the presence in certain jurisdictions of very developed systems of admissibility control in public law claims, for instance, reflects success on the part of the administration in influencing the production of law (here administrative procedure) rather than the greater general good.

One of the most powerful interest groups is the legal profession: in fact, it can be argued that it represents the main driving force for maintaining divergence, especially under the pretence of 'legal culture'. The conceptual device of 'legal culture' allows the legal profession to keep the tensions and debates alluded to above within its ranks, and hide behind a monolithic façade, which moreover is made opaque to outsiders by being presented as a

---

[15] GJ Stigler, 'The Theory of Economic Regulation' (1971) 2 *Bell J of Economics*, 3; G Becker, 'A Theory of Pressure groups for Political Influence' (1983) 98 *Quarterly J of Economics*, 371; DC Mueller, *Public Choice* (2nd edn, Cambridge: Cambridge University Press, 1989); and DA Farber and PP Frickey, *Law and Public Choice: A Critical Introduction* (Chicago: University of Chicago Press, 1991).

'culture'. The legal profession can then protect and perpetuate its 'monopoly' on its legal 'culture'.[16] This also helps to explain the lawyers' asymmetric attitude towards 'importing' foreign legal rules, as compared to 'exporting' their own legal solutions.[17]

2.4 *Concluding note*

In this section, three different lines of argument were explored, all of which explained why the law could be different from one place to another, and in a more convincing fashion than endless invocations of irreducible differences between legal cultures. It is inaccurate to consider that the state of a legal system at a given moment is the single and unavoidable outcome of a monolithic legal culture pertaining to that system. Rather, each legal system is rife with tensions and debates (at least at an academic level). Legal systems are open to many potential directions, and their state at a given moment is simply the outcome of certain policy choices—deliberate or not—that are neither predetermined nor irreversible over time.

It will be noted that these lines of argument do not require a specific level of comparison. They can explain differences between legal systems, of course, but they could also explain differences within a single legal system. Their point of reference is not a geographical territory or a hierarchical entity (legal system), but rather a legal epistemic community.

More importantly, these three lines of argument can explain conceptual divergence equally as well as explicit divergence. It makes no difference whether a common term is used or not.

3 When is there divergence?

In the light of the foregoing, there appears to be ample reason for divergence (explicit or conceptual) to occur. A foray into methodology is then necessary

---

[16] See A Ogus, 'Competition between National Legal Systems: A Contribution of Economic Analysis to Comparative Law' (1999) 48 ICLQ 405; Ogus, see n 8 above; and GK Hadfield, 'The Price of Law: How the Market for Lawyers Distorts the Justice System' (2000) 98 Michigan L Rev, 953.

[17] To be sure, if it can be argued that national lawyers prefer divergence for the sake of their own local interest, in the same way and on the basis of the same public choice arguments, it can also be observed that comparatist lawyers represent another—albeit far less powerful—pressure group with the opposite interest in favouring harmonization.

to ensure that divergence will only be found where it really exists.[18] First of all, a specific remark is made concerning conceptual divergence specifically and the 'keyword trap' (section 3.1), before going more generally into the methodology used to assess divergence (section 3.2).

3.1 *The keyword trap*

In the case of conceptual divergence, there could be a methodological trap at work to do with the focus on keywords (including short key phrases of a few words). Jurists like to work with keywords, since it simplifies their task considerably by enabling them to put a shorthand label on subsets of the law in a given legal system. A whole piece of legal architecture is subsumed under one keyword: for instance, the set of rules and concepts concerning cases where a decision maker has some degree of freedom in reaching an outcome becomes 'discretion'. The meaning of 'discretion' as a keyword can only be found by retrieving the subset of the law which it is meant to represent. Accordingly, that meaning will be linked with the rest of the legal system in question (and the broader context within which this system operates). Unfortunately, keywords tend to take on a life of their own. They then cease to be treated as shorthand labels whose meaning is to be found by looking at the underlying subset of law which the keyword is intended to represent. Instead, jurists will then believe that the keyword has an inherent meaning in and of itself, ie that the meaning of the keyword resides in the keyword itself.[19]

Under those circumstances, there is a fair chance that misunderstandings can occur. Two persons from different legal systems use the same keyword—or rather, what appears to be the same keyword in different linguistic versions—and expect it to mean one and the same thing, since it is assumed that the meaning is in the keyword. What they fail to realize is that, on a proper view, where the meaning is found by referring to the subset which the keyword represents, the same keyword can have different meanings. Conceptual divergence lurks.

It is therefore crucial that jurists beware of the keyword trap. The mere fact that the same keyword, the same shorthand label, is found in two different systems (or appears to be found once translated) does not imply convergence. To use the example given above, 'discretion' as a keyword is found in most

---

[18]   This part of the paper is based more on research experience in comparative law and interdisciplinary work with economists than on standard law and economics literature.

[19]   See on this point H Hart, 'Definition and Theory in Jurisprudence' (1954) 70 L Q Rev, 37 and A Ross, 'Tu-tu' (1957) 70 Harvard L Rev, 812.

administrative law systems. It does not take extensive research to notice that it has significantly different meanings from one system to the other.

On a proper view, one must consider keywords as shorthand labels and look beyond them to the subset of the legal system which they are meant to represent. Only then can a conclusion be reached as to whether or not there is convergence. Presumably, the same keyword used in two different legal systems will often actually represent a different subset in each system. Does that then necessarily imply conceptual divergence?

3.2 *A functional methodology to ascertain divergence*

At this juncture, it is interesting to digress briefly into a comparison with economics. Jurists work only with language, which suffers from an inherent degree of indeterminacy. Economists, on the other hand, rely on more formal tools—namely mathematical models, empirical measurements, etc—in addition to language. Nevertheless, language remains the prime means of communication between economists and, like jurists, economists use keywords to simplify communication. When two economists differ in opinion in discussion (using language), they go back to the underlying theories and models (and formal mathematical language). They check their conclusions against these theories and models, verifying that assumptions are satisfied and that the theories and models being used are really applicable to the situation at hand. In the end, perceived divergences at the so-called 'intuitive' level, using language and keywords, can be tested against theories and models whose formalism enables a conclusion to be reached. Either the divergence is removed, or it is attributed to gaps or open issues in economics. These can then be addressed as such.

Coming back to law, there is no set of formal tools which could be used to reach a conclusion on a perceived divergence across legal systems. Nevertheless, jurists have developed comparative law methods to test for divergence (and, in the case of conceptual divergence, to avoid the keyword trap).

A number of contemporary comparative law methodologies—for instance the study of legal transplants—would take a point from within the law (typically a keyword) as a basis for comparison. Each legal system will be entered into from that point. Typically, that point will be put in context with its immediate surroundings and even with the legal system as a whole.[20]

---

[20] In the case of conceptual divergence, this amounts to looking beyond the keyword and retrieving the subset that this keyword represents.

Very often, a finding of divergence will be returned. The conclusion will tend to be that (even if there is an apparent similarity in keywords) the underlying legal concepts and legal reasoning differ. An even more radical approach would go further into 'legal cultures' as a source of irreducible divergence. Very often, the civil law/common law divide will bear the blame for this (when the sample of legal systems under study allows for it).

Yet ascertaining differences in legal concepts, reasoning, and 'culture' should not be enough to warrant a finding of divergence. After all, such an inquiry offers no objective test to support its conclusion. A more solid methodology is needed, namely a form of functionalism.[21] This involves looking beyond the 'middle layer' of legal concepts and reasoning to incorporate in addition the 'upper layer' of policy considerations and the 'bottom layer' of practical outcomes. Instead of beginning the inquiry via an endogenous point in the law, the starting point is rather found outside the law, by way of a practical problem, for example. The practical problem chosen is common to all legal systems under study (eg, 'two cars collide at an intersection'). The aim of the inquiry is then to ascertain whether legal systems, seen broadly with their respective three layers, produce the same or a similar outcome on the basis of roughly the same policy considerations. Whether the legal concepts and reasoning used in doing so are similar should not be of prime relevance. Only when the outcomes differ (usually because the policy issues have been settled differently) is there sufficient basis for a finding of divergence.

For instance, the laws of France, Germany, and England do diverge on the treatment of pure economic loss under the law of liability. However, within that sample, the laws of Germany and England tend to converge both at the policy and at the outcome level,[22] even if they evidence differences in legal concepts and reasoning. French law differs fundamentally from both, however, in policy and outcomes. The divergence is thus mainly between German and English law, on the one hand, and French law, on the other. In all of this, the civil law/common law divide is of secondary significance as an explanatory factor.[23]

---

[21] For more on this and on the functionalist approach in general, see the work of the Ius Commune Casebook Project, in particular W van Gerven, J Lever, and P Larouche, *Casebook on Tort Law* (Oxford: Hart, 2000).

[22] Save for the fact that Germany tends to make greater use of contract law devices to soften the impact of the disallowance of recovery for pure economic loss.

[23] Other examples where taxonomy creates divergence though practical solutions (the operating rule) are the same are described in R Sacco, 'Diversity and Uniformity in the Law' (2001) 49 American J of Comparative L, 171.

Such a functionalist approach enables an objective test. Indeed the starting point is not an unreliable endogenous point within the law, but rather a constant exogenous point (a practical problem arising in each legal system). Furthermore, the conclusion is reached on the basis of outcomes, which are usually easier to quantify and compare (it is either one or the other outcome) than rules and concepts. In the end, if a difference in outcome is measured for the same starting point, then one cannot escape the conclusion that the legal systems do diverge. If they originally appeared to converge because of common or similar keywords, then we have a proven case of conceptual divergence: despite common keywords, the legal systems produce different outcomes when examined from a single common starting point.

Against this methodology, a number of objections are frequently voiced. First of all, questions are raised as to whether it can appropriately be called 'functionalist'. It is true that functionalism covers a number of different and sometimes conflicting concepts, as was pointed out by Michaels.[24] Yet what is put forward here is a methodology, without any teleological element: in this sense, it falls under what Michaels describes as 'equivalence functionalism', namely the idea that 'similar functional needs can be fulfilled by different institutions'.[25] Only through a functionalist method, which seeks to ascertain how various legal systems deal with a similar functional need, can the scope of convergence or divergence be properly assessed: if legal systems reach different outcomes (as mentioned above, often because of different policy choices), then there is truly divergence. If they do not reach different outcomes, then the systems are functionally equivalent. Differences in the path to that outcome matter, of course, but they do not result in significant divergence. Beyond enabling a more accurate assessment of convergence or divergence, the functionalist method advocated here cannot provide guidance at a more normative level, as regards what should be done about the divergence.[26] As will be seen in the following section, we would argue that the economic analysis of law offers a solid method to deal with those normative issues.

Second, the functionalist methodology set out above is often said to denature legal systems by preventing their spirit—their 'genius'—from

---

[24] R Michaels, 'The Functional Method of Comparative Law' in M Reimann and R Zimmermann (eds), *The Oxford Handbook of Comparative Law* (Oxford: Oxford University Press, 2006) 339.

[25] ibid, 357.

[26] A point which Michaels, see n 24 above, who considers equivalence functionalism as the most robust version of functionalism, also underlines at 373ff.

properly shining through the discussion. It forces the structuring of the discussion along the exogenous comparison point, and ignores or even does violence to the internal coherence of each system (or even to the various 'legal cultures').[27] This criticism is accurate to some extent: functionalism does not easily allow for legal systems to be comprehended above and beyond the set of discrete and exogenous entry points which are used in the research. At the same time, it can also be argued that functionalism highlights the 'genius' of legal systems by forcing them to be expressed within the constraints of these entry points. Functionally equivalent solutions are just that—equivalent, not identical: presumably, these solutions each encapsulate the characteristics of the respective legal systems—for instance, the pithiness and aestheticism usually attributed to French civil law or the doctrinal rigour often associated with German law.

A third, more radical criticism would deny the very possibility of defining an exogenous starting point for the comparison. According to this view, problems do not exist in the abstract. Functionalism is either circular, in that its exogenous point is not truly exogenous but actually a construct of the same community of meaning which administers a legal system to deal with that problem.[28] On this account, it is impossible to find a starting point which would be common to different communities. Alternatively, functionalism is value-laden and simply substitutes an exogenous rationality for the one which would be found within the system:[29] it is then impossible to deliver on the promise of a comparison that would allow each system to 'express itself' and that would separate significant divergence from functional equivalence.

On the one hand, this criticism stands as a warning to, and a challenge for, the researcher. The functionalist method must be used cautiously, and great care must be taken to ensure that the exogenous starting point is stripped as bare as possible from any influence of the legal systems to be studied. Yet on the other hand, when taken to its logical extreme, this criticism would deny

---

[27] This line of criticism is particularly sharp in the area of public law (constitutional and administrative law), where the link with the nation–State—and by extension at least in Western Europe with the national 'legal culture'—is strongest, and the belief in the specificity of national solutions most widespread. See for instance R Teitel, 'Comparative Constitutional Law in a Global Age' (2004) Harvard L Rev, 2570.

[28] This would be in line with the autopoeitic theory put forward by G Teubner, *Law as an Autopoeitic System* (Oxford: Blackwell, 1993) on the basis of the work of N Luhmann.

[29] See for instance the criticism directed at Marxist functionalism by C Castoriadis, *L'institution imaginaire de la société* (Paris: Seuil, 1975) 159ff.

functionalism and ultimately comparative law altogether. By way of example, if the exogenous starting point is a car accident,[30] of course it could be said that a car accident is not exogenous to the legal system, since it presupposes an industrialized society, with private car ownership, a public road system, and so on and so forth. With all due respect, it seems to us that this does not disqualify the functionalist methodology at all. The situation would be different if functionalism were used in a more teleological fashion, in which it is presumed that the functions give the institutions a purpose and a meaning. As was mentioned above, such is not the case in this chapter, where equivalence functionalism serves as a methodological and epistemological device.

How can a starting point be defined then? The functionalist method usually relies on a set of facts as a starting point. Within the EC context, however, it is also possible to use as a starting point a piece of EC legislation, most often a directive. Even if the directive itself—contrary to a carefully distilled set of facts—is not devoid of values and choices, at the same time it is definitely common to all legal systems. It applies in every Member State[31] and by its very nature it places all systems under the same constraint. All Member States must implement the directive, ie achieve its results, while keeping some discretion as to form and method. In this sense, the directive is an ideal canvas against which to study the possibility of functional equivalence. It is then interesting to examine how each legal system receives and implements that piece of EC law.

If the methodology just described is used, we venture that the number of cases of divergence—explicit or conceptual—is likely to be lower than might appear at first sight.

4 What is wrong with divergence?

In the previous two sections, we have seen that divergence can be explained rationally, and that, on a proper methodological approach, it is probably less frequent than suspected. Once there is a finding of divergence, the discussion is naturally drawn to the more normative question of whether it is undesirable.

[30] Or a subset of car accidents defined by the number and type of vehicles involved, the number of victims, etc.

[31] At Art 249, the TEC provides for directives to be addressed to less than all Member States, but in practice this is rarely the case.

In section 2 of this chapter, three lines of argument were set out to explain why divergence can occur. It should be noted that of the three, only the 'local preference' argument—section 2.2—provides a stable (and strong) explanation for divergence. Still, local preferences can evolve. The first line of argument (rational but not deliberate, section 2.1) implies that divergence can disappear over time, if information imperfections are removed. Network effects can work in favour of one or another outcome and would not prevent divergence from disappearing.[32] The third line of argument (rational, deliberate, but less benign, section 2.3) implies that divergence results in part from different power configurations which are not necessarily stable.

Even then, the mere fact that divergence is not stable over time does not mean that it is undesirable. Beyond purely legal arguments against divergence that are inconclusive, there are some economic reasons why divergence should be addressed.

4.1 *Convergence as a value in and of itself*

Here, we jurists sometimes fall into the classical trap of thinking that convergence (and ultimately unity) in the law is a value in and of itself.

First of all, convergence has enormous intellectual appeal, but that of course is not a sufficient justification.

Second, jurists sometimes put forward rights-based arguments for convergence: it is everyone's right to have similar situations treated in the same way across legal systems or communities. Given the arguments made above to explain why there might be divergence, we do not think that a mere assertion of rights is a sufficient trump card.[33] On the same line of reasoning, it is also somewhat hasty to advance the political argument that the call for a uniform system of law is dictated by the need to support a common European identity.[34]

---

[32] In fact, in network markets, network effects can be overcome and a new solution can replace the one previously in place, not necessarily by means of a top-down intervention, but also through bottom-up provision of incentives to transition.

[33] In J Bhagwati, 'The Demand to Reduce Domestic Diversity among Trading Nations' in J Bhagwati and R Hudec (eds), *Fair Trade and Harmonization* (Boston: MIT Press, 1996) 9ff a survey of the arguments against diversity is presented, by highlighting (i) the philosophical arguments (basic human rights beyond national borders, distributive justice and fairness); (ii) the structural arguments (globalization); (iii) the economic arguments (domestic decisions impairing international trade; distributive concerns and predation); and (iv) the political arguments (protectionism and the need for a common set of standards within an integrated union).

[34] A discussion of this point with respect to drafting a European civil code can be found in S Grundmann and J Stuyck (eds), *Academic Green Paper on Contract Law* (Deventer: Kluwer, 2002).

A third but related argument is paramount in EC law, namely the need to ensure the effectiveness of the law (here, EC law). This argument pertains more to conceptual divergence within a larger system such as EC law: it is essential to ensure that EC law is interpreted, applied, and enforced the same way throughout the EU, lest it lose its effectiveness. After all, the European Court of Justice (ECJ) has construed the EC Treaty in a very purposive fashion, which naturally leads to an emphasis on effectiveness.

At the same time, throughout its case law, the ECJ is also willing to accept a degree of divergence in the laws of the Member States. For instance, it might appear that the case law on the internal market is naturally favourable to convergence, given the ease with which the ECJ will conclude, often without empirical evidence, that a specific provision in a given Member State constitutes a barrier to the free movement of goods, workers, services, or capital or to the freedom of establishment of firms and self-employed persons. At the same time, the 'rule of reason' developed to save restrictions on the free movement of goods in *Cassis de Dijon*[35] and subsequently extended to other freedoms enables vast areas of law to remain divergent across Member States. Similarly, in the line of case law including *Keck*[36] and *Gourmet International*,[37] the ECJ retreats from its earlier statements and leaves potentially divergent Member State laws outside the realm of Article 28 EC.

More recently, the judgment in the *Tobacco Advertising* case[38] provides a useful reminder that convergence is not a value in and of itself. Writing about the availability of Article 95 EC as a legal basis, the Court stated that:[39]

[i]f a mere finding of disparities between national rules and of the abstract risk of obstacles to the exercise of fundamental freedoms or of distortions of competition liable to result therefrom were sufficient to justify the choice of Article [95] as a legal basis, judicial review of compliance with the proper legal basis might be rendered nugatory.

In the *Tobacco Advertising* case, the ECJ laid down the foundation for a more economic approach to the use of Article 95 EC as a legal basis. Indeed from an economic perspective, the mere fact of divergence is not undesirable.

---

[35] Case 120/78 *Rewe-Zentral* [1979] ECR 649.
[36] Joined Cases C-267/91 and C-268/91 *Keck* [1993] ECR I-6097.
[37] Case C-405/98 *Konsumentombudsmannen* [2001] ECR I-1795.
[38] Case C-376/98 *Germany v Parliament* [2000] ECR I-8419. Following a series of cases where that judgment seemed to have been weakened, the Court (Grand Chamber) has reaffirmed its approach in Case C-380/03 *Germany v Parliament*, Judgment of the Court of 12 December 2006, nyr.
[39] Case C-376/98 *Germany v Parliament* [2000] ECR I-8419, para 84.

In order to come to a normative conclusion, our assessment must look more broadly at the costs and benefits of divergence (and in a later step, discussed below in section 5, at the costs and benefits of removing divergence).[40]

4.2 *The costs associated with divergence*

Starting point: benefits, but no costs

The benefits of divergence flow from the lines of argumentation put forward earlier. They are strongest when divergence is explained by local preferences. Each legal system is then better attuned to its respective reality: when they reflect differences in the preferences of different communities, divergences are in principle preferable to a unified solution since the latter will not, by definition, match every community's needs equally well.[41] Since variety increases utility, social welfare is enhanced.

Moreover, since the most suitable solution is hardly, if ever, known in advance, the existence of different solutions can enable a learning process towards the discovery of the most appropriate one.[42]

In principle, divergence as such does not create costs. To be sure, in the presence of a divergence between legal systems, acknowledging it and being aware of alternative solutions can help to highlight the possible costs associated with a certain legal choice within a given legal system. However, in such cases, costs are not due to divergence but are caused by unsatisfactory choices made in the past. This is especially true when divergence is explained not by local preferences but rather by non-deliberate factors (information asymmetries, network effects) or via public choice theory (pressure of interest groups).[43] In such cases, the existence of divergence does not constitute a ground for harmonization, but may prompt a domestic revision of one's own inefficient legal choices, and eventually lead to a change.

The more realistic case: benefits, but also costs

Positive costs are usually generated, however, when diverging systems are actually communicating with each other. Communication can take place

---

[40] An obvious point for economists. See, eg, in the context of discussions concerning harmonization, JM Sun and J Pelkmans, 'Regulatory Competition in the Single Market' (1995) 33 *J Common Market Studies*, 67.

[41] Save for what is discussed in the subsequent section.

[42] FA Hayek, 'Competition as a Discovery Procedure' in FA Hayek (ed), *New Studies in Philosophy, Politics, Economics and the History of Ideas* (London: Routledge, 1978) 179.

[43] See nn 7–18 and the accompanying text above.

through various means, be it trade in goods, movement of persons, etc. Certainly this kind of communication can be considered as an increasingly recurrent feature when markets are integrating.

More specifically, when diverging systems communicate, the following costs might arise:

1. *Externalities*: Normally, the state of the law should reflect the choices made in a given jurisdiction in the light of the various trade-offs involved. It is possible, however, that the choices made in a jurisdiction impose costs which are borne by another jurisdiction, in which case the choice of the first jurisdiction is not based on a complete picture of costs and benefits (trade-offs) involved. A typical example is environmental legislation in the presence of cross-border effects (water and air flows across boundaries). In the presence of externalities, there is no reason to respect divergence arising from local preferences (eg, minimal pollution controls upstream), since they can result in sub-optimal results overall (eg, unwanted pollution downstream). A similar problem may arise if a state has a lax competition policy that allows the formation of cartels which then negatively affect consumers in other jurisdictions to the benefit of domestic firms.

2. *Transaction costs*: When there is trade between jurisdictions, divergence creates transaction costs. Indeed participants in trade—sellers as well as buyers—must acquire knowledge about the legal situation in other jurisdictions in order to engage in trade efficiently (otherwise, they incur risks). They must incur the costs necessary to draft contracts according to each legal system in which they are doing business, and they must incur the costs of possible litigation under multiple legal regimes. The risks associated with unexpected changes in each of the legal systems concerned by the transaction also represent costs for cross-border economic actors and so on.[44] On the seller side, for example, this means that products, terms, and conditions, etc must be adapted to meet the legal requirements of a number of jurisdictions, thereby increasing the cost of production, and consequently the price. On the buyer side, not only is the price higher due to these extra costs, but also the cost of buying can be increased; more likely, however (especially with consumers), buyers would refrain from buying outside their jurisdiction. The same applies to

---

[44] On the costs of diversity, see LE Ribstein and BH Kobayashi, 'An Economic Analysis of Uniform State Laws' (1996) 25 J of Legal Studies, 138ff.

business transactions other than selling and even to personal endeavours (employment, family matters). Beside these 'static' effects, dynamic ones can also be identified on a macro-economic level, namely a reduction in international trade volume, in the level of investment, consumption, and income, and ultimately in economic growth.[45]

Transaction costs offer a very powerful argument against divergence. With respect to consumers and individuals in general, transaction cost analysis can reinforce rights-based arguments: the right of a person to be treated the same way irrespective of the legal system in question can be justified because it is deemed unacceptable that individuals should bear the transaction costs associated with divergent legal systems.

Externalities and transaction costs are the standard arguments used to support the conclusion that a given instance of divergence is undesirable. These arguments apply equally to conceptual or explicit divergence. Presumably, transaction costs are higher in the case of conceptual divergence, since the precise scope of the divergence is harder to ascertain.

In addition, a third type of cost could be associated with conceptual divergence only, namely costs arising from *information imperfections*. Indeed, conceptual divergence differs from explicit divergence in that, on the surface, the same term is used, but for diverging concepts. Ideally, if acquiring information were costless, individuals and firms would dedicate sufficient resources to ascertain the legal situation and would come across conceptual divergences as well. Since, unfortunately, obtaining information is costly, parties will invest resources in such activity only until its marginal cost equals the marginal benefit.[46] There is therefore a risk that they will not look beyond the surface and will then take decisions based on the assumption that the same term is conceptualized in the same way in every jurisdiction, only later to find out that their assumption was wrong (to their cost, but perhaps also to their benefit). They could thus be misled into taking decisions which they would not have taken with complete information on the status of the law. This can lead to inefficiencies in the form of unsuspected losses or extra costs to undo mistakes. In the end, the uncertainty and the risk of hidden conceptual divergences arising only after the transaction has been

---

[45] More extensively on this, see H Wagner, 'Economic Analysis of Cross-border Legal Uncertainty: The example of the European Union' in J Smits (ed), *The Need for a European Contract Law: Empirical and Legal Perspectives* (Groningen: Europa Law Publishing, 2005).

[46] This is referred to as rational ignorance: I will spend on information only to the point when the last bit of information I have acquired allows me to reap net additional benefits.

entered into, if too extensive, could result in economic actors refraining from cross-border trade.

In sum, divergence is not undesirable as such. Yet in many cases it engenders significant costs, such as externalities, transaction costs, and (in the case of conceptual divergence) costs arising from information imperfections. These costs can exceed the benefits from divergence and thus justify the conclusion that divergence should be addressed. However, the inquiry does not end here. It must still be ascertained whether change would lead to an improvement.

5   What can be done about divergence?

A number of options are available to deal with a situation in which divergence would be undesirable.

5.1   *Do nothing and leave the market to deal with it*

At the outset, it must be remembered that markets typically provide 'private' solutions for dealing with certain costs associated with diverging legal systems. Such solutions do not in fact eliminate divergences but constitute a way to factor them into the choices of economic actors.

First of all, if parties can influence the law through contract, they will likely do so. In commercial contracts, for one, parties can either opt for one or the other legal system (or a third one) or define the law *inter partes* themselves.

Second, the legal profession can assist market players in reducing the costs of divergence by providing accurate advice, thereby minimizing transaction costs and the costs of information imperfections linked with conceptual divergence. In fact, through their work, legal professionals contribute to identifying cases of conceptual divergence. Over time, once these cases become common knowledge, the information imperfections are eliminated and conceptual divergence becomes equivalent to explicit divergence in economic terms.

Third, in commercial but also in consumer relationships, the insurance market can offer a possibility of translating divergence into quantitative terms, ie an insurance premium. In the case of liability laws, in particular, insurers have superior knowledge of the state of the law in each market and can provide a lower-cost alternative to endless inquiries, product modifications, etc. If a firm wants to keep relatively uniform prices, it can then equalize the cost of insurance over all of its customers.

In addition, large and multinational companies are generally familiar with dealing with multiple legal systems and have developed the necessary structures for cost-minimizing information-gathering, thanks also to economies of scale. In fact, they might find it worthwhile to develop international standards for contracts and products: those standards could bring about some sort of 'harmonization'.[47] In such cases, the interest of Member States (or of the European Commission) would rather lie in making sure that such standard-setting activities do not conceal competition law infringements.

These solutions can only work in certain cases: for instance, divergences in administrative procedure cannot be compensated via contract or insurance. Moreover, for small to medium enterprises (SMEs)[48] and consumers, such solutions might be less affordable or practicable. In situations where they are available, however, these market-based solutions can be attractive, especially if there are no externalities involved and the costs associated with divergence (transaction costs, information imperfections, as the case may be) are limited in comparison with the value of the overall activity.

Market-based solutions apply equally to explicit and conceptual divergence. It can be added, however, that when parties themselves draft in the contract the law applicable to their transaction, they must be aware of the existence of a conceptual divergence and explicitly address the problem, otherwise the contract will itself become the source of the hidden divergence, instead of removing it.

5.2 *Top-down harmonization*

Jurists tend to be less sanguine than economists about divergence between legal systems, and they readily see it as a problem. What is more, they often propose to remedy that problem with a fairly drastic solution, namely harmonization or even unification of the law. In such a process, the respective laws of each legal system, in the area where divergence is deemed problematic, are replaced by a single law common to all systems.

---

[47] In this sense, Wagner, see n 45 above, and the references contained therein.

[48] It has been noted, however, that in the debate launched by the Commission on the harmonization of contract law at the European level, some associations of SMEs have expressed their opposition to full harmonization.

Looking back at the costs associated with divergence, as they were identified above, the case for harmonization is most compelling when divergence leads to externalities. In such cases, given that market players and national legislators are unable to decide on the basis of a complete picture of costs and benefits, it is unlikely that an efficient outcome will be reached. Indeed, externalities are a typical form of market failure that requires intervention by public authorities.

The benefits of (successful) harmonization, including uniform implementation, are that the costs of divergence are removed:

- Externalities are addressed and removed.
- Transaction costs are eliminated, since cross-border activities will be subject to the same set of rules in all the relevant legal systems.
- Information imperfections disappear, since parties can rely on the common legal framework thus established.

As a consequence, cross-border activity would be boosted and so also would investment, consumption, and growth.

Furthermore, there might be occasions where economies of scale are possible, thus justifying the need for a uniform solution. This might be the case of problems of a complex technical nature that are more cheaply dealt with in a one-stop-shop setting.

As mentioned at the outset, however, jurists tend to ignore the benefits of the current situation and the costs associated with change. Even if divergence leads to costs, it is conceivable that harmonization would generate even higher costs.[49]

A superficial cost-benefit analysis of harmonization

At a superficial level, harmonization removes the benefits associated with divergence, first and foremost so that the law is better attuned to local preferences. Presumably, if divergence is found to be a problem, it is because the costs flowing from divergence exceed the benefits it provides. Therefore if harmonization could remove these costs, it would still produce an overall benefit even if the benefits of divergence were removed by the same token.

On that count, harmonization will always be beneficial, and indeed jurists would be right to focus solely on the costs of the current situation and the benefits of change.

---

[49] There is a shared presumption in the literature that full harmonization generally brings about higher costs than those caused by maintaining diversity.

A more complete cost-benefit analysis

The above analysis is incomplete on two accounts: harmonization itself generates costs (as opposed to the mere removal of the benefits of the current situation), and the benefits of harmonization must be discounted to reflect uncertainty as to realization.

Harmonization generates costs of its own, which must also be taken into account. First of all, the production of harmonized legislation is costly, involving as it does extensive background studies and discussions. Costs also arise because of the need to 'develop [. . .] new bureaucracies or demolish [. . .] old structures'.[50] Further costs are incurred in adapting to the new rules, in terms of information spreading and re-training.

Second and more fundamentally, it is a rare occurrence that the area to be harmonized is relatively autonomous within the law as a whole. More frequently, this area interacts with the rest of the law. For instance, product liability or State liability for breaches of EC law are part of the law of liability and more generally of private and/or public law. Ahead of harmonization, each legal system is in an equilibrium of sorts: the various areas of the law are supposedly seamlessly integrated into the legal system. Top-down harmonization, coming from the outside, implies a break within the legal system, ie the creation of a specific 'harmonized area' which co-exists with other remaining areas. In the ideal situation, implementing (incorporating) the harmonized law should be done seamlessly, without distorting the legal system. For instance, under EC law, the mechanism of the directive is designed to allow Member States some room in adapting the harmonized law to their legal system and thereby to minimize distortions. The ideal being an ideal, more often than not harmonization will generate distortions within the legal system or miss its goal because harmonization is undone at the implementation stage (as mentioned above), or sometimes both.

When faced with such distortions as a result of harmonization, legal systems can react in two ways. First, via a kind of ripple effect, the changes introduced in the harmonized area can induce further changes outside the harmonized area in order to restore the system to equilibrium. There are numerous examples of Member States using the implementation of a directive as an opportunity to change a broader area of their law (often in a spirit of 'cleaning up'). Such a ripple effect generates costs, but they are limited in

---

[50] Wagner, see n 45 above.

time. Second, the legal system can treat the harmonized area as a form of foreign body (*Fremdkörper*) and seek to isolate it. For an example, see the reaction of German courts and writers to the introduction of State liability for breaches of EC law via the *Francovich* and *Brasserie du Pêcheur* judgments. The ensuing tension within the legal system generates costs on a lasting basis.

Moreover, the need to legislate in many languages—leading to often-lamented inaccuracies, even within the same language[51]—may facilitate the reproduction of the divergence in the implementation phase.

The above analysis applies to explicit as well as conceptual divergences. However, given the complexity of the law, harmonization exercises sometimes end up replacing explicit divergence with conceptual divergence or merely pushing conceptual divergence deeper, so that harmonization does not deliver all the expected benefits. There is an illusion of convergence in terminology and presumably a fair amount of conceptual overlap, but somewhere at the conceptual level undesirable divergence remains. If this happens as the result of a harmonization effort aiming at removing the externalities and costs of an existing divergence, then it will instead merely replace such costs with new ones, perhaps adding those peculiar to conceptual divergences.

In addition to the above costs of harmonization, by implication, the benefits of harmonization must be discounted with a higher degree of uncertainty as to the results. By the same token, it is more likely that harmonization will induce significant distortions and thus costs. Accordingly, top-down harmonization efforts must be analysed as a trade-off between the benefits of harmonization and the costs associated with inducing distortions within legal systems.

5.3 *Bottom-up alternatives: 'regulatory emulation' and the marketplace of legal ideas*

Between doing nothing and introducing top-down harmonization, there is a third option, namely relying on bottom-up processes to bring about convergence when needed.

If legal systems diverge but do communicate with each other through trade and other forms of exchange, they will also communicate at the intellectual level, in the proverbial marketplace of ideas. If the various legal epistemic communities are introduced to each other's ideas, one could expect that they

---

[51] See, eg, B Pozzo, 'Harmonisation of European Contract Law and the Need of Creating a Common Terminology' (2003) 11 Eur Rev of Private L, 754.

will compare them. Over time, they might adopt the policies, concepts, reasoning, or outcomes of another community if they are convinced that they are preferable. A certain amount of convergence will then result.

Of course, if divergence echoes local preferences, one could object that local law will remain in place even after the comparison. However, in many cases, the need to reduce transaction costs and improve trade will act as a counterweight and will provide an incentive to move away from a law based strictly on local preferences.[52]

This view builds on the theory of *regulatory competition*[53] but complements that theory, hence the name 'regulatory emulation'. Regulatory competition theorists make a parallel between product markets and lawmaking: they consider legal rules as a sort of 'product' and depict lawmakers in the different legal systems[54] as the suppliers of this product. On a given topic,[55] different lawmakers compete with each other for the provision of the legal rules that are more attractive to their 'customers'—individuals as well as firms. Those 'customers', in turn, respond by relocating in the jurisdiction with the set of rules that best suits their preferences.[56] In this way, lawmakers are pushed to experiment and try to find the best legal rules (in a so-called 'race to the top'). This process of trial and error can generate further divergence but can also lead to a certain amount of convergence as 'good' rules are discovered and replicated. In this case, convergence will not have been imposed by any superior authority but chosen bottom-up by the legal systems on the basis of their own cost-benefit analysis of changing an existing rule. In this way, some of the costs of top-down harmonization are avoided.

The theory of regulatory competition has been used extensively to explain developments in American company law,[57] one of the topical legal fields

---

[52] It has been remarked, however, that some areas of law might be deeply connected with local preferences and therefore less subject to 'regulatory emulation' and that this might in particular be the case of 'interventionist' law, as opposed to 'facilitative' law. See Ogus, see n 8 above.

[53] R van den Bergh, 'Towards an Institutional Legal Framework for Regulatory Competition in Europe' (2000) 53 *Kyklos*, 435; D Esty and D Geradin, 'Regulatory Competition and Co-opetition' in D Esty and D Geradin (eds), *Regulatory Competition and Economic Integration: Comparative Perspectives* (Oxford: Oxford University Press, 2001) and Ogus, see n 16 above.

[54] Or at different levels in a single legal system with a federal structure.

[55] It is assumed that legislatures, each within its respective geographical borders, have the power to regulate the same kind of situations.

[56] The so-called 'voting with their feet' as developed by CM Tiebout, in relation to the provision of public goods, in his influential article 'A Pure Theory of Local Expenditures' (1956) 64 *J of Political Economy*, 416.

[57] R Romano, 'Law as a Product: Some Pieces of the Incorporation Puzzle' (1985) 1 J of L, Economics and Organization, 225.

where legislators compete to attract the incorporation of businesses within the boundaries of their jurisdiction. The ECJ judgments in the *Centros*[58] and *Überseering* cases,[59] by affirming the incorporation principle,[60] are often referred to as the starting points for the same kind of competition in the European setting.[61] In addition, environmental law and tax law are often analysed through the lens of regulatory competition.[62]

To be sure, critics of the theory have argued that such competition may easily lead to the degradation of legal standards in the interests of attracting more business (by, for instance, relaxing the protection of shareholders to the managers' advantage—the so-called race to the bottom or 'Delaware effect').[63] This critique, however, has been questioned on theoretical as well as empirical grounds.[64] It has also been remarked that the concepts of 'top' and 'bottom' are not very clear, being based on value judgements, and therefore that the concept of a race is not able to provide univocal policy guidance.[65] It is not to be taken for granted either that there will in fact be a 'race'.[66]

In fact, what is important for regulatory competition to work effectively are the assumptions on which it is based, in particular:

- a sufficiently large number of divergent legal systems among which to choose;

---

[58] Case C-212/97 *Centros* [1999] ECR I-1459.

[59] Case C-208/00 *Überseering* [2002] ECR I-9919.

[60] According to this principle, the legal existence and capacity of a company depends on the law of the State in which it is incorporated. What the Court has ruled is that any company, once incorporated in one Member State, is free to establish itself and do business in another Member State—even if this implies transferring its 'real seat'—without having to comply with the host country's legislation.

[61] Discussion of this issue can be found, amongst others, in K Heine, 'Regulatory Competition between Company Laws in the European Union: The Überseering Case' (2003) 38 *Intereconomics*, 102 and EM Kieninger, 'The Legal Framework of Regulatory Competition Based on Company Mobility: EU and US Compared' (2004) 6 German L J, 742.

[62] See, amongst others, R Revesz, 'Federalism and Regulation: Some Generalisations' in Esty and Geradin, see n 53 above, 3.

[63] L Bebchuk, 'Federalism and the Corporation: The Desirable Limits on State Competition in Corporate Law' (1992) 105 Harvard L Rev, 1443.

[64] See D Vogel and RA Kagan, 'National Regulations in a Global Economy: An Introduction' in D Vogel and RA Kagan (eds), *Dynamics of Regulatory Change: How Globalization Affects National Regulatory Policies* (Berkeley: University of California Press, 2004) and CM Radaelli, 'The Puzzle of Regulatory Competition' (2004) 24 *J of Public Policy*, 1.

[65] ibid.

[66] Heine, see n 61 above, and M Kahan and E Kamar, 'The Myth of State Competition in Corporate Law' (2002) 55 Stanford L Rev, 679.

- mobility or, more generally, reactivity on the part of individuals and firms in response to differences in the rules;
- reactivity on the part of the lawmakers to the choices made by their 'customers';
- a full understanding of the legal rules adopted in the different systems;
- no externality problems.

The first of these assumptions contains a clear policy indication against top-down harmonization: uniform legal systems do not provide alternatives and would therefore nullify the 'discovery' procedure.

The mobility issue, at first glance, might seem problematic, as it might imply very high relocation costs. However, in relation to many legal areas individuals do not need to move geographically in order to express their preferences: for instance, in the presence of mutual recognition, free movement of goods replaces the necessity of relocating; a choice of foreign law made by parties to a contract also reflects individual preferences without actual relocation. As has been emphasized, in many cases this is a question of private international law, ie whether legal systems will recognize and enforce the choice of law rule made by the parties to a transaction.[67]

Some doubts have been cast as to the reactivity of lawmakers to the preferences of individuals and firms.[68] However, so far, there seems to be no conclusive evidence one way or the other.[69]

The problem of knowledge of alternative legal rules and their effects seems to be a more severe one. The circulation of ideas between legal communities is obviously a condition *sine qua non*. At this juncture, in Europe such exchanges are still in their infancy. While EC law fosters the free movement of ideas (among others), there are still vast areas of law (and the legal community) that remain generally shielded from any confrontation with ideas from other legal communities. National legislation and the judgments of national courts are not disseminated beyond national borders, and only a small group of academics actually looks across these borders. Recently created networks of regulatory authorities such as the European

---

[67] See FJ Garcimartín Alférez, 'Regulatory Competition: A Private International Law Approach' (1999) 8 Eur J of L Economics, 251.

[68] Radaelli, see n 64 above, 7 and A Harcourt, 'Institution-driven Competition: The Regulation of Cross-border Broadcasting in the EU' EUI Working Papers, RSCAS no 2004/44, although one might doubt whether the broadcasting sector is the most representative example.

[69] See, for instance, on reactivity of legislators in the 'competition' for incorporations, Kieninger, see n 61 above, 766ff.

Competition Network (ECN), the European Regulators Group (ERG), or the European Regulators Group for Electricity and Gas (ERGEG) may be seen as examples of institutional devices for boosting circulation of information among legal systems. Furthermore, the creation of these networks prompts the development of technical tools and fora whereby information is made available across borders.

Lastly, the presence of market failures and in particular of externalities can effectively prevent the development of healthy regulatory competition, or generate a race to the bottom. Economics teaches us that in such situations, unco-ordinated actions of individuals (in the present case, of individual Member States) do not lead to the best outcome, the one that maximizes social welfare. This can justify some degree of co-ordination or some sort of top-down intervention.

In fact, it seems clear that we are never really faced with a binary choice— full harmonization or bare regulatory competition—but that there is a whole range of possibilities with variable degrees of competition and co-operation.[70] The necessity of a certain regulatory harmonization at the procedural level or at an *institutional meta-level* is generally advocated in order to allow regulatory competition to take place and avoid the risk of a race towards the bottom.[71]

In fact, as mentioned at the beginning of this section, the form of bottom-up solution suggested in this chapter is broader than the theory of 'regulatory competition' and market actors 'voting with their feet'. It also extends to a 'marketplace of legal ideas' where law is central and members of the legal community are looking for the best solution to the issues with which they are confronted.

There are at least three dimensions of this 'marketplace of ideas' that can work in favour of the elimination of harmful divergences among legal systems in the sense advocated by this chapter.

---

[70] In this sense, Esty and Geradin, see n 53 above; AO Sykes, 'Regulatory Competition or Regulatory Harmonization? A Silly Question?' (2000) 3 J of Int Economic L, 257 and Radaelli, see n 64 above.

[71] See, among others, C Barnard and S Deakin, 'Market Access and Regulatory Competition' in C Barnard and J Scott, *The Law of the Single European Market: Unpacking the Premises* (Oxford: Hart, 2002); Heine, see n 61 above and Garcimartín Alférez, see n 67 above. It is sometimes also argued that harmonization is indispensable when diverging terminology exists across legal systems (in this sense, Van den Bergh, see n 53 above). However, if we adopt the functionalist approach suggested above in section 3, the purely terminological problem loses much of its relevance.

1. The free movement of persons and goods, choice of law rules;
2. The circulation of legal ideas by academics or new forms/institutions of cooperation;
3. The role of the ECJ and the principle of proportionality.

The first point refers to the classical view of regulatory competition, but takes into account the alternatives to the physical relocation of economic agents, as noted above.

The second dimension broadens the idea of regulatory competition to a more general phenomenon of regulatory emulation by circulation not among economic actors but among legal actors and the regulators. At this level, legal rules do not evolve as a sort of 'side-effect' of the choices of economic actors and citizens; instead, they are compared and chosen directly by legal actors. Increasingly, the law is subject to review, benchmarking, impact assessment, etc, all of which typically involve a comparison with other jurisdictions. In some cases, institutions have been developed for the purpose, including networks such as the ECN and the ERG. In such networks there is a permanent flow of information about the experiences of and the rules applied in the different jurisdictions, and 'best practices' are continuously accessible. In this type of system, the various regulators can both experiment with new solutions and freely replicate those tried out by others. This model could be extended successfully to other areas outside the competition and network industries sectors.

Of course, the academic community performs a similar role, although this could indubitably be enhanced by increased cross-border cooperation and exchange. The various attempts at drafting 'common principles' and casebooks in different areas of law have been of great assistance in disseminating information on existing legal solutions and their characteristics.[72]

The third dimension emphasizes the role of the ECJ in the circulation of legal ideas and legal solutions. In this context the Court can be seen as a 'coordinator of information'.[73] Parties to the proceedings may refer to practices in other Member States and the Court itself may evaluate the proportionality of particular legal rules (such as mandatory requirements) in the light of what is done in other Member States. As a result, just as in the previous dimension, legal actors (attorneys and judges as well as national authorities convened for the alleged infringement of European Law or acting in support

---

[72] This quite apart from the question of rendering them binding instruments.
[73] Barnard and Deakin, see n 71 above, 223.

of another party) are exposed to the rules adopted in a different jurisdiction in an adversarial setting in which, for the purpose of winning the case, its relative advantages and disadvantages are singled out.

The kind of bottom-up process that we have described can help to explain the move towards convergence in the field of competition law. The Member States of the EU have very similar competition laws today but this has not always been the case. This convergence was not the result of a harmonization effort,[74] and it is possible that the previous regimes may have been better attuned to local preferences, but the benefits of convergence in terms of the reduction in transaction costs (including administrative costs) have played an important role in the drive towards change.

6 Conclusion

By looking at what we have discussed in the previous sections, we can attempt to draw some conclusions.

Bearing in mind that the mere existence of divergence is not a problem in itself, it is worth noting that none of the alternatives described above seems to be a panacea for all forms of 'problematic' divergence.

If the divergence problem is one of trans-boundary externalities, then, as has been highlighted, unco-ordinated actions might result in failure. In such cases, therefore, both explicit and conceptual divergence are probably best cured by harmonization. This does not necessarily imply that a uniform substantive rule should be imposed on all the jurisdictions involved. As we have mentioned, there are various degrees of inter-jurisdictional cooperation that can be established, relative to the problem at hand and the jurisdictions involved. Thus, harmonization could also take the form of a procedural framework,[75] within which it would be possible to come to an agreement or aim at establishing an appropriate (uniform) private international law rule.[76]

If the problem is caused by the presence of transaction costs, the solution will probably not be the same in every case. In some cases, the 'do nothing'

---

[74] Of course this is not meant to deny that some adaptations were not the fruit of choice, but rather the consequence of certain obligations, but the described convergence was certainly not a deliberate act of harmonization.

[75] In this direction, Barnard and Deakin, see n 71 above, 220.

[76] In favour of this alternative, Garcimartín Alférez, see n 67 above.

approach might work well. Full harmonization is generally prone to bringing about very high costs, without there being any certainty about the overall result. Moreover, in the case of conceptual divergence, it might push the problem deeper, thus reinforcing the costs specific to this type of divergence.

'Regulatory emulation'—a broader version of regulatory competition extending to the 'marketplace of legal ideas'—offers a valid alternative to the above-mentioned solutions. It could bring about a certain degree of convergence without many of the costs of top-down harmonization and only where this appears to be desirable because economic actors have revealed their preferences for a superior legal rule or because regulators have been exposed to (or forced to take into account) a legal rule in force in a different jurisdiction.

Moving back to conceptual divergence, in general the use of economic analysis tends to reduce the sense of urgency that might be felt when conceptual divergence is detected. Indeed, by and large, the various tools of economic analysis used to examine explicit divergence are applicable to conceptual divergence as well. As is the case with explicit divergence, they show that divergence can be explained rationally, that it does not really occur that often, that it may not always be undesirable, and that attempts to remove it can sometimes make the situation worse.

21

Towards an Internally Consistent Doctrine on Invoking Norms of EU Law

Koen Lenaerts and Tim Corthaut

1 Introduction

Divergence within the EU legal order has many causes. Several of these relate to the fact that EU law operates in interaction between the central institutions of the European Union and the legal orders of the twenty-seven Member States. The most notable remedy is the Union's judicial architecture, which allows the Commission and the Member States to act against divergence through the infringement procedure laid down in EC Treaty, Articles 226–228 and allows individuals to rely on EU law before national courts, which can be uniformly instructed through preliminary rulings by the European Court of Justice (ECJ). Another reason for divergence, however, is precisely the product of this centralized system of interpretation of EU law. First, the ECJ can act against divergence only to the extent that the Commission or national courts refer cases to it, thus leaving many issues unresolved. Second, and more importantly, the ECJ itself bears the responsibility of seizing the opportunities that do occur to respond in a consistent manner to the issues raised.

In this chapter these aspects come together in a discussion of the way in which EU norms can be invoked. In section 2 we aim to determine how, in dialogue with national courts, the ECJ has sent out diverging signals as to when norms of EU law can be invoked. On the one hand, divergence flows from conflicting conceptual approaches to invocability; on the other hand, it can be linked to the piecemeal construction of case law. Moreover, the introduction of the Third Pillar instruments has created further uncertainty. In our opinion, however, that divergence can be overcome. Therefore, in section 3 we will restate an alternative reading of case law, which recalls the role played by primacy in invoking norms of EU law.[1]

2   A doctrine shaped in dialogue with national courts

2.1   *Setting the stage: three areas of possible confusion*

If one looks at various cases involving the invocability of norms of EU law a somewhat confusing picture appears. On the one hand, there seems to be a thread that limits the possibilities of invoking norms of EU law to norms having 'direct effect', ie binding norms that are sufficiently clear, precise, and unconditional to confer rights on individuals. On the other hand, it turns out that these strict conditions are often eroded in practice, resulting in the possibility of raising EU instruments, with seemingly little or no binding force,[2] without any reference to rights,[3] or without much precision.[4] Moreover, with the introduction of the framework decision, a legal instrument was created without 'direct effect', but which clearly produces legal consequences which individuals can rely on in court.[5]

In the following paragraphs some landmark cases are recalled and the apparent divergence as to their outcomes highlighted. It will be suggested in section 2.2 that this divergence may be partly the result of the way in which the preliminary rulings procedure operates. At the same time, these landmark cases form both the building blocks and a litmus test for the model proposed in section 3, in that we submit that despite the ostensible divergence in the case law, it is possible to reconcile these cases with our approach.

---

[1] A more elaborate version of our thesis can be found in K Lenaerts and T Corthaut, 'Of Birds and Hedges: The Role of Primacy in Invoking Norms of EU Law' (2006) 31 ELR, 287–315.

[2] Such as a recommendation, see Case C-322/88 *Grimaldi* [1989] ECR 4407, paras 13 and 16 or the Charter of Fundamental Rights of the European Union, see Case C-540/03 *European Parliament v Council* [2006] ECR I-5769, para 38.

[3] Case C-344/04 *IATA* [2006] ECR I-403, para 39.

[4] Case C-58/89 *Commission v Germany* [1991] ECR I-4983, para 14.

[5] Case C-105/03 *Pupino* [2005] ECR I-5285 and see also the Opinion of Advocate General Ruiz-Jarabo Colomer in Case C-303/05 *Advocaten voor de Wereld* Judgment of the Court of 3 May 2007, nyr

A first area of seemingly diverging case law concerns the relationship between international law and internal norms of the EU legal order. First of all, there is the well-known strand of cases relating to the invocability of the law of the World Trade Organization (WTO). The ECJ has so far, subject to two minor exceptions,[6] denied both individuals[7] and Member States[8] the possibility to rely on the provisions of the WTO agreements, no matter what the purpose of invoking WTO law. Accordingly, the ECJ has refused to use WTO law as a yardstick for judicial review of EC law[9] and has rejected its use in actions for damages involving alleged breaches of WTO law.[10] Systematically, the ECJ recalls that the WTO legal instruments such as the WTO, TRIPS, and TBT agreements 'are not in principle, having regard to their nature and structure, among the rules in the light of which the Court is to review the lawfulness of measures adopted by the Community institutions'[11] and are 'not capable of conferring on citizens of the Community rights which they can invoke before the courts'.[12]

By contrast the ECJ does not seem to have much difficulty in allowing individuals to rely on other provisions of international law. Accordingly, the ECJ has accepted that individuals rely on fundamental norms of customary international law,[13] even if the exact scope of these norms is often difficult to ascertain. Likewise, the ECJ (or Court of First Instance, CFI) has allowed individuals to rely, against national and Community authorities, on provisions of a whole series of agreements with third countries ranging from the EEA agreement[14] to the Association Agreements with the Eastern European countries[15] to the Partnership and Cooperation Agreement with Russia[16]—even though most of the provisions relied on were arguably no more clear, precise, and unconditional than those of, for instance, the GATT.

---

[6] Case 70/87 *Fediol* [1989] ECR I-1789 and Case C-69/89 *Nakajima* [1991] ECR I-2069.

[7] Joined Cases C-300/98 and C-392/98 *Parfums Christian Dior* [2000] ECR I-11307 and Case C-377/02 *Van Parys* [2005] ECR I-1465.

[8] Case C-149/96 *Portugal v Council* [1999] ECR I-8395.

[9] ibid.

[10] Case C-94/02 P *Biret v Council* [2003] ECR I-10565.

[11] Case C-377/98 *Netherlands v European Parliament and Council* [2001] ECR I-7079, para 52.

[12] Joined Cases 21/72 to 24/72 *International Fruit* [1972] ECR 1219, para 27.

[13] Case C-162/96 *Racke* [1998] ECR I-3655.

[14] Case T-115/94 *Opel Austria* [1997] ECR II-39.

[15] For an overview, see K Lenaerts and P van Nuffel, *Constitutional Law of the European Union*, ed R Bray(2nd edn, London: Sweet & Maxwell, 2005) 742, n 390.

[16] Case C-265/03 *Simutenkov* [2005] ECR I-2579.

Moreover, when these international agreements are used as a yardstick for judicial review, reference is no longer made to the conferral of rights.[17]

A similar debate concerns the invocability of directives. The point of reference is *Faccini Dori*.[18] In this case the ECJ denied a consumer the right to reconsider her purchase made in the Milan train station, as Italian law, in contravention of Council Directive (EEC) 85/577, did not grant her this right. The ECJ stressed that 'a directive cannot of itself impose obligations on an individual and cannot therefore be relied upon as such against an individual',[19] even though 'the directive on contracts negotiated away from business premises is undeniably intended to confer rights on individuals and it is equally certain that the minimum content of those rights can be identified by reference to the provisions of the directive alone'.[20] Crucially, the ECJ indicated that directives create obligations for Member States only and are thus constitutionally different from regulations, through which the Community may enact obligations for individuals with immediate effect when the Treaties empower it to do so.[21] The sole alternative open to individuals, even if this is rather imperfect,[22] is a *Francovich* action for damages against the Member State that failed to implement the Directive in a correct or timely manner.

However, the case law has never been entirely straightforward. Ever since *Marleasing*,[23] which even predates *Faccini Dori*, the ECJ has urged national courts to draw on non-implemented or incorrectly implemented directives while interpreting national law such as to let one individual prevail over another.[24] The ECJ has since accepted that a directive may have the effect of setting aside a piece of Italian legislation on labelling that stood in the way of the normal implementation of a contractual relationship between individuals.[25] Moreover, the ECJ has also come close to legitimating a form of the horizontal effect of directives in allowing one individual, Ms Wells, to rely

---

[17] Case C-344/04 *IATA* [2006] ECR I-403, para 39.

[18] Case C-91/92 *Faccini Dori* [1994] ECR I-3325.

[19] ibid, para 20.

[20] ibid, para 28.

[21] ibid, para 24.

[22] T Tridimas, 'Horizontal Effect of Directives: A Missed Opportunity?' (1994) 19 ELR, 634.

[23] Case C-106/89 *Marleasing* [1990] ECR I-4135. More recent examples are Case C-456/98 *Centrosteel* [2000] ECR I-6007 and Joined Cases C-397/01 to C-403/01 *Pfeiffer* [2004] ECR I-8835.

[24] See in this respect T Corthaut, case note under Joined Cases C-240/98 to C-244/98 *Océano Grupo Editorial*, Case C-215/97 *Bellone* and Case C-456/98 *Centrosteel* (2002) 8 Columbia J of Eur L, 293–310.

[25] Case C-443/98 *Unilever* [2000] ECR I-7535.

on a directive, in order to contest a licence given to another individual, the owner of the neighbouring Conygar Quarry.[26]

At the same time *Berlusconi*[27] makes clear that there may be two fundamentally different approaches to the problem of invocability. Advocate General Kokott had opined that as a directive is at least binding on the Member State, it could be used to block the application of later legislation undoing the correct implementation of a directive in national law, as a matter of primacy.[28] By contrast, the ECJ refused to follow this path, expressing a genuine concern about the principle of the retroactive application of the more lenient penalty.[29] Indeed, in spite of language in the judgment suggesting that the Advocate General might well be right in principle,[30] the outcome which she suggested crossed a line by increasing the criminal liability of individual defendants as a result of invoking the—now incorrectly implemented—directive.[31]

The debate on the invocability of directives, especially in criminal matters, has moreover taken a new turn with the introduction of the framework decision. The drafters of Article 34 TEU, aware of the ECJ's position on the direct effect of directives, have explicitly excluded any 'direct effect' of framework decisions, also in vertical relations. However, framework decisions may still be invoked in national courts. First, this was foreseen by these same drafters, who provided for the possibility of preliminary rulings on the validity and interpretation of framework decisions. This only makes sense if framework decisions can be relied upon in a national court.[32] Second, the ECJ has already decided a case involving a framework decision invoked in national court proceedings to affect the national rules on evidence in a criminal trial to the detriment of the defendant and to the benefit of the victim, both of them individuals. Notwithstanding concerns about the compatibility of doing so with Article 6 ECHR, the ECJ has, as a matter of principle, indicated that the national court was to construe the internal legislation, so far as possible, in line with the object and purpose of the framework decision, despite the effects this might have on the respective legal positions of the parties to the case.[33]

---

[26]   Case C-201/02 *Delena Wells* [2004] ECR I-723.

[27]   Joined Cases C-387/02, C-391/02, and C-403/02 *Berlusconi* [2005] ECR I-3565.

[28]   See the Opinion of Advocate General Kokott in Joined Cases C-387/02, C-391/02, and C-403/02 *Berlusconi* [2005] ECR I-3565.

[29]   ibid, paras 66–69.

[30]   ibid, para 72.

[31]   ibid, paras 73–77.

[32]   See by analogy Case 6/64 *Costa v ENEL* [1964] ECR 1203.

[33]   Case C-105/03 *Pupino* [2005] ECR I-5285.

2.2 *A dialogue with national courts*

It is no coincidence that most of the landmark cases discussed above reached the ECJ through preliminary references. In the ensuing paragraphs our focus shifts to the interaction between the ECJ and national courts in shaping a doctrine of invocability. The analysis aims to identify two possible causes of perceived divergence in the ECJ case law, ie first, the number and content of requests for preliminary rulings and, second, the fact that, like any court, the ECJ decides 'one case at a time'.[34]

The more questions, the merrier?

Arguably, the primary goal of the system of preliminary rulings is the uniformity of Community law. However, there may be limits as to how much uniformity is to be expected from the exchange between national courts and the ECJ.[35] There are several reasons for this, both in respect of the national courts and the Court of Justice itself.

As to the national courts, issues relating to the invocability of EU law are undoubtedly at the forefront of a wider tendency towards ever more detailed questions being referred to the ECJ for a preliminary ruling. Having formulated the main principles about primacy and direct effect early on in its existence, the ECJ is indeed increasingly faced with rather concrete issues, both legally and factually. Once litigants came to realize the full potential of the principles of primacy and direct effect, new questions arose in the national courts, in particular about the procedural consequences of bringing EU law into the debate and about remedies in cases where Member States had failed to implement EC law.[36] The development of the *Francovich* doctrine of state liability[37] and the explicit rejection of horizontal direct effect of directives in the *Faccini Dori* case[38] are illustrations of this development.

But matters did not end there. Sometimes, ECJ judgments themselves led to further questions being raised. An example is offered by the *Centrosteel*

---

[34] The expression is coined by C Sunstein, *One Case at a Time: Judicial Minimalism on the Supreme Court* (Cambridge, MA: Harvard University Press, 2001).

[35] See in this respect also K Lenaerts and T Corthaut, 'Rechtsvinding door het Hof van Justitie' (2006) 55 Ars Aequi, 581–588.

[36] For an elaborate analysis of this evolution, see HW Micklitz, *The Politics of Judicial Co-operation in the EU* (Cambridge: Cambridge University Press, 2005); see also M Poiares Maduro, *We the Court: The European Court of Justice & the European Economic Constitution* (Oxford: Hart, 1998) 25–30.

[37] Joined Cases C-6/90 and C-9/90 *Francovich* [1991] ECR I-5357.

[38] Case C-91/92 *Faccini Dori* [1994] ECR I-3325.

case,[39] where the national court sought a way around an Italian rule that apparently ran counter to a limited list of grounds for nullity contained in a non-implemented Directive. The issue had already been decided in *Bellone*.[40] However, the latter judgment could be (mis)interpreted as requiring the national court to accord horizontal direct effect to the Directive. The national court in *Centrosteel*, aware of the ECJ's stance on the matter, therefore thought it wise to refer the issue to the ECJ again. This time the ECJ—helped by a ruling of the Italian *Corte Suprema di Cassazione* reversing its previous interpretation of Italian law—was able to solve the issue as a classic case of interpretation of national law in conformity with EC law.[41]

Furthermore, the increase in legal and factual complexity of preliminary references is a steady phenomenon. Nowadays national courts know about *Faccini Dori*,[42] *Francovich*,[43] *Marshall*,[44] or *Marleasing*.[45] But they seek to reconcile those doctrines with the particularities of national laws and the facts of the case before them. The ECJ's role changes accordingly. It no longer needs to tell a national court to set aside conflicting legislation as a matter of primacy, but rather whether and how this can be reconciled, for instance, with the principle of retroactivity of the milder penal law.[46] The ECJ no longer has to proclaim *in abstracto* that national law must be interpreted, so far as possible, in conformity with non-implemented or incorrectly implemented directives. The importance of *Pfeiffer*[47] accordingly does not lie so much in its reiteration of this principle, but in the way in which it calls on the national court to consider all aspects of the internal legal order[48] and to apply every interpretative tool available.[49]

---

[39] Case C-456/98 *Centrosteel* [2000] ECR I-6007.

[40] Case C-215/97 *Bellone* [1998] ECR I-2191.

[41] Case C-456/98 *Centrosteel* [2000] ECR I-6007, para 9. Interestingly the national court also suggested a totally different approach, based on the direct effect of the underlying treaty provisions.

[42] Case C-91/92 *Faccini Dori* [1994] ECR I-3325.

[43] Joined Cases C-6/90 and C-9/90 *Francovich* [1991] ECR I-5357.

[44] Case C-271/91 *Marshall* [1993] ECR I-4367.

[45] Case C-106/89 *Marleasing* [1990] ECR I-4135.

[46] Joined Cases C-387/02, C-391/02, and C-403/02 *Berlusconi* [2005] ECR I-3565.

[47] Joined Cases C-397/01 to C-403/01 *Pfeiffer* [2004] ECR I-8835.

[48] ibid, para 115.

[49] ibid, para 116. For an analysis of the interpretative tools known in the German legal order and available to the national court in *Pfeiffer*, see K Riesenhuber and R Domröse, 'Richtlinienkonforme Rechtsfindung und nationale Methodenlehre' (2005) 51 Recht der Internationalen Wirtschaft, 47, 51 and 52–53.

This new role creates new problems. On the one hand, there may be a problem as to the degree of factual involvement. In principle, fact-finding is the province of the national courts. With preliminary references becoming more detailed, there is, however, a risk that the boundary between law and fact may get exceedingly blurred.[50]

On the other hand, the tendency to steer away from abstract principles may have an effect on the internal consistency of the case law itself. There is, of course, the prohibition on the ECJ[51] deciding issues of national law or fact. Yet, 'hard cases, it is said, make bad law'[52] and the ECJ does not fully escape that fate. Hard cases occur where the national court indicates that it knows the basic framework but is in need of further guidance as to how the framework interacts with the intricacies of national law. A case like *Berlusconi*[53] is not hard because the basic framework is initially in doubt, but because every step the ECJ takes in the application of that framework becomes visibly outcome-determinative and may, in turn, have an impact on the basic framework itself. And though it is undoubtedly wise to seek inspiration for the solution of peripheral problems by refreshing principles, the Court cannot afford to do so in every case. Therefore, attempts such as in section 3 hereinafter to search for some coherent theory behind the case law outside the interest-laden context of the odd case are increasingly important to support the further development of jurisprudence in the face of new hard cases coming up in future.

This is, of course, not a problem that is exclusive to the ECJ. For example, after having struck down a series of federal laws based on s 5 of the Fourteenth Amendment for lack of congruency between these laws and the breach of fundamental rights by state authorities to be remedied,[54] the US Supreme Court recently created some confusion when it started to apply its

---

[50] Compare, eg, Case C-206/01 *Arsenal Football Club* [2002] ECR I-10723 with the judgment of Laddie J in *Arsenal Football Club Plc v Reed* (No 2) [2002] EWHC Ch 2695; [2003] 1 CMLR 13 and the reversal on appeal in *Arsenal Football Club Plc v Reed* [2003] EWCA Civ 96; [2003] 2 CMLR 25. For more, see the case note of A Arnull (2003) 40 CML Rev, 753–769.

[51] The ECJ sometimes explicitly introduces a preliminary paragraph indicating its understanding of the findings of the referring court, see Case C-199/05 *European Community* [2006] Judgment of the Court of 26 October 2006, nyr, para 17 and Case C-168/05 *Mostaza Claro* [2006] Judgment of the Court of 26 October 2006, nyr, paras 21–23.

[52] John Campbell Argyll (1678–1743).

[53] Joined Cases C-387/02, C-391/02, and C-403/02 *Berlusconi* [2005] ECR I-3565.

[54] *City of Boerne v Flores* 521 US 507 (1997) and *Florida Prepaid Postsecondary Education Expense Board v College Savings Bank* 527 US 627 (1999).

new test in various contexts with different outcomes.[55] If we assume that, in the absence of any statement in that direction, there is no intent of the US Supreme Court to overturn precedent, the explanation may just be that the US Supreme Court has reached a state of equilibrium where the principles have been spelled out and the even-handed application of those principles results in outcomes which go both ways, with some federal statutes meeting the new test and others being invalidated. However, there is a major difference in EU law. Once such state of equilibrium has been reached, the US Supreme Court can easily turn its attention away from the matter and leave the application of the new test to the Circuit Courts of Appeals.

In contrast, the ECJ may time and time again be drawn into the debate because of new references seeking further clarification. Some important nuances are nonetheless in order. The first is that national courts, when properly instructed by the ECJ on the principles underlying a field of the law, can play a filtering role similar to that of the US Circuit Courts of Appeals, and exercise their discretion, however limited for the courts of last instance, not to refer the issue to the ECJ.[56] Second, the ECJ has its own filtering mechanisms in place to cope with repetition. Increasingly such cases are disposed of by Chambers of the Court composed of five or even just three Judges,[57] often without oral proceedings,[58] and occasionally even by a simple order, rather than a judgment.[59] As a result, one could even argue that the cases which the Grand Chamber decides every year are similar to the case load of the US Supreme Court.

The enlargement of the EU has added a further dimension in this respect. As the Full Court will rarely be convened to decide cases,[60] the major cases are virtually always dealt with by the Grand Chamber. However, the Grand Chamber is composed of only thirteen Judges, apart from the President and the four Presidents of the Chambers of five Judges, allocated through a rotation system.[61] It remains to be seen whether this will affect the stability

---

[55] Compare the outcome in *Kimel v Florida Board of Regents* 528 US 62 (2000) or *Trustees of the University of Alabama v Garrett* 531 US 356 (2001) with *Nevada Department of Human Resources v Hibbs* 538 US 721 (2003) or *Tennessee v Lane* 541 US 509 (2004).

[56] Case 283/81 *CILFIT* [1982] ECR 3415 and Case C-461/03 *Schul* [2005] ECR I-10513.

[57] Art 11(c) and 44(3) Rules of Procedure of the Court of Justice.

[58] Art 44(2) and 44(a) Rules of Procedure of the Court of Justice.

[59] Art 104(3) Rules of Procedure of the Court of Justice.

[60] See Opinion 1/03 *Lugano Convention* [2006] ECR I-1145 and Case C-432/04 *Commission v Cresson* [2006] Judgment of the Court of 11 July 2006, nyr.

[61] Art 11(b) Rules of Procedure of the Court of Justice. In accordance with the principle of the *gesetzliche Richter*, the rotation list of Judges is published in the Official Journal.

of the case law, and if so to what extent. To cope with this challenge, the President and the Presidents of the Chambers of five Judges bear particular responsibility. As they are permanent members of the Grand Chamber they should contribute to ensuring coherence in the case law by drawing attention to precedents or—in absolutely exceptional cases of threatening conflict between Grand Chamber precedents—by urging referral to the Full Court.

Another, closely related consequence of the tendency to steer away from abstract theories lies in the shifting perception of the role of the ECJ. When dealing with cases like *Berlusconi*[62] or *Pfeiffer*,[63] the ECJ comes within an inch of deciding the case as such. Thus, the ECJ increasingly risks being perceived as deciding cases, not in the grand sense of establishing landmark principles (which in their application, of course, result in 'winners' and 'losers'), but in the sense of directly determining who wins and who loses. Admittedly, it has never been the case so that the 'parties' to a preliminary rulings procedure were only there to assist the ECJ almost detachedly in finding the correct answer to the question asked by the national court. In reality, the parties before the national court vigorously continue their debate before the ECJ, and rightly so. However, the lines of the debate have traditionally been drawn quite clearly, as the roles of the ECJ and the national court are different. If, however, these lines are somehow blurred, a series of knock-on effects may affect the coherence of the case law. Indeed, in such circumstances one would expect more pressure on national courts to refer questions,[64] and thus more cases, before the ECJ. As argued above, this alone may result in more divergence. Furthermore, when parties realize that it actually is the ECJ that decides whether they win or lose, they will be even less interested in the formulation of general principles, the application of which they can still steer before the national court, but will merely focus on getting a decision in their favour from the ECJ. Given the fact that in deciding a concrete case additional policy concerns may enter the debate beyond those relating to the interpretation of the underlying principles of EU law as such, there is a risk that such additional policy concerns will confuse matters, since the

---

[62] Joined Cases C-387/02, C-391/02, and C-403/02 *Berlusconi* [2005] ECR I-3565.

[63] Joined Cases C-397/01 to C-403/01 *Pfeiffer* [2004] ECR I-8835.

[64] A tendency that may even be strengthened by the introduction of State liability in cases where national courts of last instance failed to refer, see Case C-224/01 *Köbler* [2003] ECR I-10239 and Case C-173/03 *Traghetti del Mediterraneo* [2006] Judgment of the Court of 13 June 2006, nyr.

rationale for any given answer to a preliminary reference may be inspired to a far greater extent by the peculiarities of the case at hand. This may make it difficult to avoid result-driven divergence in the case law concerning the principles of EU law involved, including in the field of invocability of norms of EU law.[65]

One case at a time

A further element flows from a crucial constitutional brake on even the most activist court: judges can only decide issues to the extent that they arise in the cases presented to them. Accordingly, the steps in the development of the doctrine of direct effect are to be traced back to the various attempts by the ECJ to formulate satisfactory answers to the specific questions asked by national courts. This implies that the ECJ may not be in a position fully to clarify the contents of that doctrine until another question arises. Of course, occasionally *obiter dicta* slip into a judgment, placing the answer given to the concrete question in a broader perspective. Nonetheless, the very nature of a case-based system brings with it some incompleteness, uncertainty, and apparent incoherence in the formulation of the doctrine.

As a side-effect, the 'wrong' case at the 'wrong' time may greatly upset the development of the case law. *Pupino*[66] was arguably the ideal case for the ECJ to attach some legal consequences to framework decisions, in spite of the statement in Article 34 TEU that framework decisions do not have direct effect. The case could be read as raising the question of whether EU law required the national court to try to give optimal protection to vulnerable child witnesses where national law was somewhat ambiguous on when non-confrontational procedures could be used. Clearly, in doing so there were some concerns about the rights of the defence, but none of these carried so much weight that they could not be brushed aside: after all, national law provided for these types of procedure, which in all likelihood were not contrary to Article 6 ECHR. Accordingly, expecting the national court to extend the use of those procedures in order to protect children in conformity with the framework decision did not really impose a burden on the accused, even if the impact on the outcome of the case might be quite real.

---

[65] The perception of result-driven divergence in this field has already given rise to strong academic criticism, see B Wegener and T Lock, 'Die Kleinen "hängt" man, die Großen lässt man laufen? Berlusconi und Niselli—Ungleiche vor dem EuGH' (2005) 40 Europarecht, 802.

[66] Case C-105/03 *Pupino* [2005] ECR I-5285.

Imagine, however, that the first case to reach the ECJ had really concerned the criminal liability of the defendant.[67] We know from *Berlusconi*[68] that directives cannot be invoked in order directly to impose additional criminal responsibility or sanctions on the defendant beyond the provision of national law. Likewise the ECJ would rightly reject any thesis that the national court was under an obligation to interpret domestic law so as to increase the criminal responsibility or the sanction to be imposed on the defendant directly on the basis of the framework decision.[69] But in doing so, the first landmark judgment in the field might have carried the message that framework decisions do not have legal consequences in the Member States if they have not been fully implemented or that they can never negatively affect the position of defendants. In such a context, arguing a case such as *Pupino*[70] would have become significantly more difficult. Of course, it would still have been possible to make the same arguments in this case. Nevertheless, the tone of the debate would have been different.

Admittedly, clever lawyers will always try to find ways out. For example, when the national court in *Centrosteel*[71] realized that *Bellone*[72] appeared a rather shaky precedent for setting aside Italian legislation, since it seemed to be based on the horizontal direct effect of directives, it made a whole series of inventive suggestions to the ECJ in order to achieve the same result by relying on the Treaty provisions underpinning the Directive. As indicated above, however, what really saved the day in *Centrosteel* was the 'switch in time' by Italy's highest court.[73] In the absence of such a happy coincidence,[74]

---

[67] For instance a case about the interpretation of the common definition of terrorism, see Art 1 of Council Framework Decision (EC) on combating terrorism [2002] OJ L164/3.

[68] Joined Cases C-387/02, C-391/02, and C-403/02 *Berlusconi* [2005] ECR I-3565.

[69] See by analogy Case C-168/95 *Arcaro* [1996] ECR I-4705, paras 41–42.

[70] Case C-105/03 *Pupino* [2005] ECR I-5285.

[71] Case C-456/98 *Centrosteel* [2000] ECR I-6007, para 9.

[72] Case C-215/97 *Bellone* [1998] ECR I-2191.

[73] Case C-456/98 *Centrosteel* [2000] ECR I-6007, para 17.

[74] Arguably, this begs the core question of how the ECJ ought to have reacted if the Italian courts had not made a 'switch in time'? To a certain extent the ECJ had answered that question already the first time around when it ruled against the Italian law in Case C-215/97 *Bellone* [1998] ECR I-2191, without making any reservation as to the effect of the Directive on private parties. But it was, of course, precisely that case which triggered the concerns of the referring court in Case-456/98 *Centrosteel* [2000] ECR I-6007. The outcome of Joined Cases C-397/01 to C-403/01 *Pfeiffer* [2004] ECR I-8835 demonstrates that it remains impossible to rely solely on the primacy of non-implemented or incorrectly implemented directives in horizontal relations. In those circumstances, the suggestion of the national court to look beyond the directive and turn attention to the underlying Treaty provisions might well have been taken up. Compare Case C-144/04 *Mangold* [2005] ECR I-9981, paras 74–77.

however, the most effective way of overcoming a perceived divergence with regard to whether a certain norm can be invoked in a particular way is by fitting each case into a consistent doctrine on invoking norms of EU law. That is what we will set out to do in section 3.

3 Overcoming divergence

Our argument is that primacy may help to overcome divergence. With this we actually mean two things. On the one hand, by giving primacy the prominent place it deserves in any discourse on invoking norms of EU law a more uniform model can be applied, irrespective of whether the norm invoked is an international agreement, a directive, or a framework decision. On the other hand, as the principle of primacy is nothing more than a conflict rule, it can only do so much. Accordingly, by recalling the different roles played by primacy and direct effect we will argue that some of the divergent outcomes, if they cannot be overcome, can at least be explained. From the outset it should be clear that what follows is not a plea for the horizontal direct effect of directives, but rather a demonstration that both *Faccini Dori*[75] and *Unilever Italia*[76] are good law, as they fall on different sides of the constitutional divide. Similarly, no position is taken on the desirability of excluding virtually all legal consequences of the WTO agreements, but rather it is submitted that the path chosen by the ECJ can be reconciled with its seemingly liberal approach to invocability of an international agreement in *IATA*.[77] Finally, it will become clear that as directives and framework decisions are constitutionally different, their legal consequences must differ as well—but only to the extent that they really are constitutionally different.

Our starting point is simple. Since the beginning of the case law, the EC legal order has had a basic conflict rule,[78] called primacy: whenever a national rule conflicts with a rule of Community law the latter is to trump the former, irrespective of the status of the national rule concerned in the domestic legal order, and irrespective of whether the Community rule is one of primary or

---

[75] Case C-91/92 *Faccini Dori* [1994] ECR I-3325.

[76] Case C-443/98 *Unilever* [2000] ECR I-7535.

[77] Case C-344/04 *IATA* [2006] ECR I-403.

[78] P van Nuffel, 'De doorwerking van het Europees gemeenschapsrecht in de Belgische rechtsorde' (2005) 53 SEW Tijdschrift voor Europees en Economisch Recht, 3–4.

secondary law. The same principle applies in the Second and Third Pillars as well,[79] which resonates with the conception of the ECJ reading a basis for the concept of *Unionstreue*[80] into the idea of an ever-closer Union laid down in Article 1 TEU. Accordingly, for the EU the following holds true as well, namely that 'the law stemming from the Treaty, an independent source of law, could not, because of its special and original nature, be overridden by domestic legal provisions, however framed, without being deprived of its character as [EU] law and without the legal basis of the [Union] itself being called into question'.[81]

One might think that only provisions of EU law enjoying direct effect could be awarded this type of precedence. On this view, only those provisions that are intended to confer rights on individuals and which are sufficiently clear, precise, and unconditional could result in blocking the application of national law. This is however not a necessity, even though primacy and direct effect are not entirely unrelated.[82] It appears from *Costa* that the real concern is consistency:[83] to the extent that a national measure is inconsistent with EC law in a situation *where both norms claim applicability*, the national measure cannot be allowed to apply over EC law. But if we take consistency seriously, there is no need at this stage of the analysis to identify whether EC law confers rights on individuals. The only thing that matters is that EC law, and by extension EU law, claims applicability and imposes an identifiable result which cannot be thwarted by incompatible national measures. This result may be to grant rights to individuals, but it may also be to create the conditions under which rights are to be granted to individuals, as will often be the case with directives. When it comes to primacy the relevant question is whether a conflict can be identified. In principle,[84] if it can, the conflicting national measure has to yield.

---

[79] For more on this, see Lenaerts and Corthaut, see n 1 above, 289–290.

[80] Case C-105/03 *Pupino* [2005] ECR I-5285, paras 41–43.

[81] Compare Case 6/64 *Costa v ENEL* [1964] ECR 1203.

[82] JM Prinssen, *Doorwerking van Europees recht: de verhouding tussen directe werking, conforme interpretatie en overheidsaansprakelijkheid* (Deventer: Kluwer, 2004) 11.

[83] 'The integration into the laws of each Member State of provisions which derive from the Community, and more generally the terms and the spirit of the treaty, make it impossible for the States, as a corollary, to accord precedence to a unilateral and subsequent measure over a legal system accepted by them on a basis of reciprocity. Such a measure cannot therefore be *inconsistent* with that legal system.' See Case 6/64 *Costa v ENEL* [1964] ECR 1203 (emphasis added).

[84] Even though a rather rigorous application of primacy is advocated in this chapter, it is to be acknowledged that the case law demonstrates that even a principle as fundamental as the primacy of EC law cannot always apply without qualification; see, for instance, the limitations

When EC law itself intends to grant rights to individuals, we are not merely concerned with removing inconsistencies from the national legal order, but with actively imposing a particular burden on an identifiable debtor for the benefit of an identifiable creditor. Only in such a setting does direct effect *sensu stricto* come into play. Direct effect is then a very particular way of invoking a higher norm in order to enforce rights that were conferred upon the applicant by that norm and which would not otherwise have existed in the national legal order. In those circumstances, it does not suffice to stop the application of inconsistent national law, as EC law must be resorted to in order to fill a gap in the national legal order. Then it does matter whether the EC norm relied on was intended to confer rights upon individuals and whether to that effect it is sufficiently clear, precise, and unconditional because, on the one hand, the norm identifies these rights and the persons who must provide them, and, on the other hand, the norm indicates when and under what conditions the rights claimed are deemed to be created in the national legal order.

In connection with this, several authors have made pleas for a renewed focus on the primacy of EU law[85] and on analysing the ways to invoke Community law rights in a Hohfeldian analytical framework,[86] resulting in a distinction between the invocability of exclusion and the invocability of substitution.[87] This distinction has been taken up by several Advocates General of the ECJ. Foremost, there is the Opinion of Advocate General Léger

---

flowing from fundamental rights in Joined Cases C-387/02, C-391/02, and C-403/02 *Berlusconi* [2005] ECR I-3565.

[85] M Lenz, D Sif Tynes, and L Young, 'Horizontal What? Back to Basics' (2000) 25 ELR, 509–522.

[86] C Hilson and T Downes, 'Making Sense of Rights: Community Rights in EC Law' (1999) 24 ELR, 121–139.

[87] PV Figueroroa Regueiro, 'Invocability of Substitution and Invocability of Exclusion: Bringing Legal Realism to the Current Development of the Case-law of "Horizontal" Direct Effect of Directives', Jean Monnet Working Paper 7/02, available at <http://www.jeanmonnetprogram.org/>; see also T Eilmansberger, 'The Relationship between Rights and Remedies in EC Law: In Search of the Missing Link' (2004) 41 CML Rev, 1213–1216. The distinction goes back on earlier, mainly French legal writing often inspired by French administrative law; see amongst others Y Galmot and JC Bonichot, 'La Cour de justice des Communautés européennes et la transposition des directives en droit national' (1988) Revue française de droit administrati, 16; T Dal Farra, 'L'invocabilité des directives communautaires devant le juge national de la légalité' (1992) 28 Revue Trimestrielle de Droit Européen, 631; P Manin, 'De l'utilisation des directives communautaires par les personnes physiques ou morales' (1994) 4 L'Actualité Juridique Droit Administratif, 259; D Simon, *La directive européenne* (Paris: Dalloz, 1997) and *Le système juridique communautaire* (2nd edn, Paris: Presses Universitaires de France, 2001).

in *Linster* describing the distinction between *invocabilité d'exclusion* and *invocabilité de substitution*,[88] following the lead of Advocate General Saggio in *Océano Grupo Editorial*.[89] Since then this approach has inspired others, including Advocate General Ruiz-Jarabo Colomer[90] and Advocate General Kokott.[91] We build further on these views and apply them also outside the context of directives in order to develop a more consistent theory of invocability which can apply to any norm of EU law and to the relationship between EU law and international law.[92]

First, the relationship between EC law and international law is to be addressed. In line with what was argued above, there is no need for direct effect *sensu stricto* when invoking international agreements to assess the validity of EC measures. Indeed, the ECJ has accepted that the validity of such measures can be reviewed in the light of international agreements, or even in the light of customary international law, without having to wonder whether these norms confer rights on individuals.[93] So why does this not extend to most cases involving WTO law? The answer lies in the fact that primacy only works to the extent that there is a conflict between two norms which both claim to be applicable.

This actually implies two qualities the norms at issue must have: first, the norms must have some identifiable content, ie it must be possible to ascertain some behavioural standard for the actor to whom the norm is addressed. Second, the norm must be binding, in the sense that it vests a legally enforceable claim in another actor to ensure compliance with that standard. The extent to which this is the case differs depending on the legal instrument relied upon. In the case of WTO law, the second factor causes difficulties.[94]

---

[88]   See the Opinion of Advocate General Léger in Case C-287/98 *Linster* [2000] ECR I-6917, paras 57ff.

[89]   See the Opinion of Advocate General Saggio in Joined Cases C-240/98 to C-244/98 *Océano Grupo Editorial* [2000] ECR I-4941, para 30. However, doubts have been expressed as to whether the claimed 'exclusion' made by Saggio really sufficed to explain the result in that case, see in this sense the annotation by Corthaut, see n 24 above, 301–310.

[90]   See the Opinion of Advocate General Ruiz-Jarabo Colomer in Joined Cases C-397/01 to C-403/01 *Pfeiffer* [2004] ECR I-8835.

[91]   See the Opinion of Advocate General Kokott in Joined Cases C-387/02, C-391/02, and C-403/02 *Berlusconi* [2005] ECR I-3565.

[92]   Lenaerts and Corthaut, see n 1 above, 292.

[93]   Case C-377/98 *Netherlands v European Parliament and Council* [2001] ECR I-7079, para 54.

[94]   This does not preclude a different form of invocability, however: the interpretation in conformity with EU law. As Case C-322/88 *Grimaldi* [1989] ECR 4407 demonstrates, even non-binding norms still form part of the legal order of the EU and they also affect the legal orders of the Member States, whether as the result of the implicit hierarchy of norms or the

In ruling that, given the political character of the obligations incurred, the WTO norms 'are not in principle, having regard to their nature and structure, among the rules in the light of which the Court is to review the lawfulness of measures adopted by the Community institutions',[95] the ECJ indicates that no matter how detailed those norms may be, they do not, unlike similar provisions of the EEA Agreement, aim to bind the Community in the above-mentioned sense of vesting a legally enforceable claim in any actor. Accordingly, no conflict can exist, making judicial review in the light of these norms to no purpose.

This also explains why there are exceptions to this rule. To the extent that the EC indicates that it nonetheless considers itself bound by these norms, it becomes possible to rely on them. This is what happened in *Fediol*[96] and *Nakajima*.[97] Moreover, this reasoning is not limited to the WTO agreements, as the ECJ used the same technique to justify review of an EC measure in the light of the Charter of Fundamental Rights of the European Union.[98]

Second, the foregoing analysis offers important lessons for the invocability of non-implemented or incorrectly implemented directives. Directives can be relied upon in national court (or by the Commission in the ECJ in an infringement procedure) to assess the compatibility of national measures if the same two conditions are fulfilled. The first condition depends on the content of the directive, but as we do not need the conferral of rights, but rather some behavioural standard, it explains why the ECJ has been able to find infringements of rather vague norms contained in a directive.[99] The second condition often causes difficulties. Directives are binding on their addressee: they set a behavioural standard for the relevant actors, the Member States, to whom they are addressed. But who is entitled to claim in court that the Member States comply with that standard? The Commission is entitled, in infringement proceedings brought in the ECJ.[100] Private parties are entitled, in a setting in which they may oppose the public authorities

---

obligation of good faith applicable in international law and specified in the First Pillar by Art 10 TEC, in the Second Pillar by Art 11(2) TEU, and in the Third Pillar by Case C-105/03 *Pupino* [2005] ECR I-5285.

[95]   Case C-377/98 *Netherlands v European Parliament and Council* [2001] ECR I-7079, para 52.

[96]   Case 70/87 *Fediol* [1989] ECR 1789, para 20.

[97]   Case C-69/89 *Nakajima* [1991] ECR I-2069, paras 26–32.

[98]   Case C-540/03 *European Parliament v Council* [2006] Judgment of the Court of 27 June 2006, nyr, para 38. See Lenaerts and Corthaut, see n 1 above, 301–302.

[99]   Case C-58/89 *Commission v Germany* [1991] ECR I-4983, para 14.

[100]   Arts 226–228 TEC.

of the Member State concerned.[101] However, matters get more complicated when there are additional private parties involved. Two situations may occur. The first involves a private party requesting judicial review of a national measure providing a benefit to another private party. An example is *Wells*.[102] In such a situation the presence in the dispute of the second private party does not prevent invocation of the directive. Indeed, the directive is not invoked against this private party, but against the government. It is not the behaviour of an individual which is assessed in the light of the directive but that of the government. However, all private parties involved must bear the consequences of the outcome of this judicial review procedure, which may be beneficial to some, like Ms Wells, and detrimental to others, like the quarry owners.

The second situation involving indirect judicial review is an even more controversial one. Here the parties are both private. This was the situation in *Unilever*,[103] where Unilever Italia was allowed to raise the incompatibility of an Italian law with a directive in a dispute opposing it to the buyer of barrels of its olive oil. As a result, the olive oil was no longer considered to be labelled in violation of the law, thus making delivery of the barrels conform to the terms of the contract. The buyer, who had initially refused to pay, thus had to pay in accordance with the underlying rule of national contract law *pacta sunt servanda*. This situation is not fundamentally different from *Wells*.[104] Where domestic law allow the raising of an exception of illegality against a national measure, the relevant actors in the dispute change:[105] what is assessed first is not the behaviour of the private parties to the contract, but the behaviour of the government in adopting the national measure in question. As the government is bound by a directive as to the result to be achieved, once the period for implementation has lapsed, the government's behaviour can be reviewed in the light of the content of the directive—irrespective of whether the directive contains procedural rules or substantive ones.[106] Just as in *Wells* 'mere adverse repercussions on the rights of third

---

[101] Case 148/78 *Ratti* [1979] ECR 1629 and Case C-188/89 *Foster* [1990] ECR I-3313.

[102] Case C-201/02 *Delena Wells* [2004] ECR I-723.

[103] Case C-443/98 *Unilever* [2000] ECR I-7535.

[104] Case C-201/02 *Delena Wells* [2004] ECR I-723.

[105] In some Member States this is to be taken literally, in that the government may intervene, or the validity question is referred to a specialist court. For a clear example see Lenaerts and Corthaut, see n 1 above, 309, n 30.

[106] The extension to substantive rules is controversial; see S Prechal, 'Case note under Joined Cases C-397/01–403/01, Pfeiffer' (2005) 42 CML Rev, 1447. However, there is at least one example where the ECJ has done just that: Case C-215/97 *Bellone* [1998] ECR I-2191.

parties, even if the repercussions are certain, do not justify preventing an individual from invoking the provisions of a directive against the Member State concerned',[107] and thus are no bar to the indirect judicial review to be carried out. It is true that individuals are not bound by a directive as such, and should not be penalized on the basis of *nemo auditur*. They can freely decide to comply only with the rules currently in force in the domestic legal order, even when those rules are incompatible with the directive. However, an individual who does not take into account a behavioural standard for a Member State laid down in a directive and tries to hide behind national legislation, cannot plead surprise at the ensuing 'adverse repercussions' when the Member State spontaneously changes that legislation or is forced to comply through the procedural mechanisms provided to that effect by the Member State's own domestic law.

In *Unilever*[108] the result was that the seller could now claim payment for the goods, as the rule that prevented them from conforming had been set aside while the rules of national contract law continued to apply: the loophole was closed and the defendant had to fulfil the contract and pay. By contrast, in *Faccini Dori*,[109] not much was to be gained by setting aside the Italian legislation. Neither the contract, nor the Italian legislation provided for a fall-back position under which a consumer could reconsider the purchase, unless one were to disregard the underlying *pacta sunt servanda* rule altogether. This, however, would go well beyond the extent of the incompatibility. What was necessary in this case was a real change in the terms of the contract or the national legislation, ie the introduction of the right to reconsider that so far existed only in the non-implemented Directive. Such direct intervention in the national legal order by creating rights and obligations between private parties is indeed restricted to norms that are directly applicable and have direct effect.[110]

One could argue that this is a capricious divide leading to arbitrary results. In fact, it is merely the consequence of the existence in the EU legal order of normative instruments with less than full legal effect: imperfect legal instruments create imperfect outcomes. Indeed, our theory accepts the constitutional difference between regulations and directives laid down in

---

[107]   Case C-201/02 *Delena Wells* [2004] ECR I-723, para 57.
[108]   Case C-443/98 *Unilever* [2000] ECR I-7535.
[109]   Case C-91/92 *Faccini Dori* [1994] ECR I-3325.
[110]   J Winter, 'Direct Applicability and Direct Effect: Two Distinct and Different Concepts in Community Law' (1972) 9 CML Rev, 425–438; see also D Edward, 'Direct Effect—Myth, Mess or Mystery?' (2002) 2 Il diritto dell'Unione Europea, 215–227.

Faccini Dori.[111] But that difference should not serve as an excuse not to apply imperfect legal instruments in situations where they do claim applicability, specifically, with a view to reviewing the compatibility of governmental acts. This is particularly relevant in respect of framework decisions, which the drafters of the Treaty further emasculated by expressly precluding direct effect. Consequently, the binding force of framework decisions is never so great as to allow an individual to rely upon them to obtain a right not provided for by national law, not even against the State. For example, if no reimbursement of costs is provided for in national law, it is useless to sue the State under Framework Decision 2001/220/JHA[112] to obtain this, whereas this would be possible if the same obligation were included in a directive.

However, by definition, framework decisions are binding on Member States as to the result to be achieved, and in this they do *not* differ from directives. Accordingly, everything that has been said in respect of direct and indirect judicial review can be transposed to framework decisions. Moreover, as any instrument of EU law, binding or non-binding, forms part of the domestic legal order, framework decisions can also be relied upon in order to offer guidance in the interpretation of national law.[113]

4 General conclusion

The current case law about invoking norms of EU law is being developed in dialogue with national courts and within the constraints of the questions they put to the ECJ. As a result, there may still be uncertainties as to when such norms can be invoked. These uncertainties are particularly unfortunate for two reasons. First, the ECJ is confronted with cases in the Third Pillar. In order to address the status of these unfamiliar legal instruments it is useful to rethink the theory on invoking norms of EU law. In particular, any theory that puts a great deal of emphasis on 'direct effect' *sensu stricto* is bound to limit the possibilities of individuals invoking Third Pillar instruments, even in circumstances where this may be the only way to protect important fundamental rights. Second, a consistent theory could

---

[111] Case C-91/92 *Faccini Dori* [1994] ECR I-3325, para 24.
[112] Art 7 Council Framework Decision on the standing of victims in criminal proceedings [2001] OJ L82/1.
[113] Case C-105/03 Pupino [2005] ECR I-5285.

guide the ECJ in its changing role. The judgment of the ECJ in preliminary reference proceedings is gradually making a more visible impact on the final outcome of cases. Thus, the ECJ may increasingly be seen to be shaping its case law on the basis of the possibility of invoking norms of EU law in the light of the outcome for one of the parties. A more nuanced approach to invocability, such as briefly sketched in section 3 above, which consistently aims to give full effect to EU legal instruments as far as their status as legally binding norms allows, may help to dispel this illusion.

INDEX

abortion
  Grogan case 305–8
absolutism
  idea behind 186
administrative law
  continuity 256
  convergence, development leading
      to 256
  discretion, after decisions 259–60
  European 257
  European Community law, influence
      of 256–8
  Europeanization
    divergence to unity 255–9
    over-simplifying 269
    public law, as subject of 259
    scepticism 258
  foreign and international developments,
      exclusion 255
  Germany, in
    Community and national law,
        divergent approaches 260
    duty to withdraw decisions 269
    ECJ judgments 258–9
    effective implementation of
        Community law, flexibility
        for 264–9
    ineffectiveness of application of
        Community law 268
    jurisprudence, crystallization of 261–2
    legitimate expectation, principle of
        protection 262–4
    legitimate interests, stability by means
        of protecting 261–4
    non-beneficial administrative
        acts 264–5
    stability, position on 266
    telecommunications licences, fees
        for 267–8
    Verwaltungsakte, cancelling 261–2, 268
    Verwaltungsakte in breach of
        Community law 268–9
  national legal systems, development
      of 255
  national, value of structure of 258
  positivism, rise of 255–6

agent
  interpretation of terms of rule 323
  legal competence 321
agricultural law
  discretion and policy in area of 333–4
Austria
  standing requirement 174–5

banking directives
  depositors, rights of 166
  individuals, rights of under 161
  supervisory measures, right to 166–7
BCCI
  collapse, damages incurred 161
Belgium
  creation of rights as condition of direct
      effect 172
  directives, transposition into national
      legislation 277
breach of contract
  inducing, tort of 75
breach of statutory duty
  infringement of Community law
      as 241–2

civil law
  Code civil, tradition of 5
  common law, divergence 5
collective interests
  protection of 175
common agricultural policy
  discretionary powers under 198–9
common law
  civil law, divergence 5
  Europe, of 39
Community institutions
  broad discretionary powers 205
  common agricultural policy,
      discretionary powers under
      198–9
  discretion of 138–41
  liability of 197–201
  liability, challenge to 200–1
  stringent review of decisions, 214
company law directives
  annual accounts, publication of 174